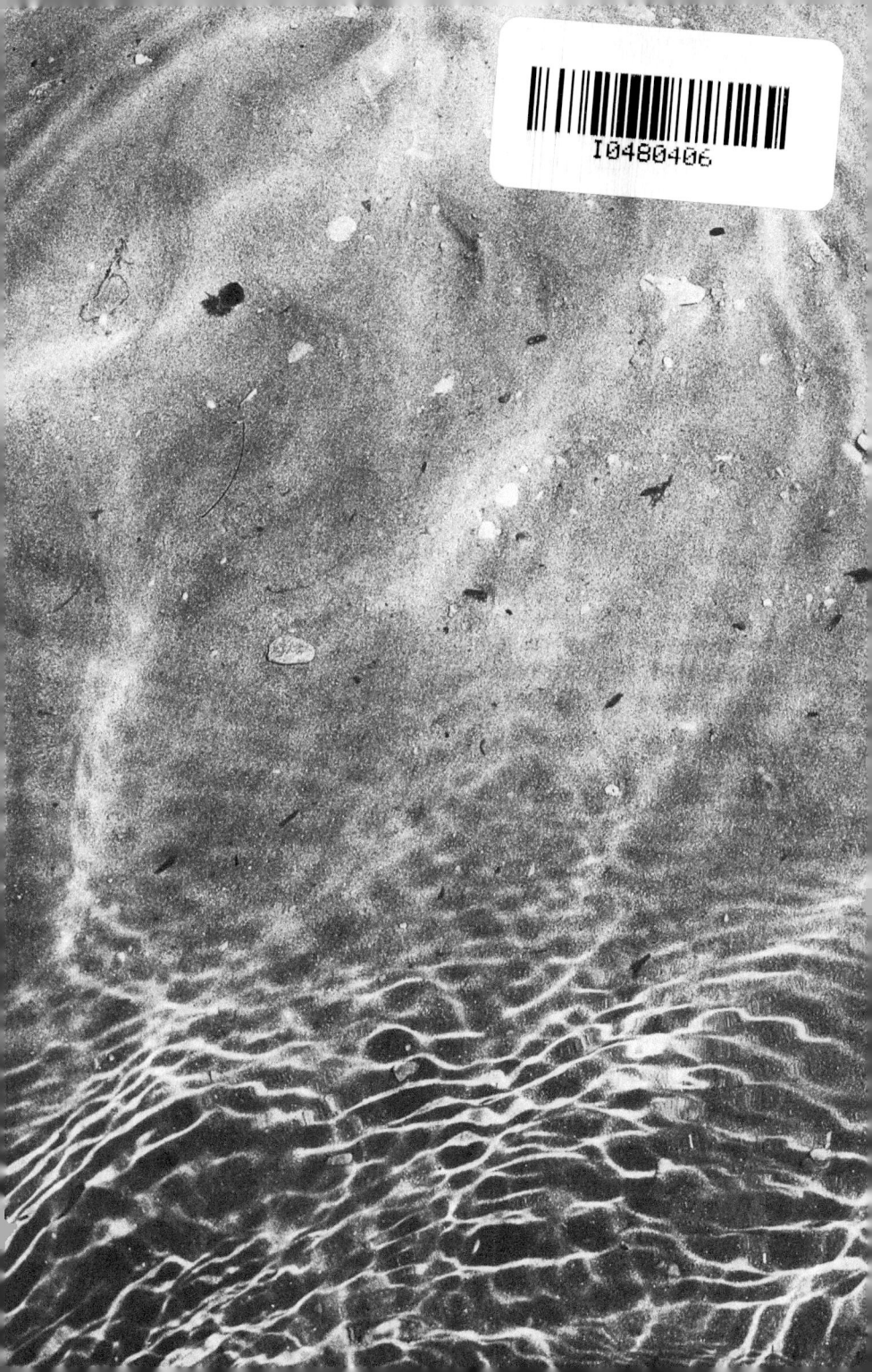

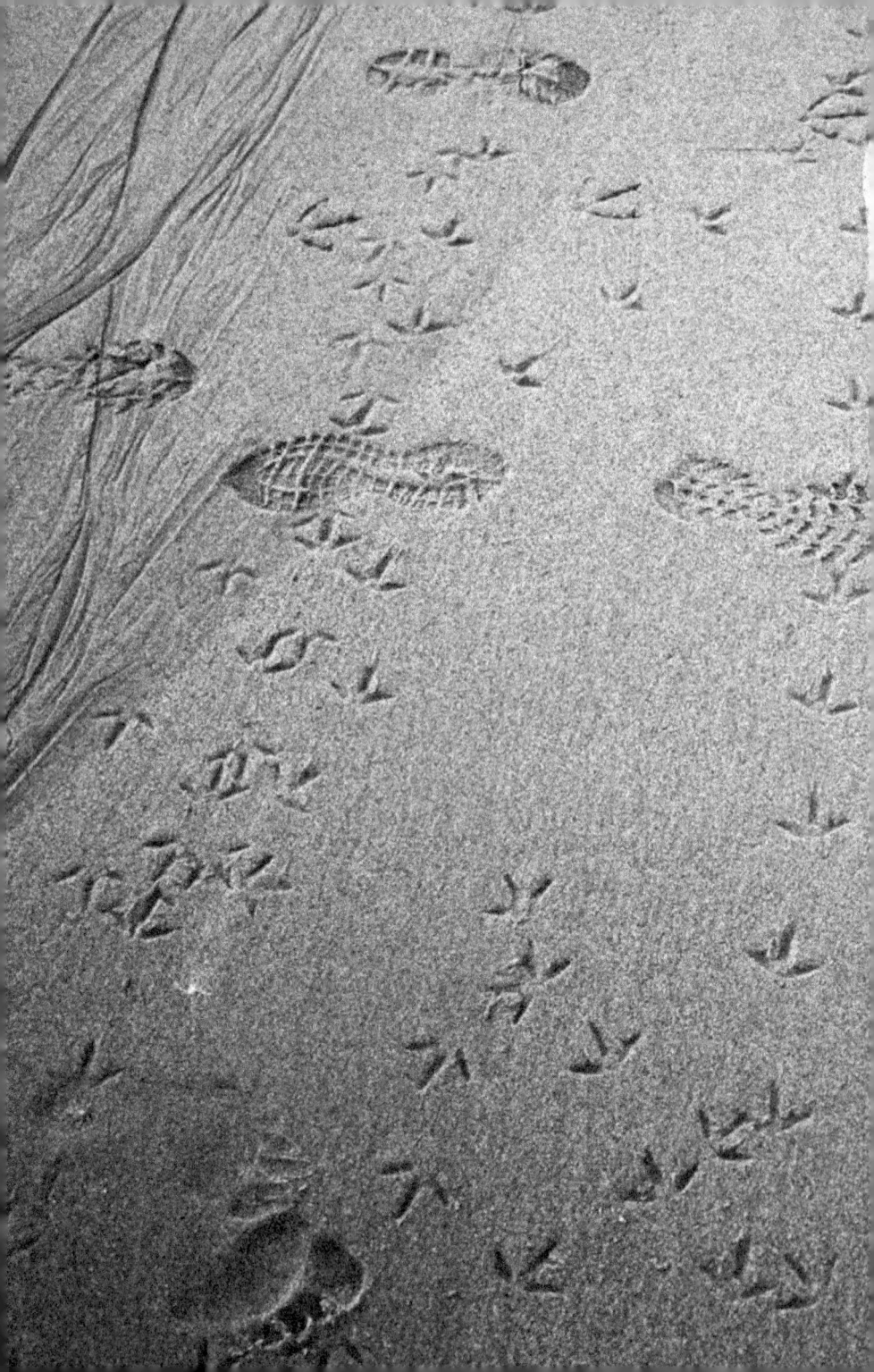

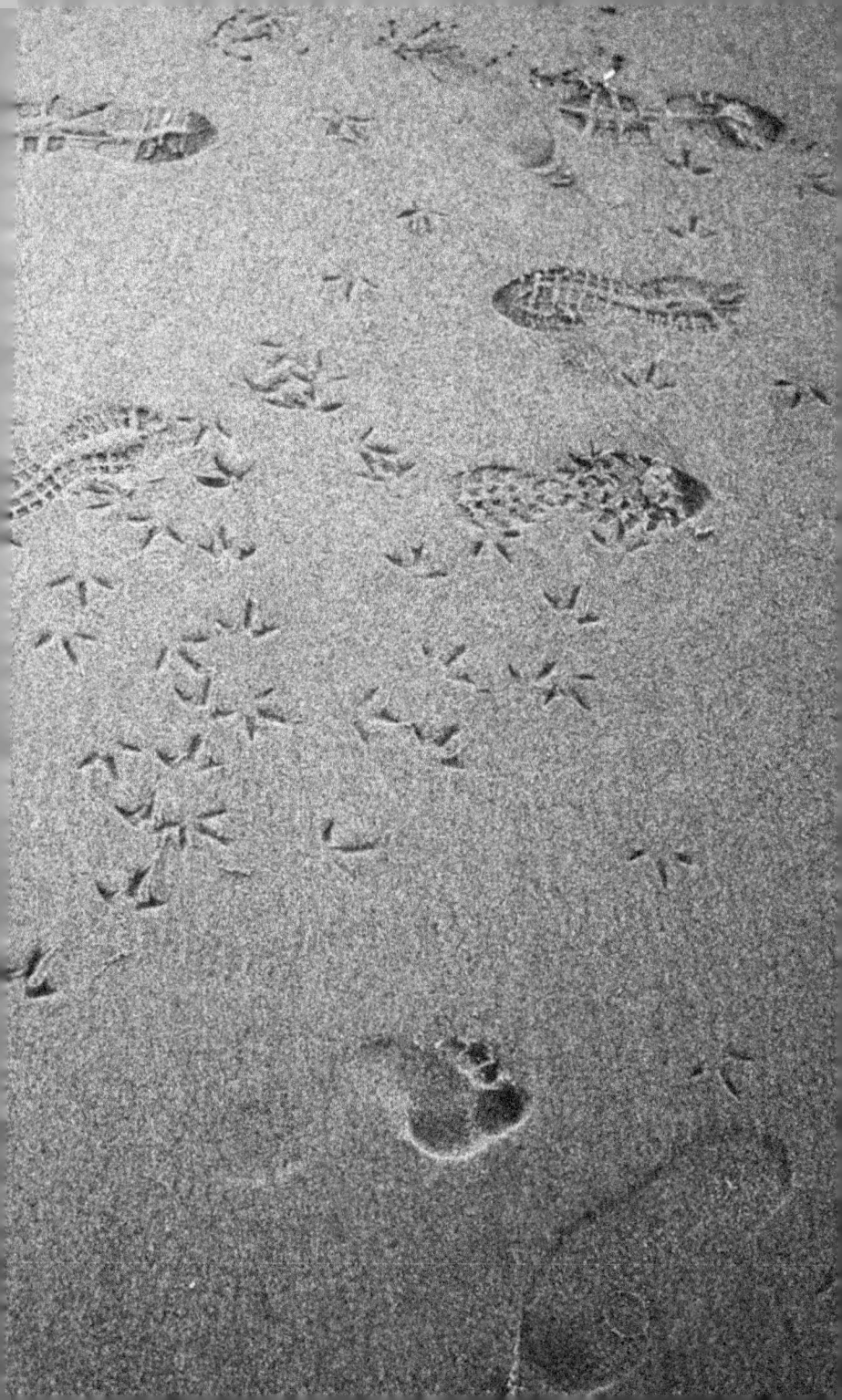

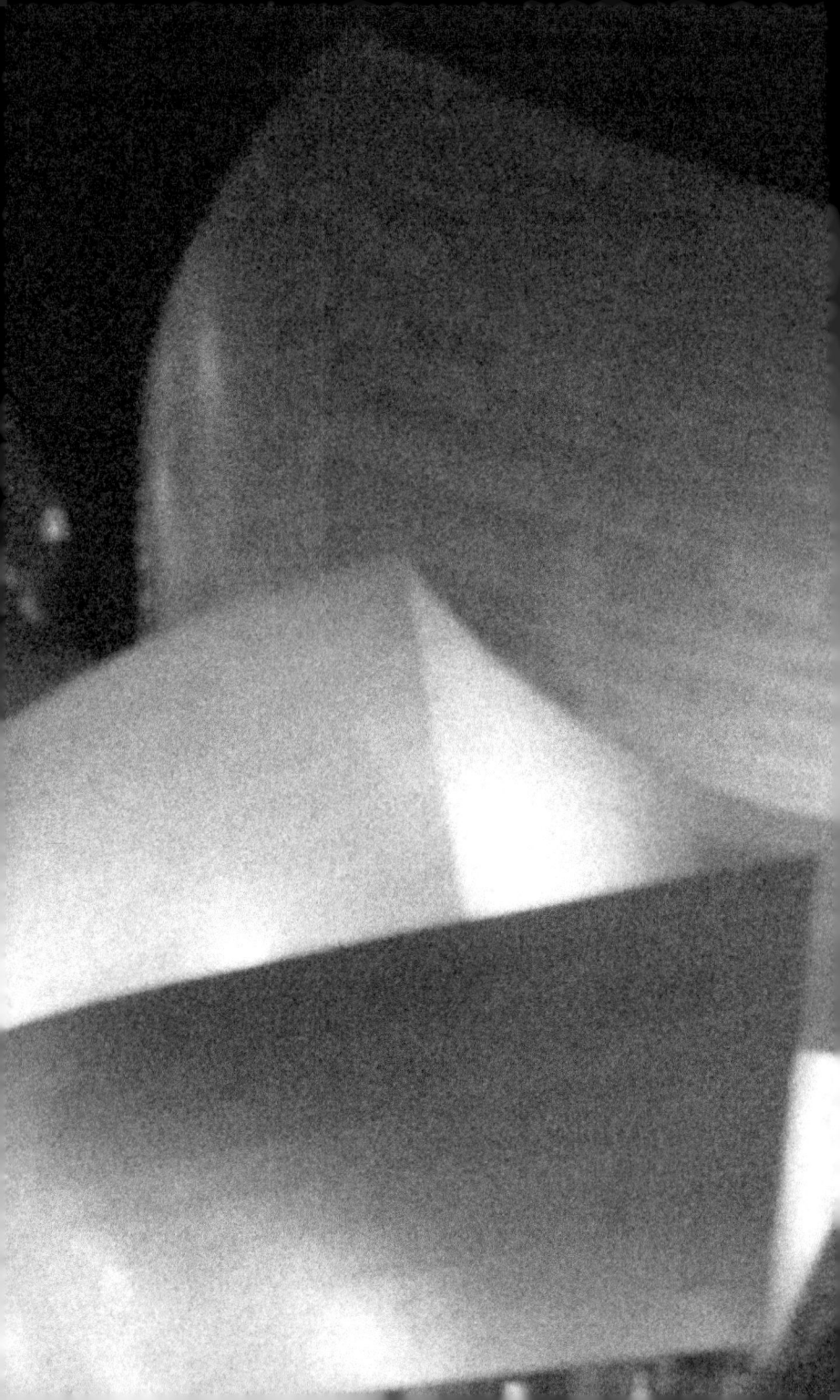

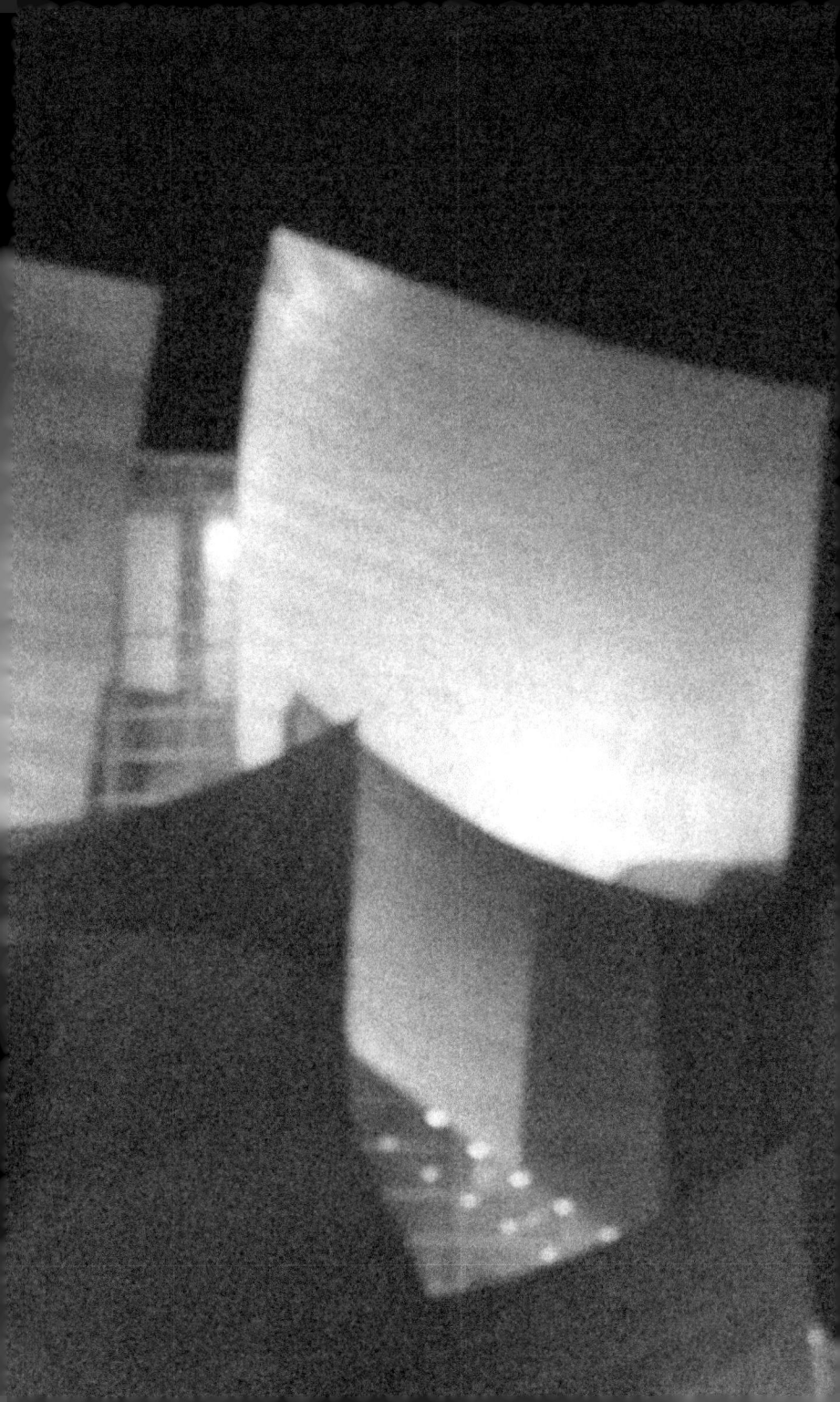

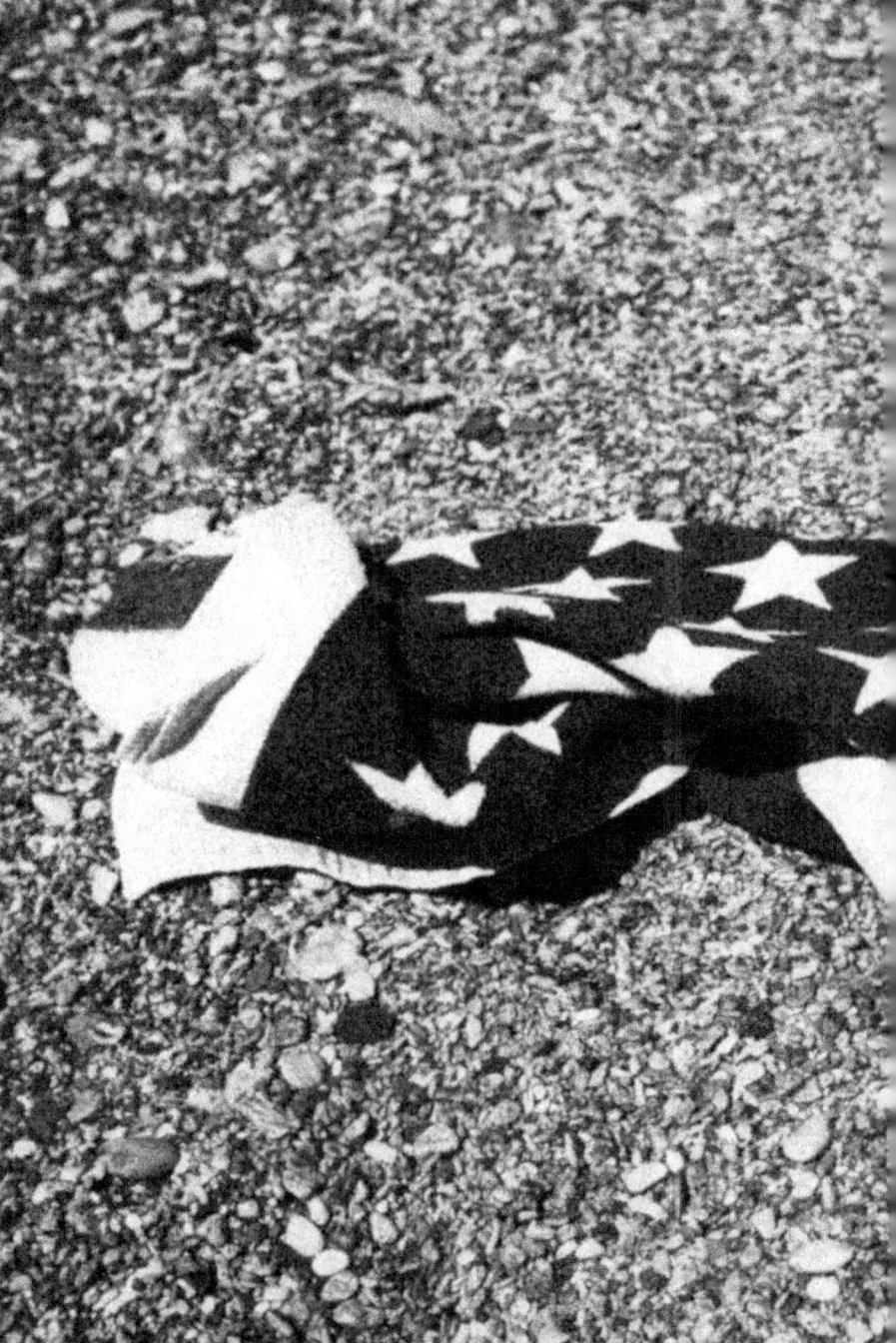

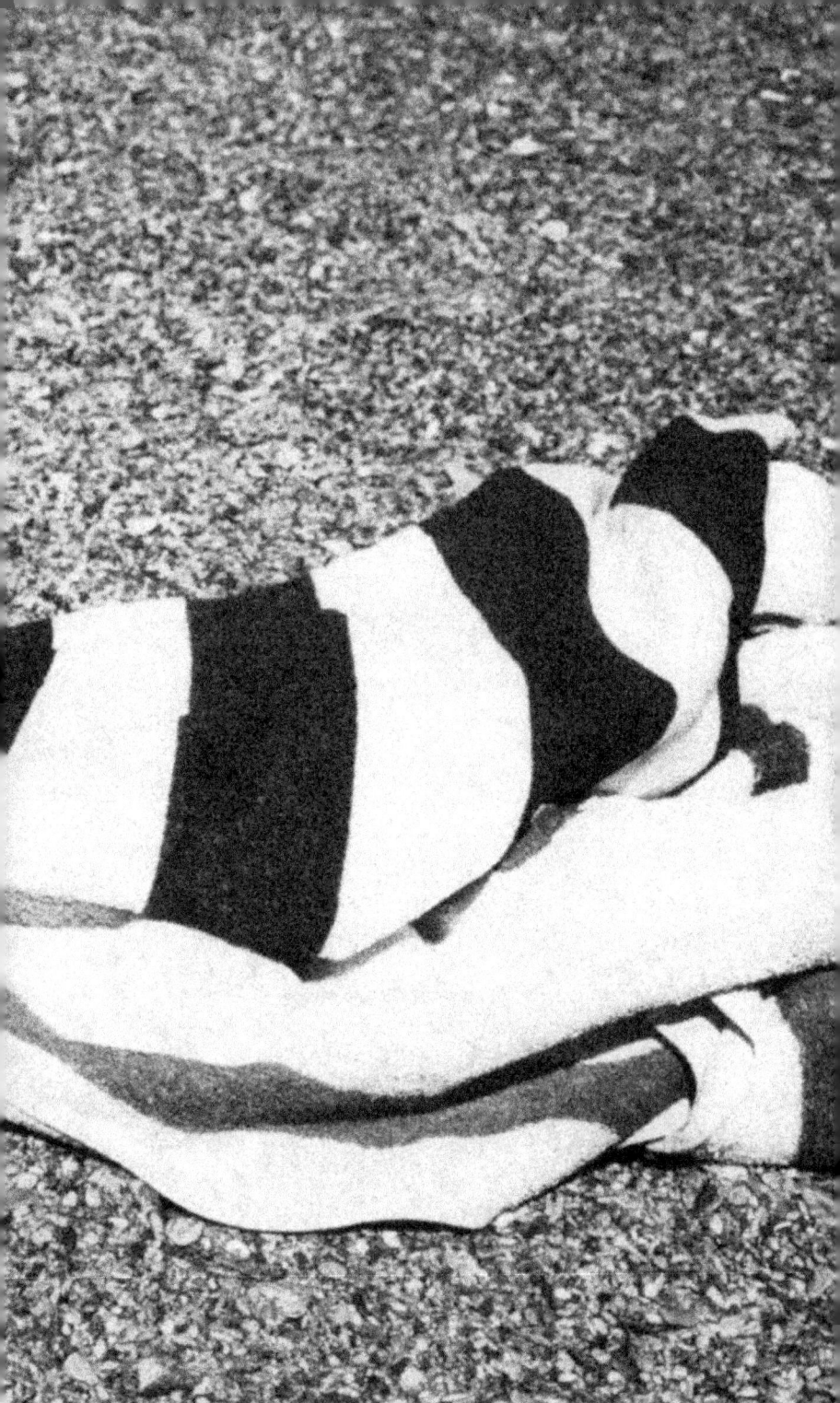

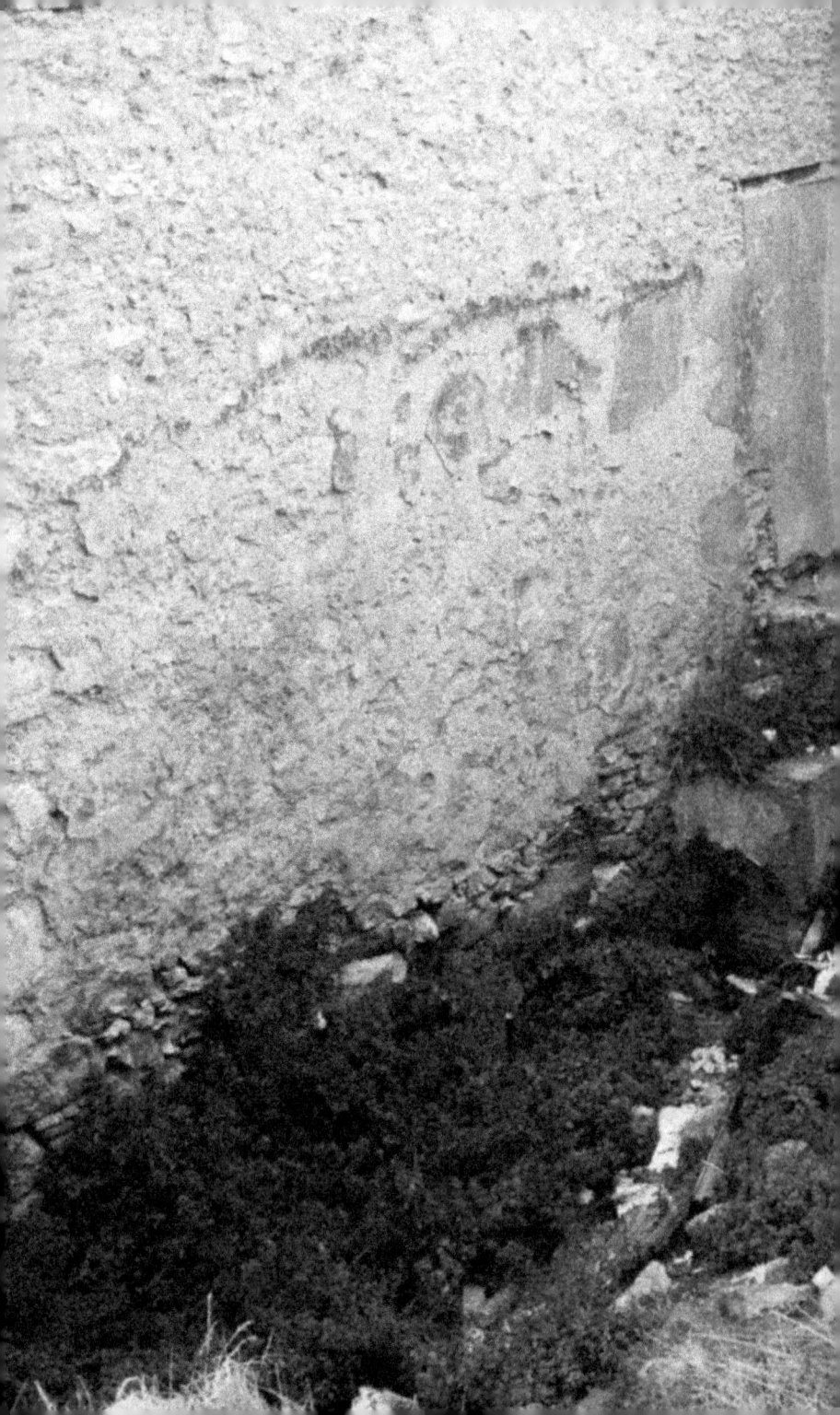

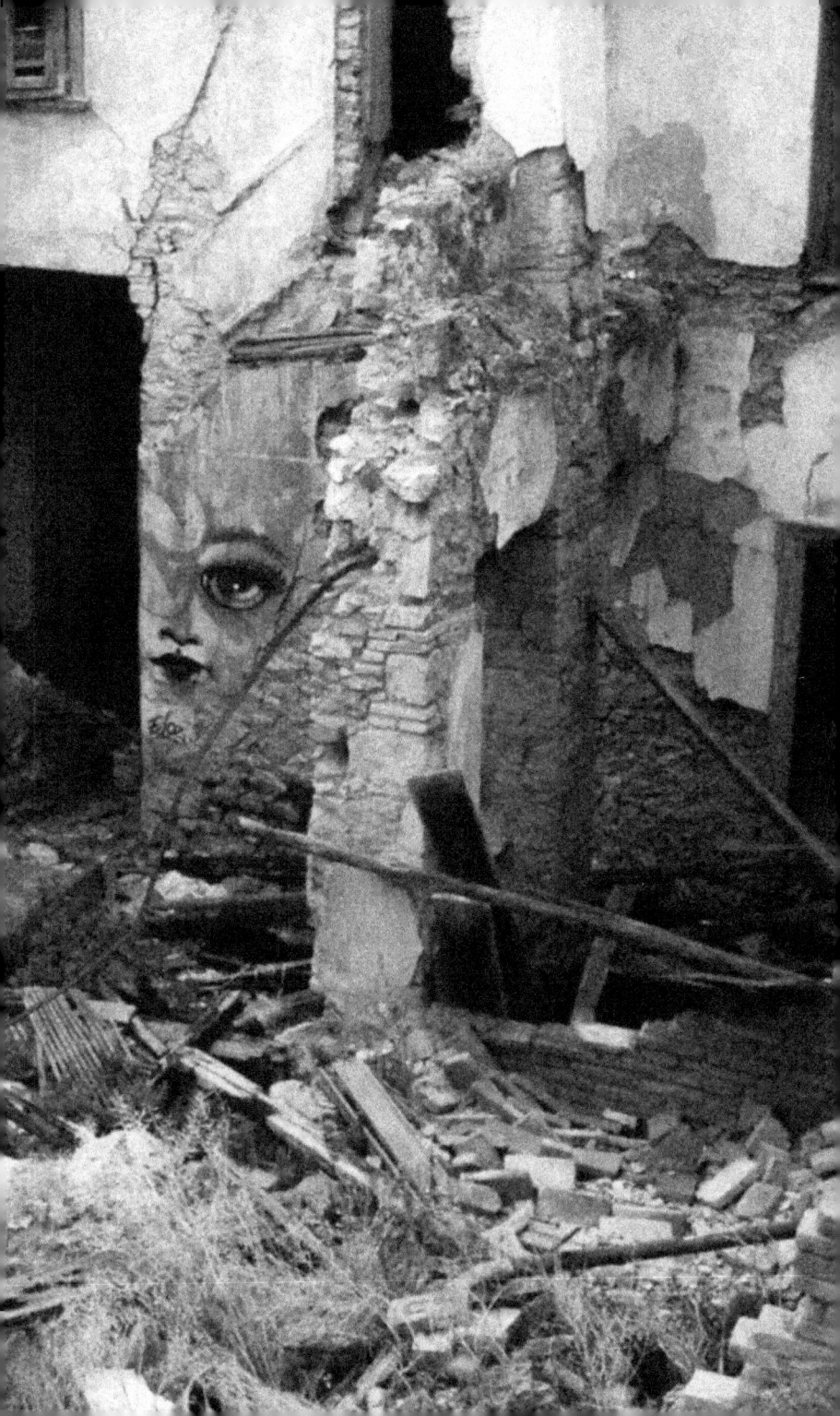

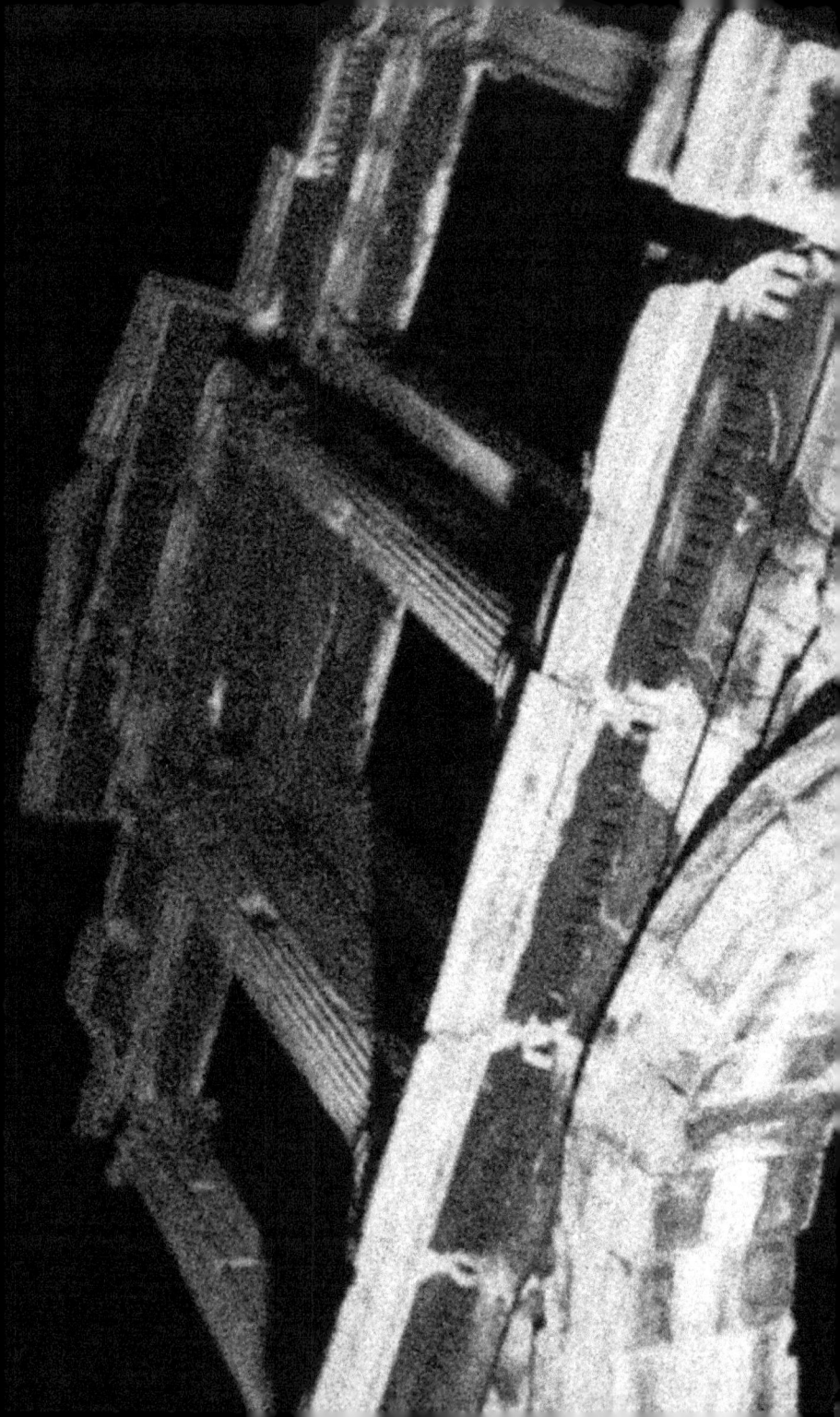

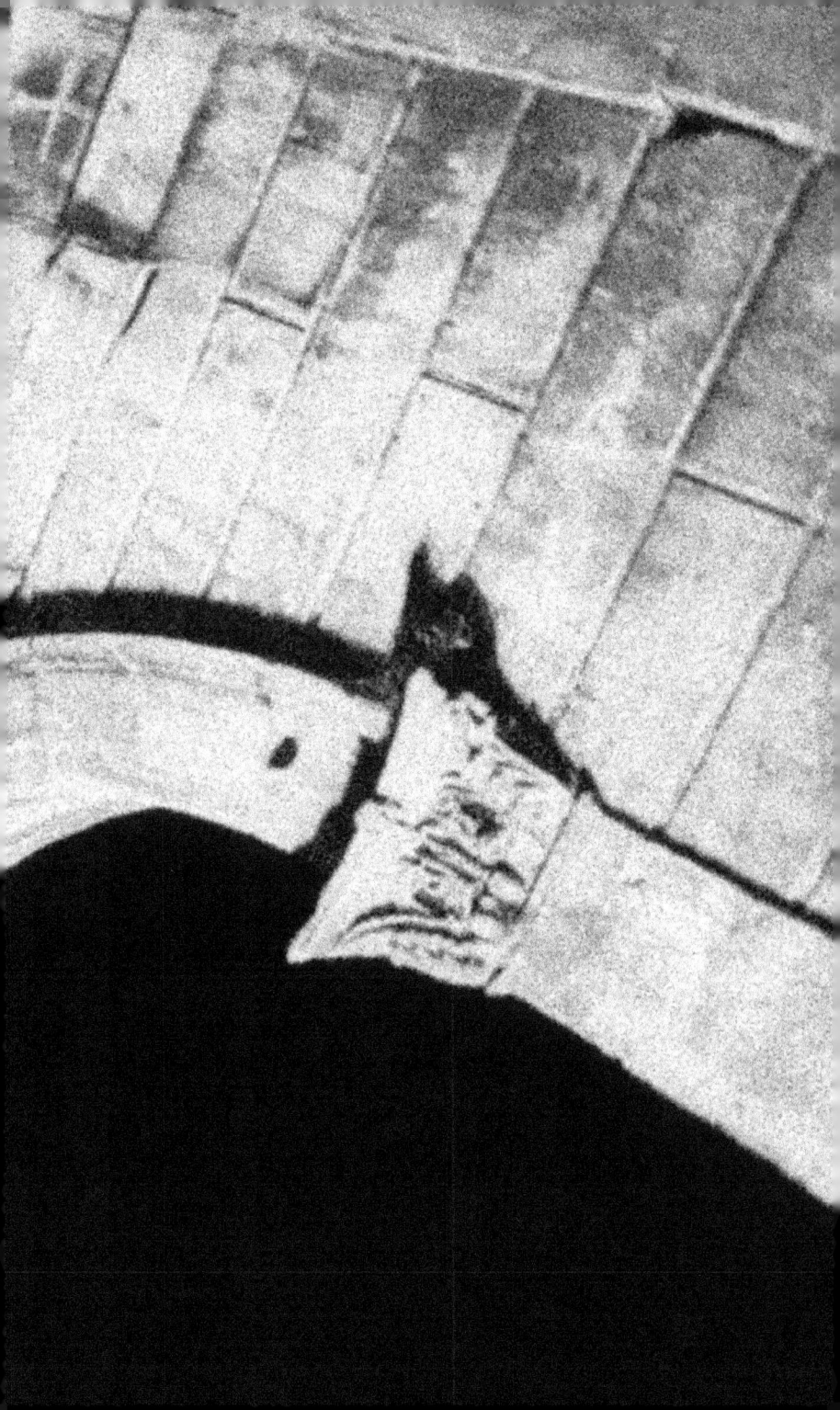

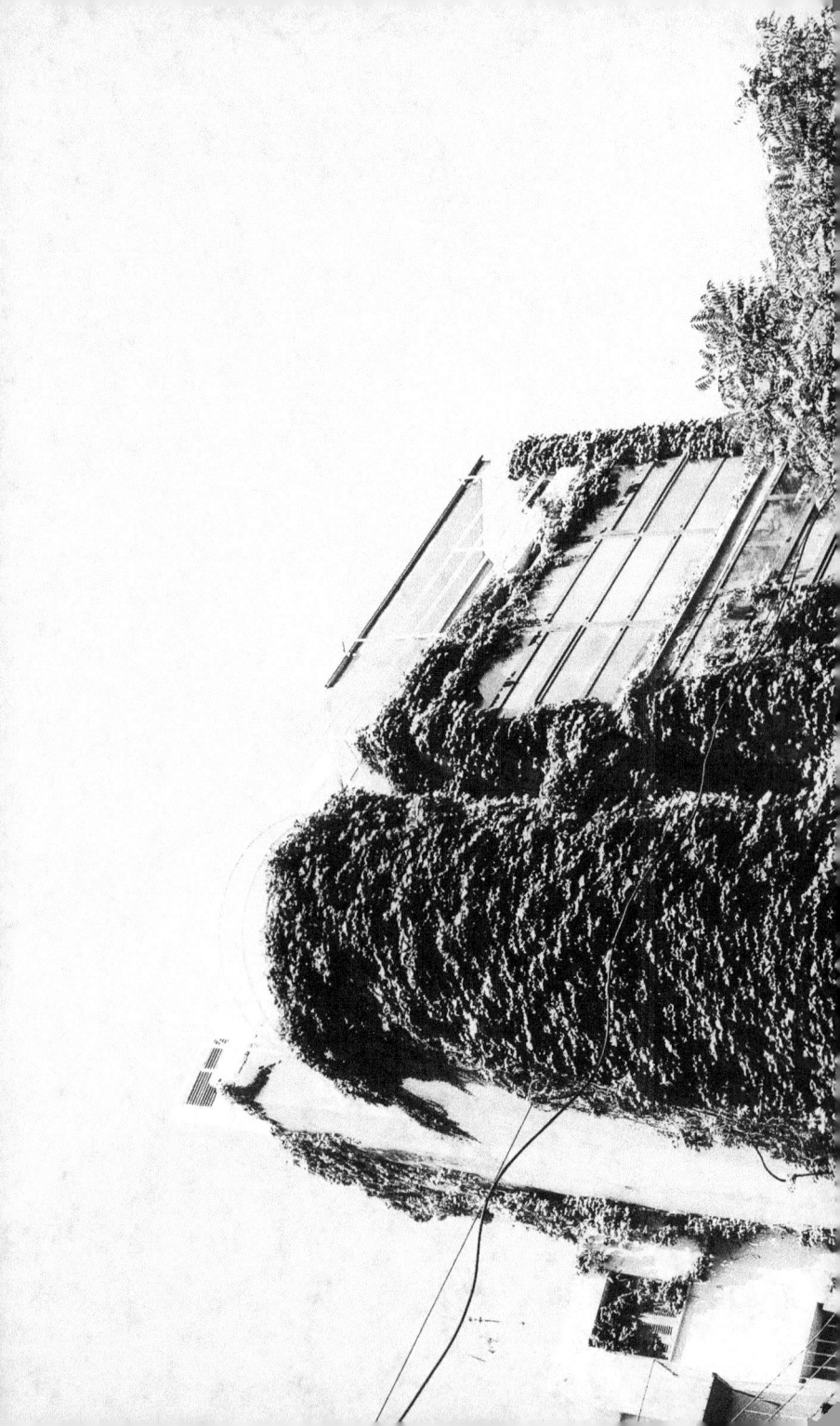

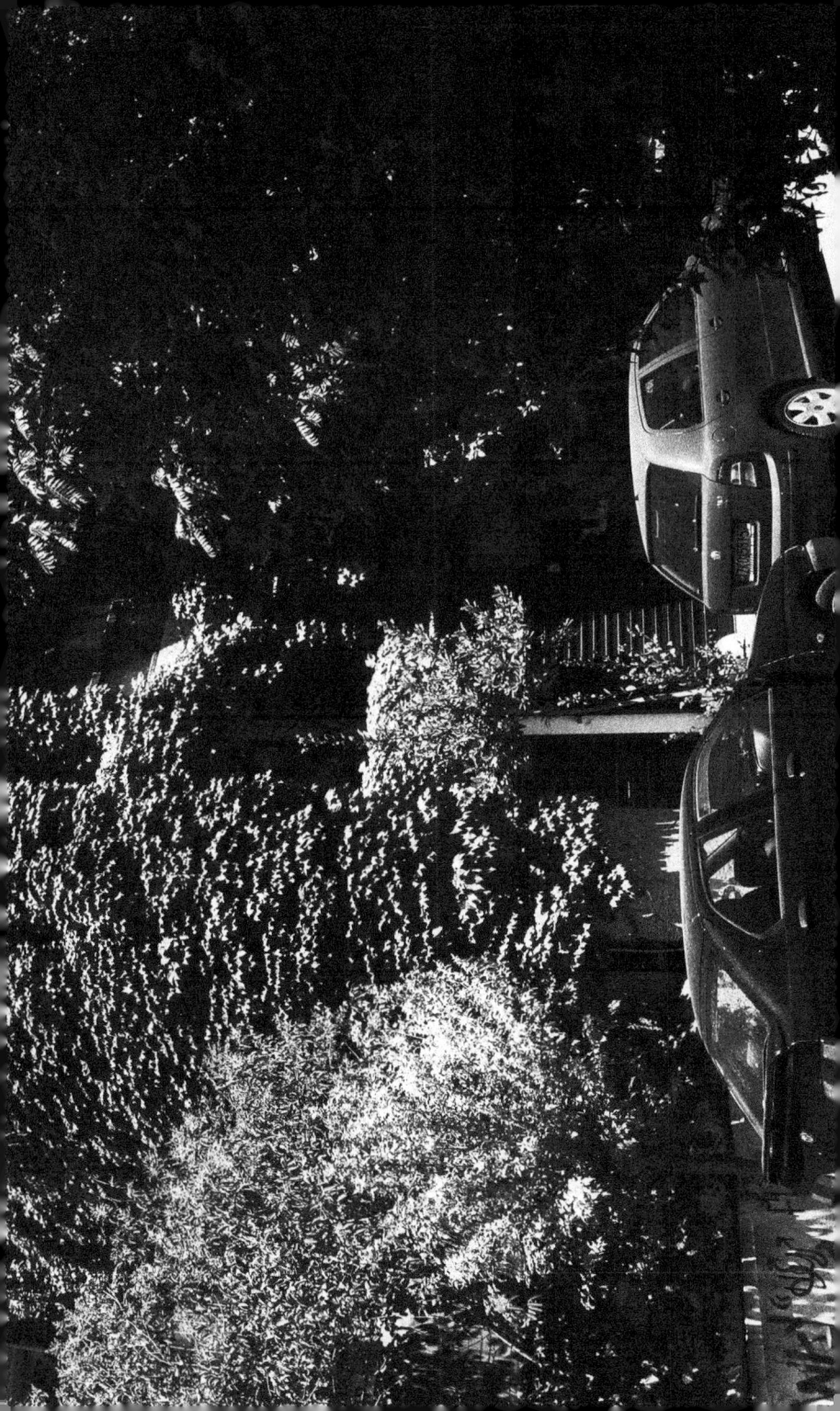

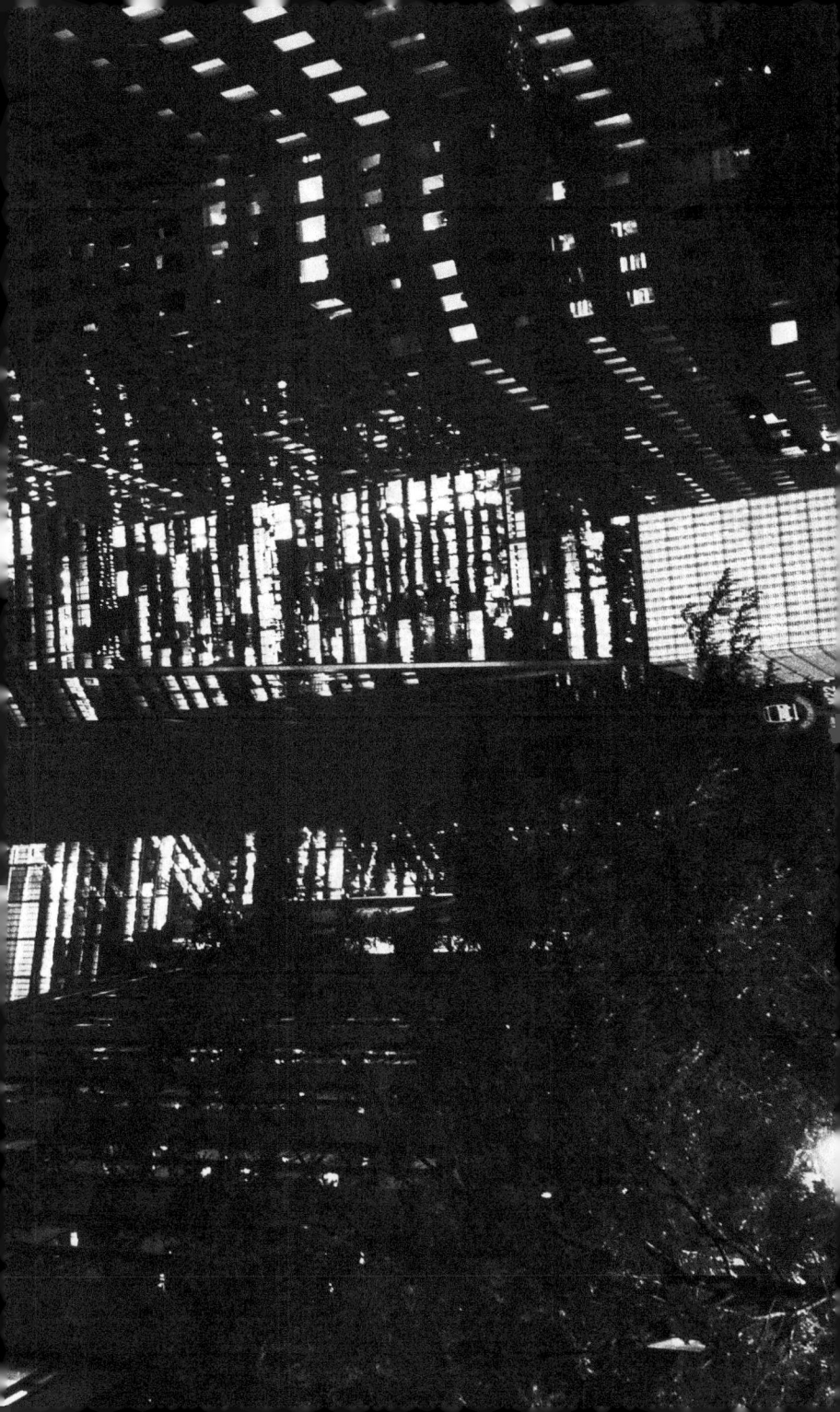

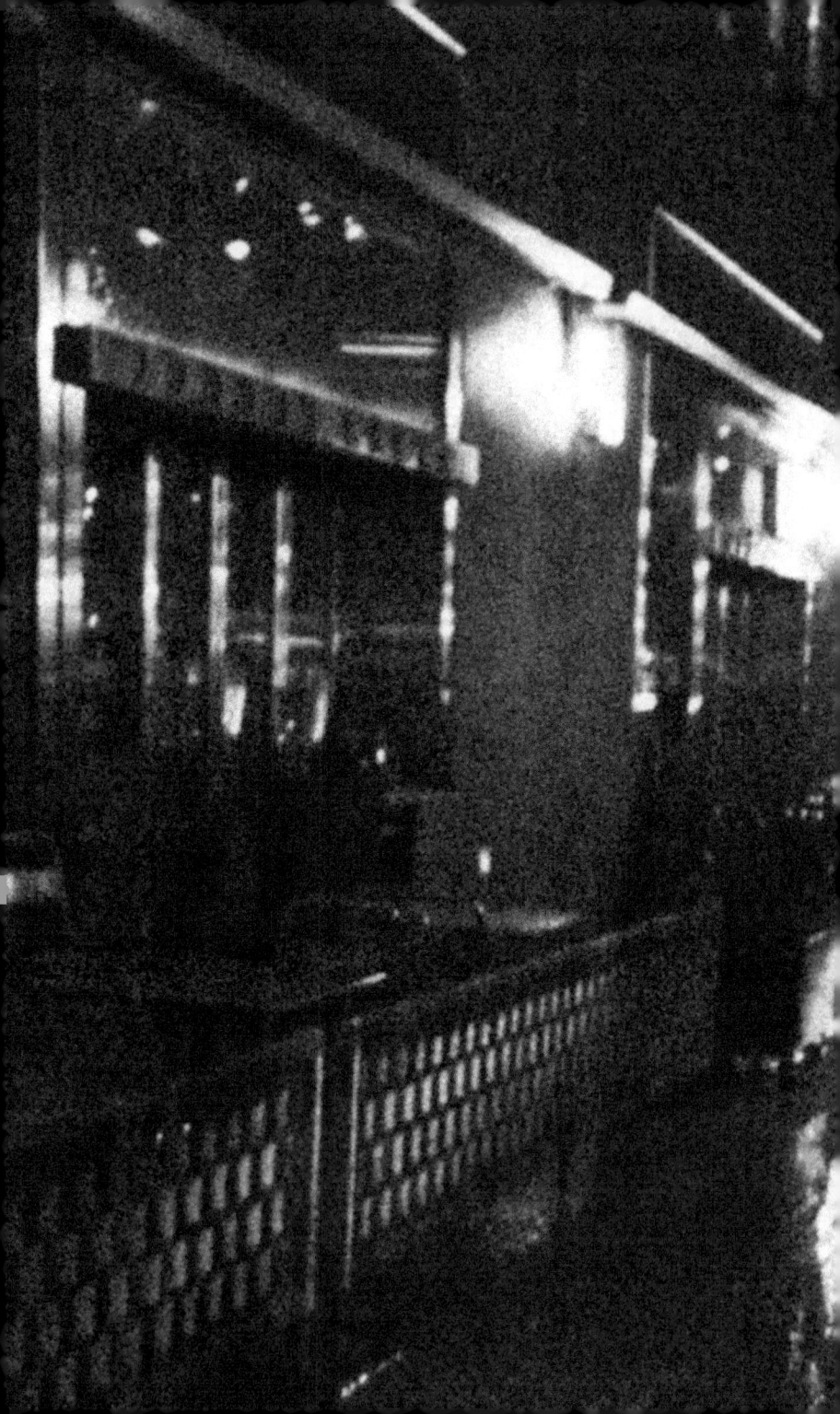

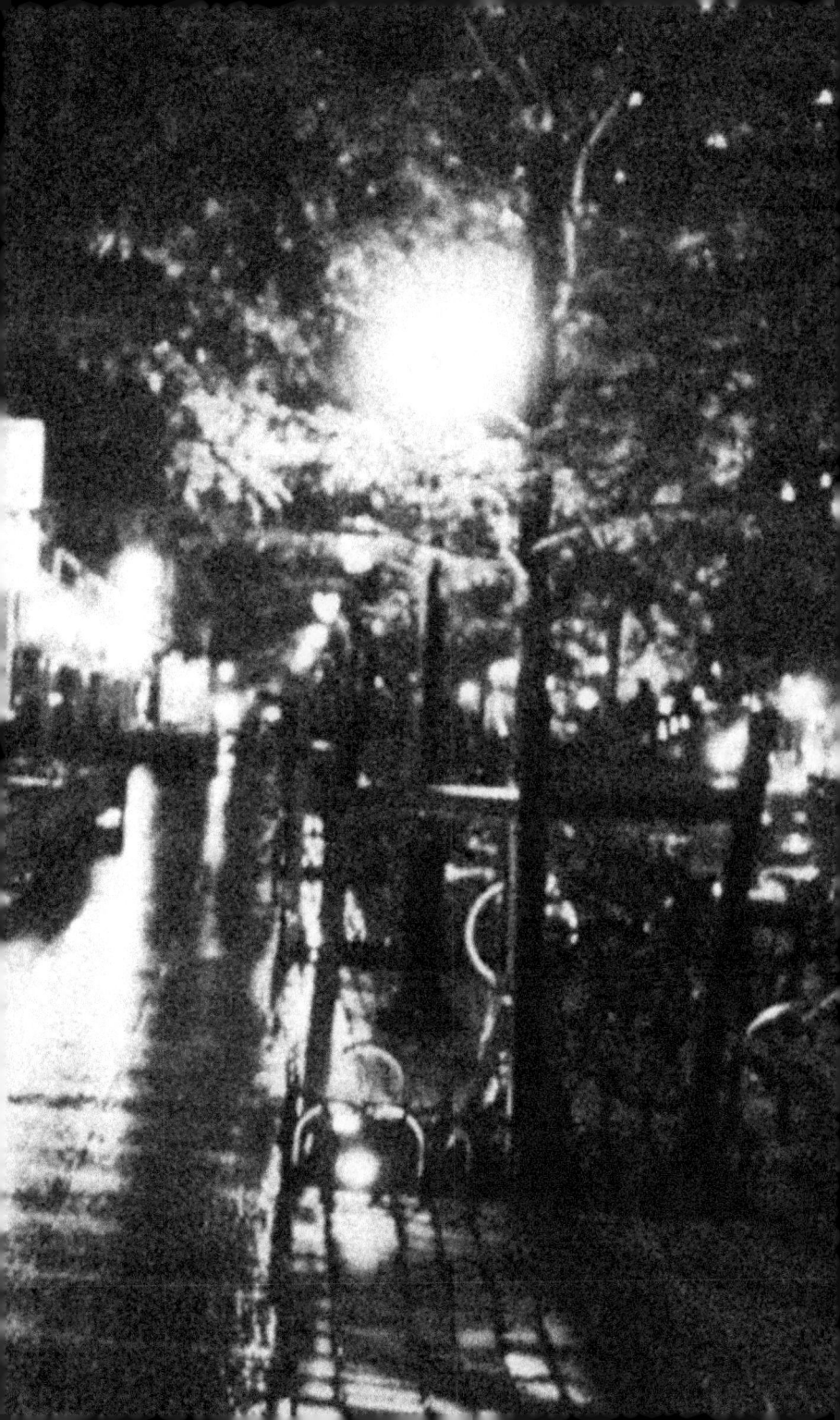

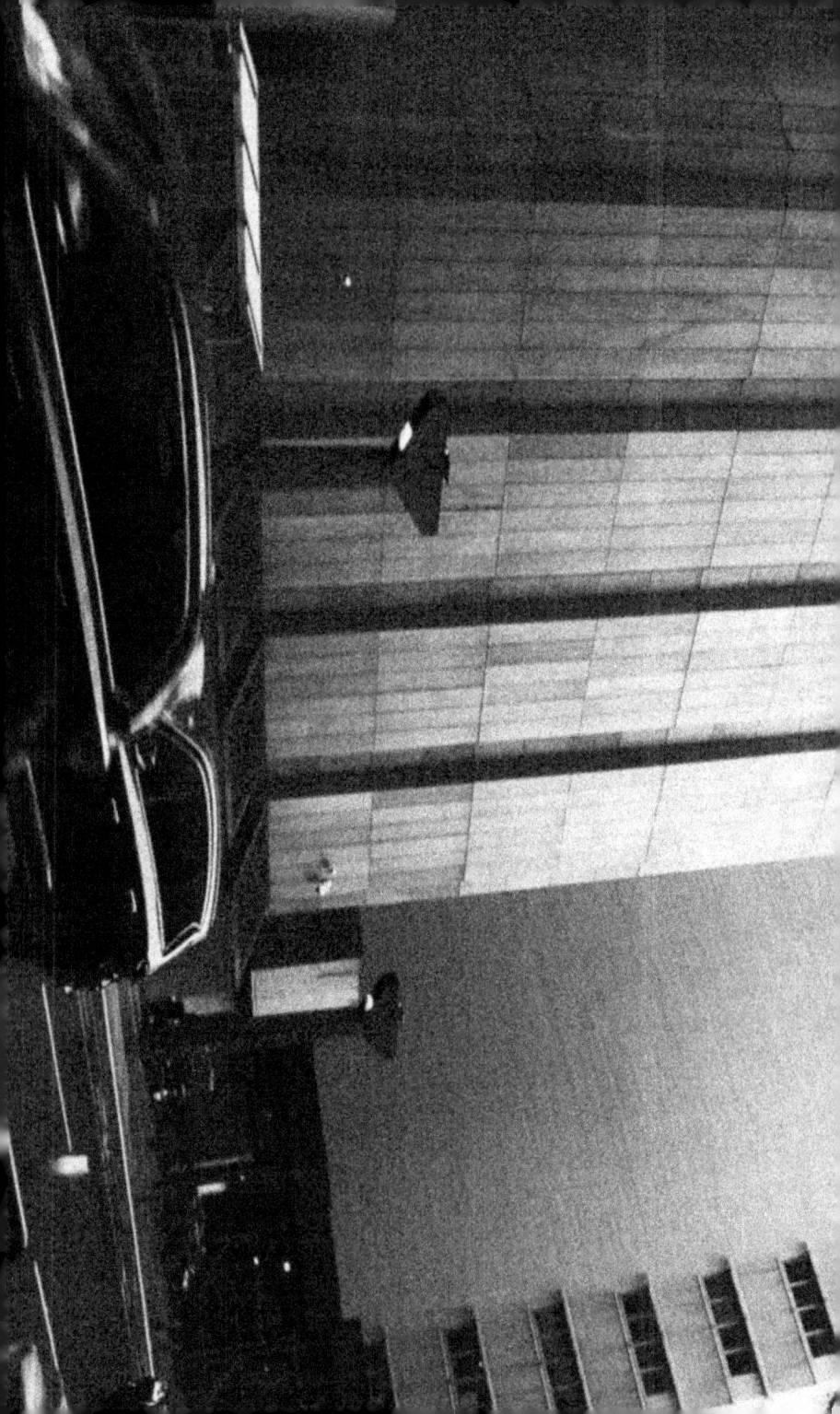

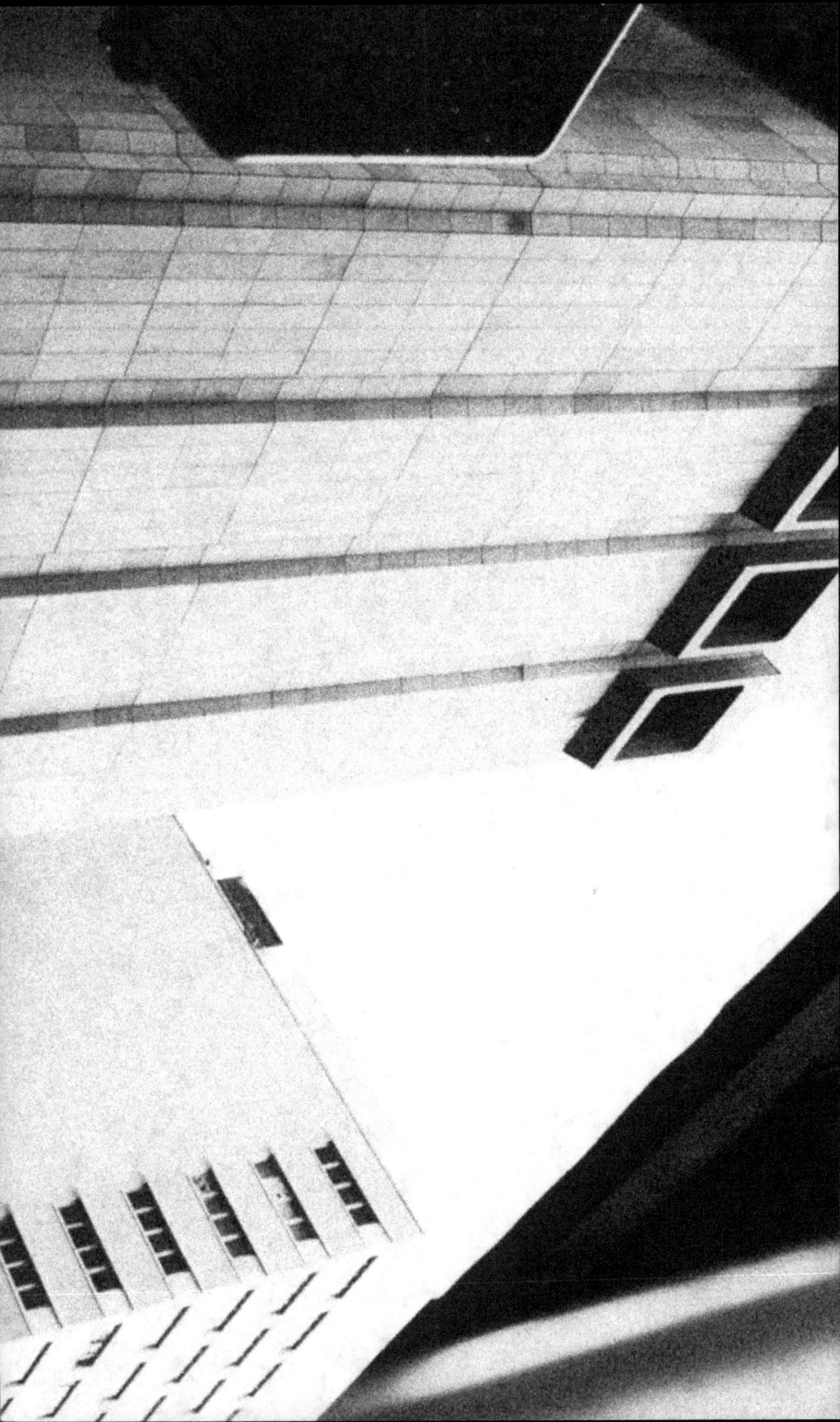

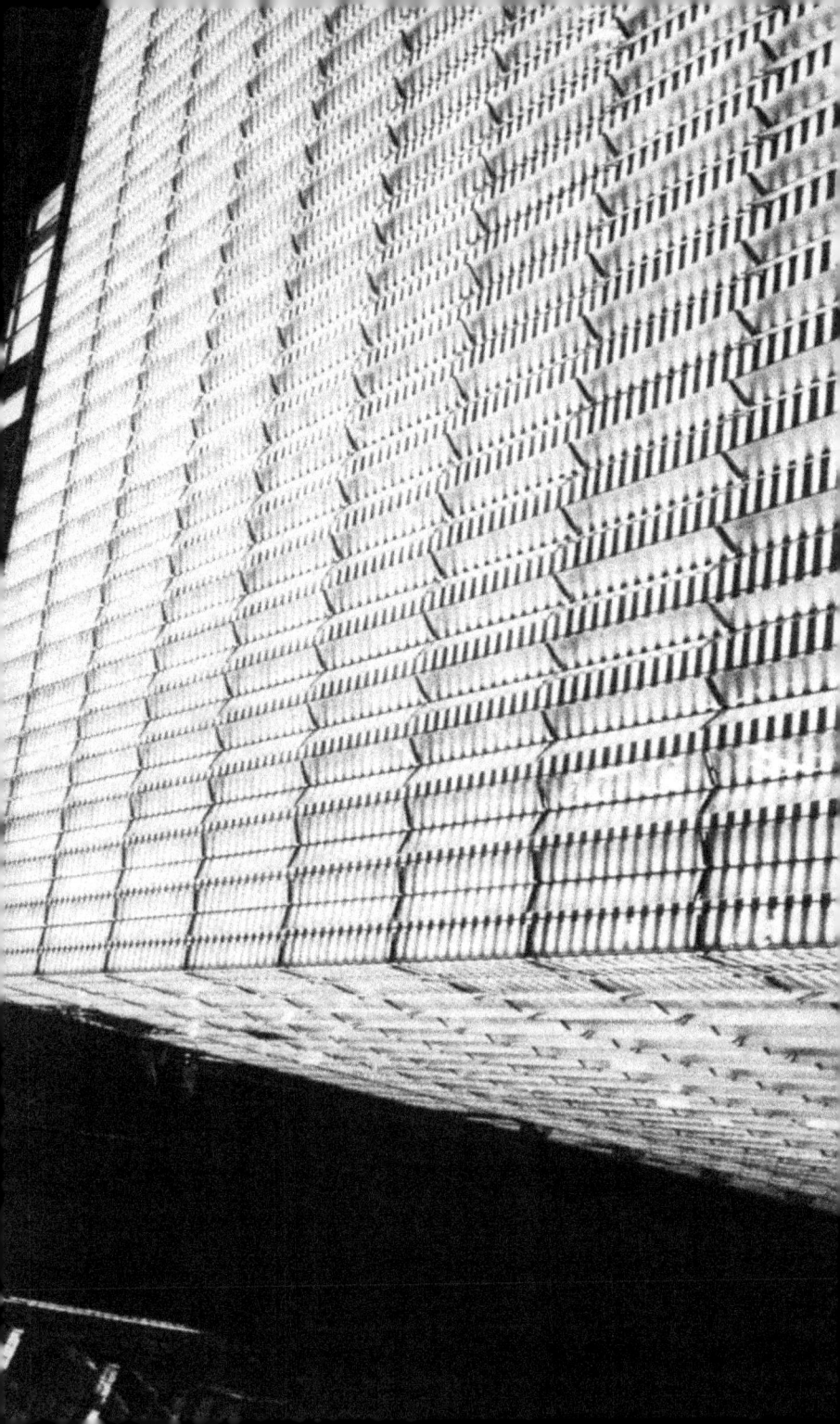

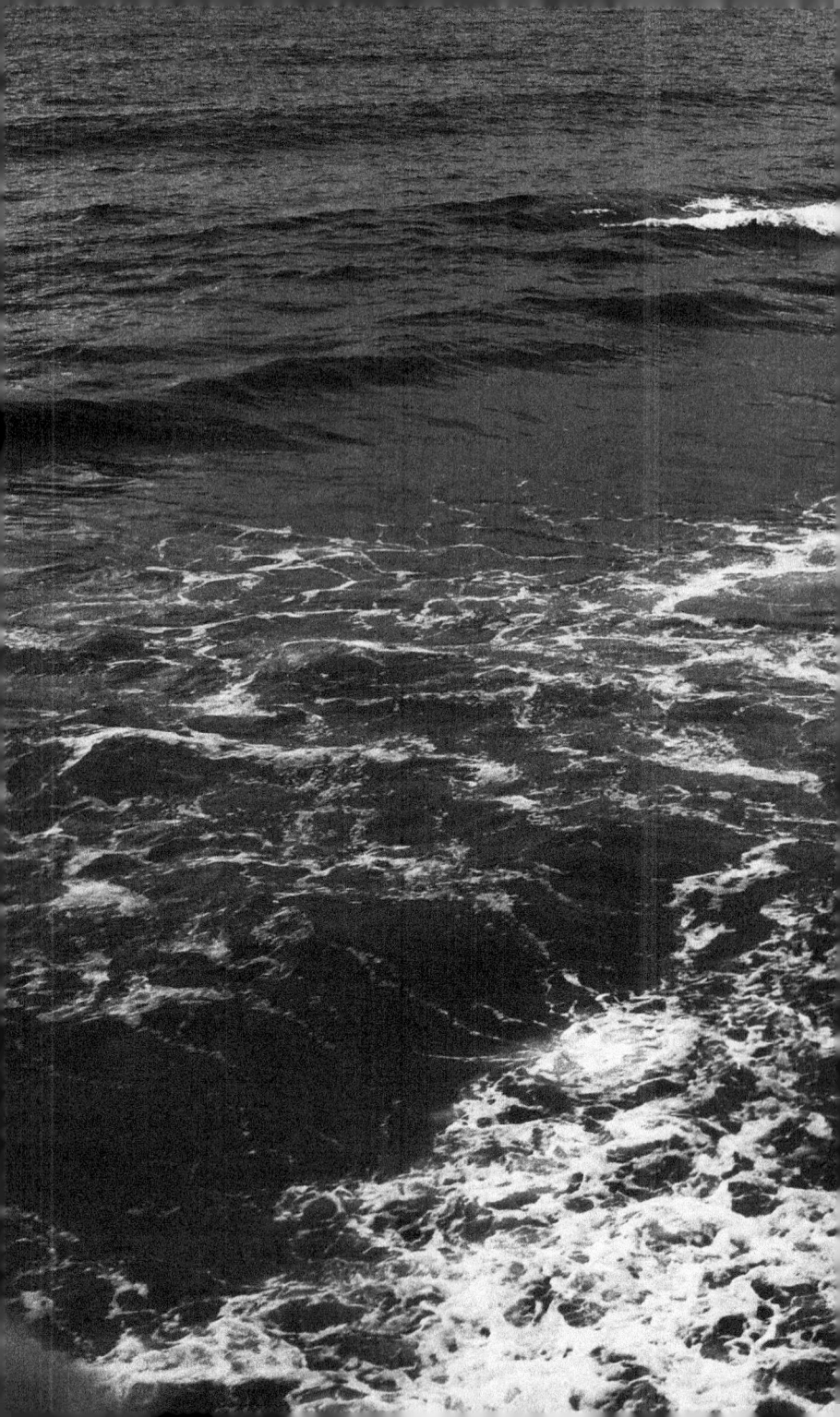

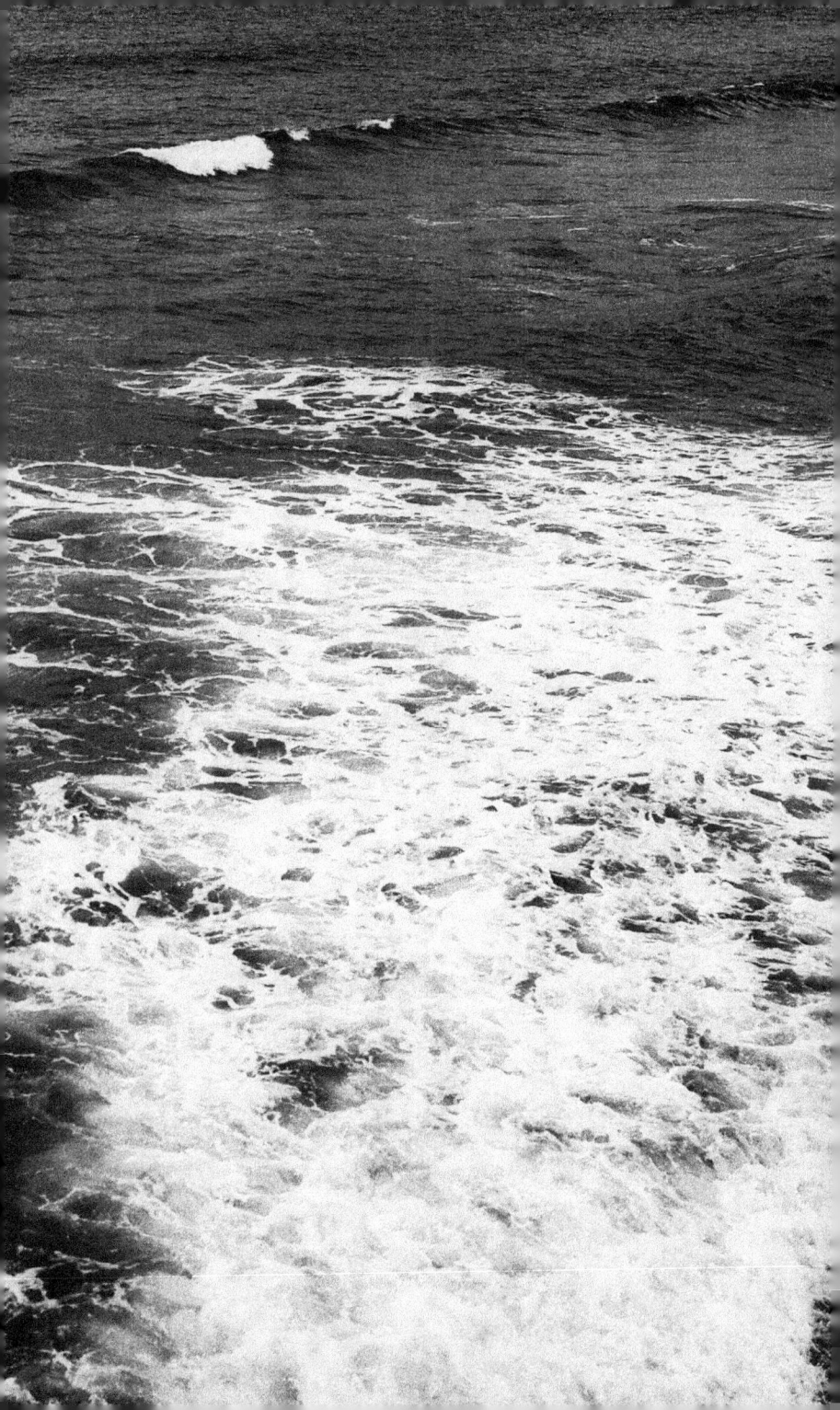

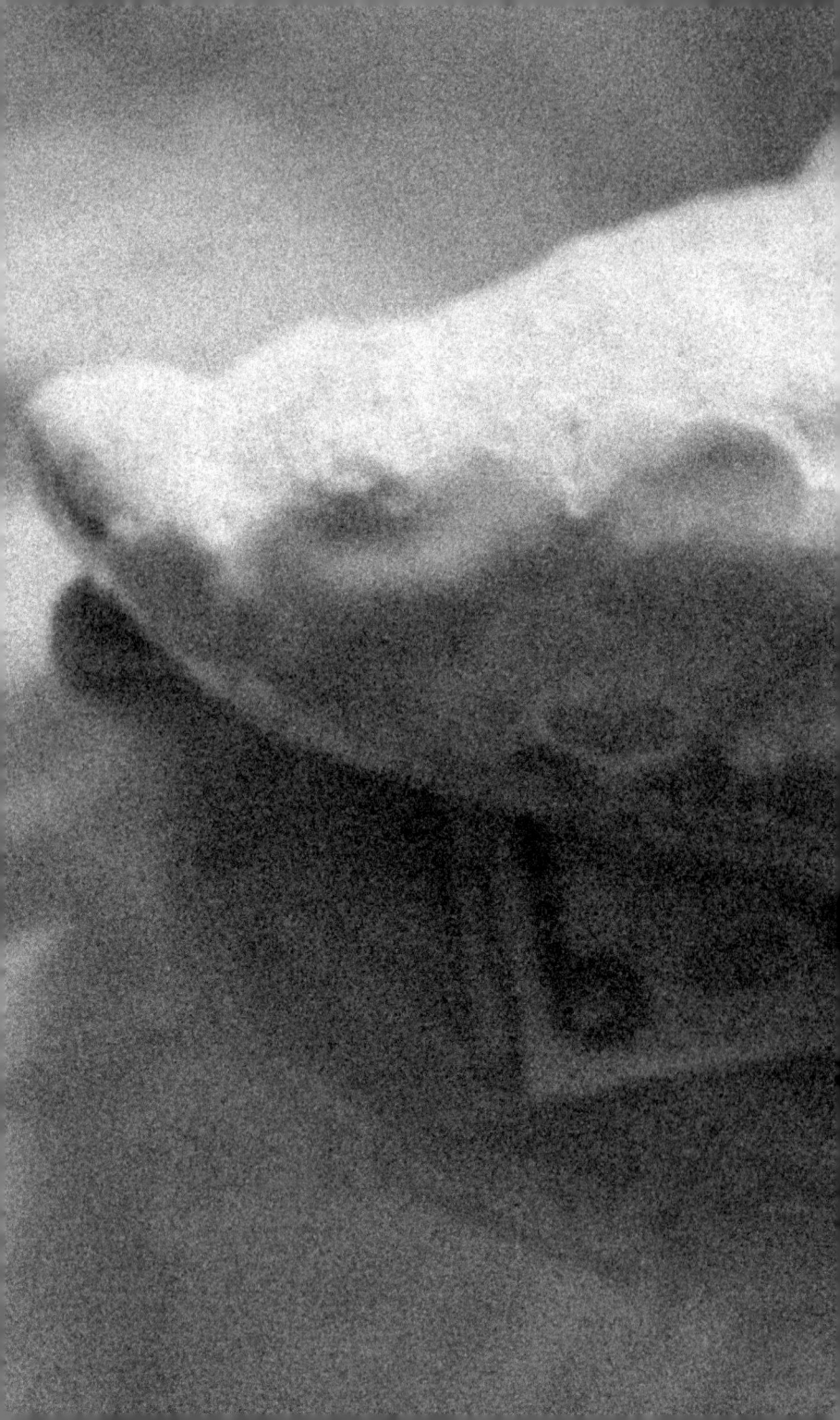

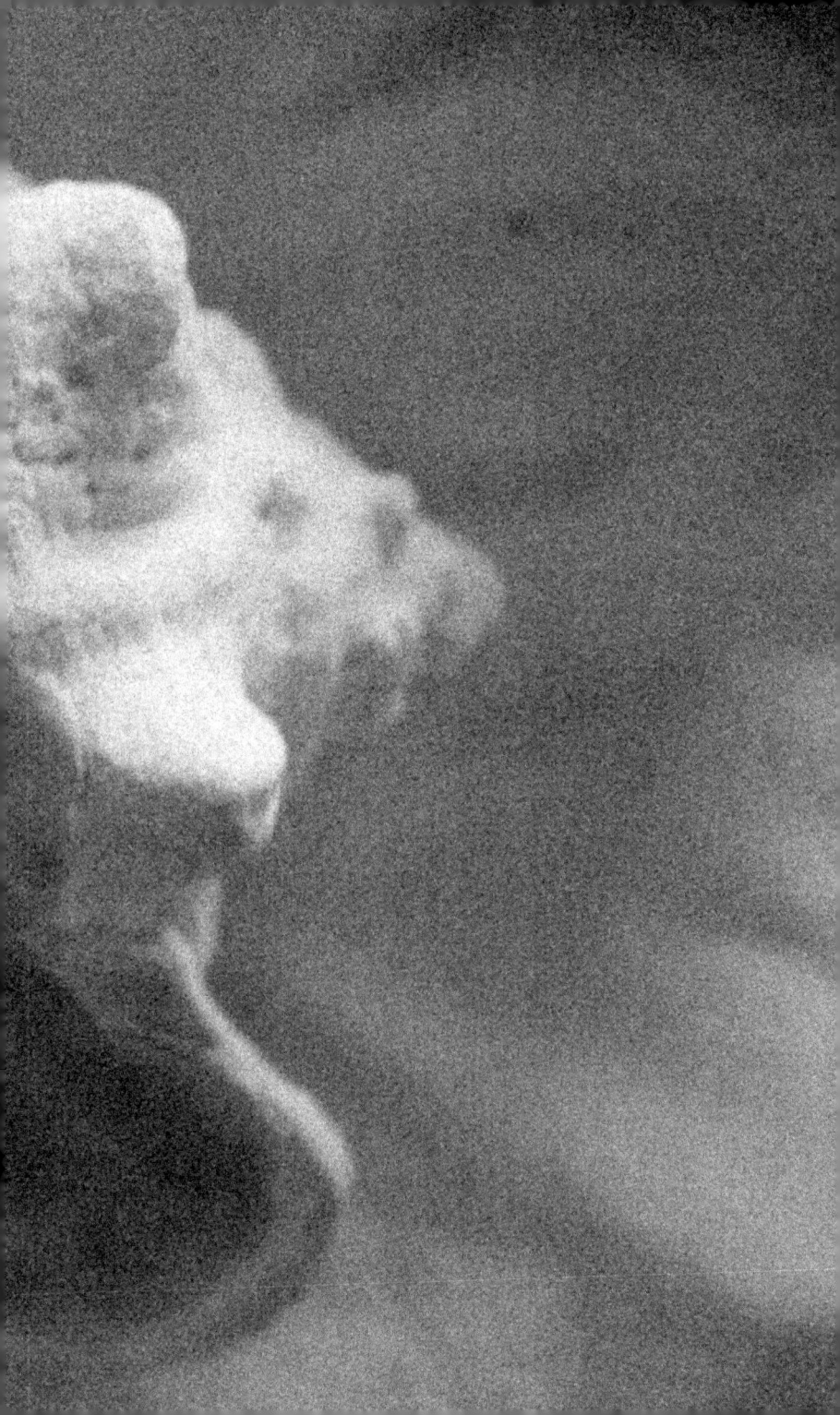

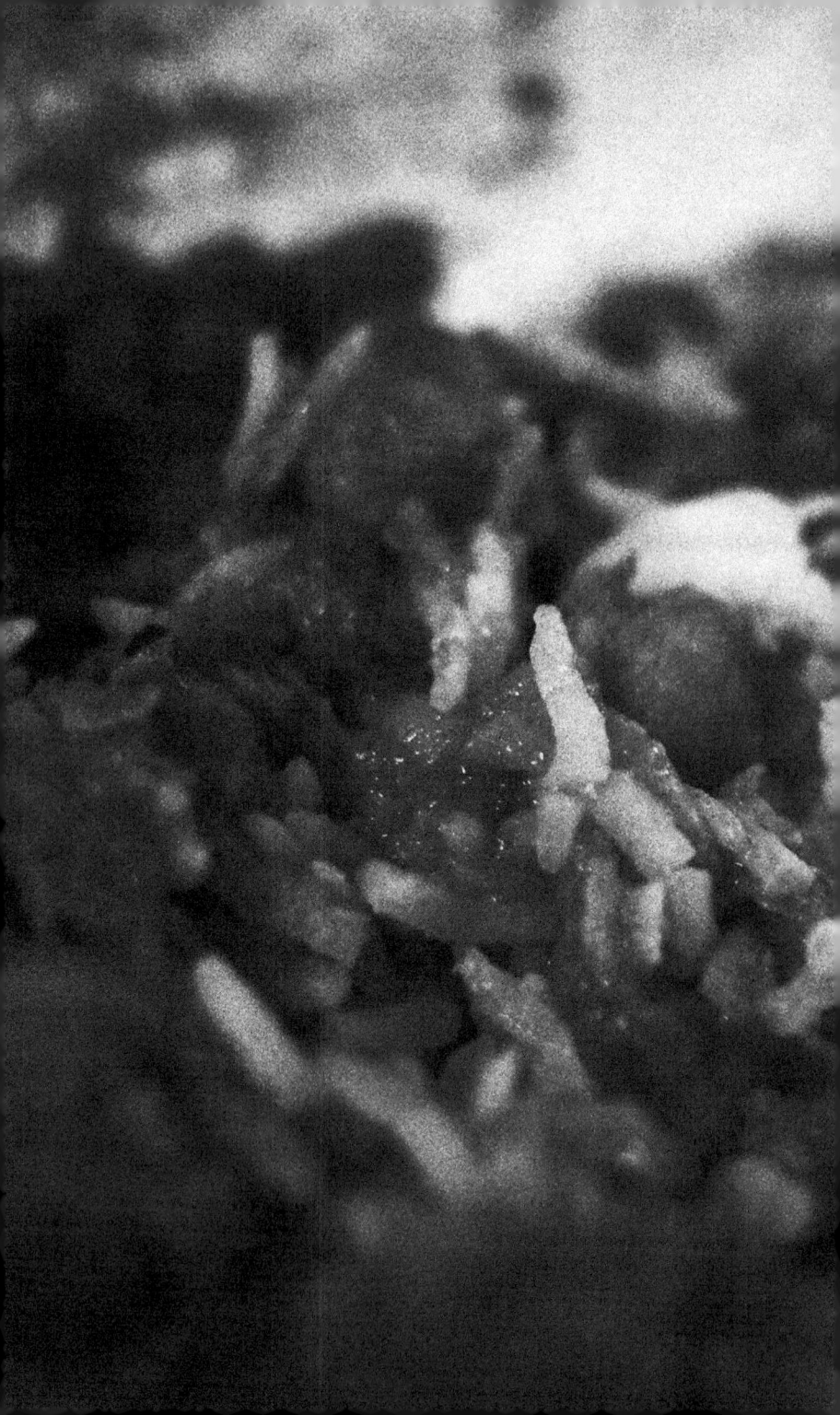

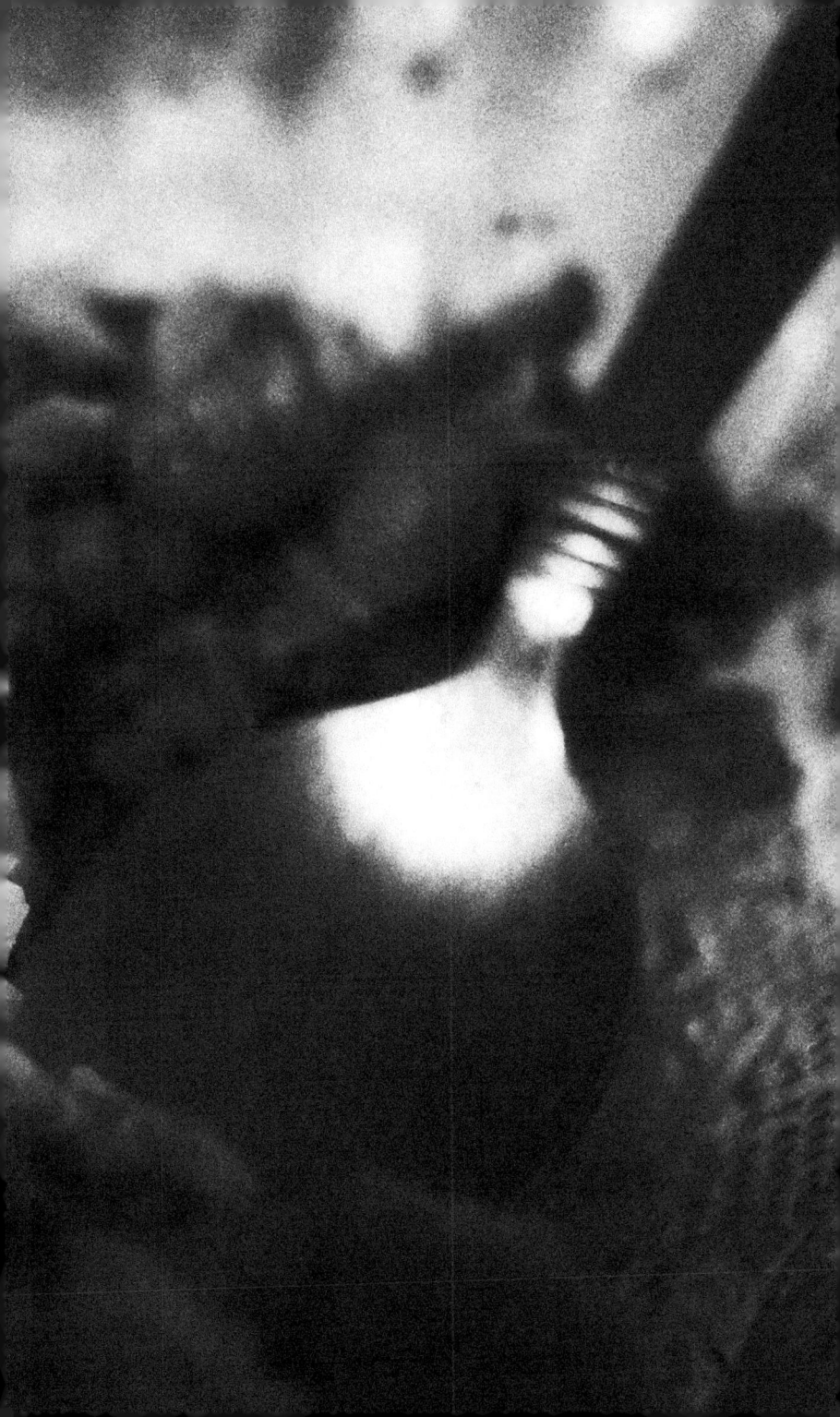

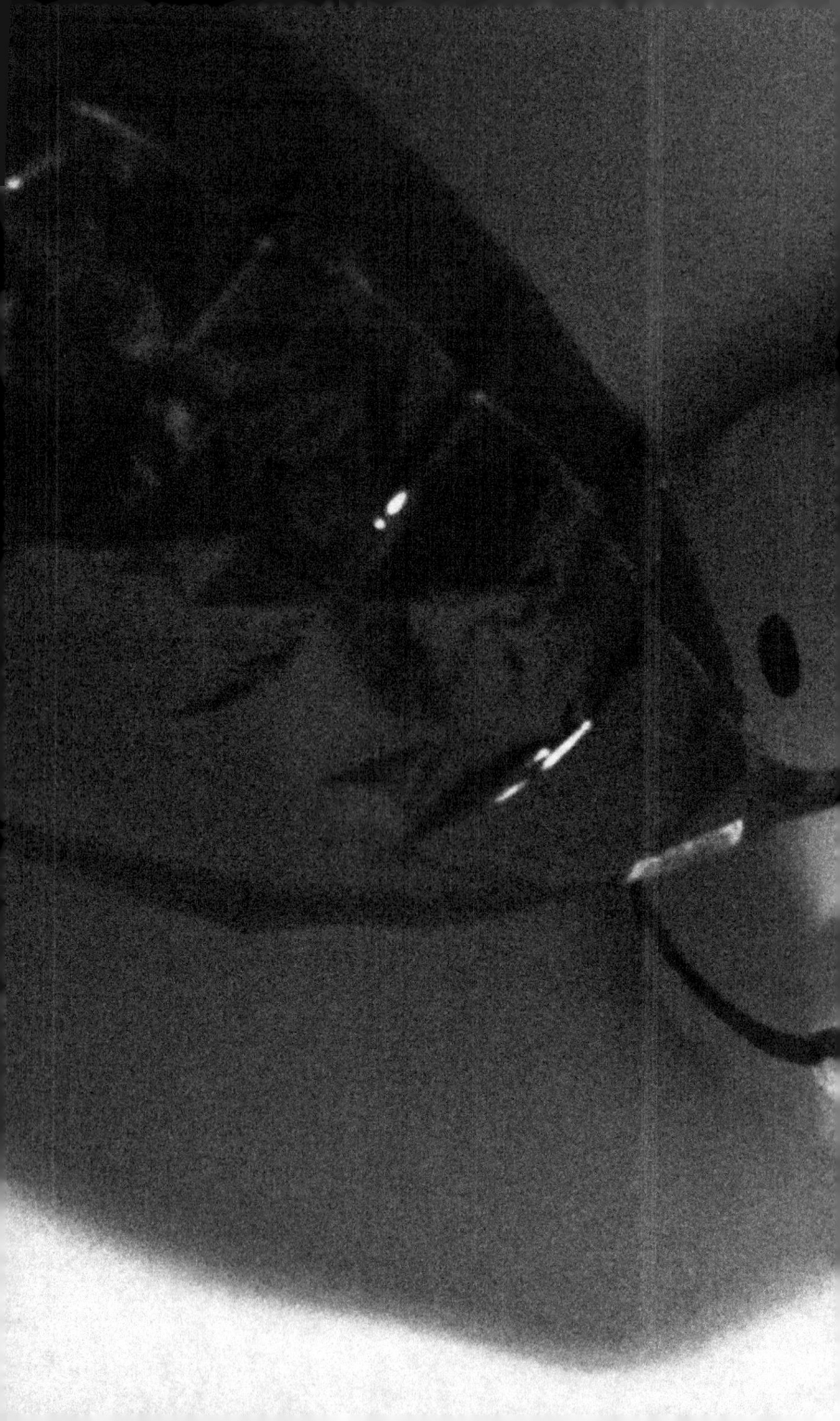

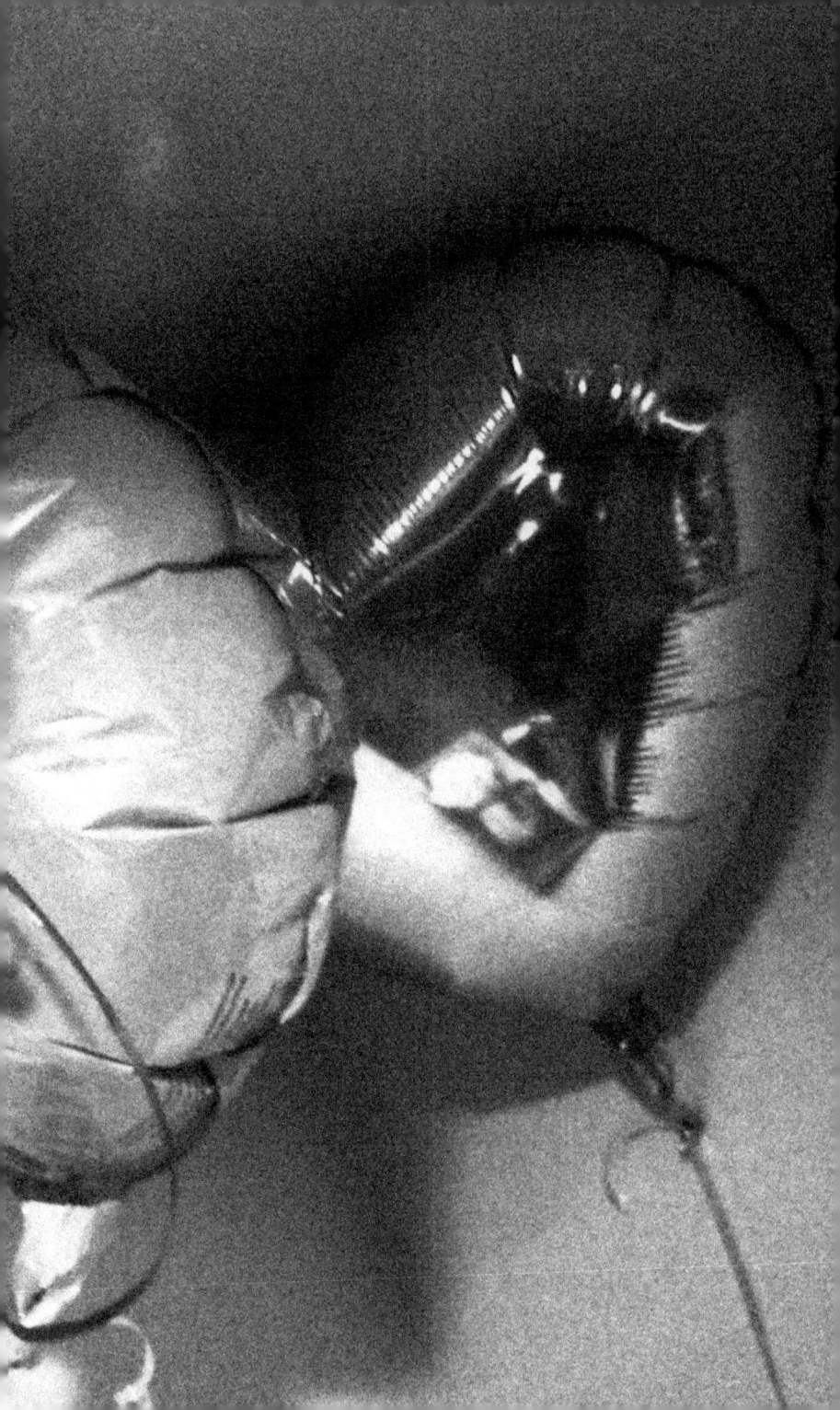

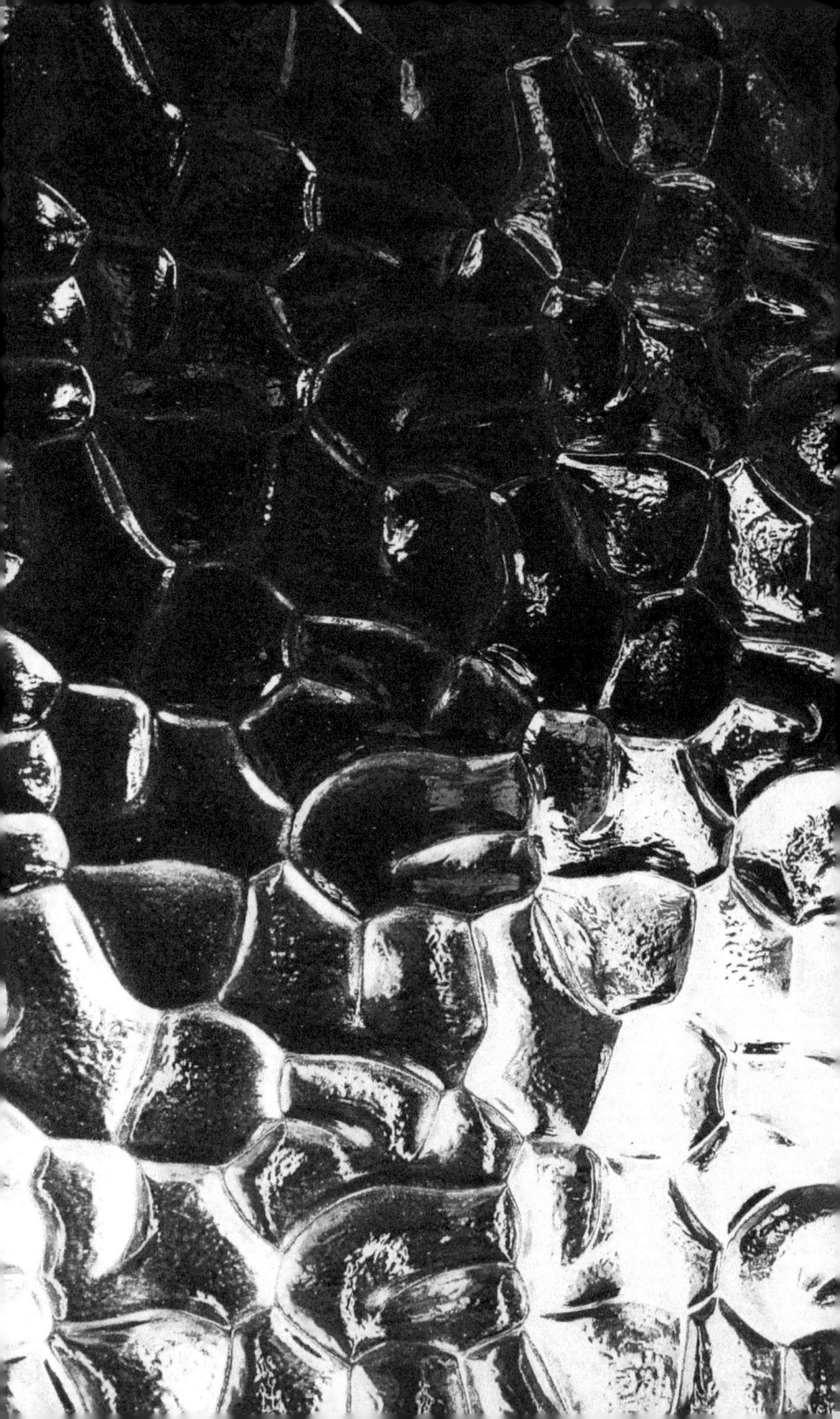

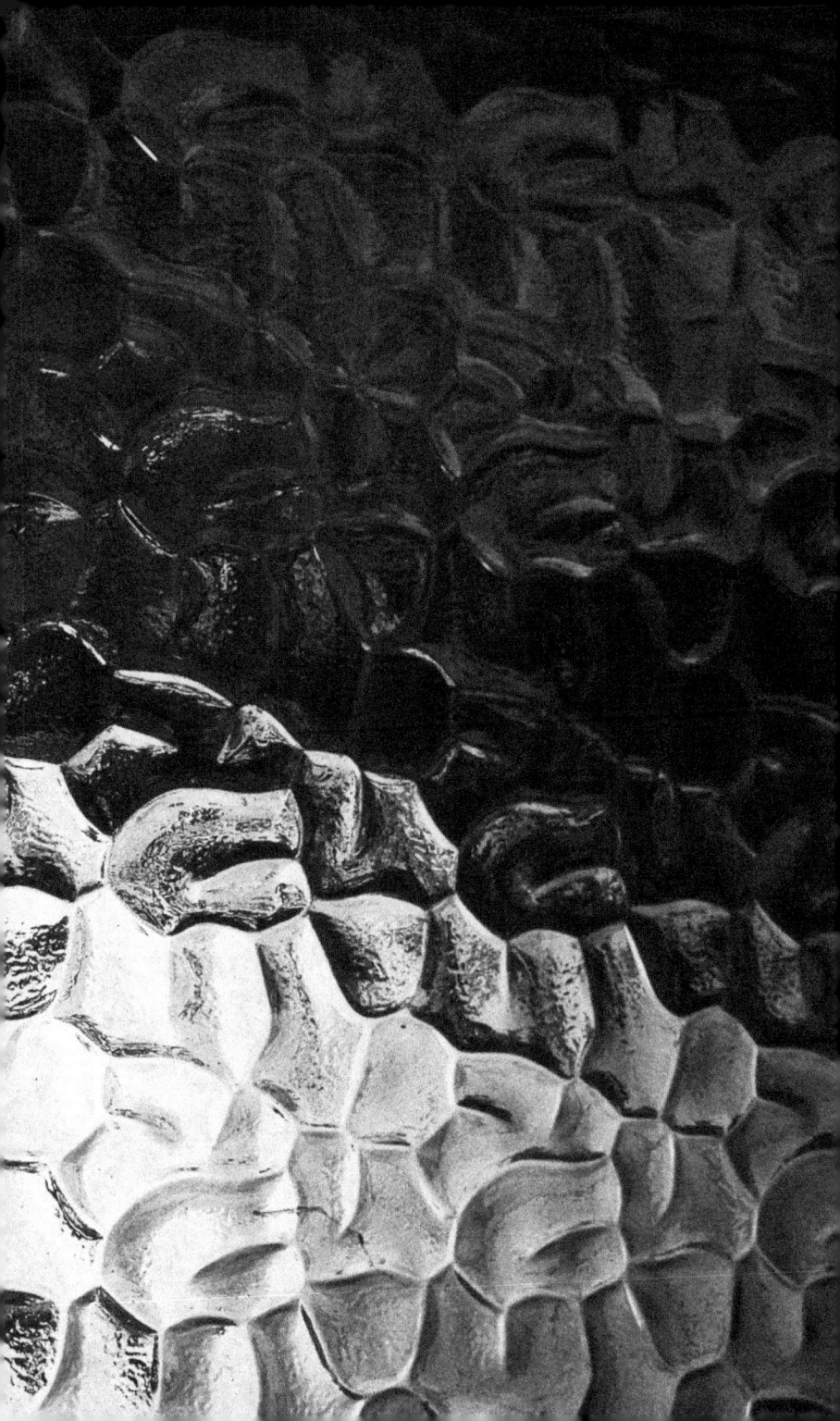

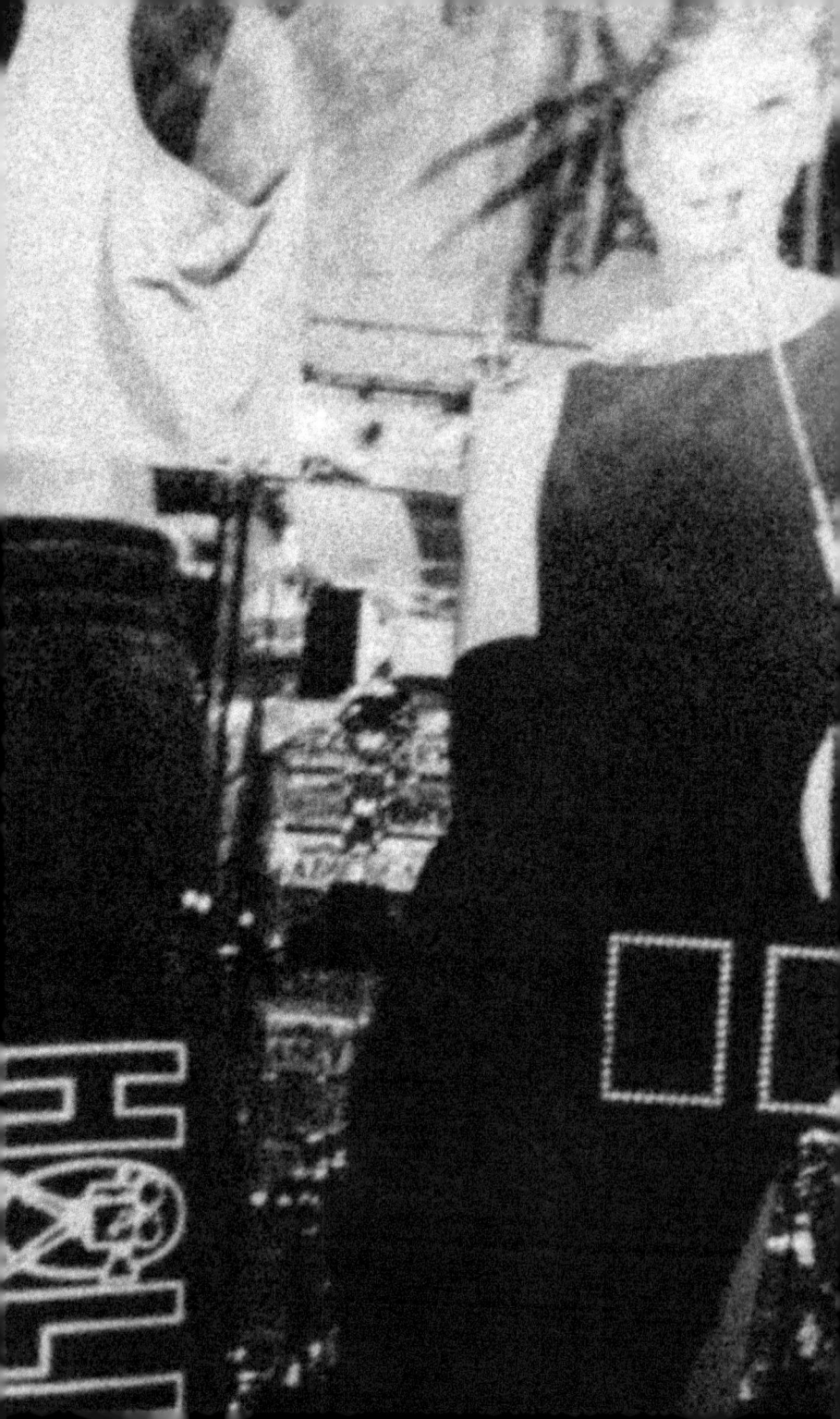

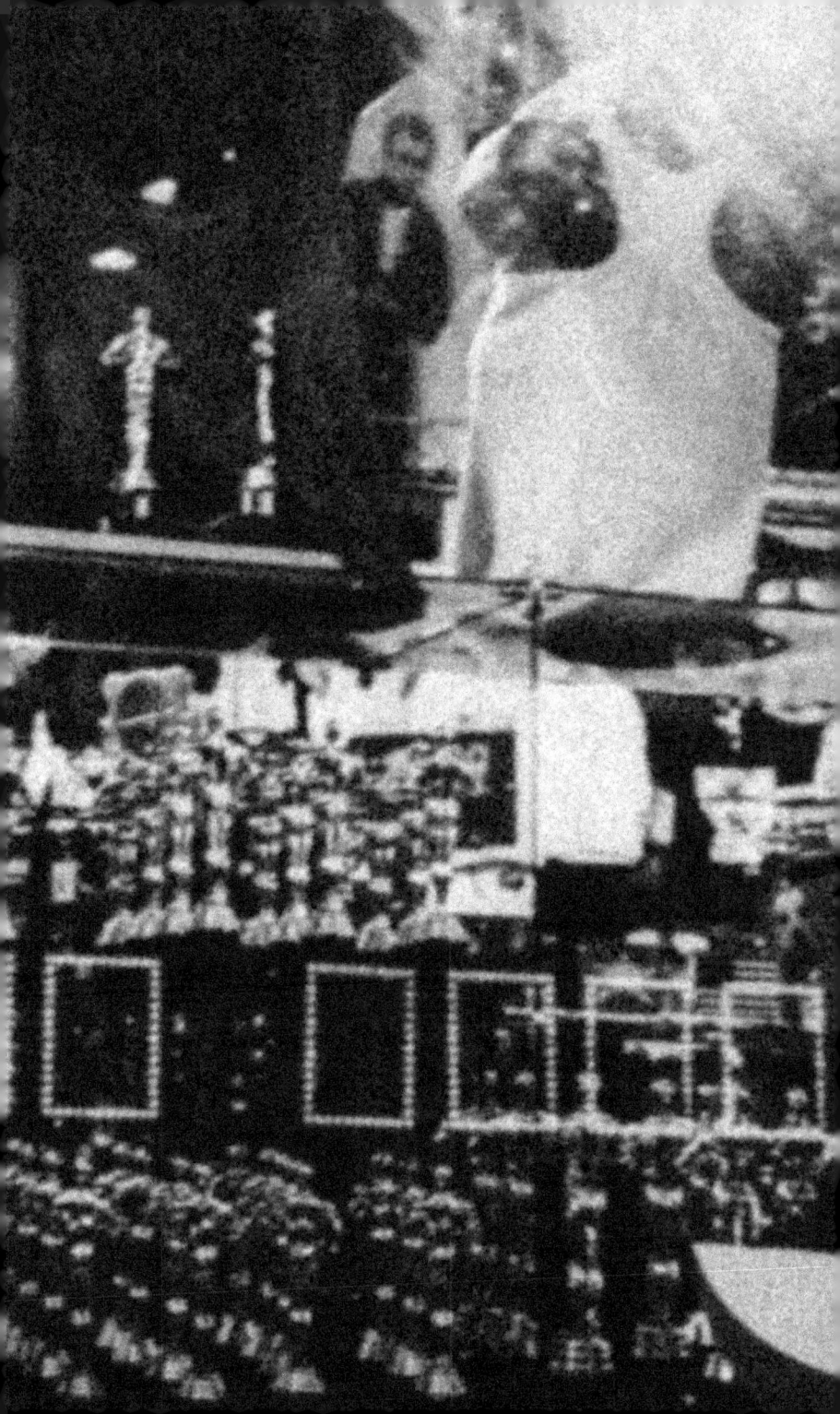

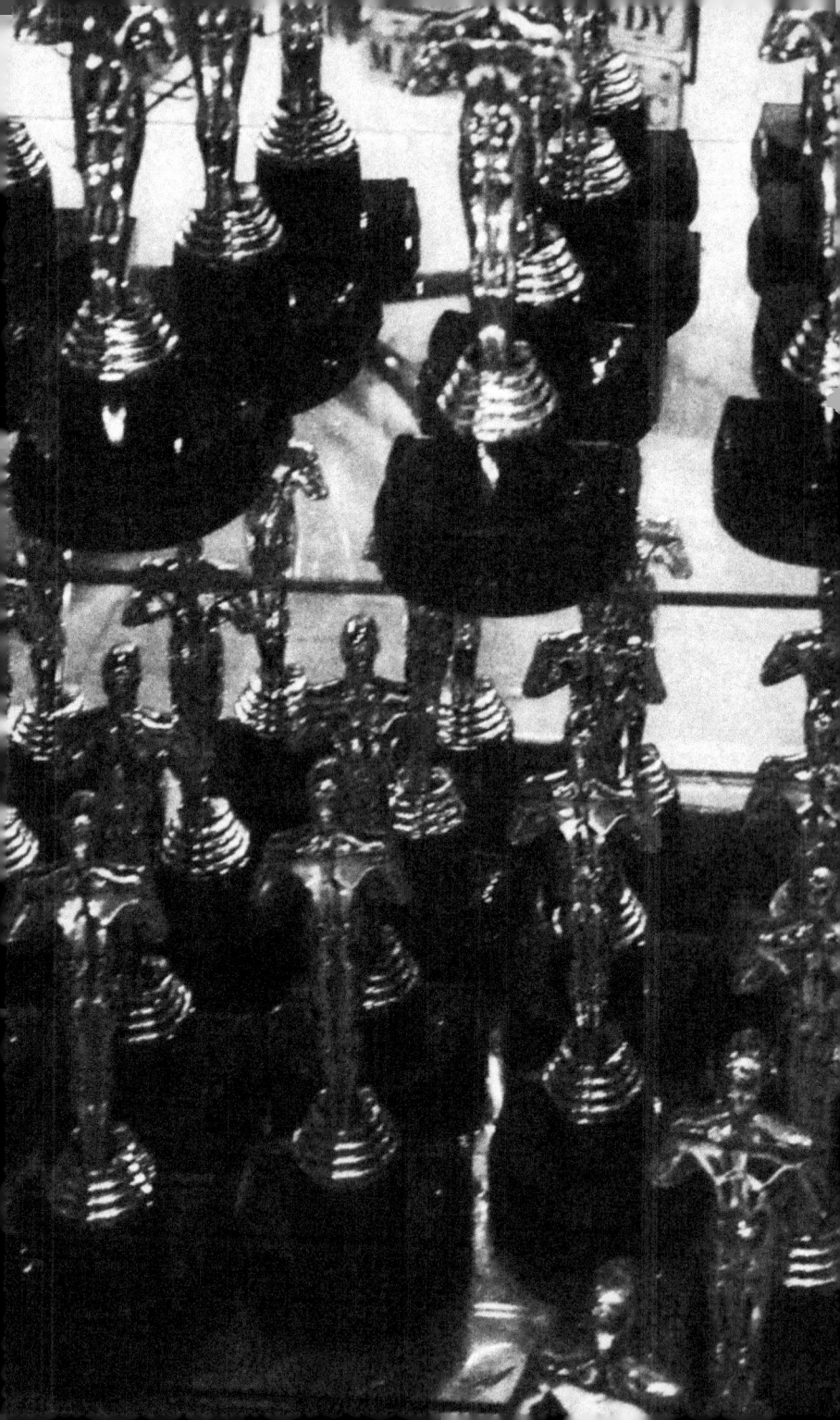

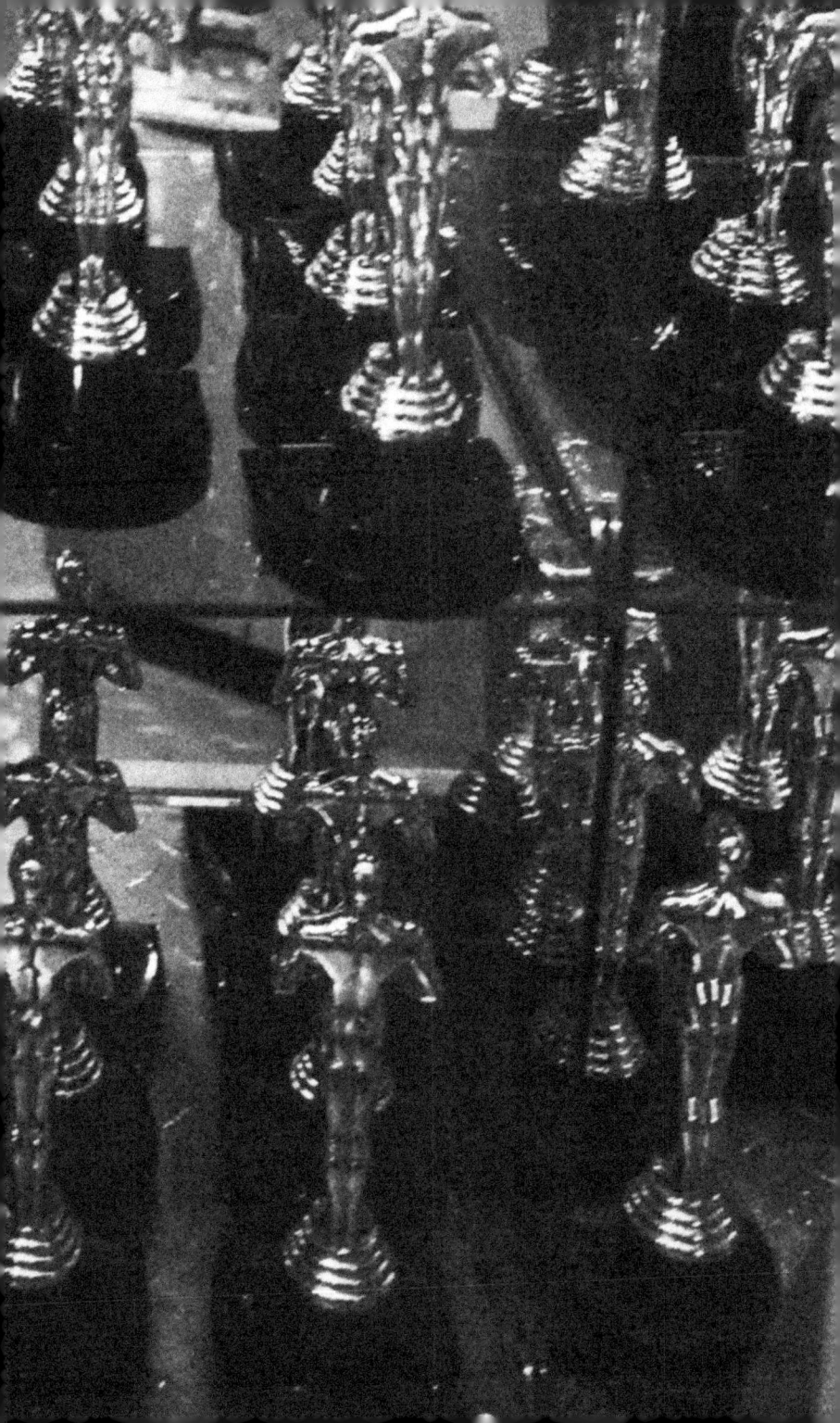

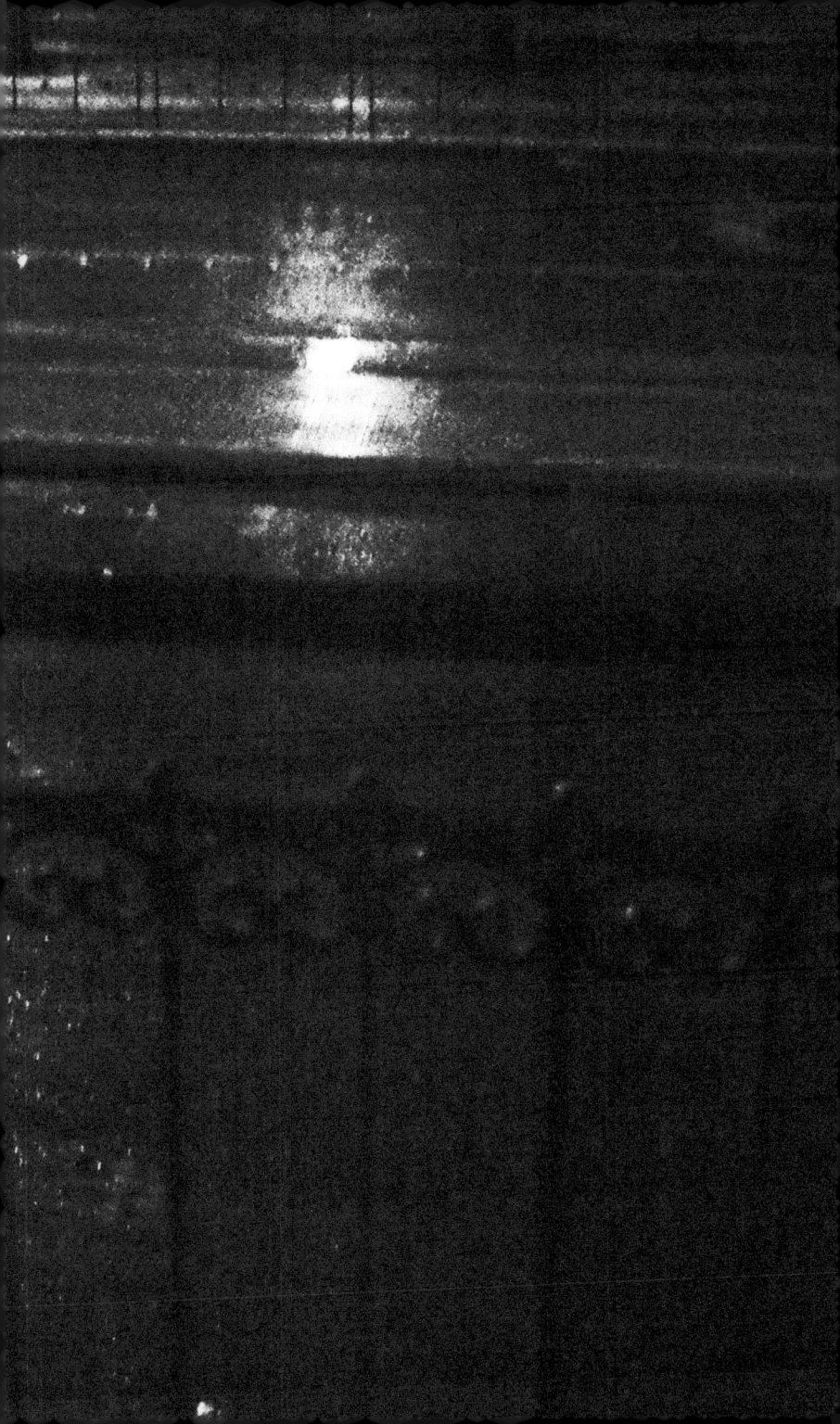

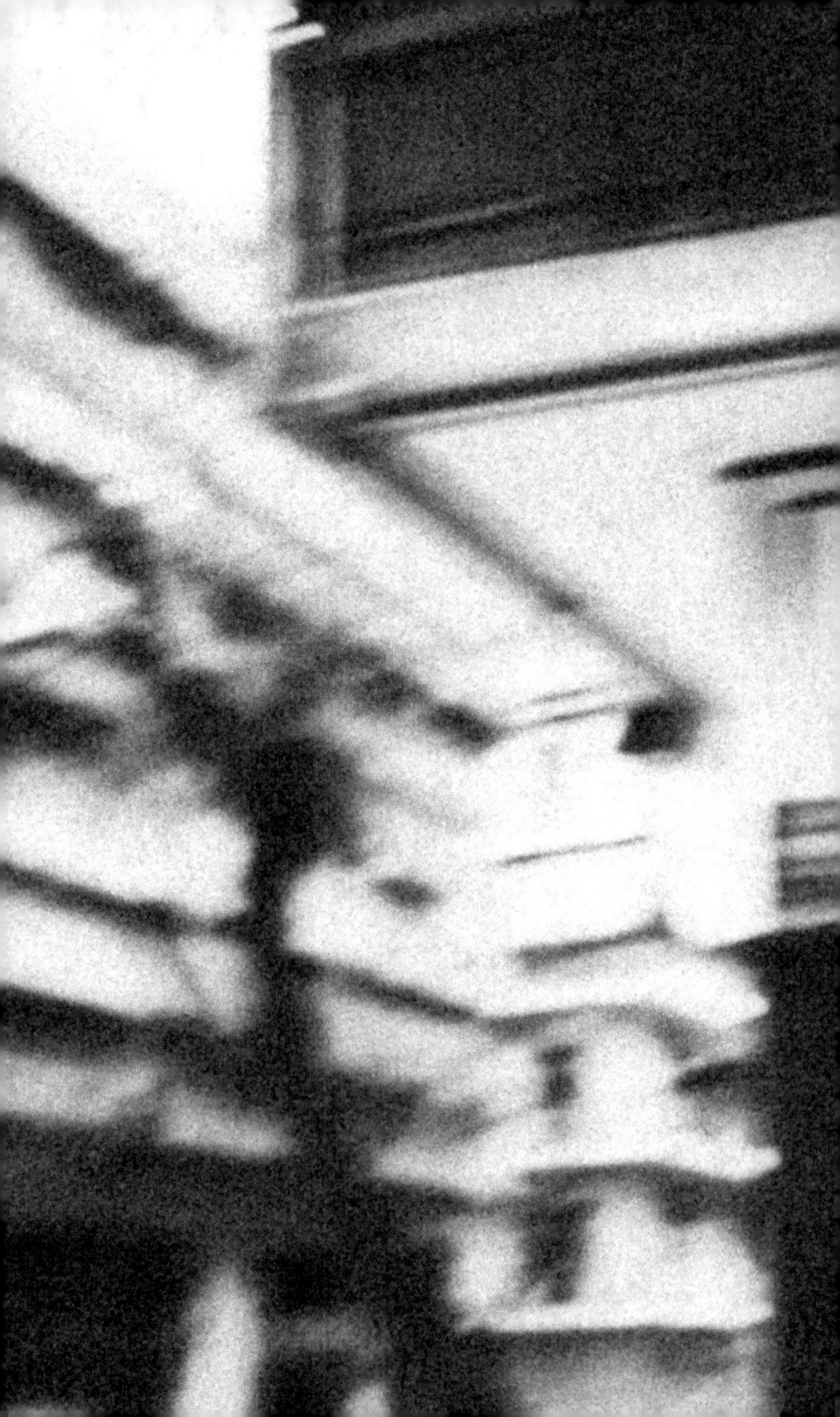

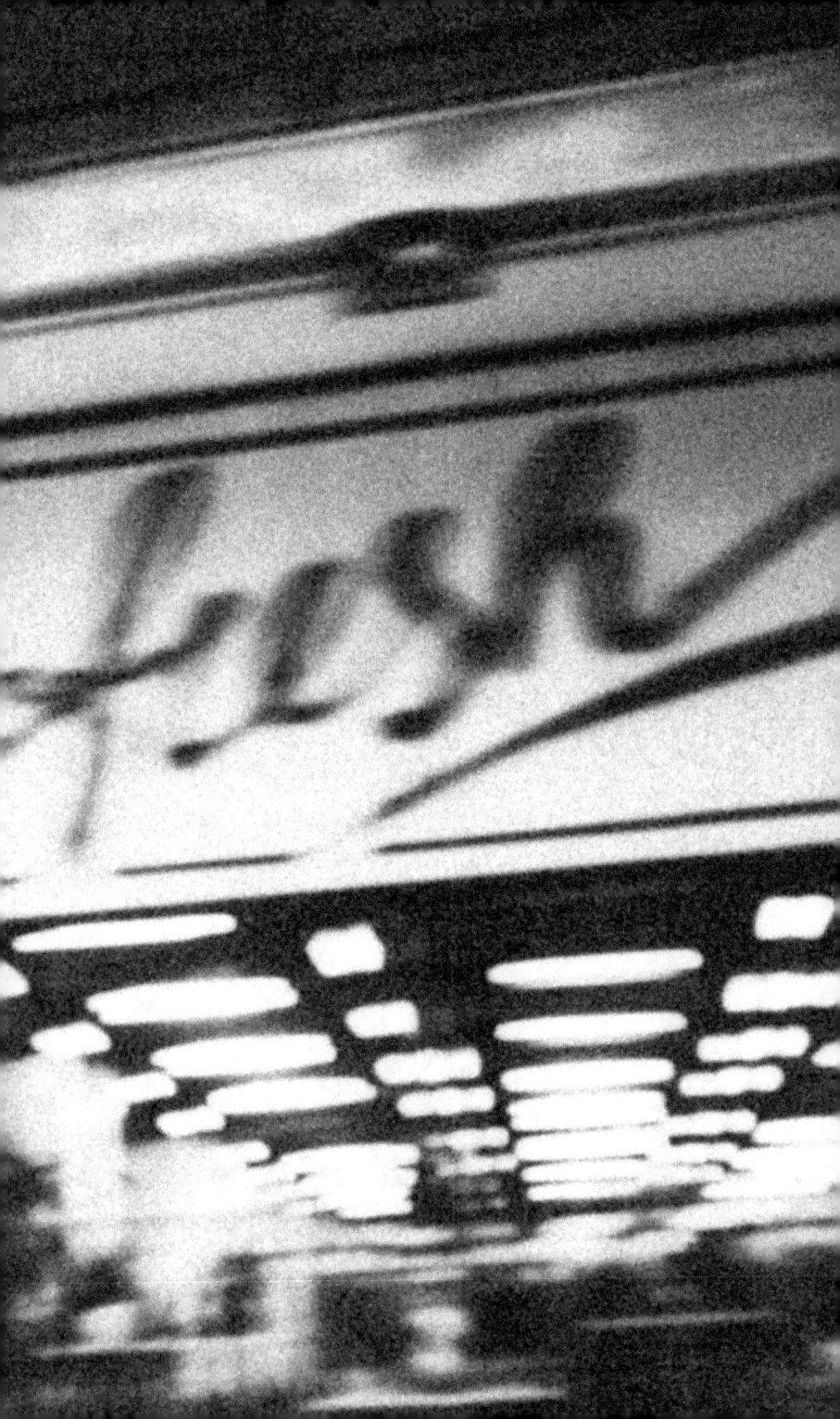

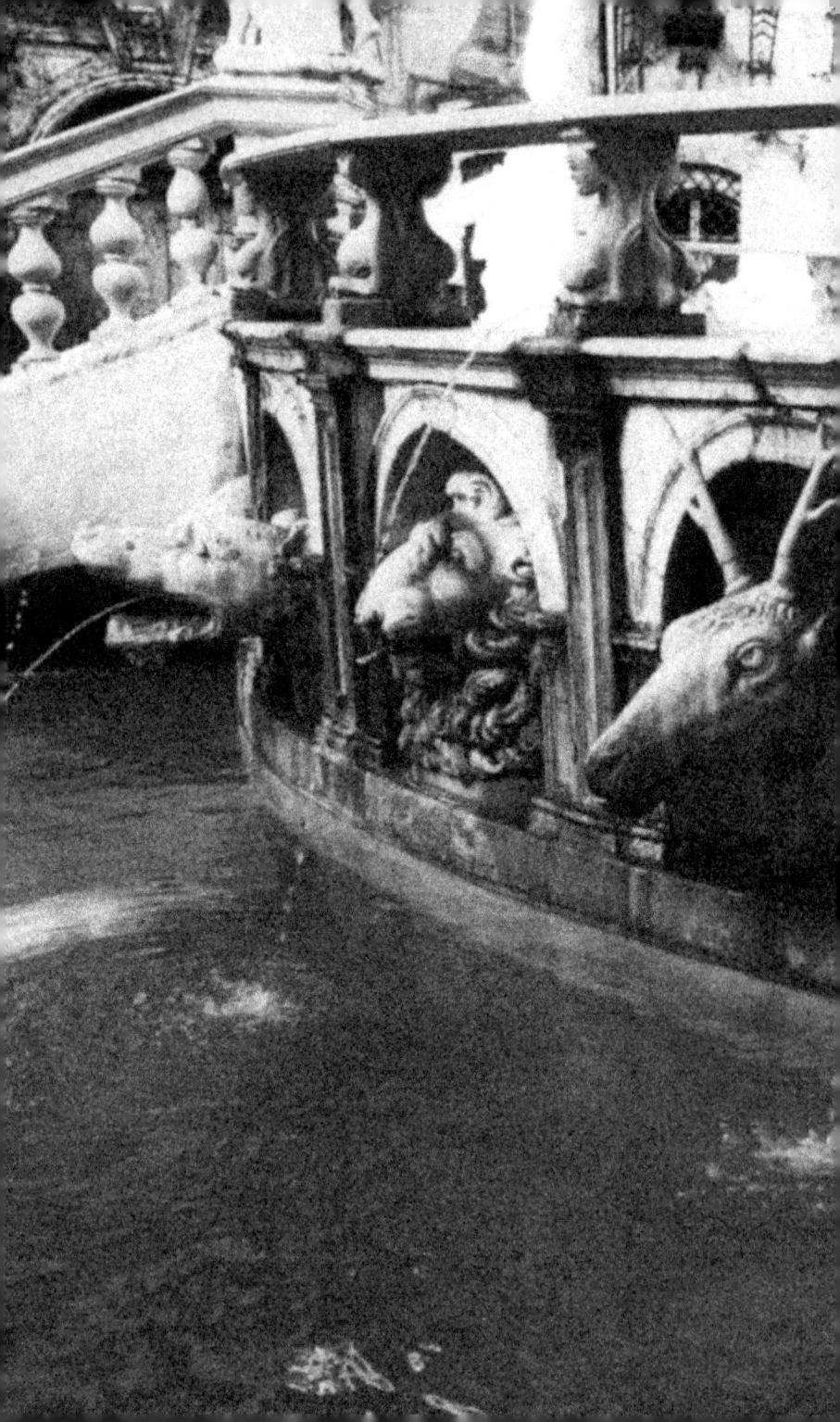

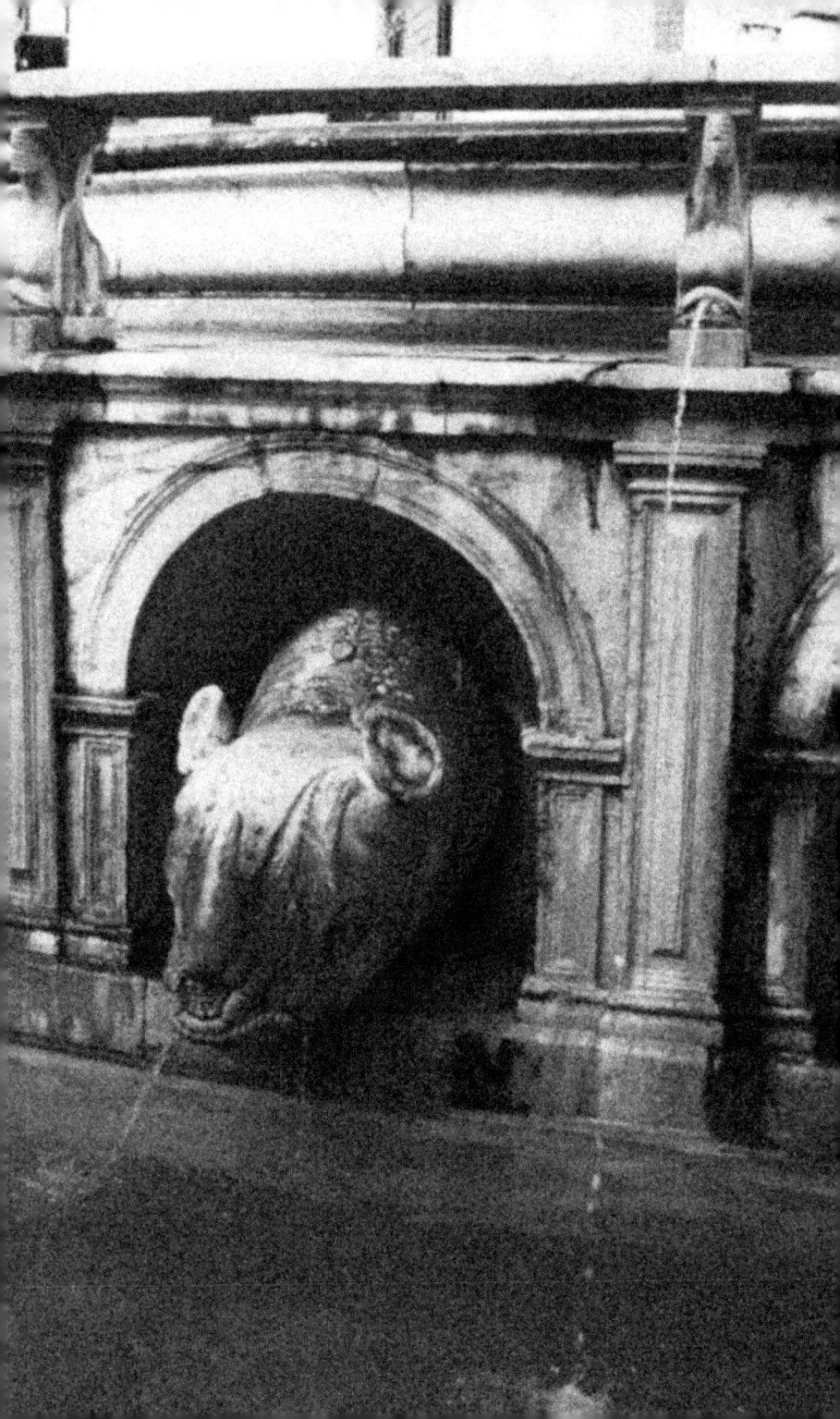

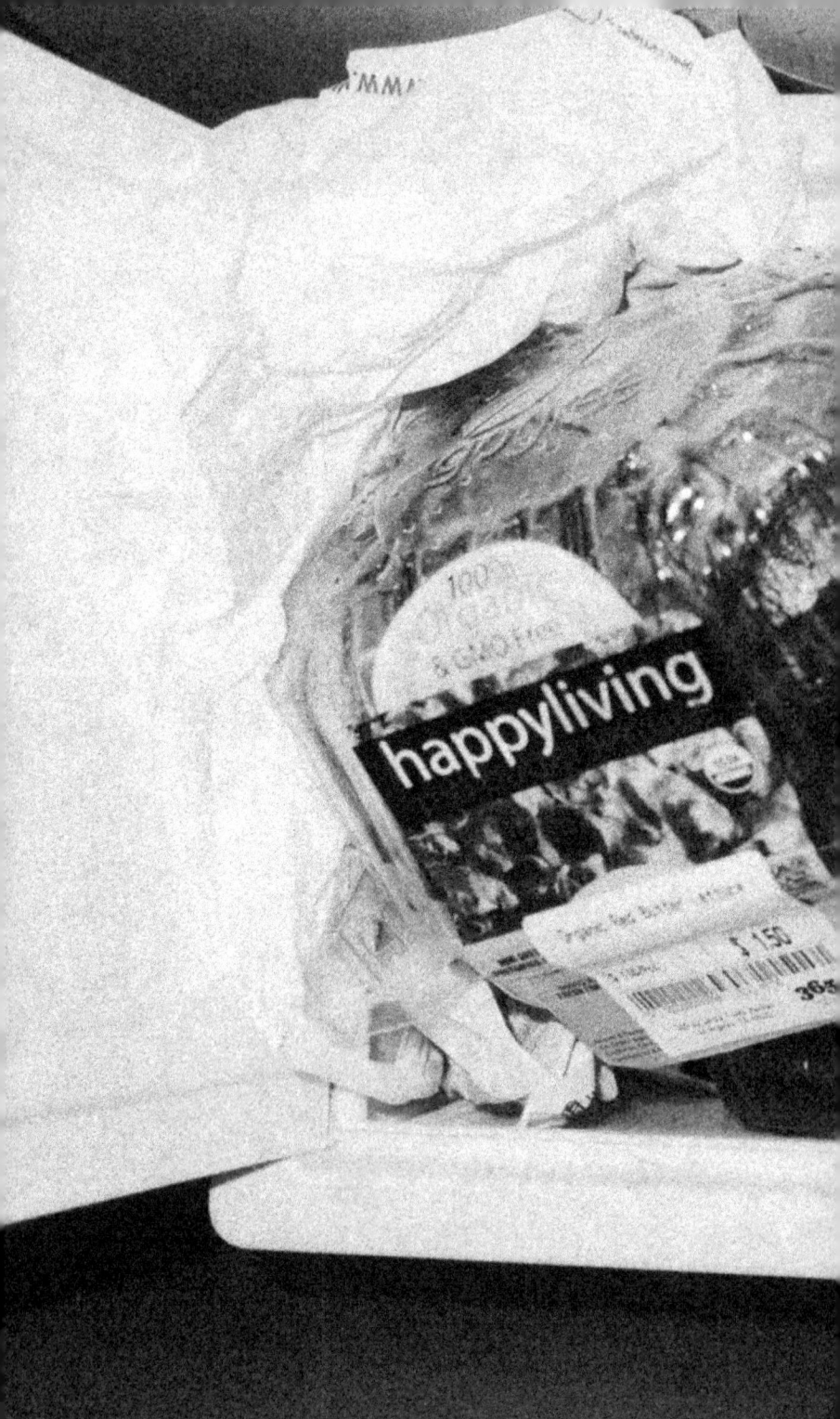

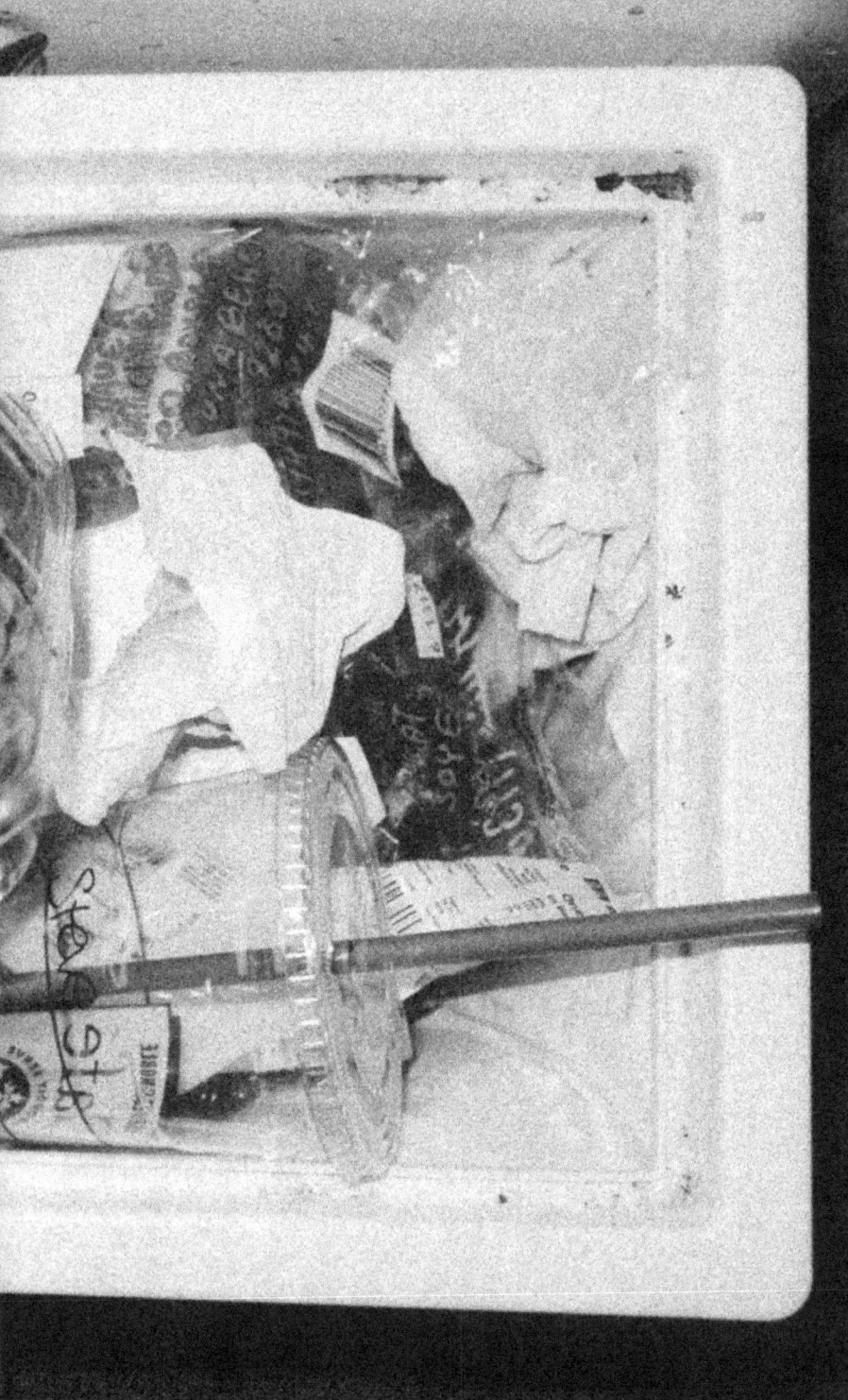

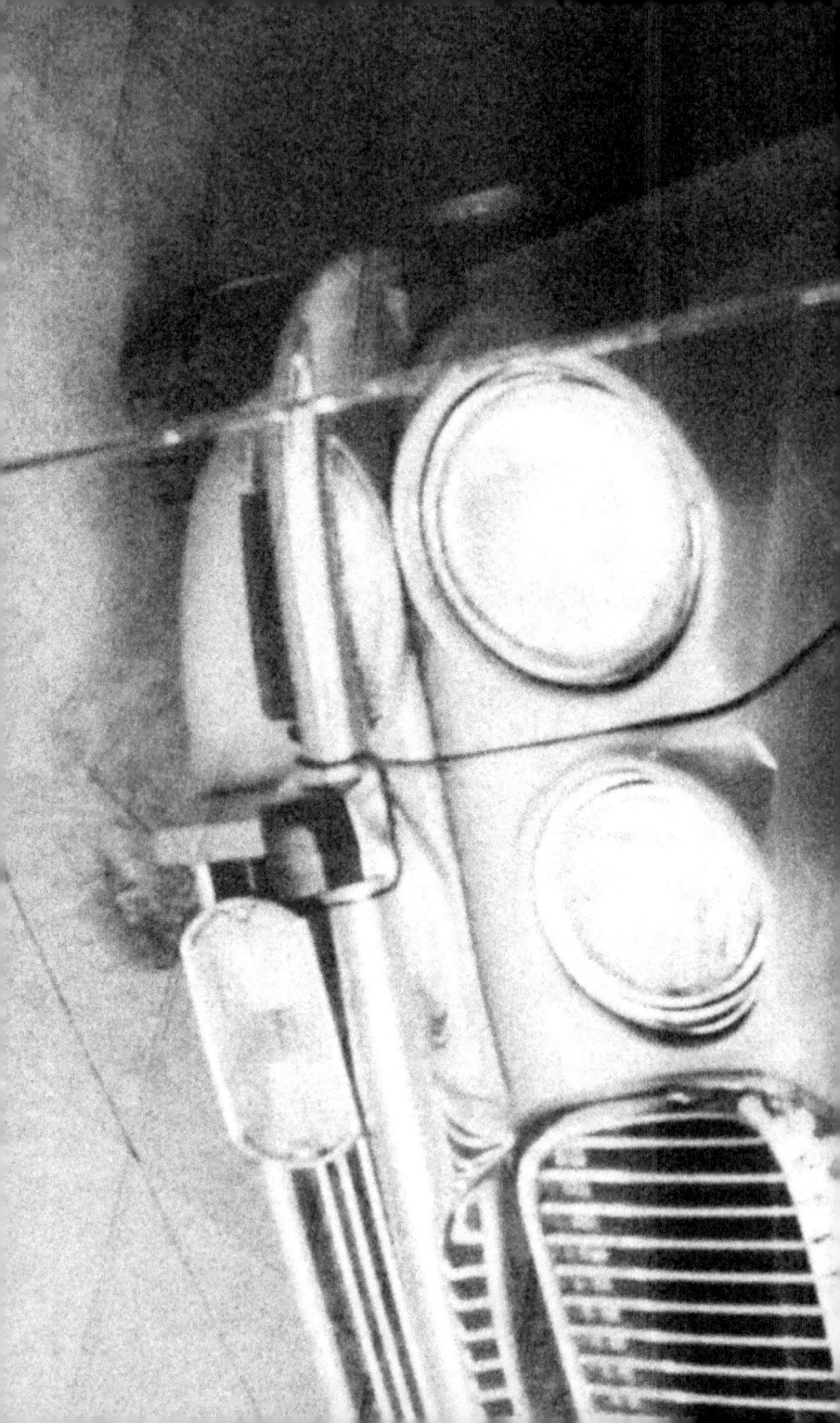

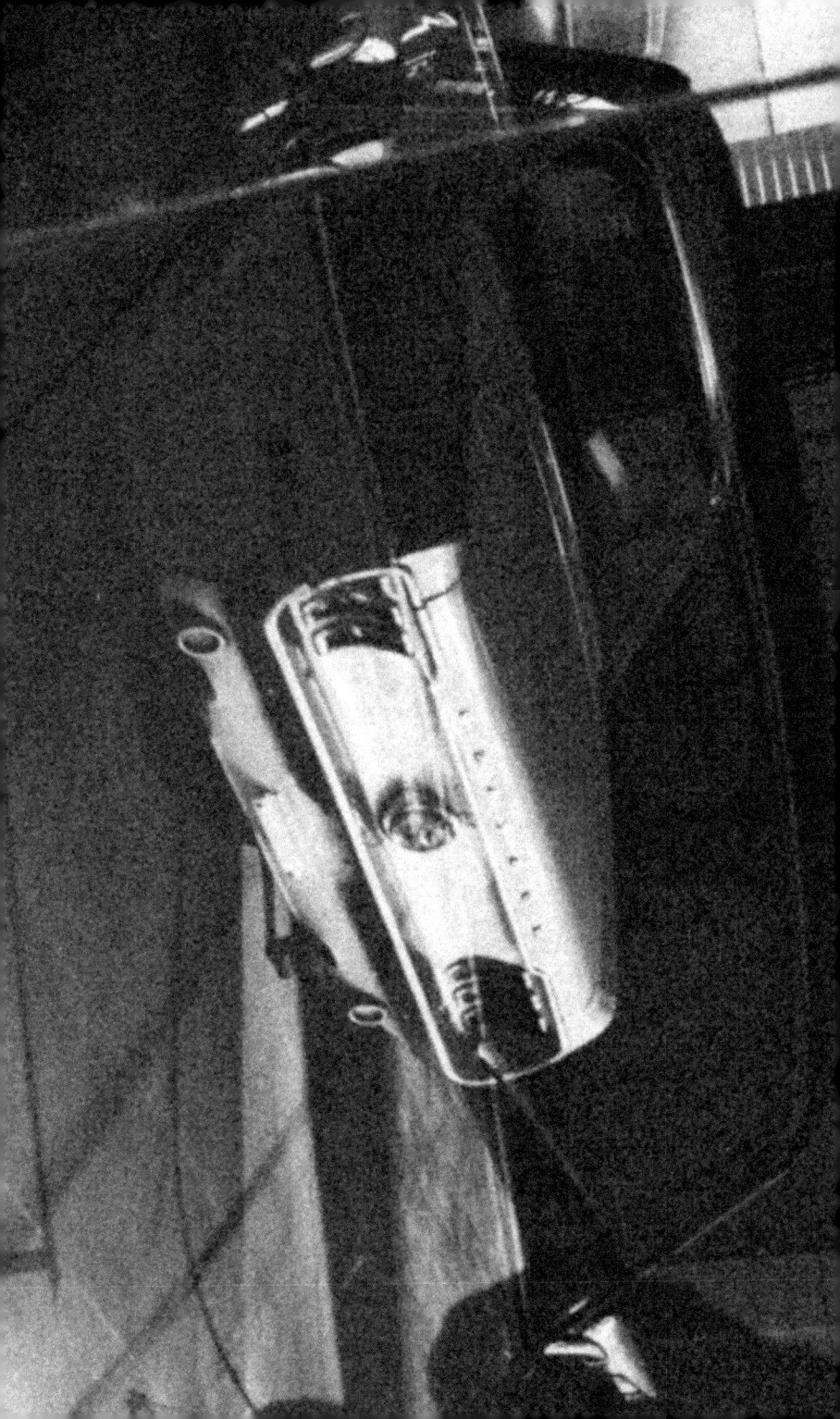

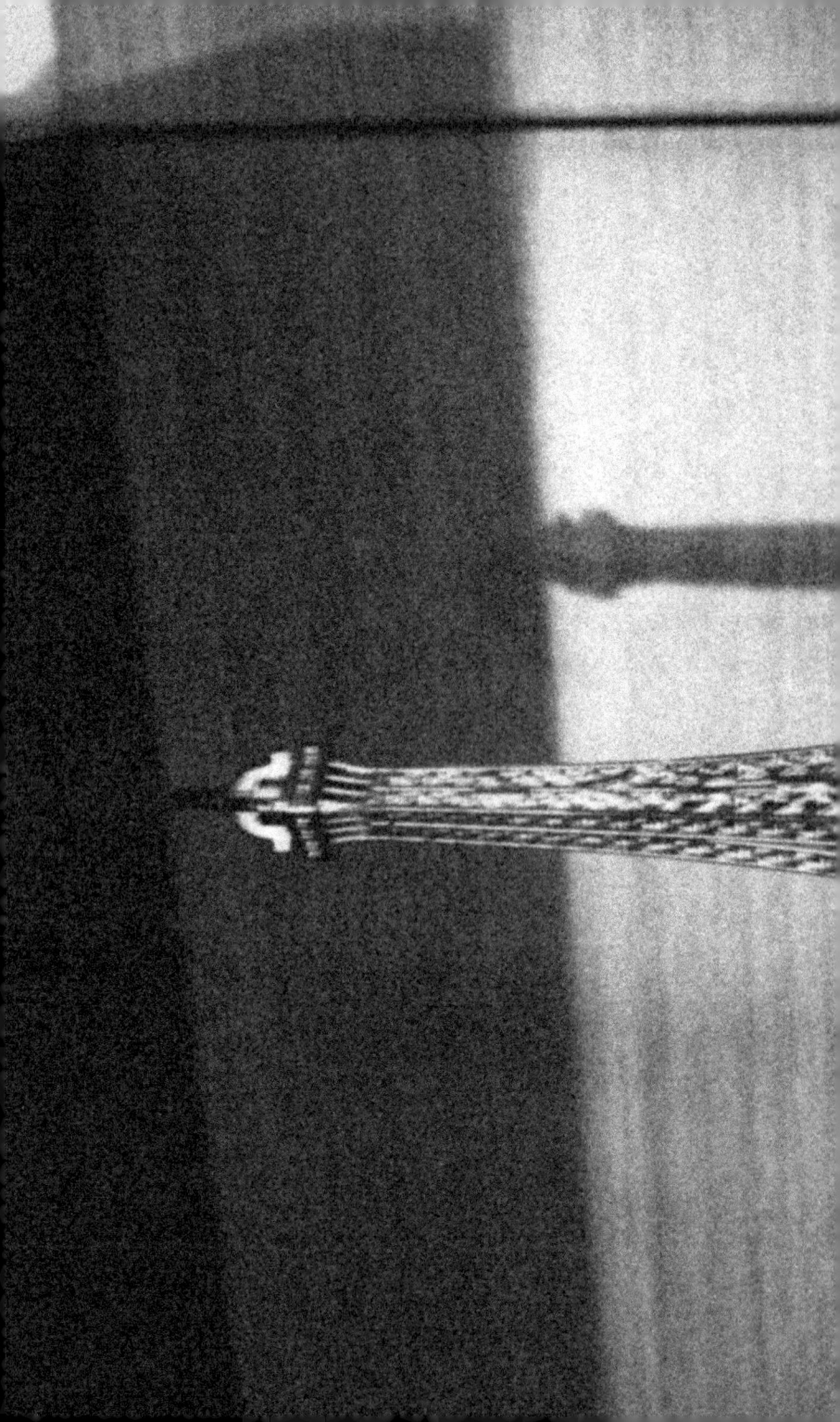

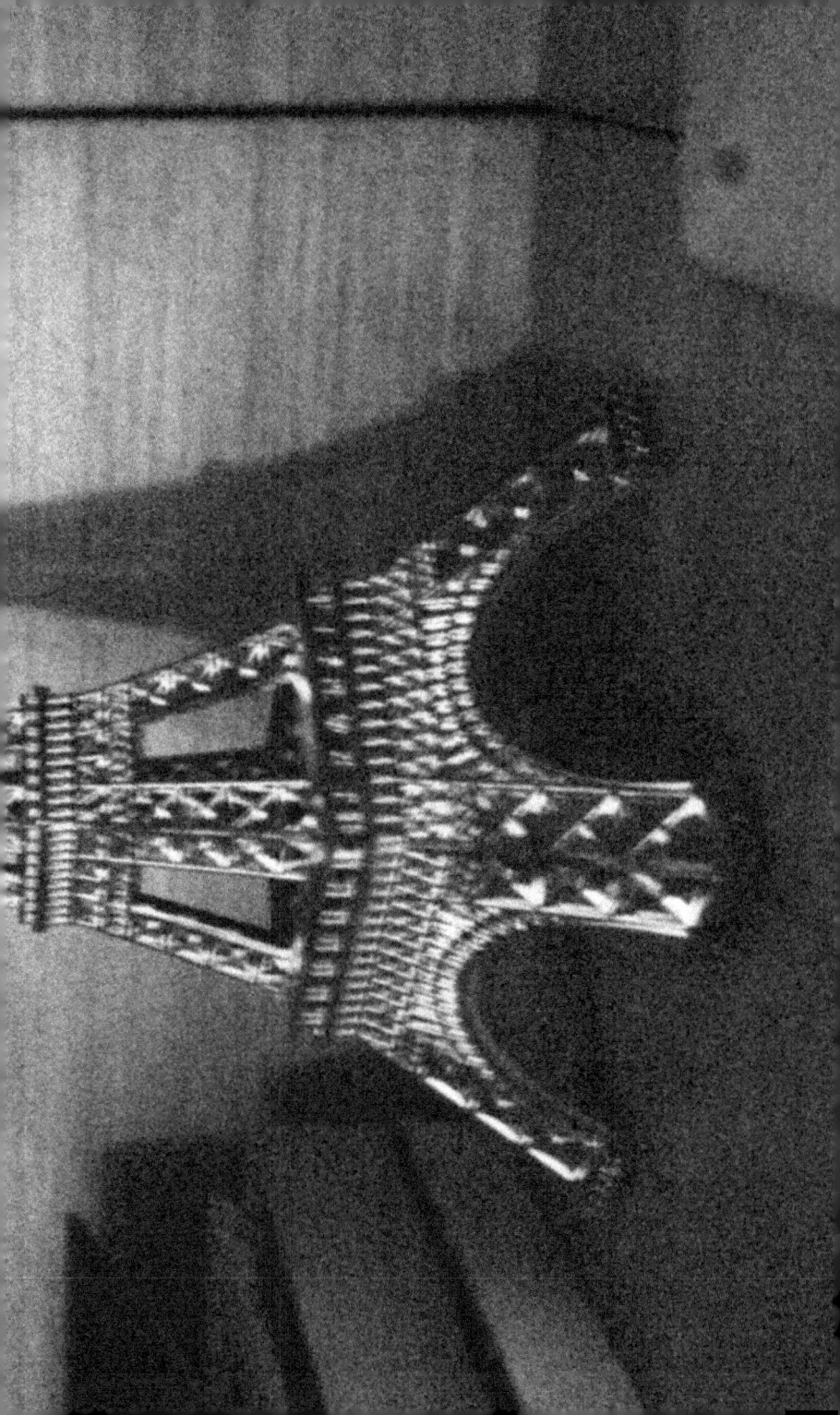

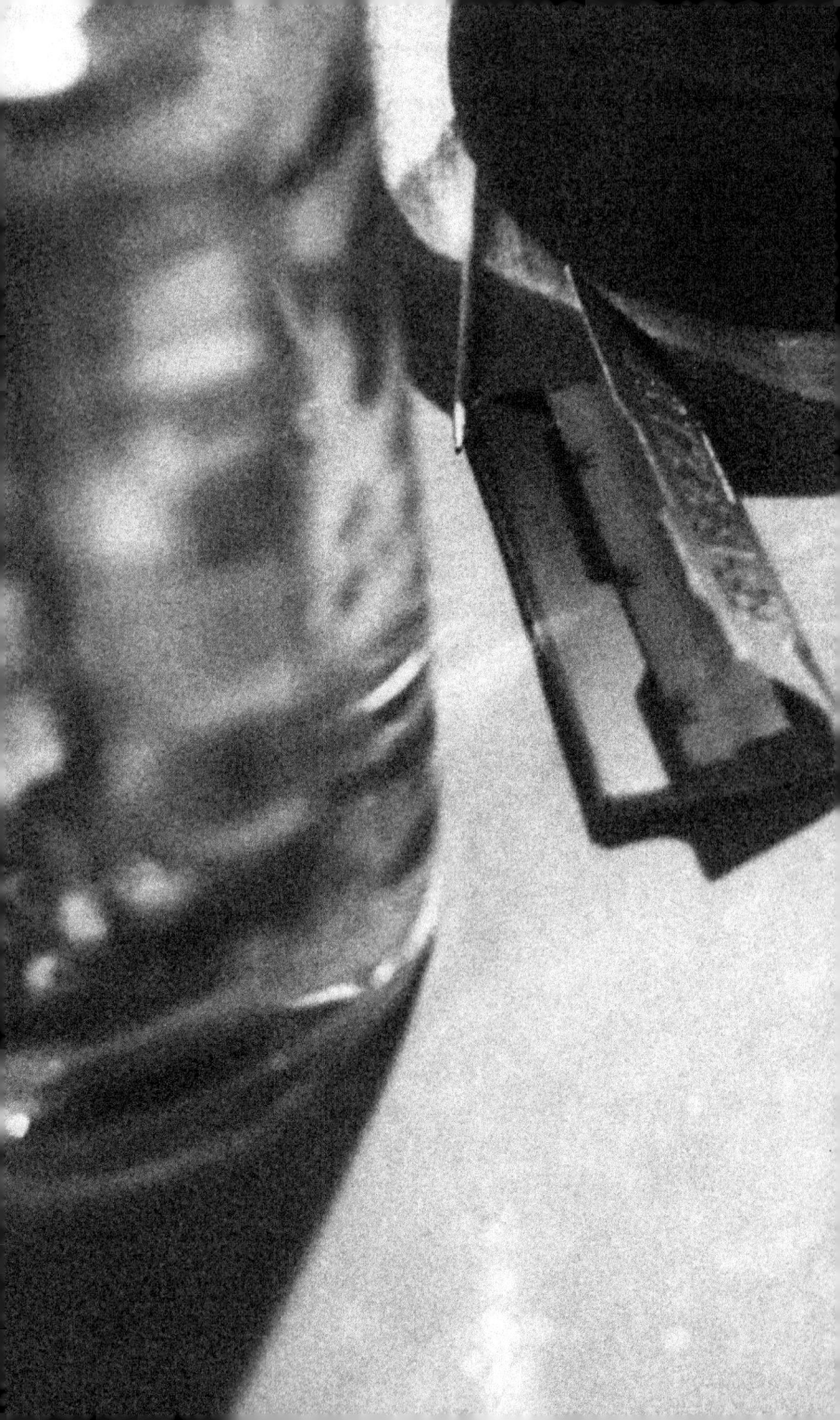

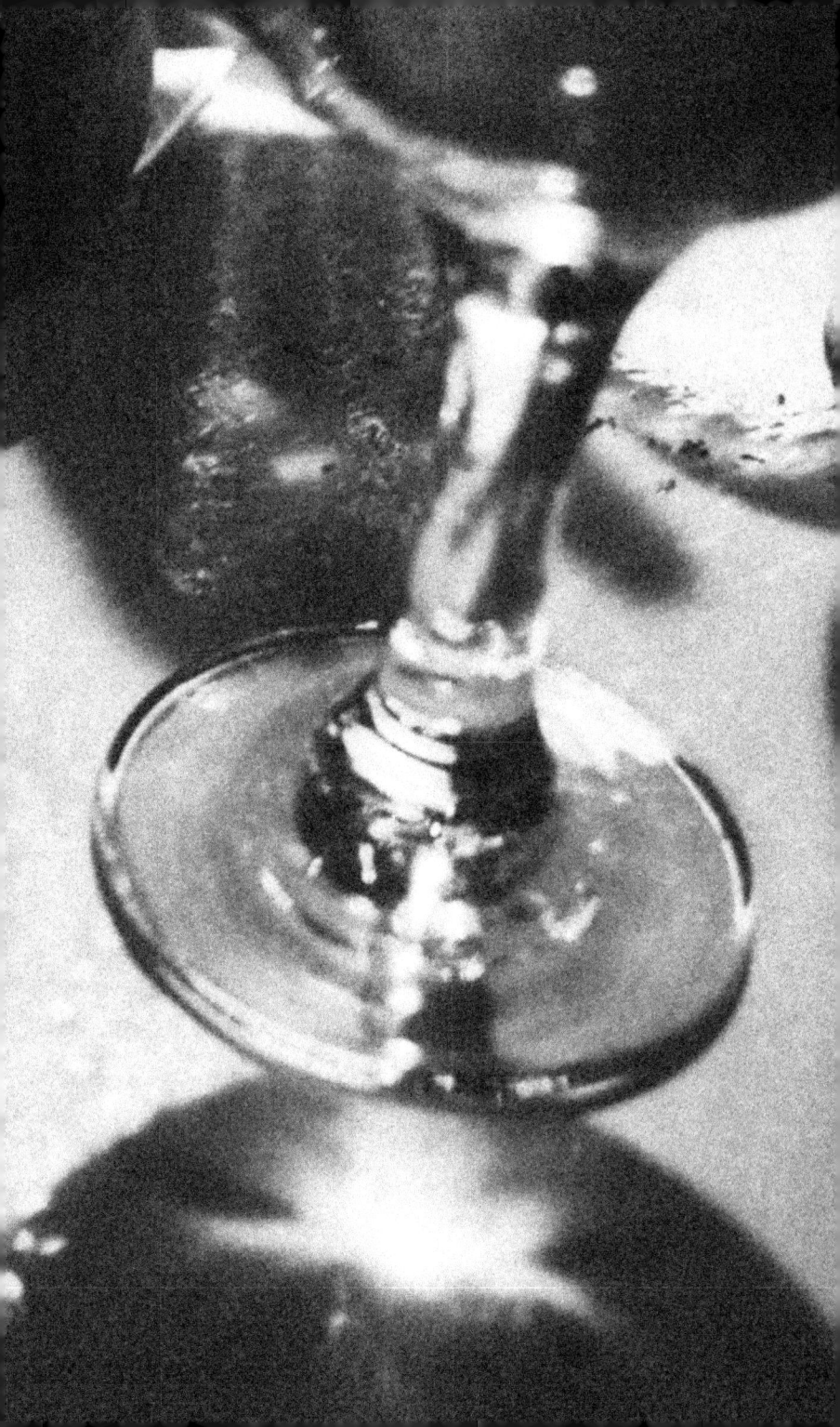

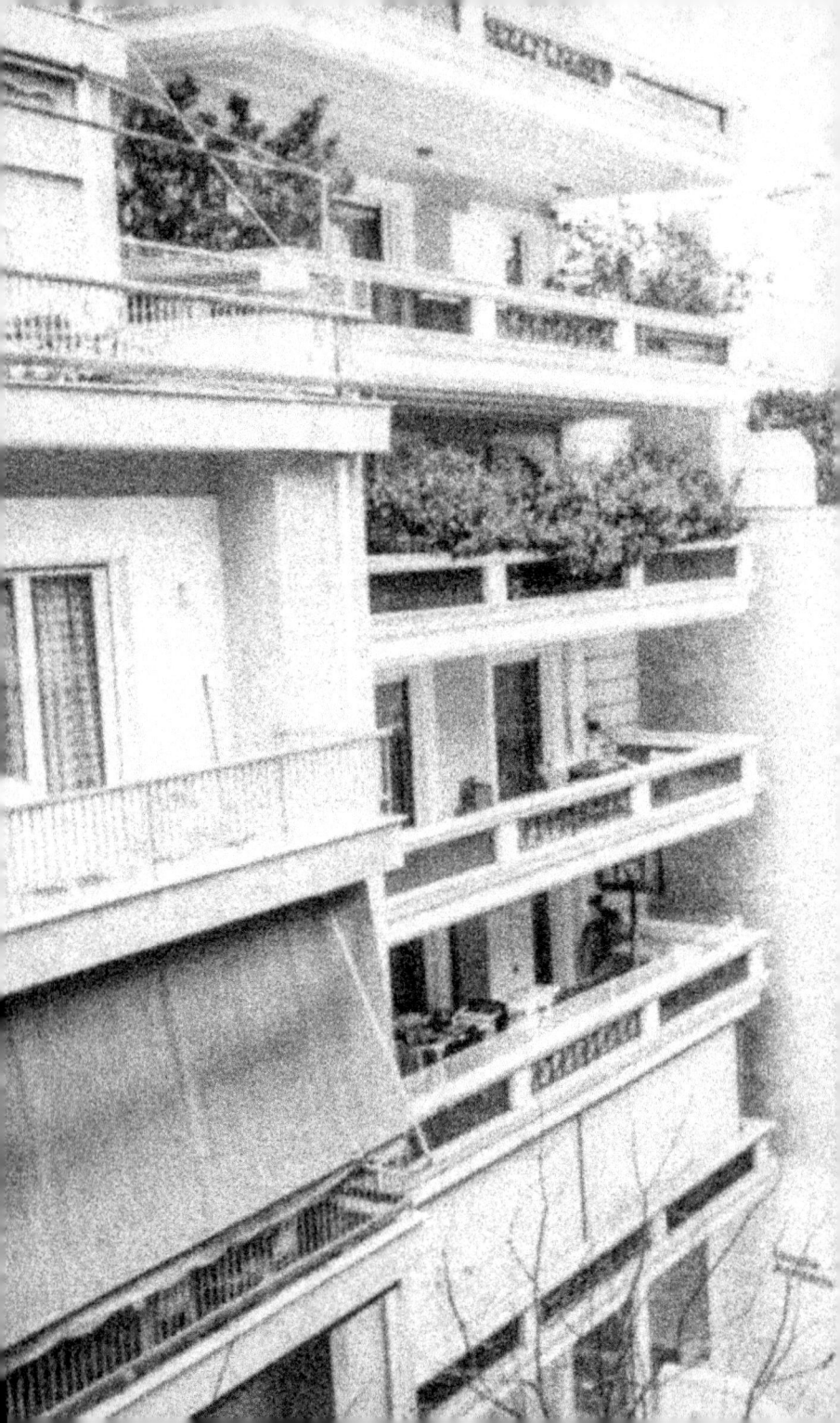

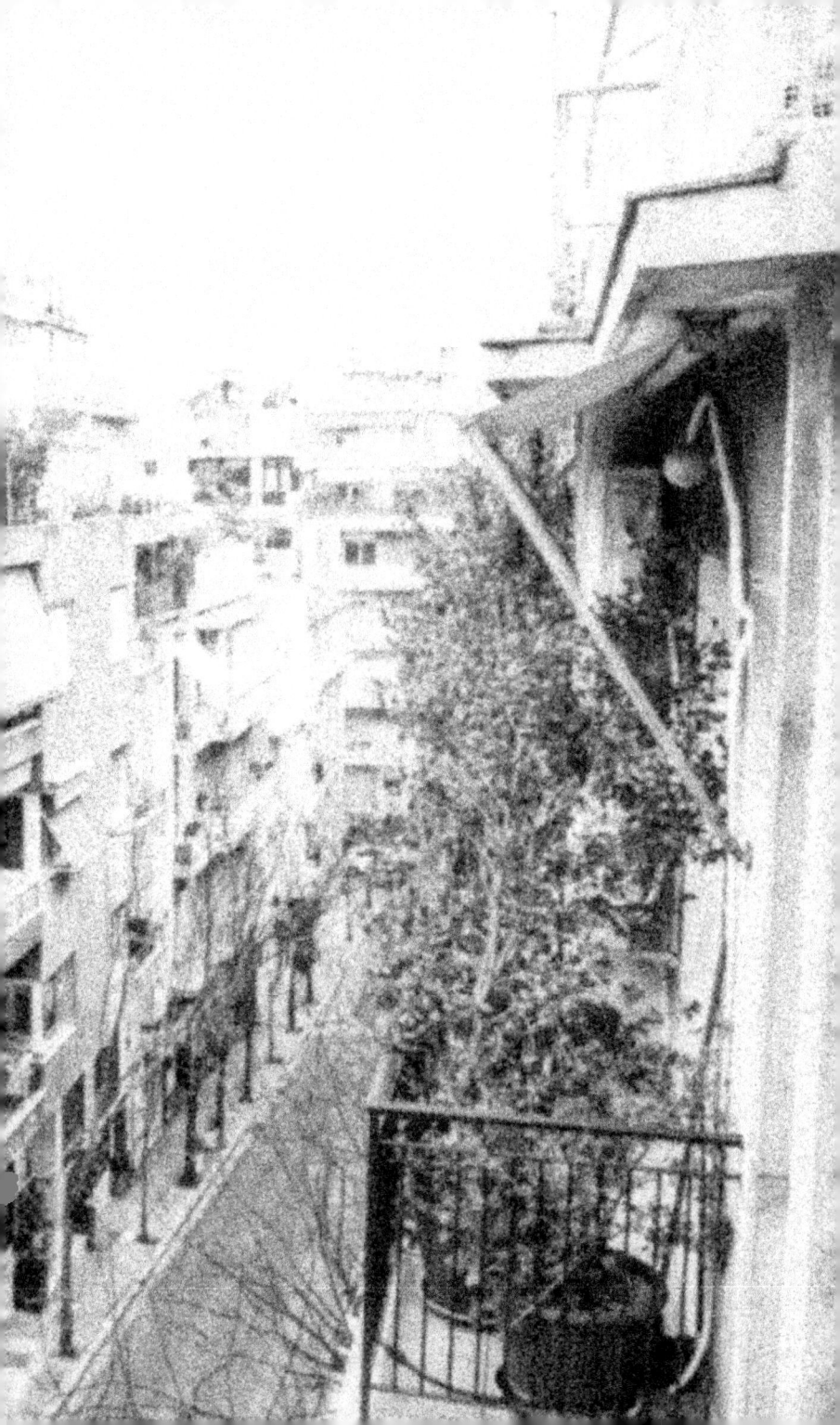

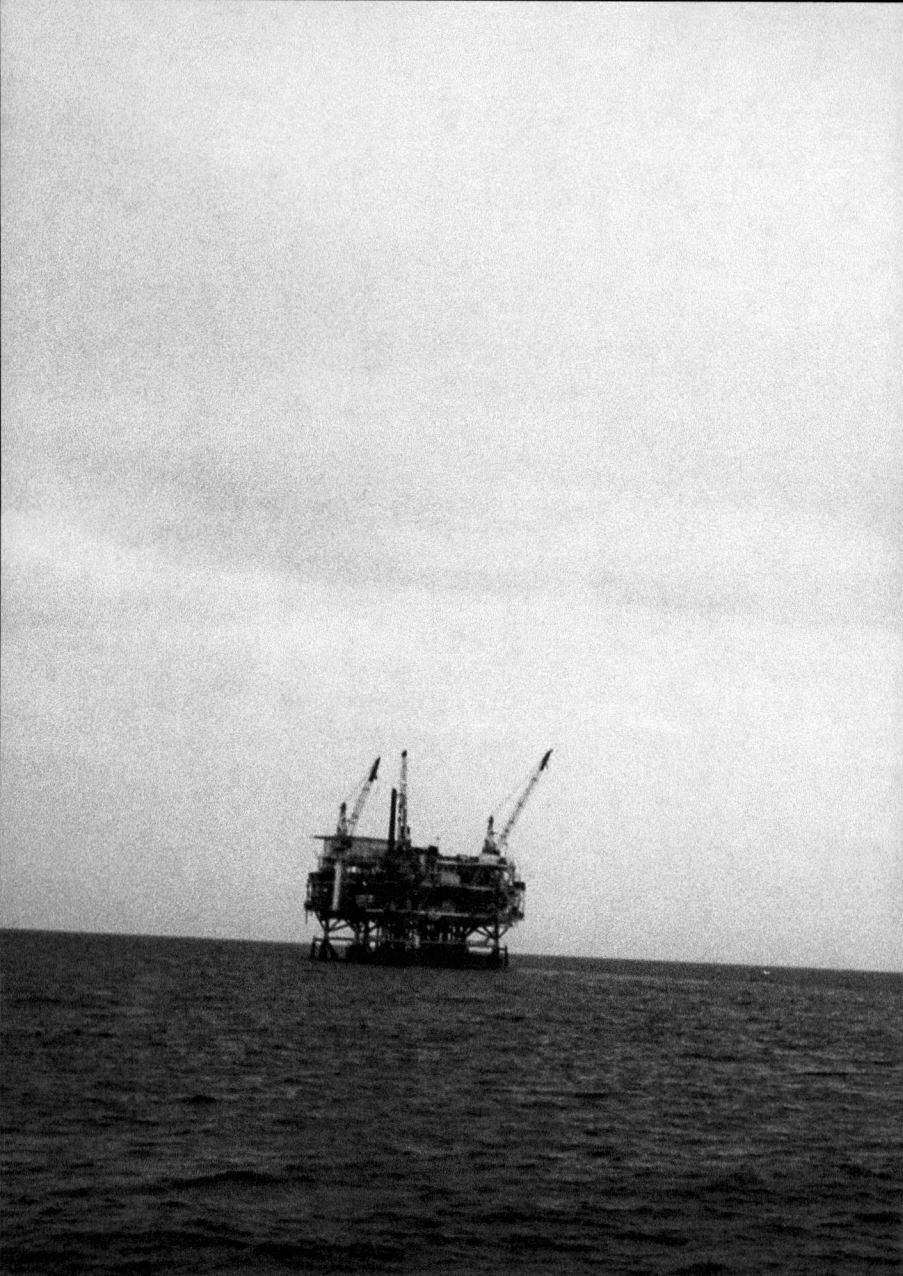

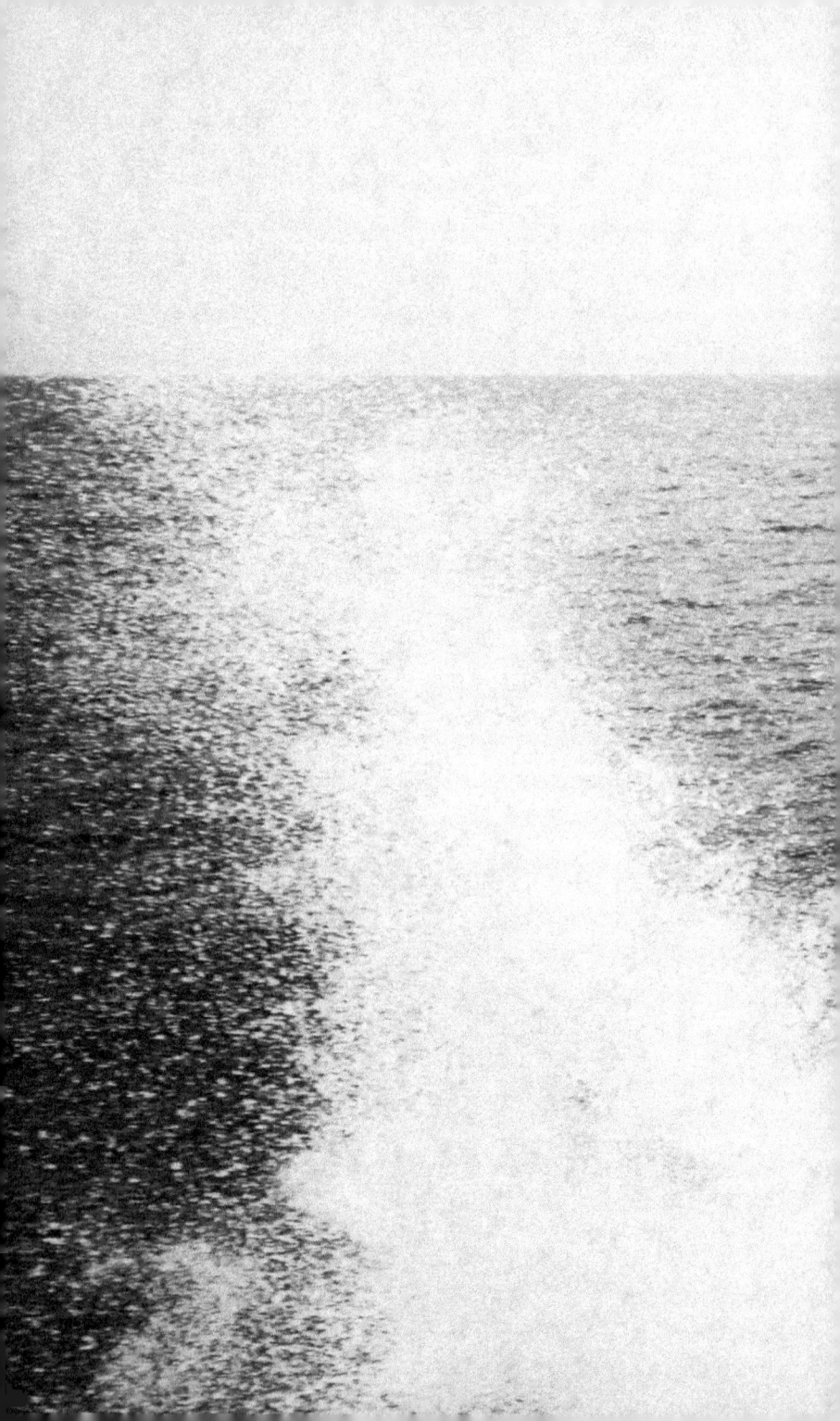

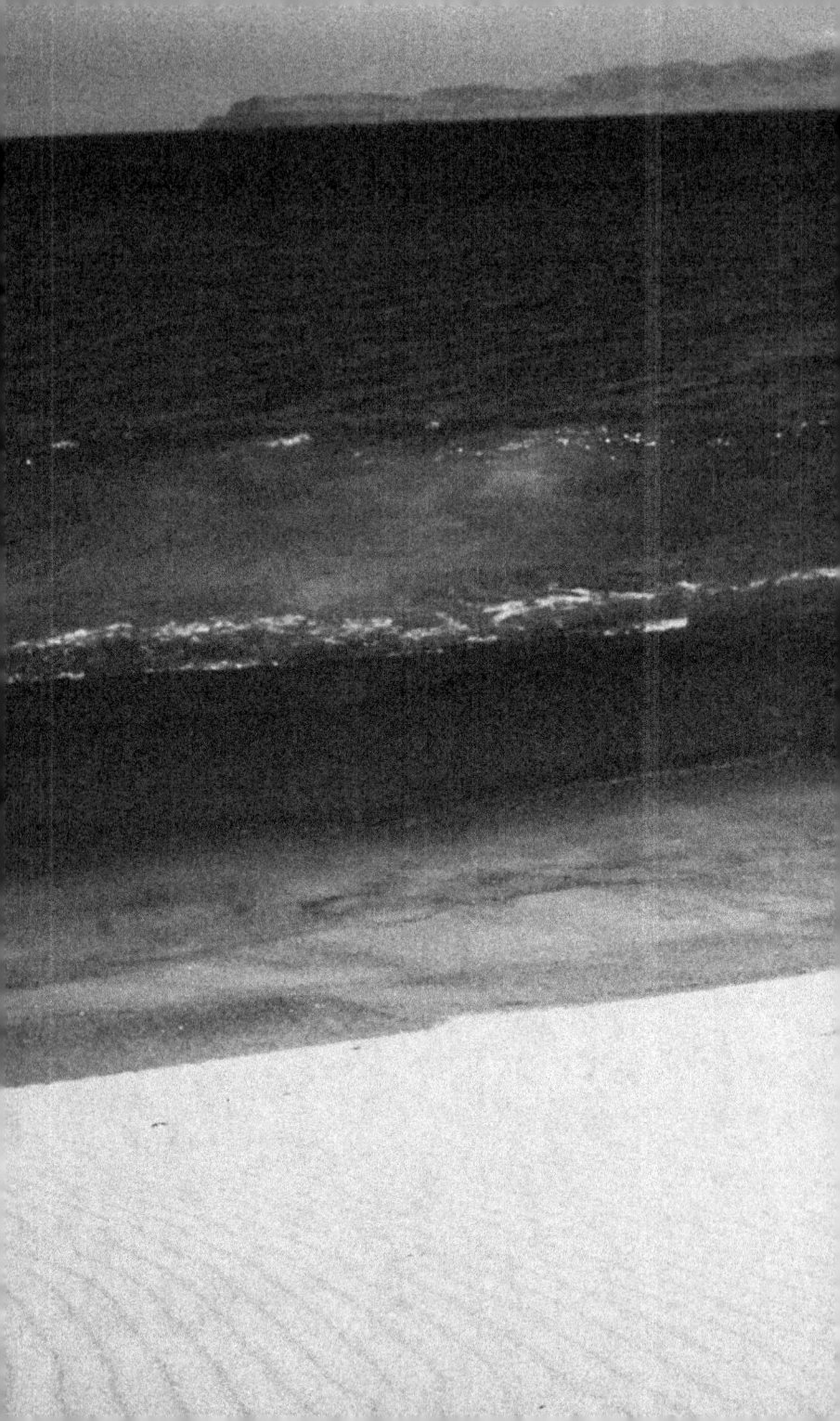

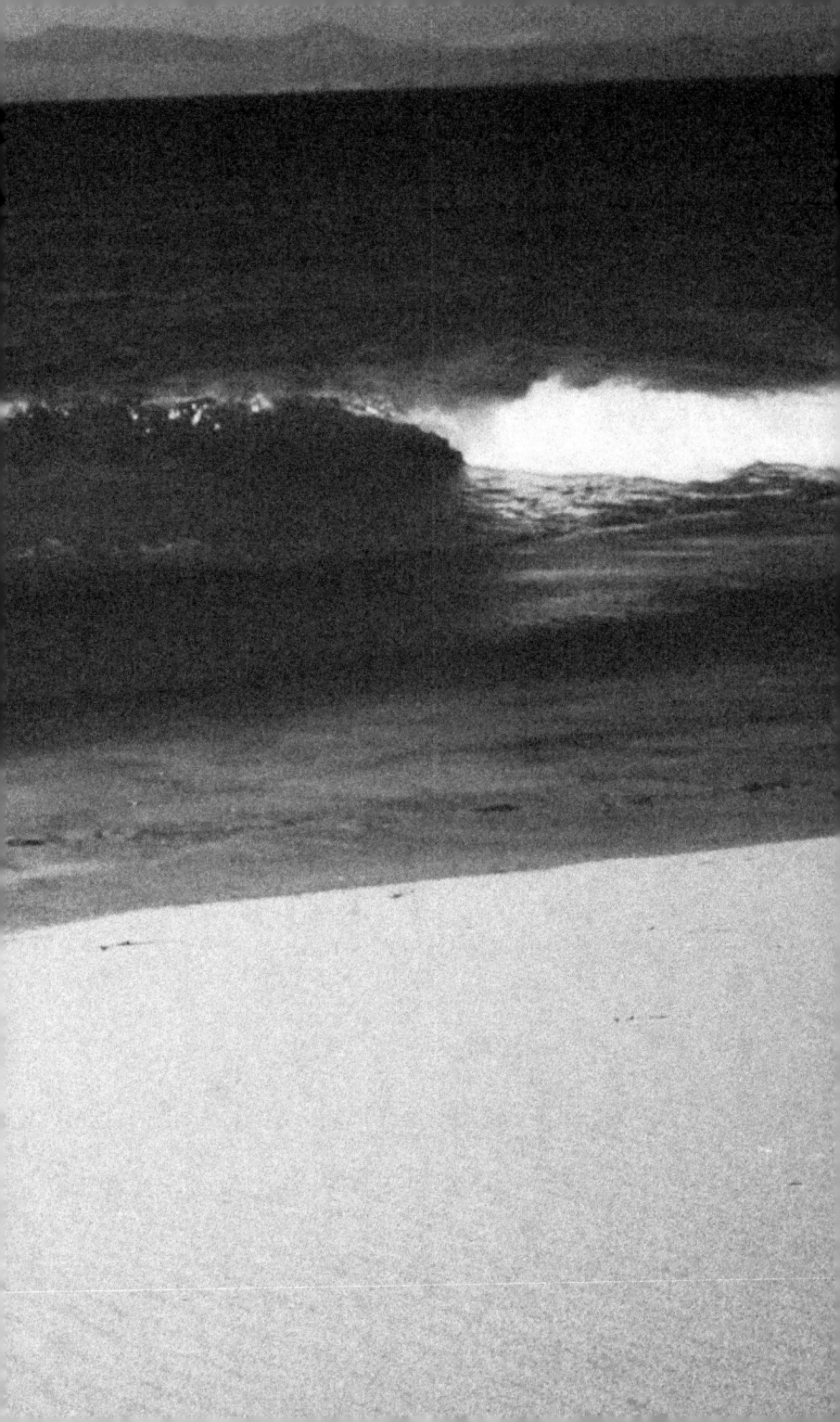

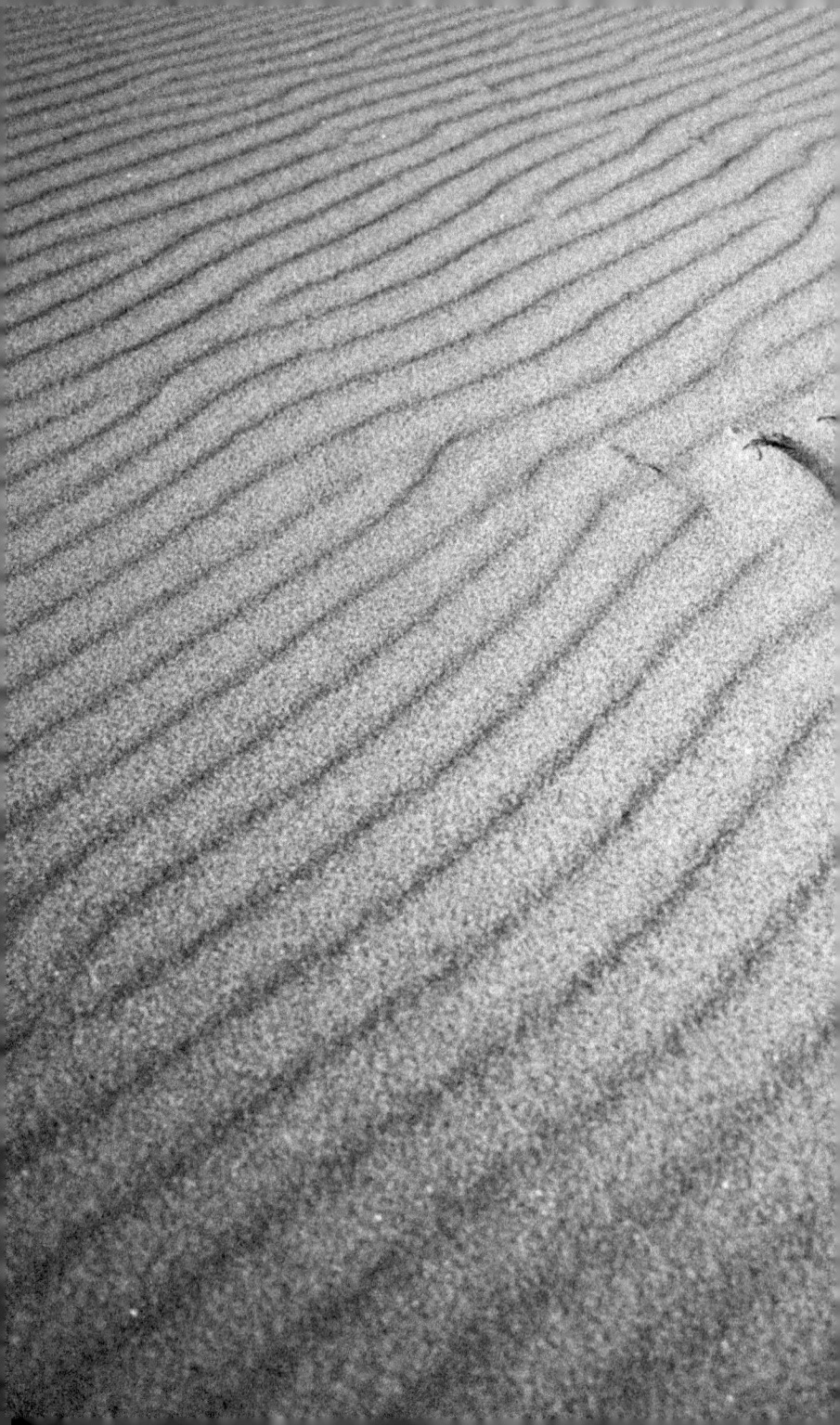

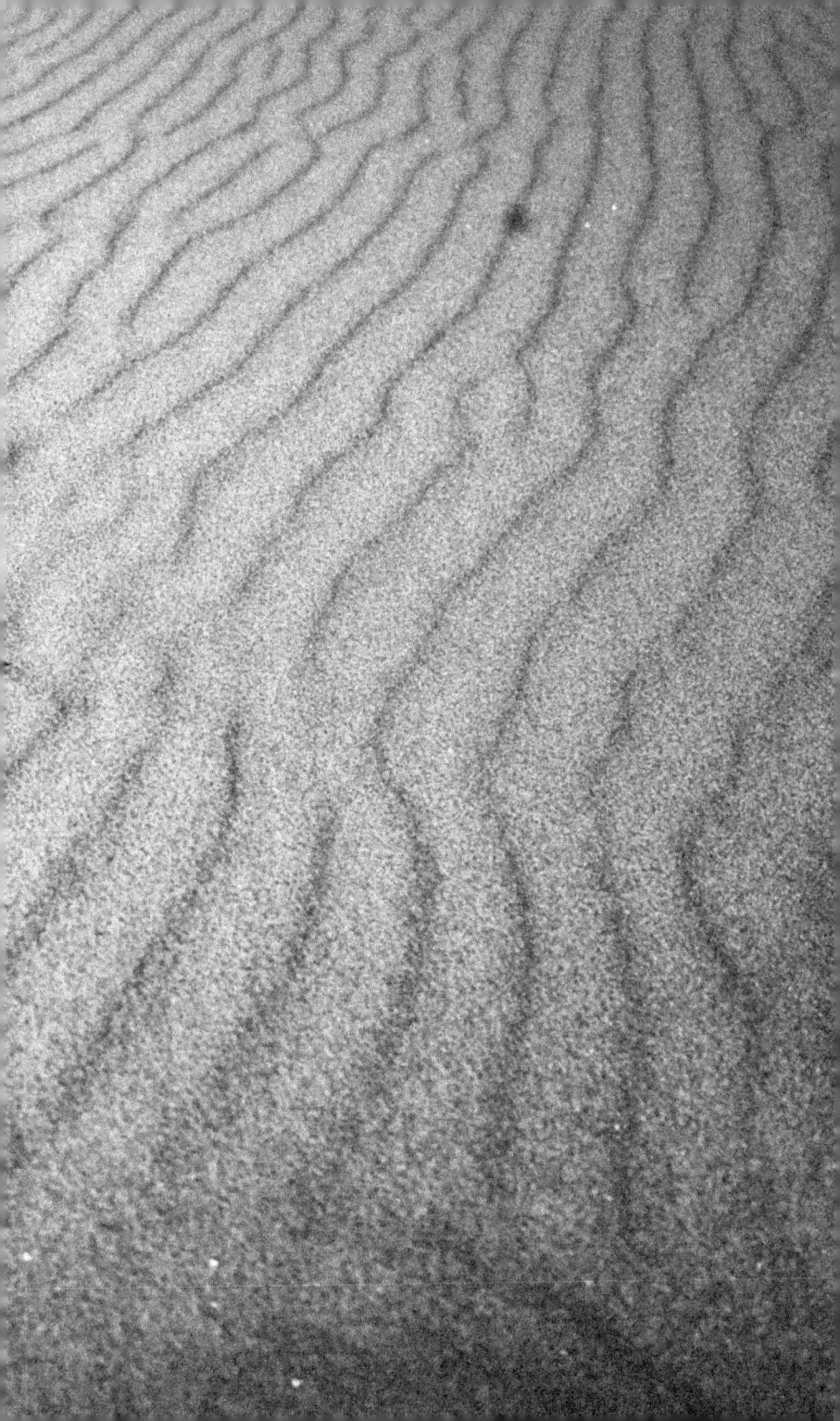

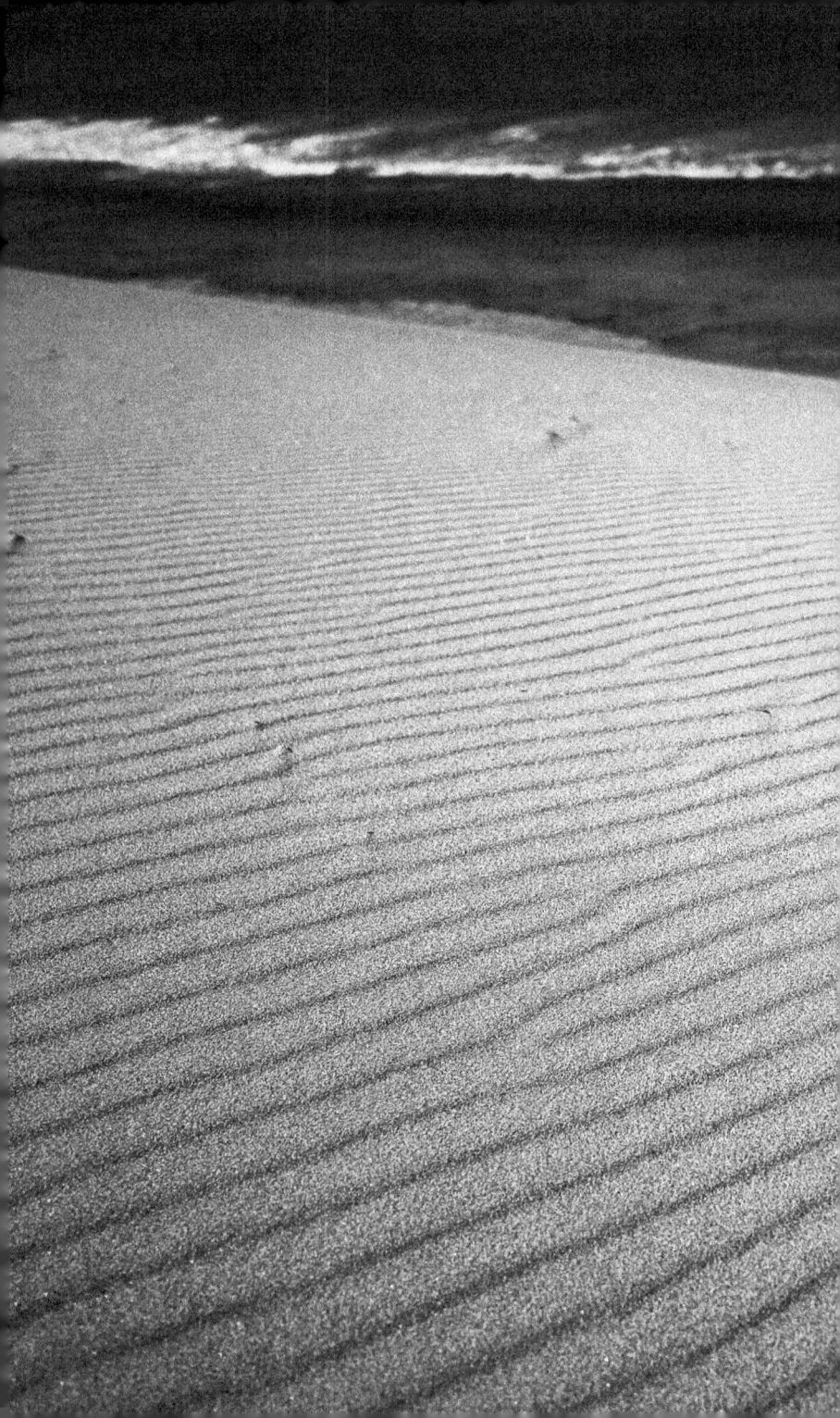

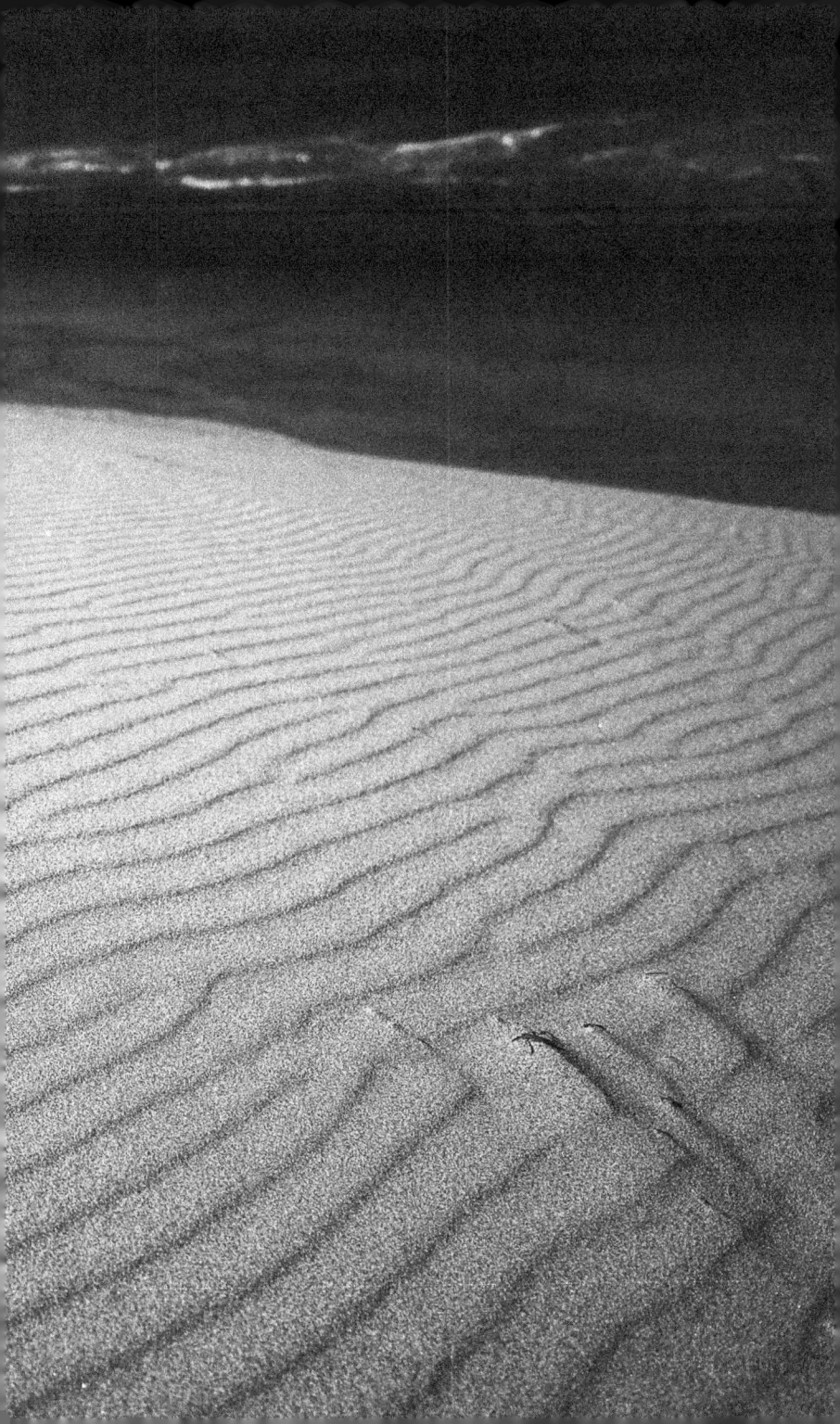

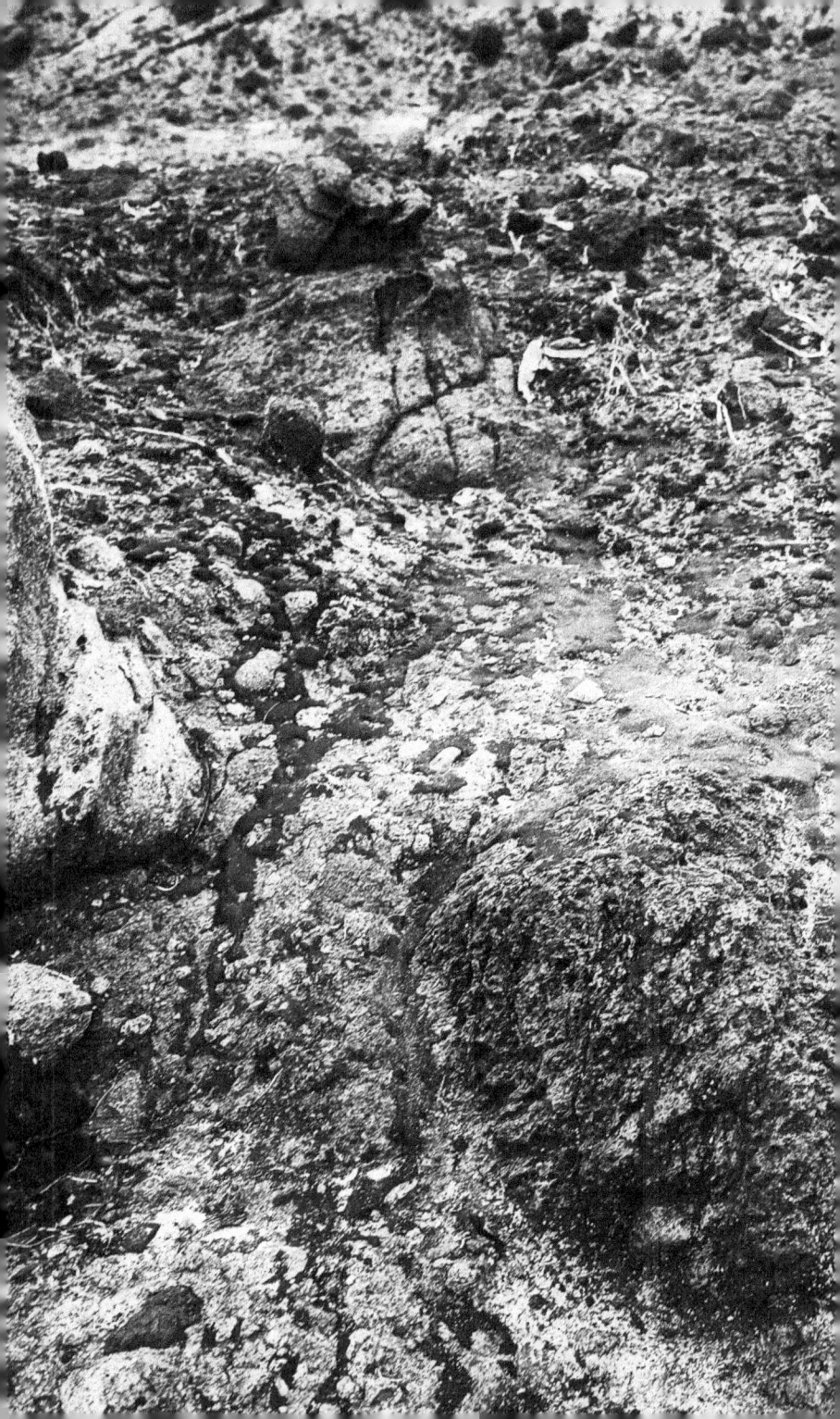

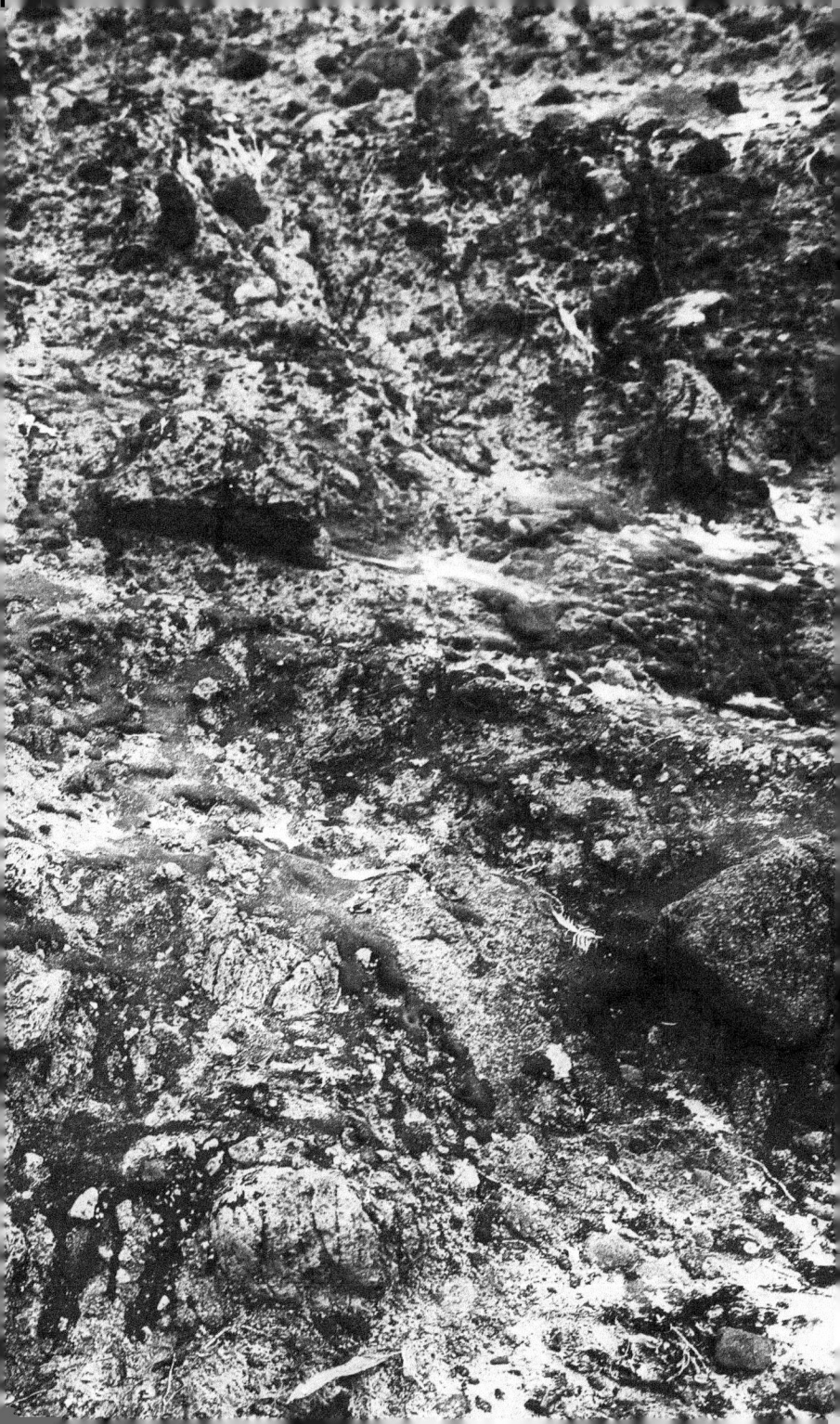

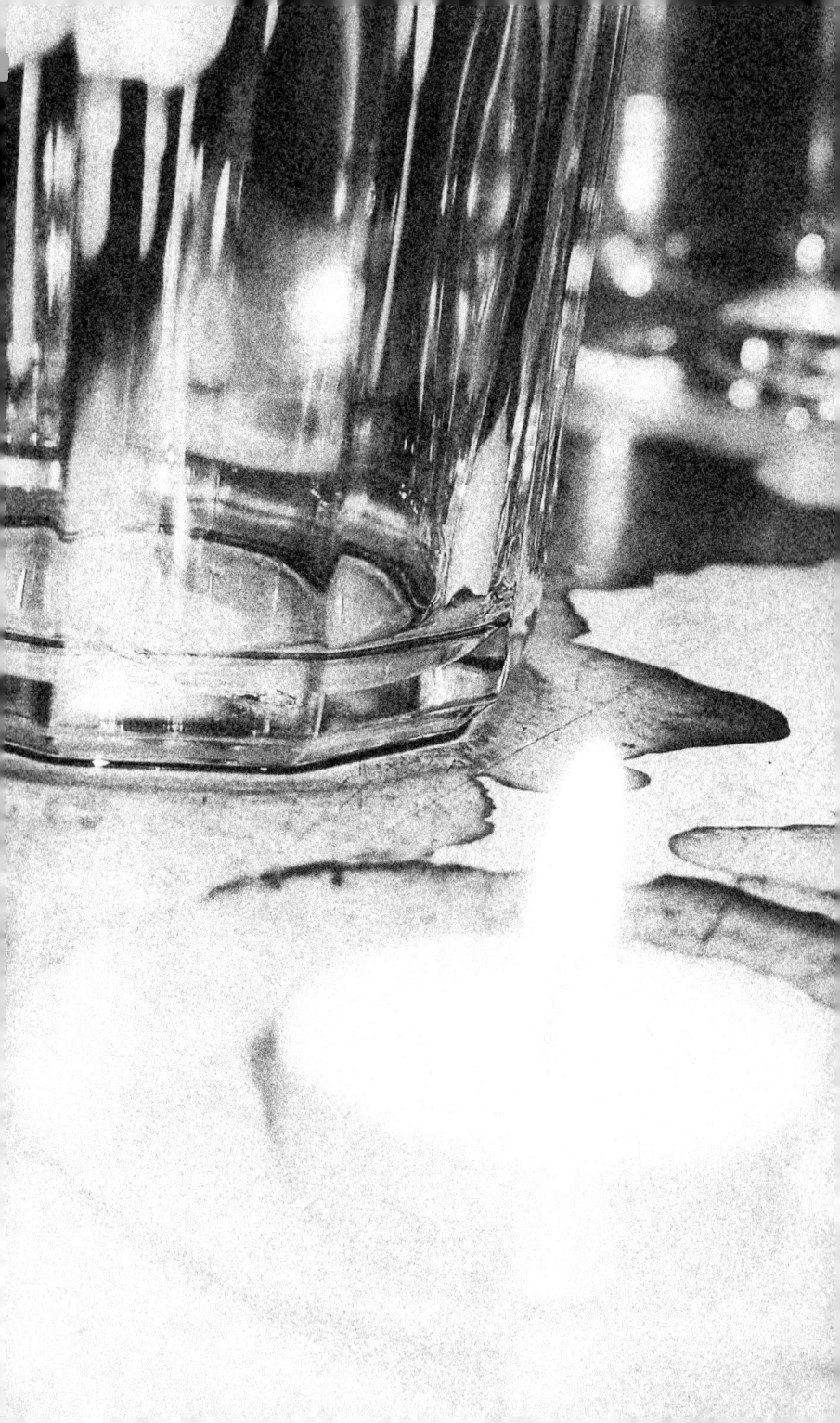

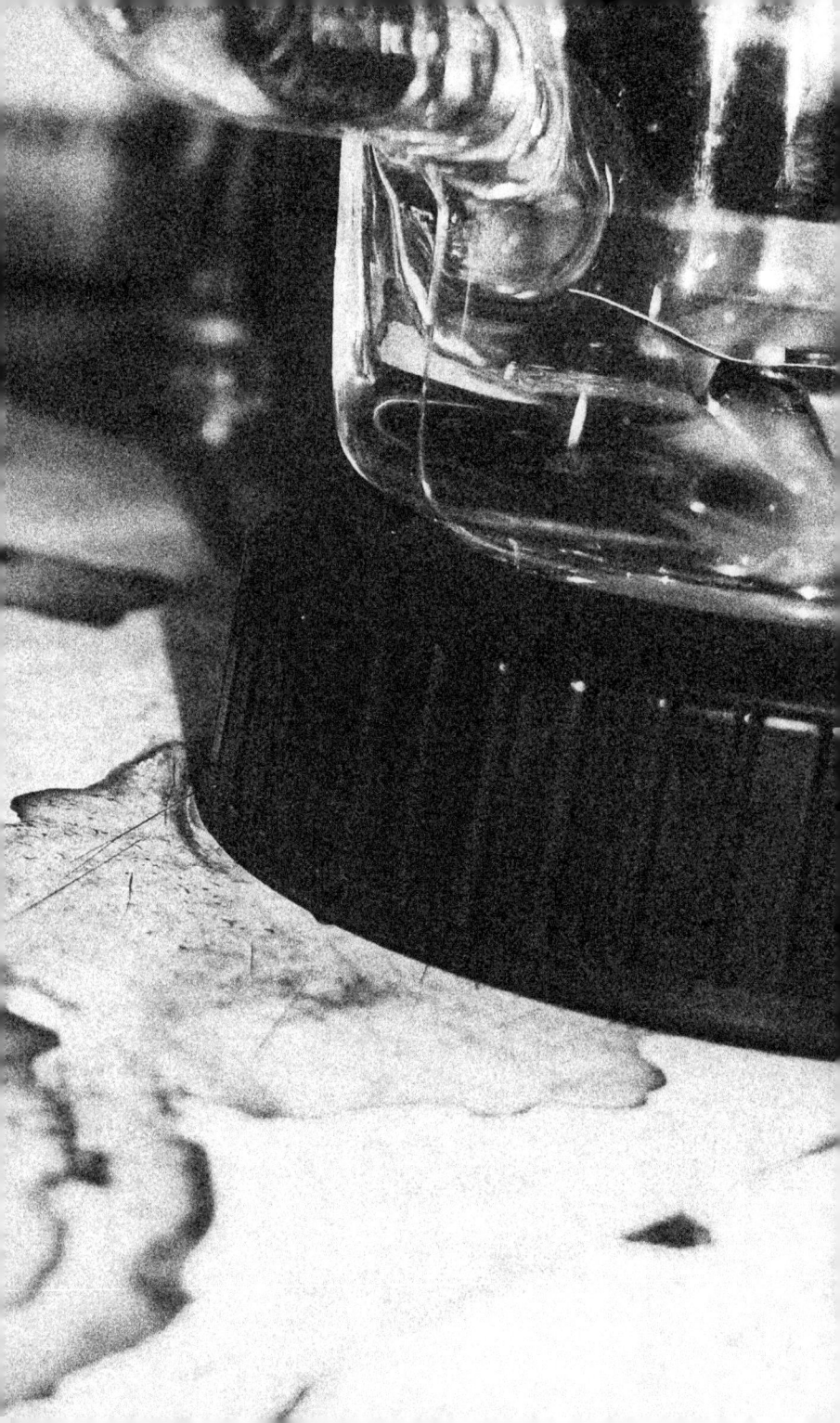

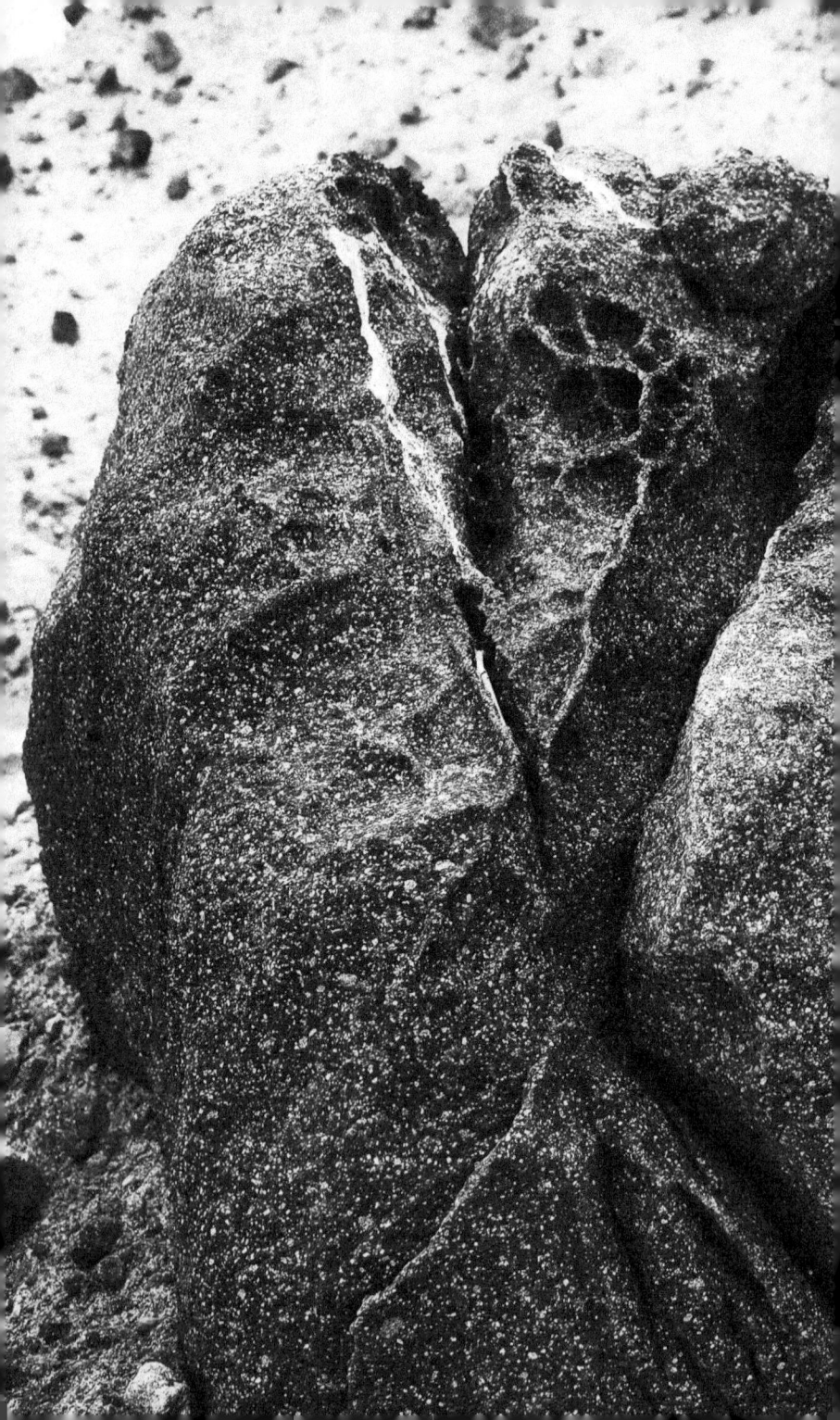

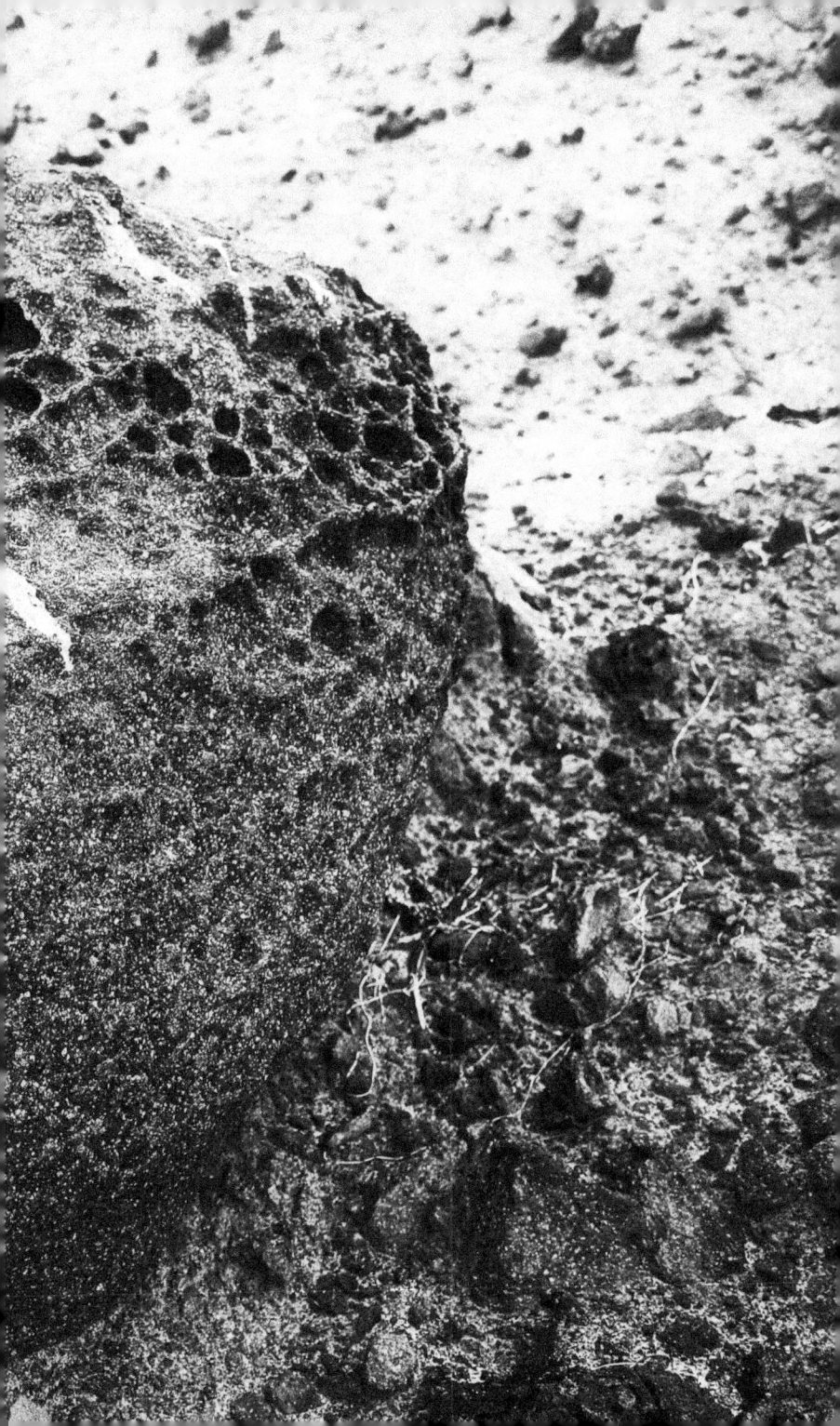

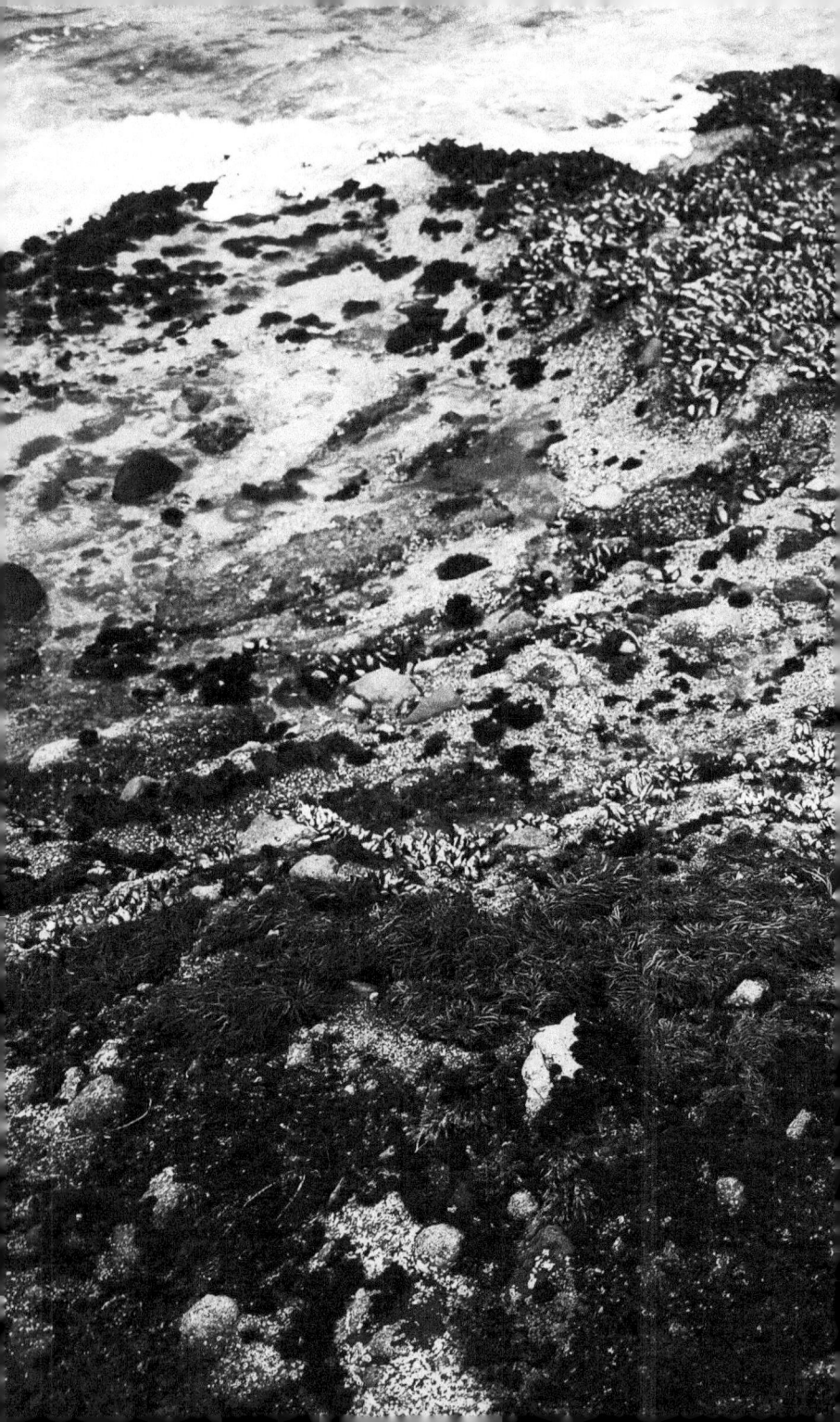

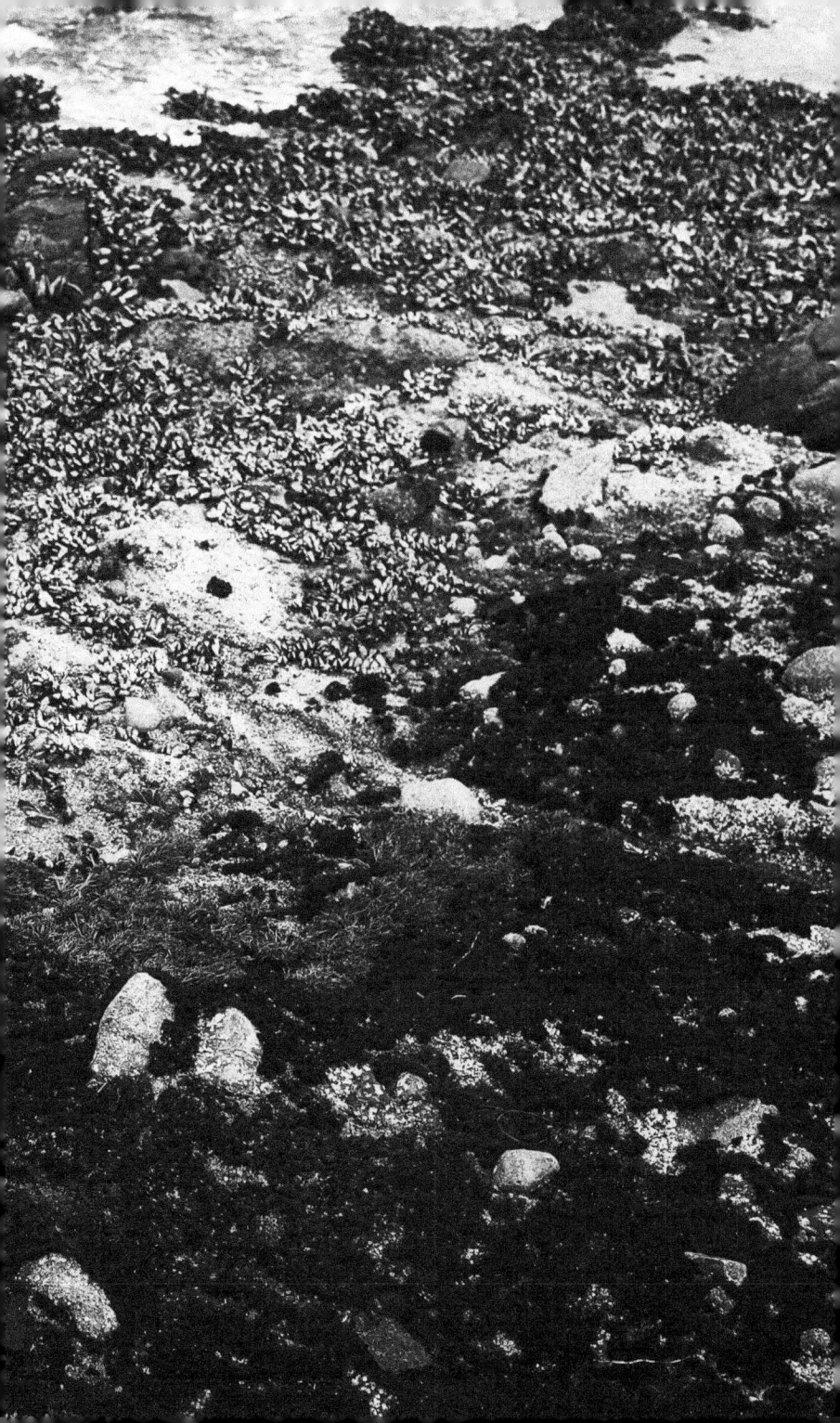

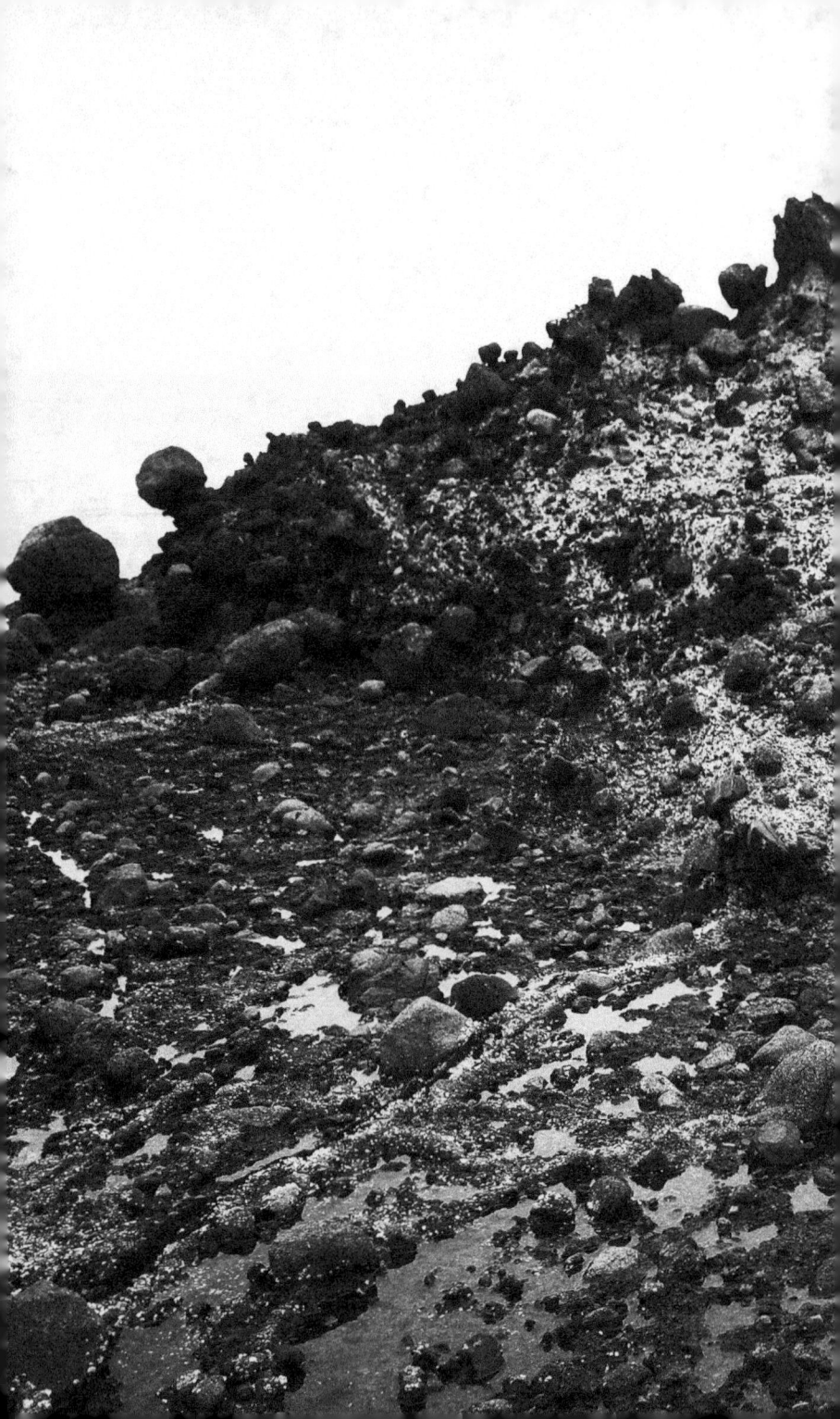

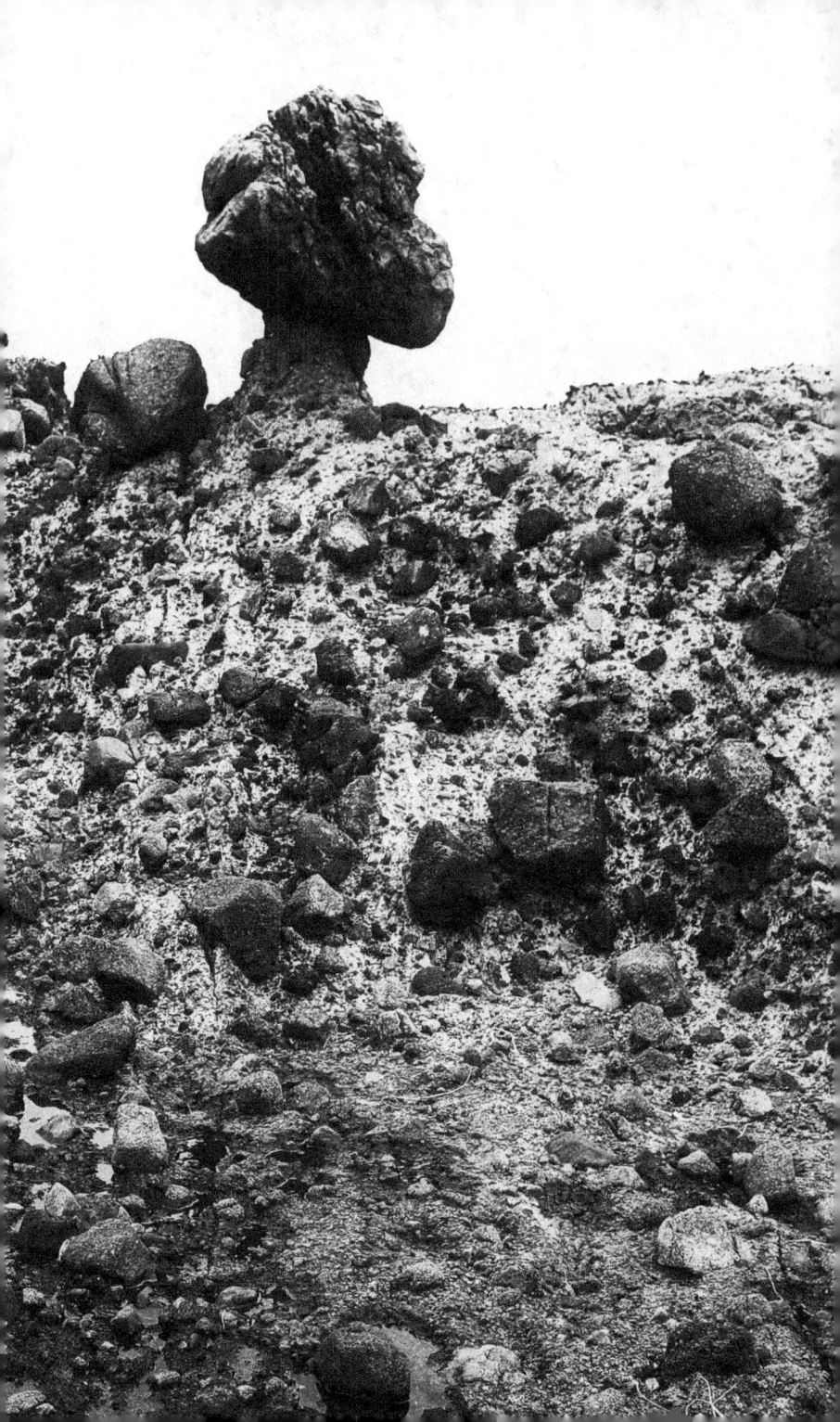

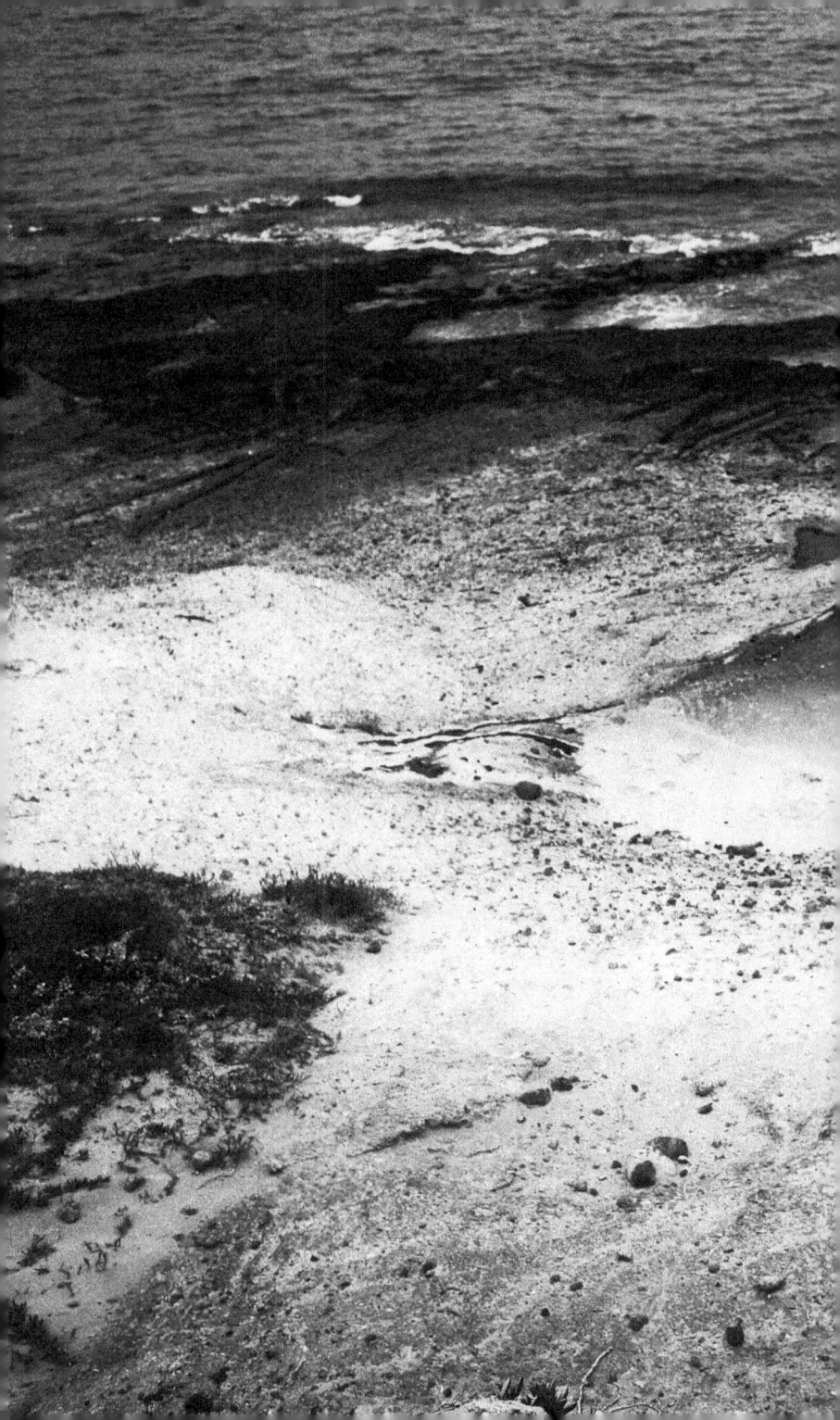

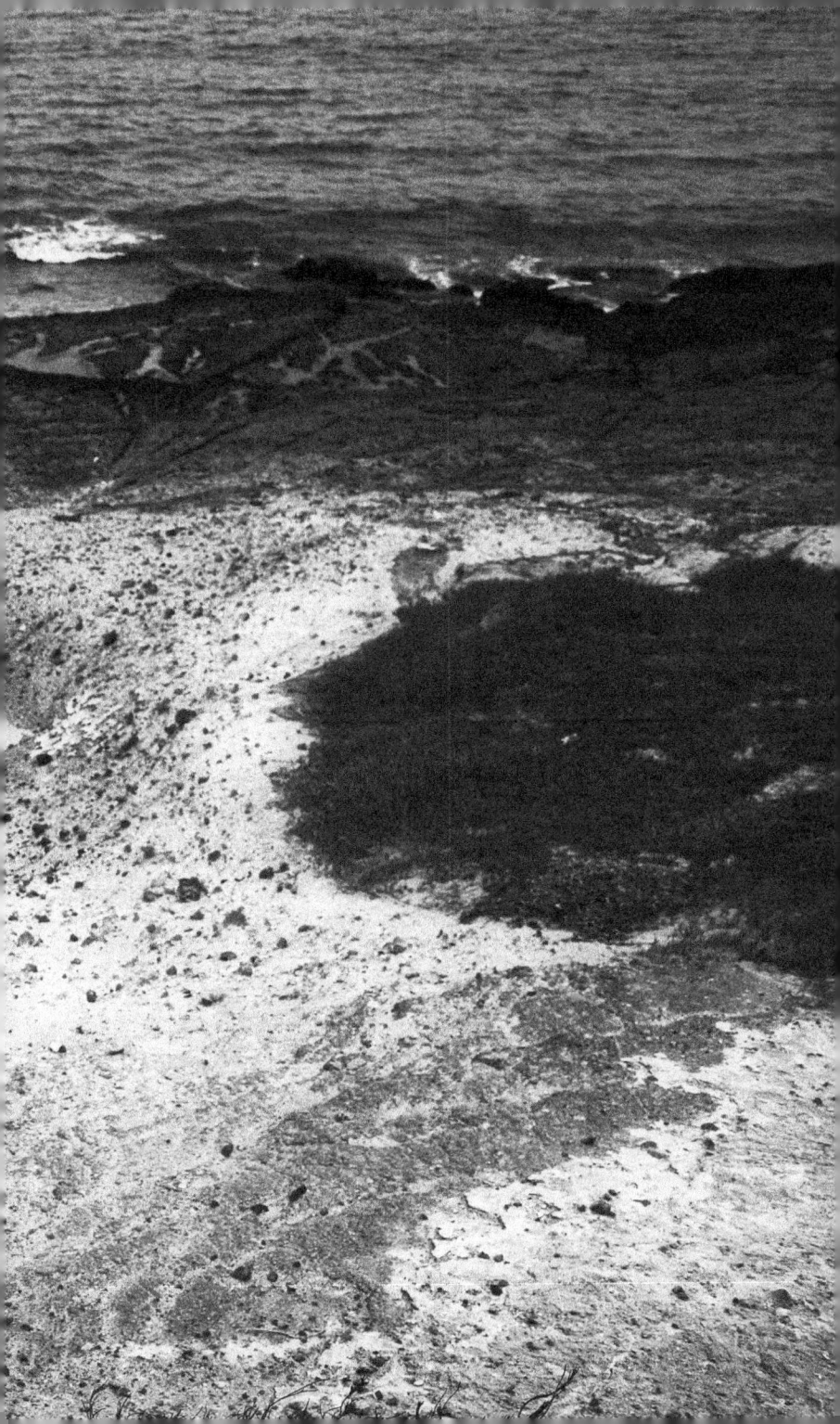

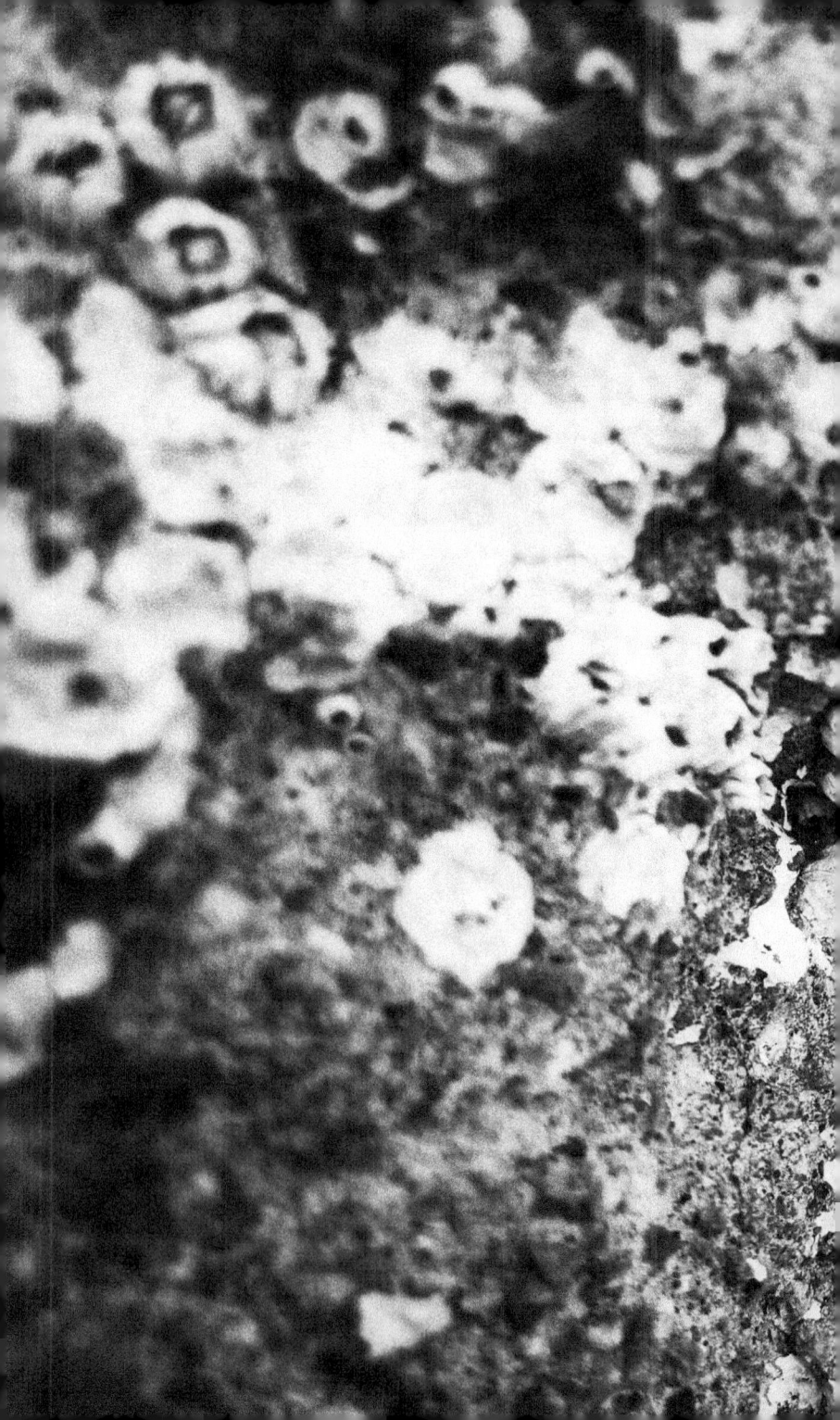

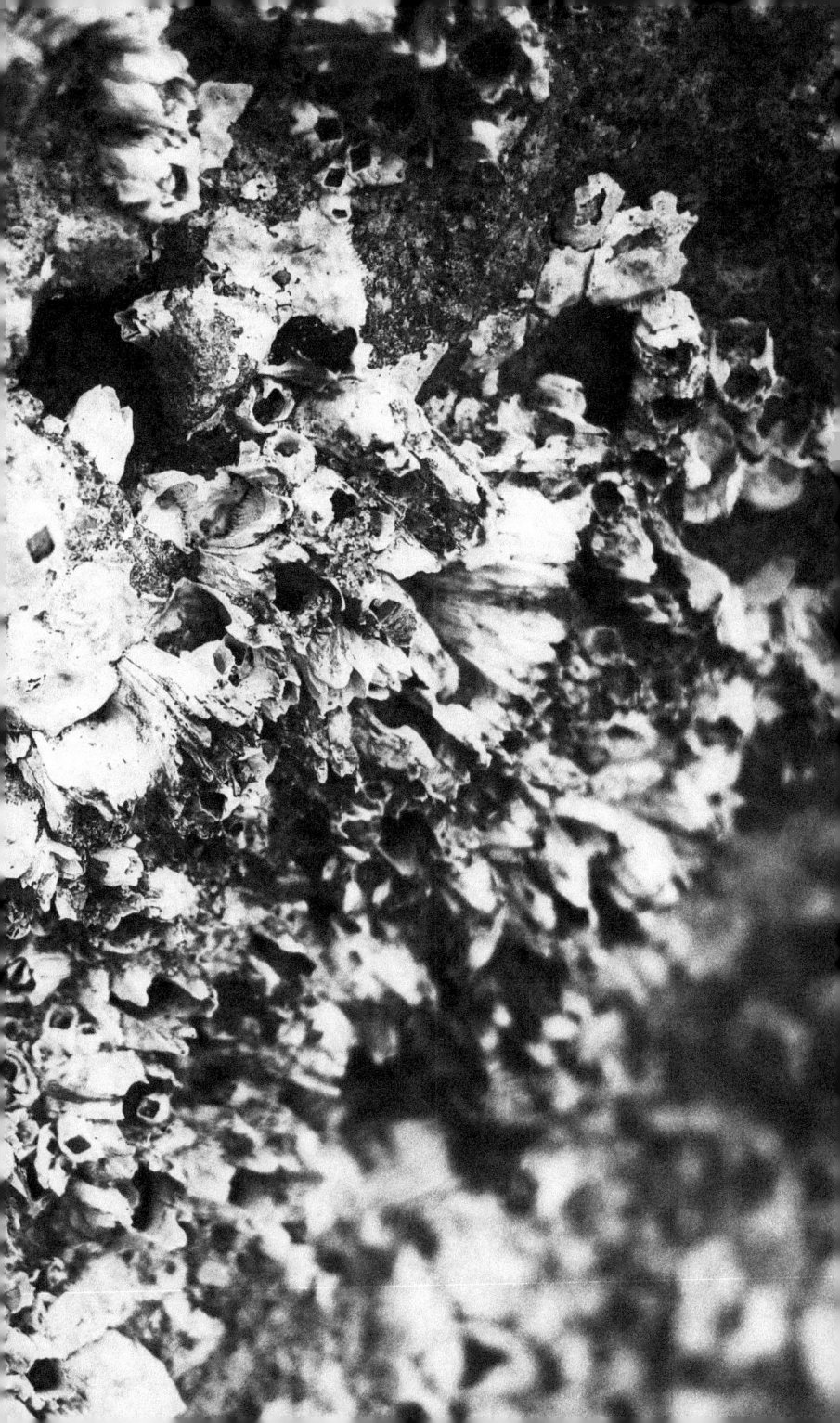

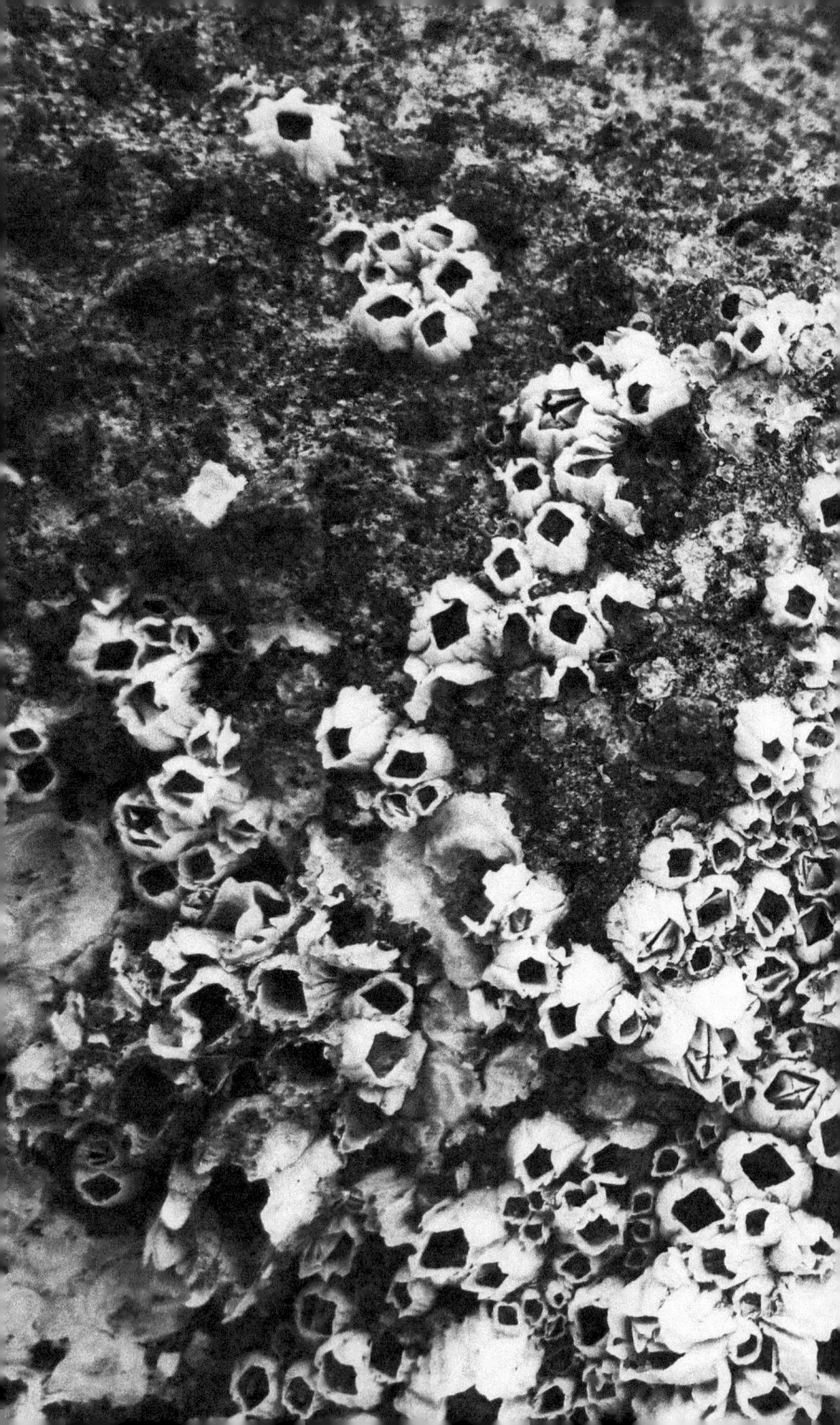

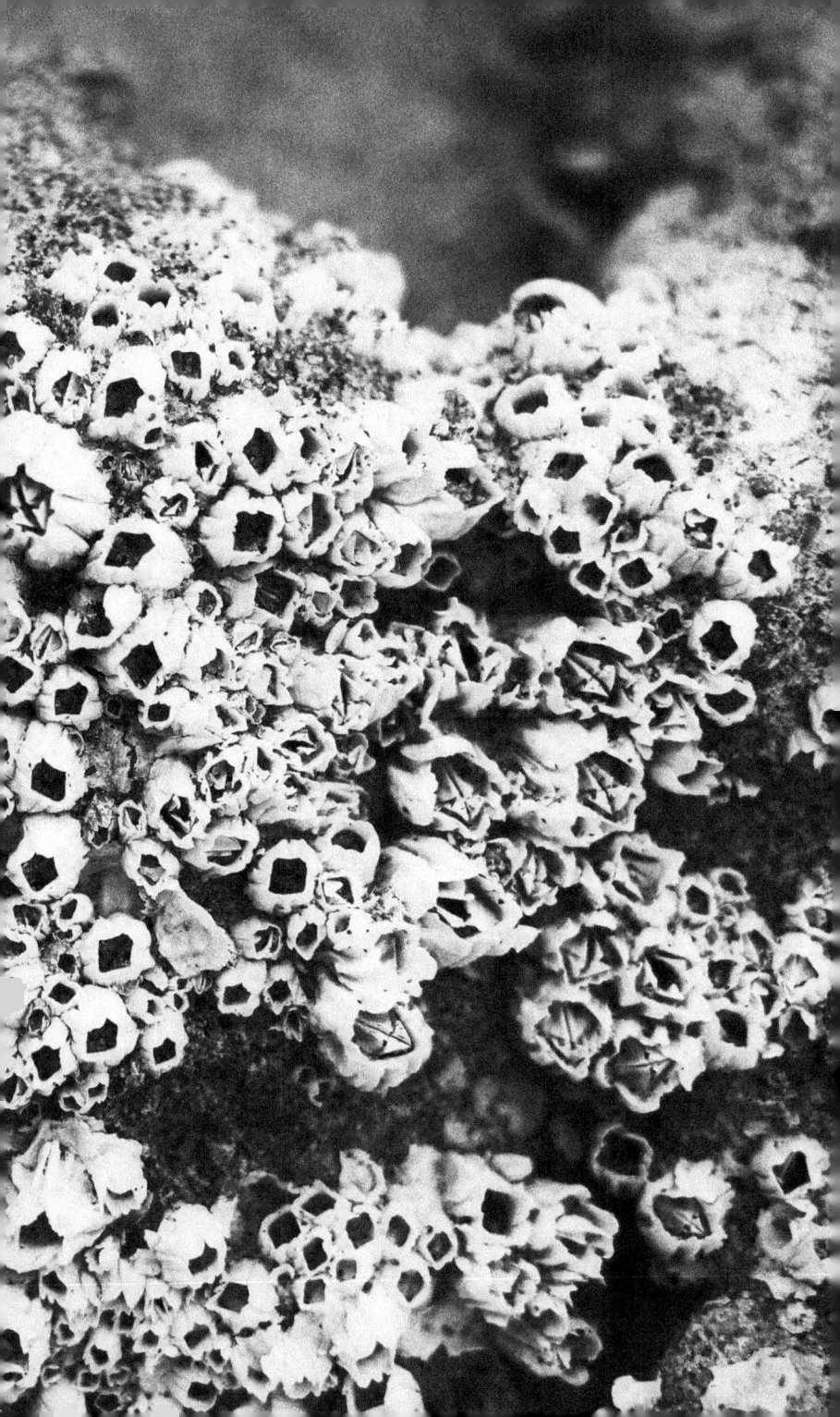

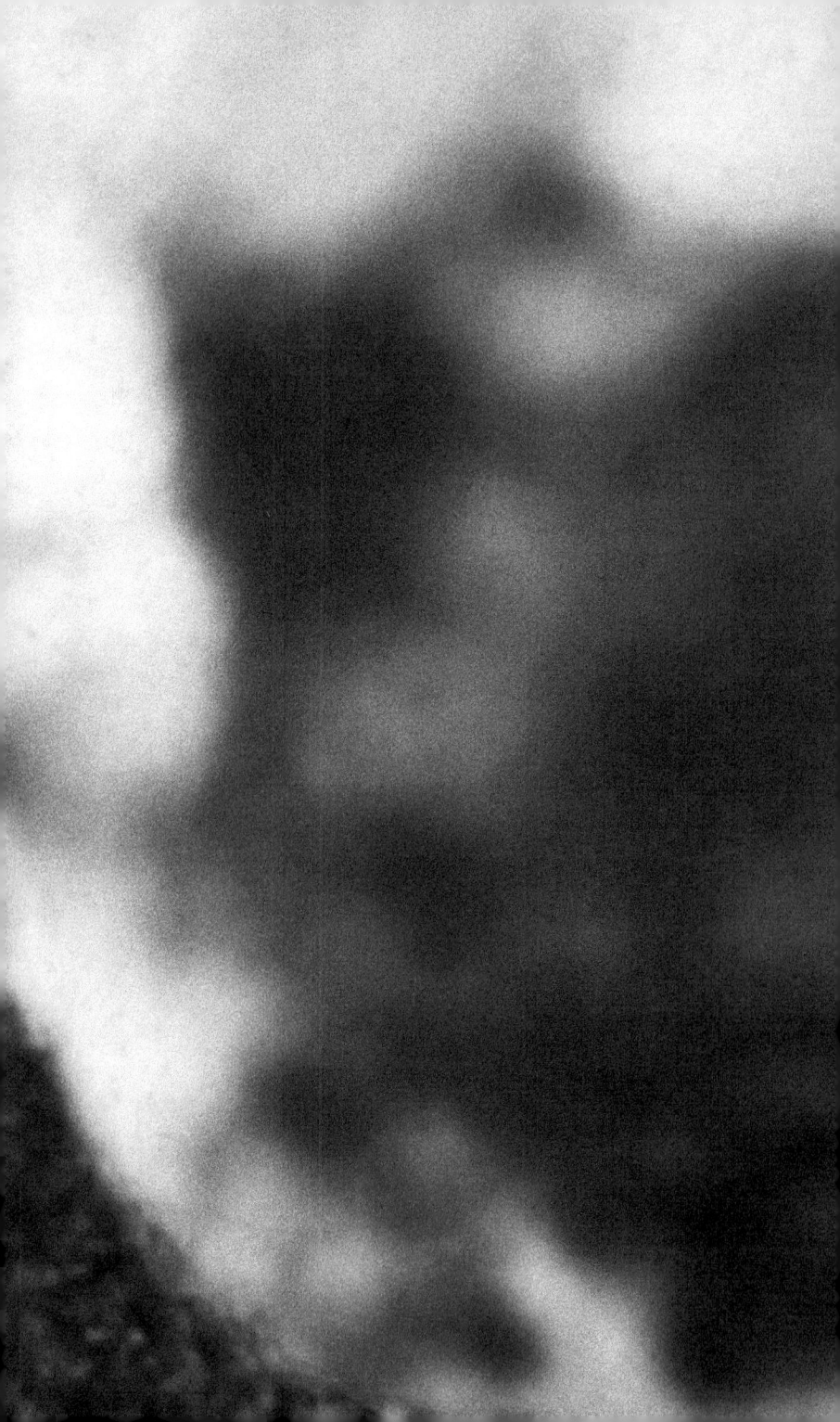

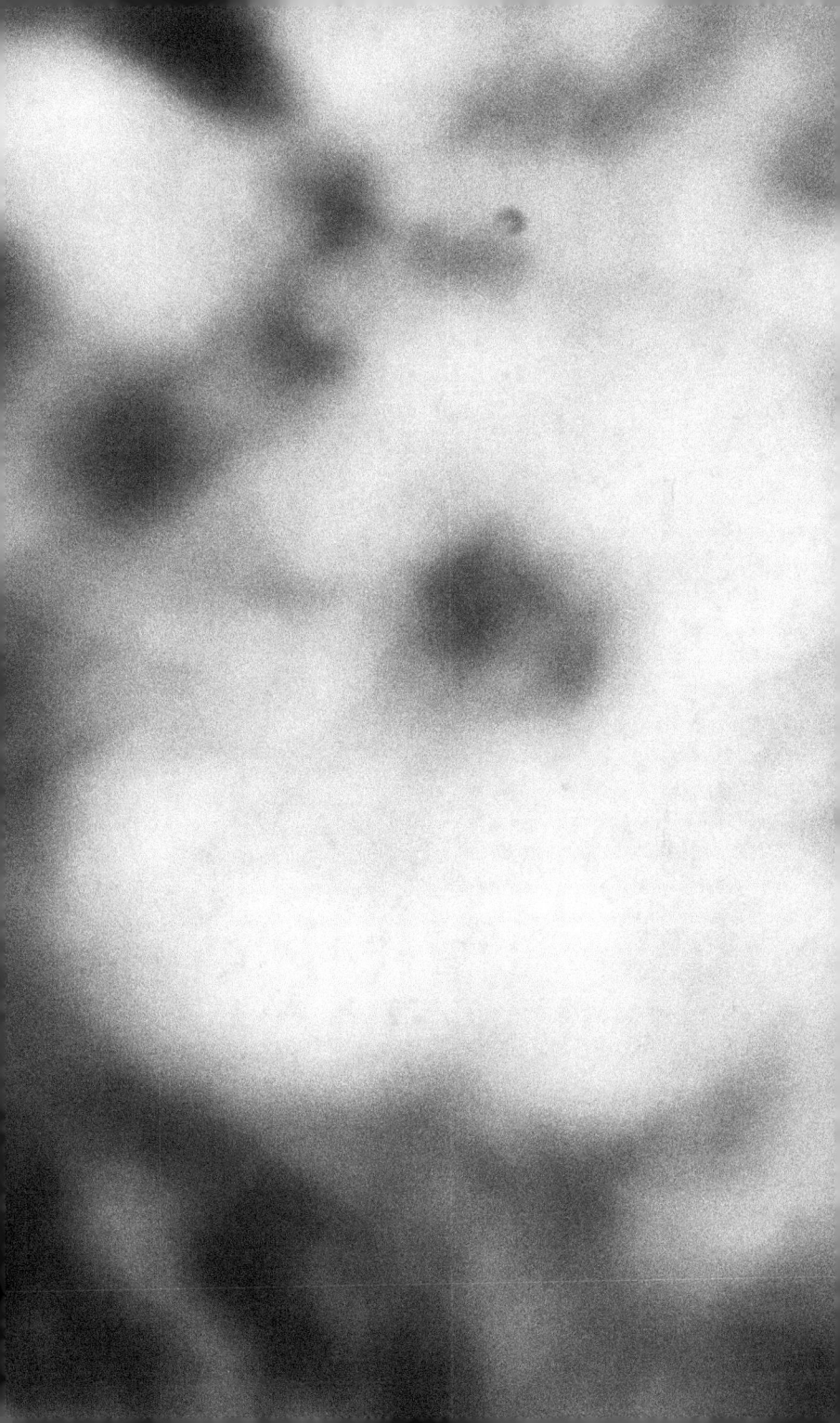

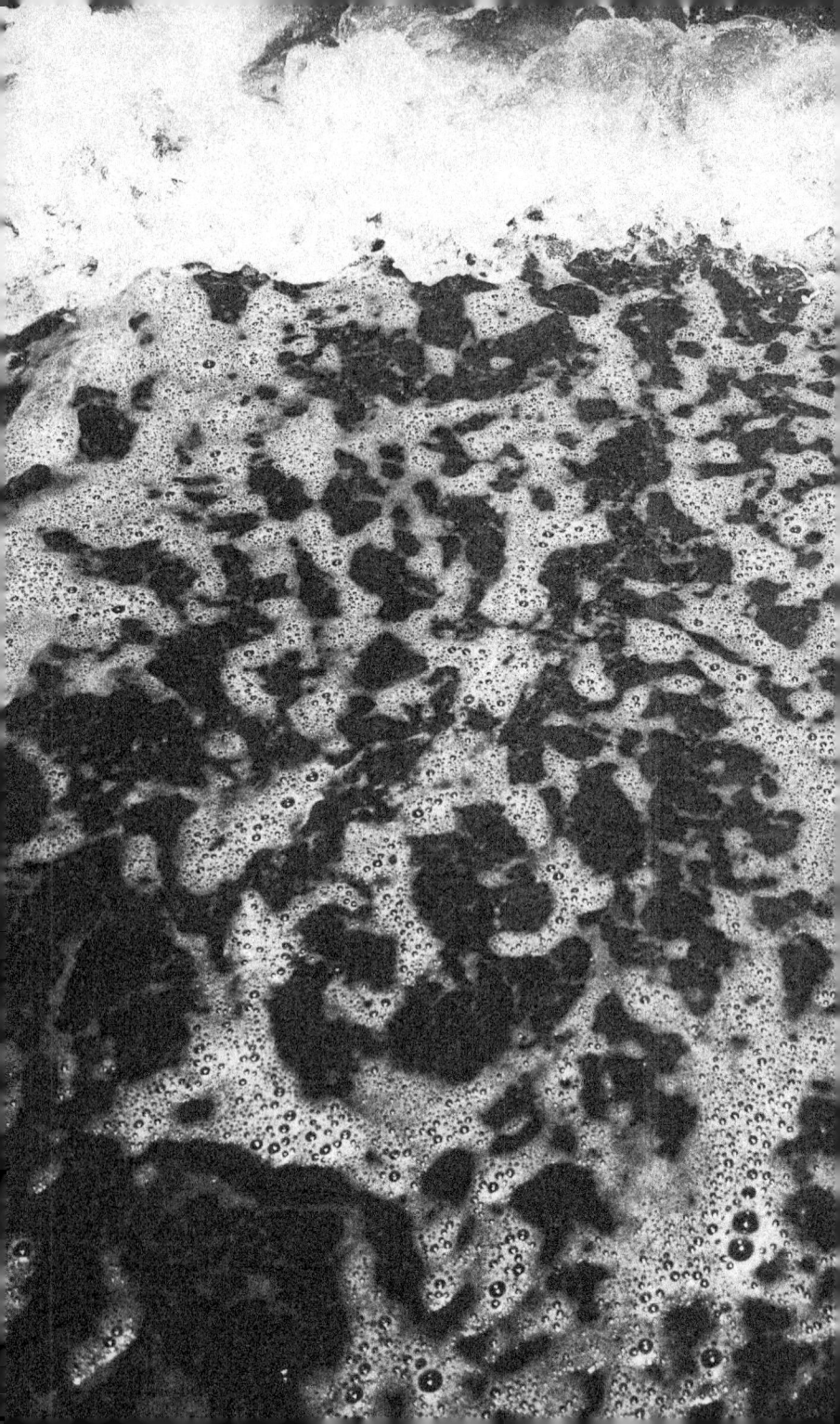

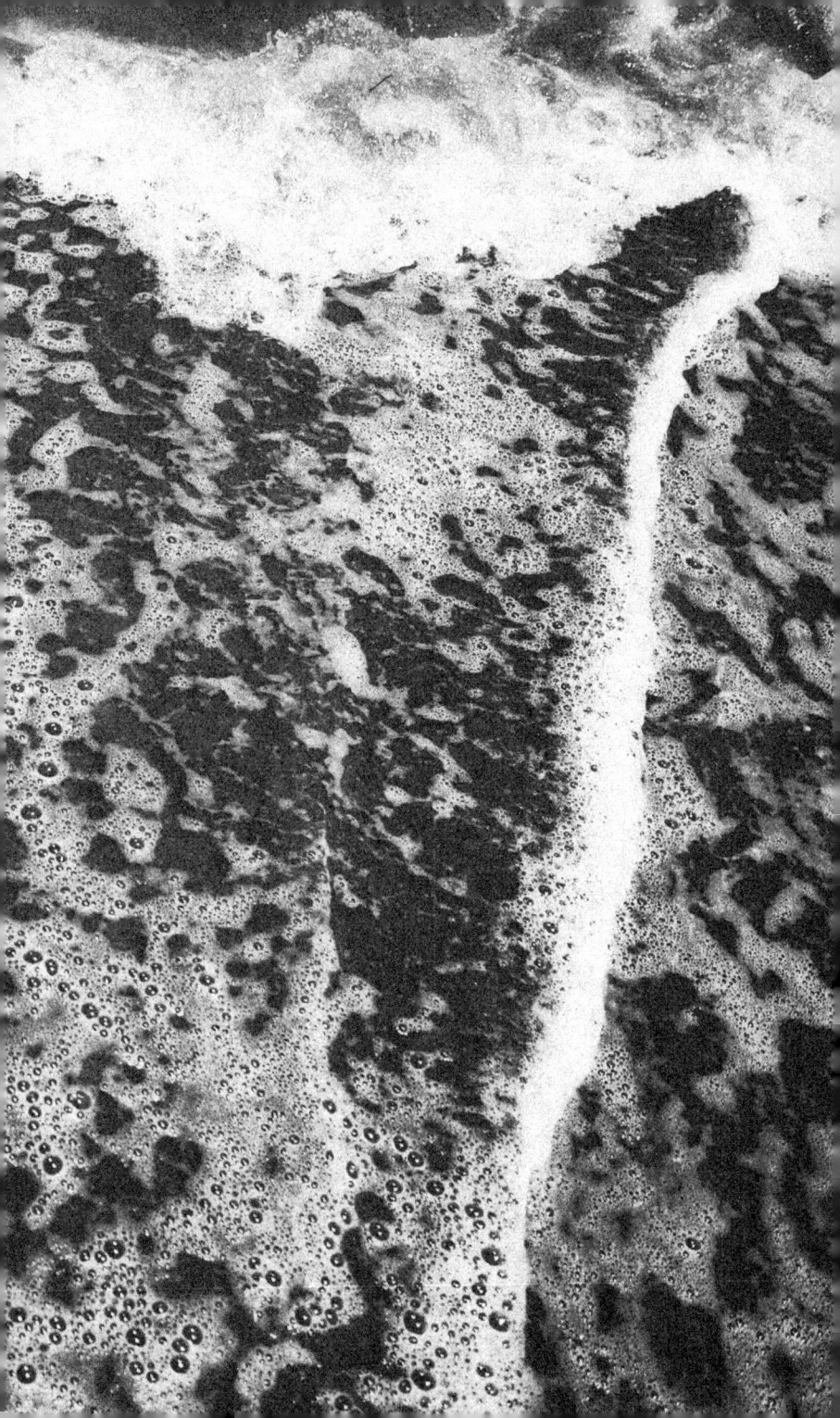

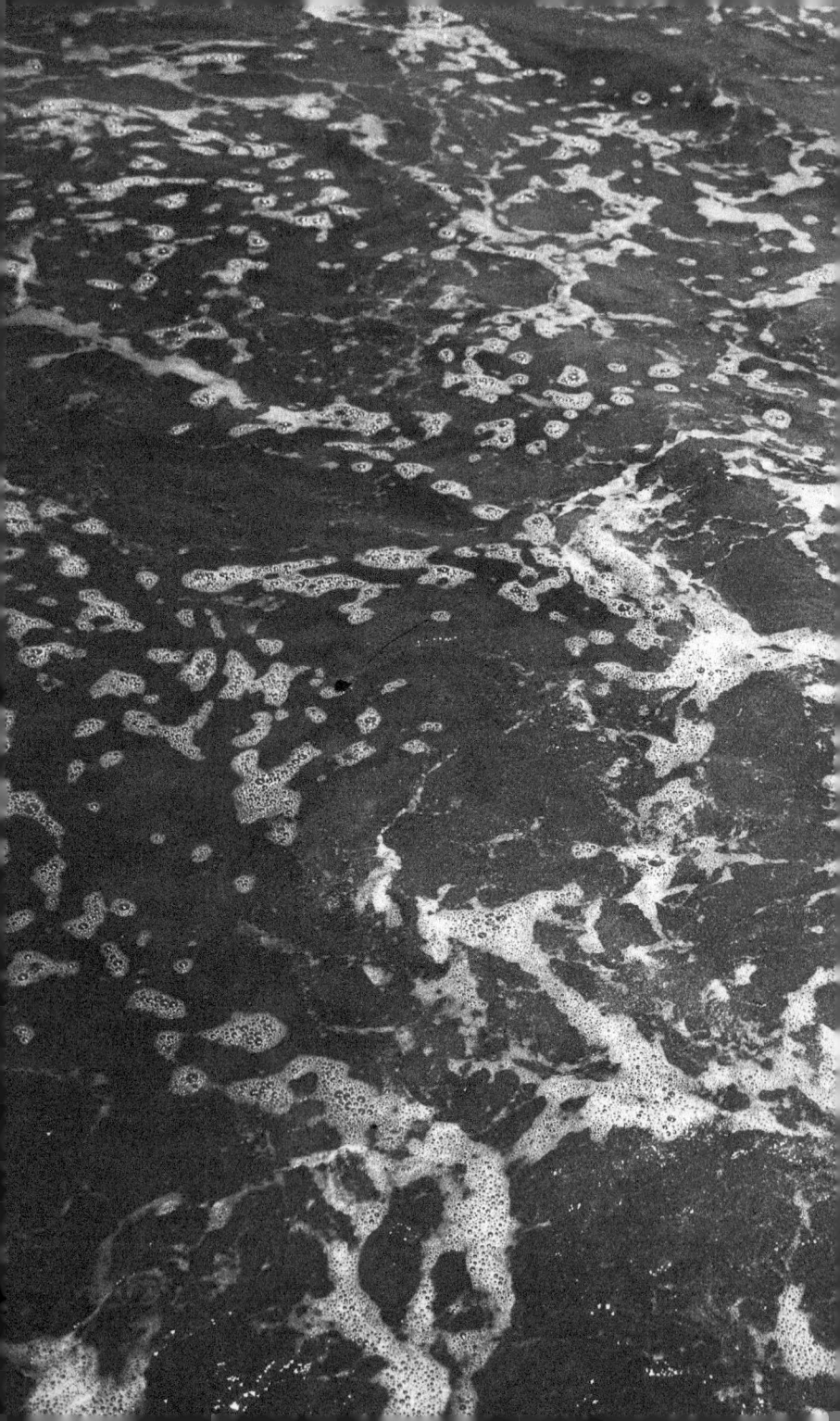

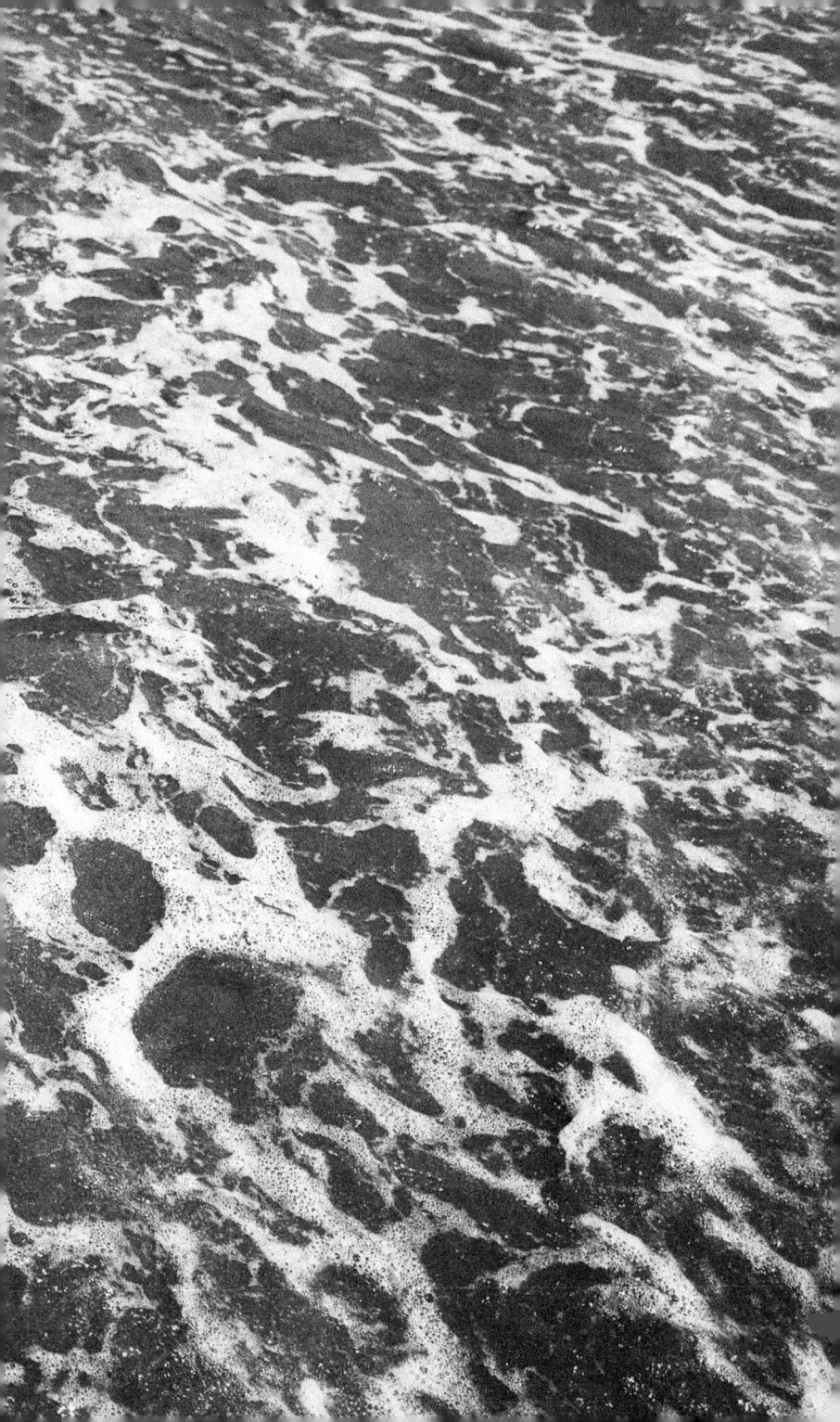

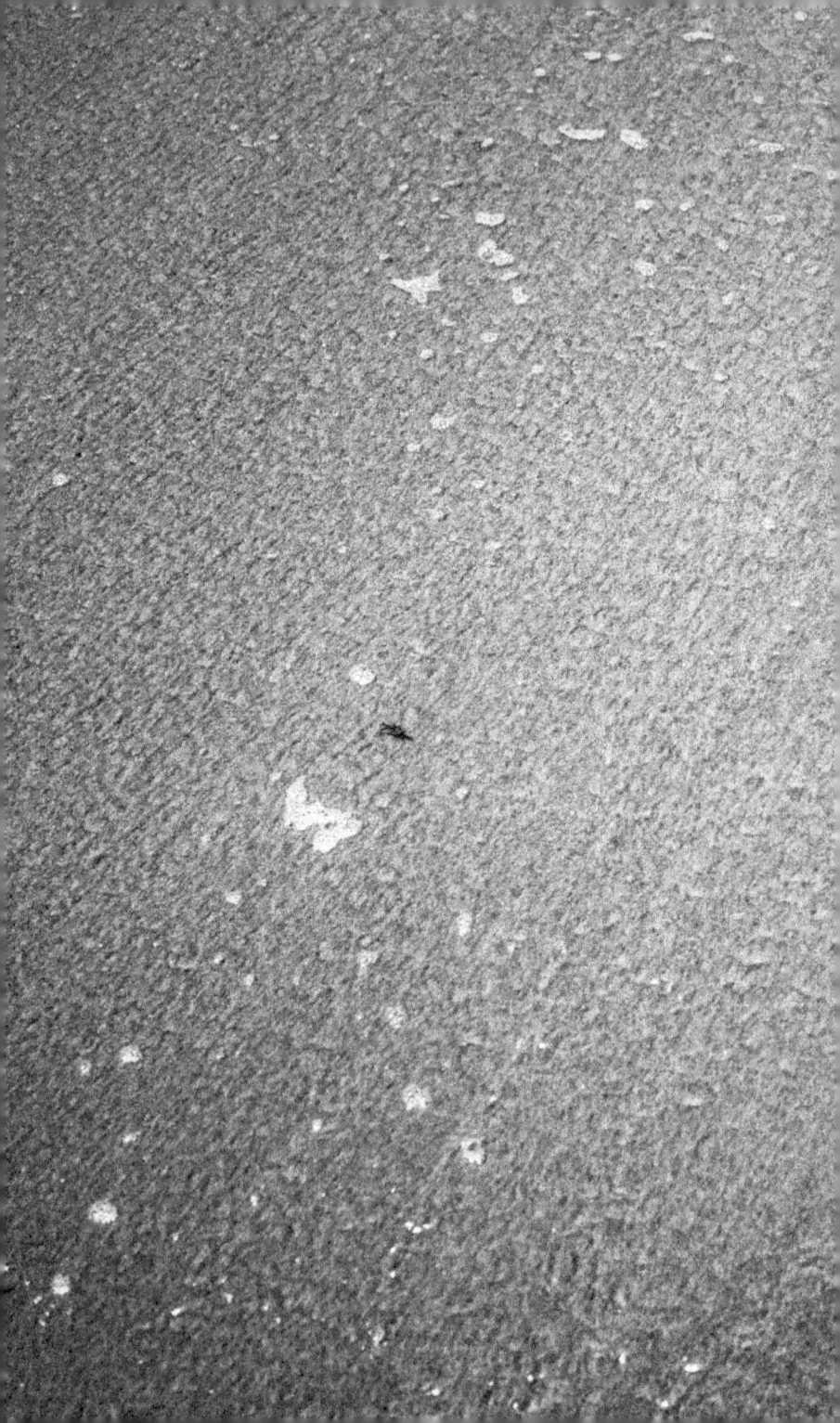

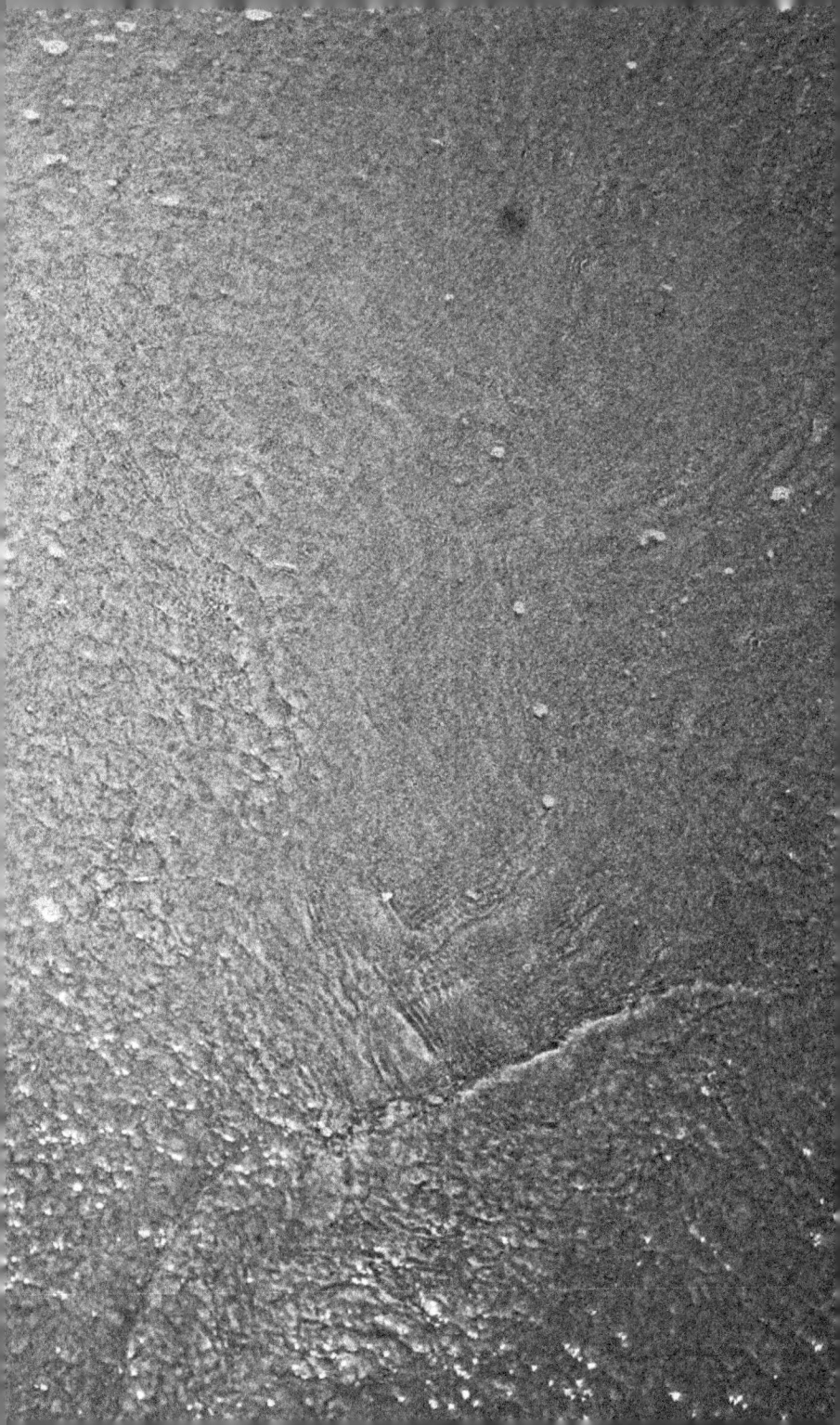

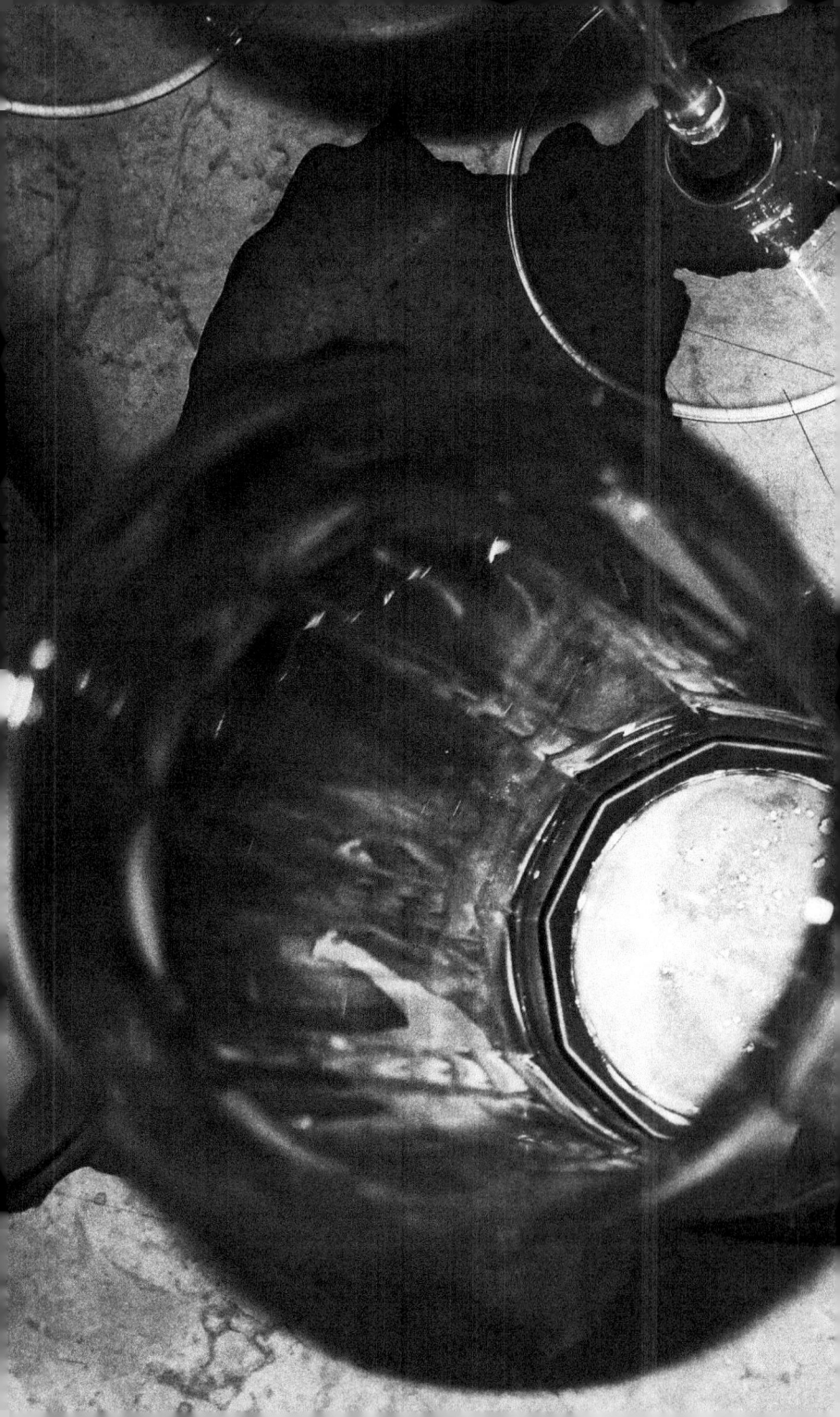

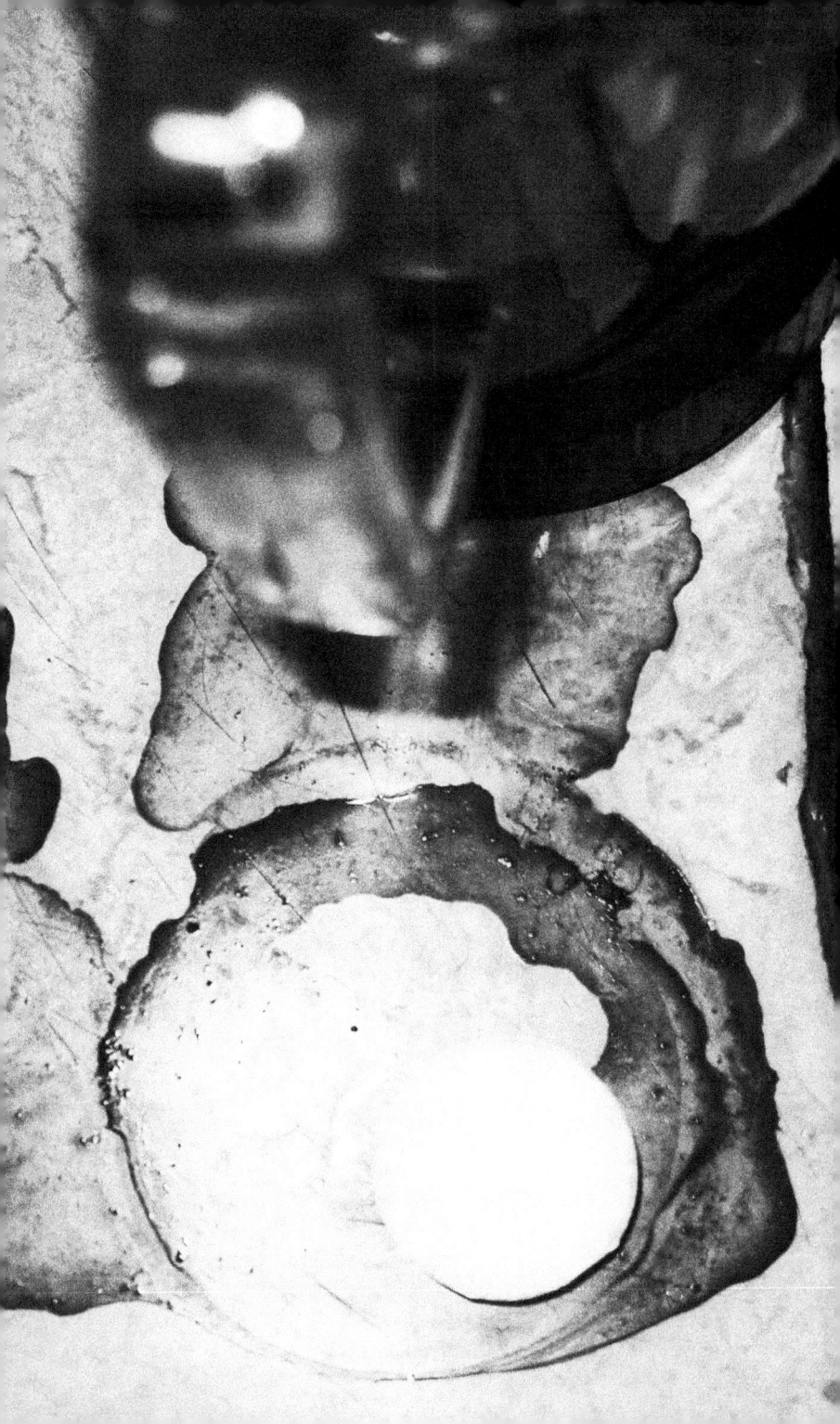

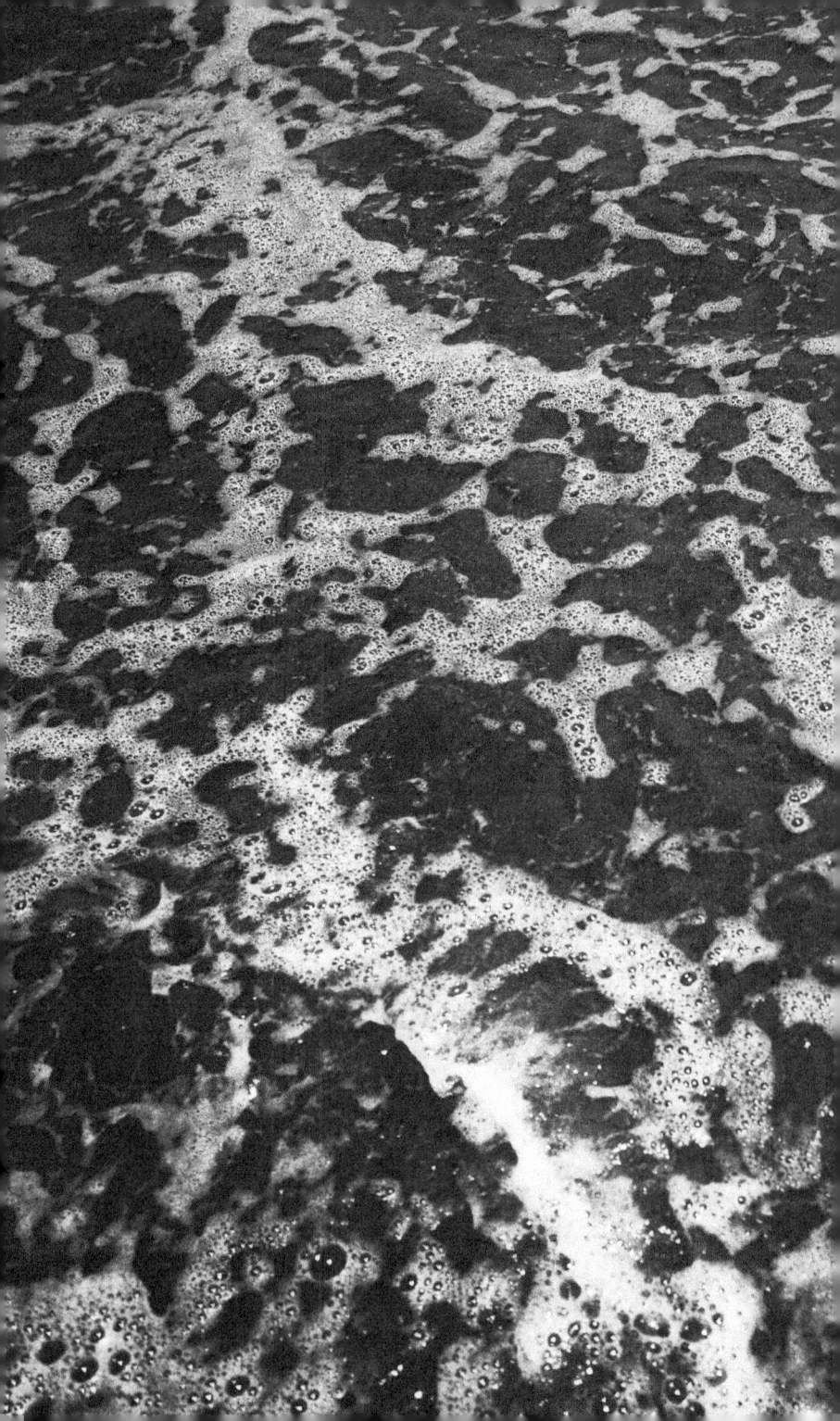

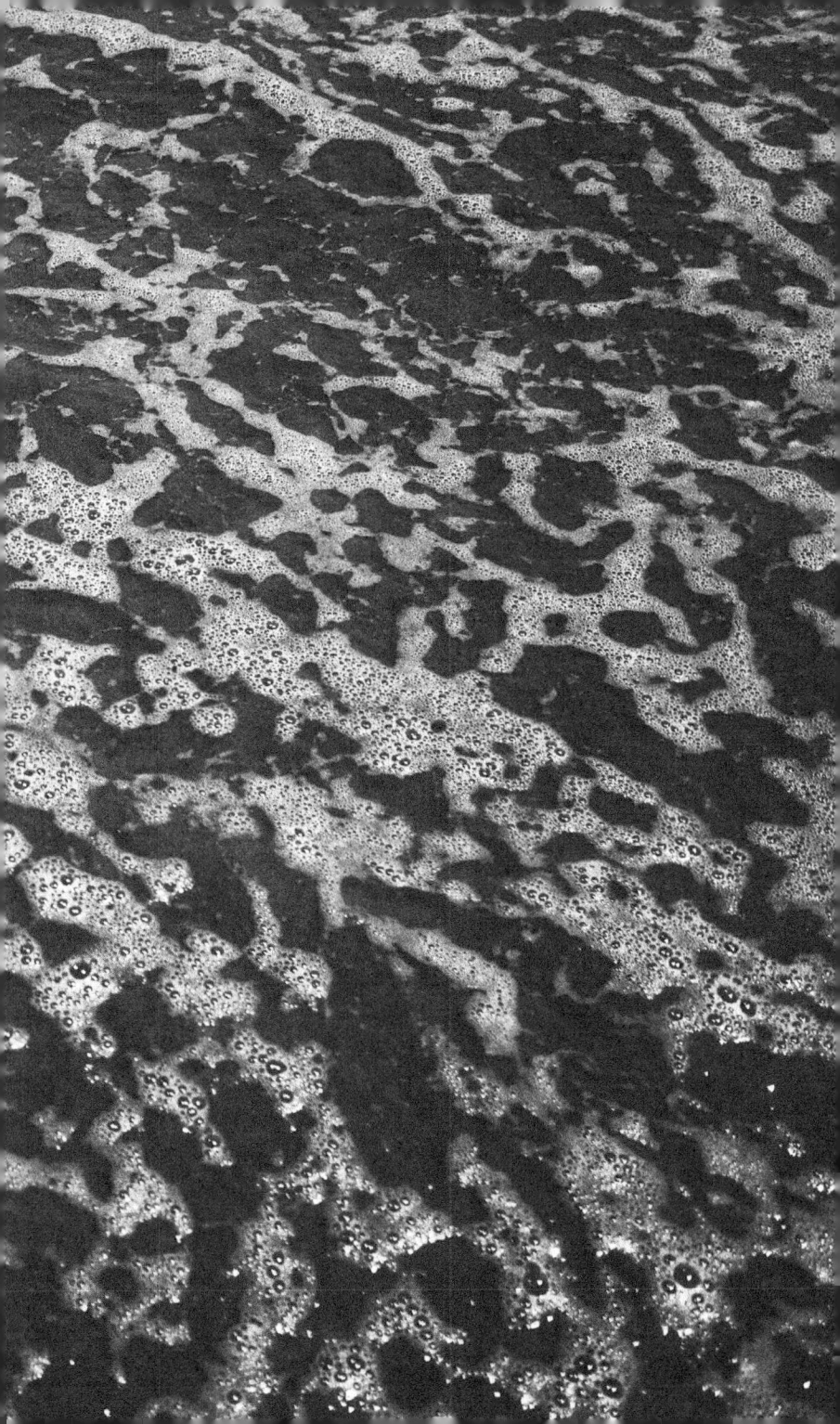

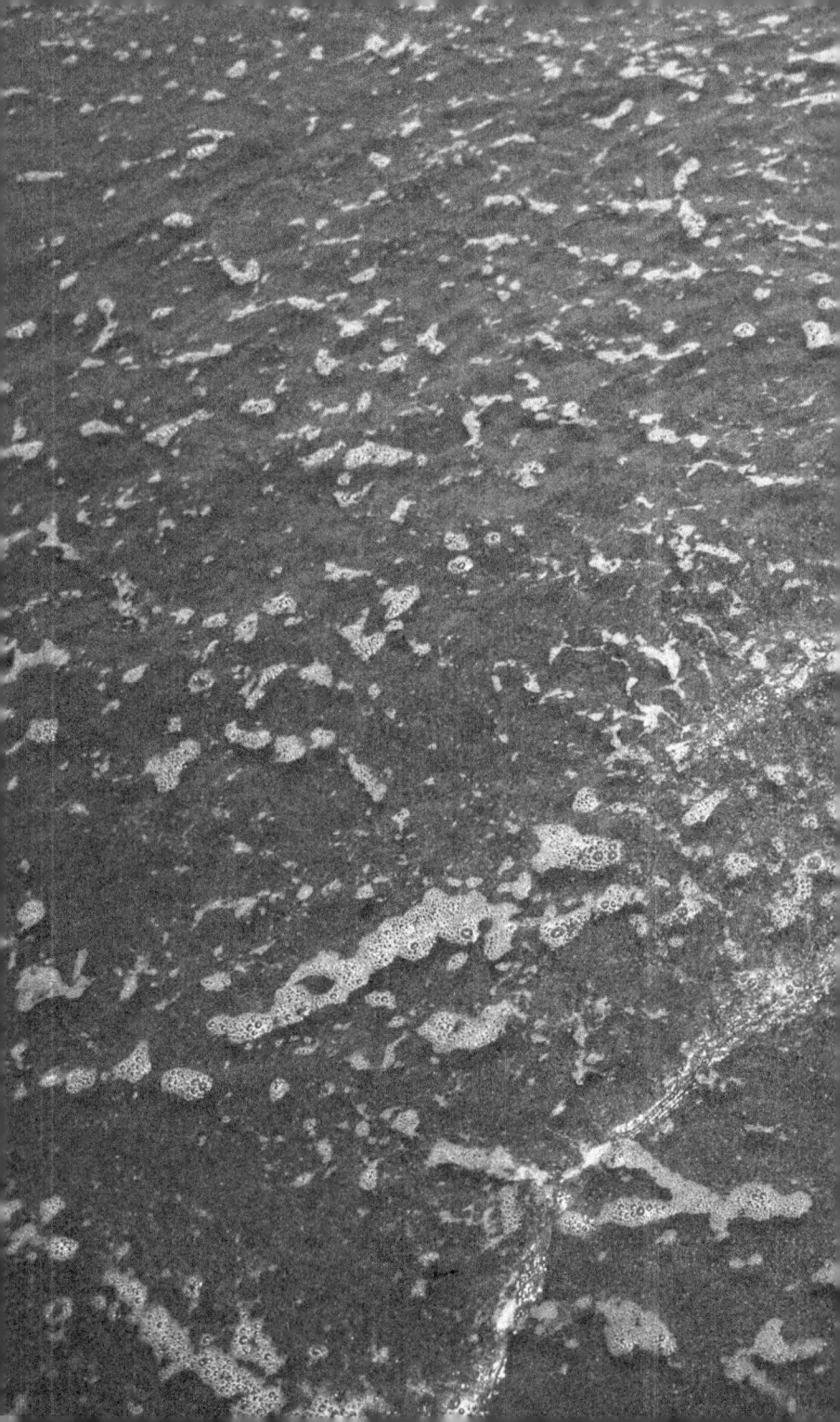

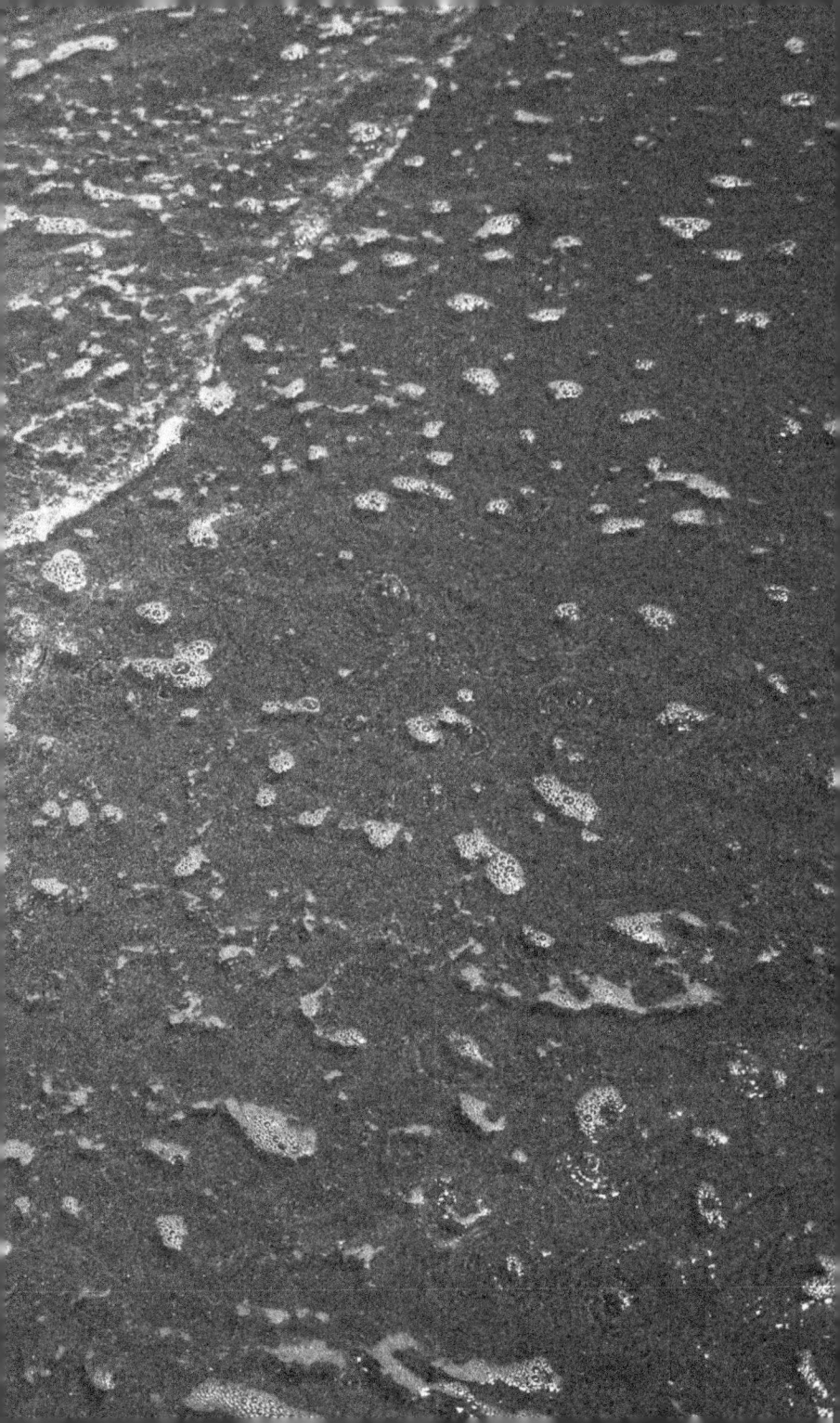

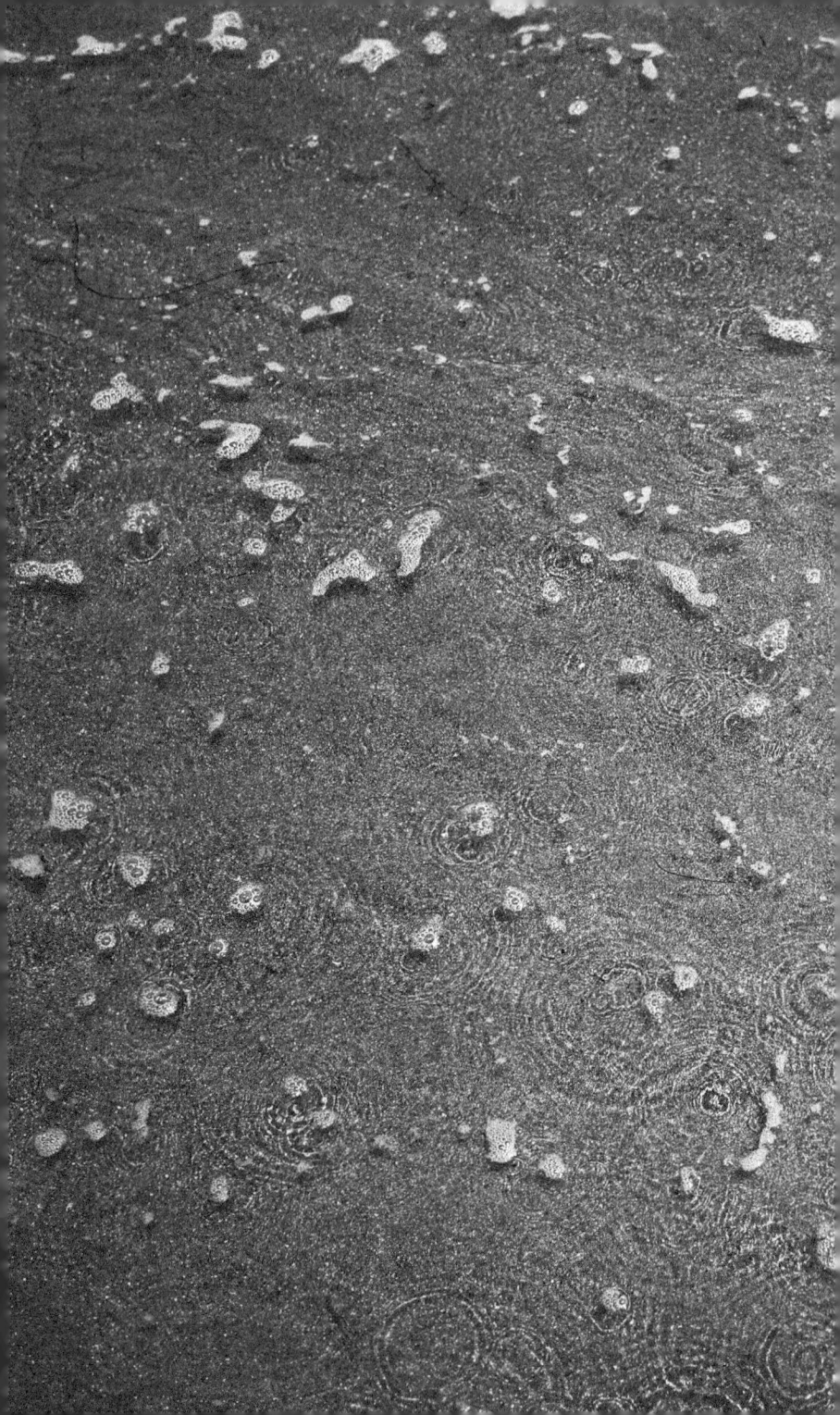

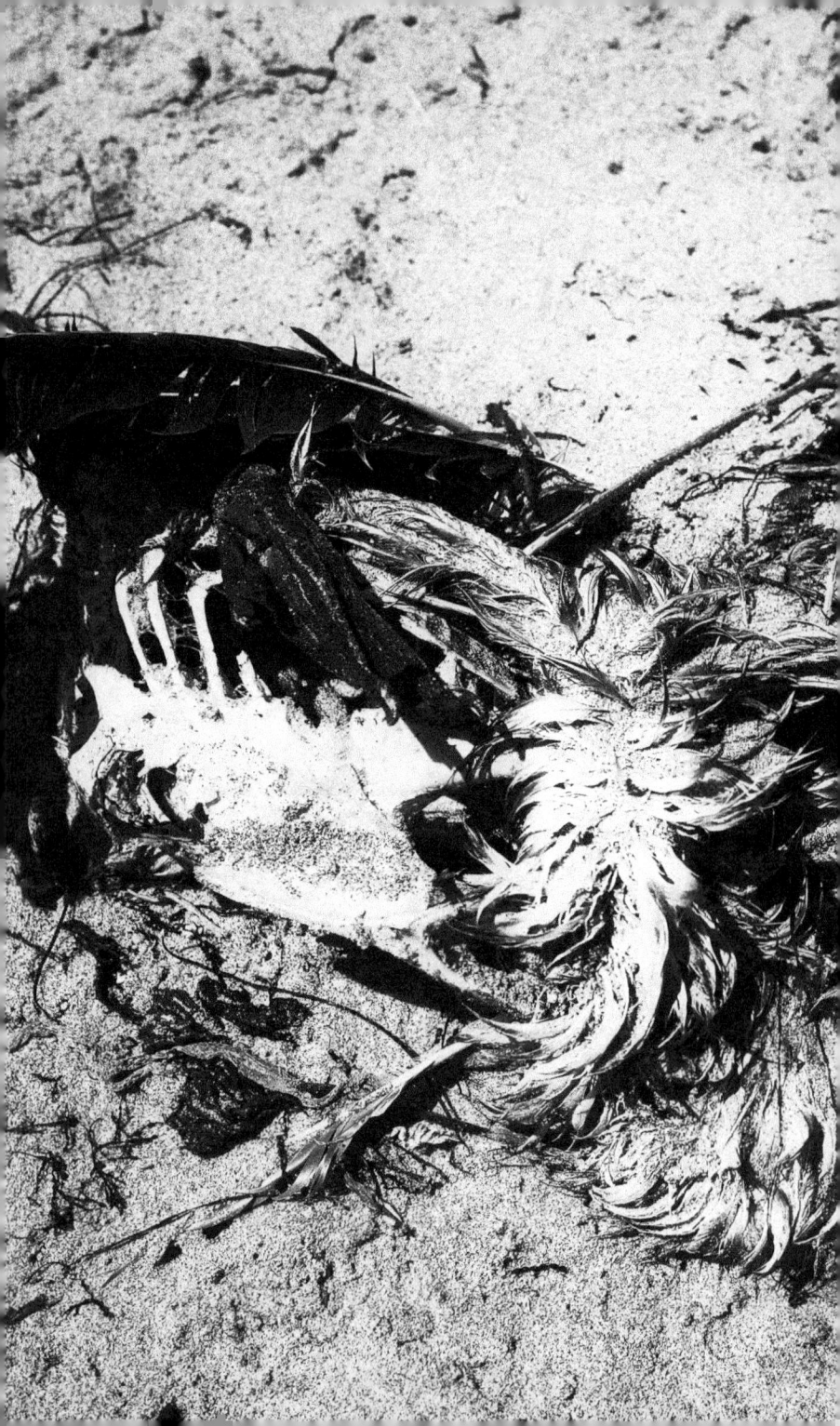

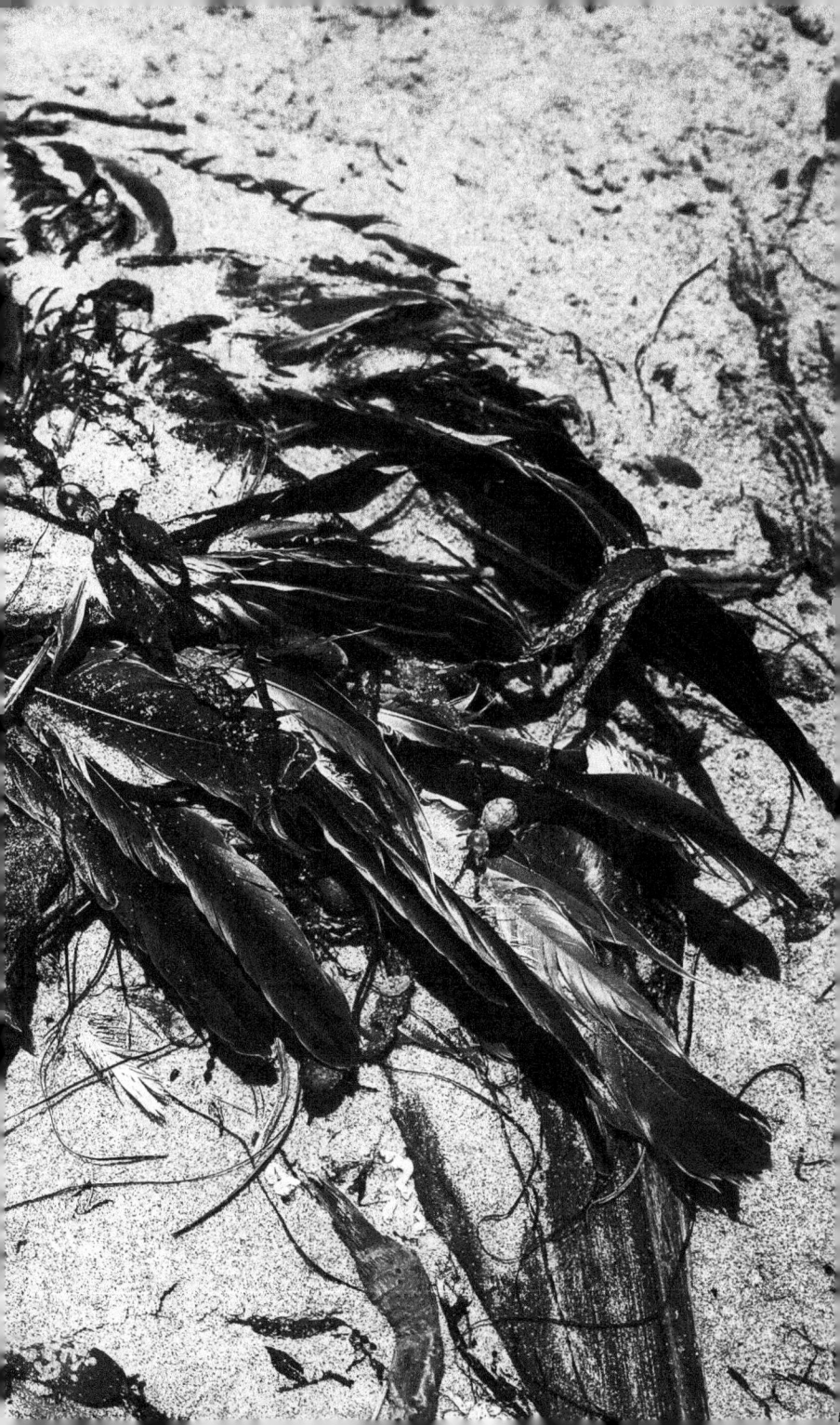

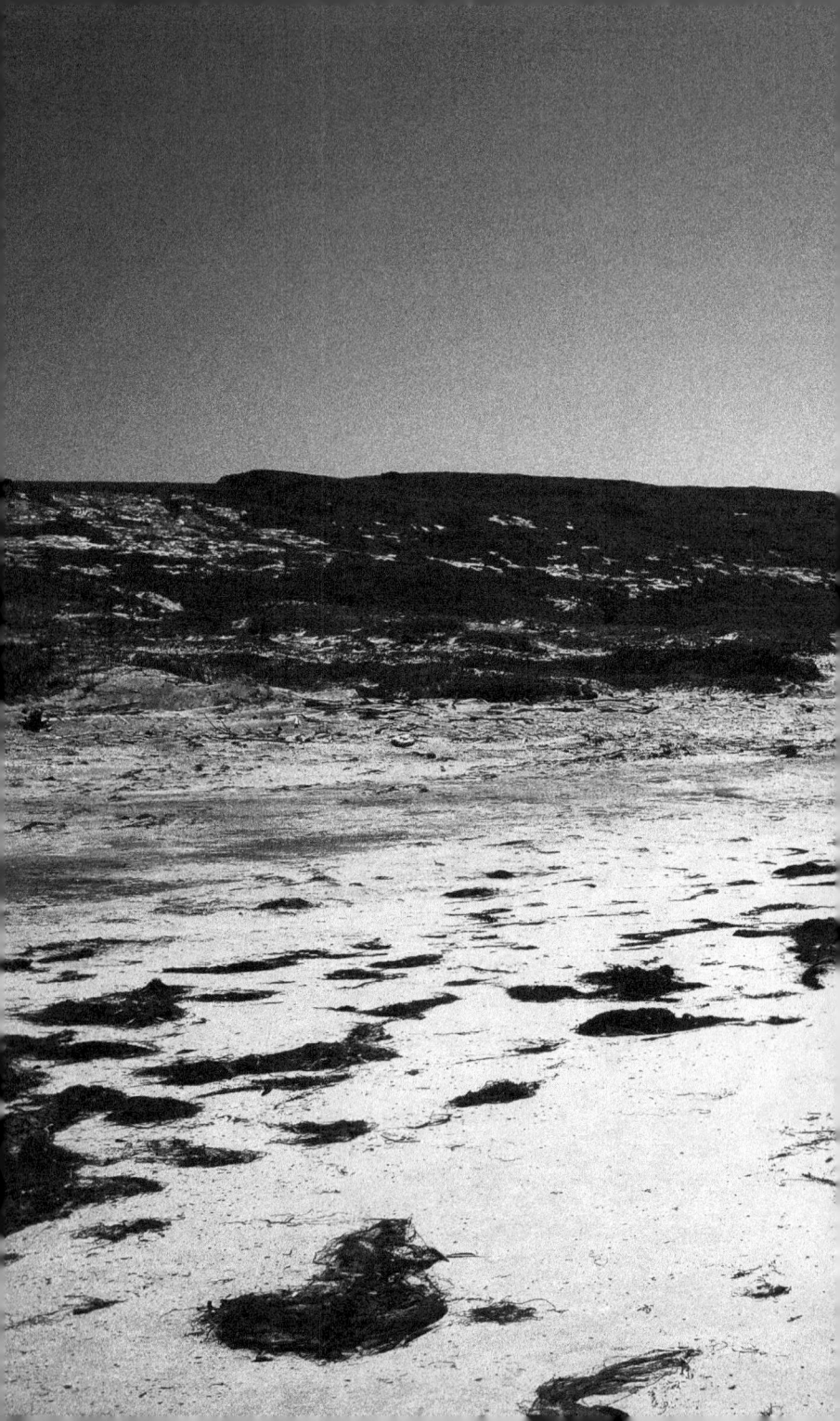

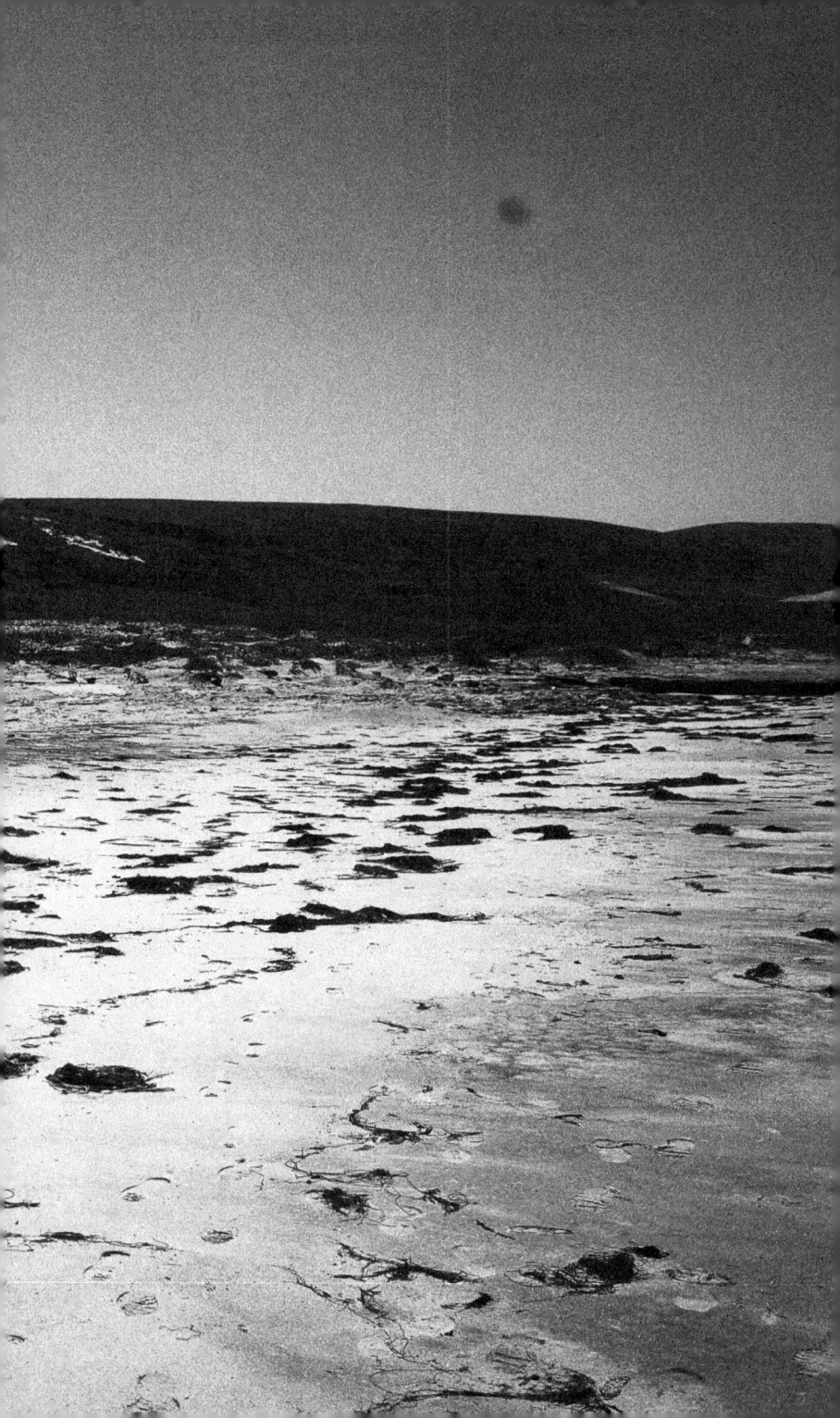

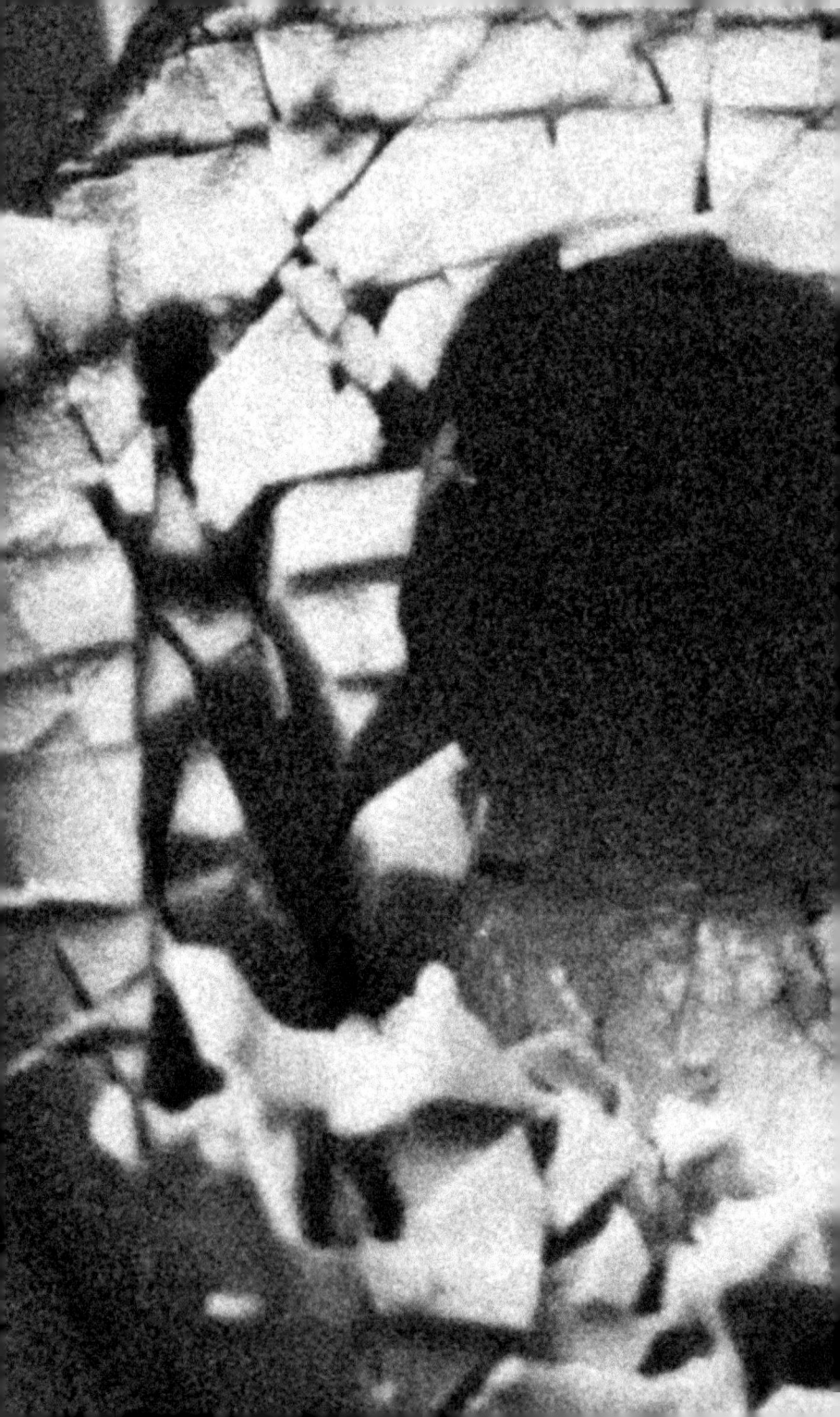

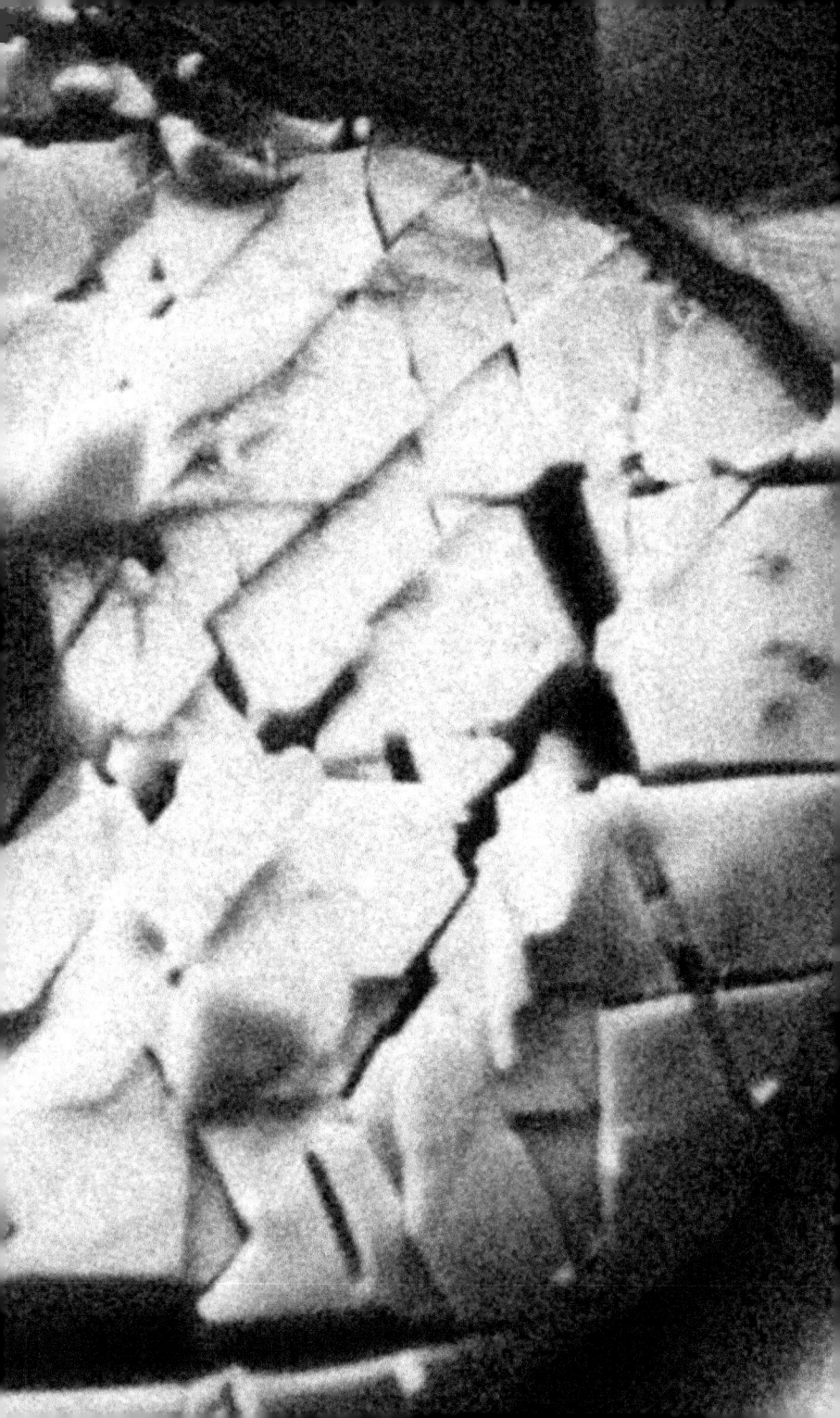

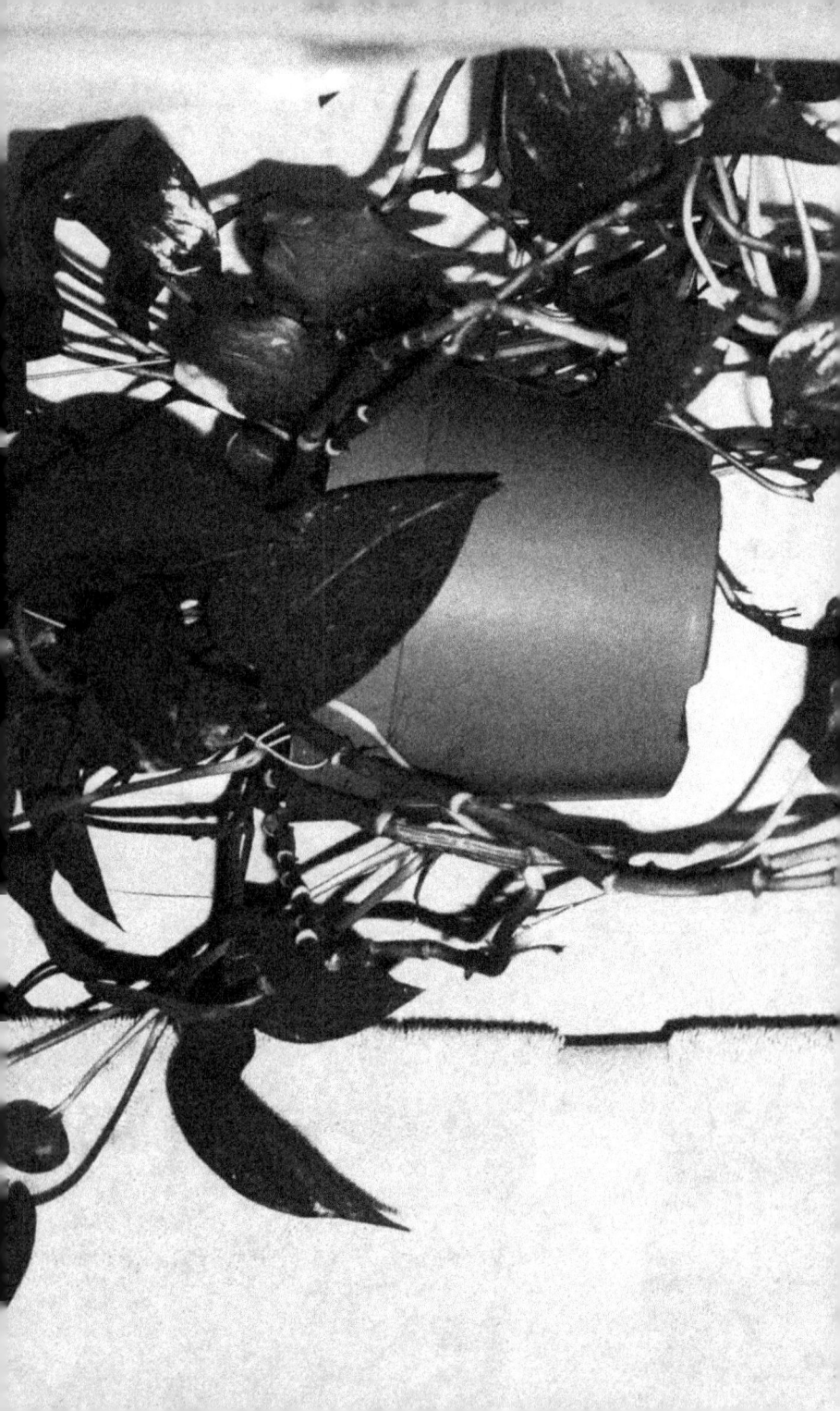

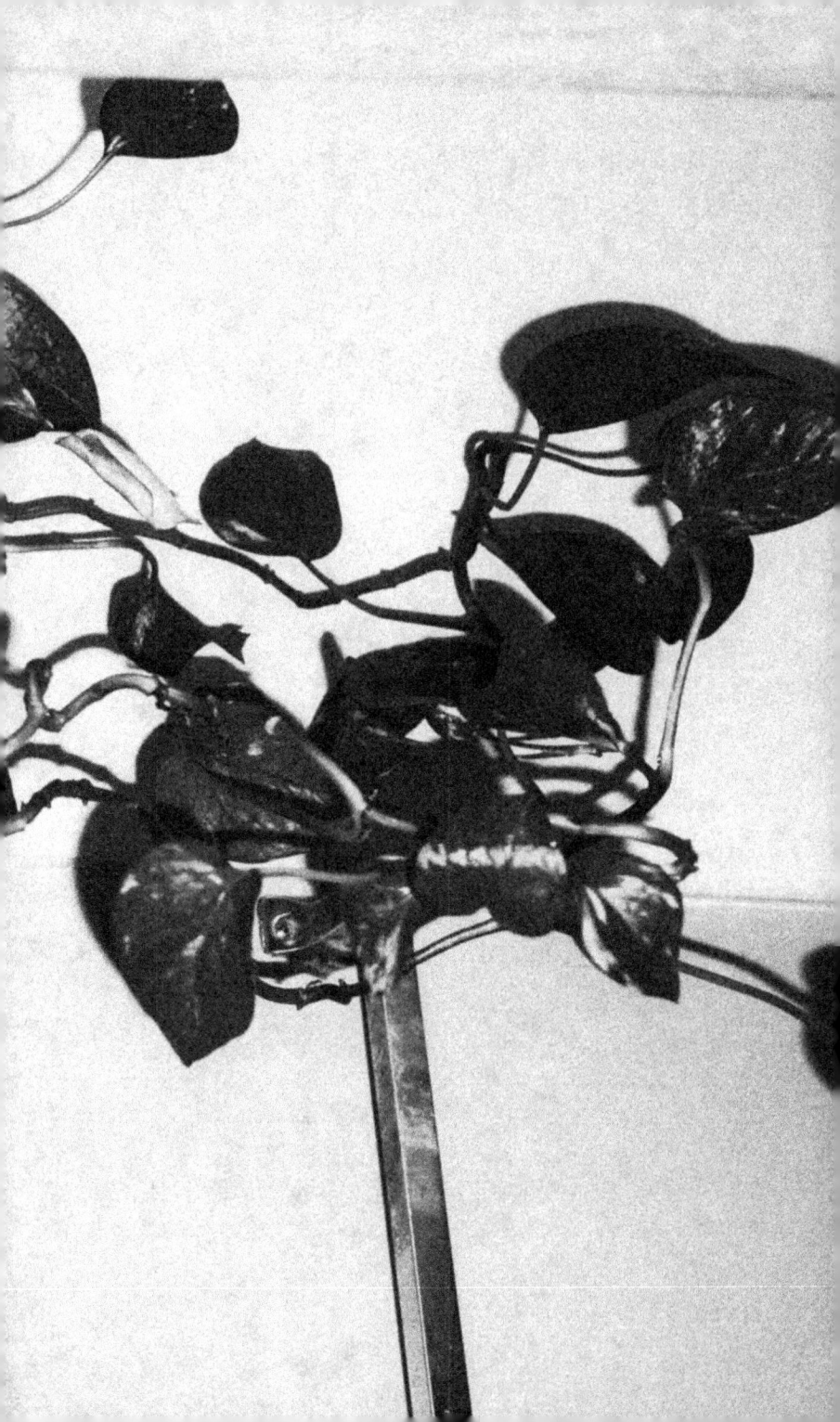

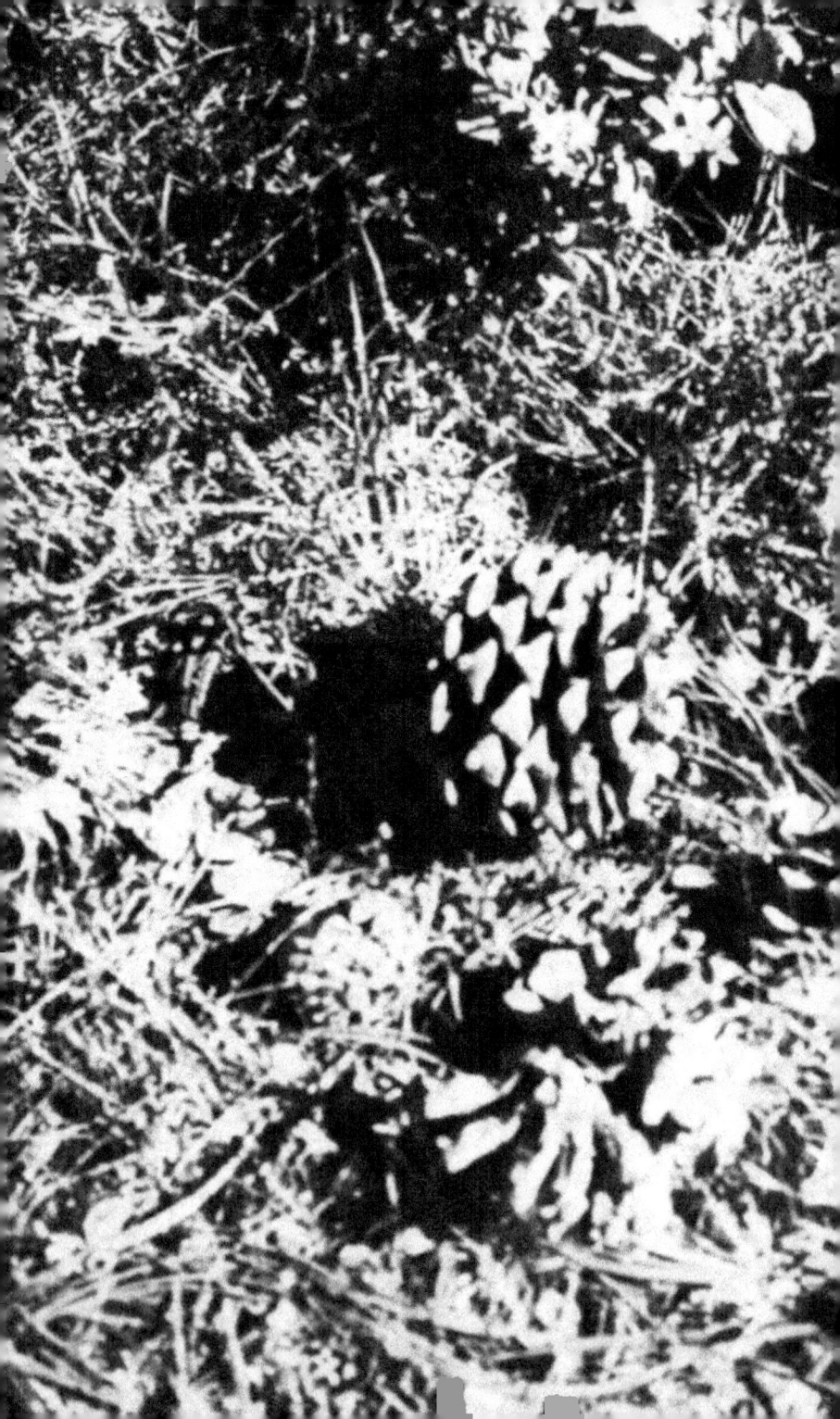

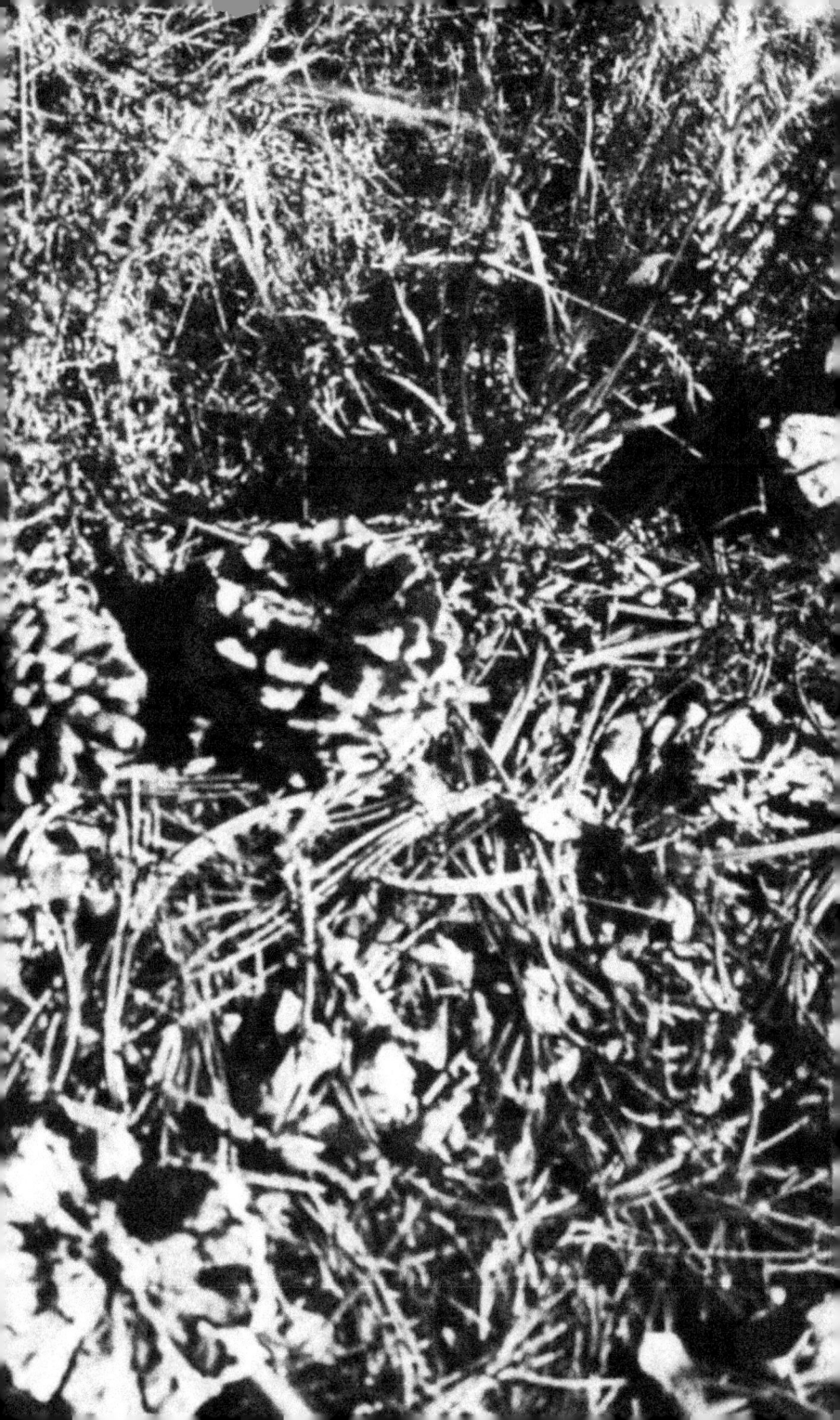

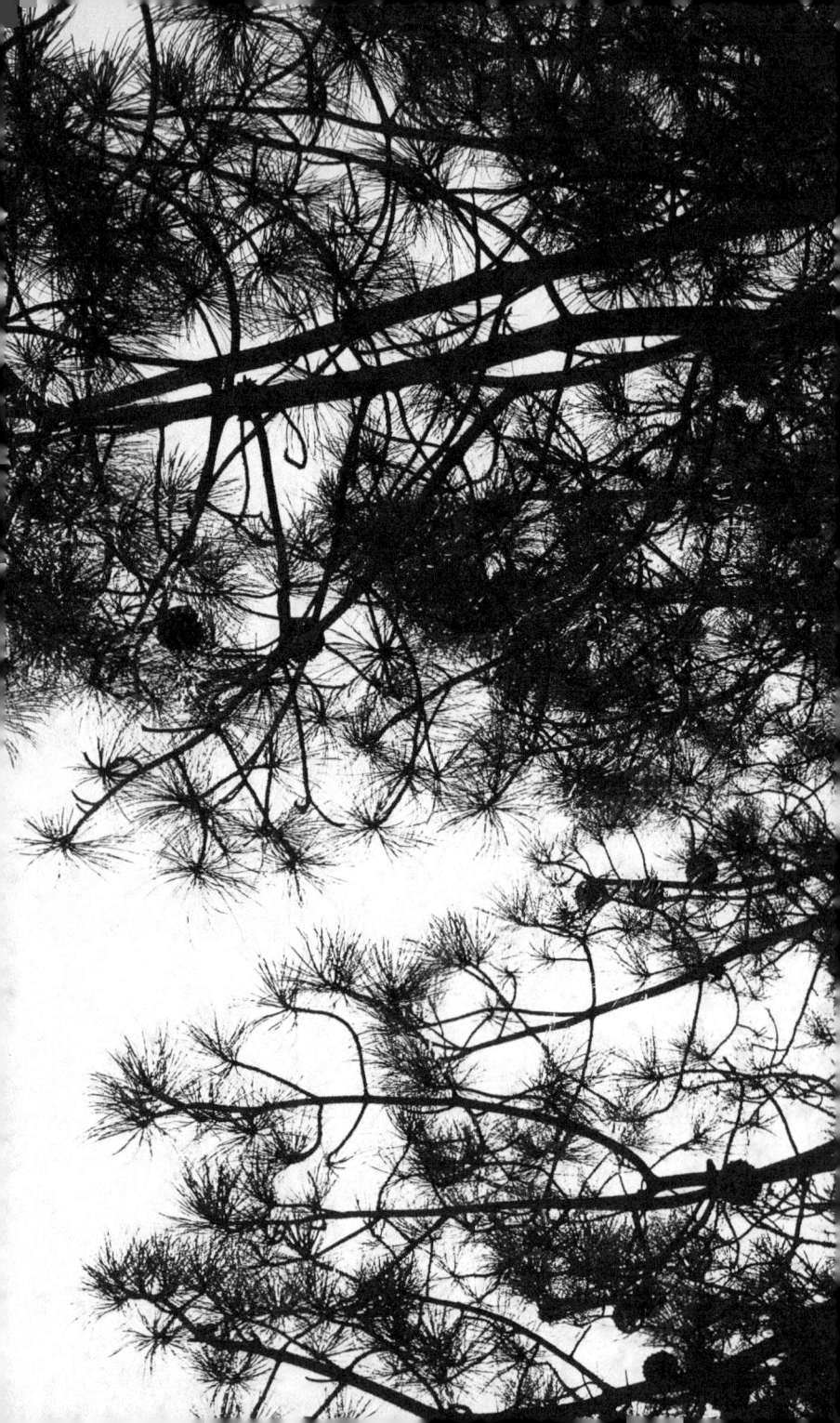

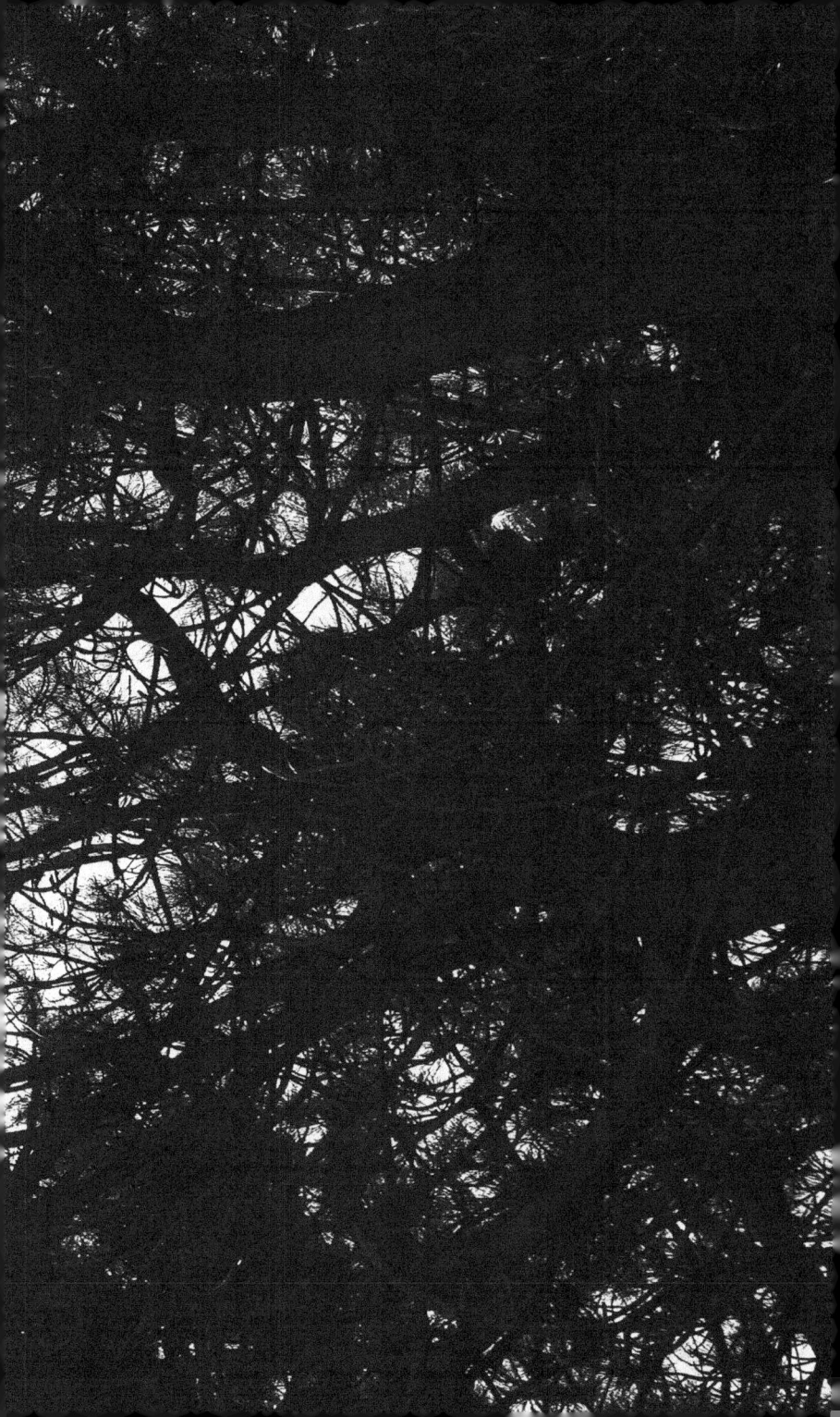

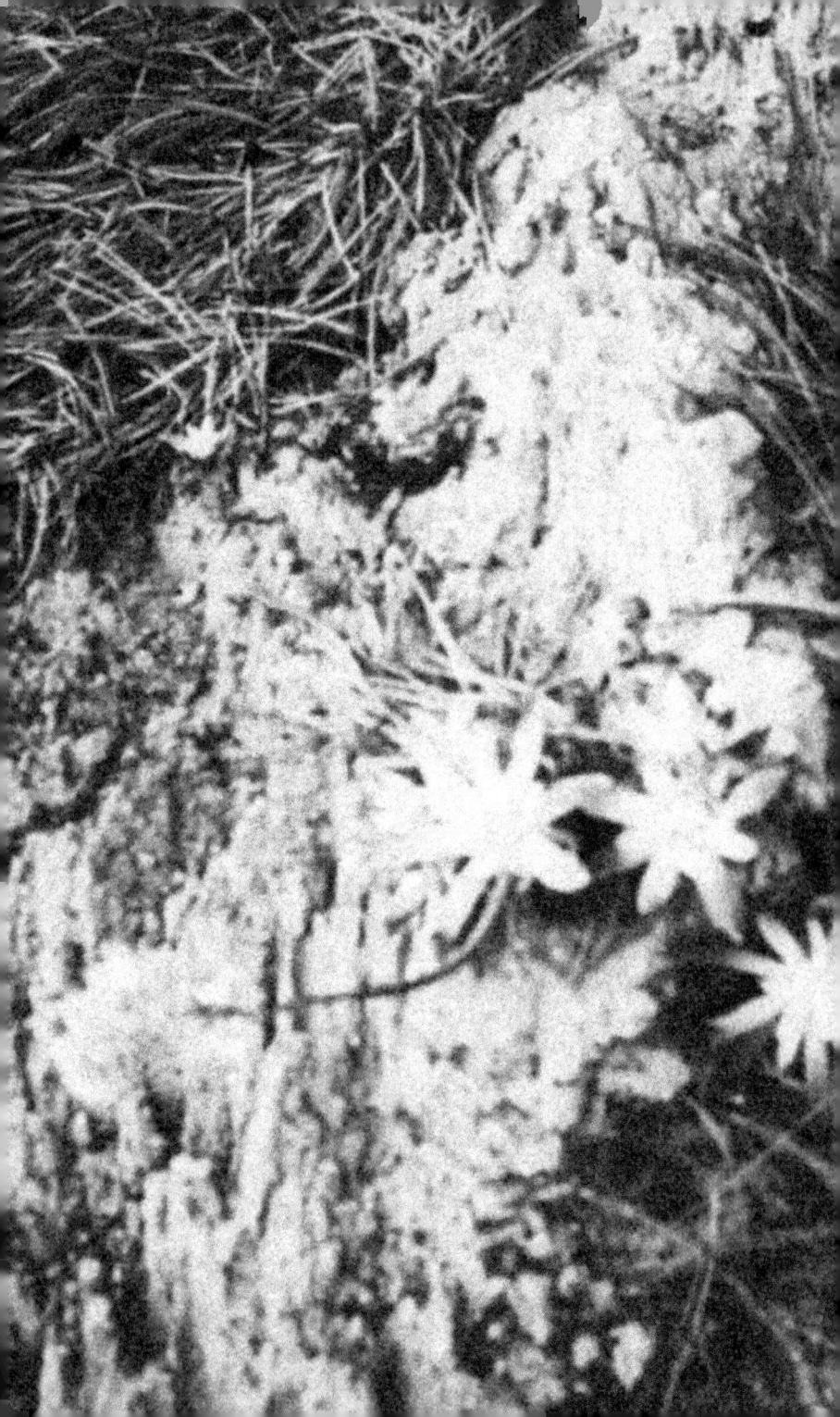

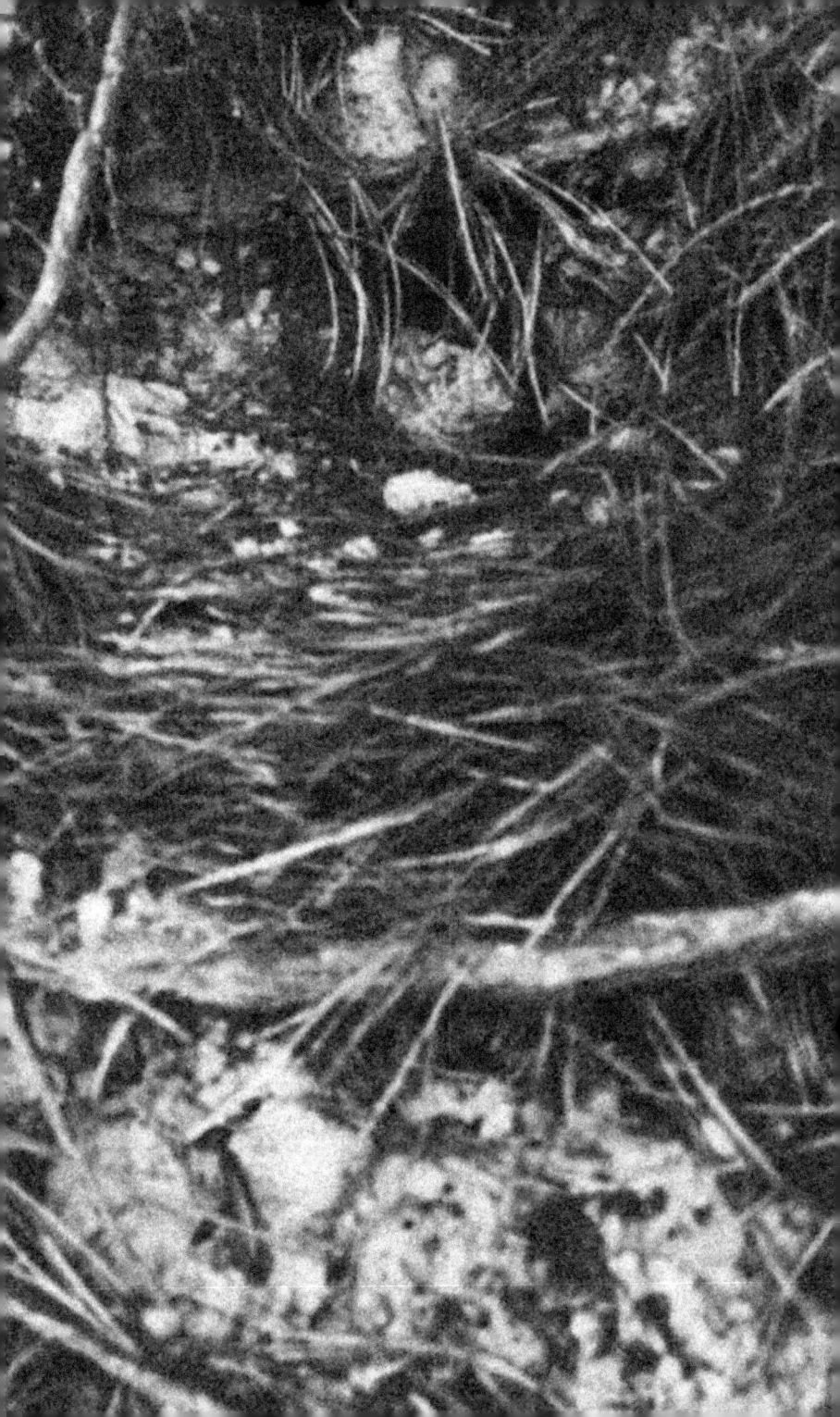

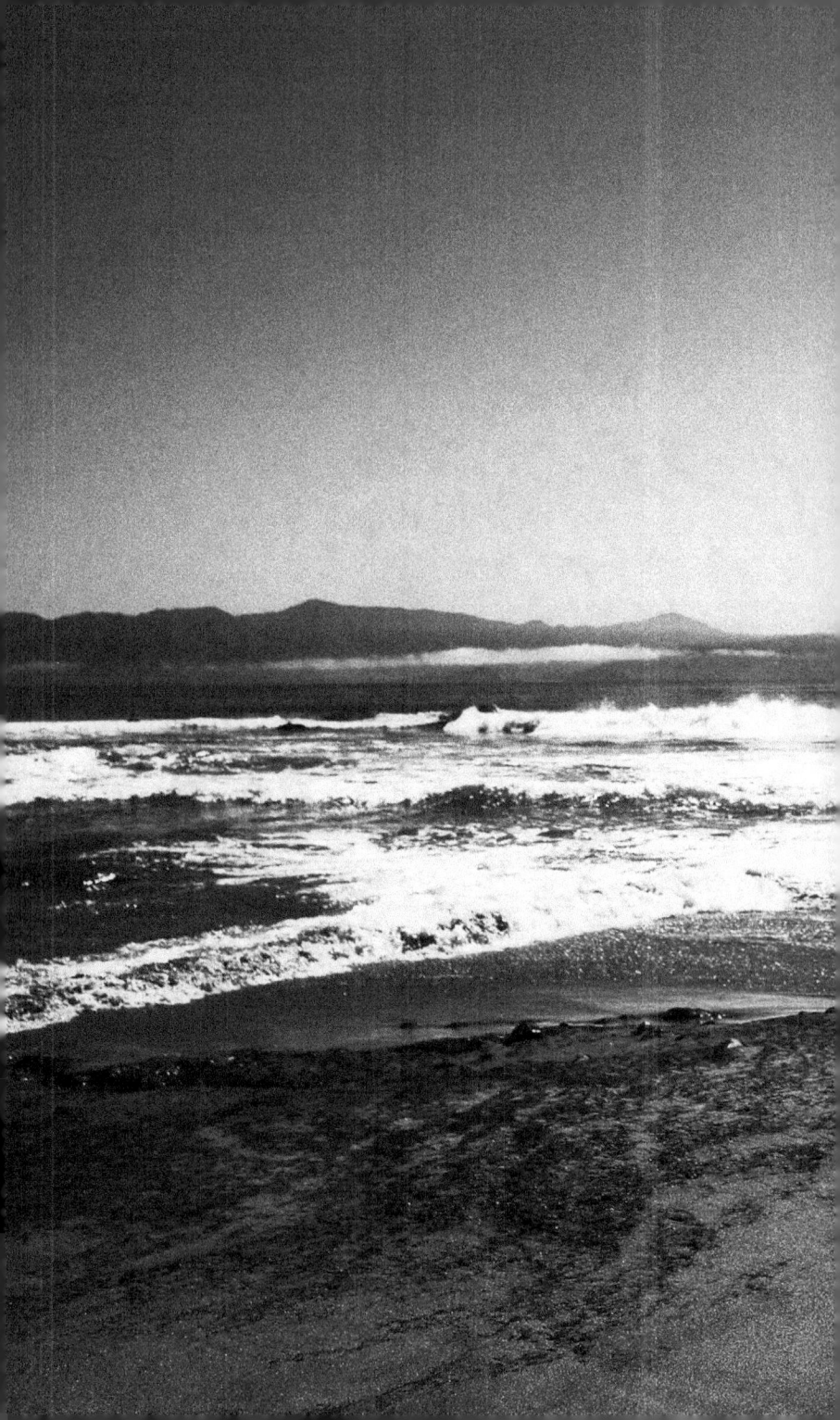

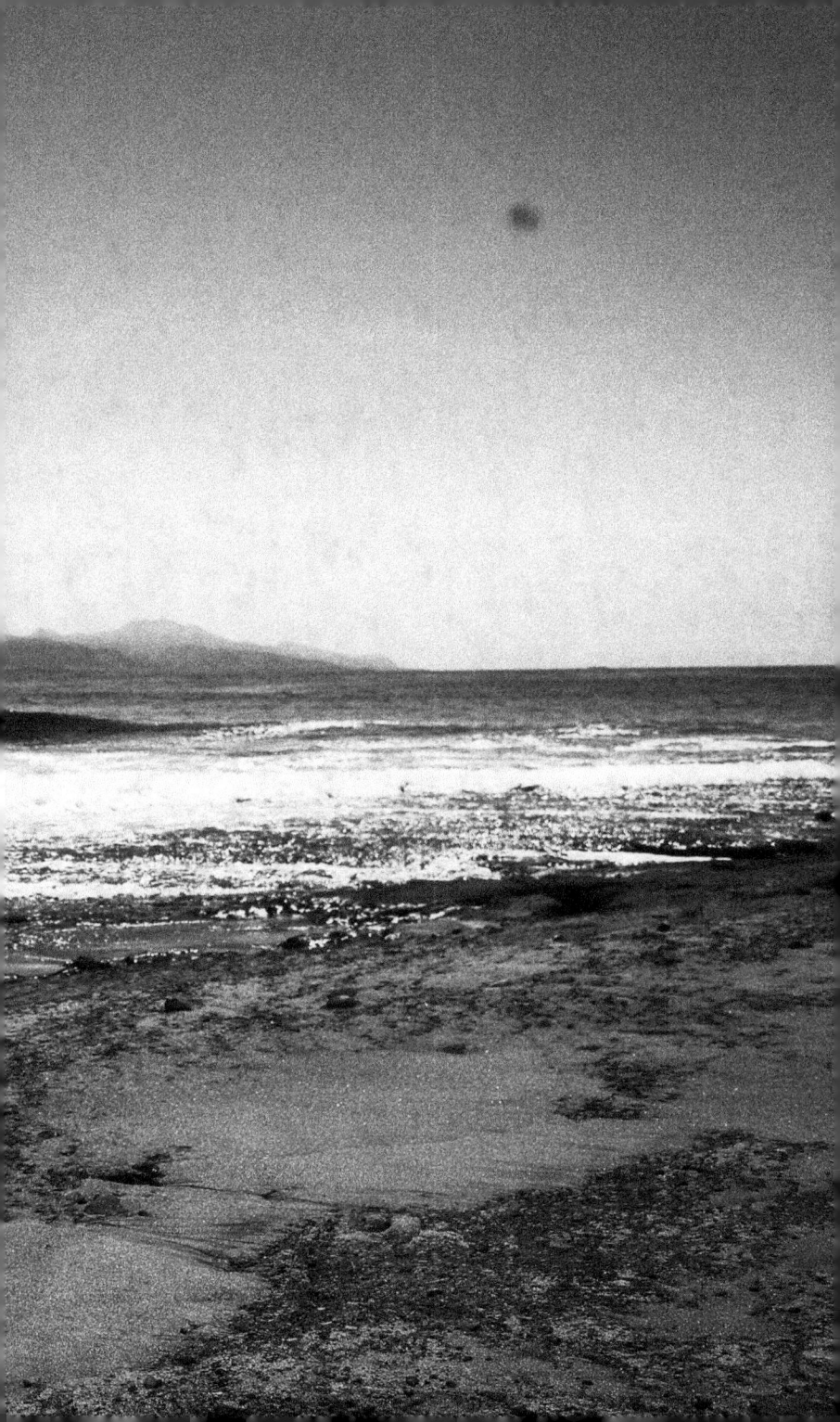

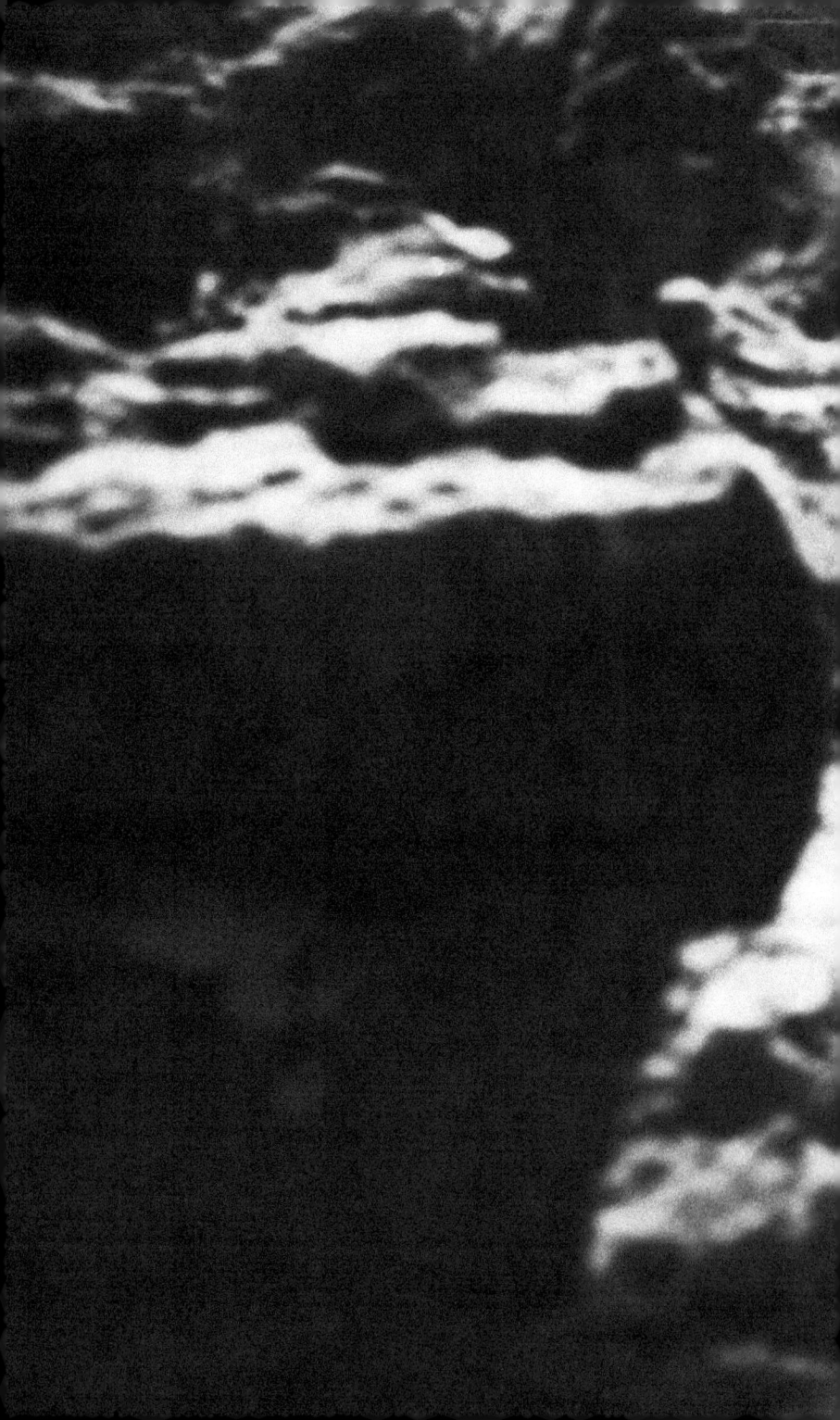

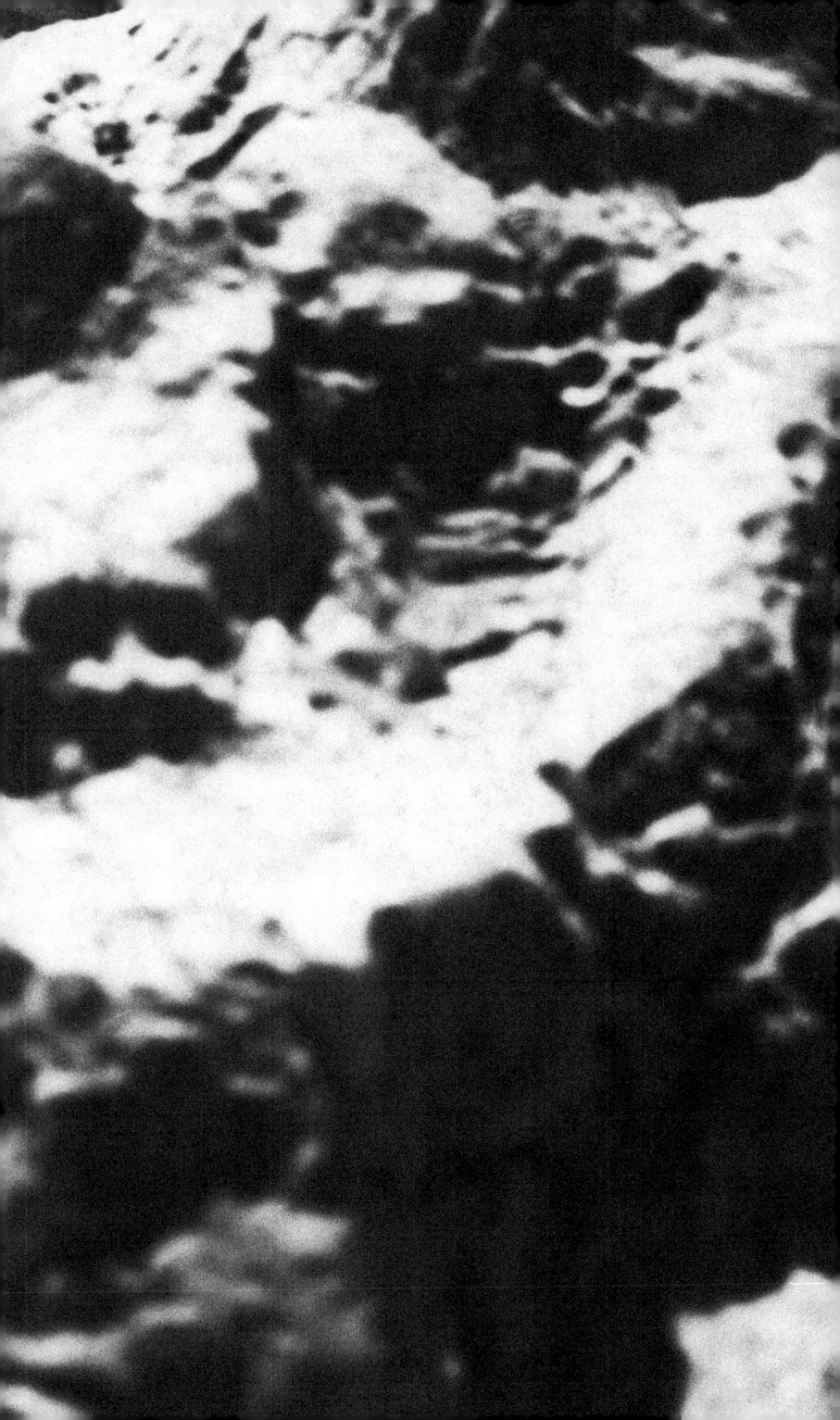

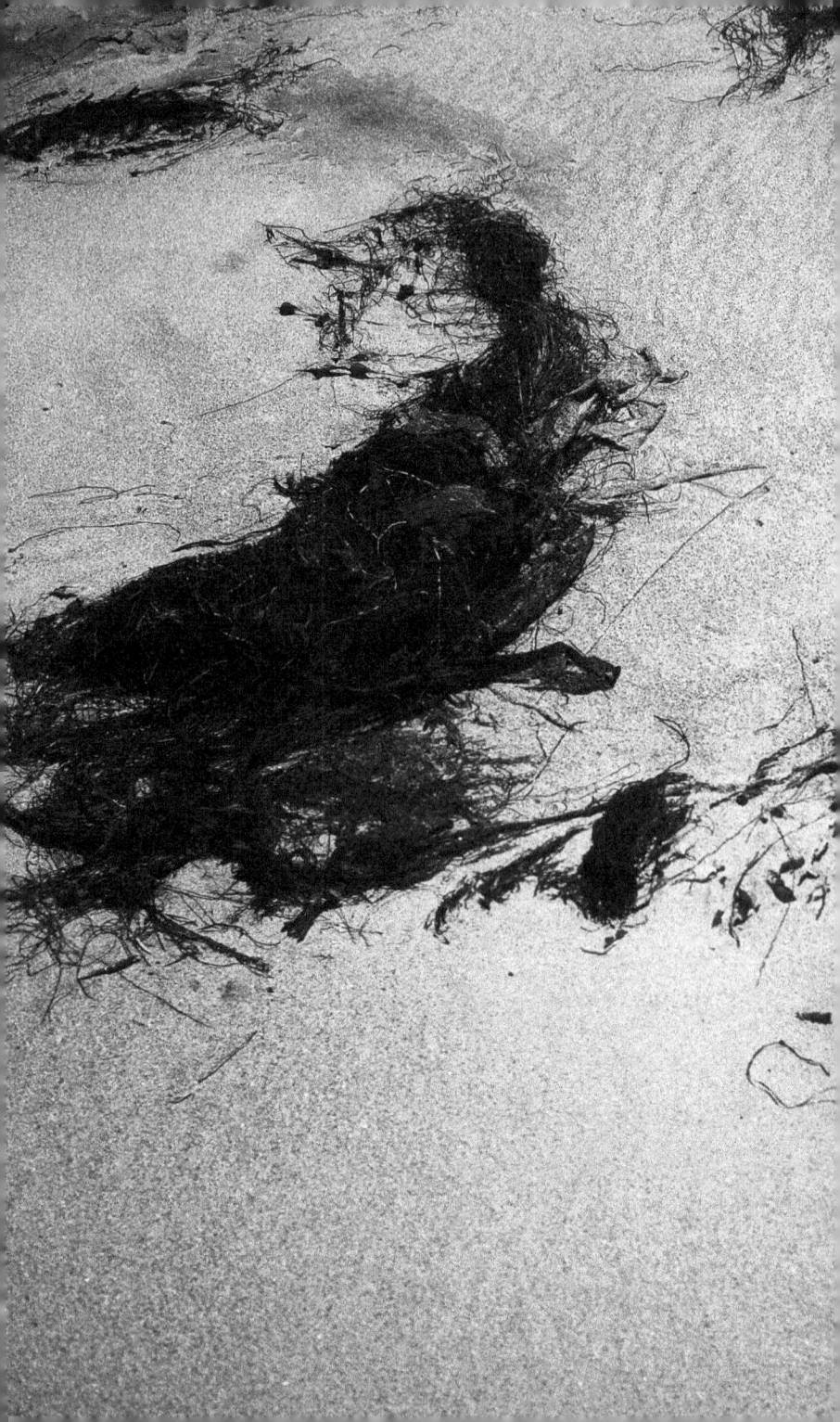

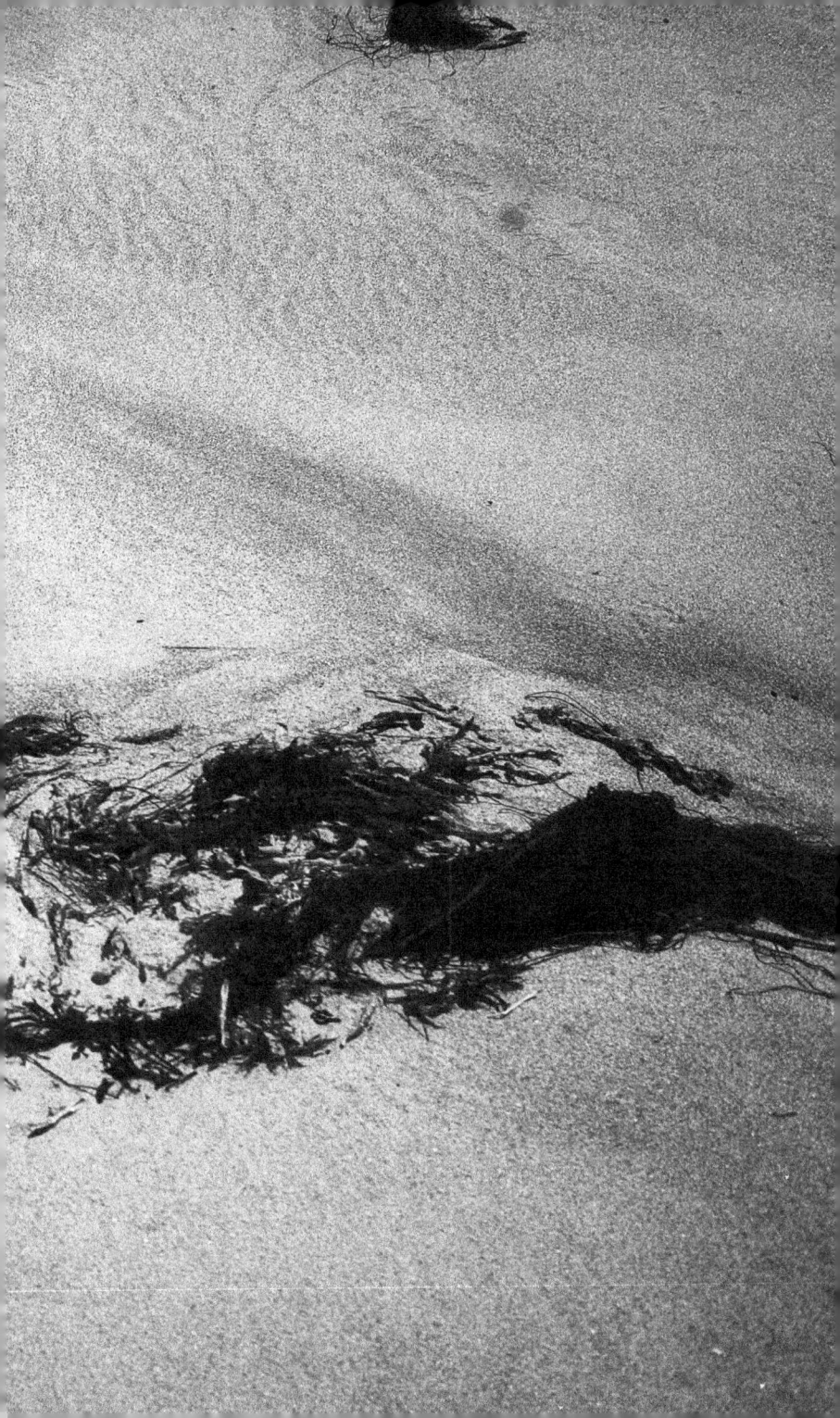

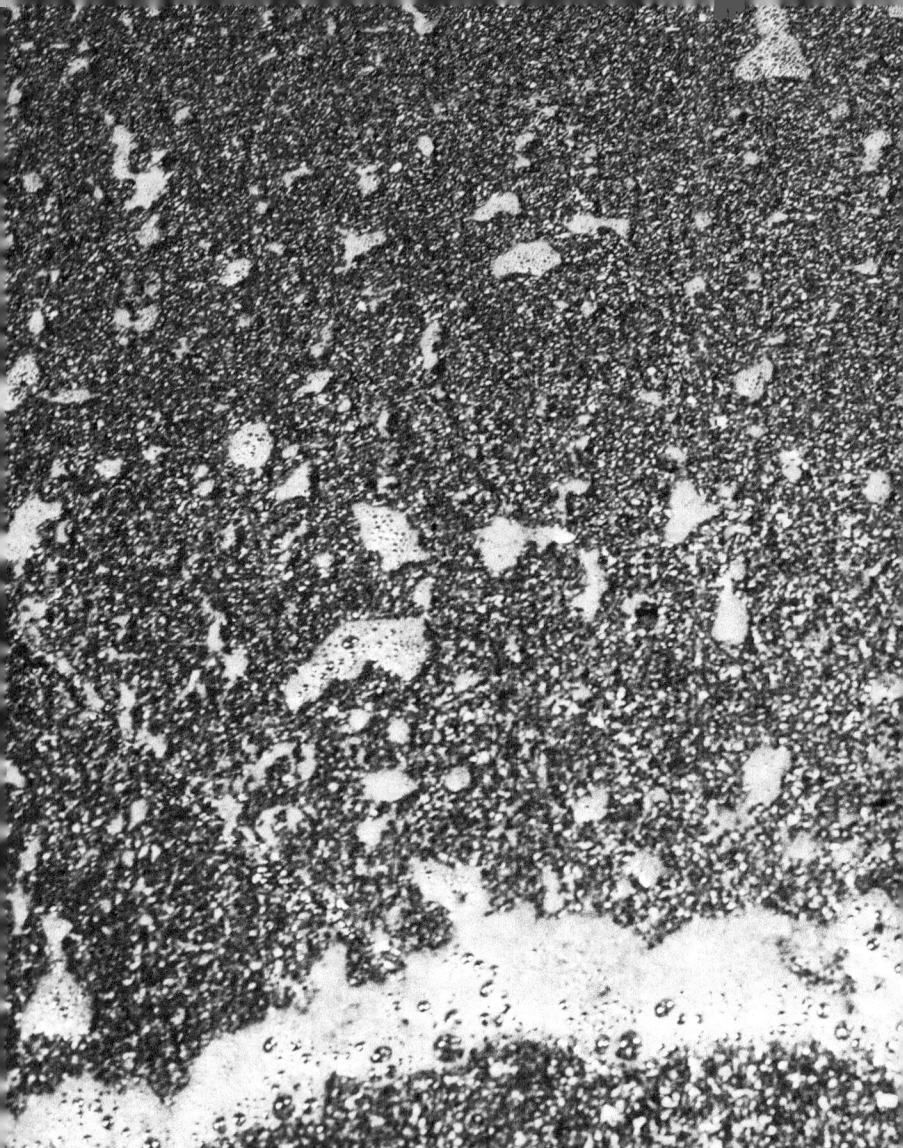

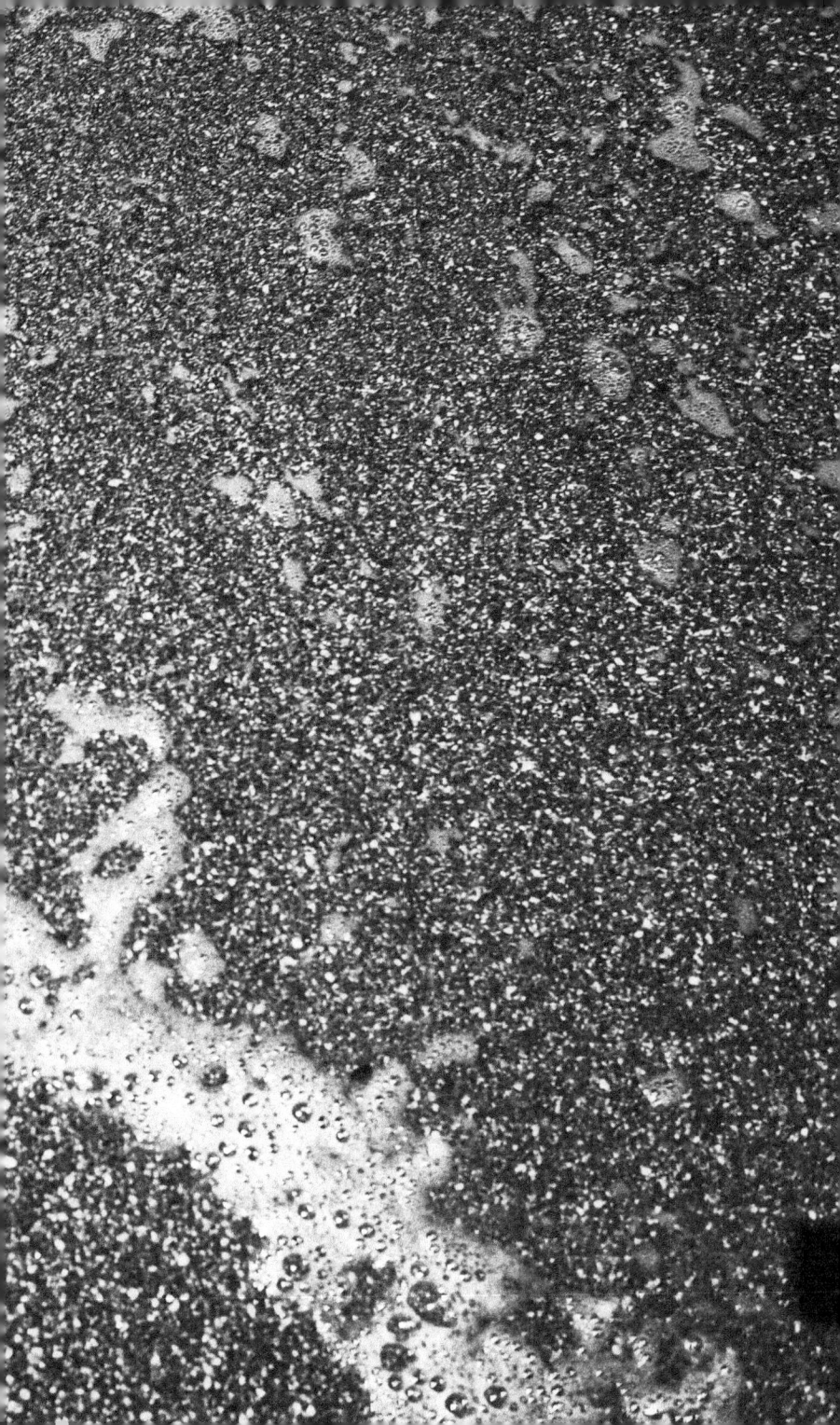

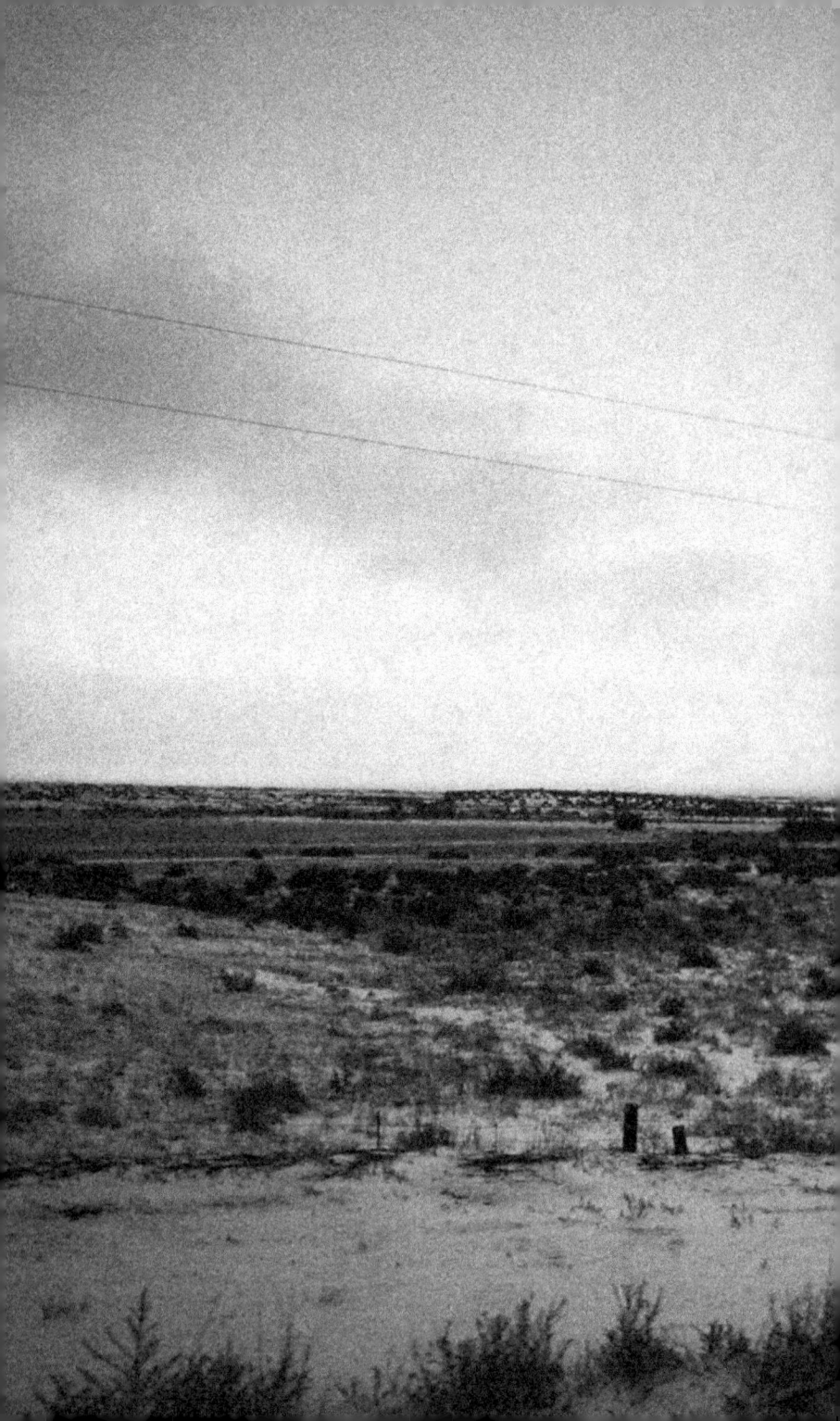

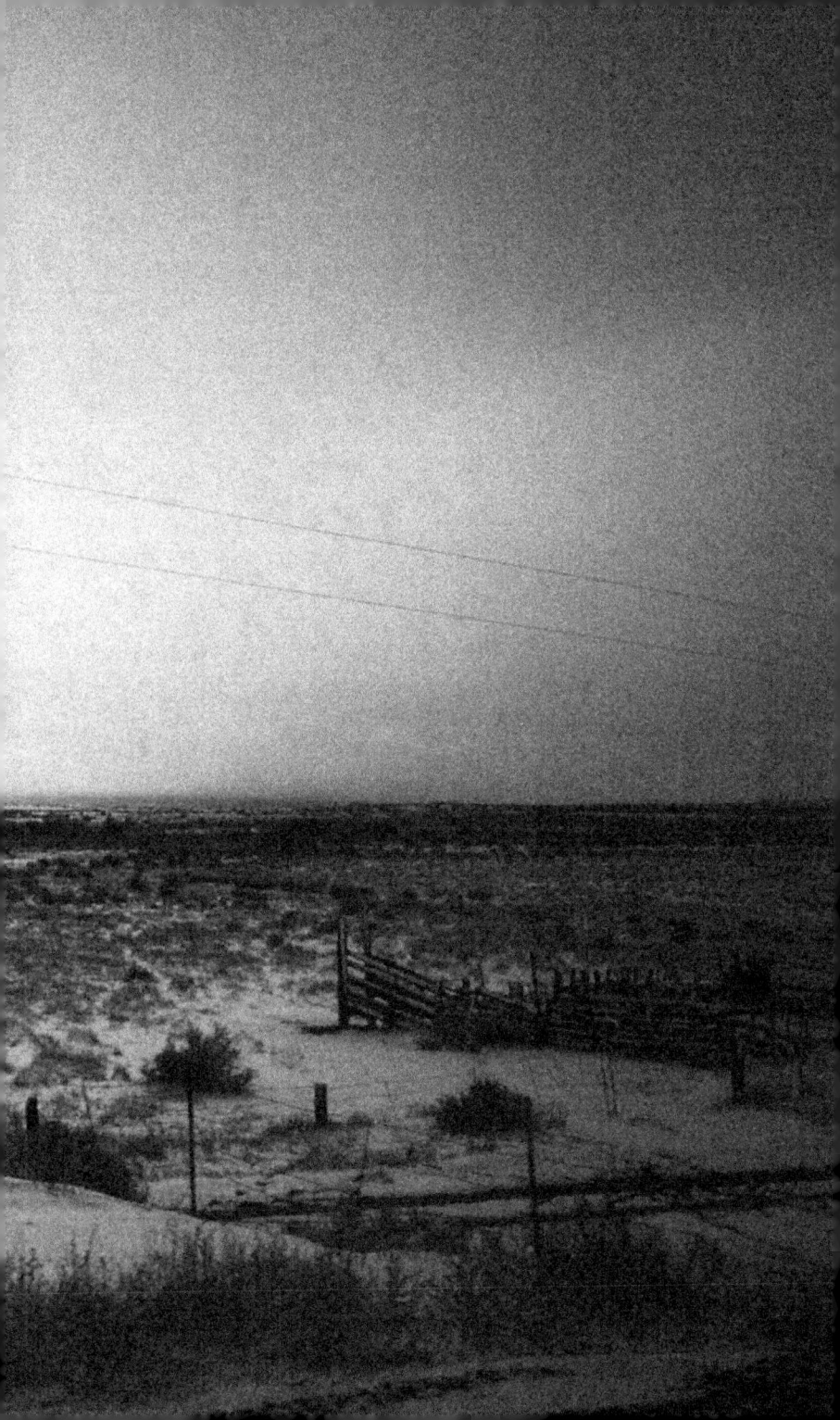

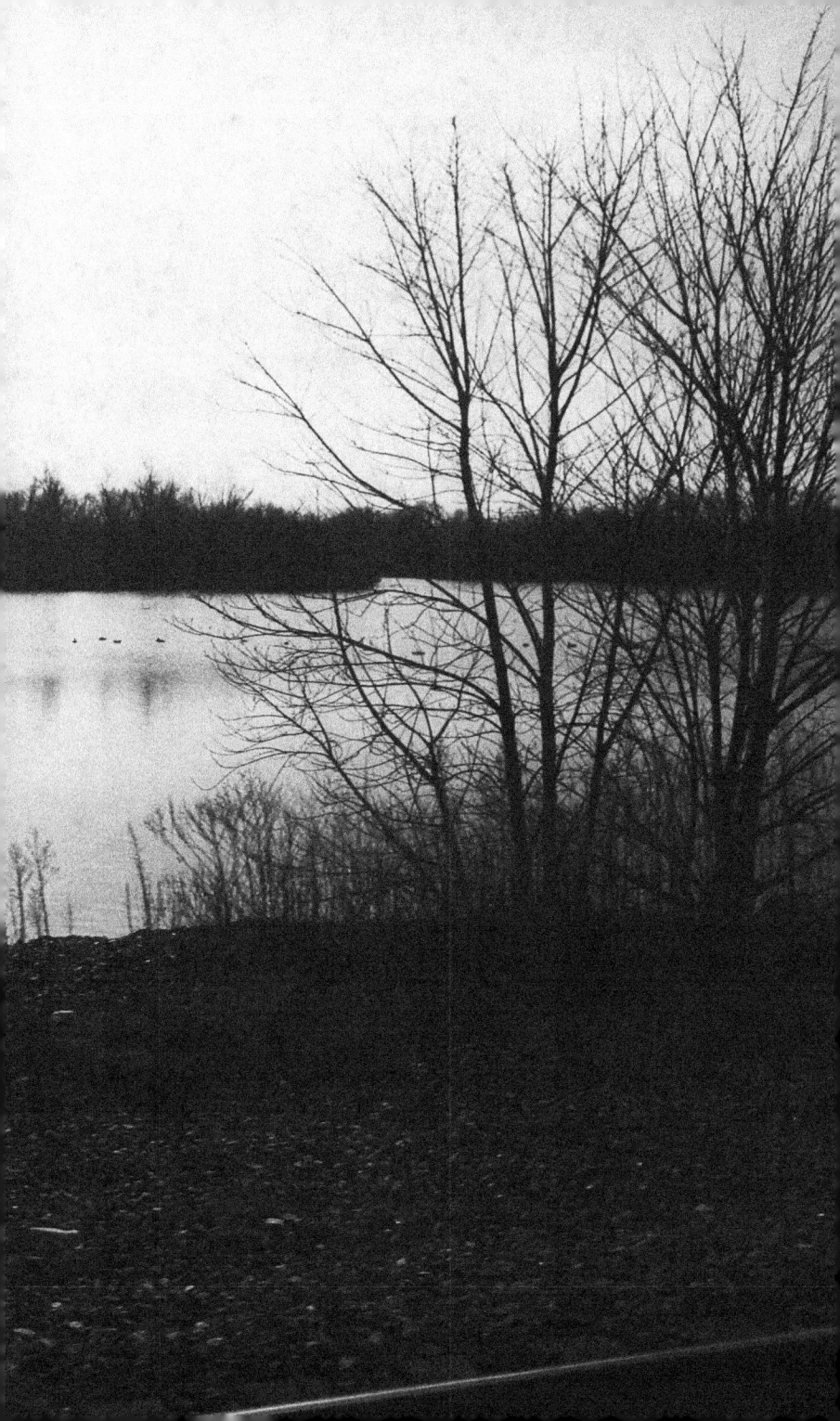

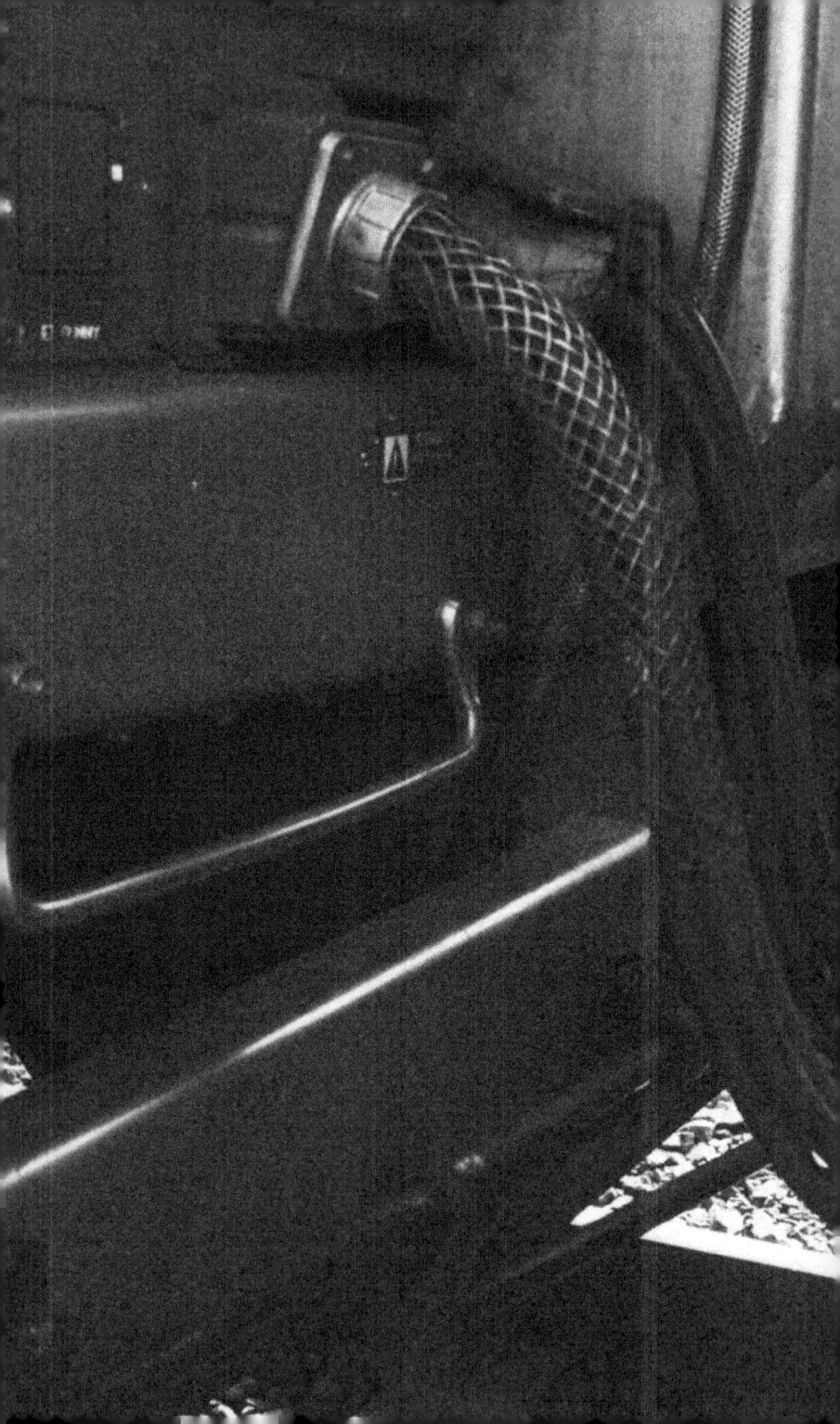

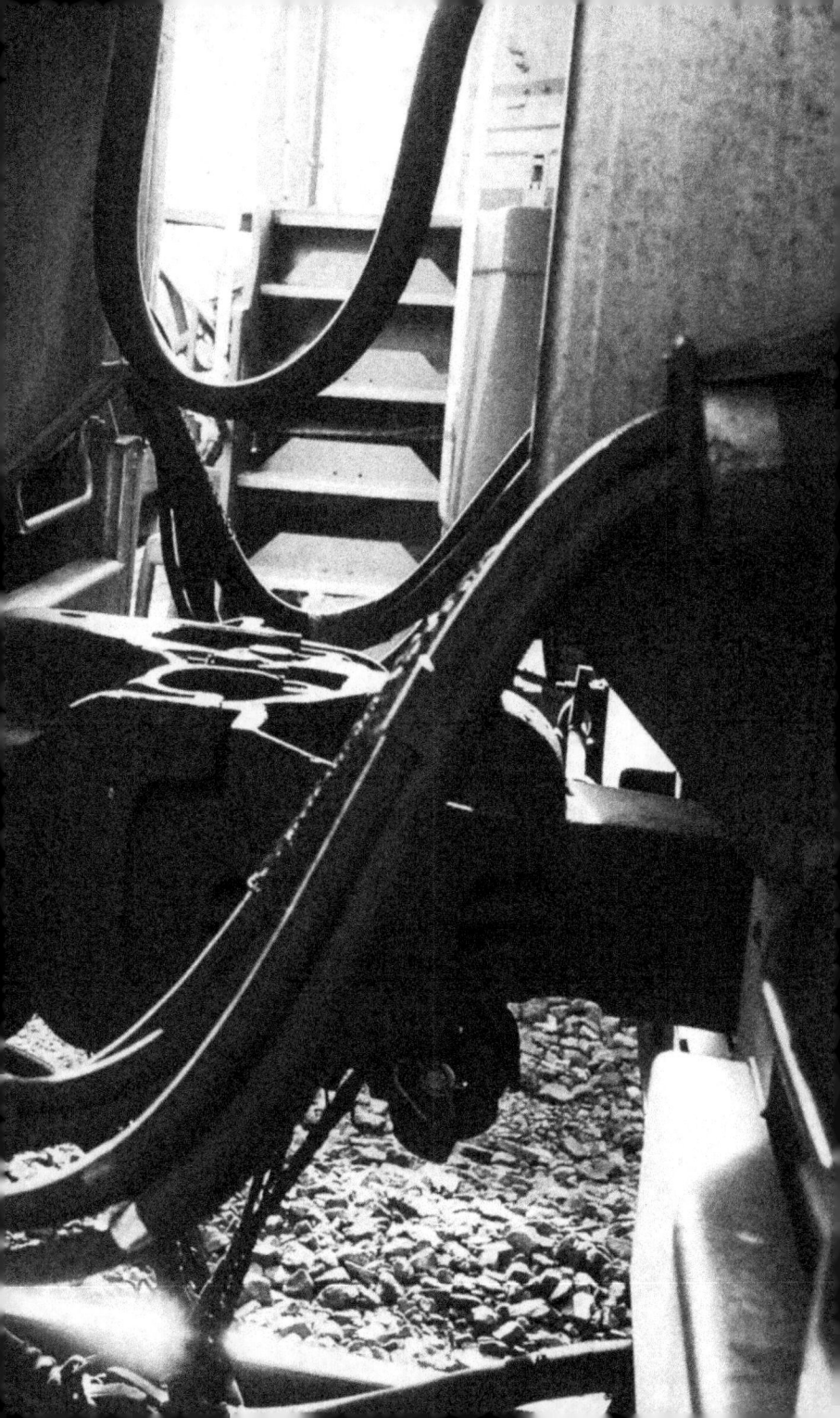

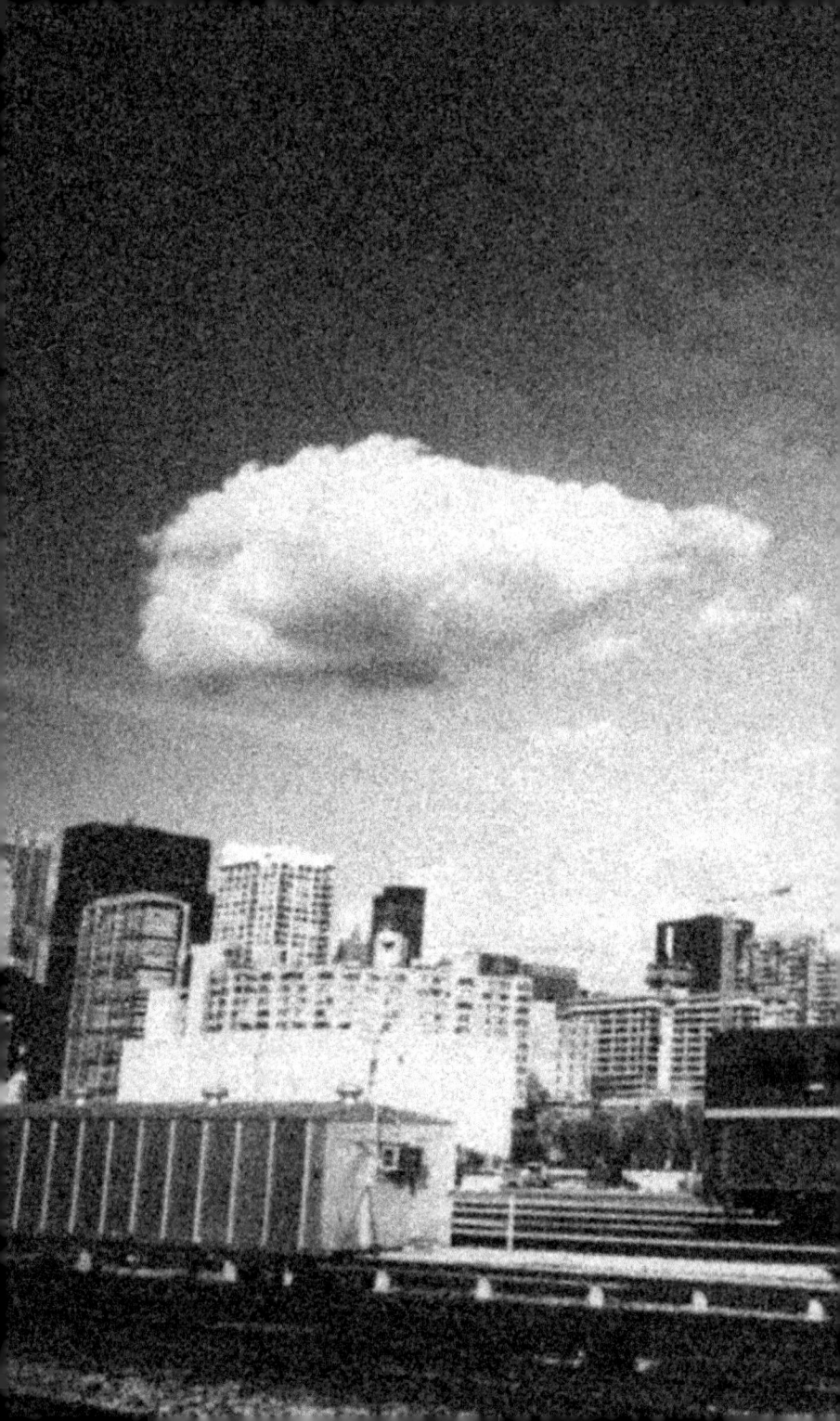

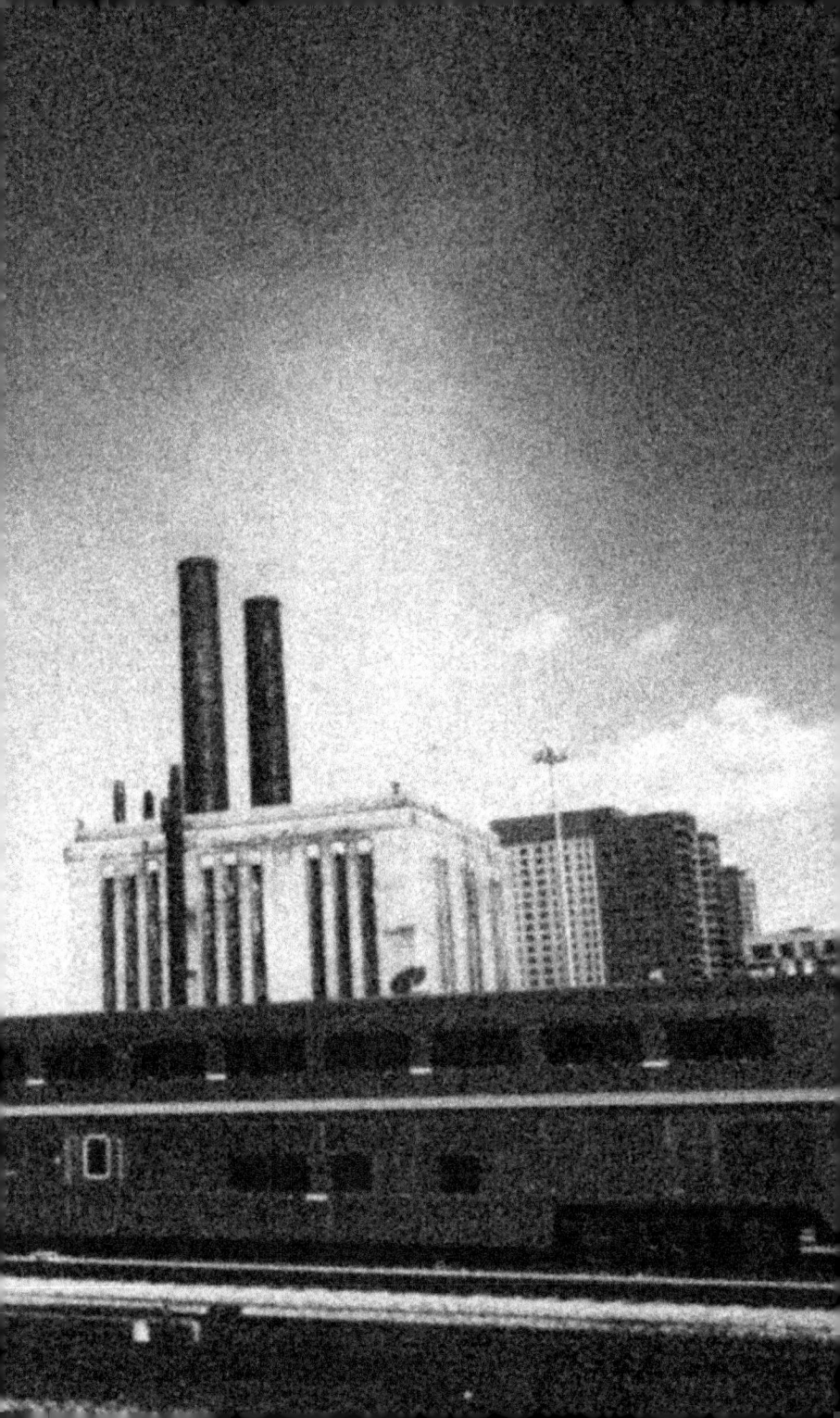

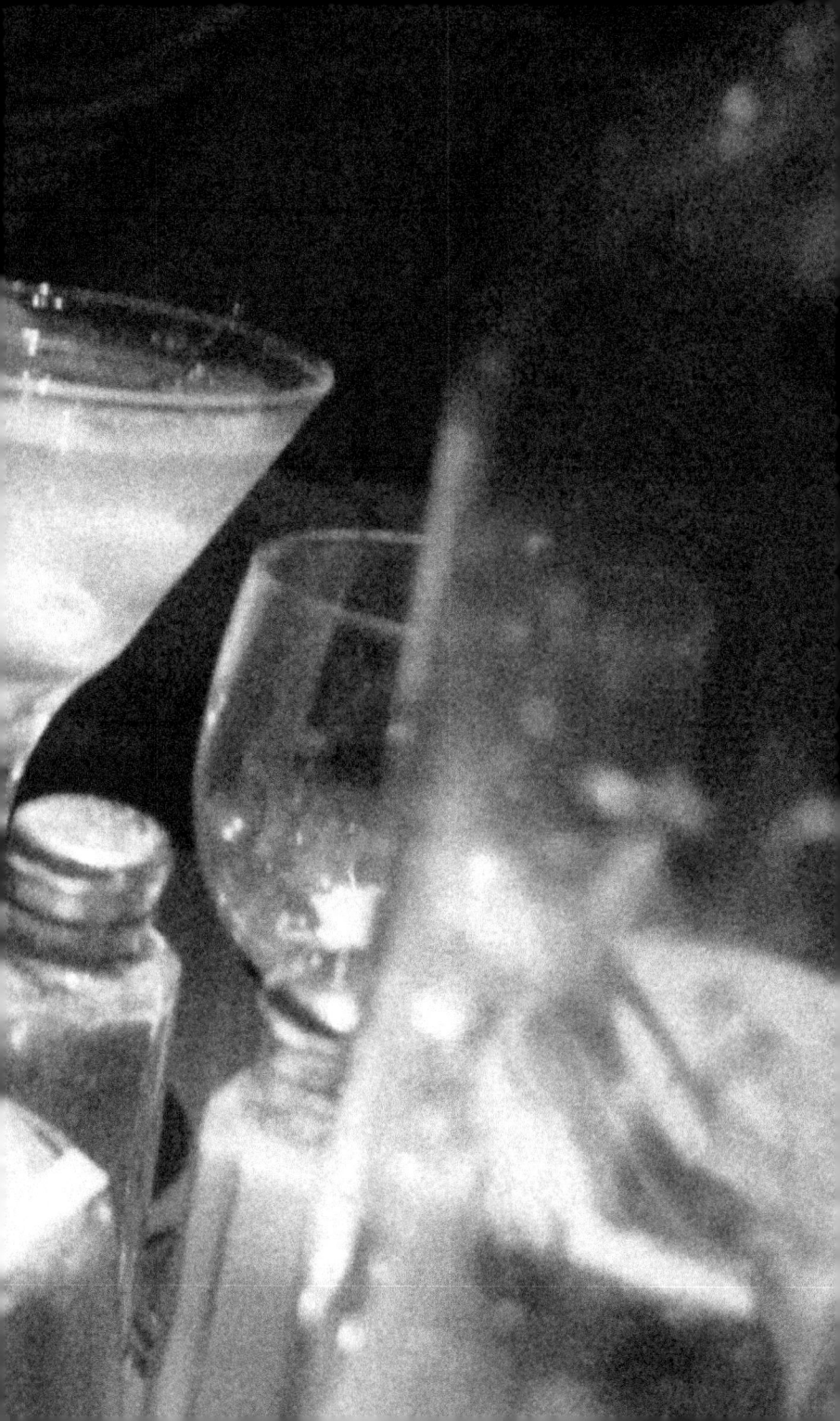

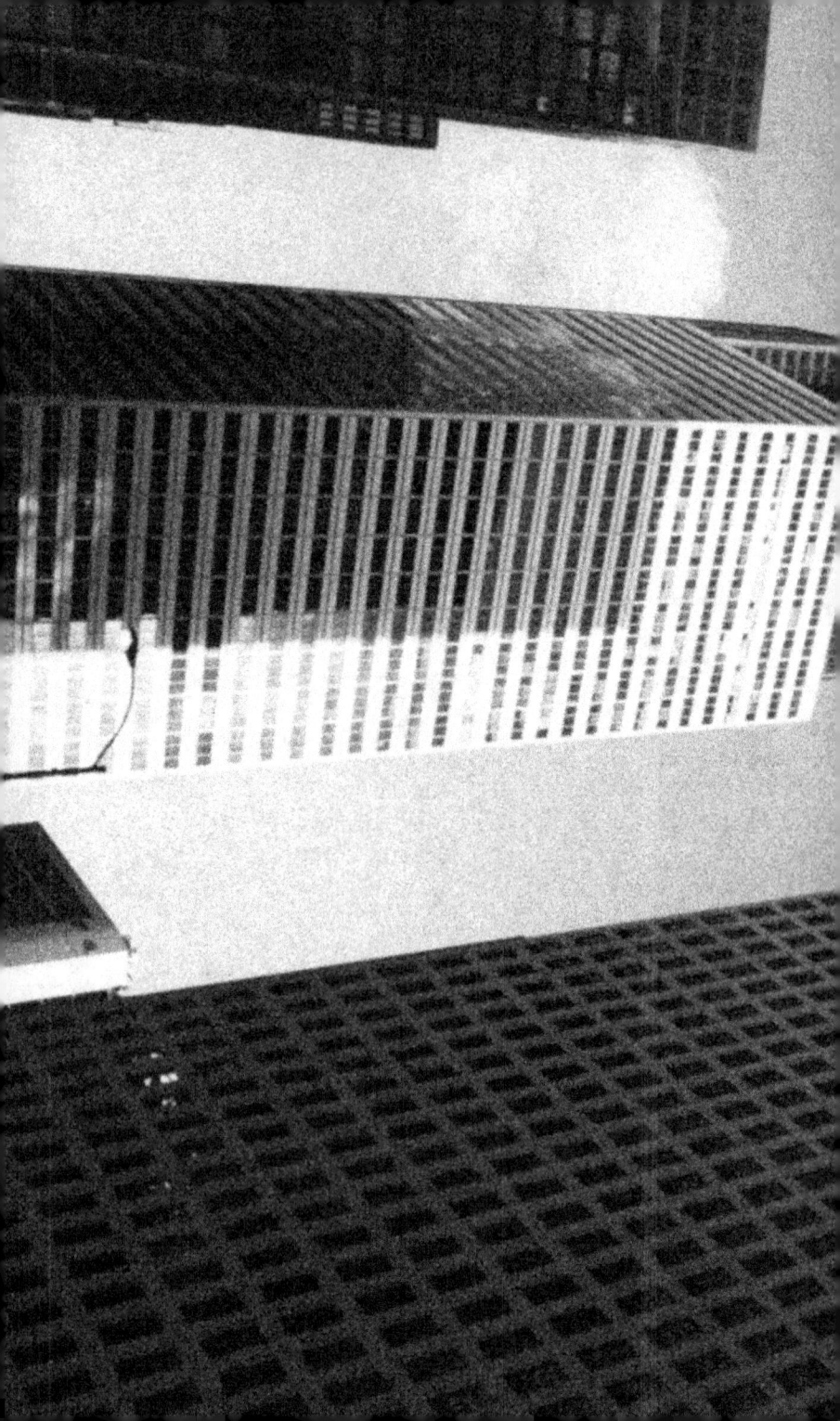

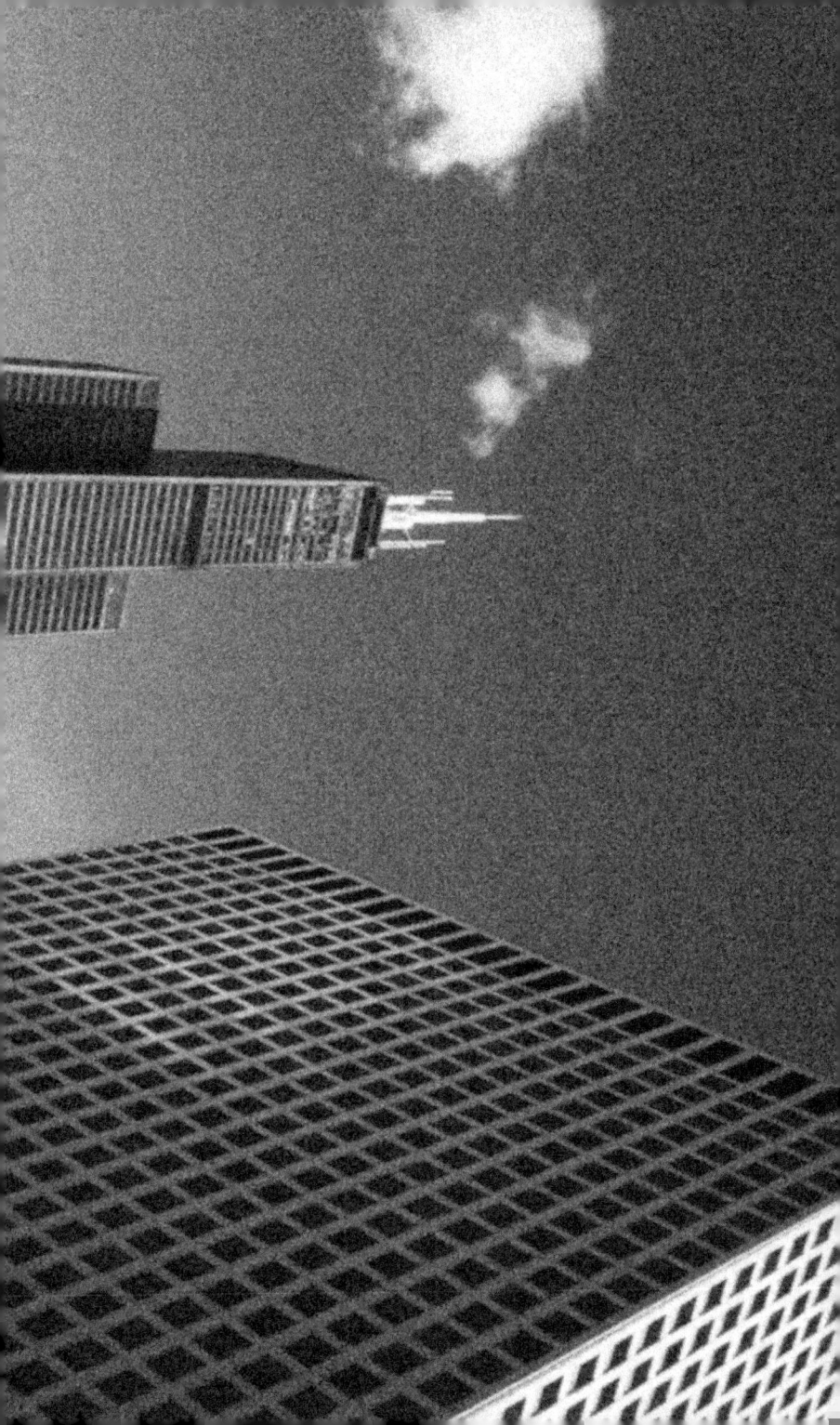

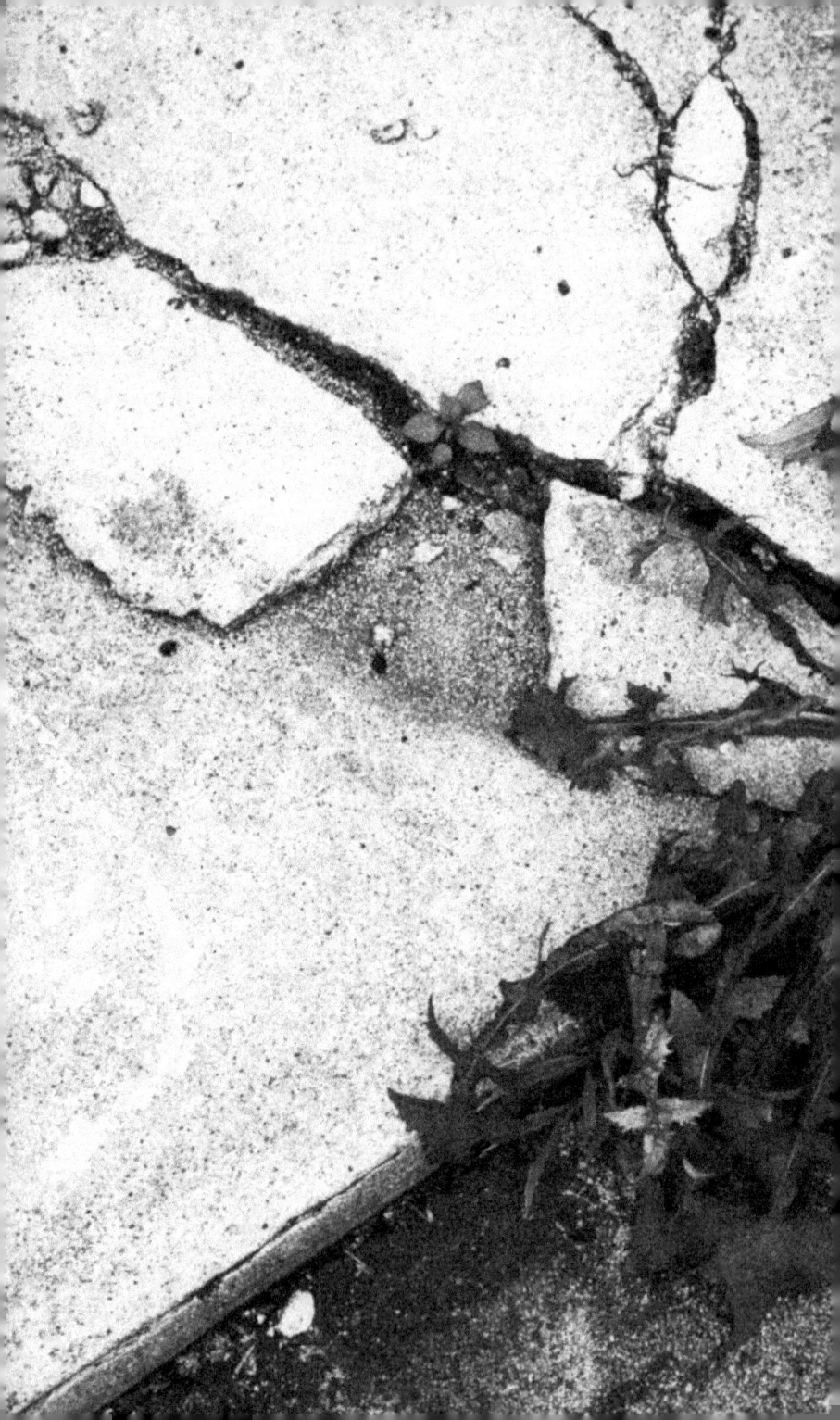

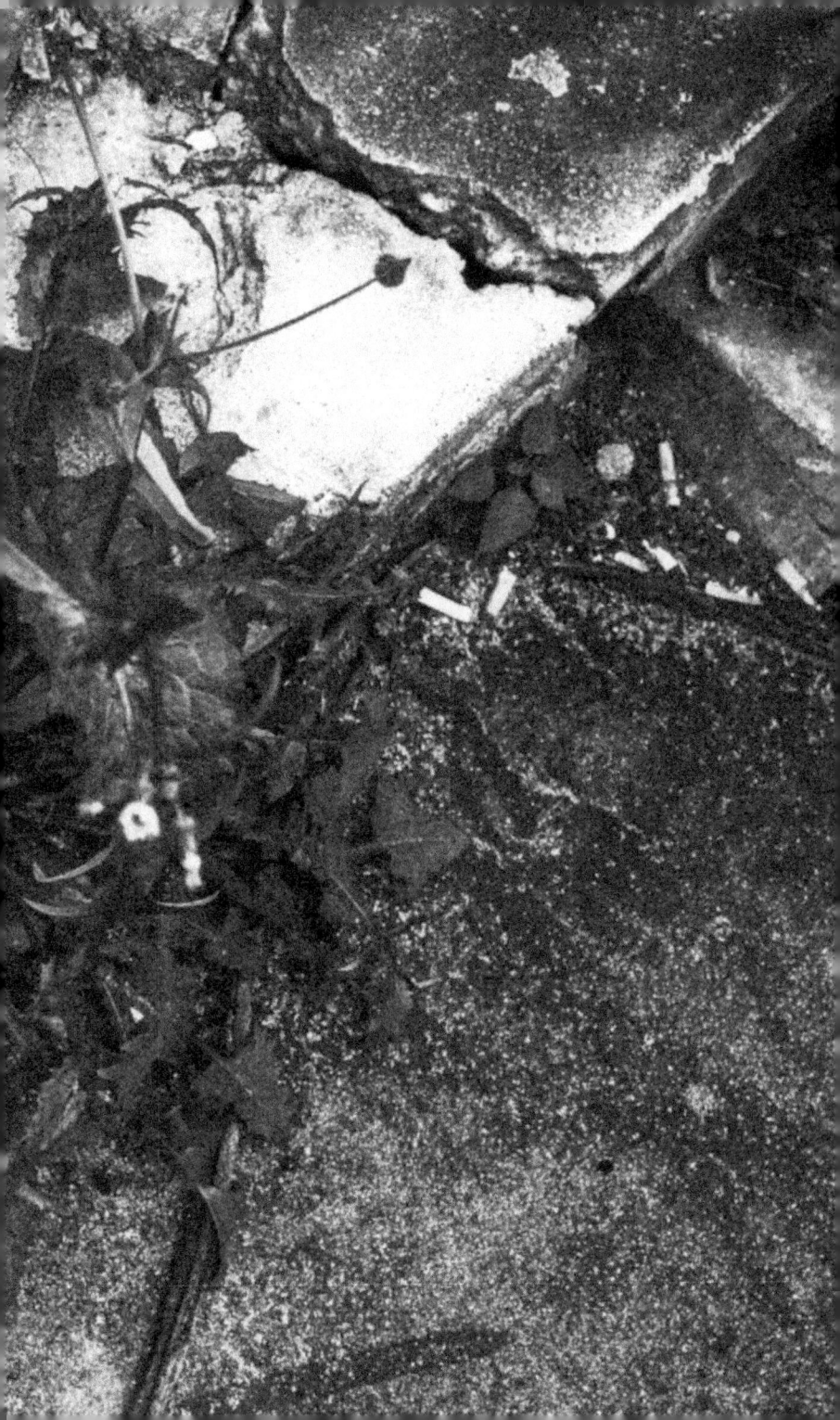

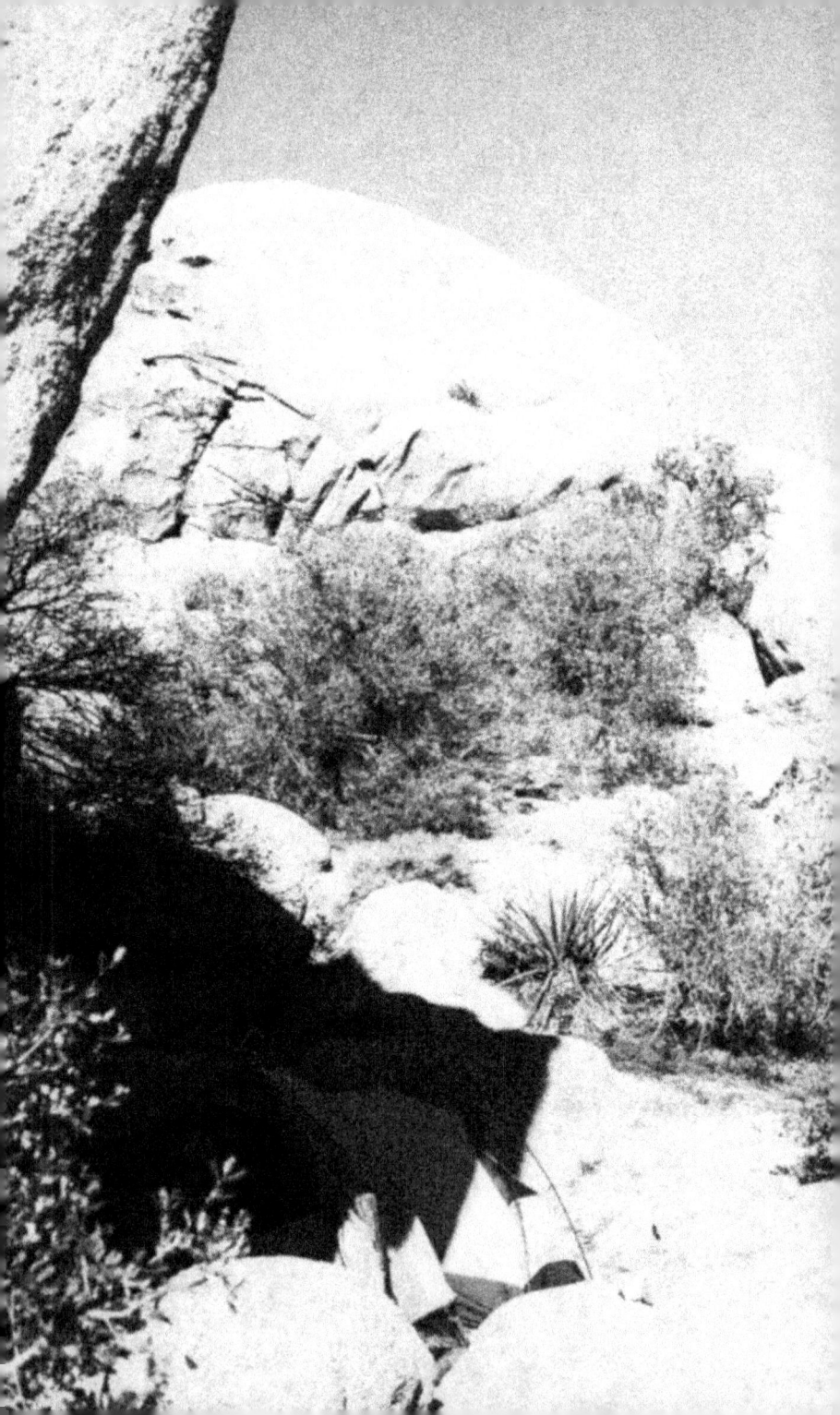

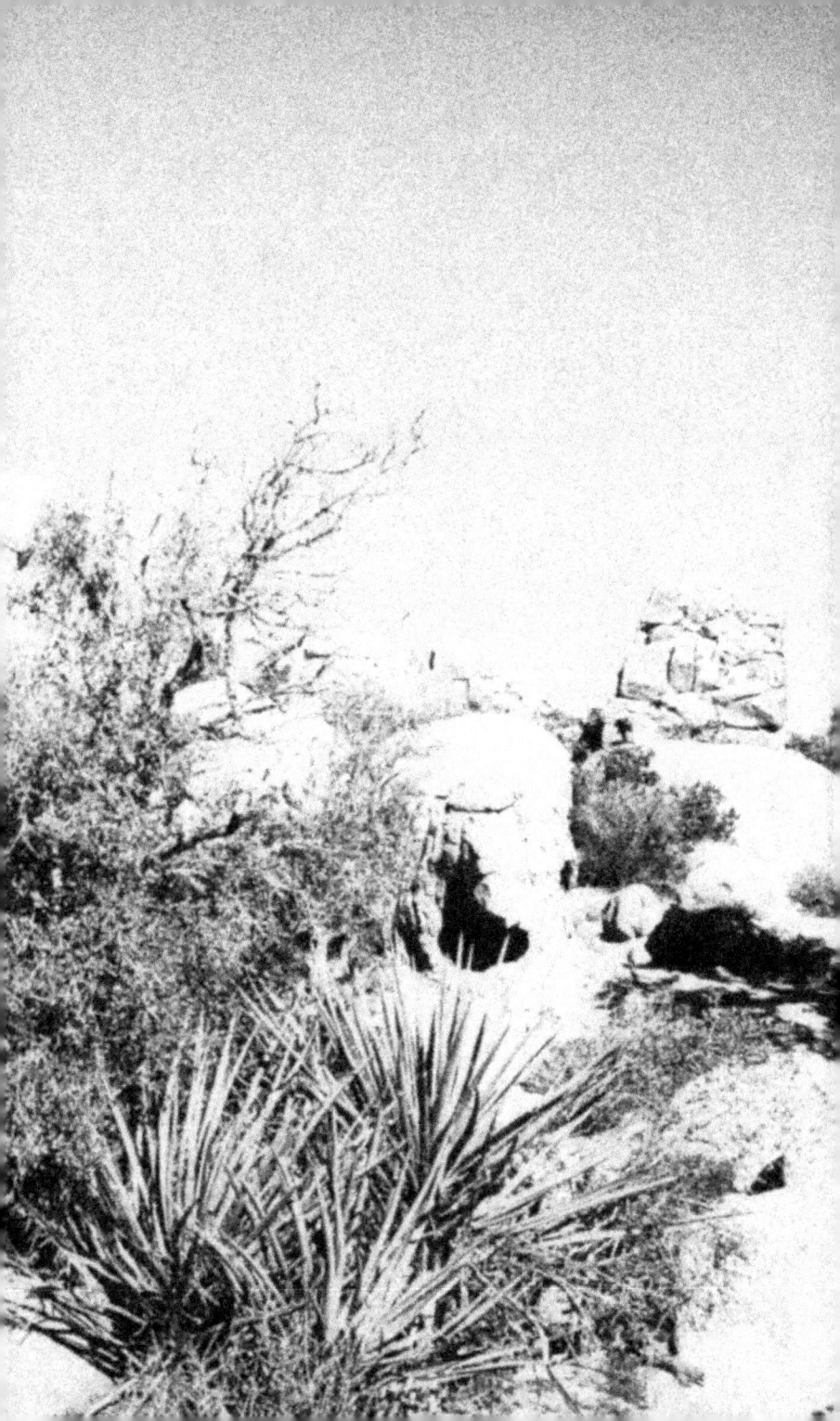

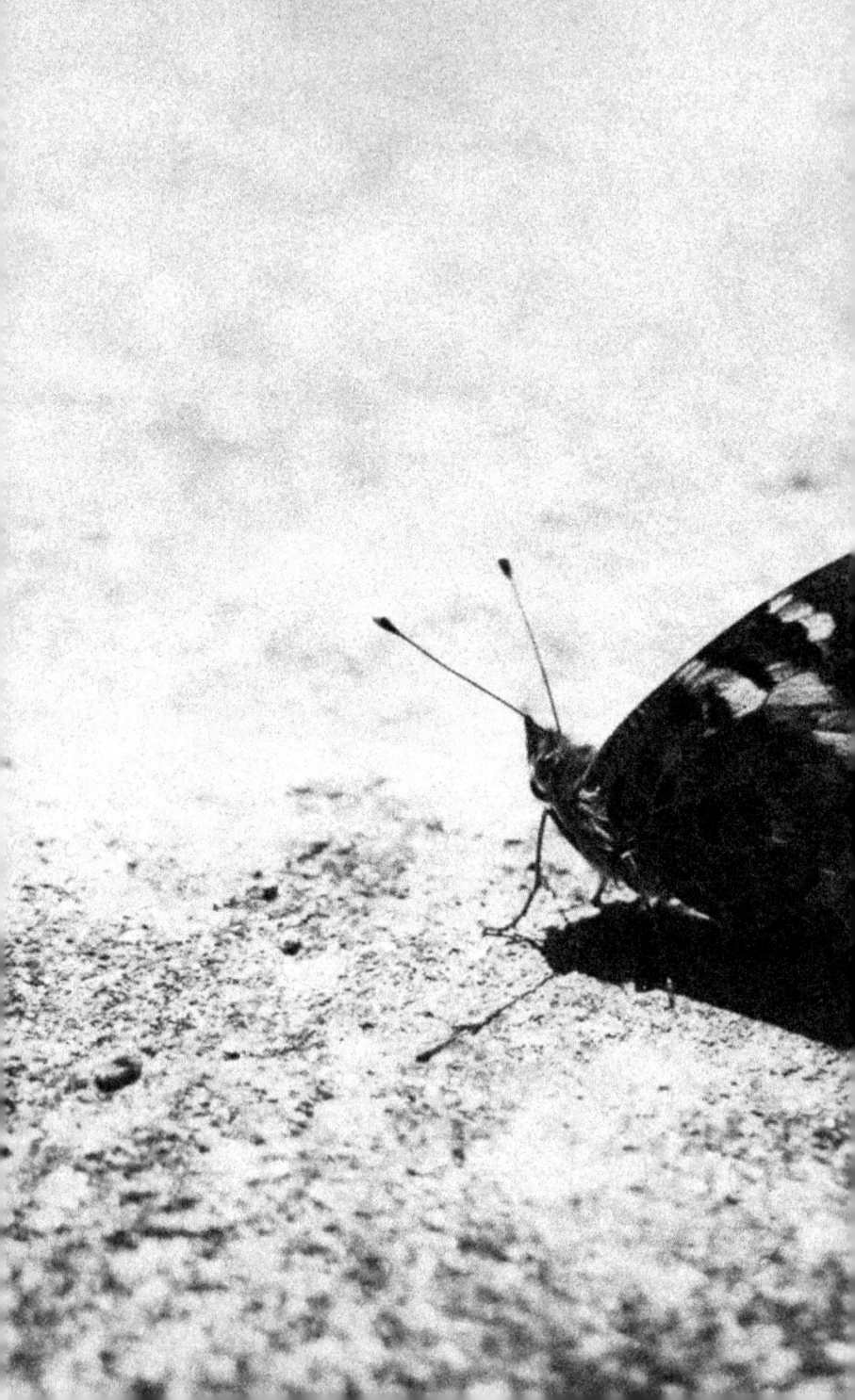

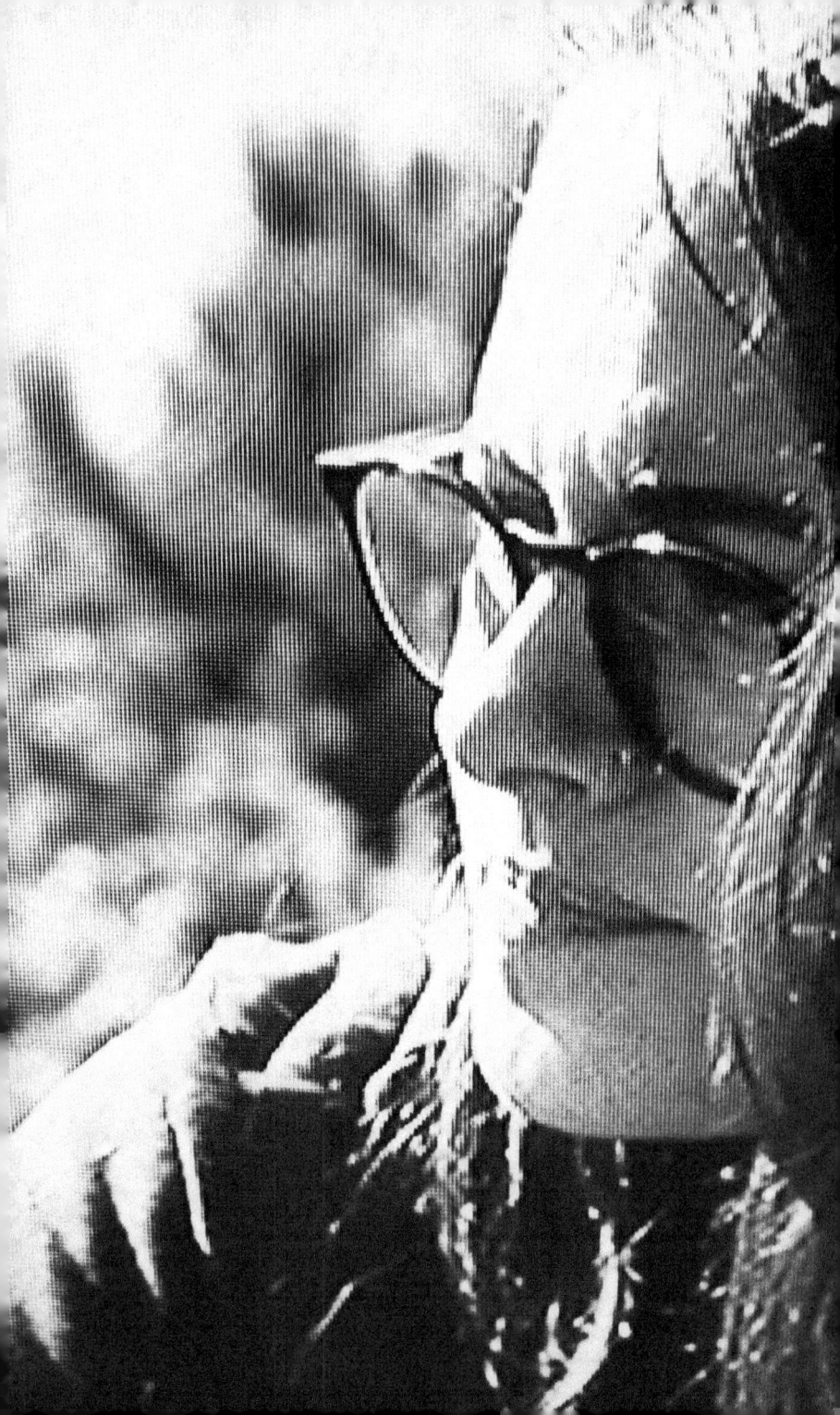

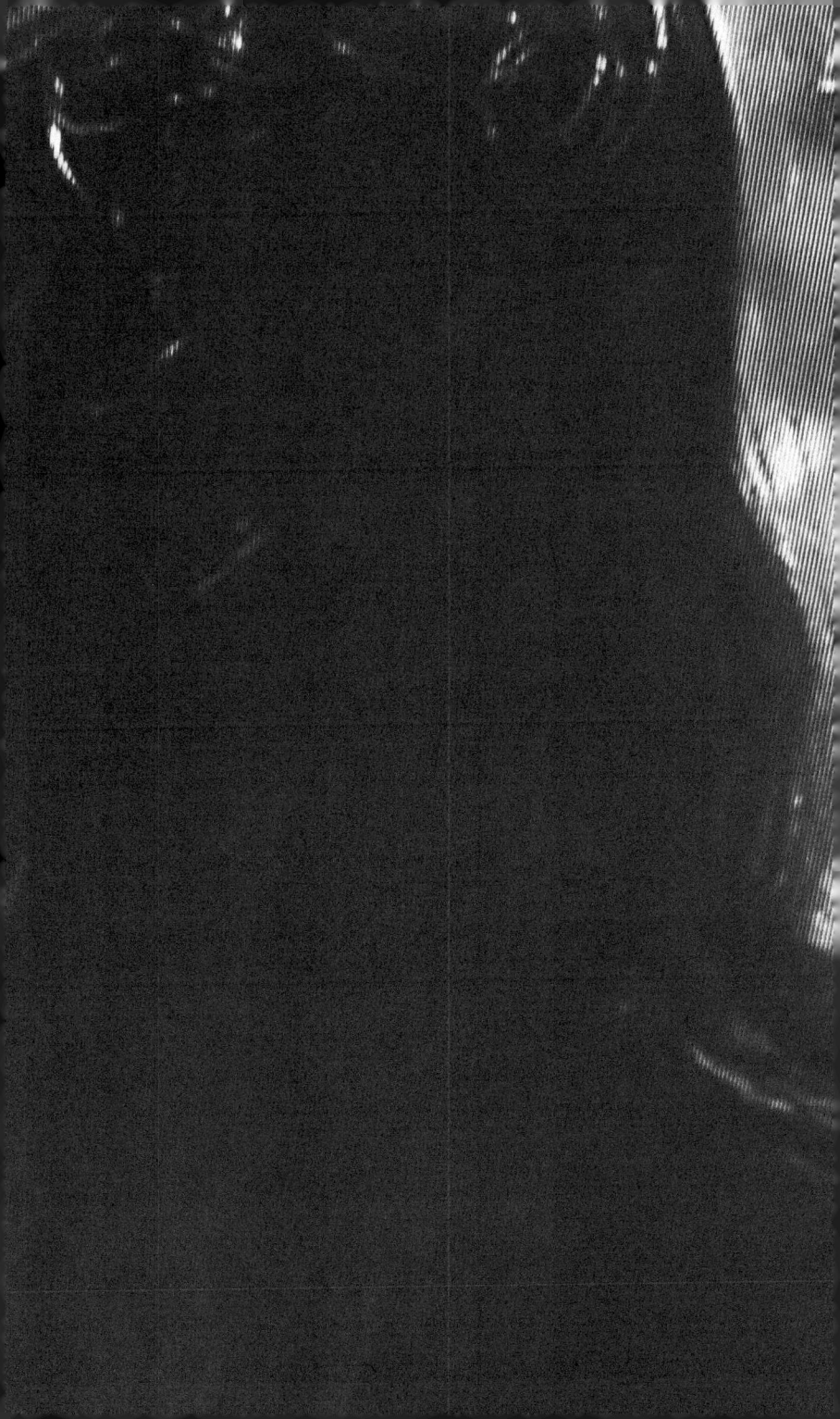

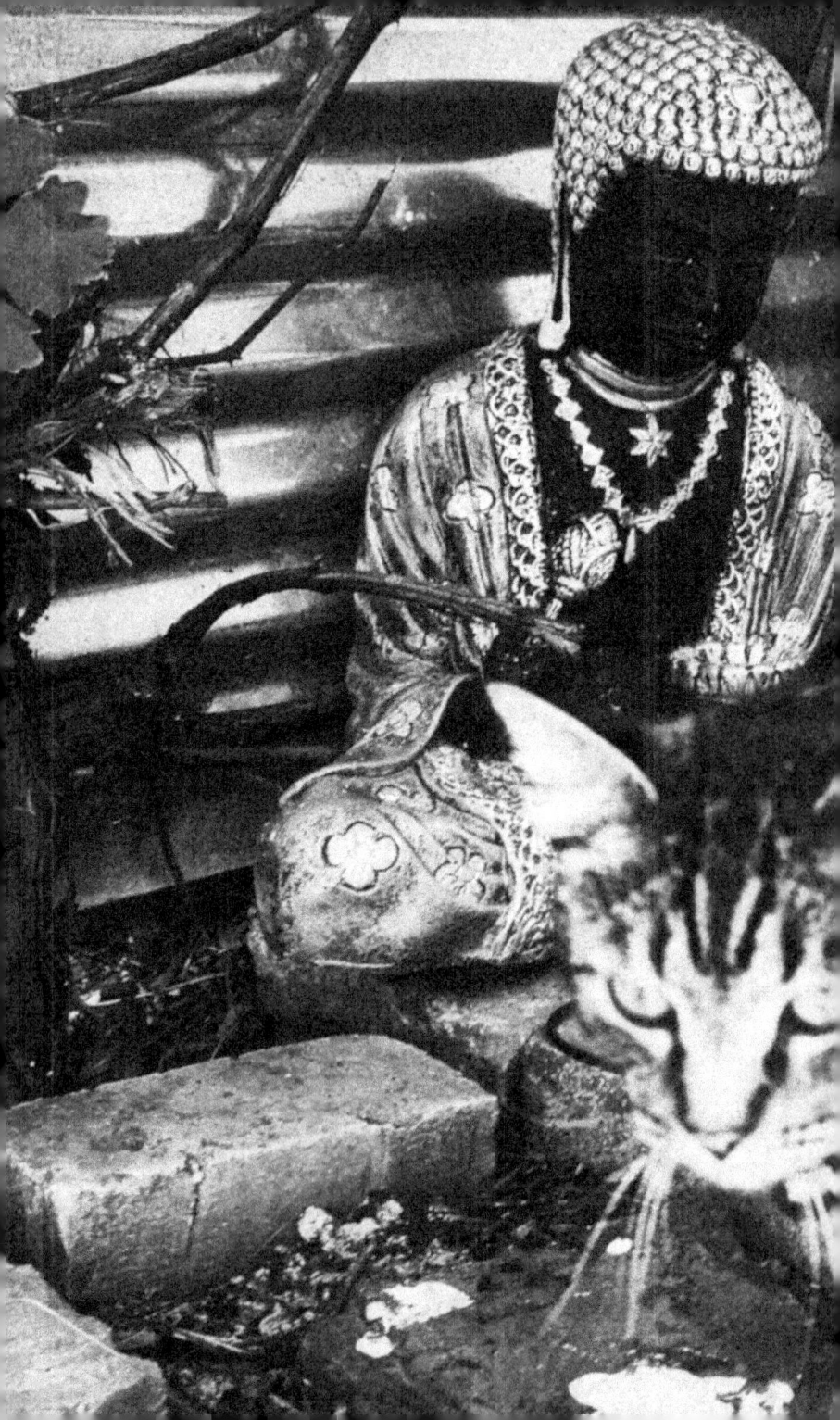

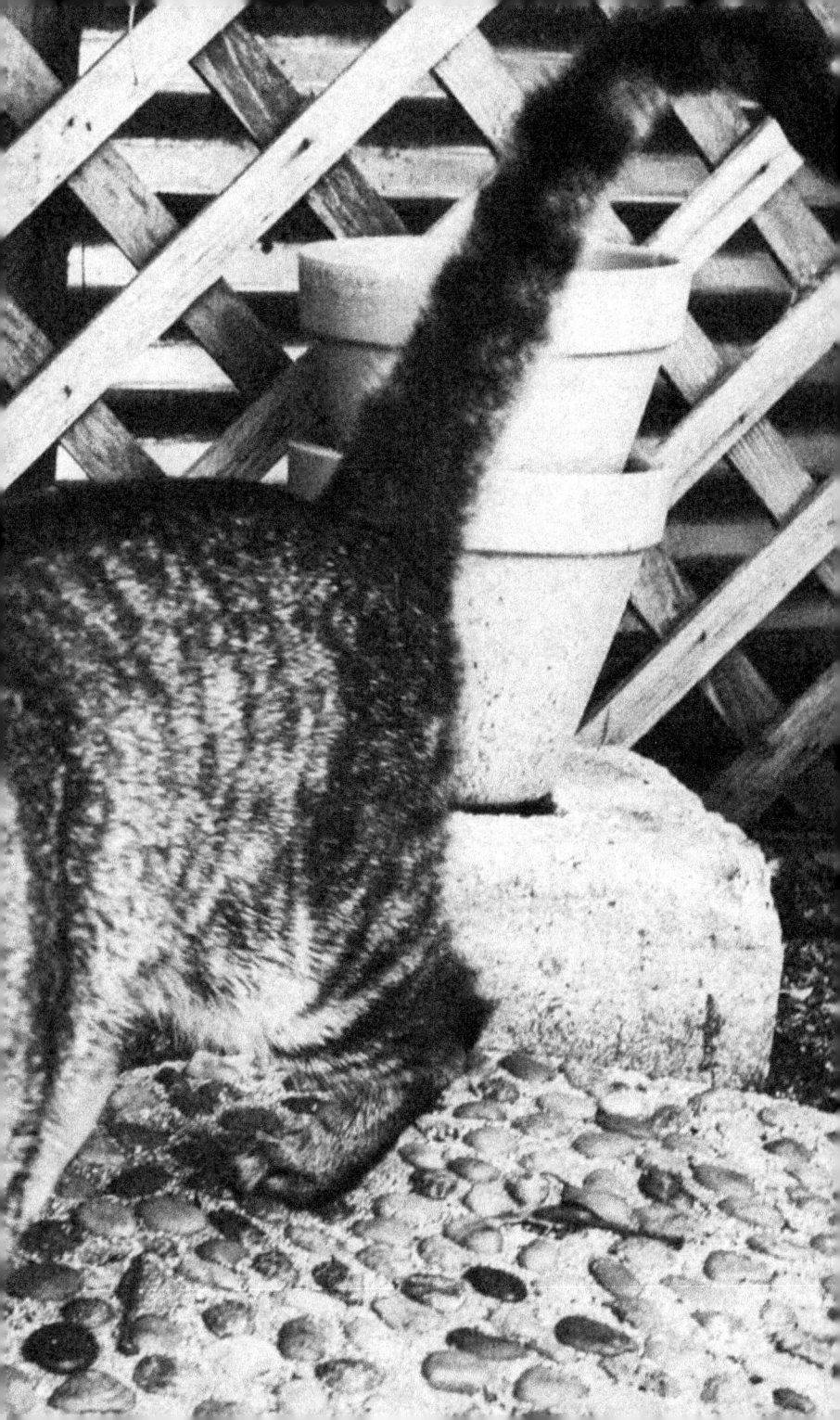

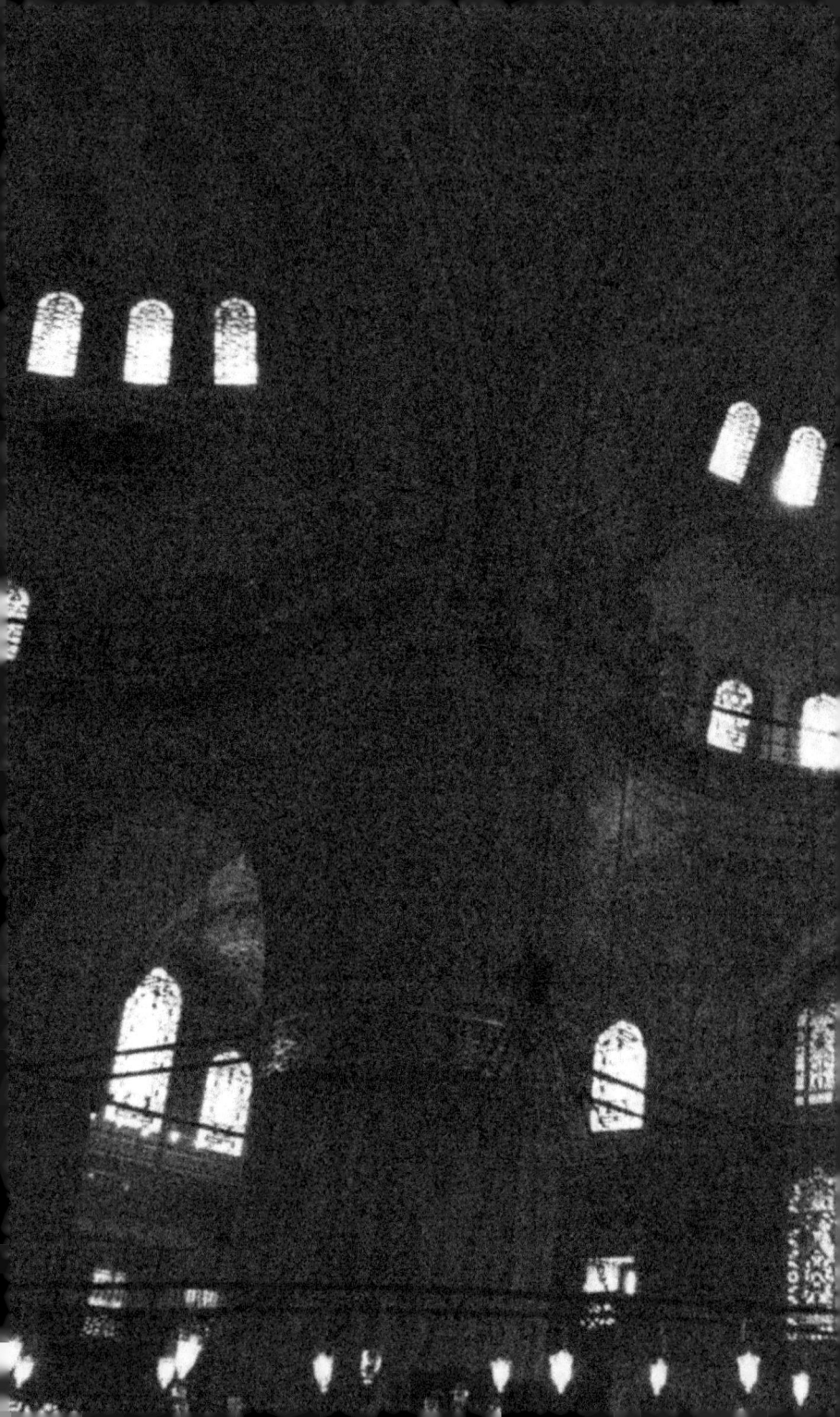

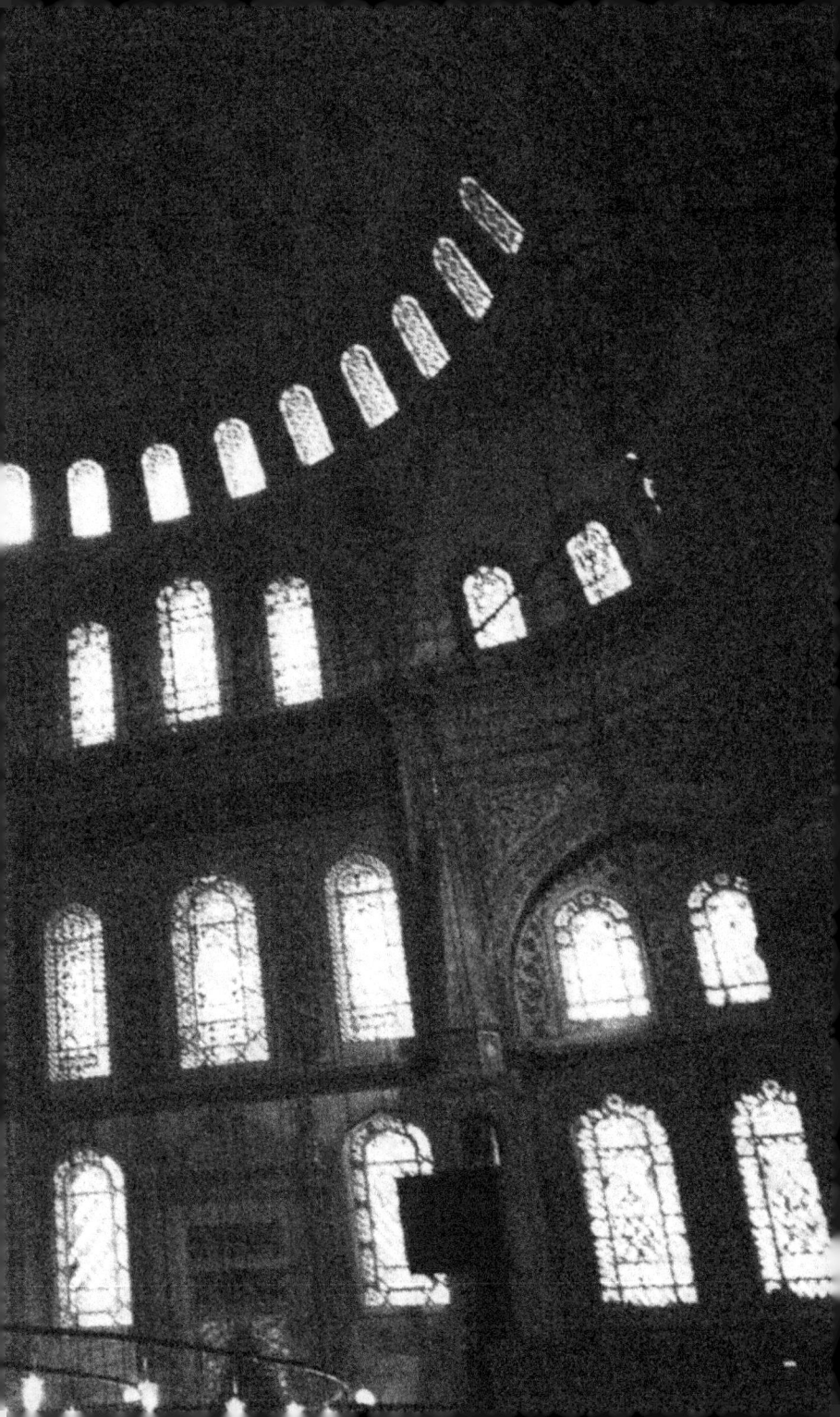

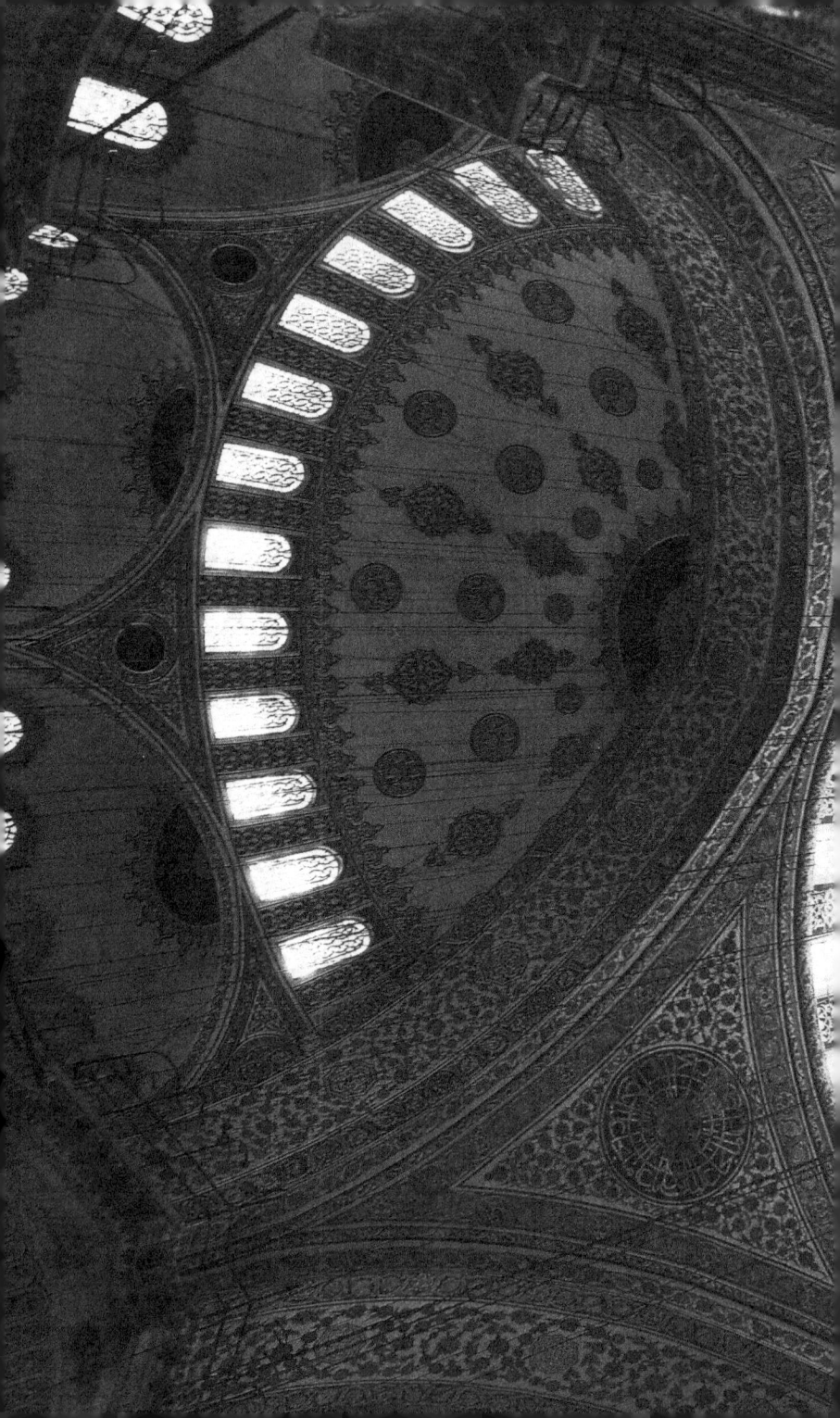

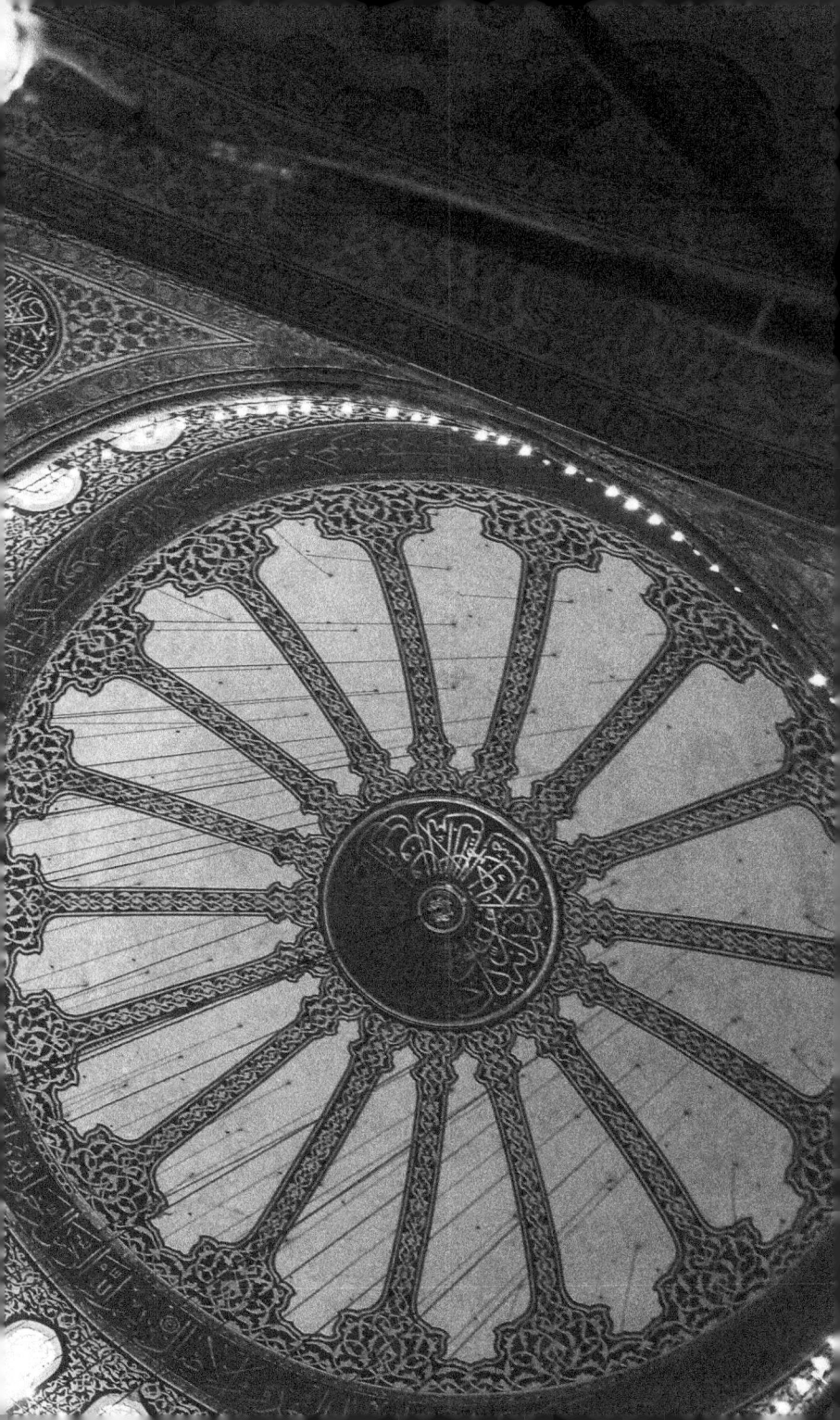

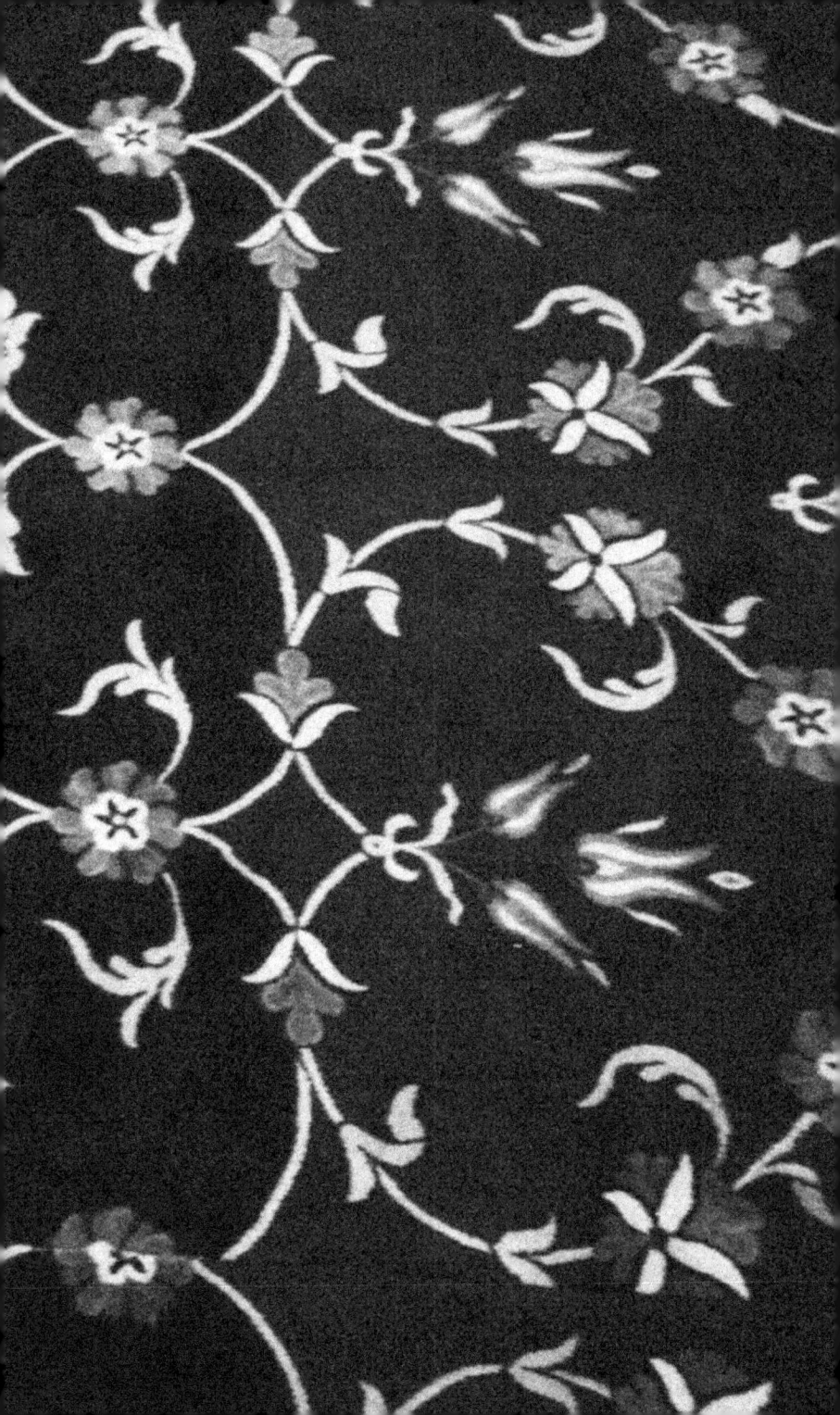

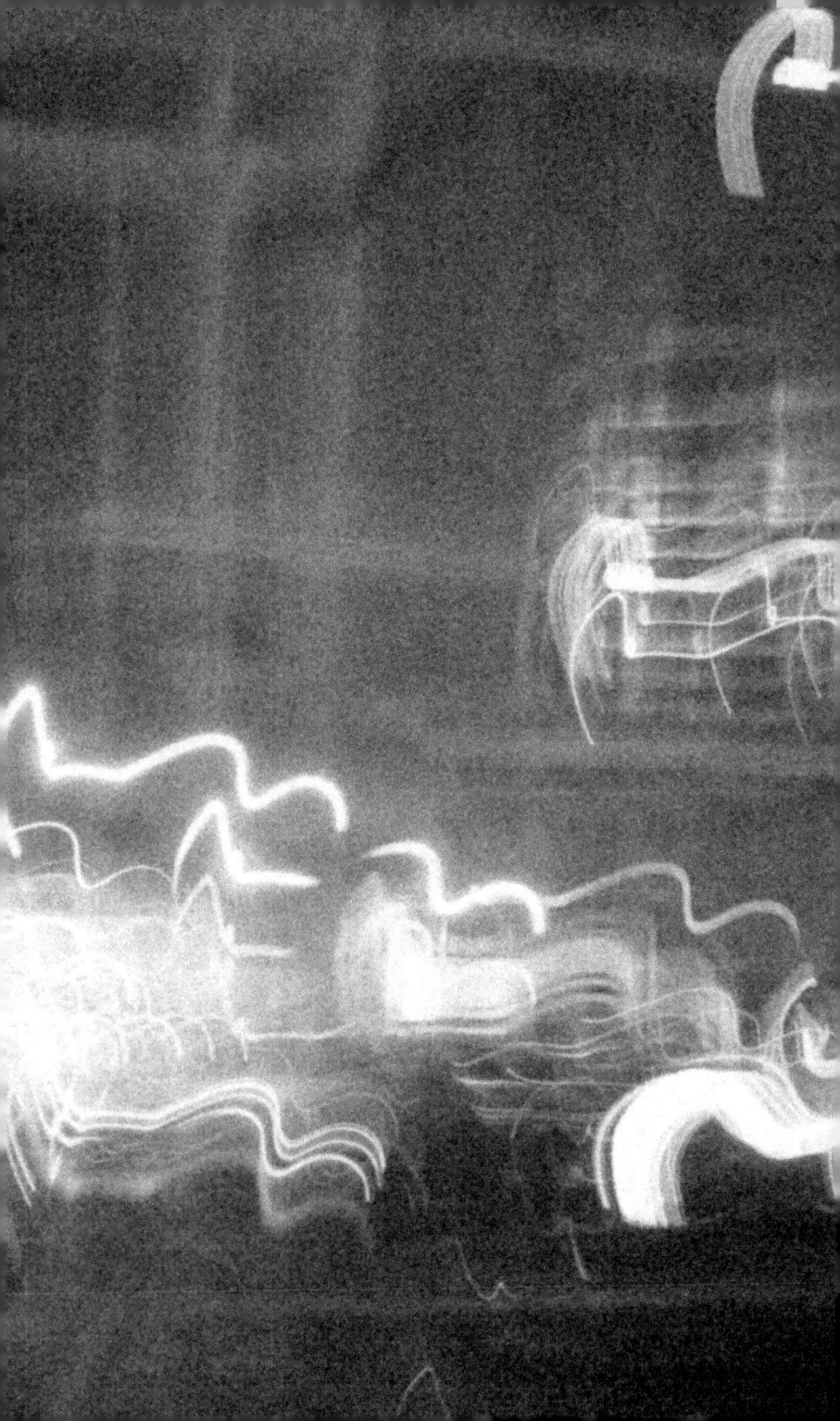

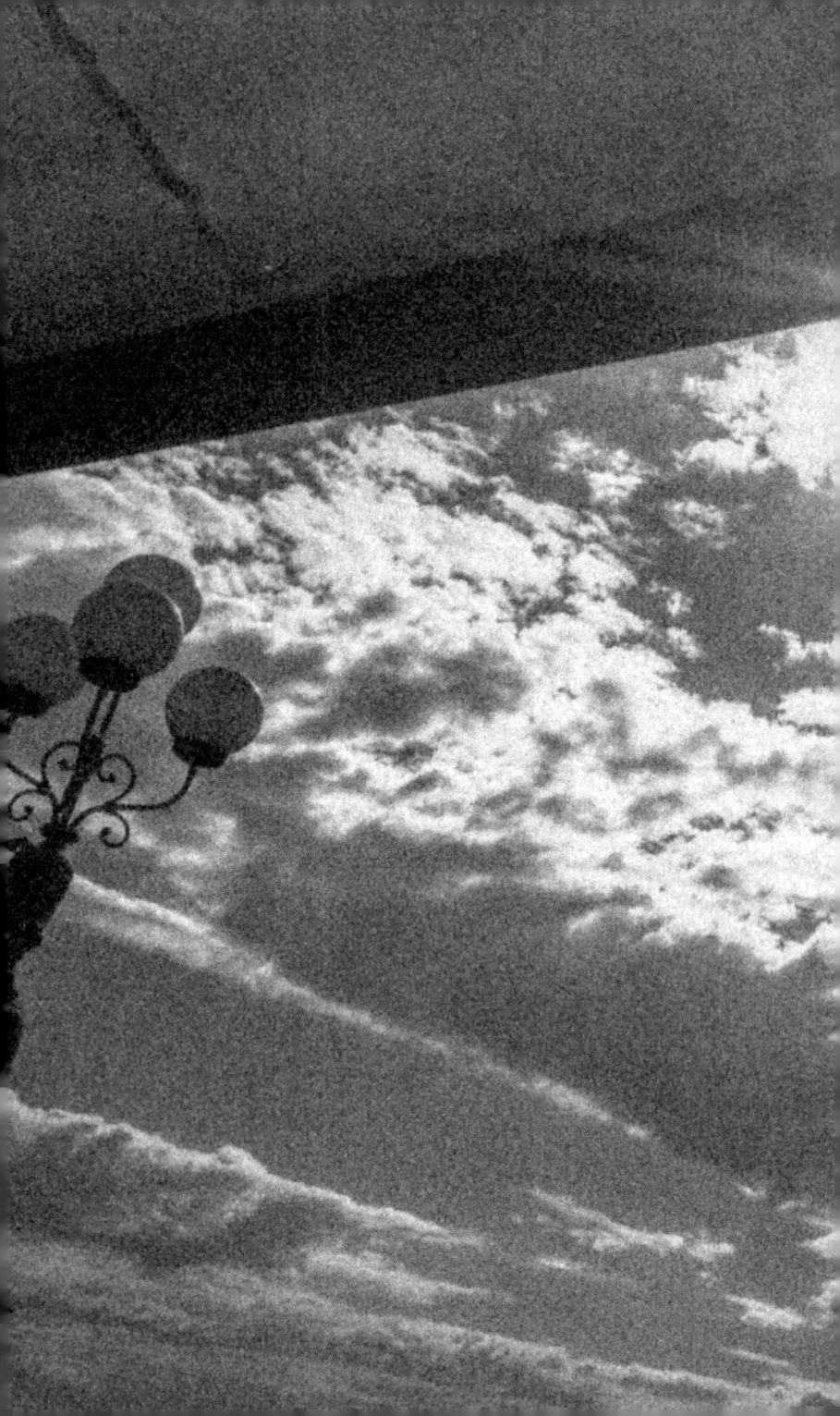

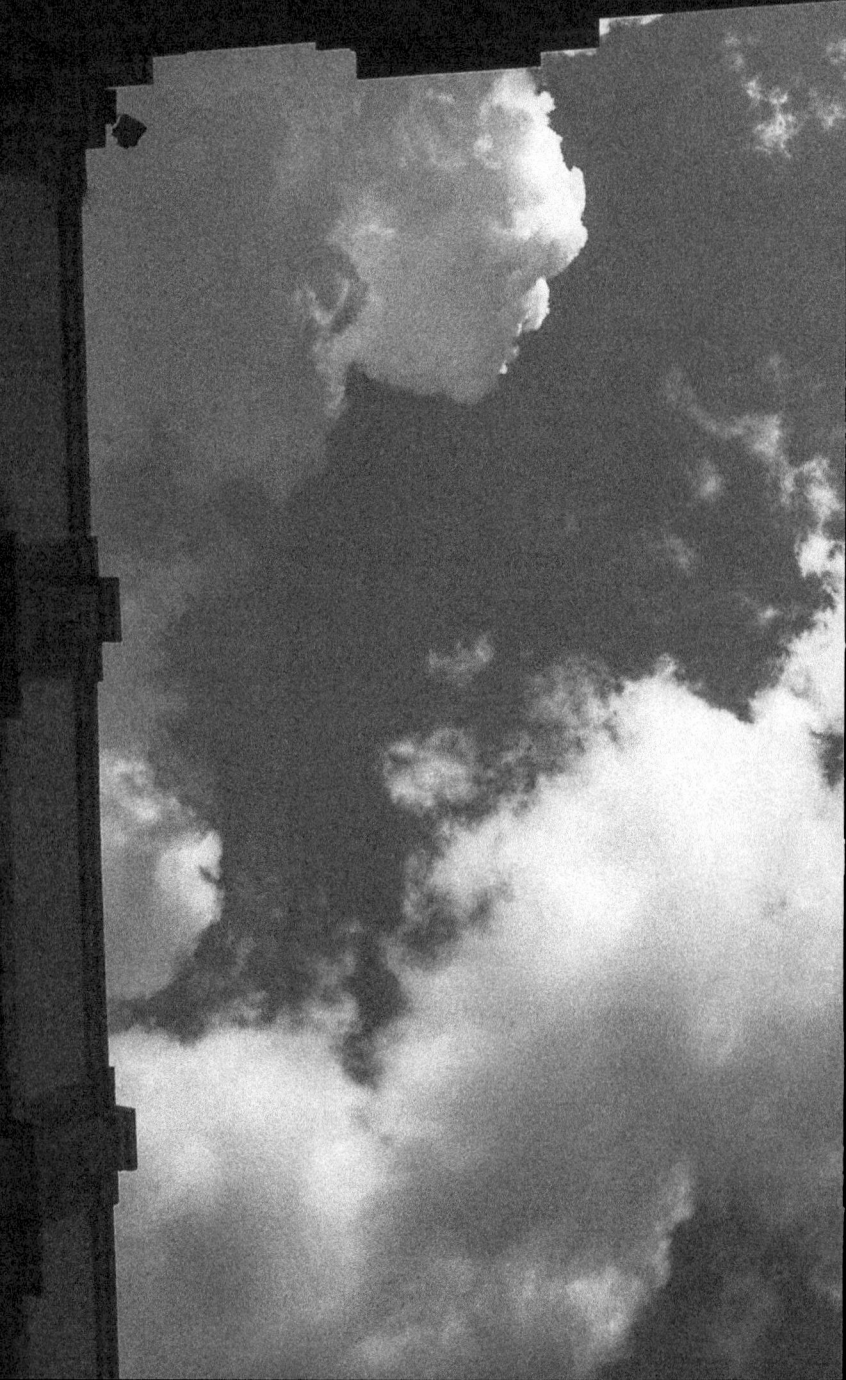

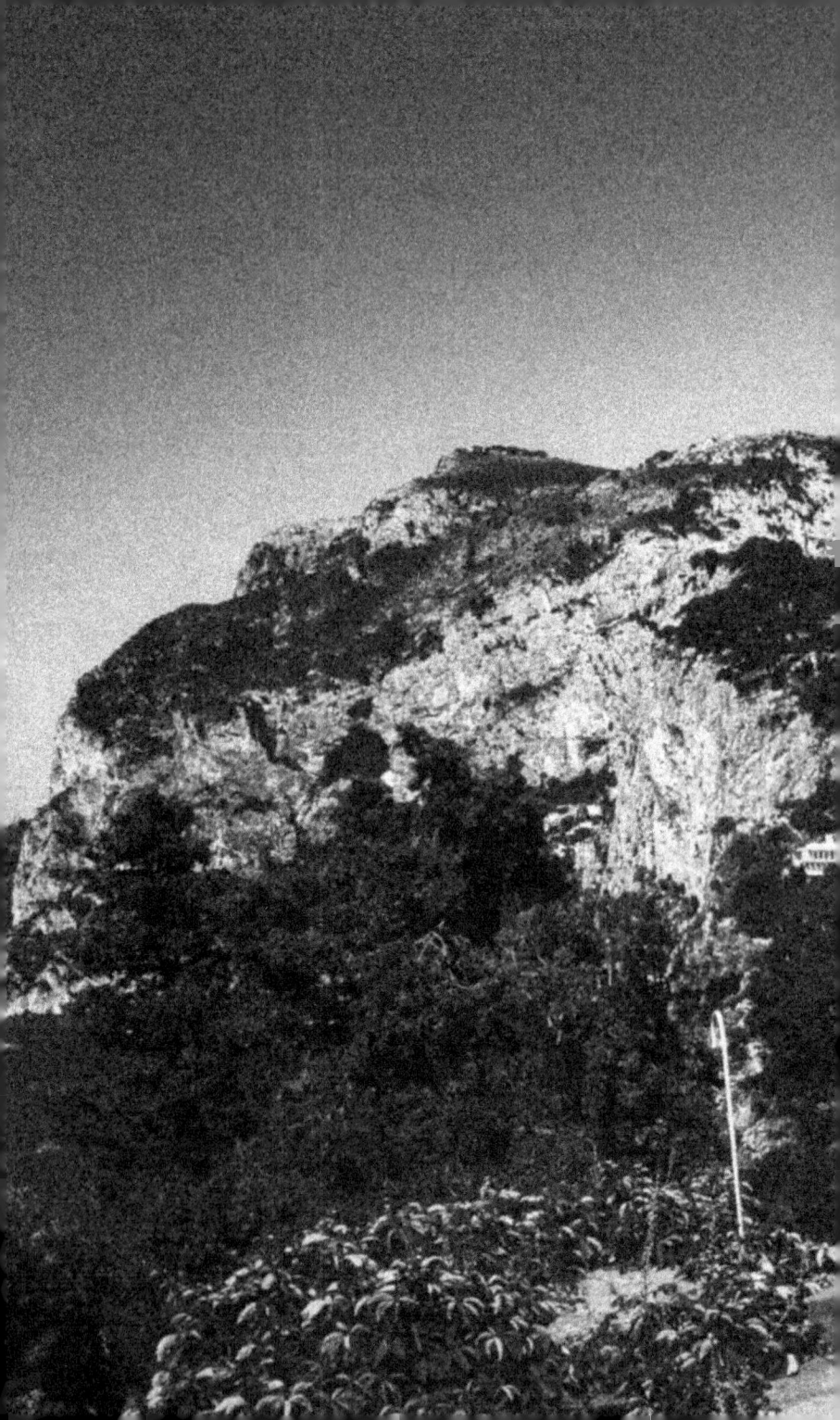

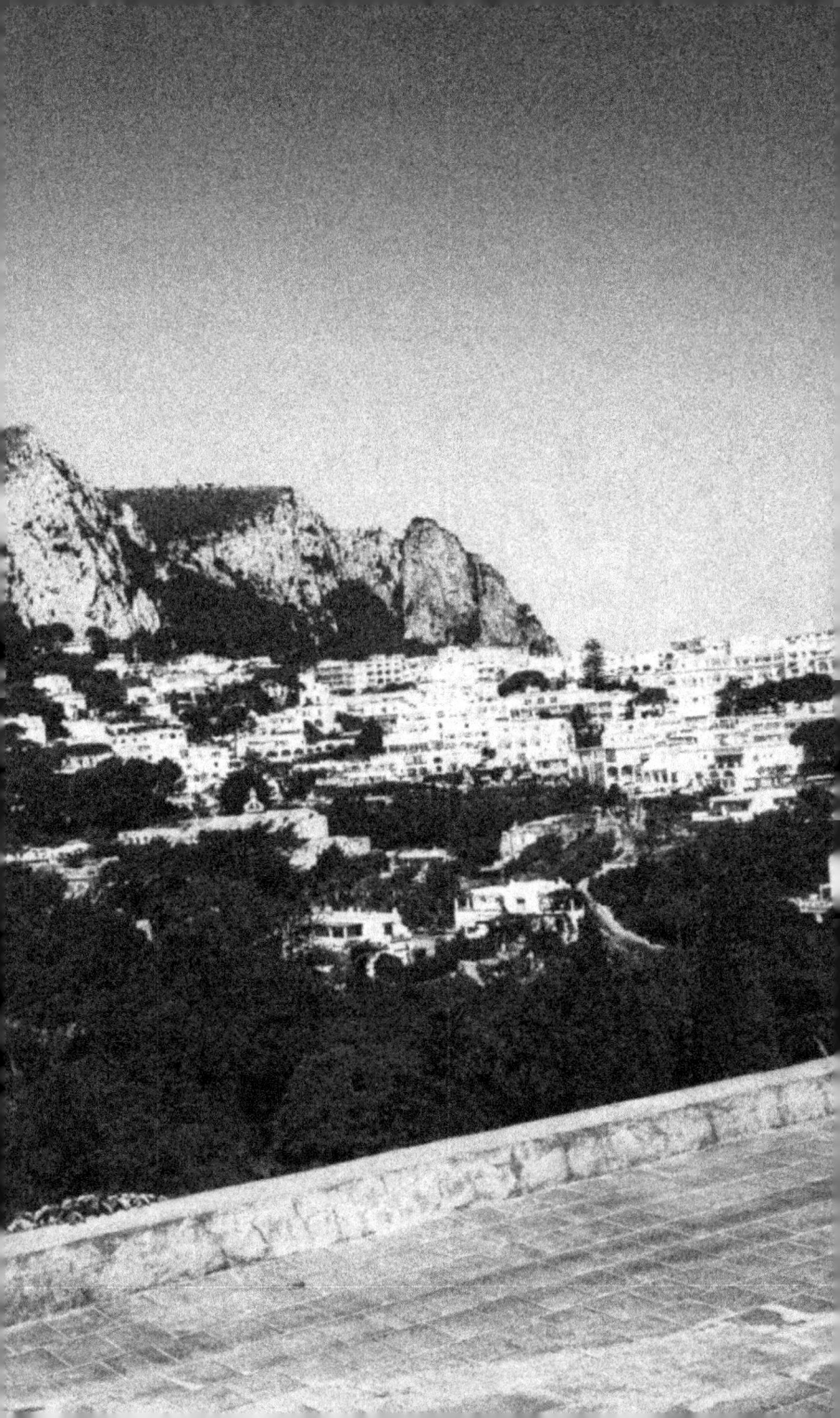

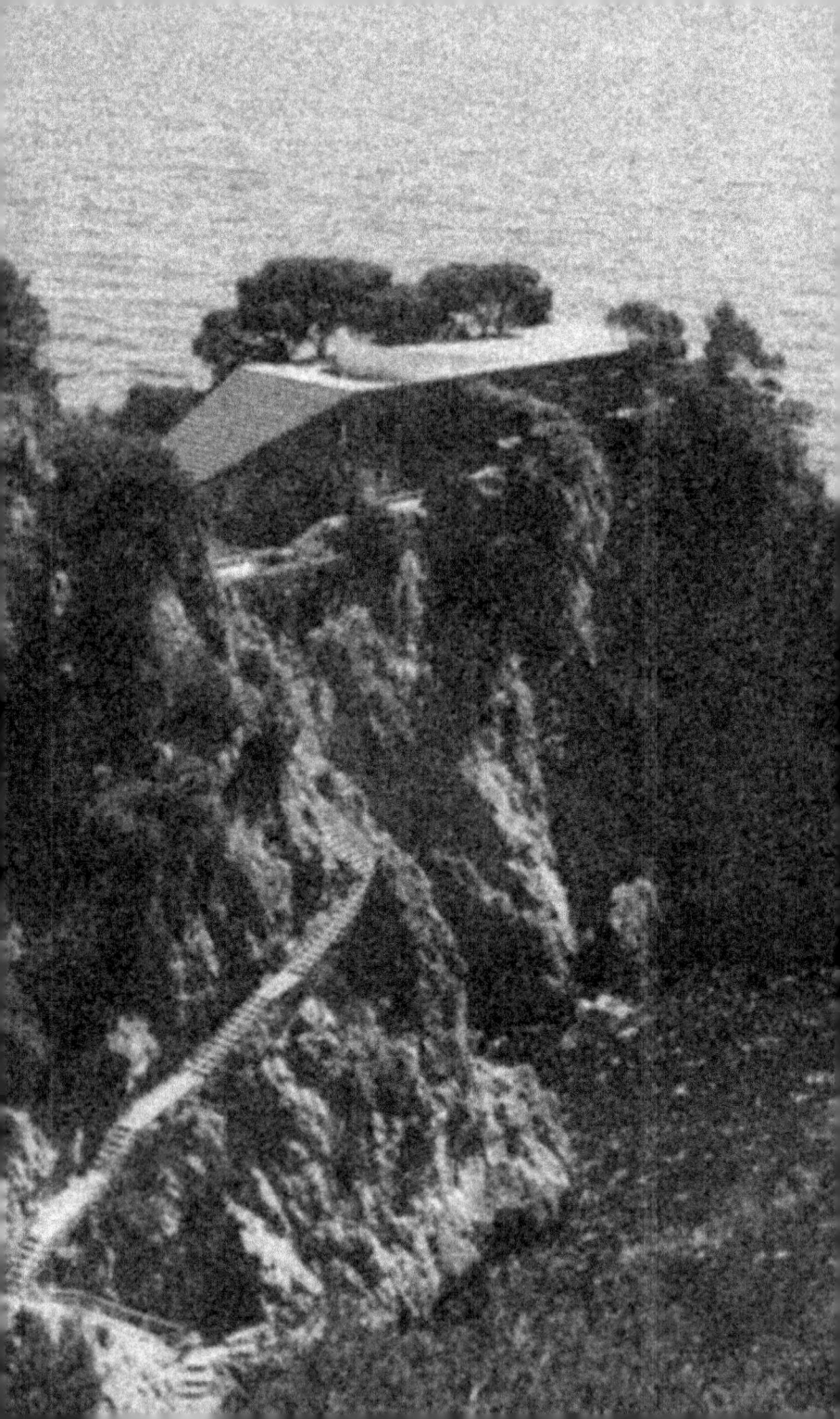

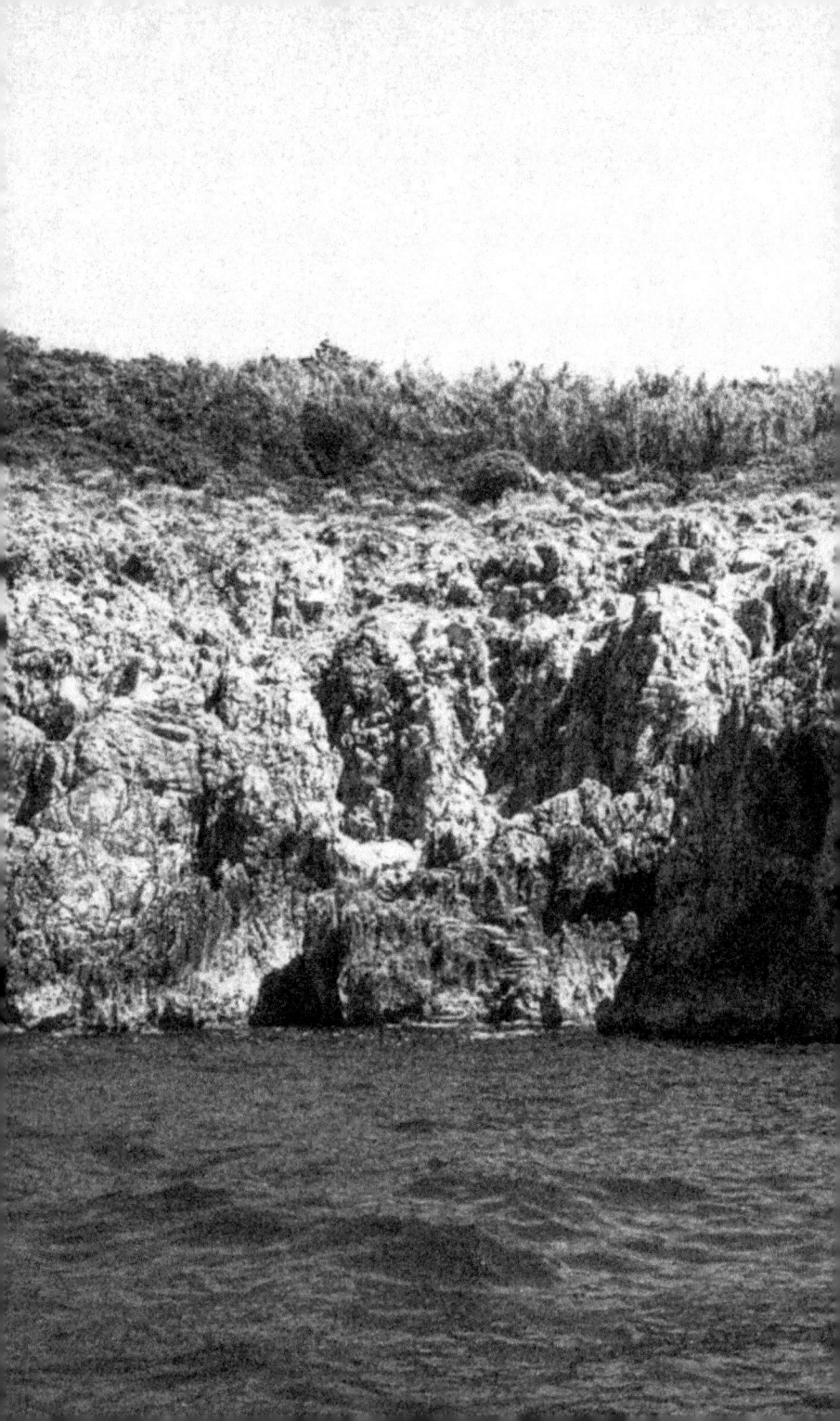

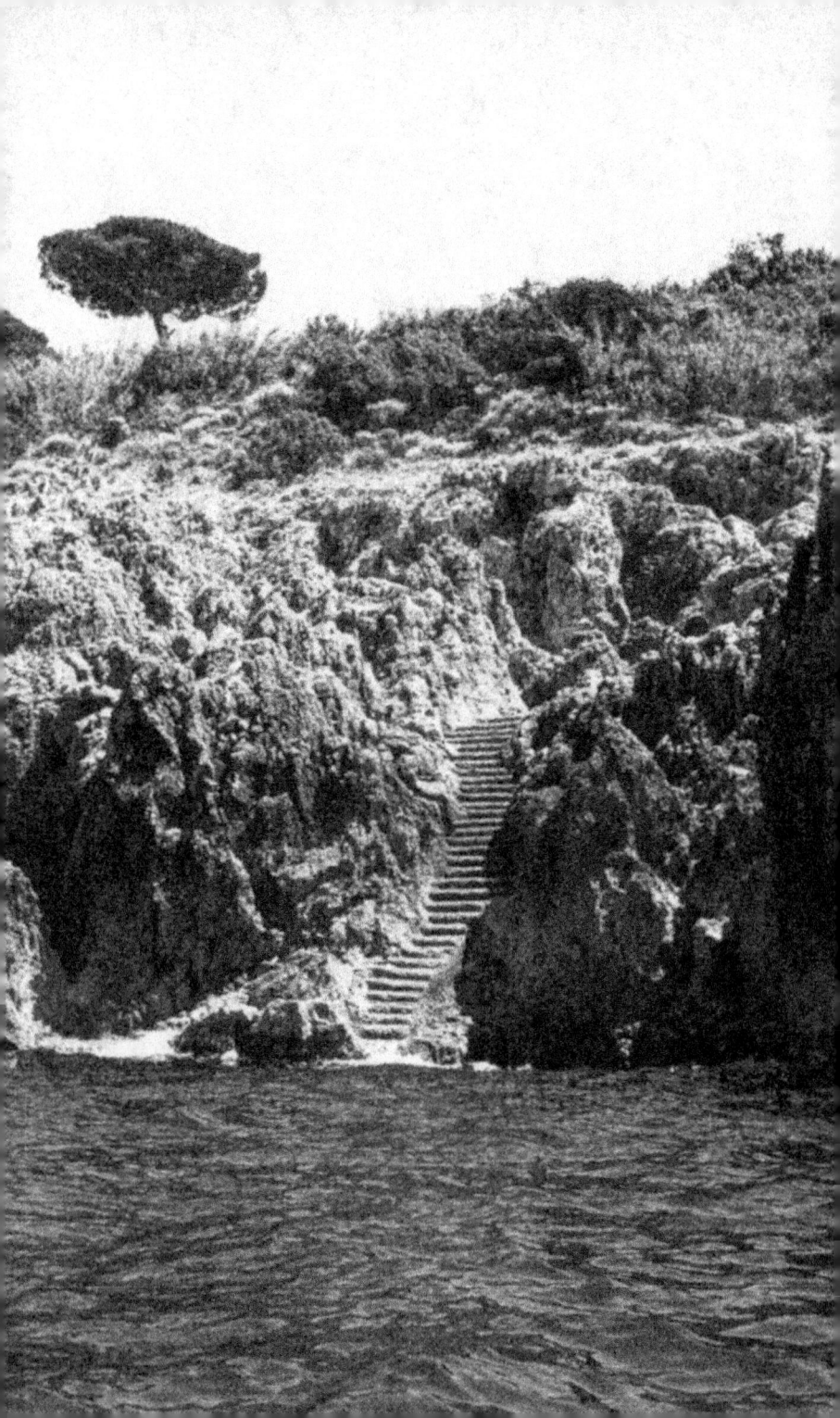

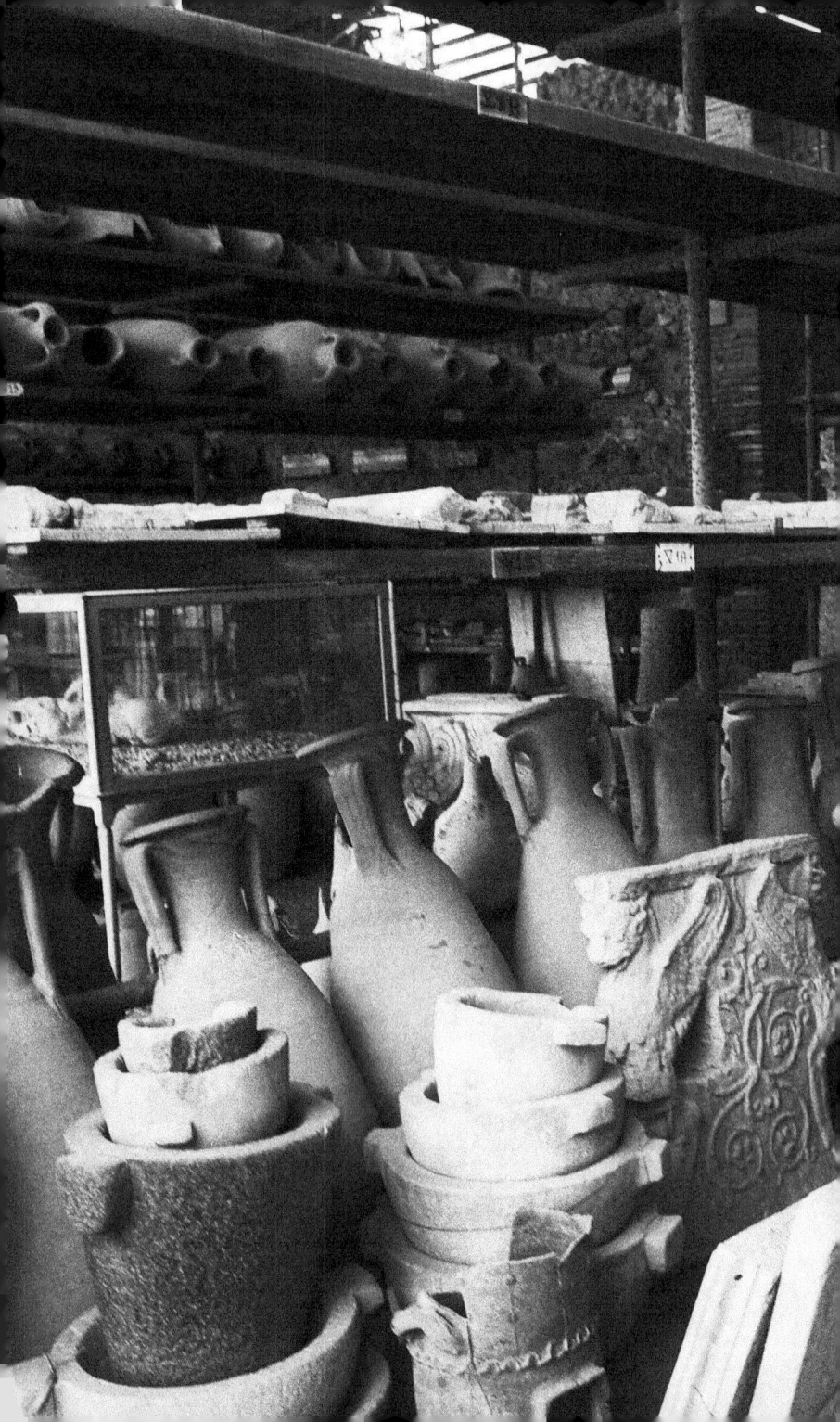

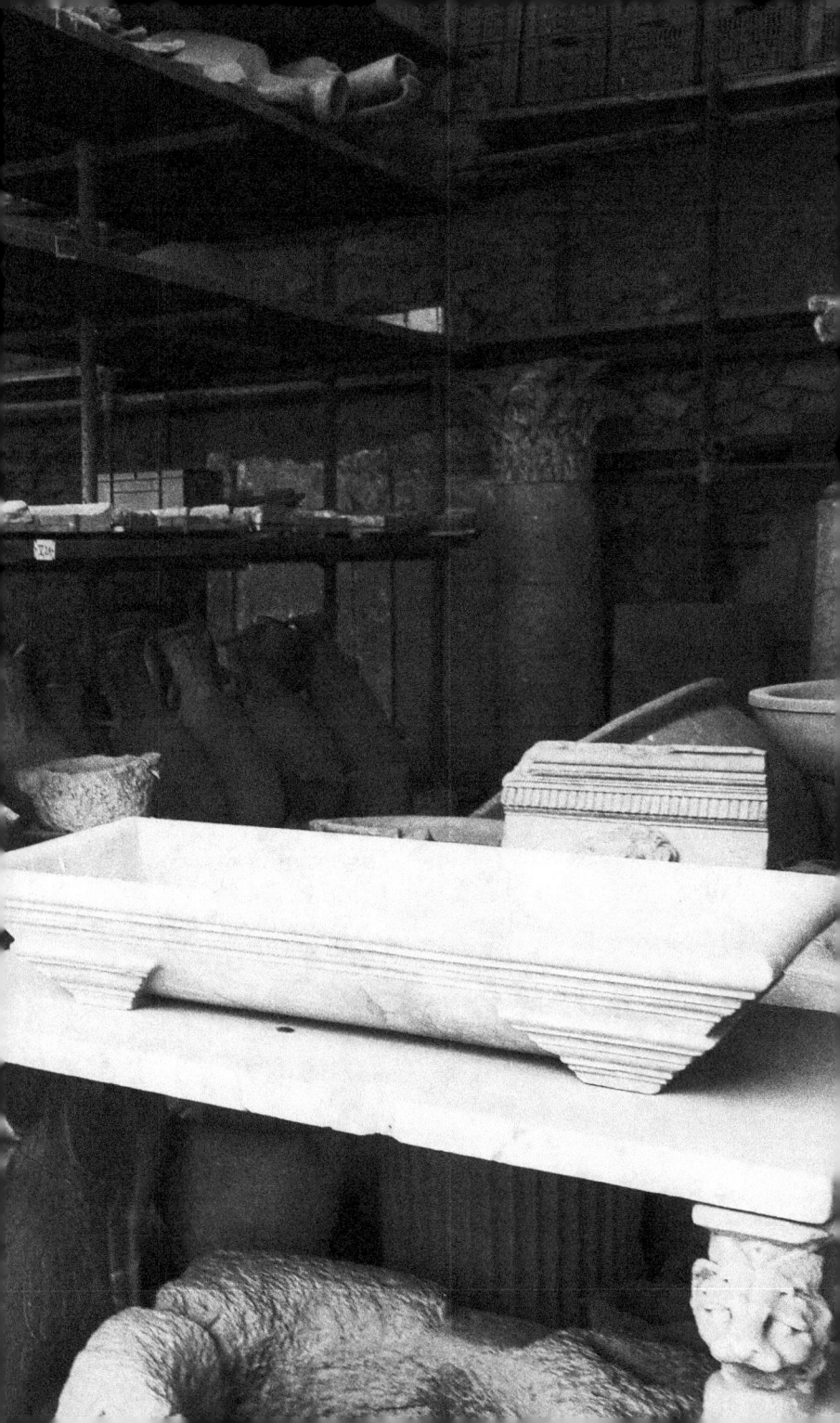

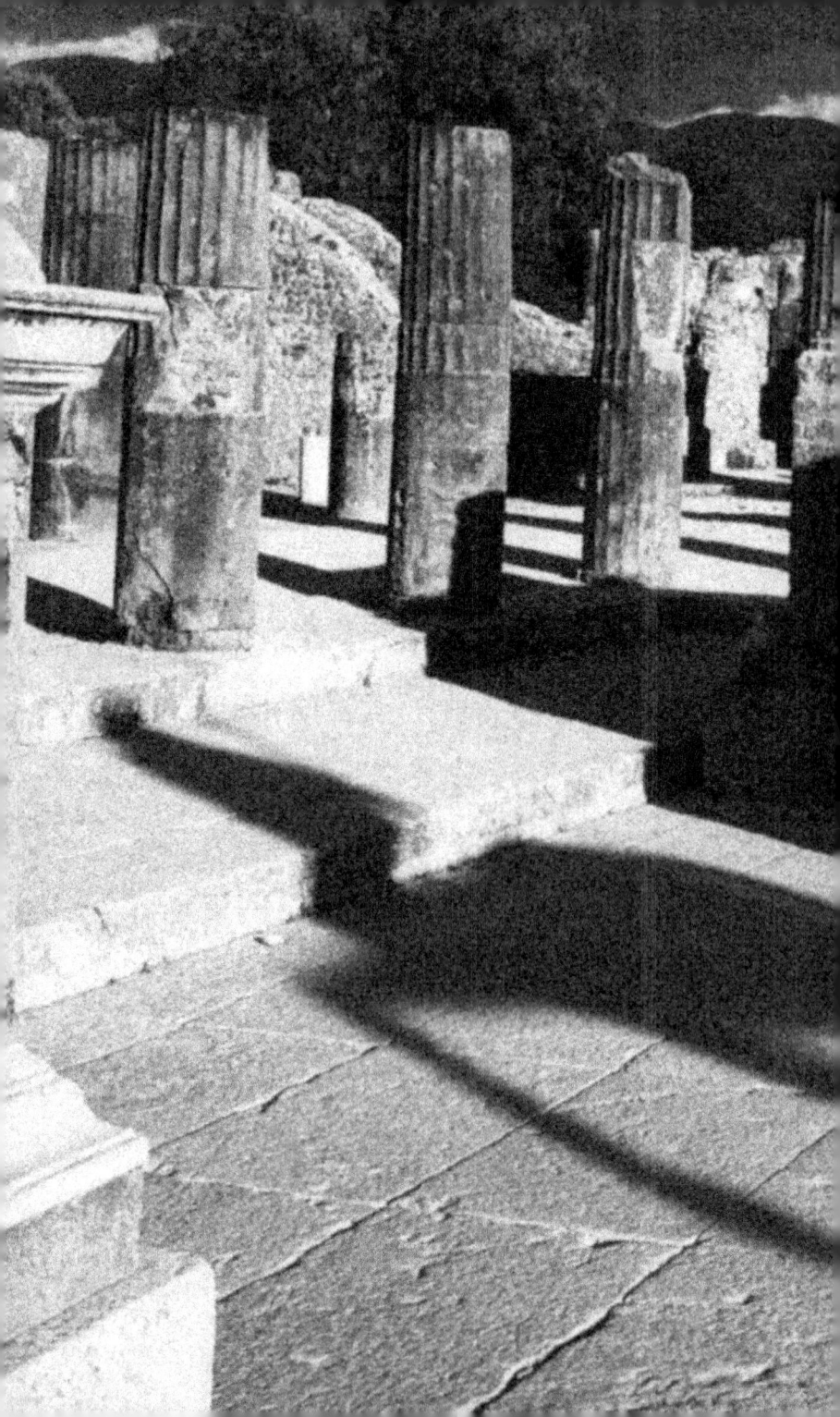

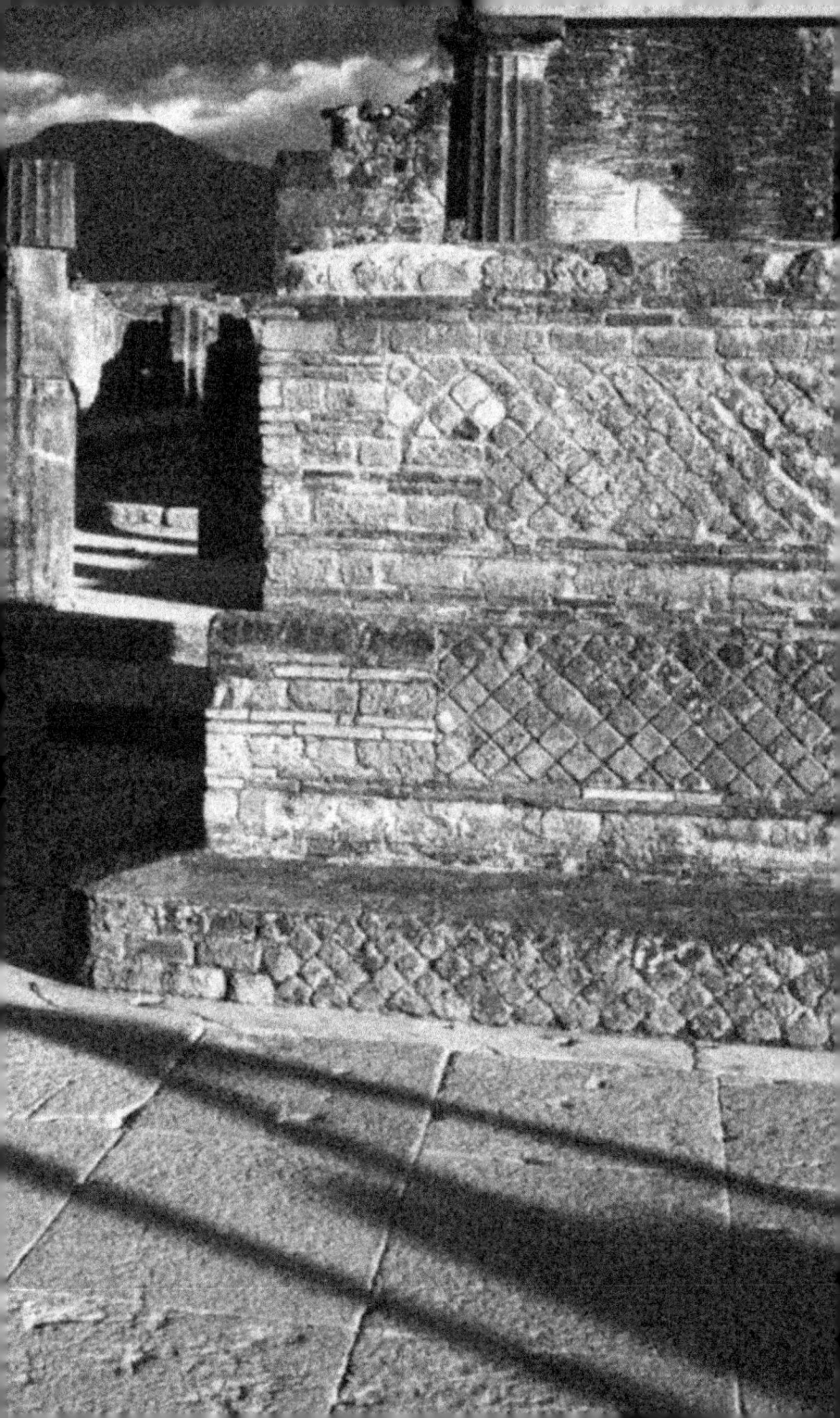

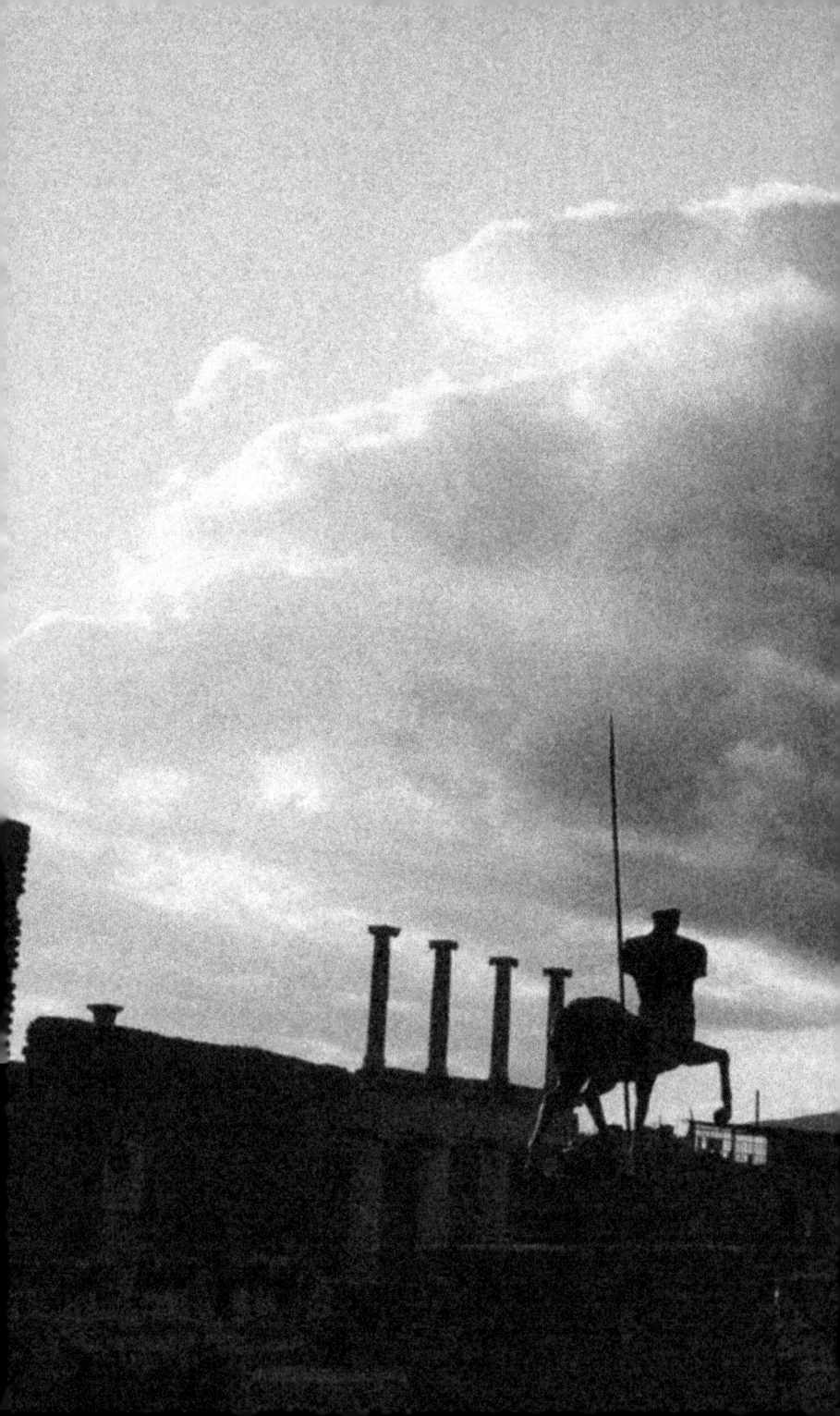

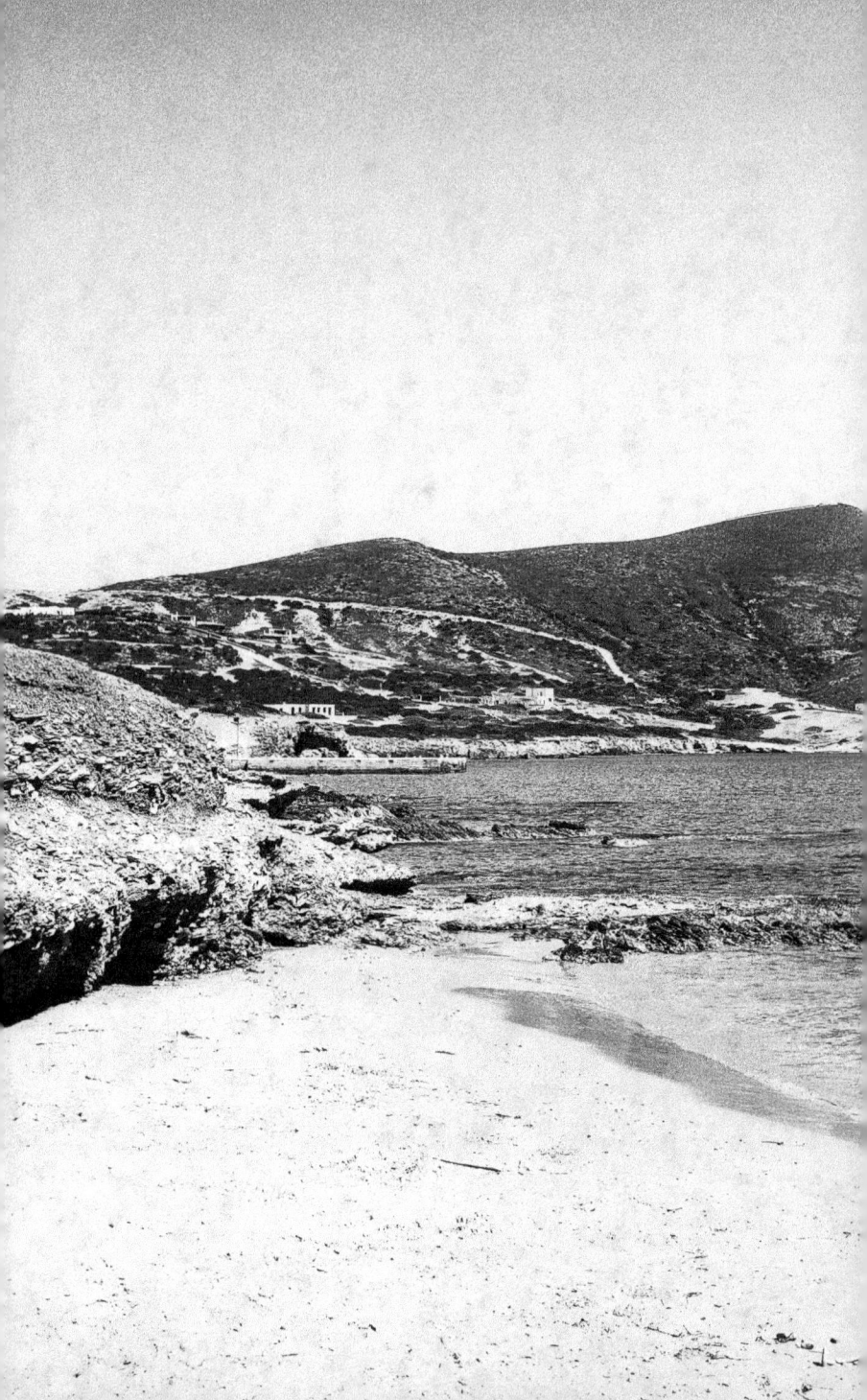

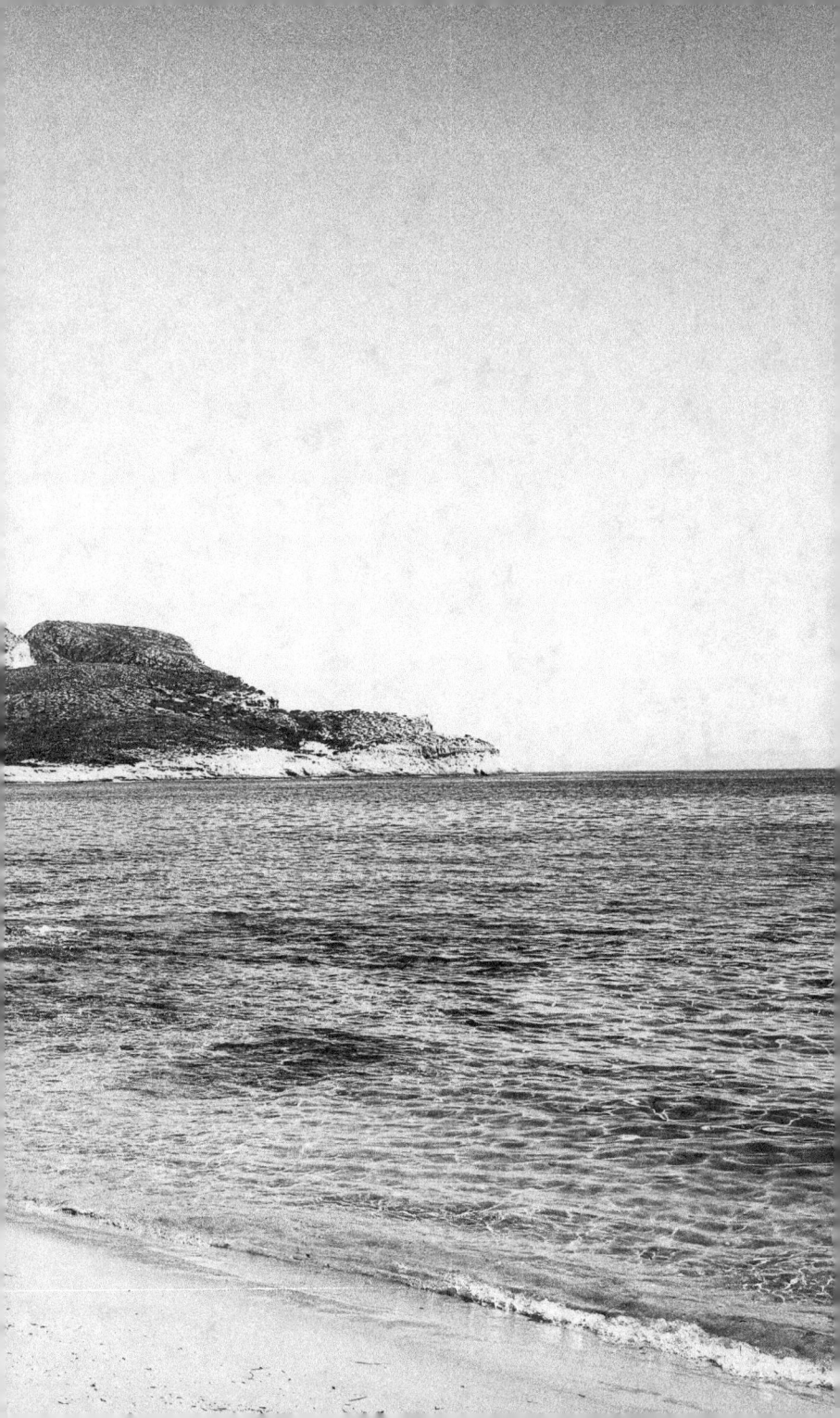

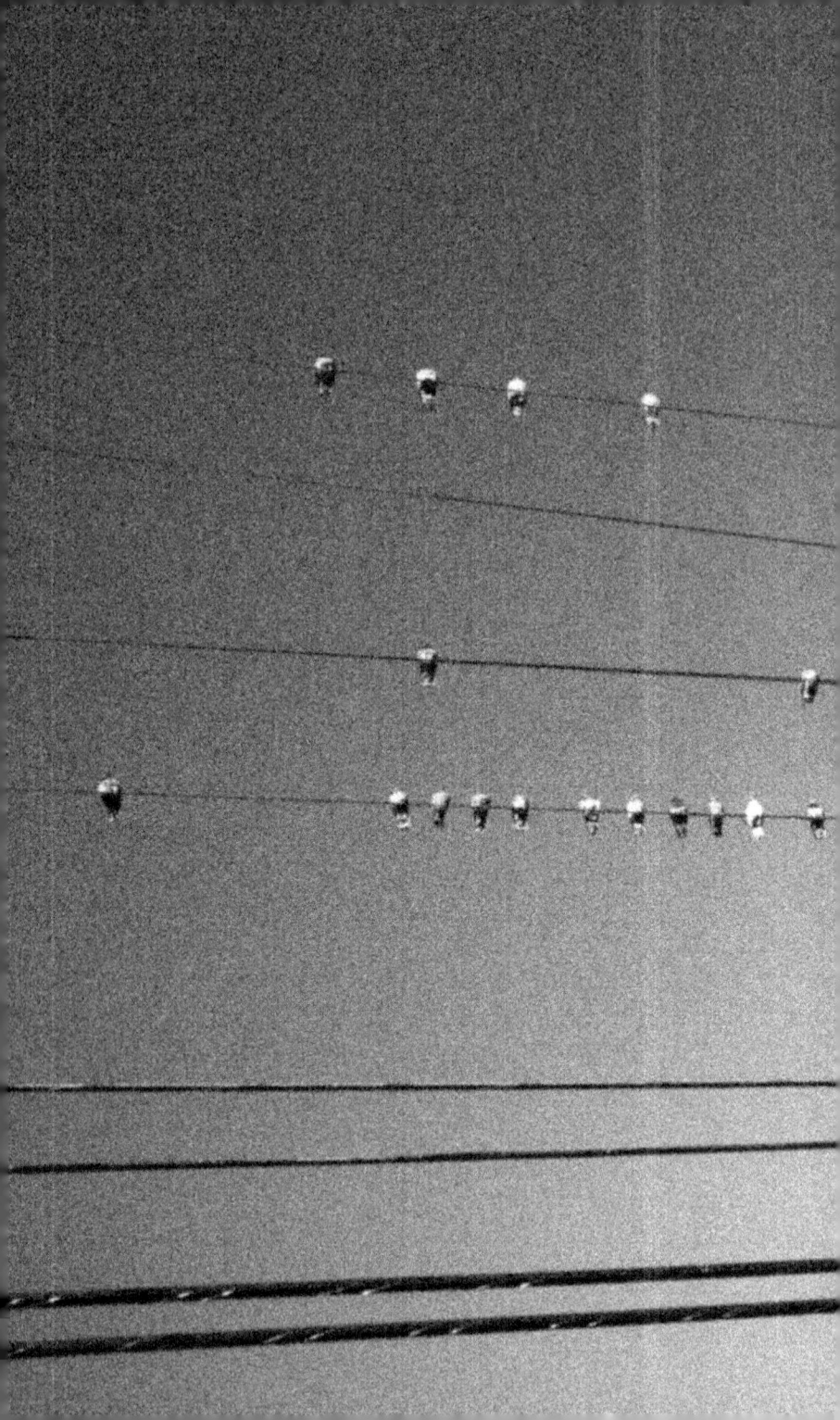

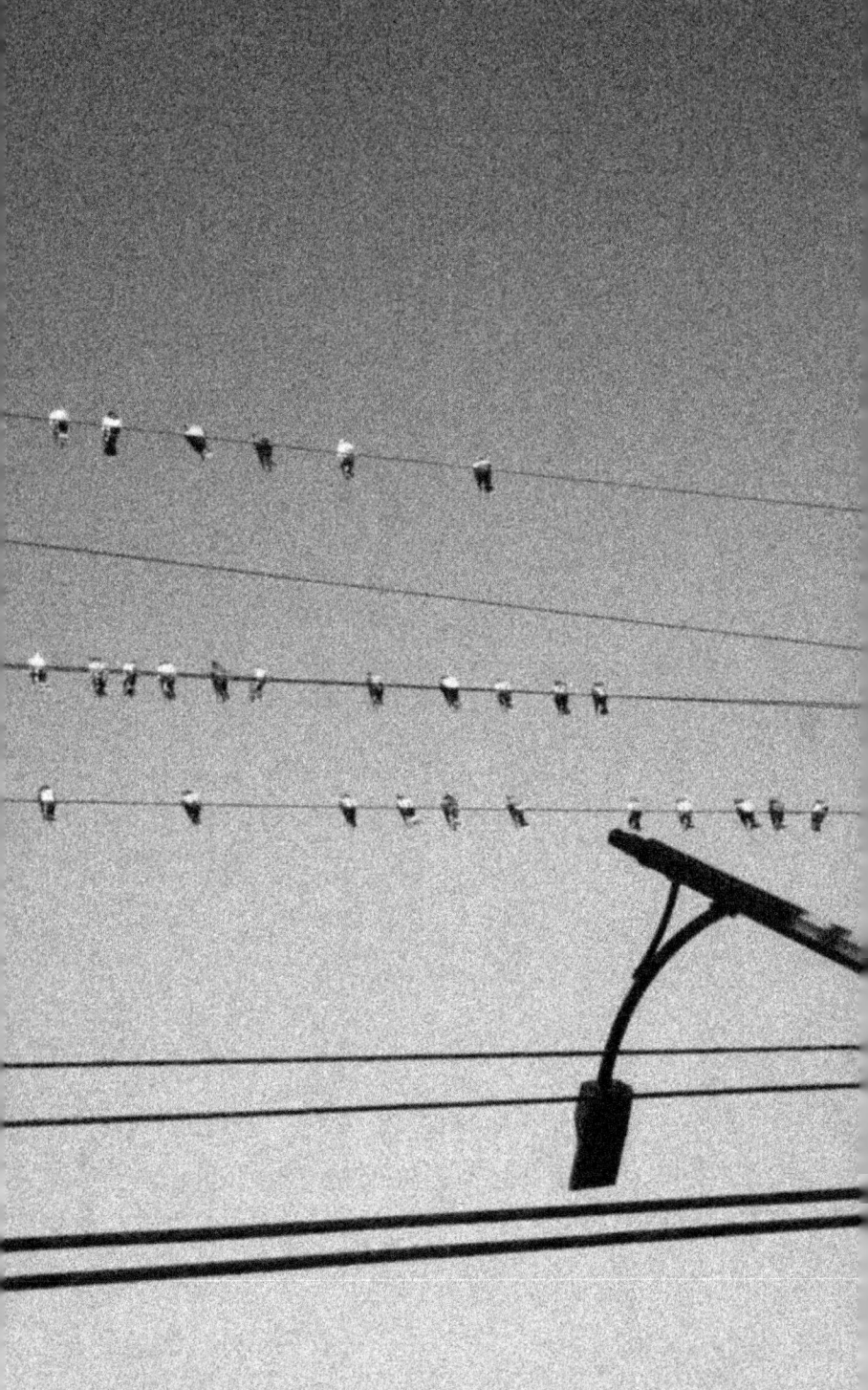

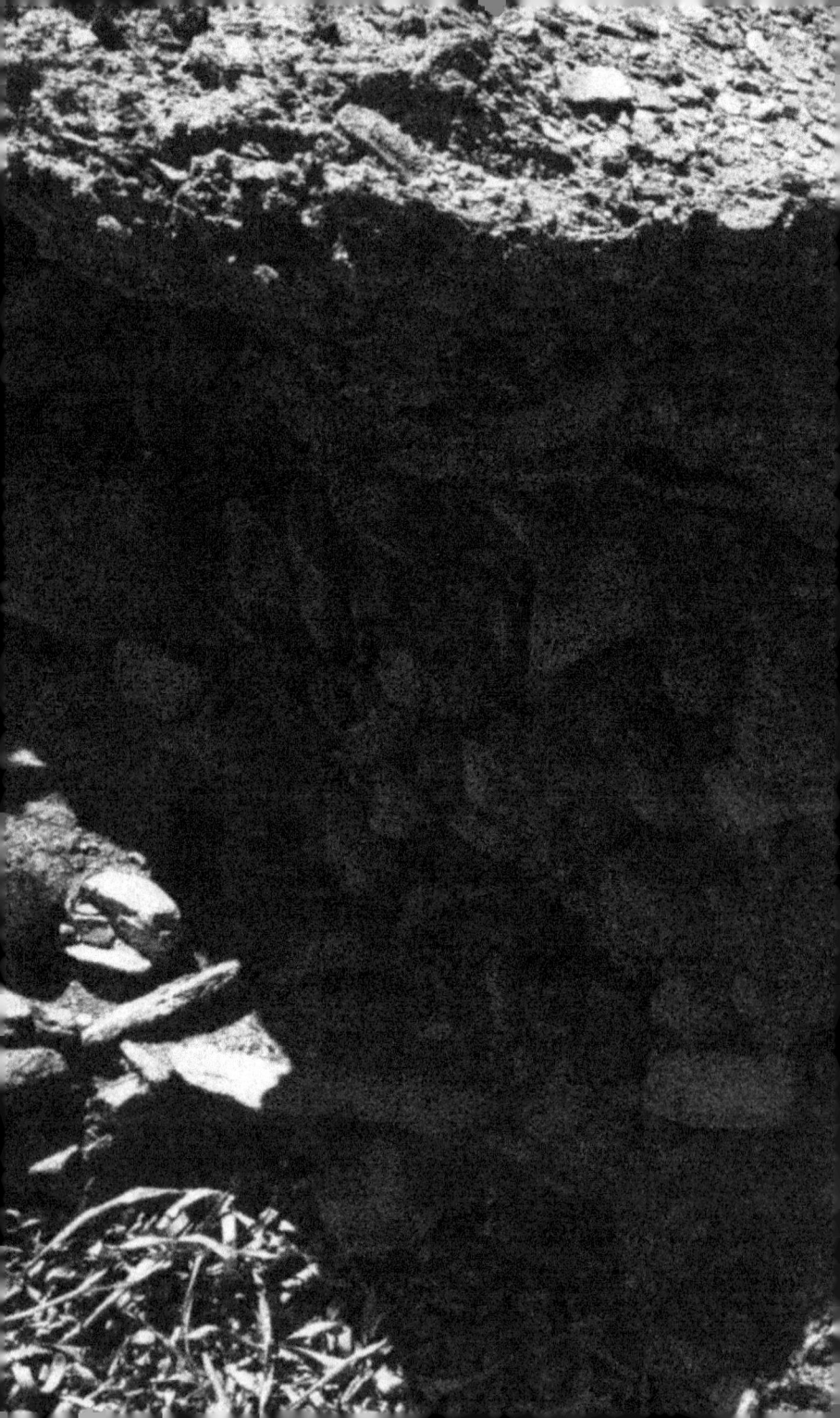

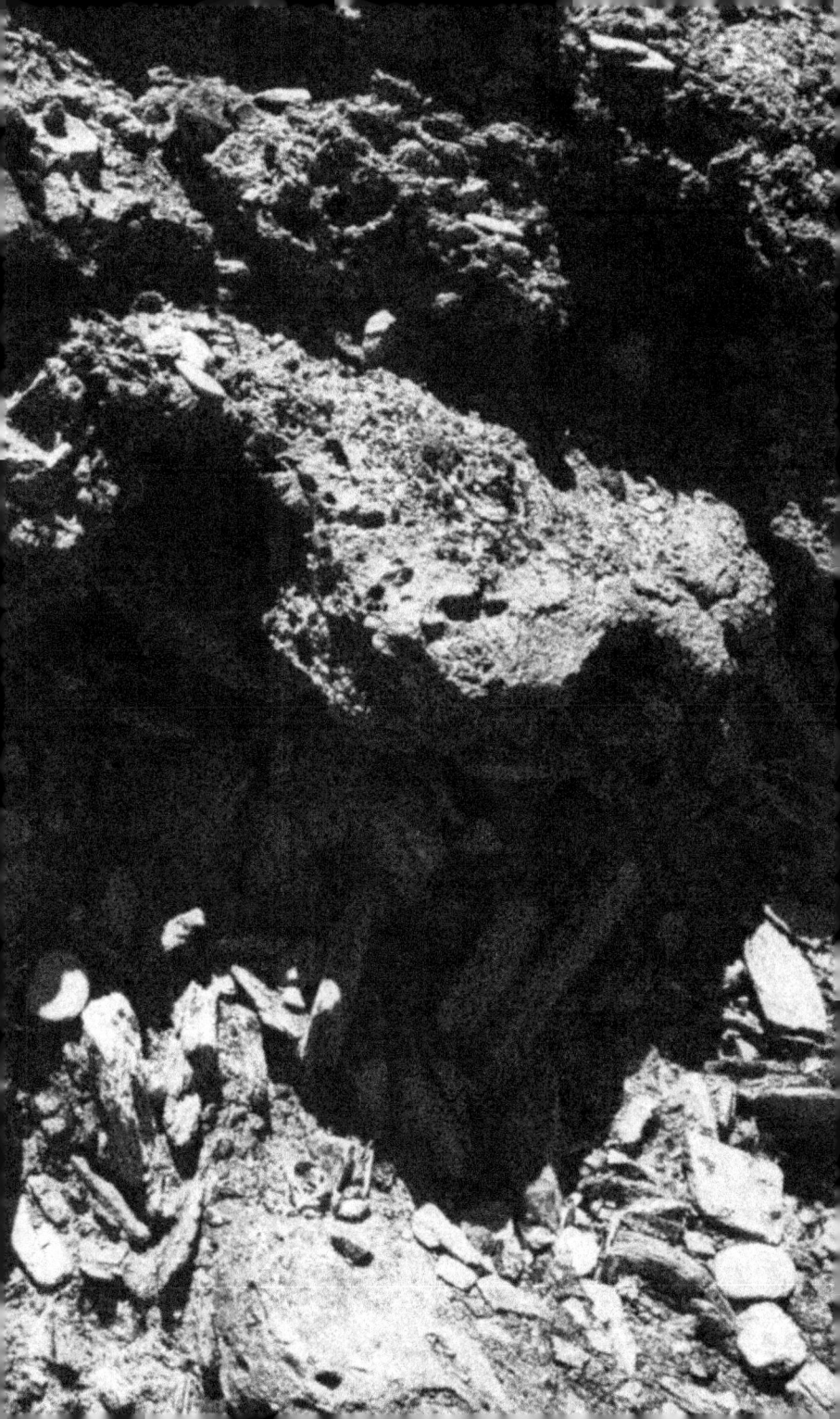

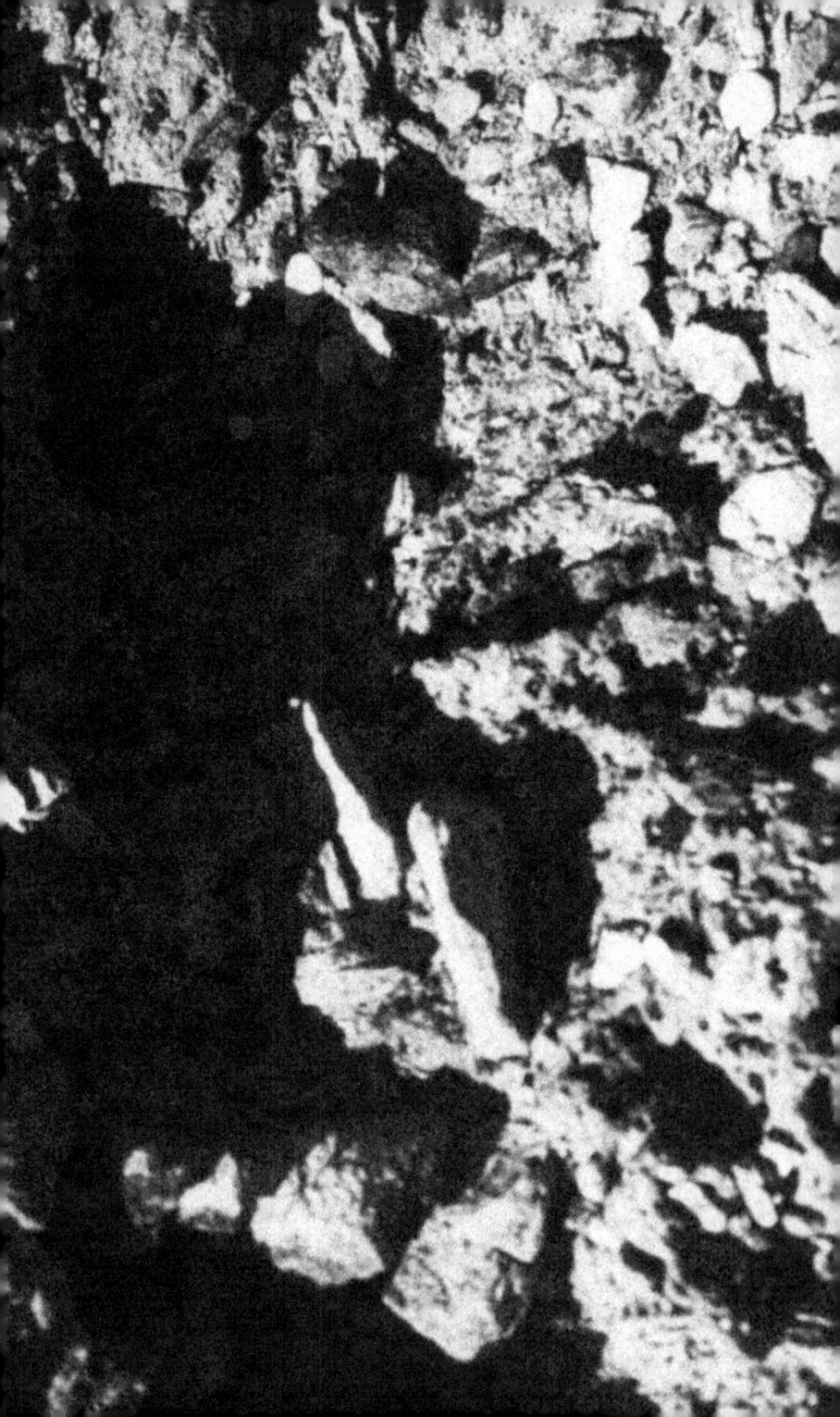

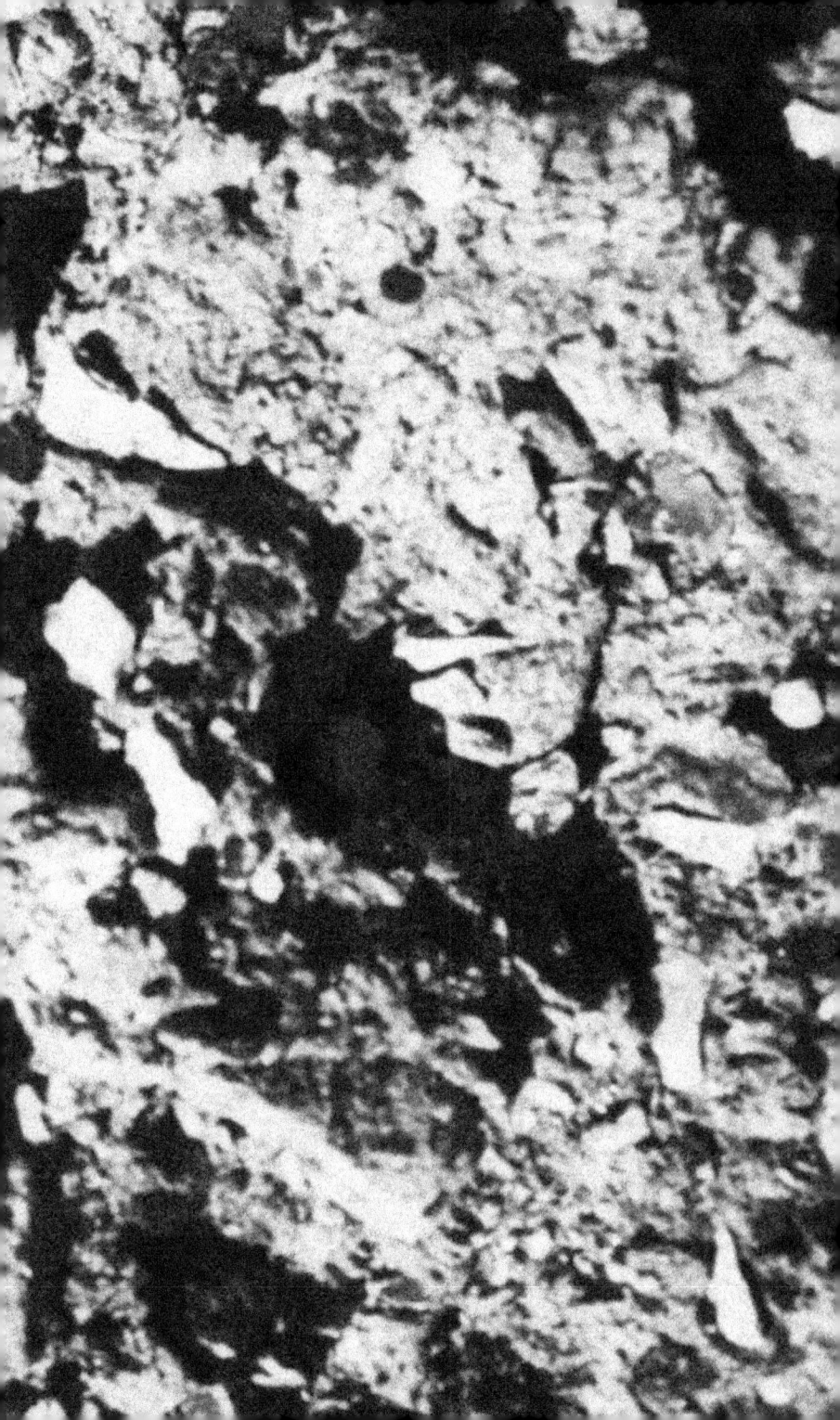

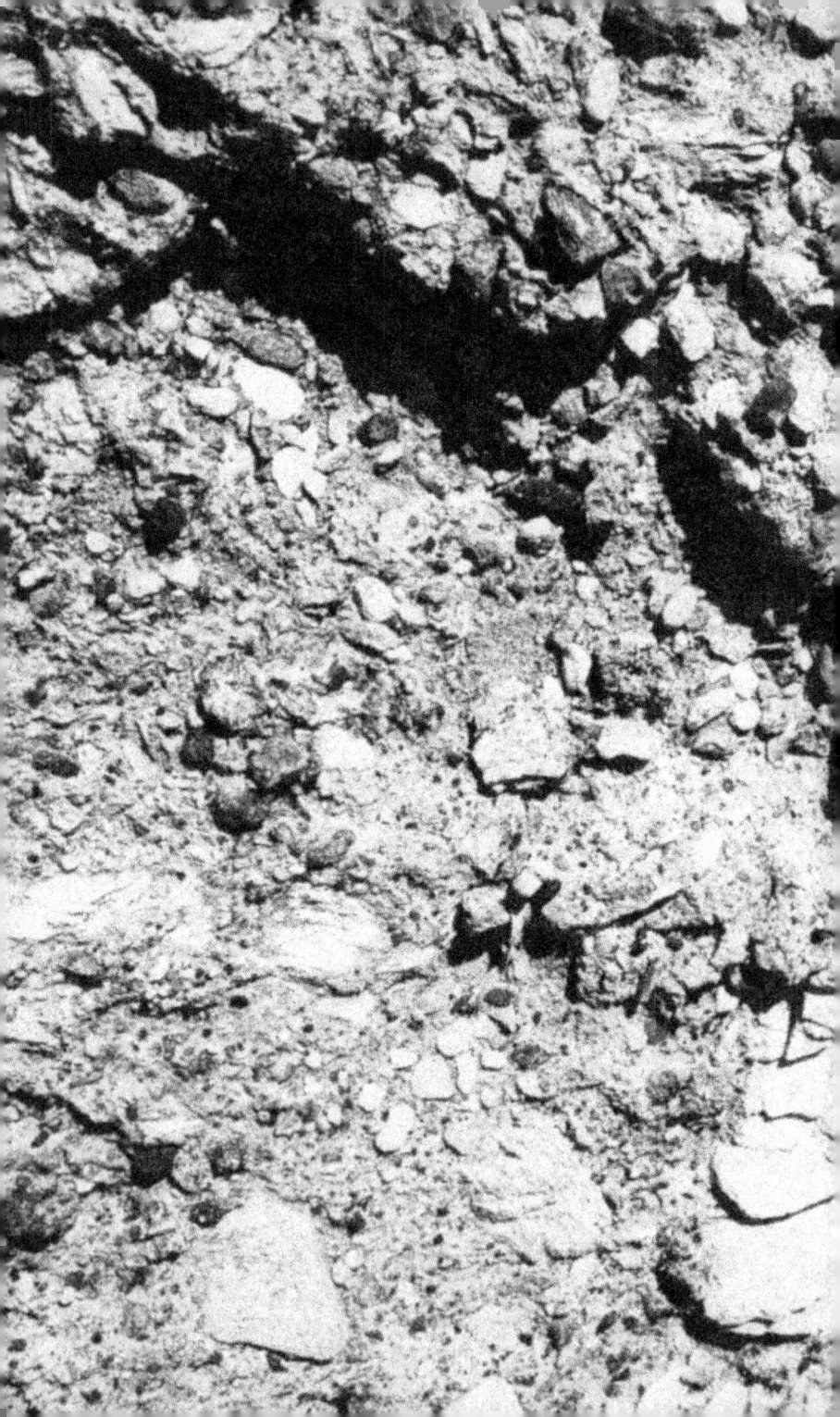

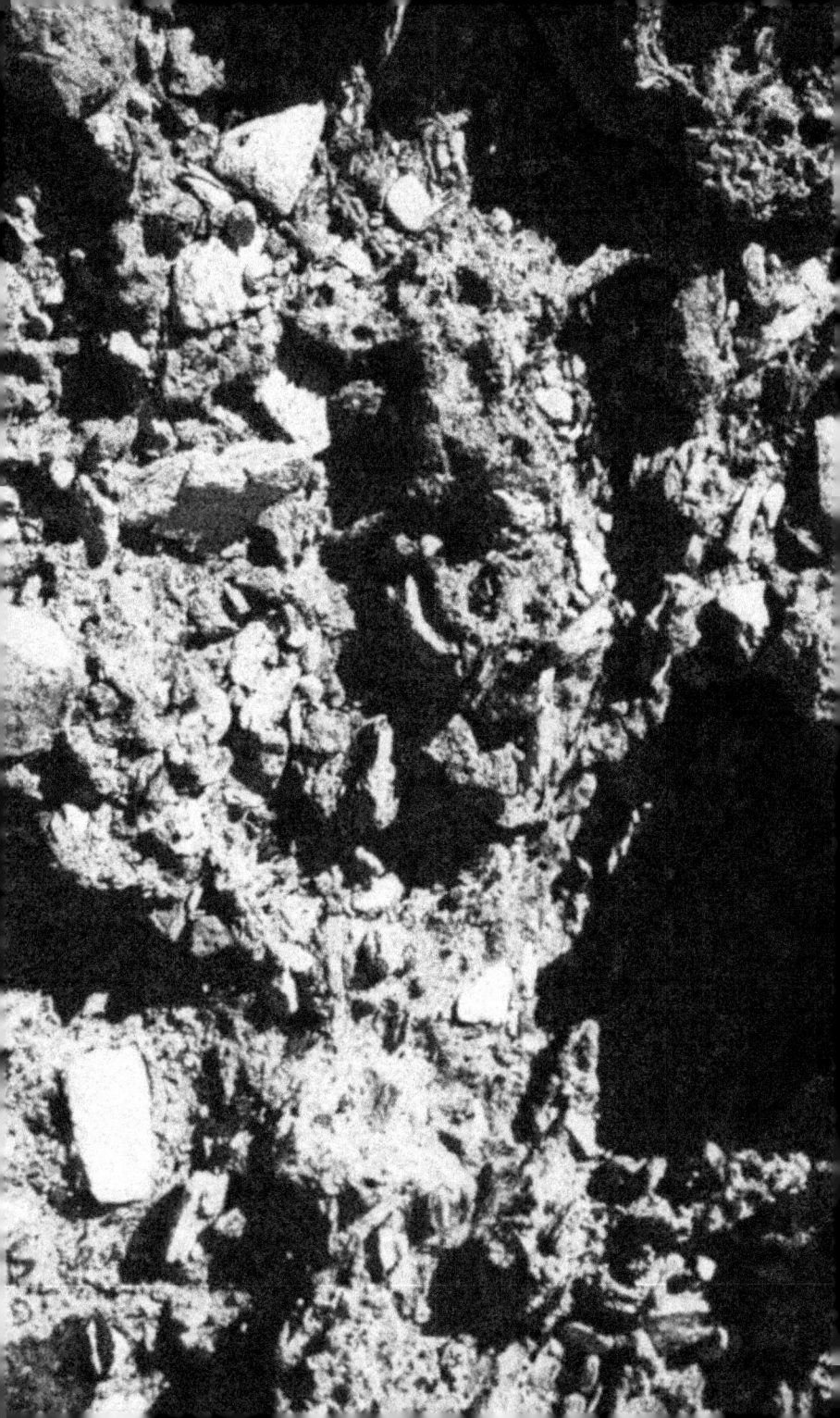

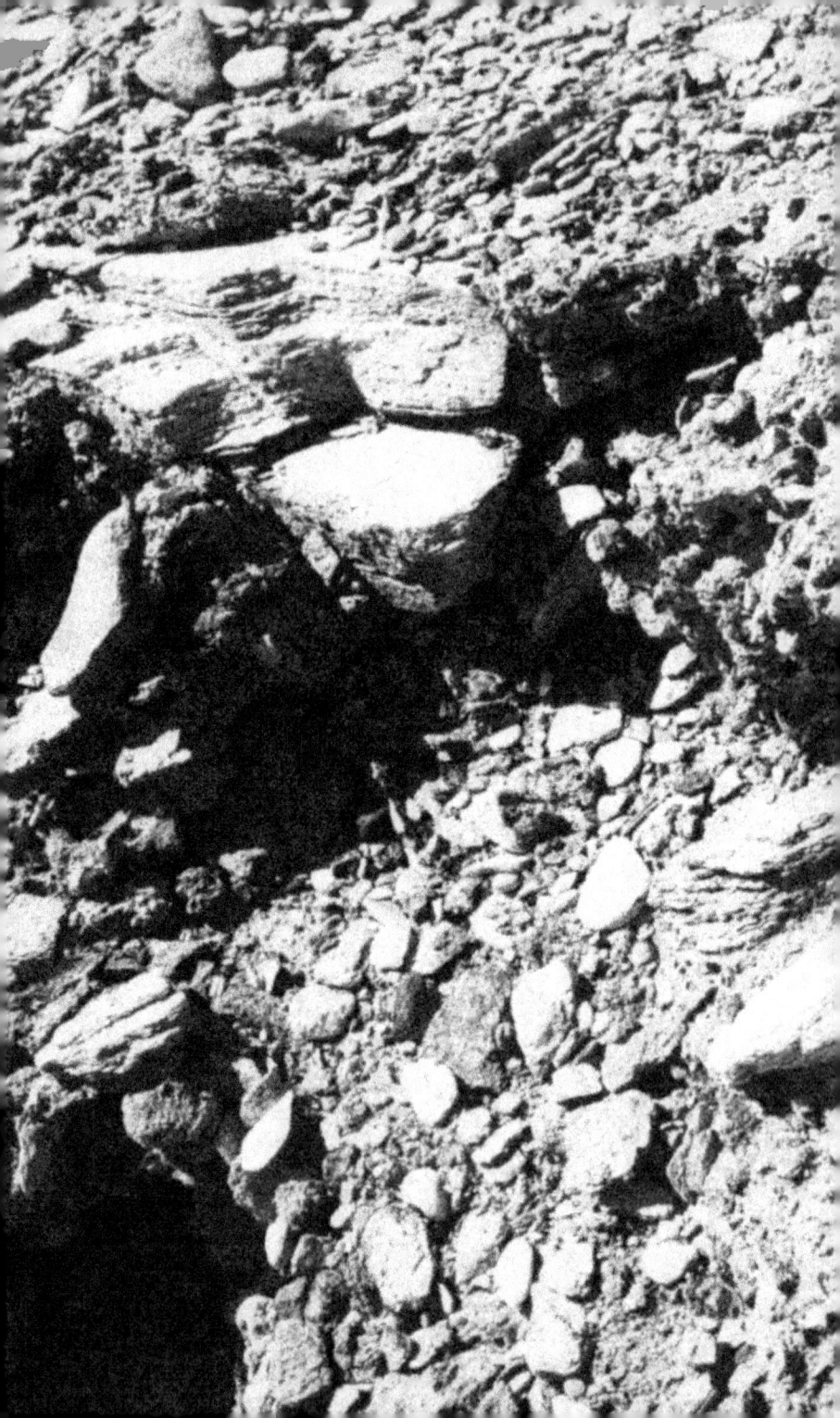

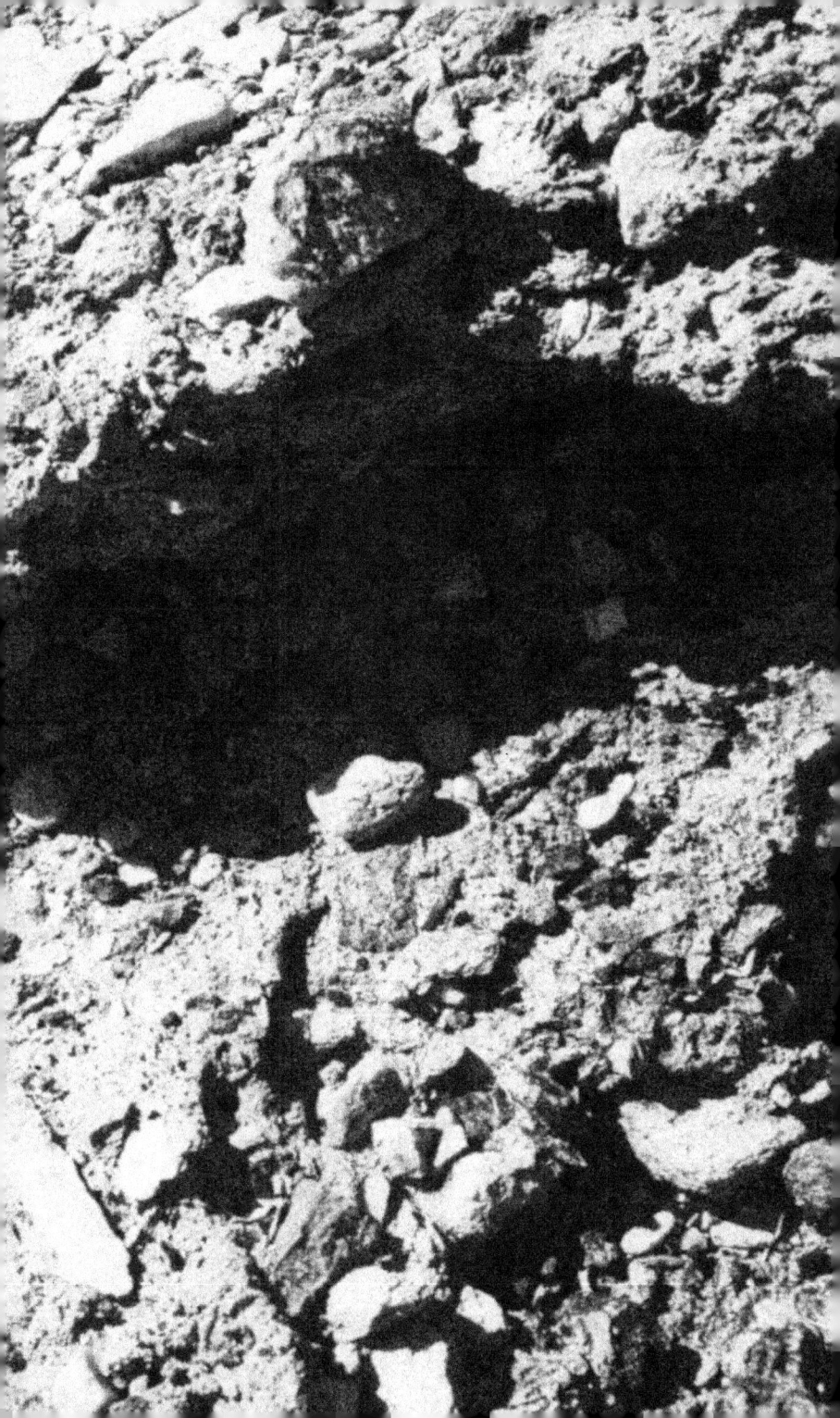

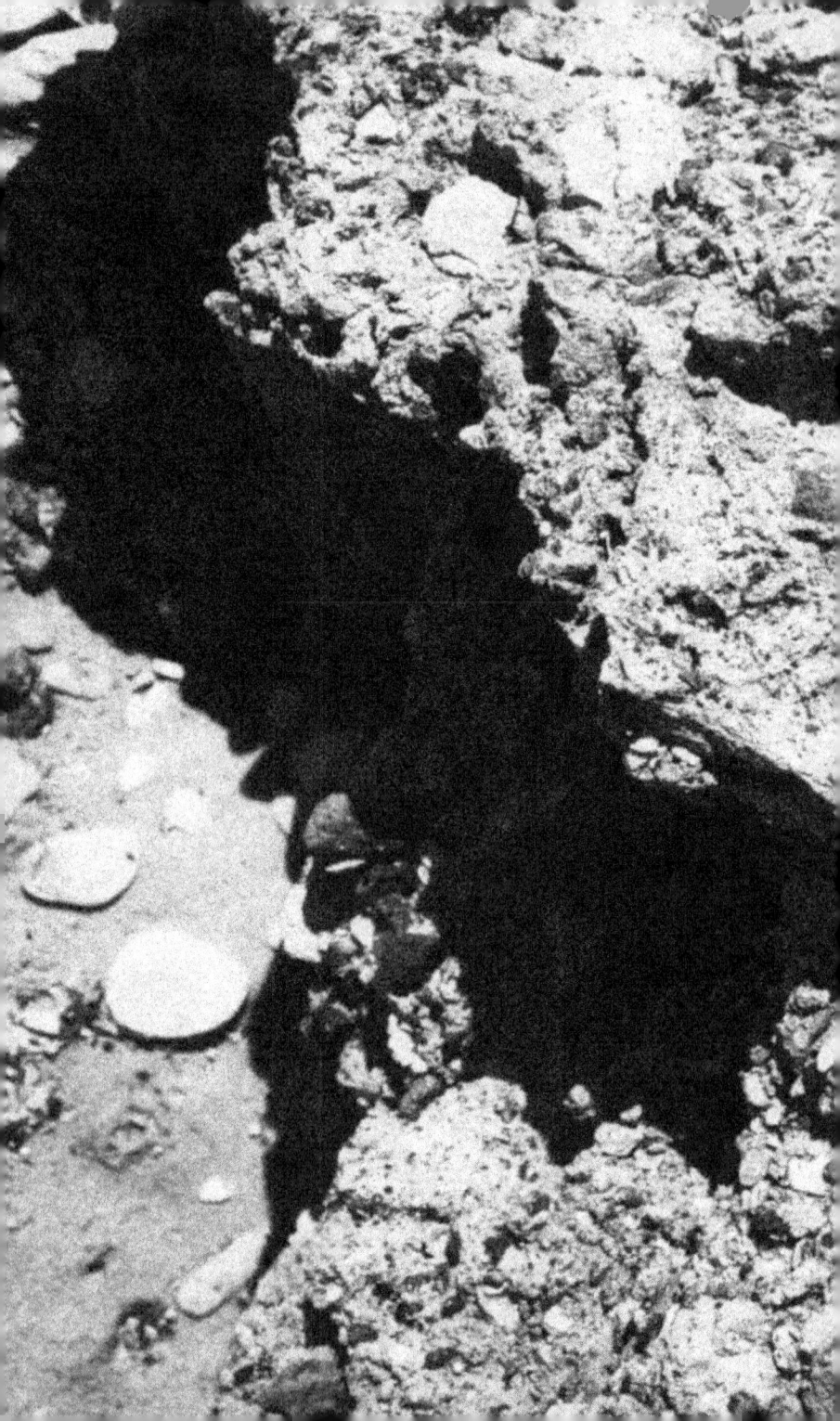

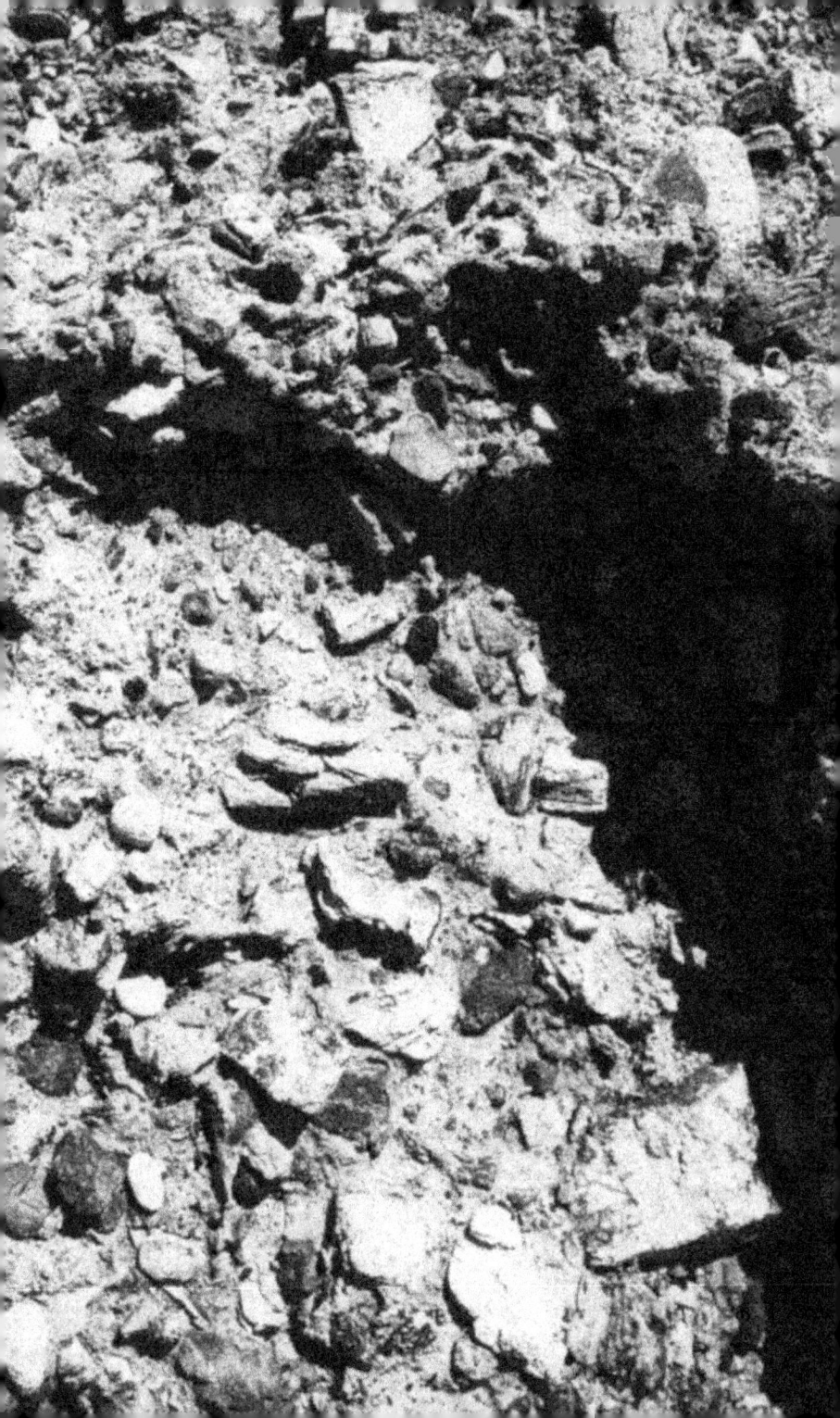

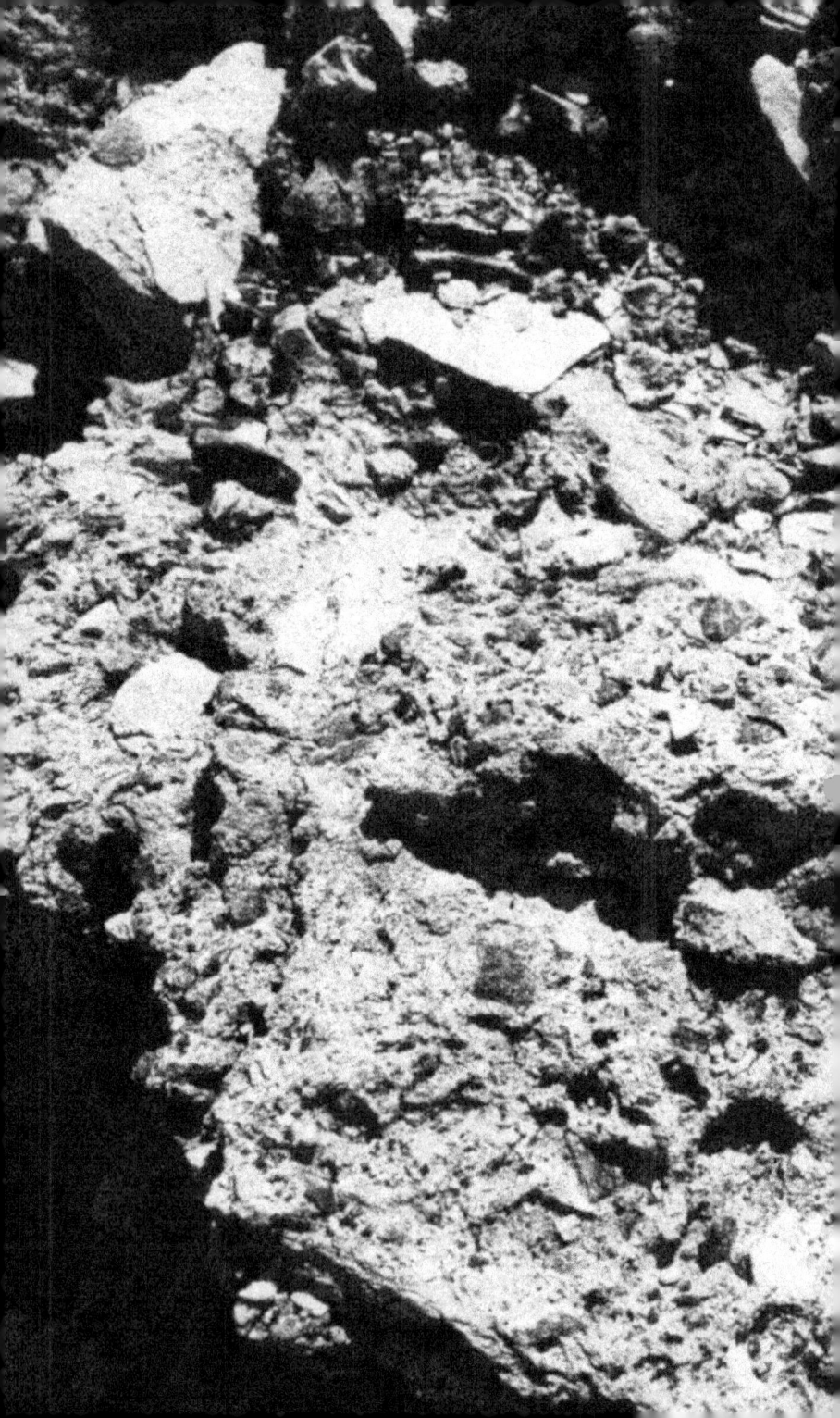

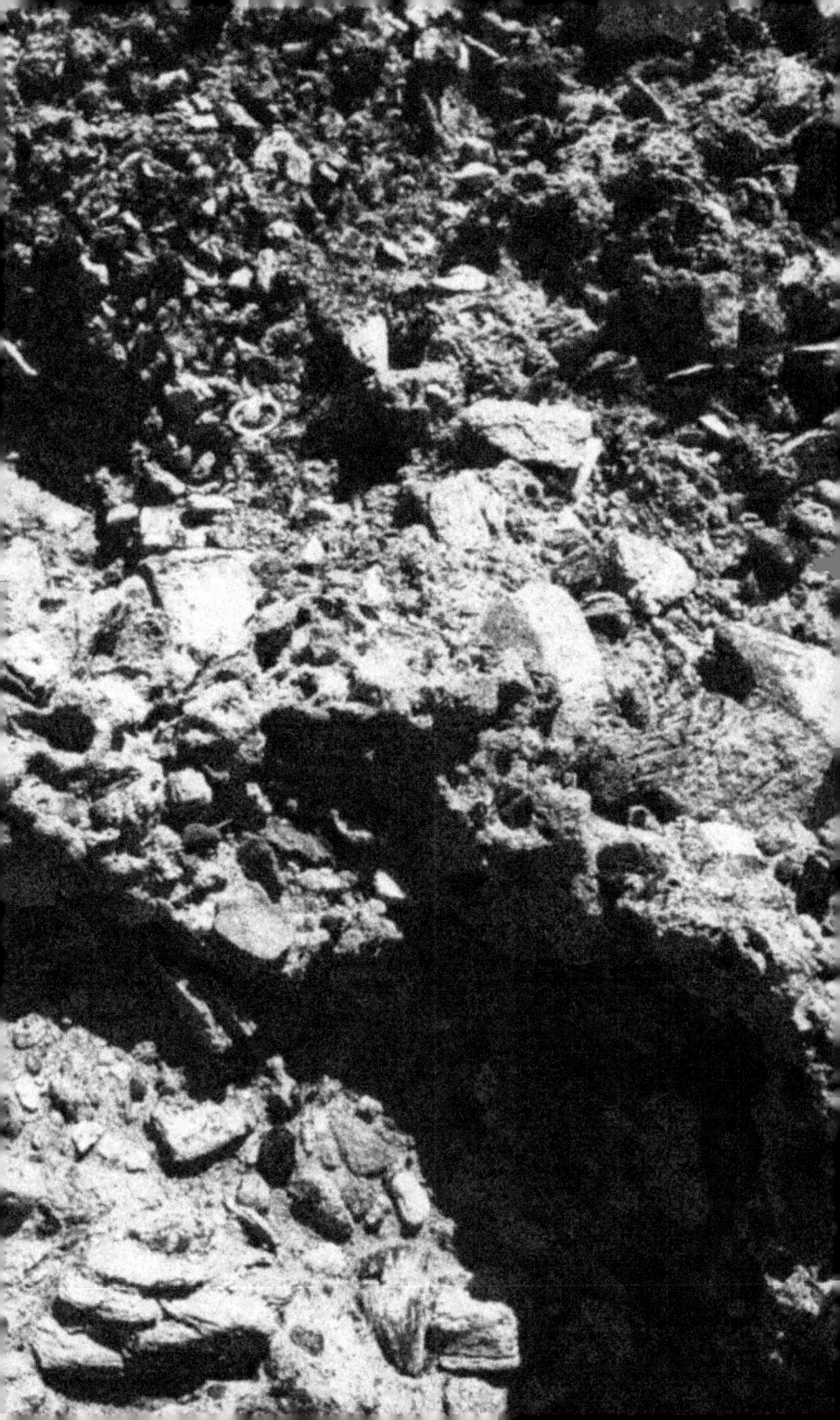

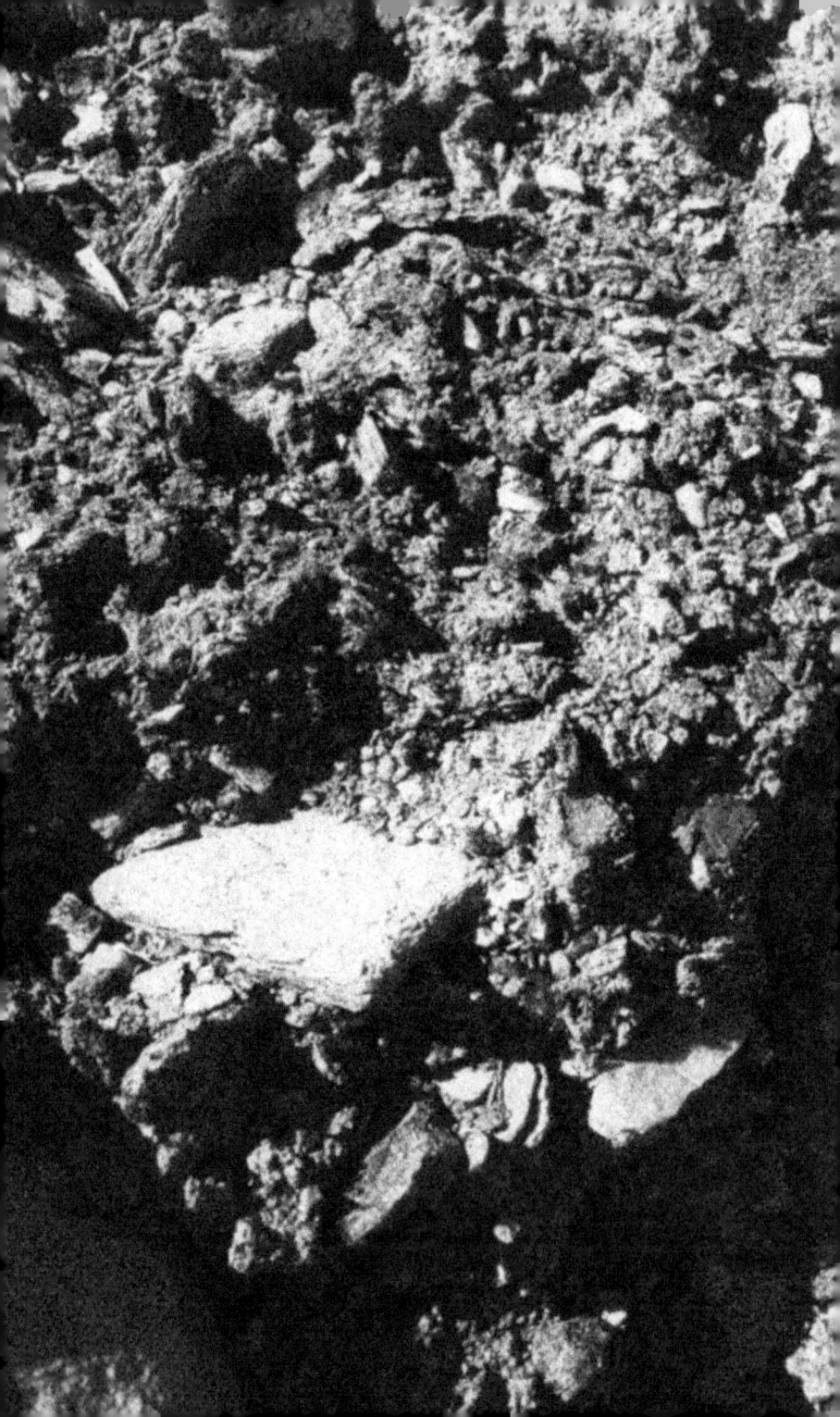

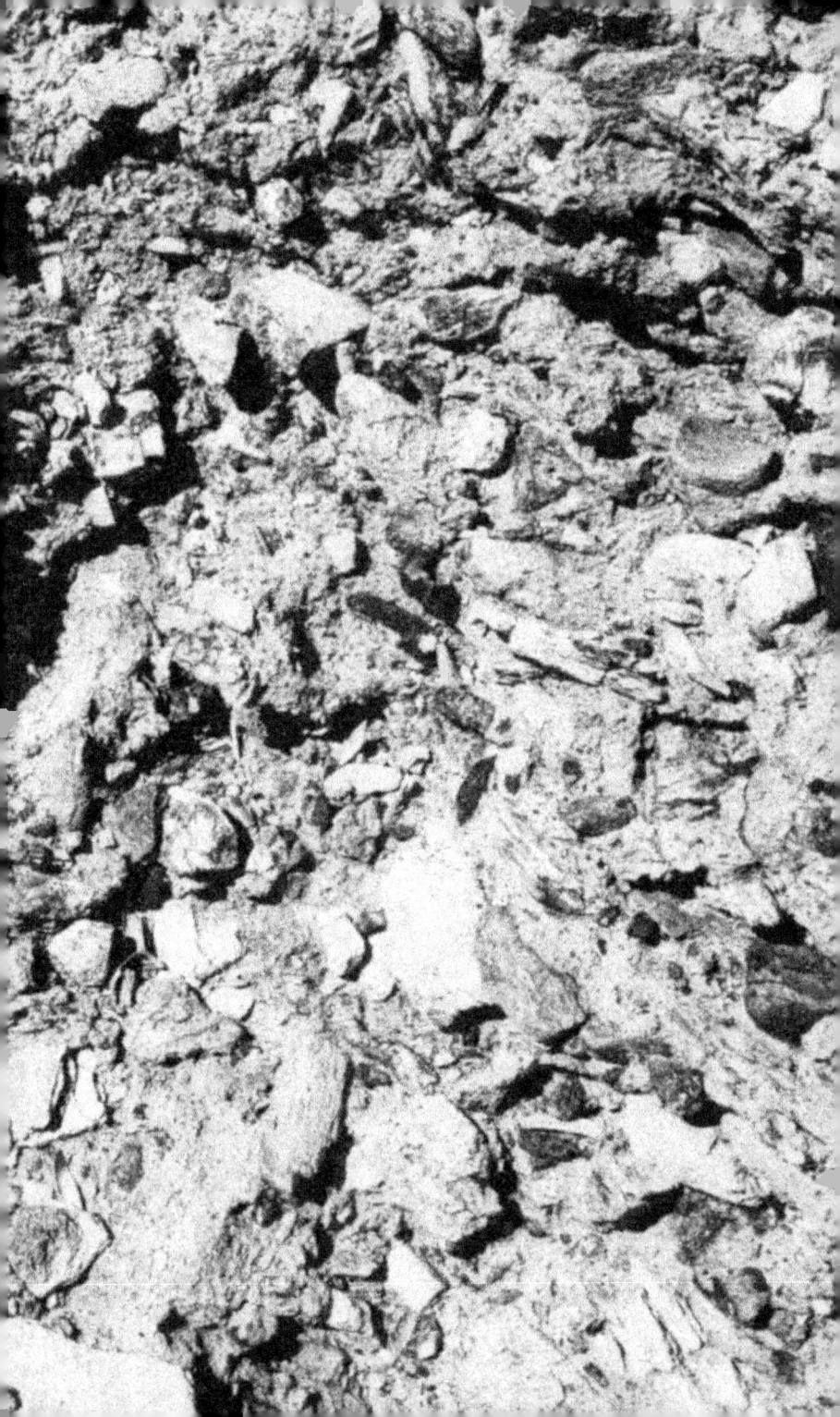

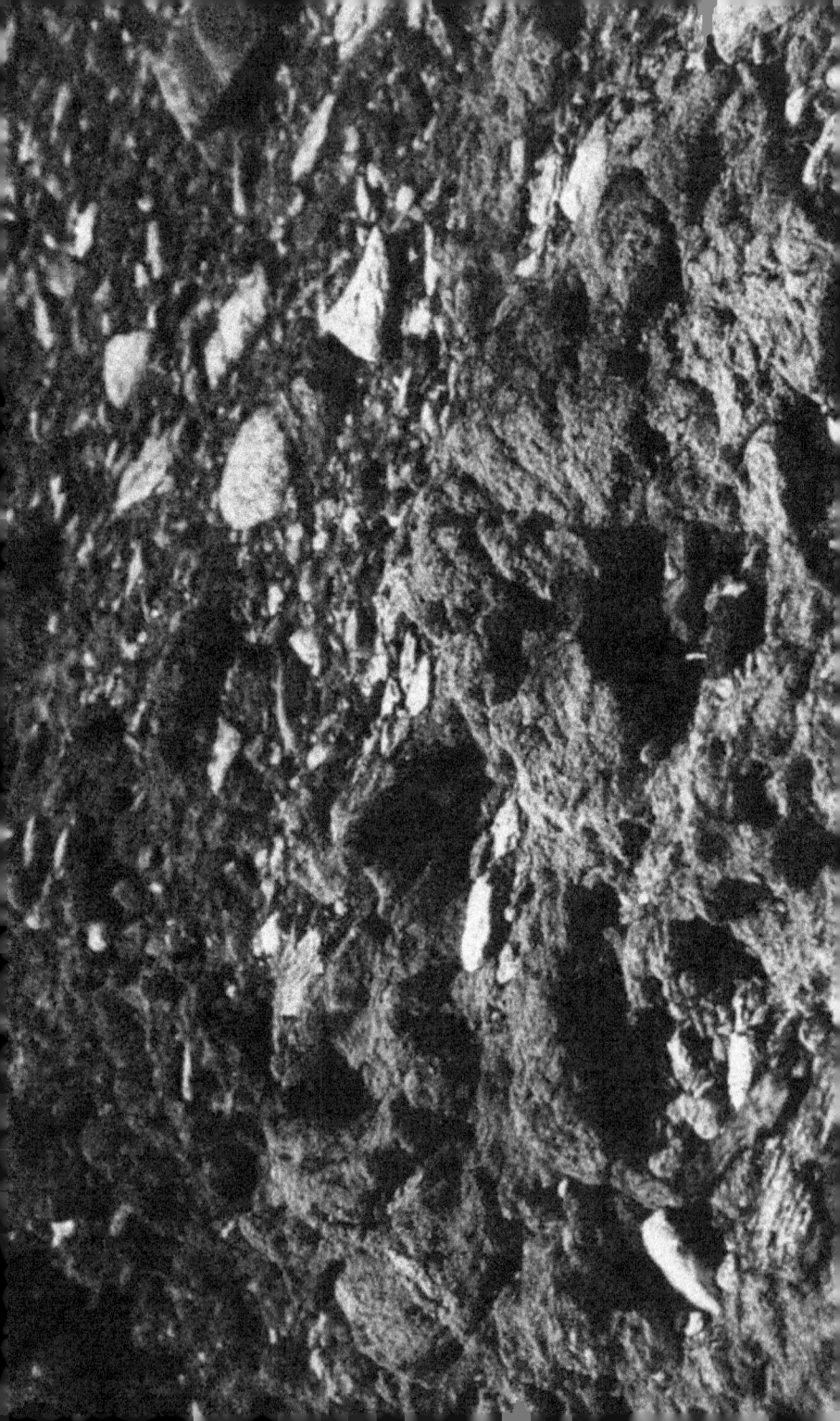

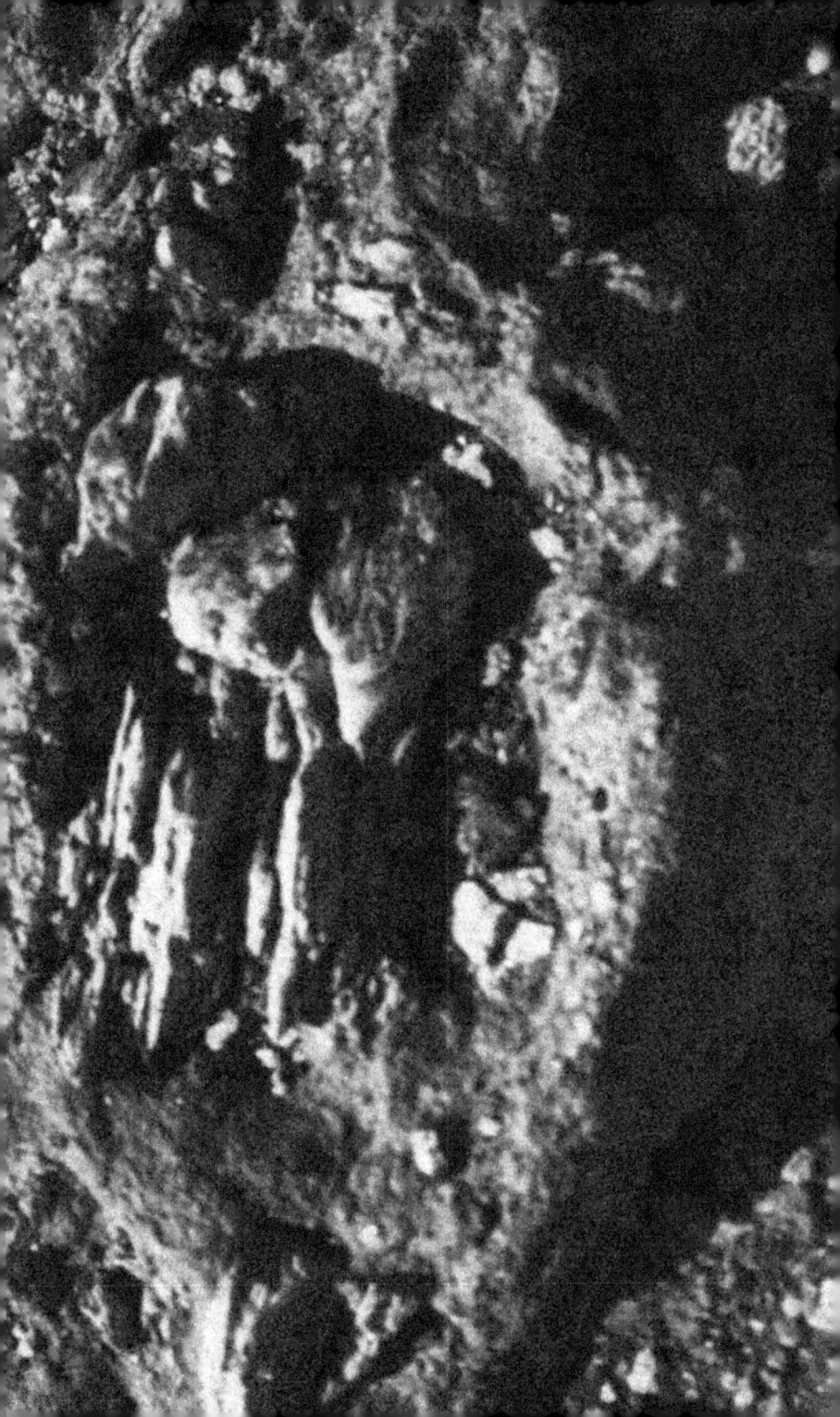

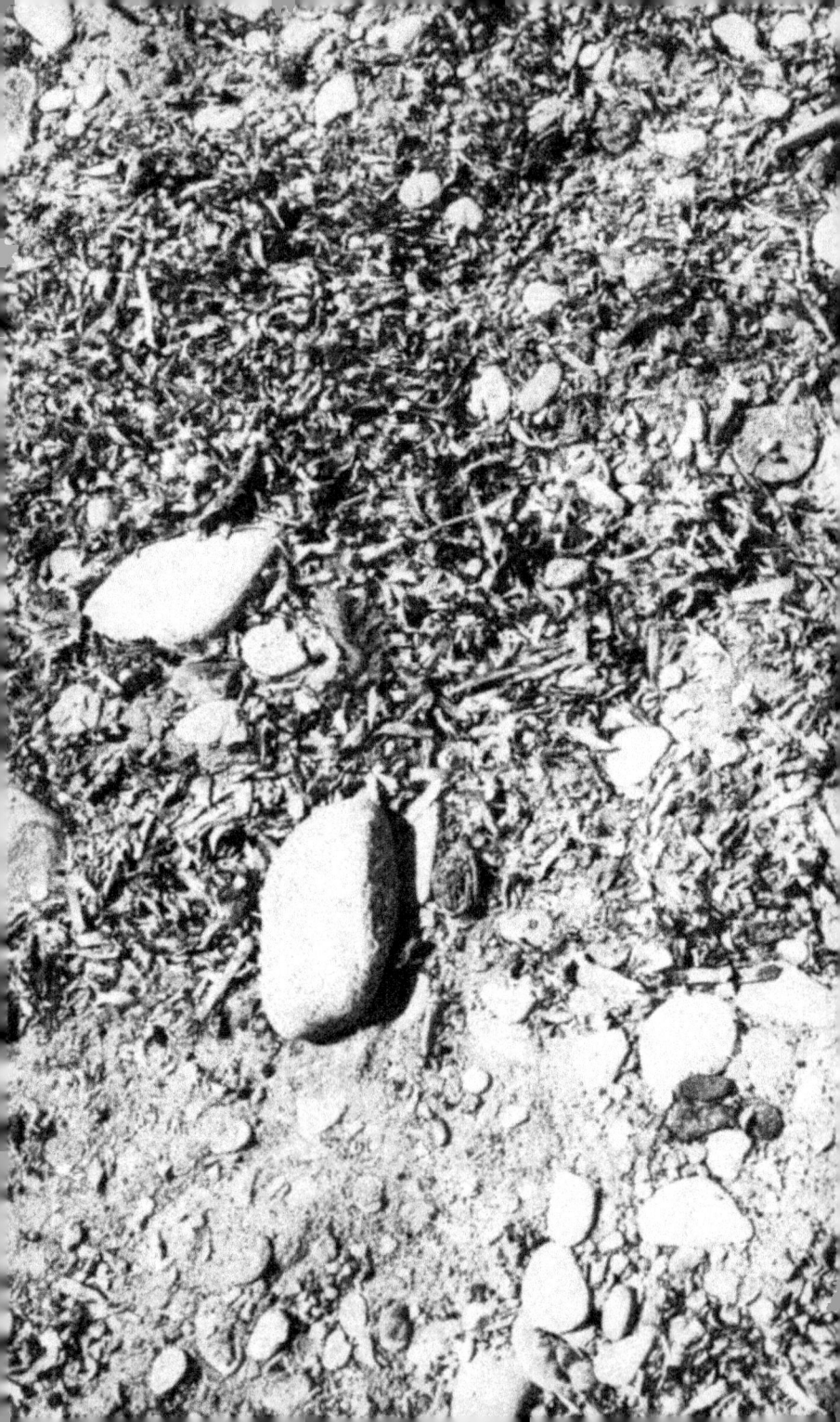

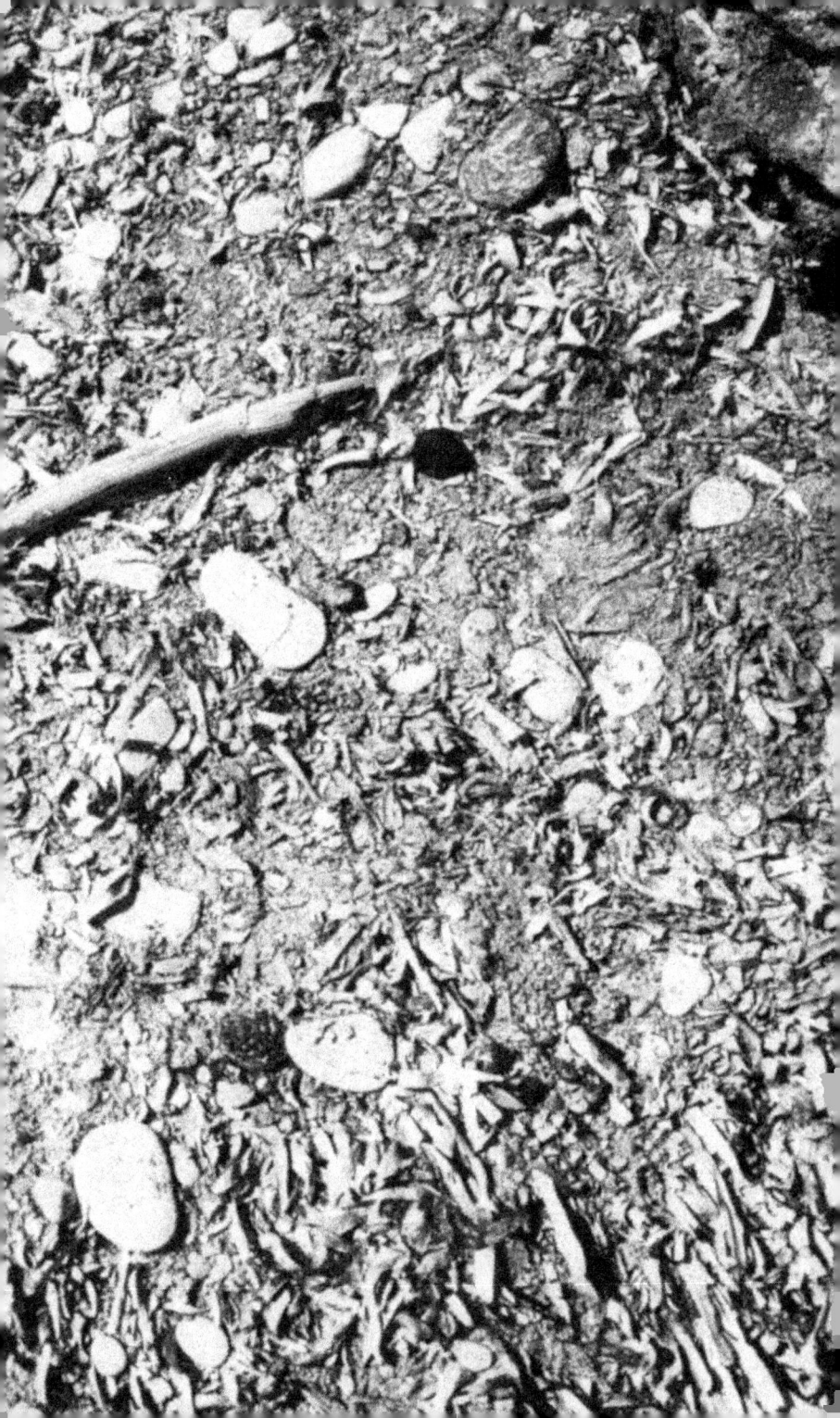

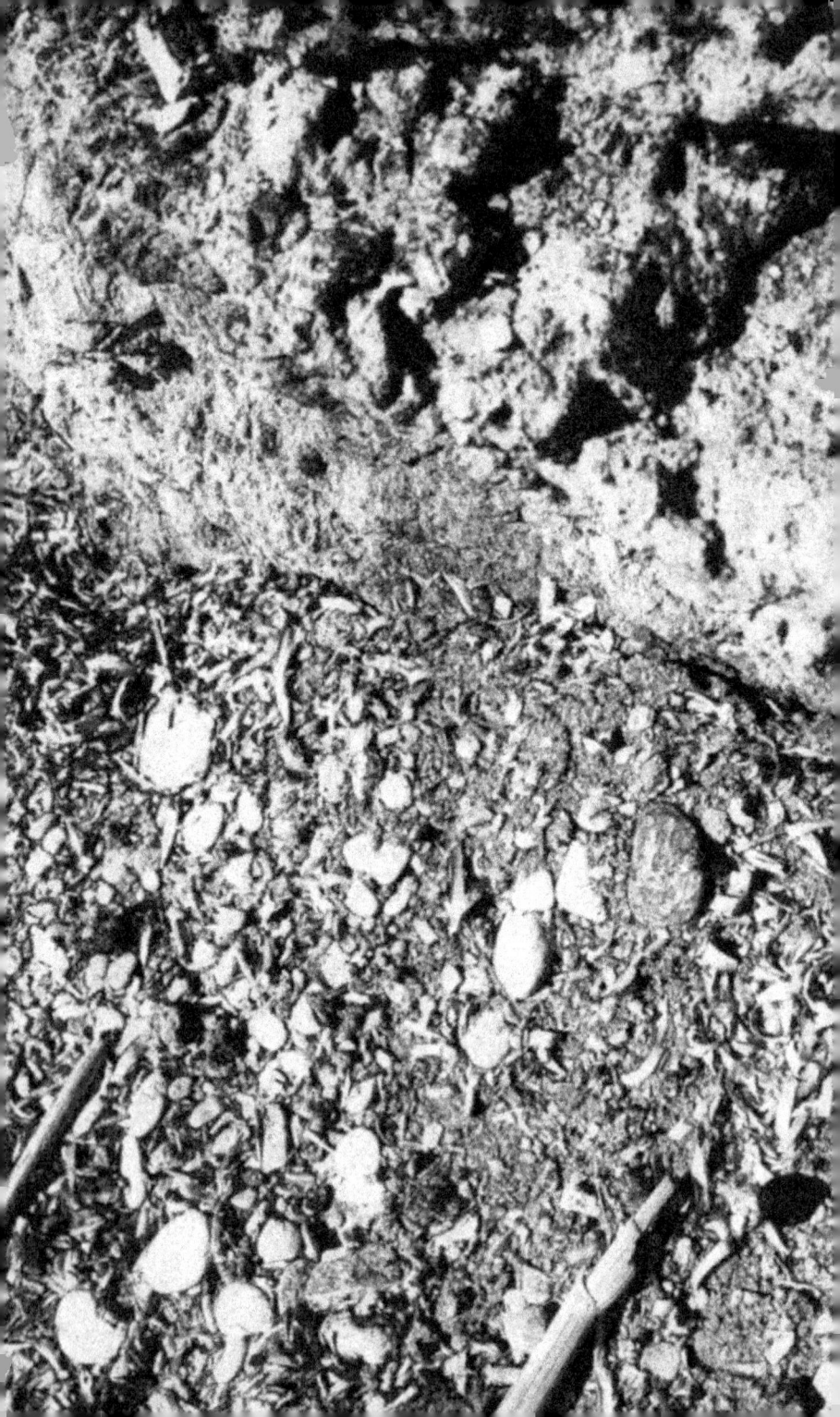

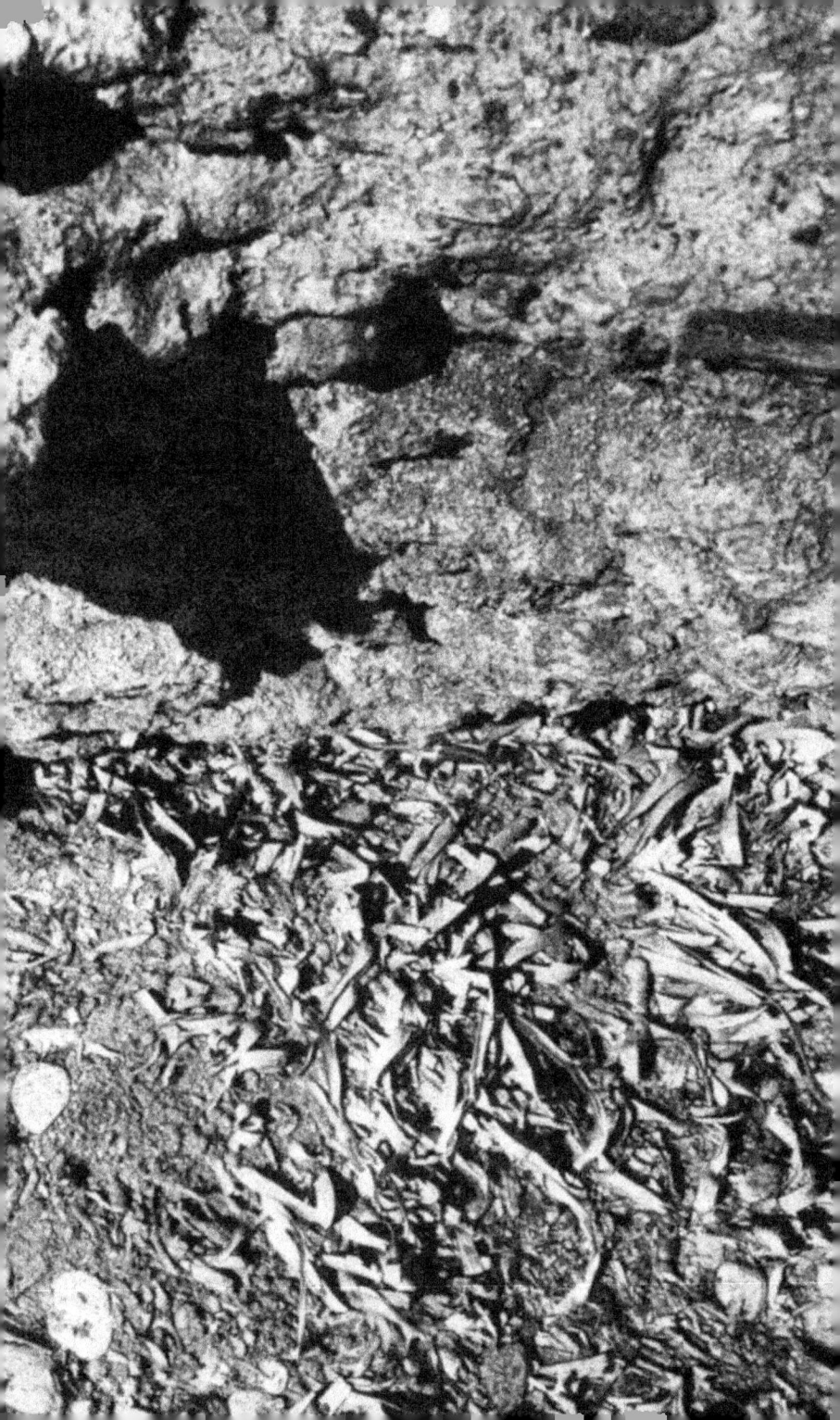

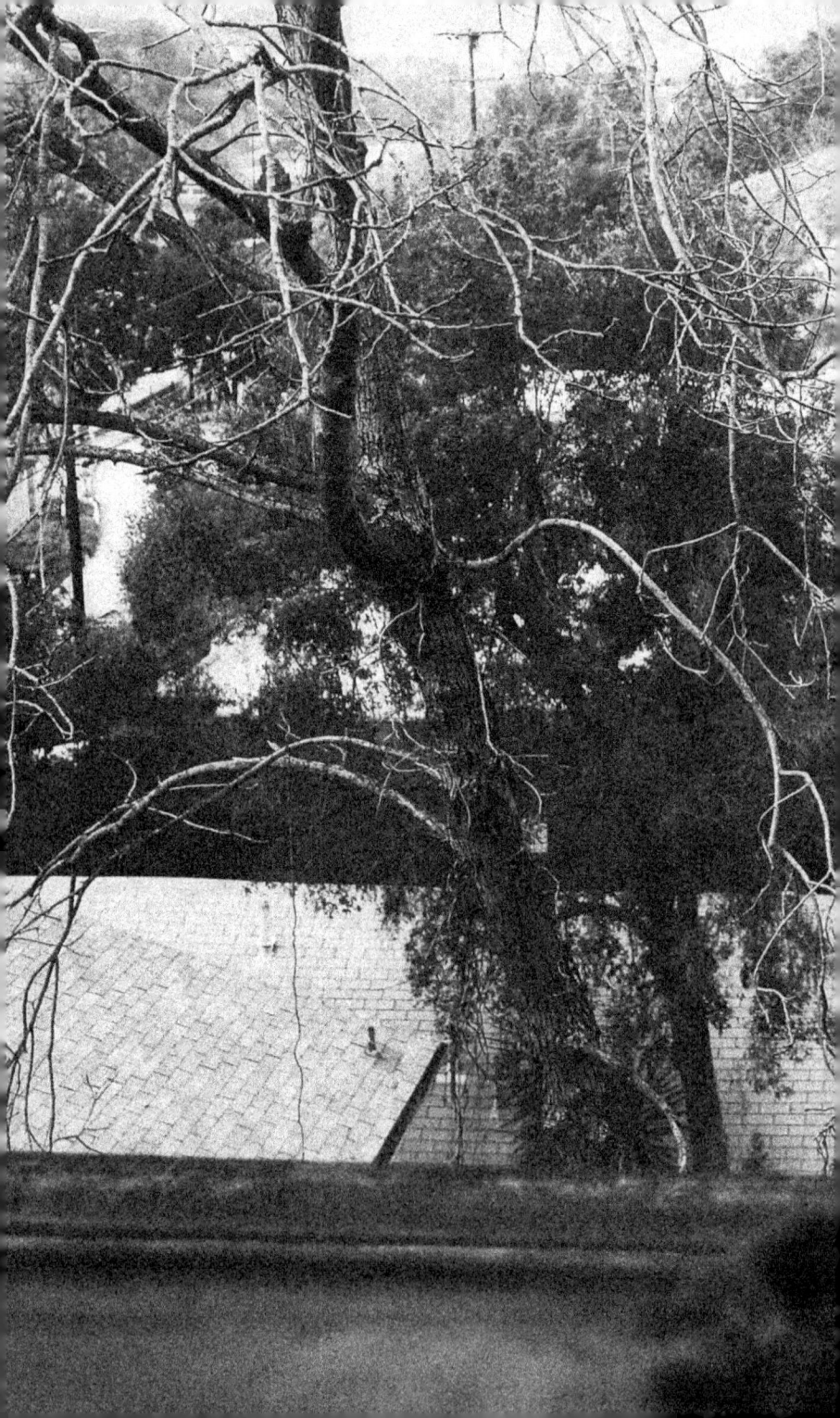

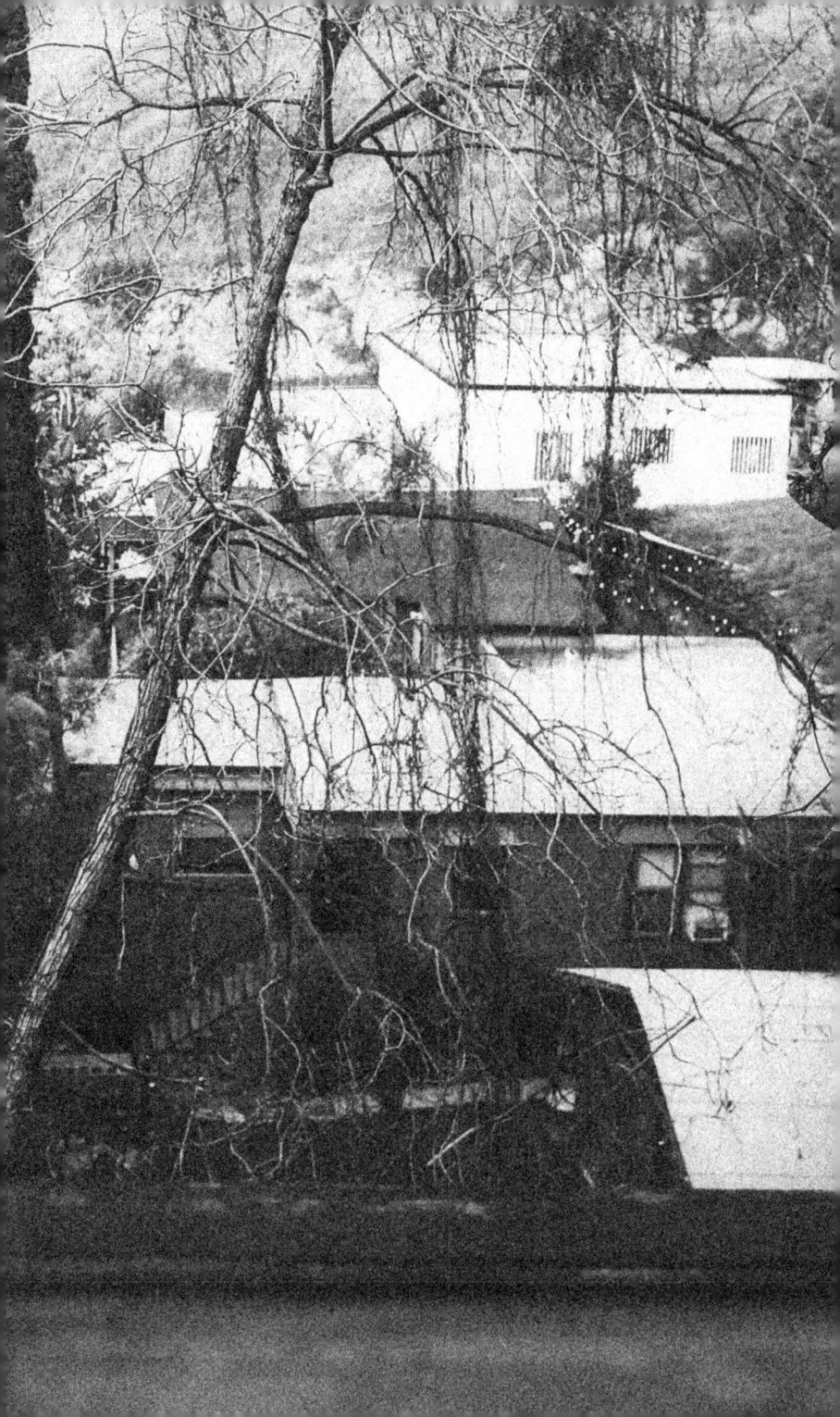

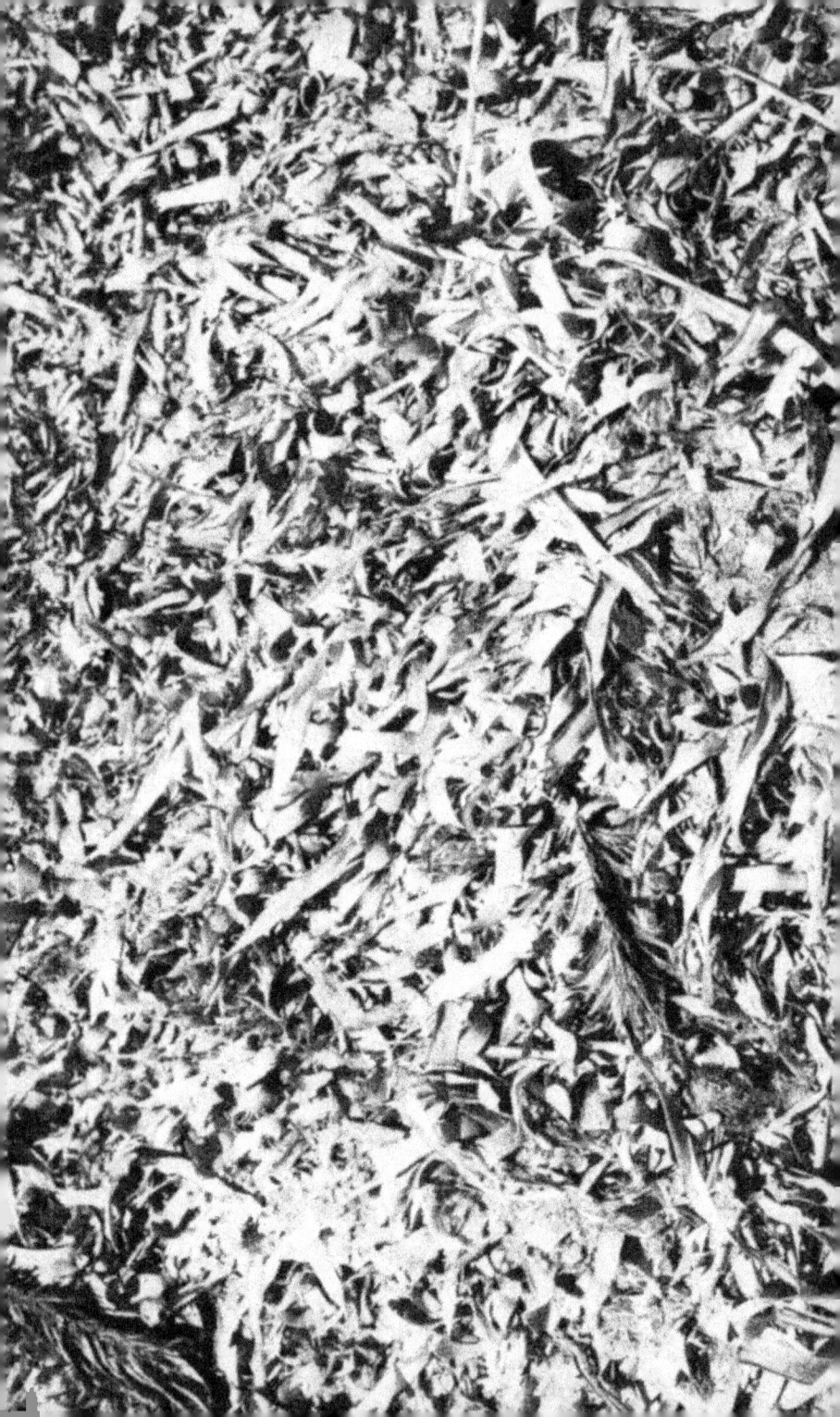

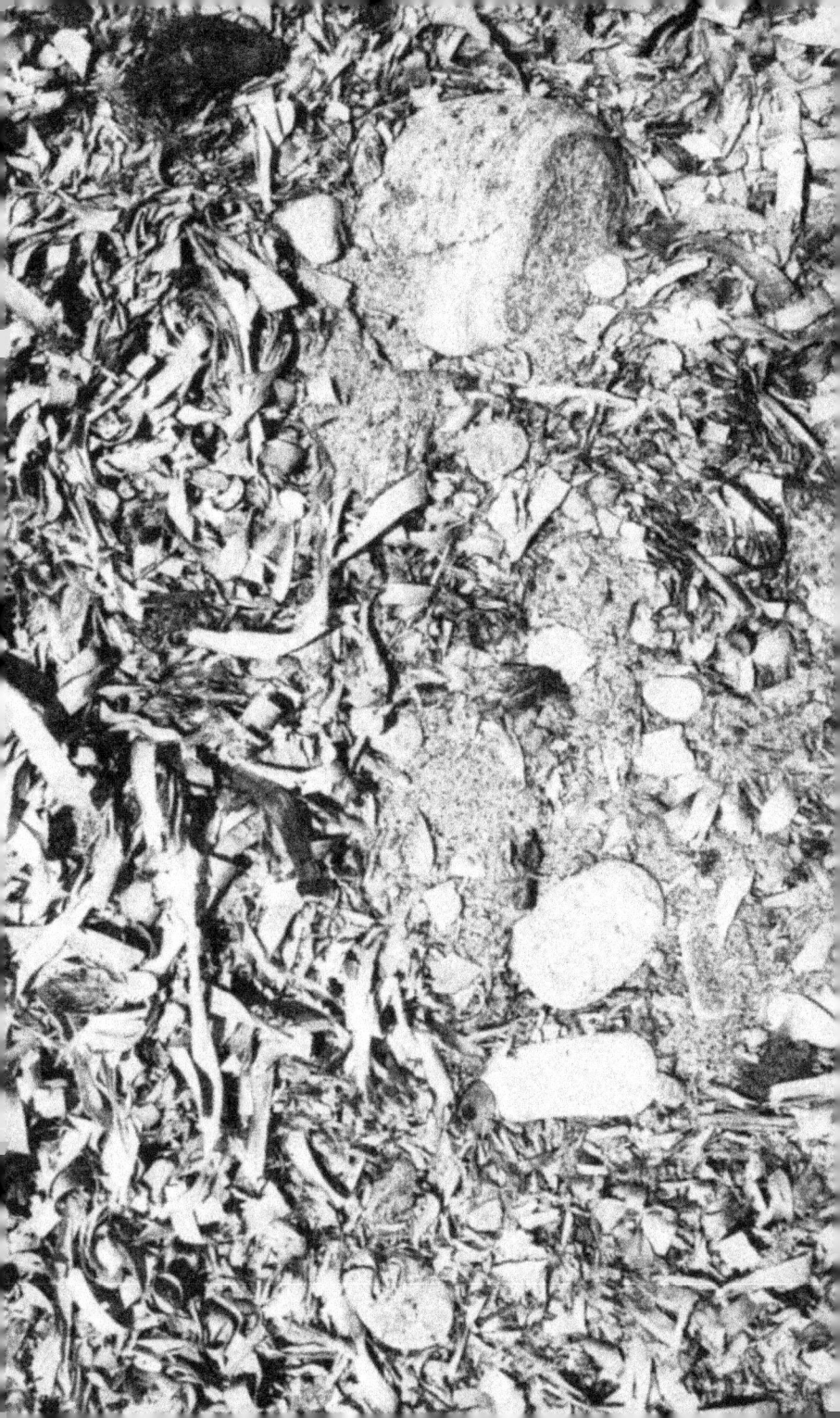

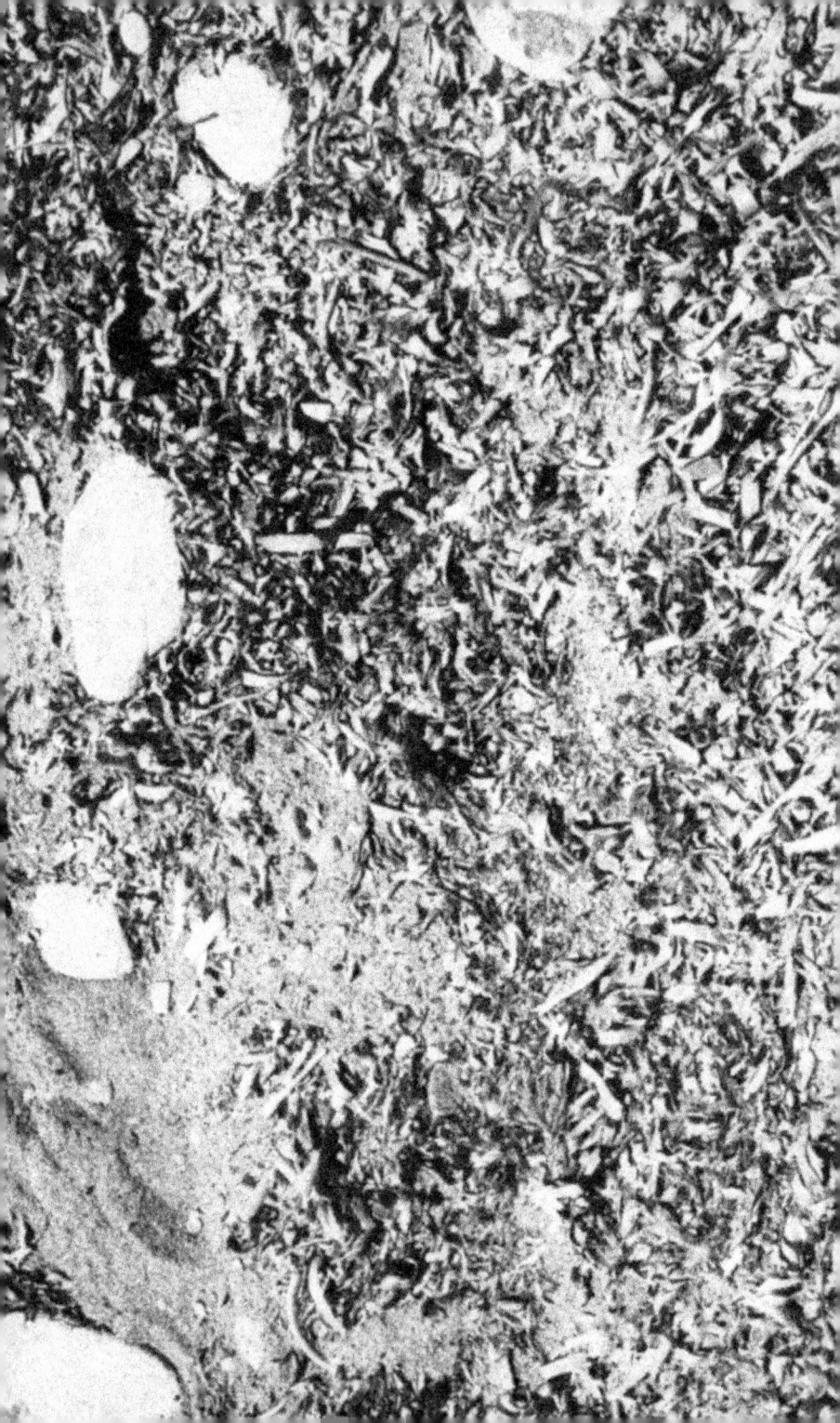

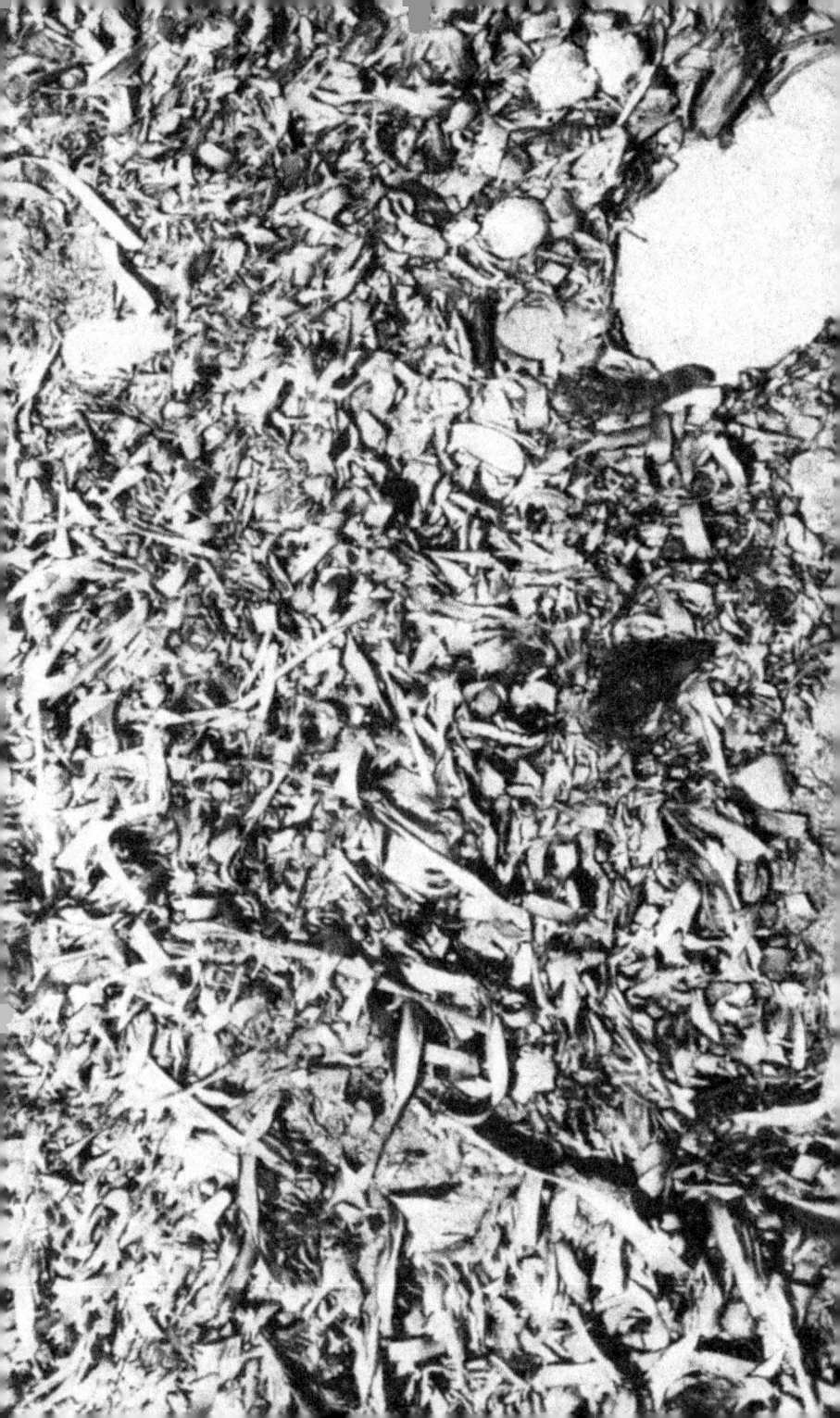

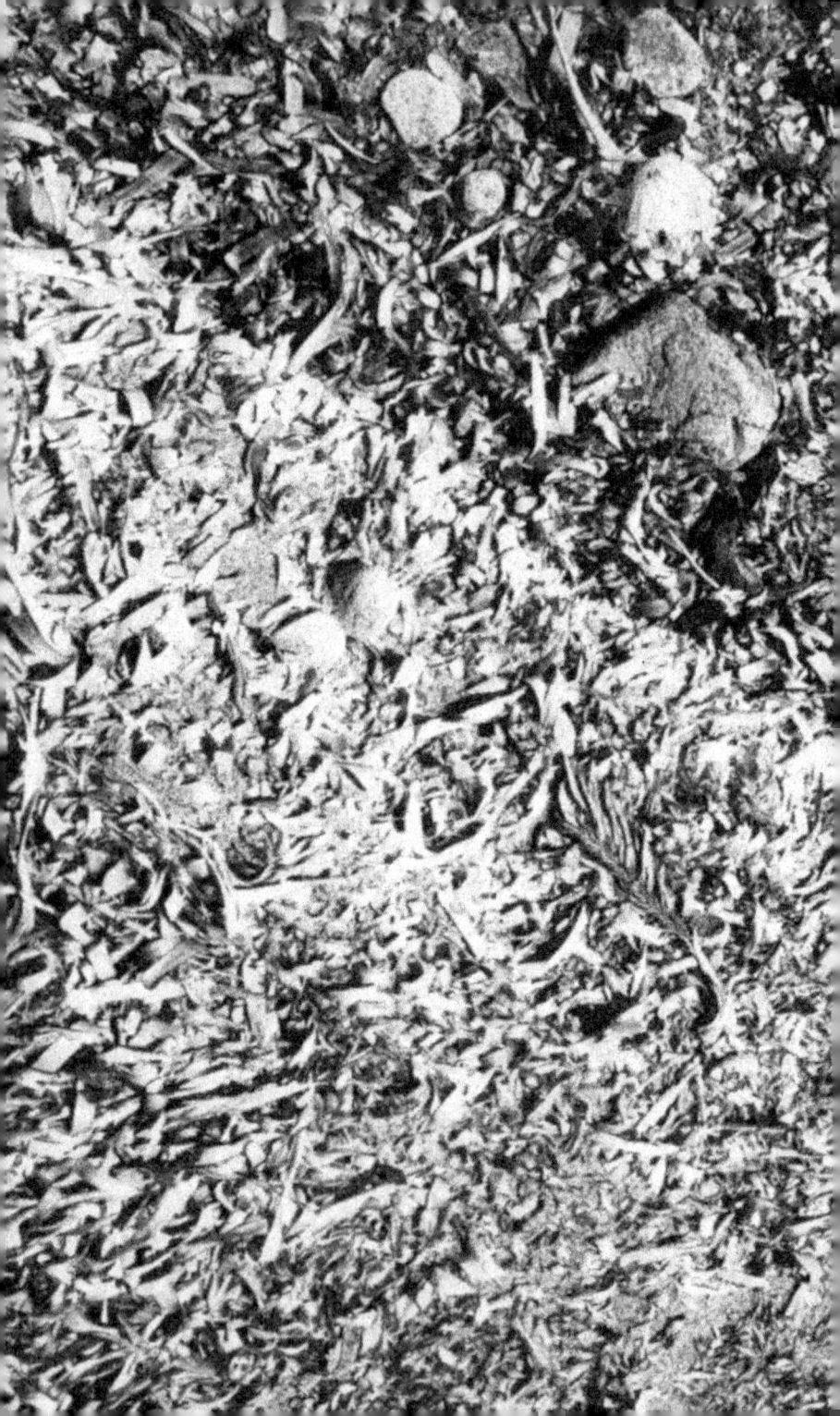

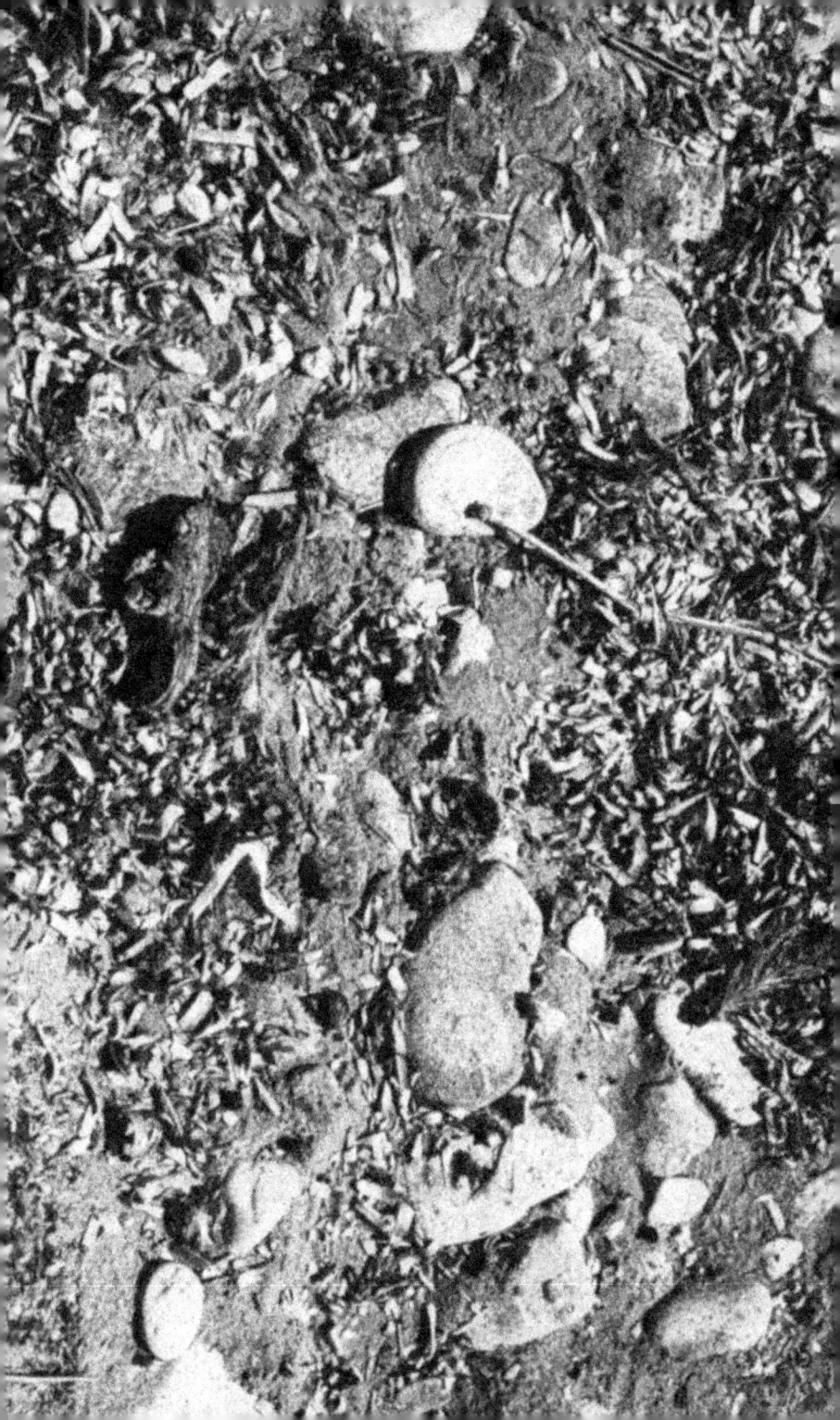

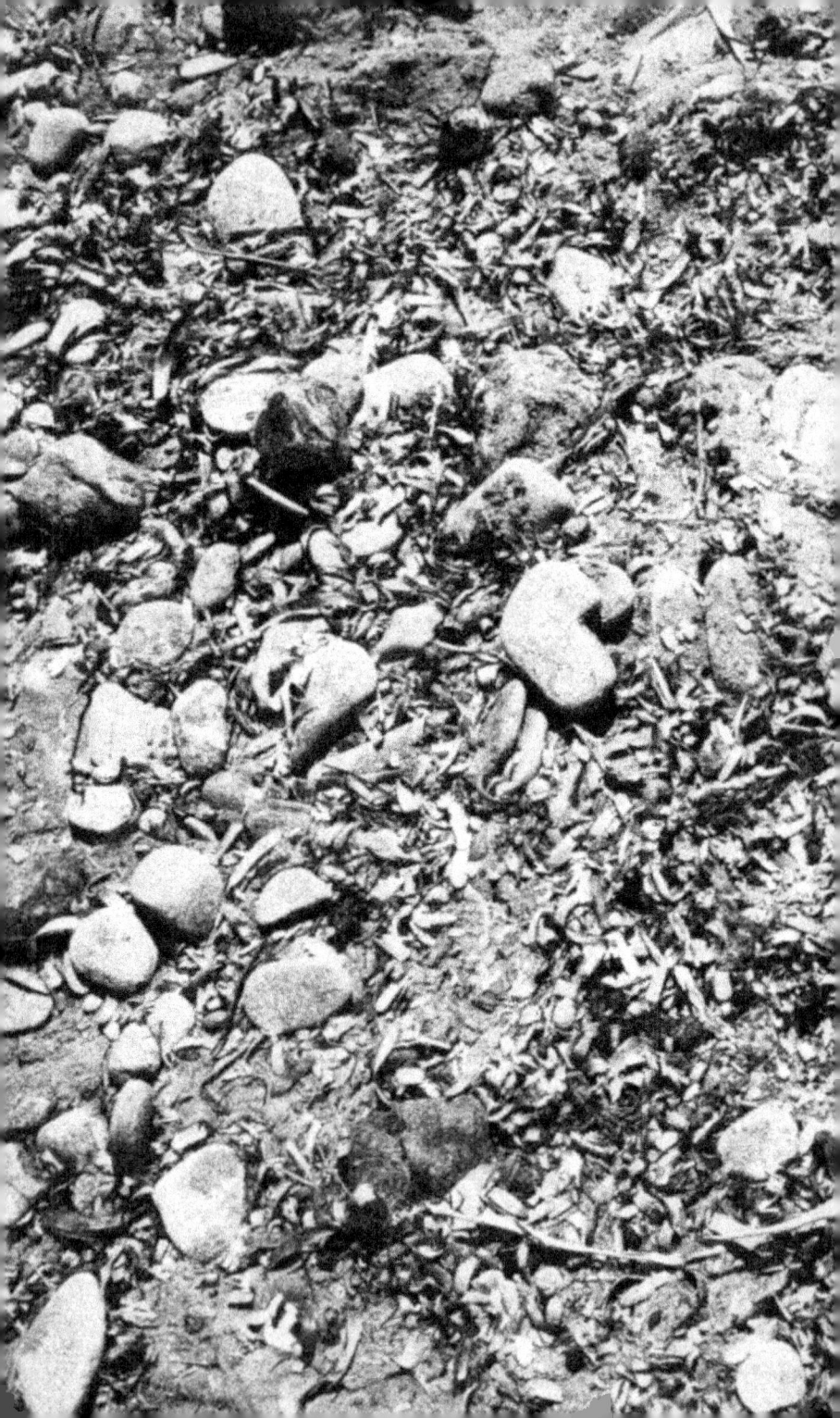

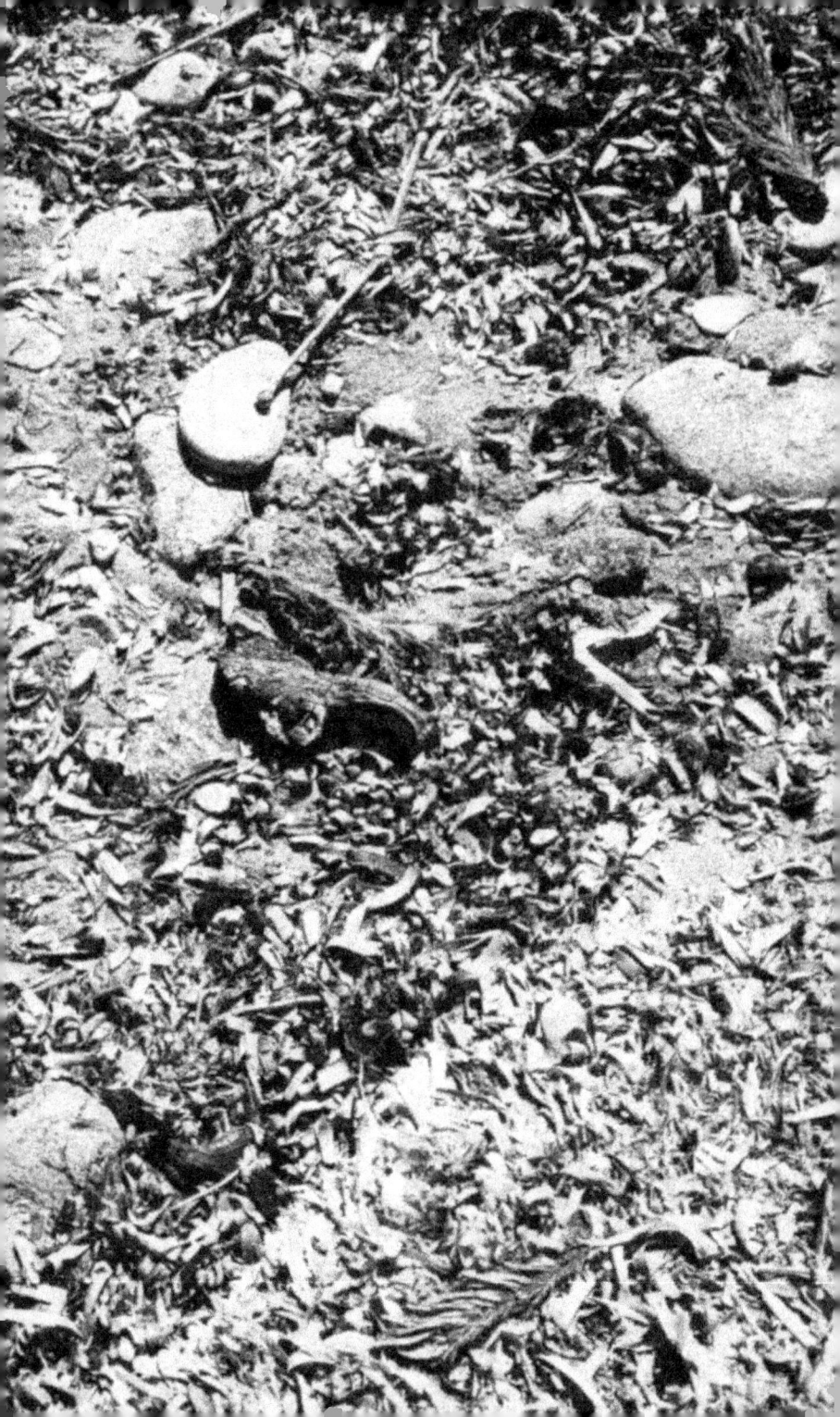

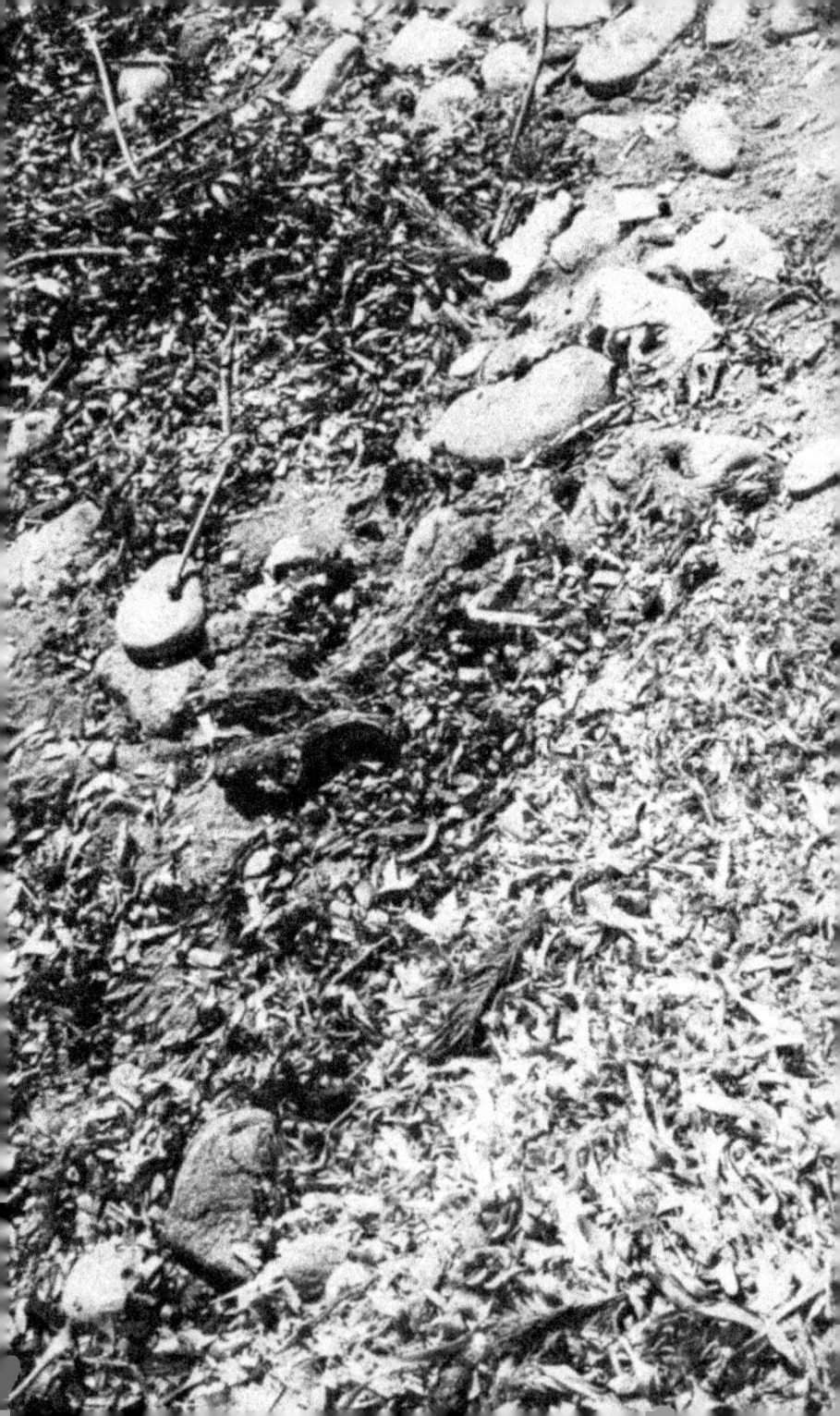

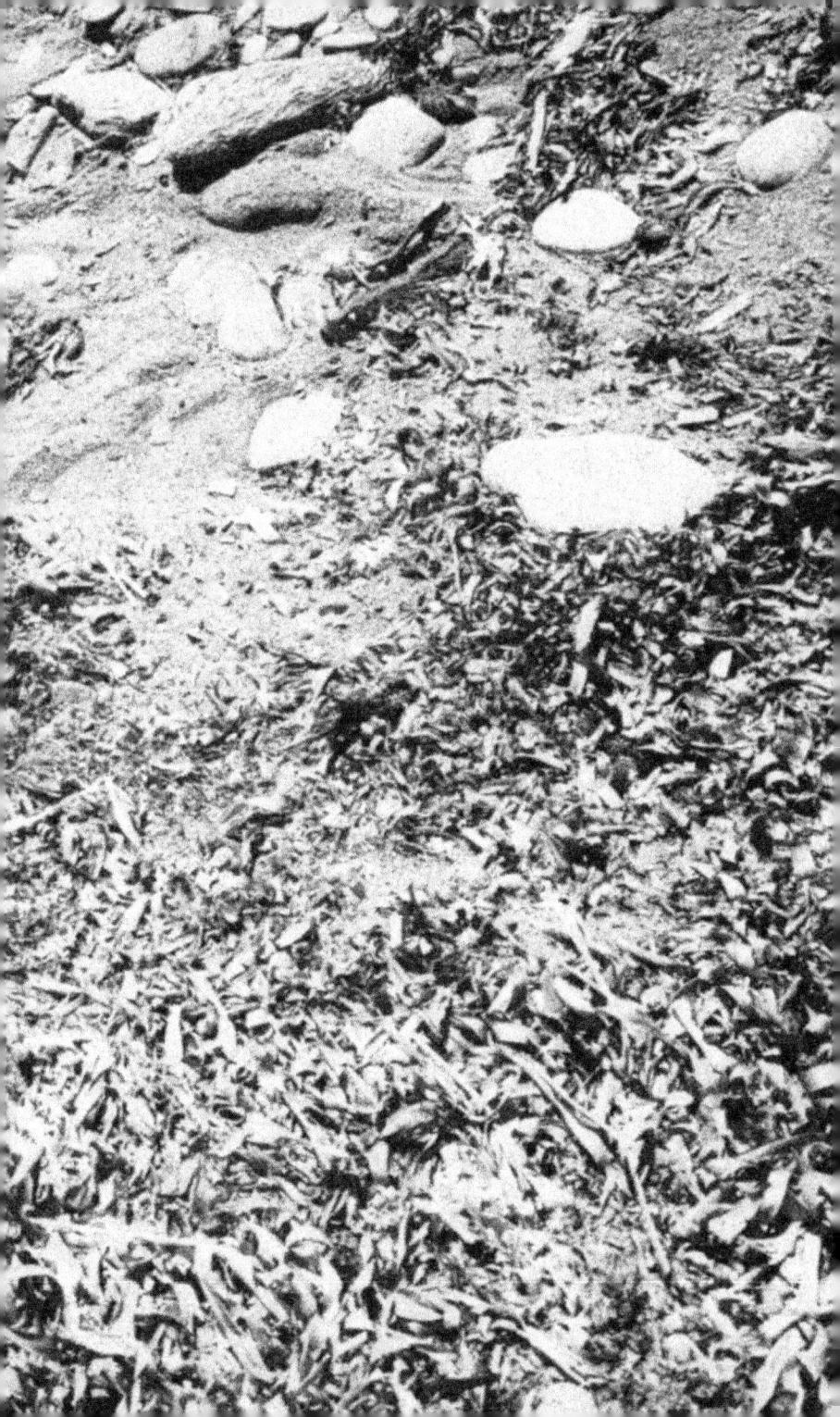

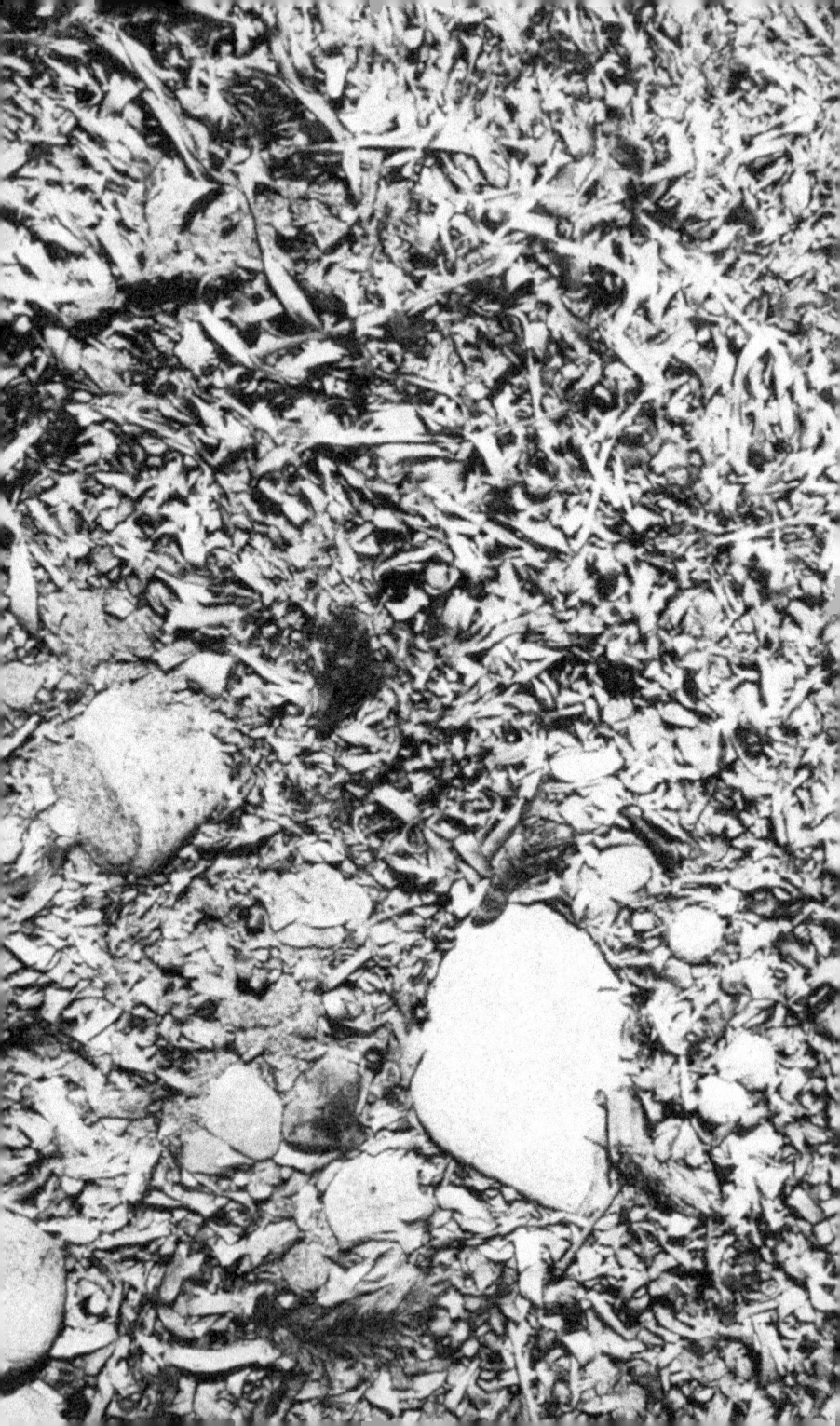

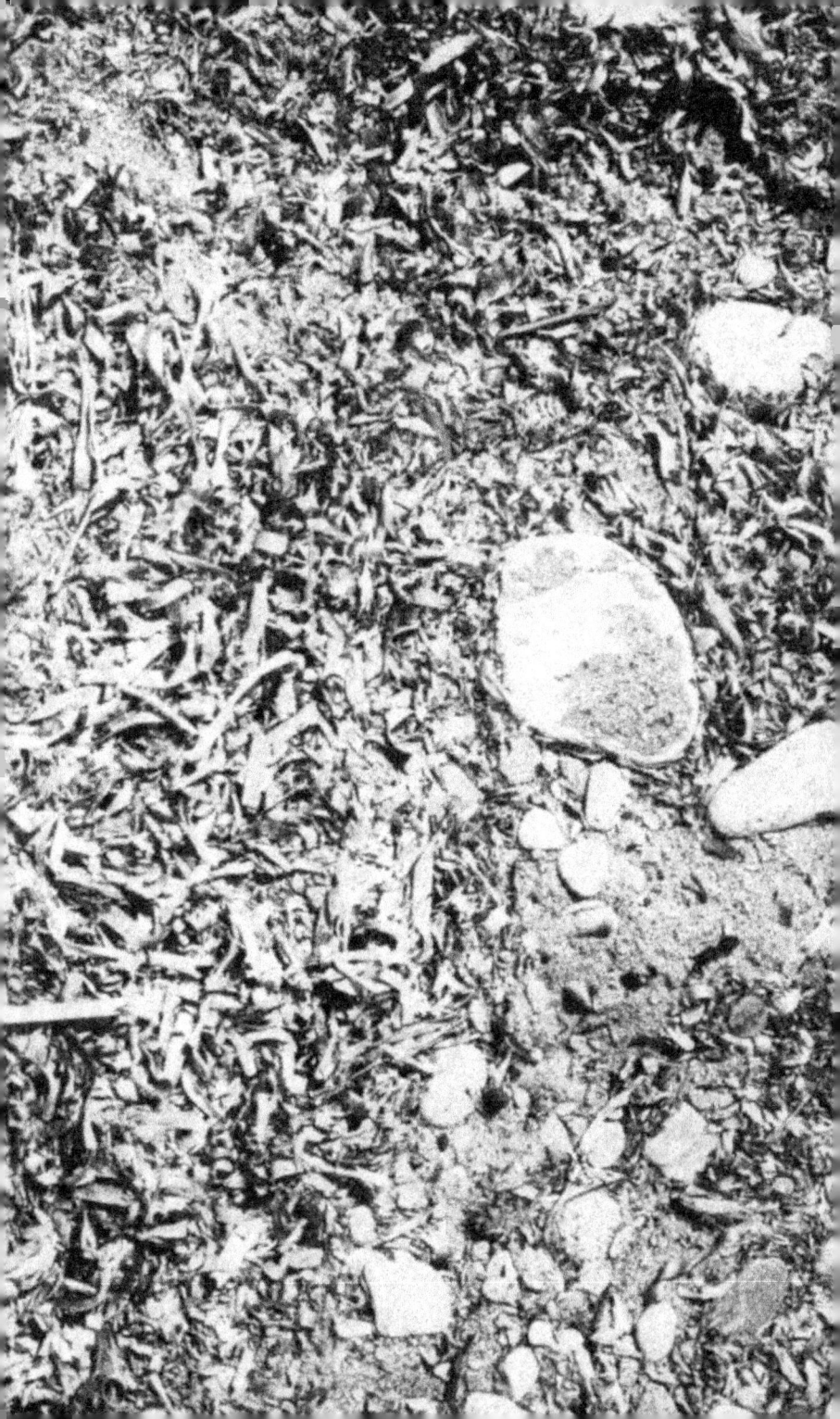

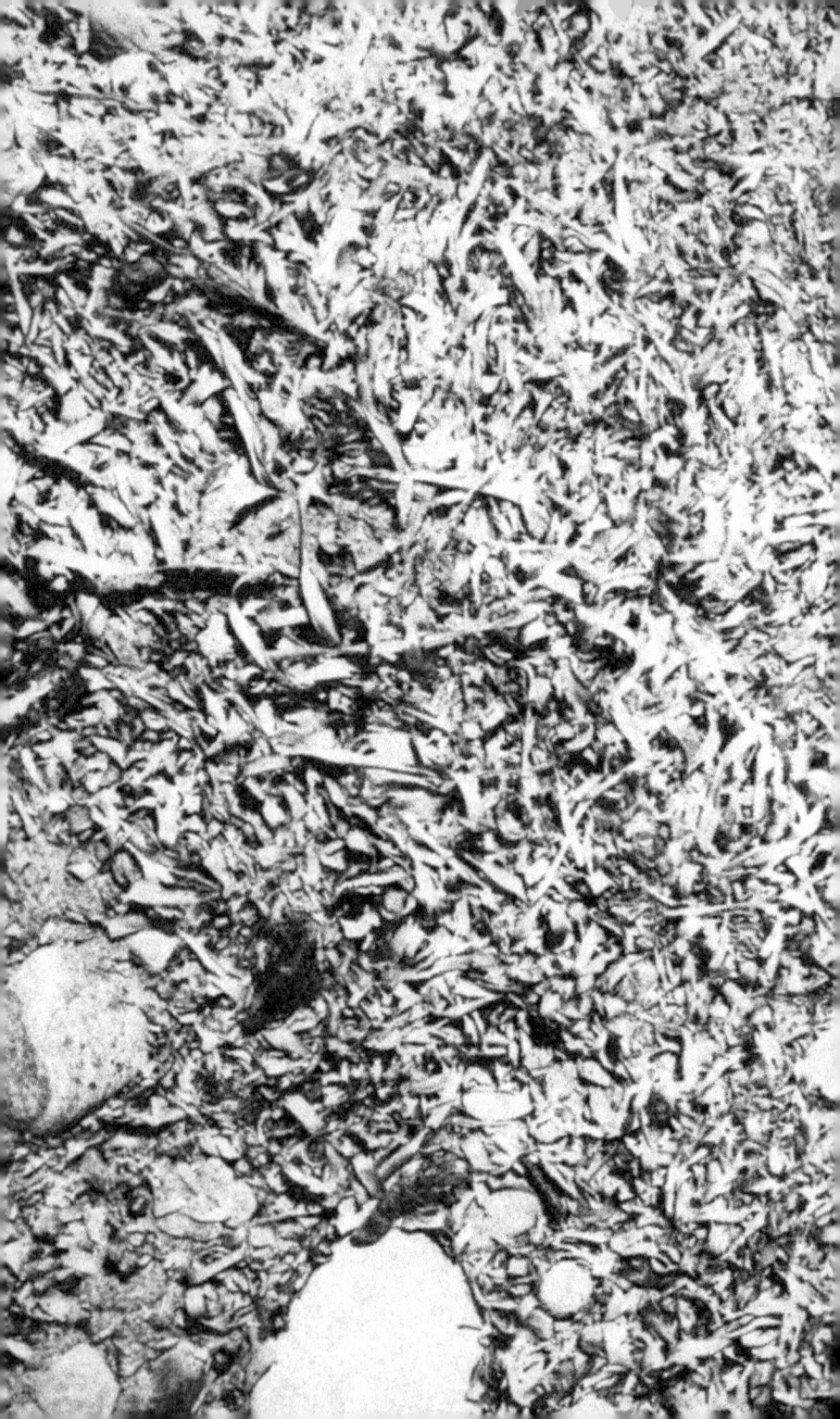

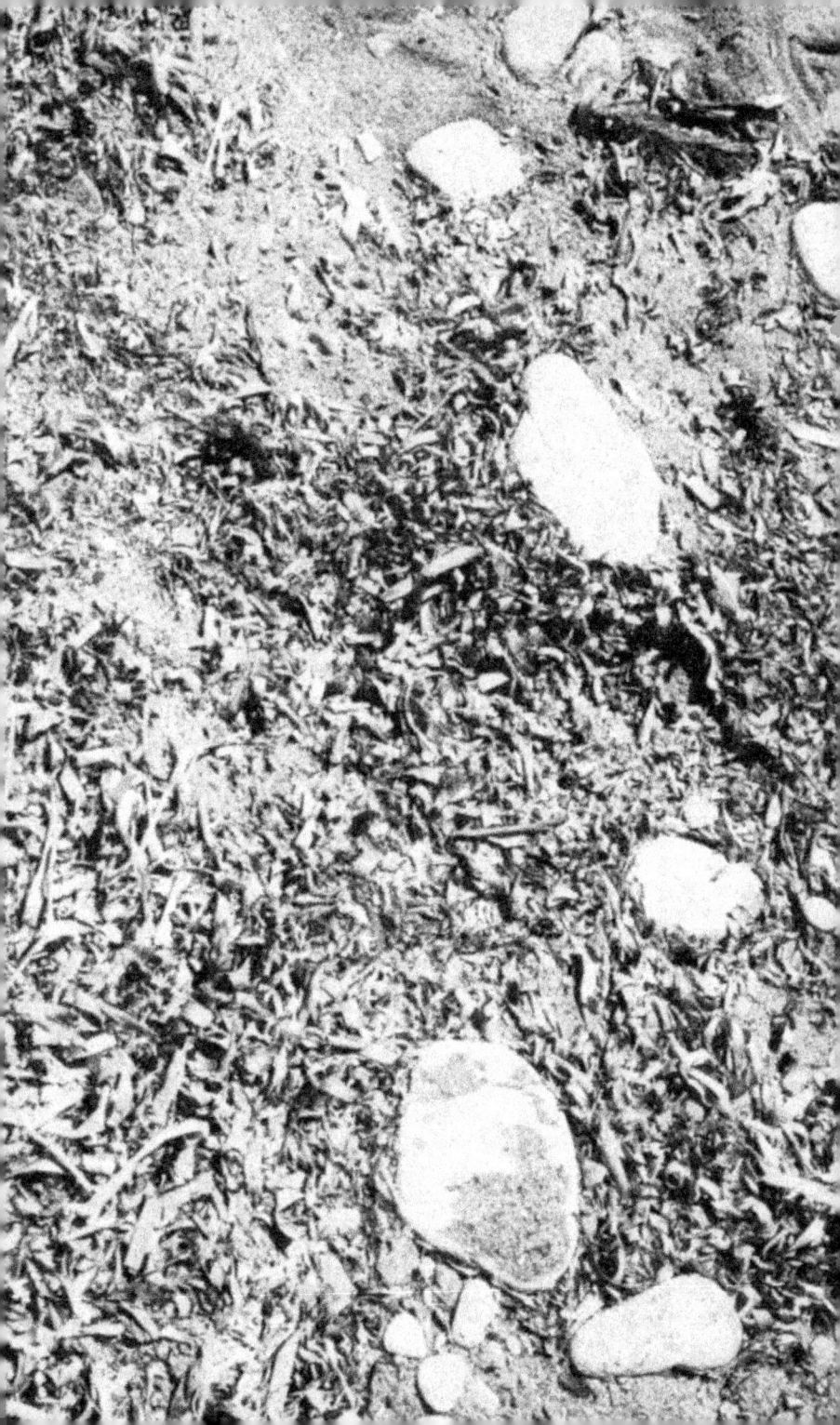

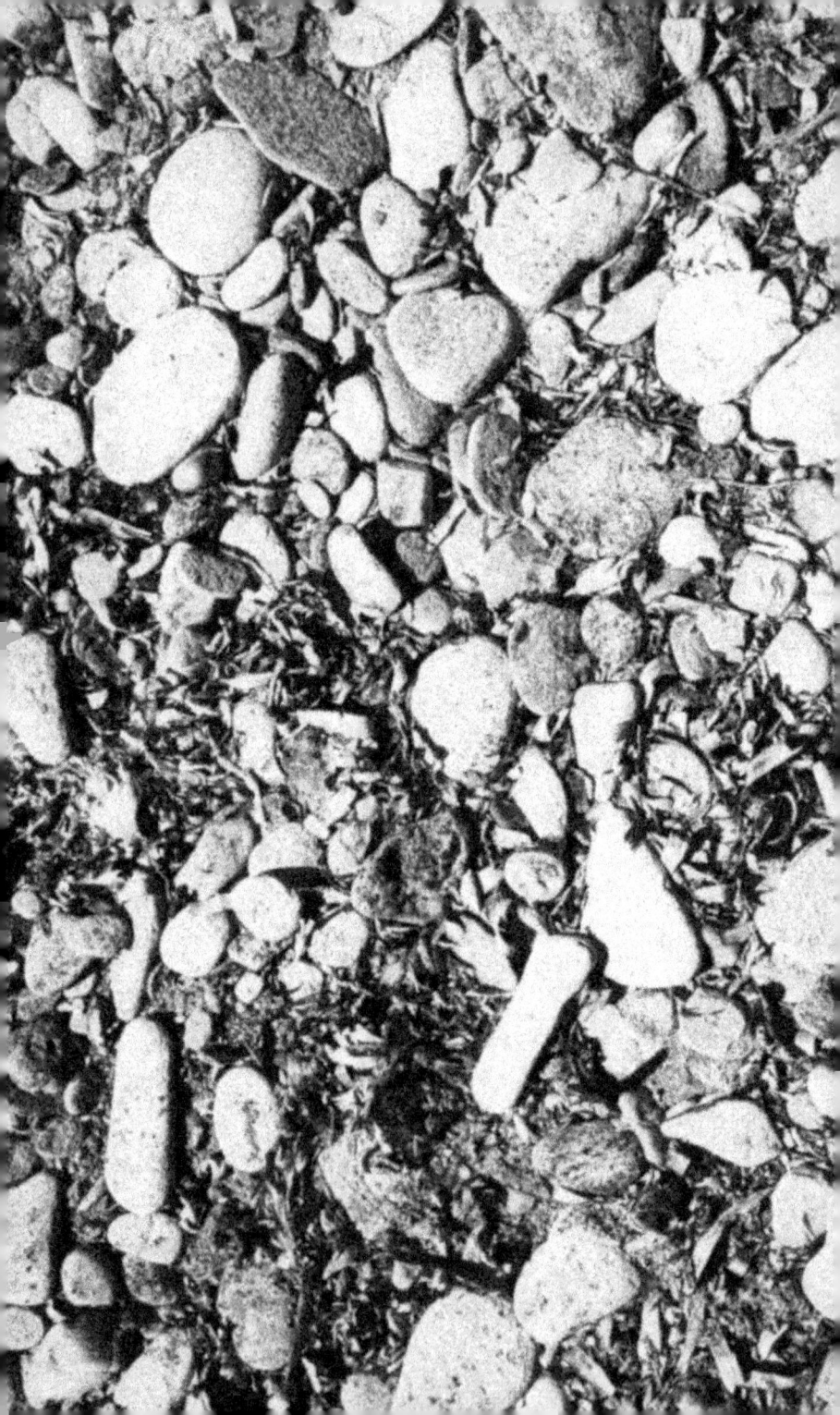

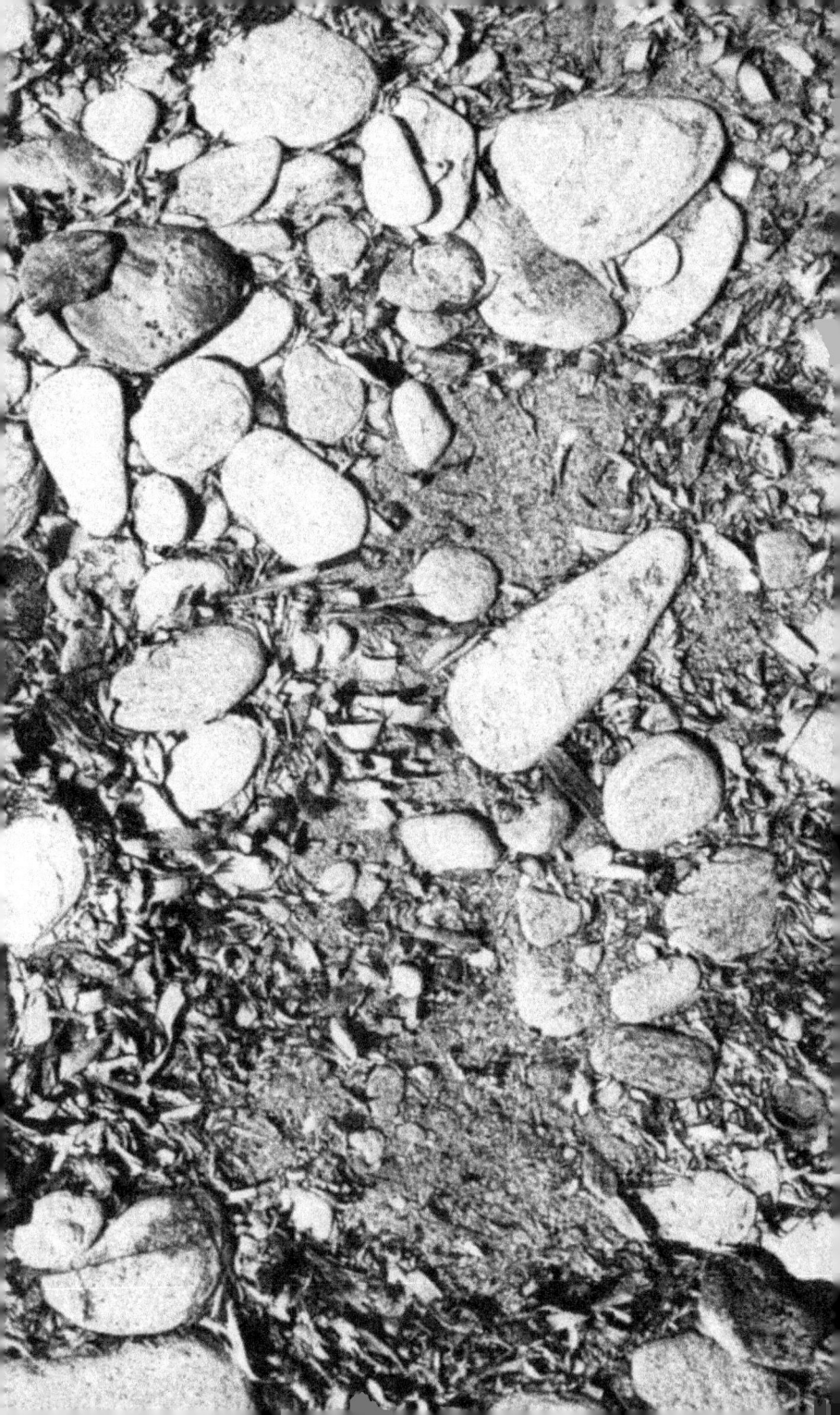

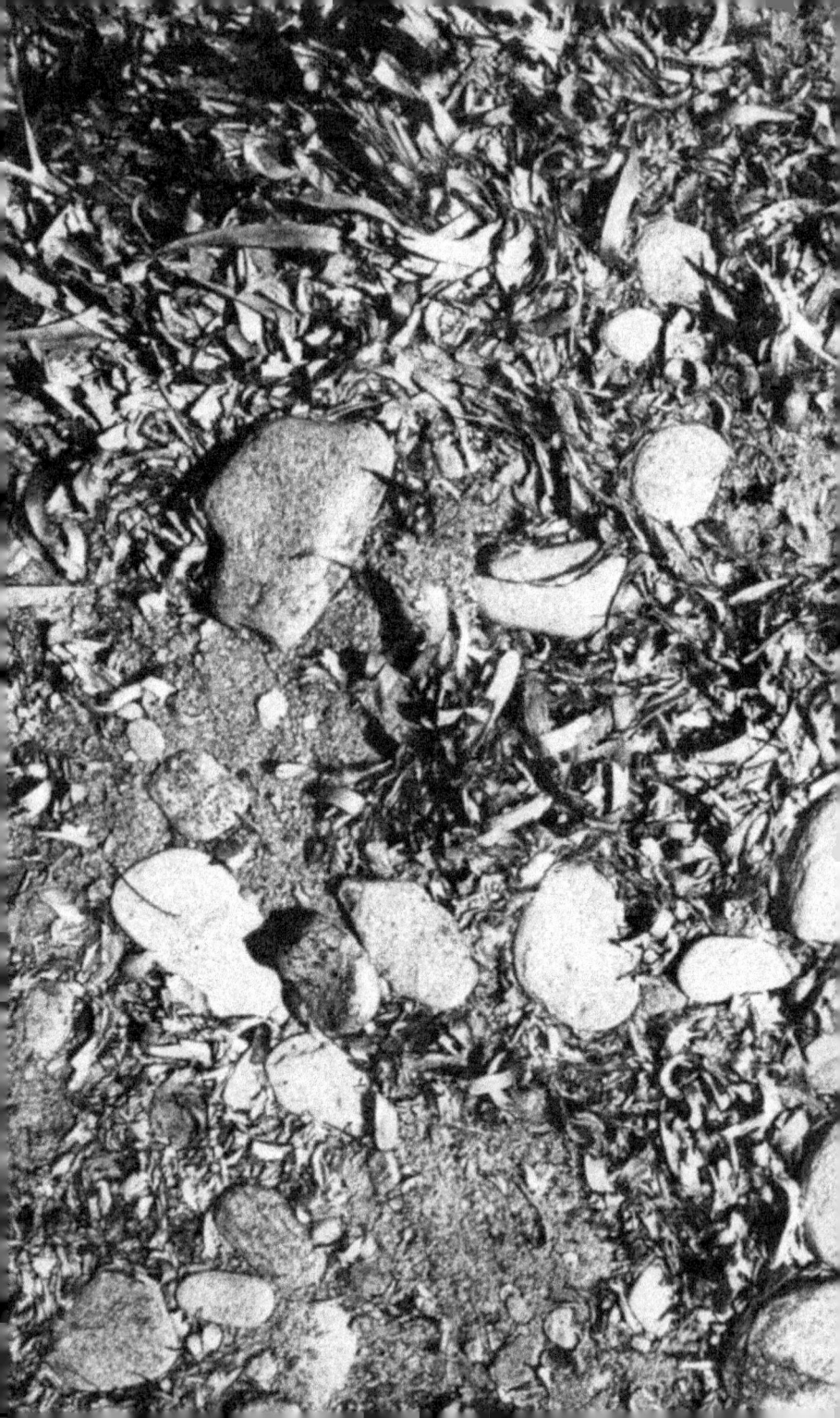

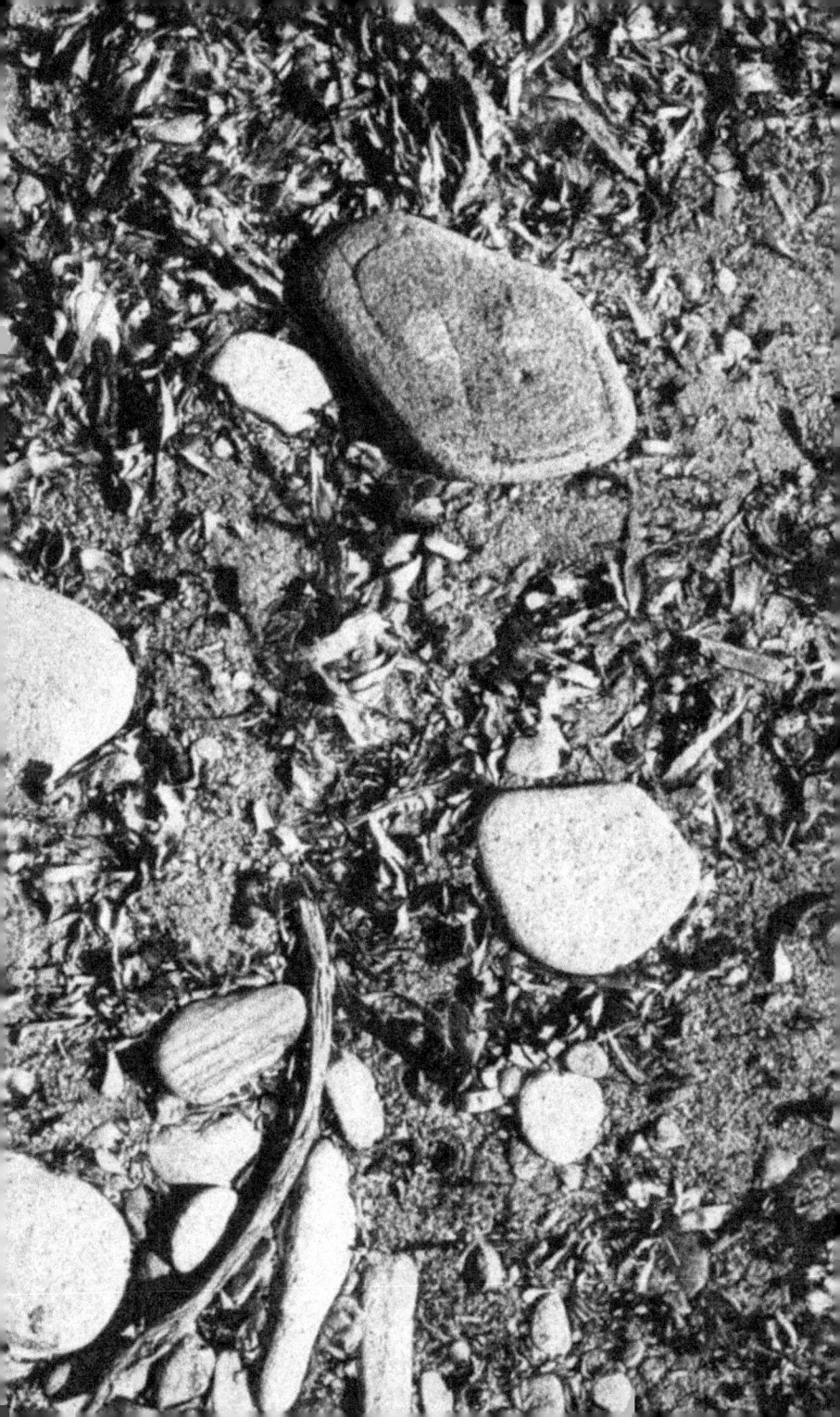

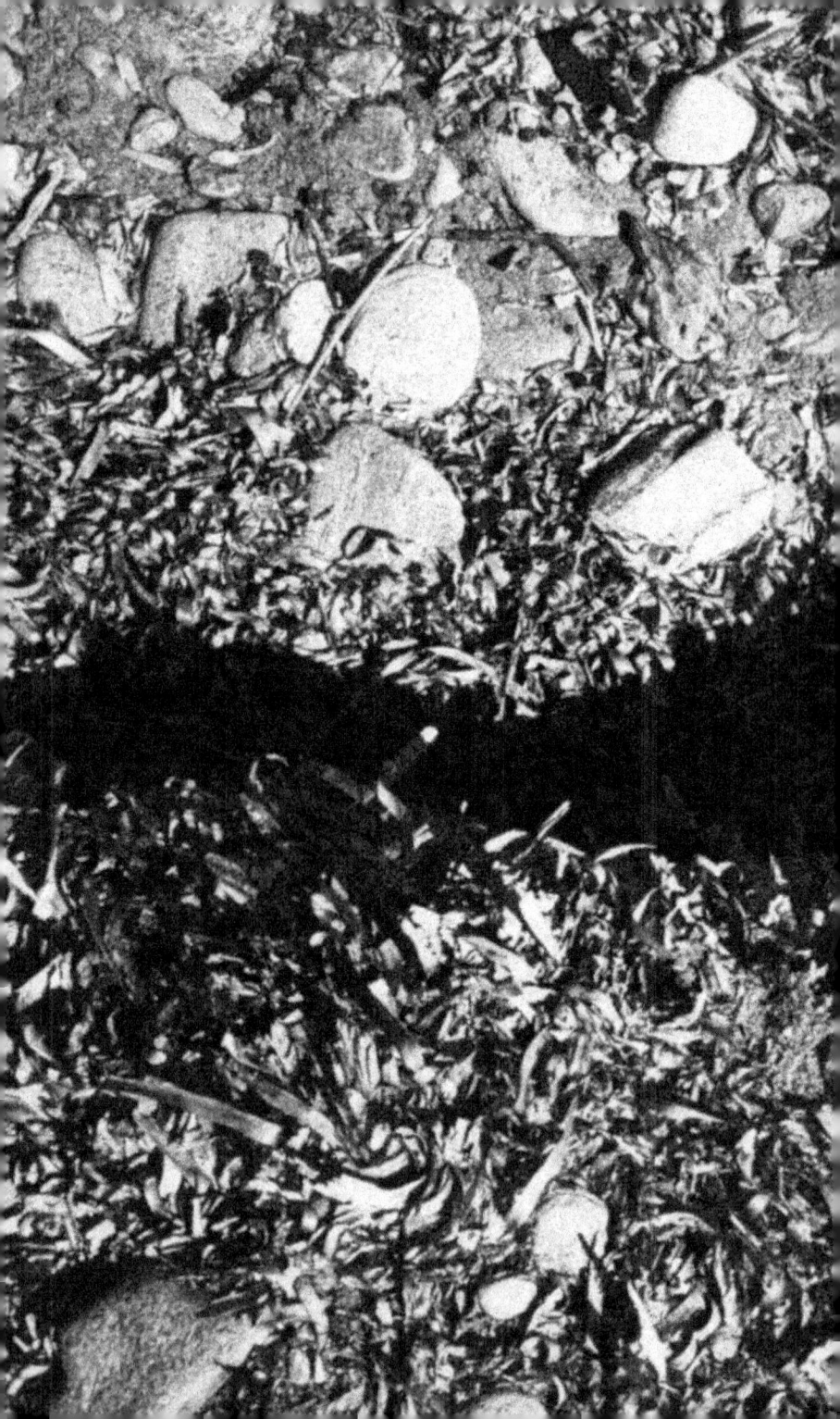

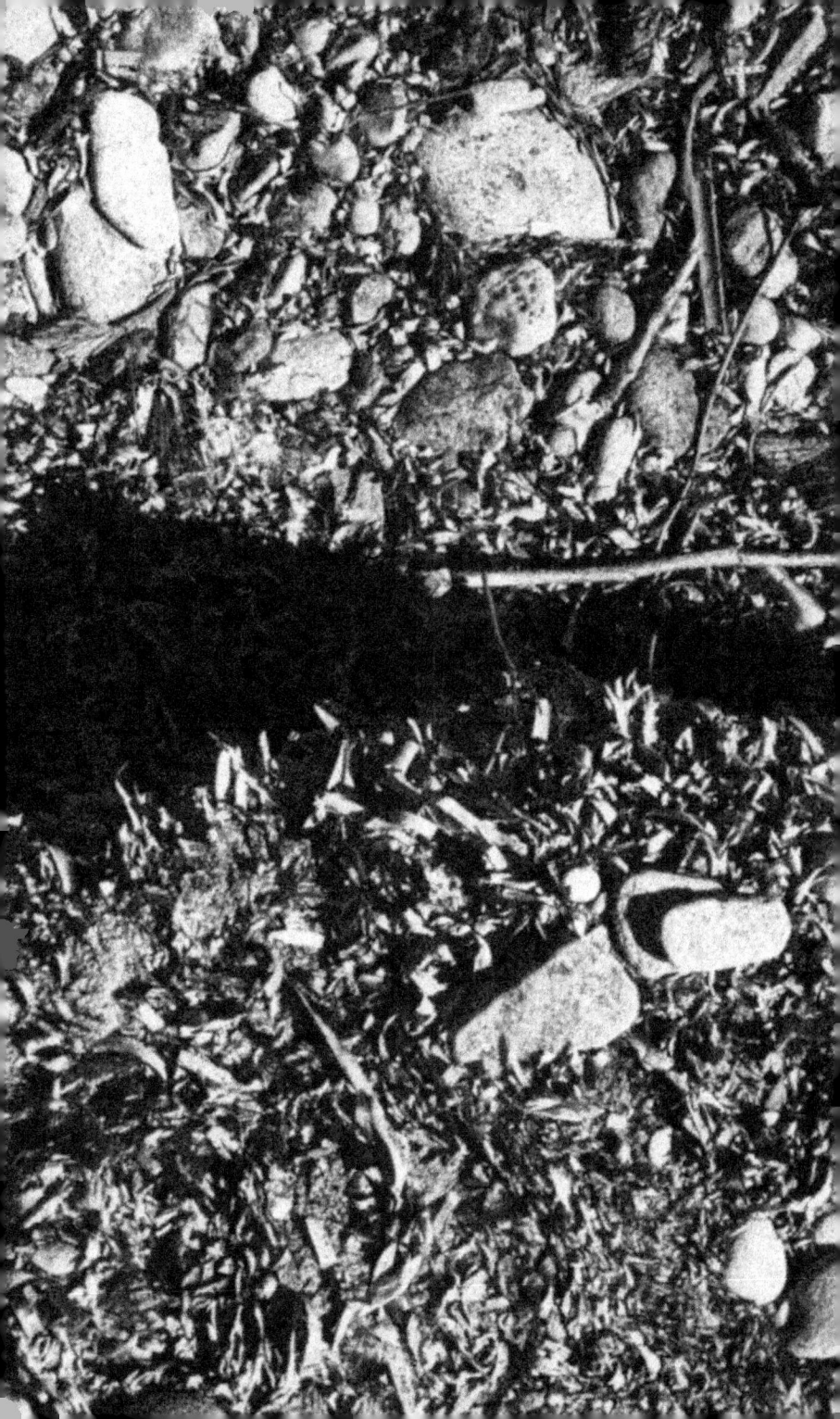

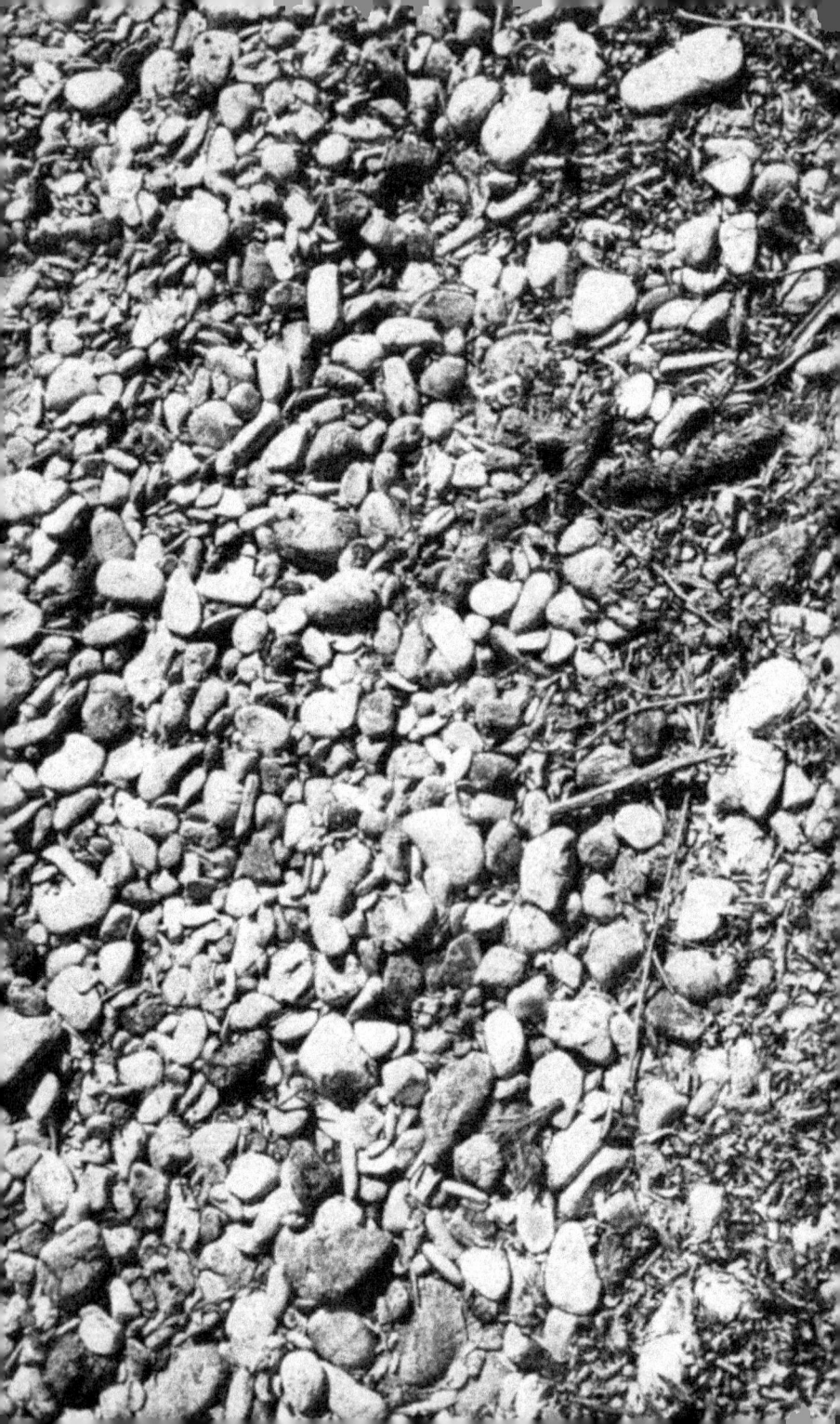

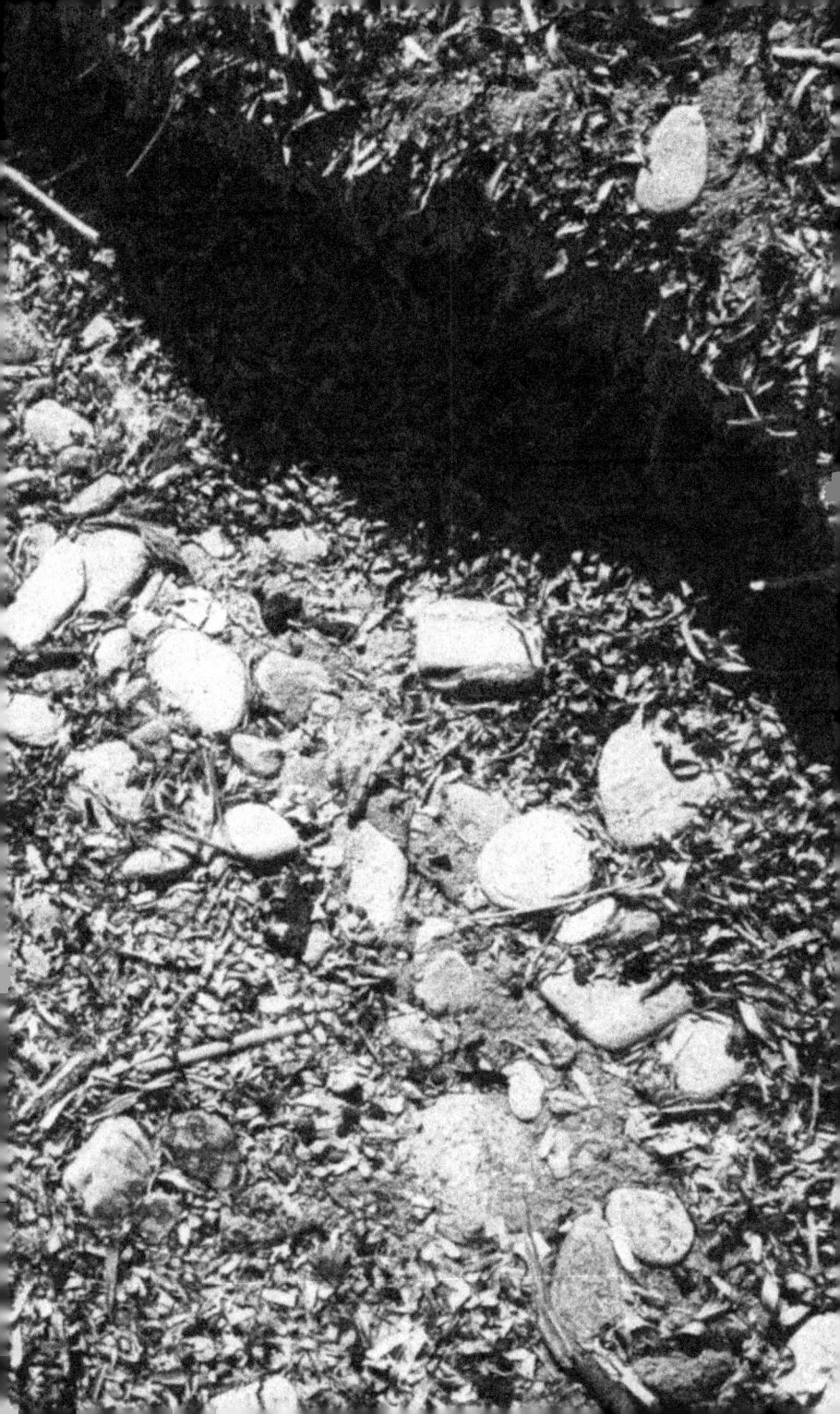

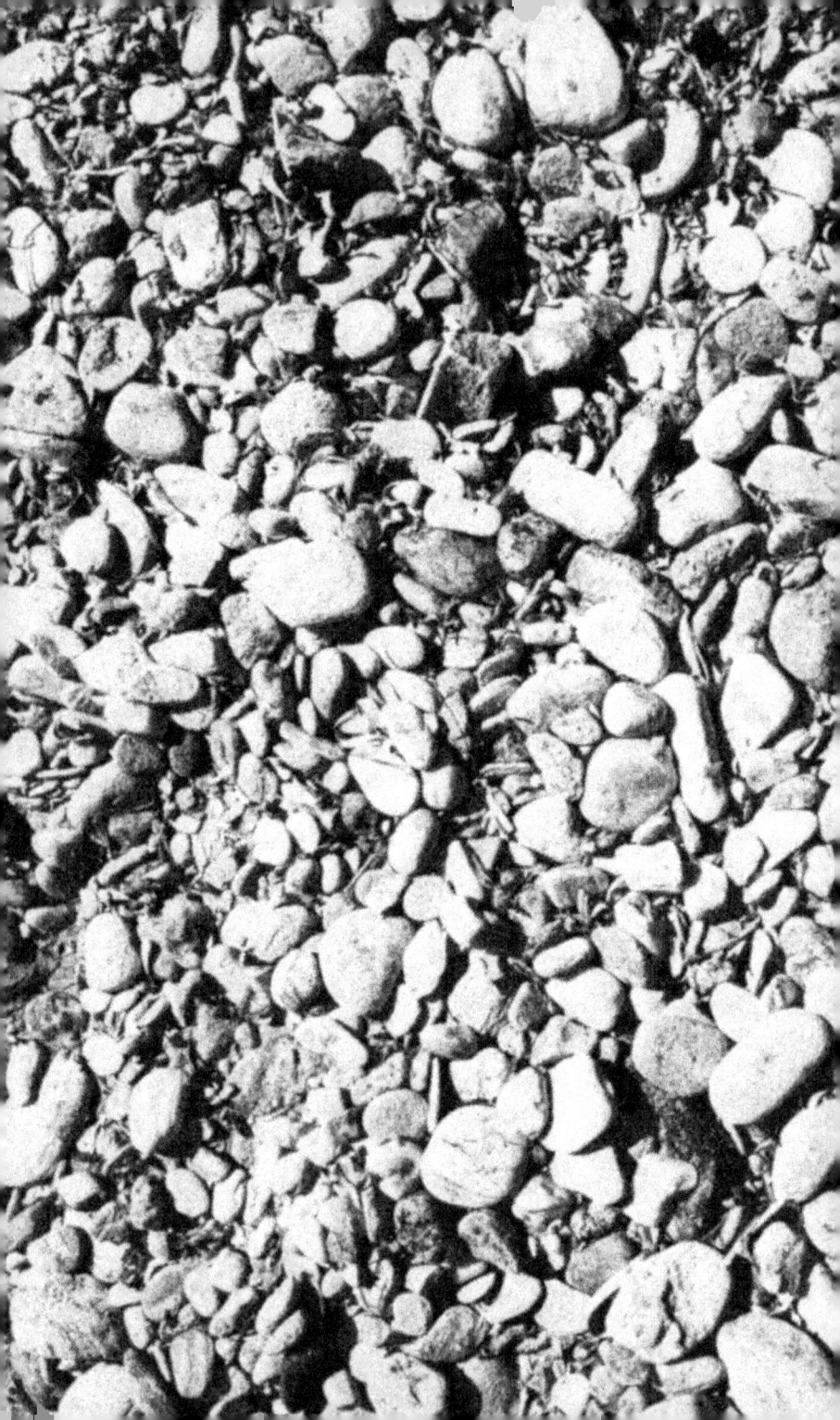

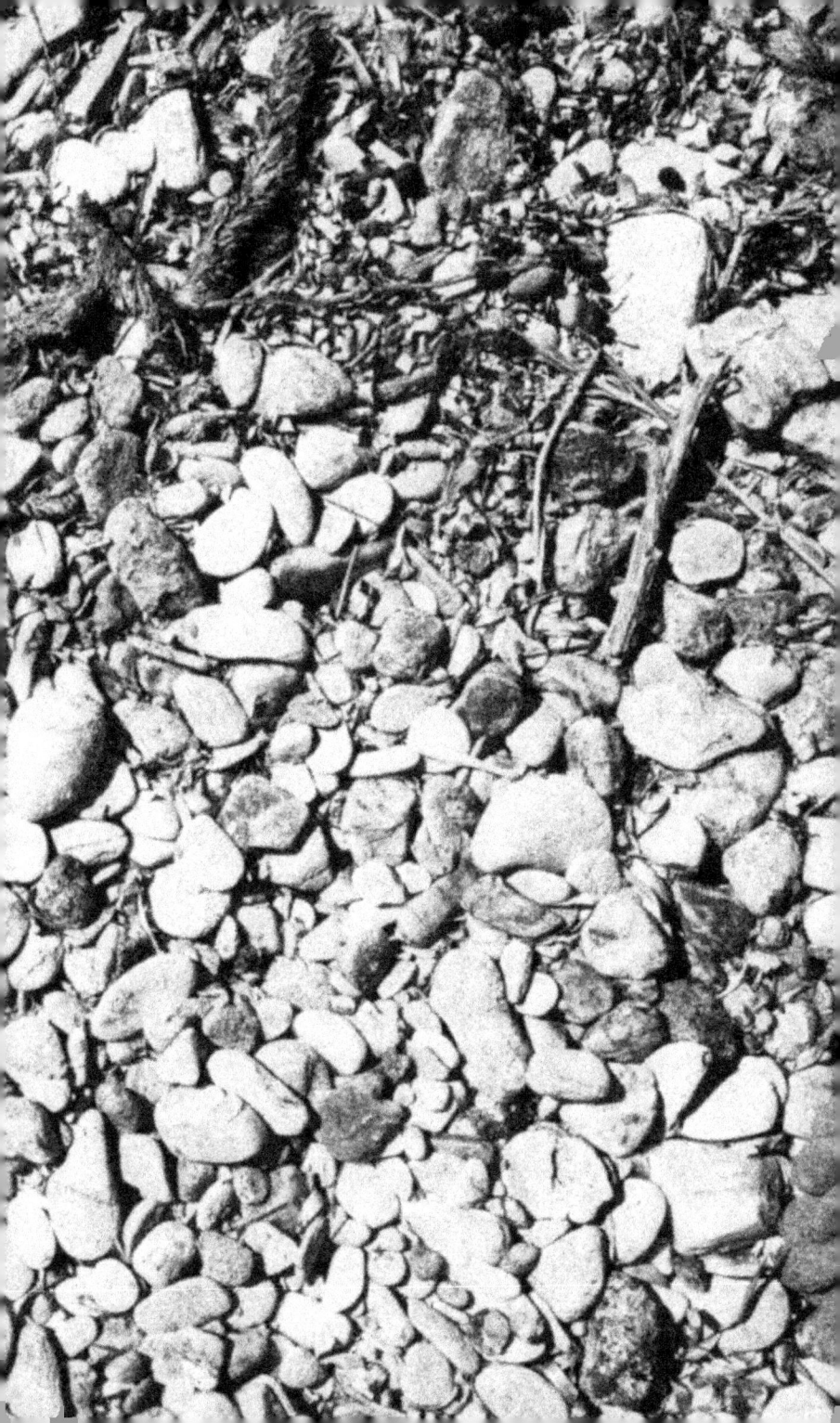

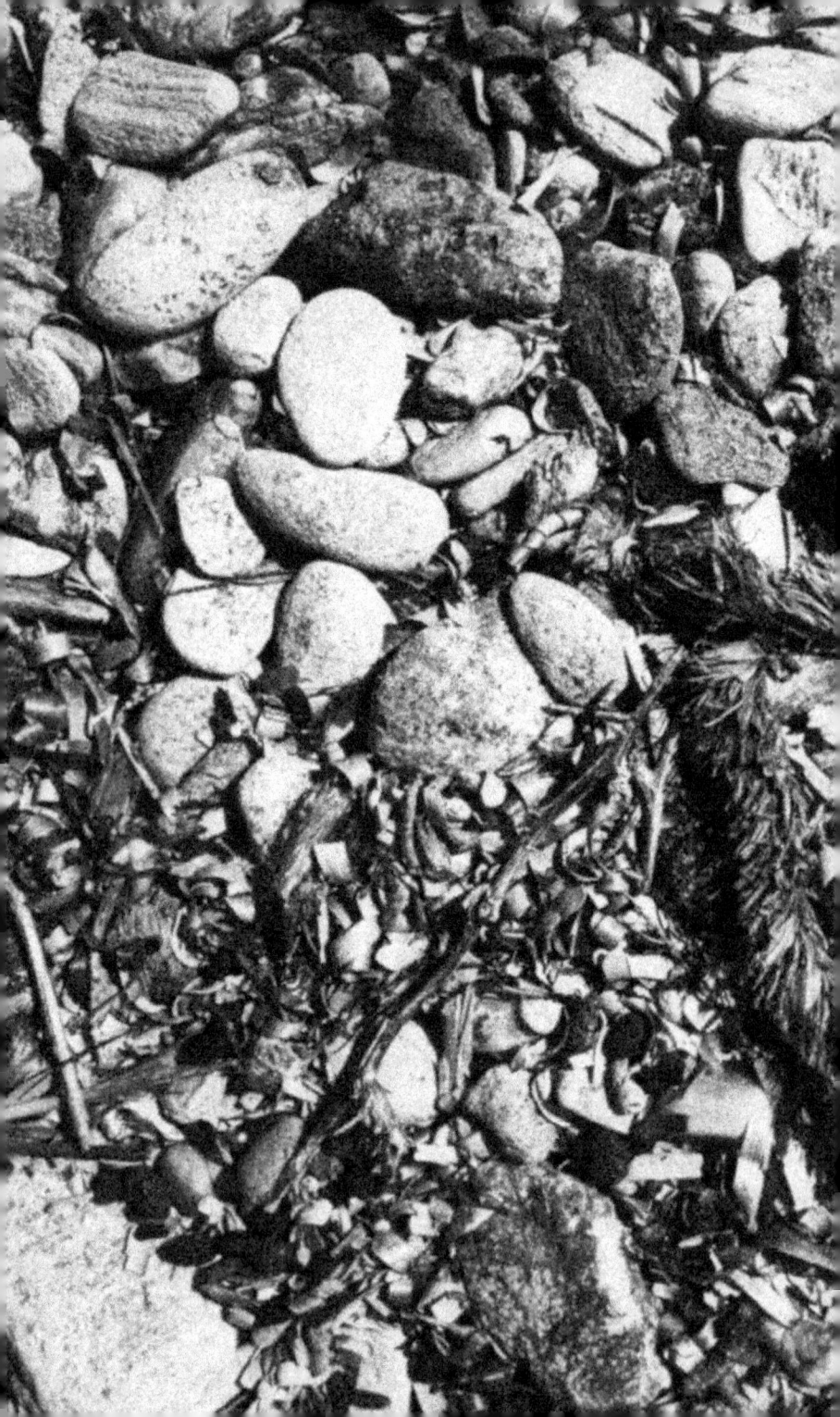

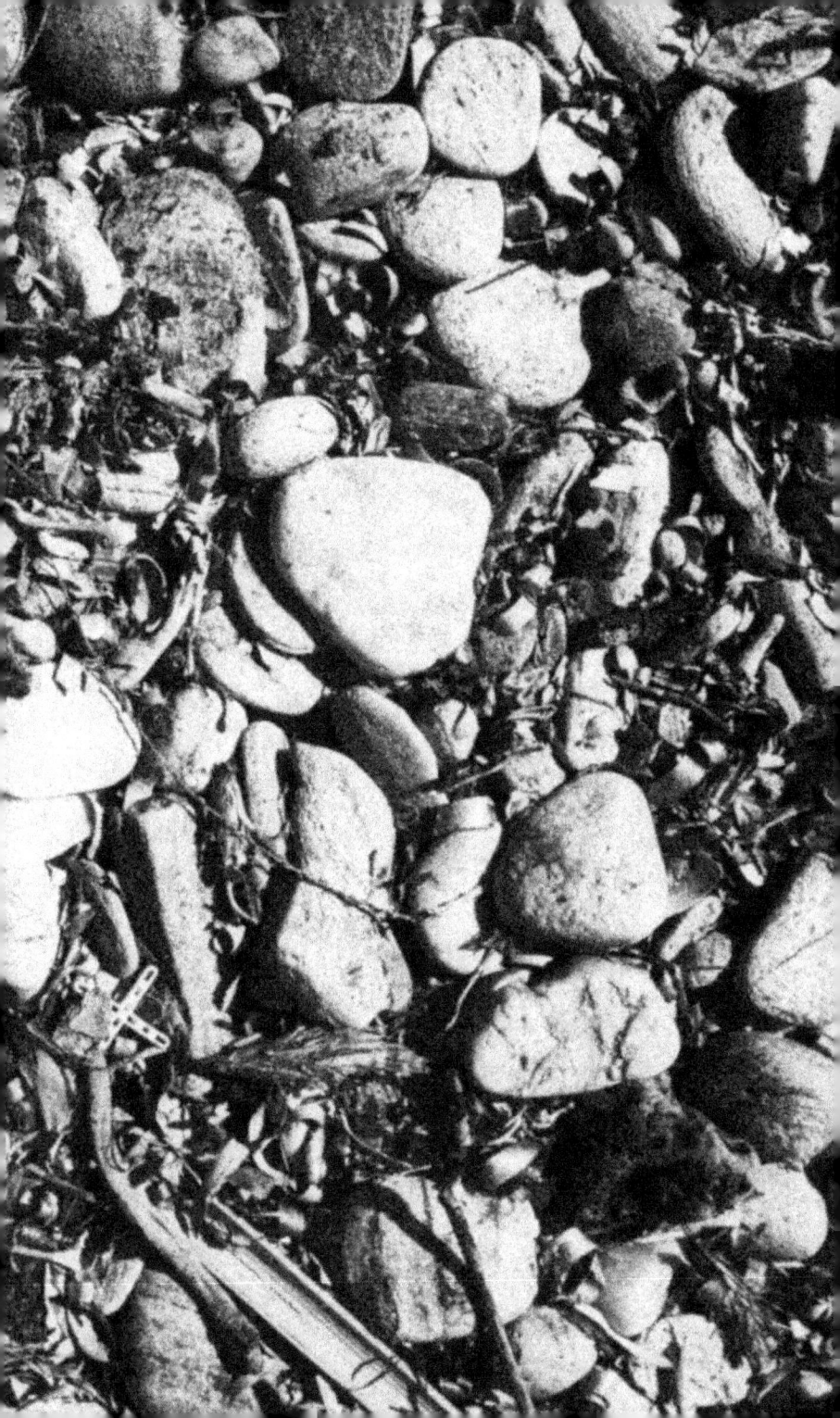

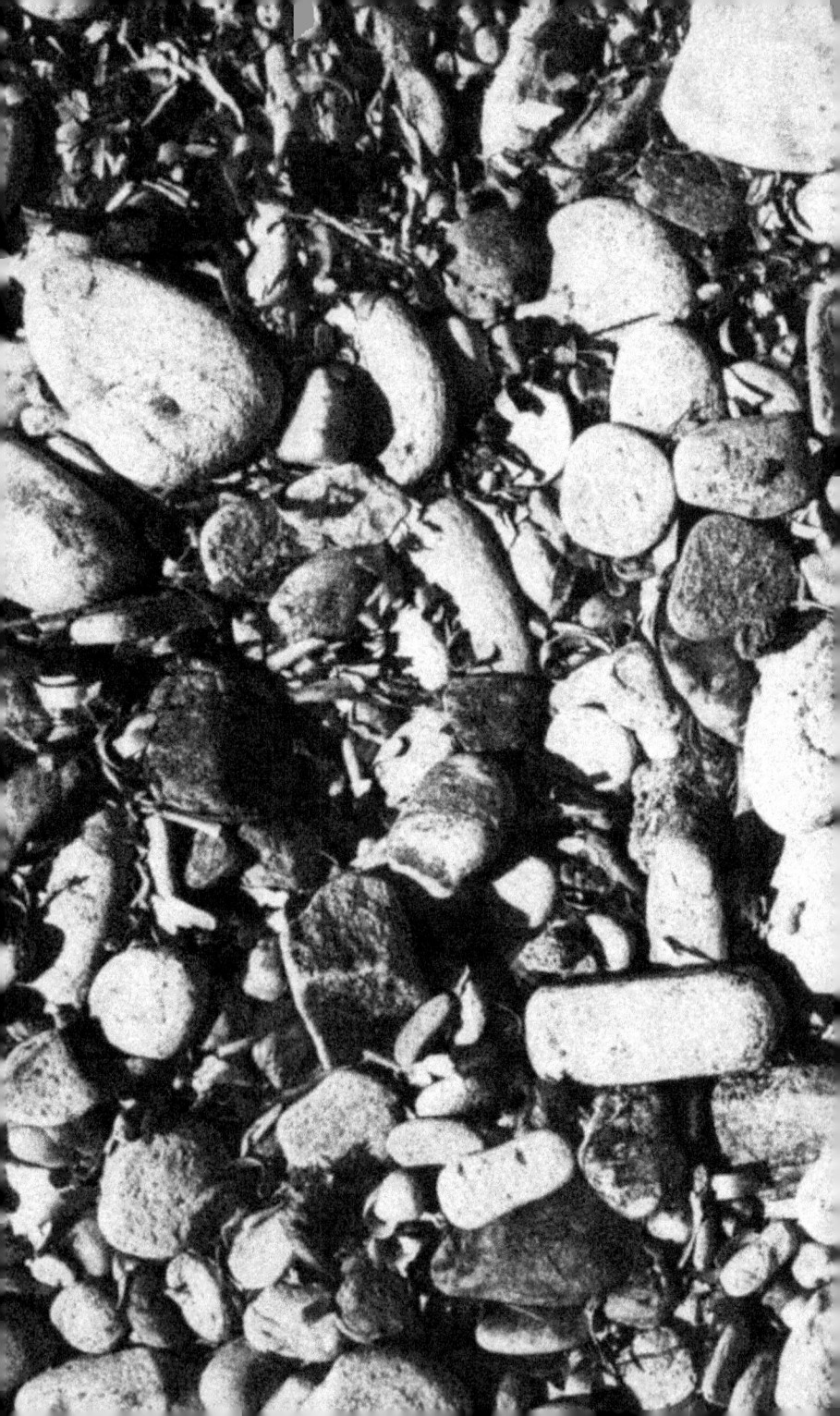

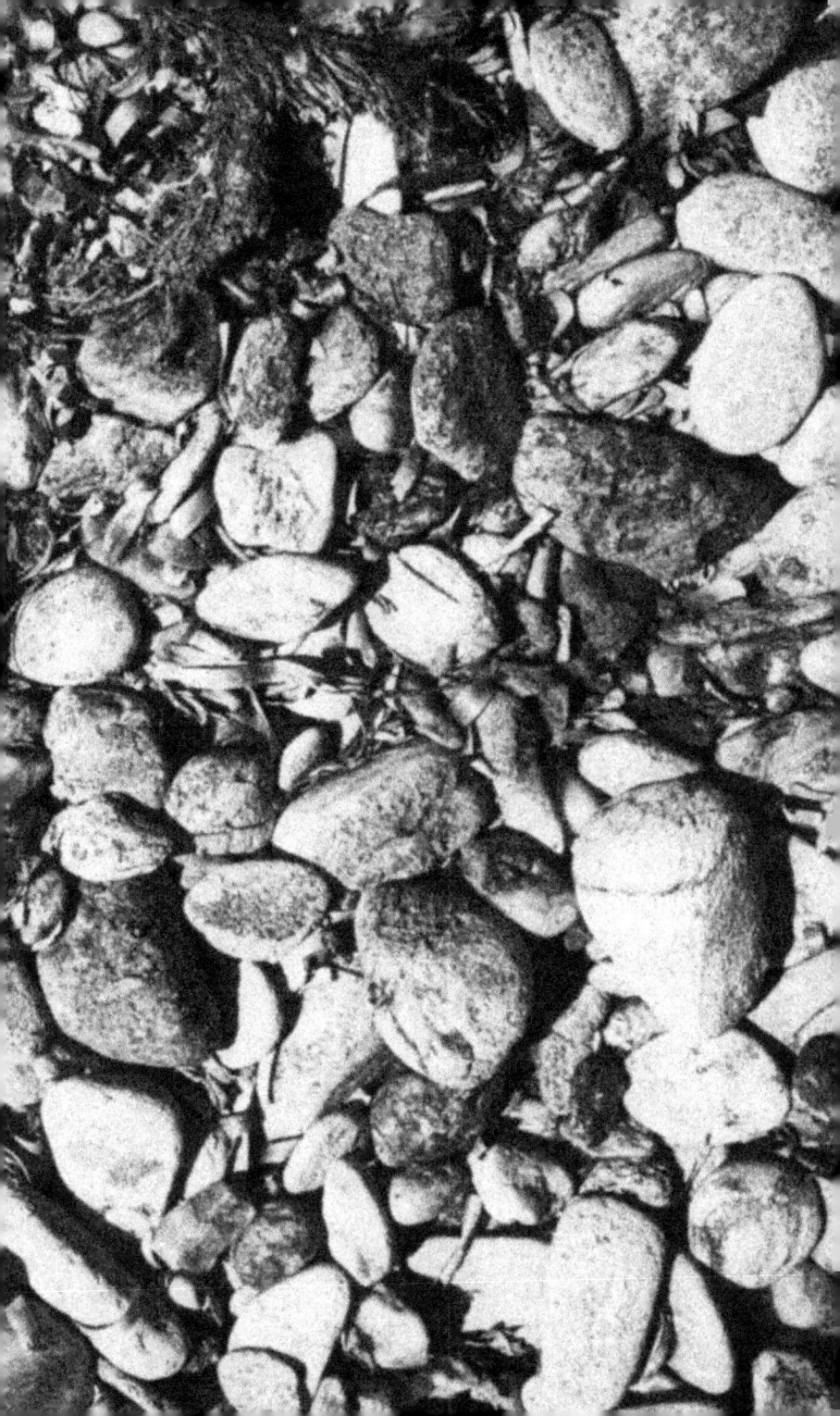

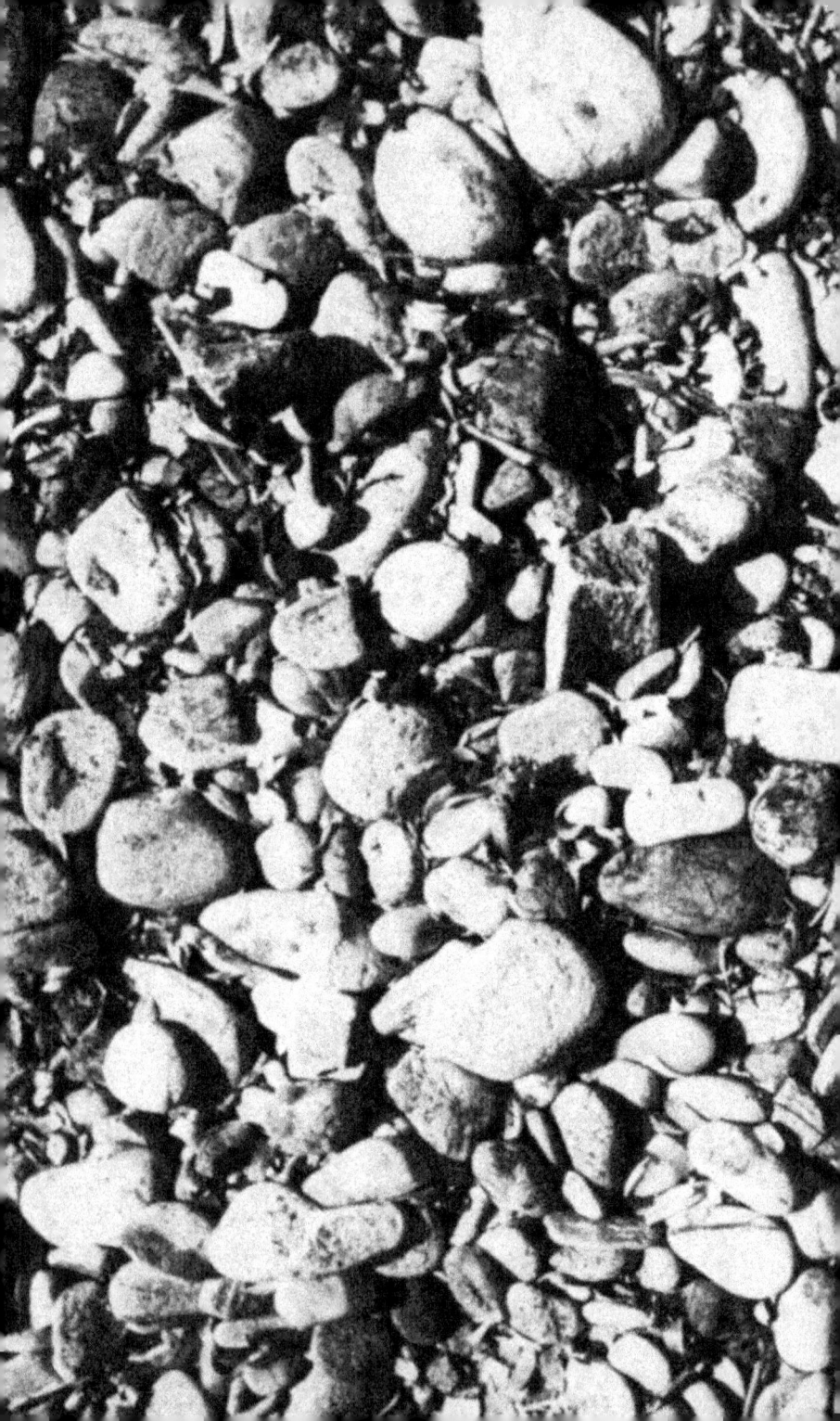

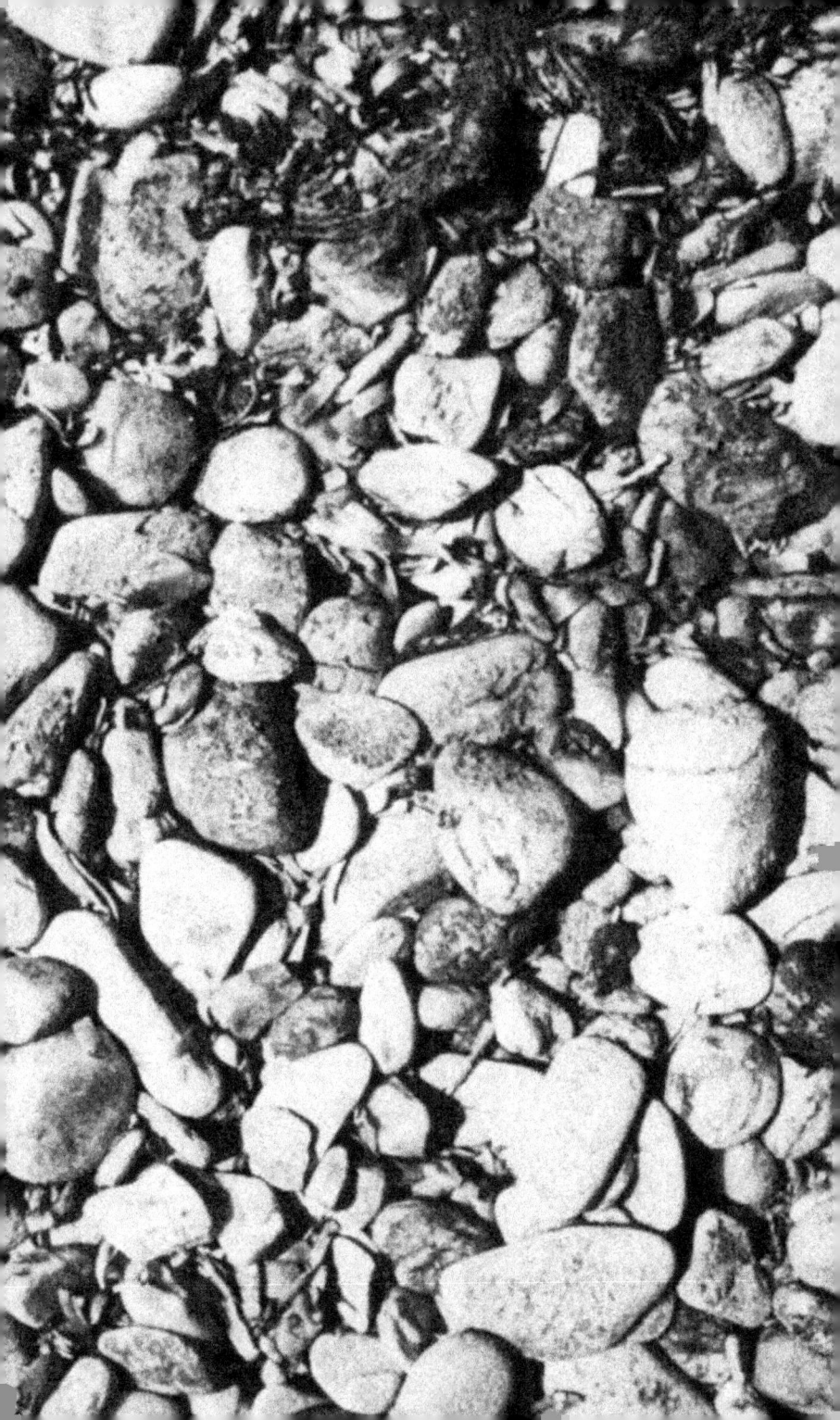

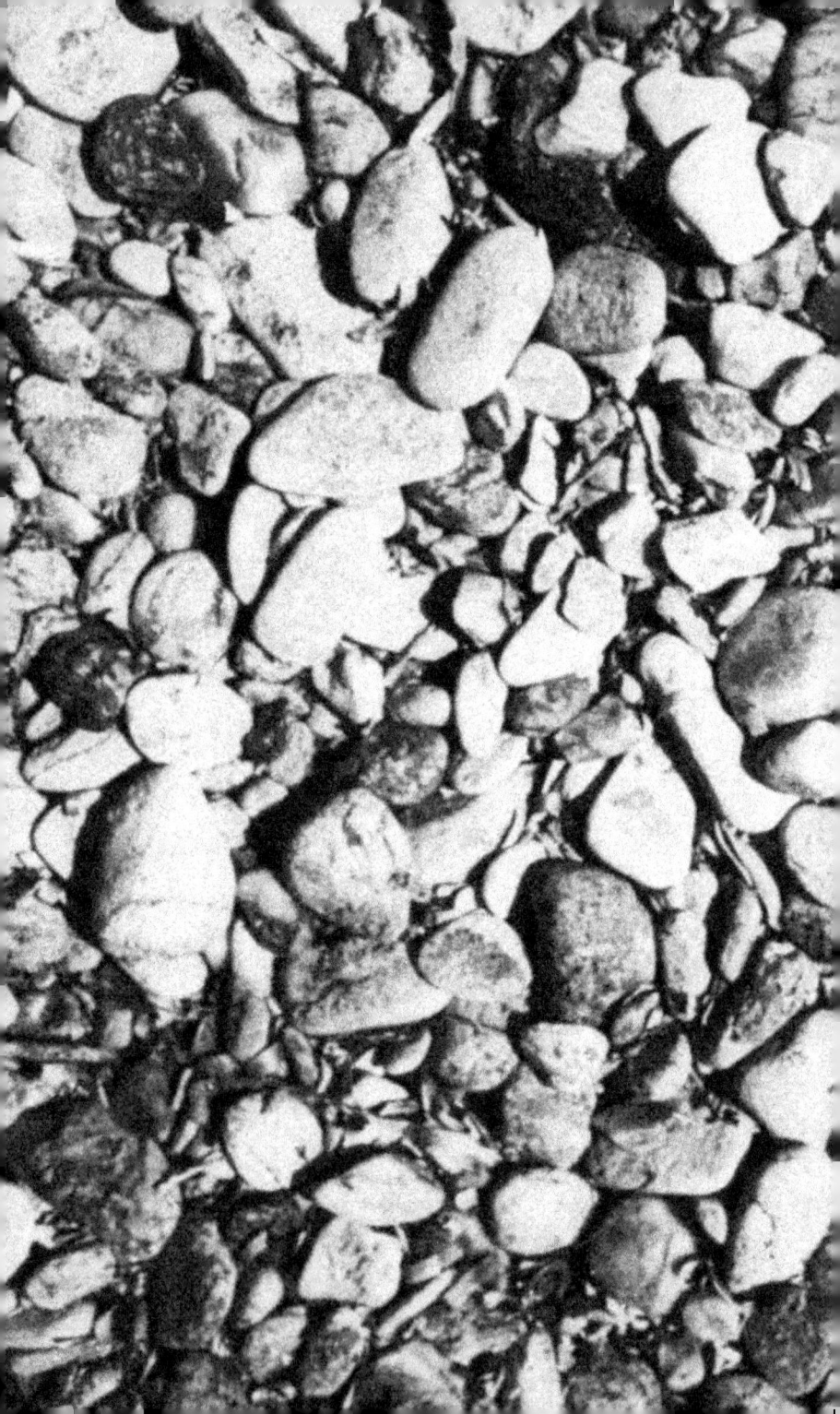

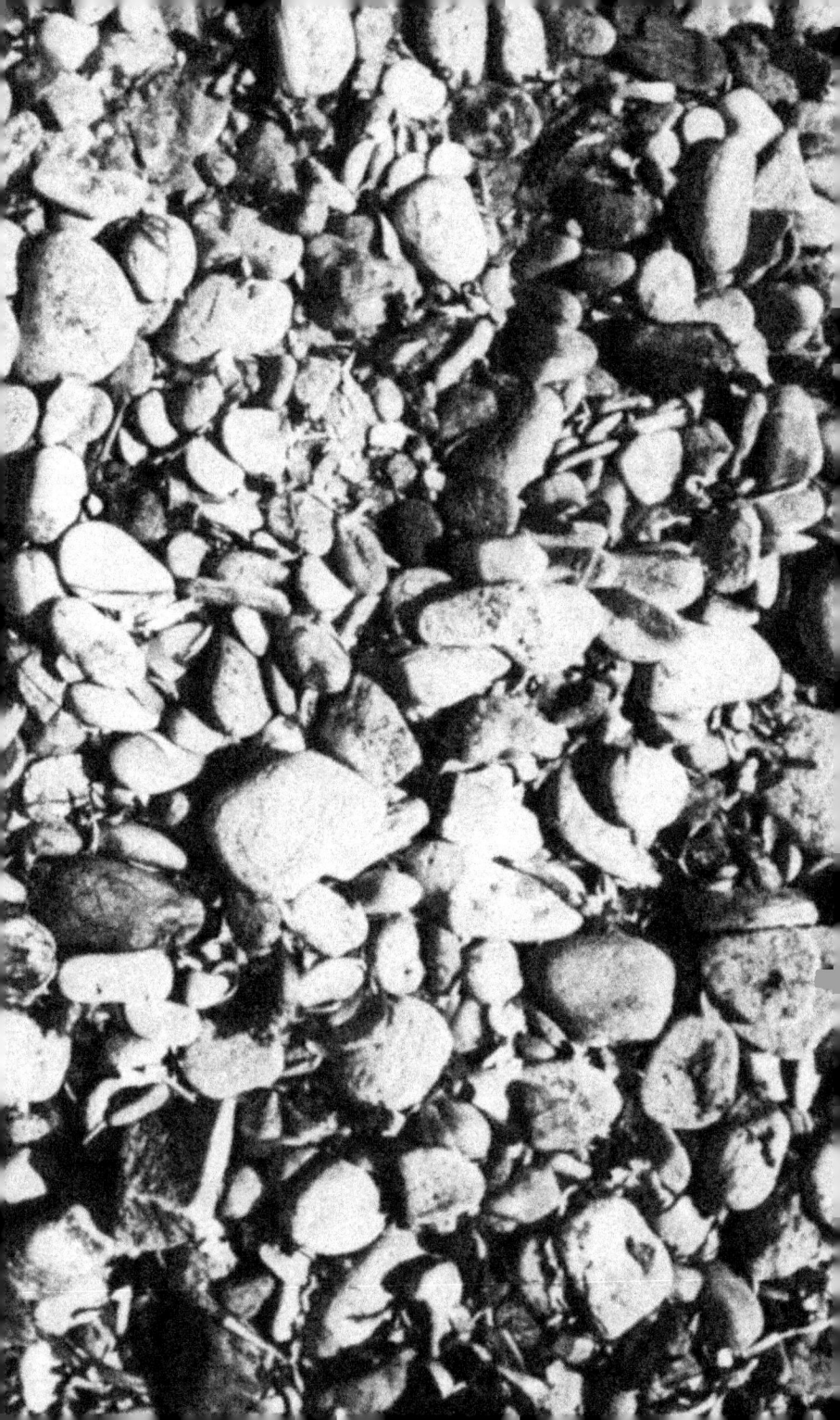

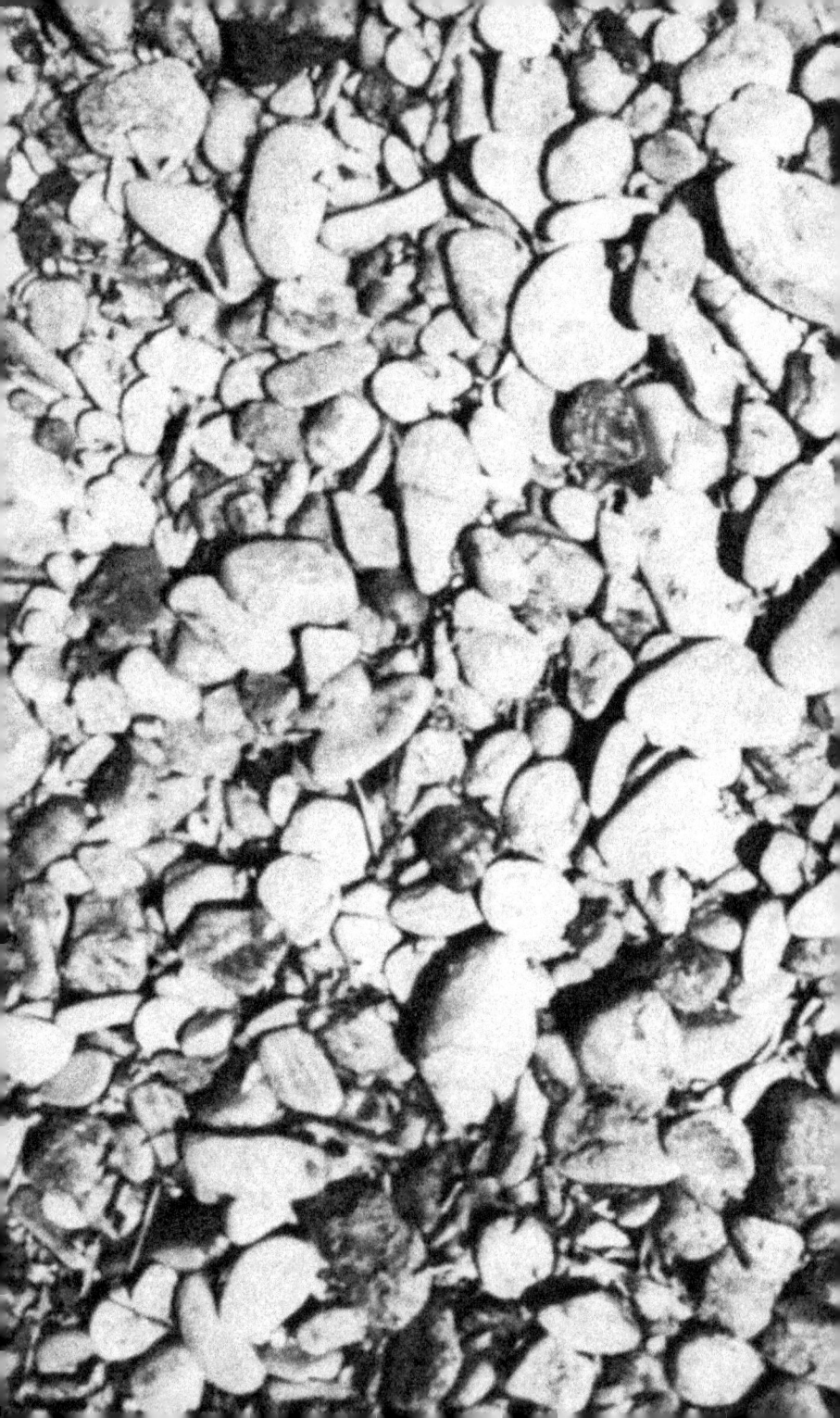

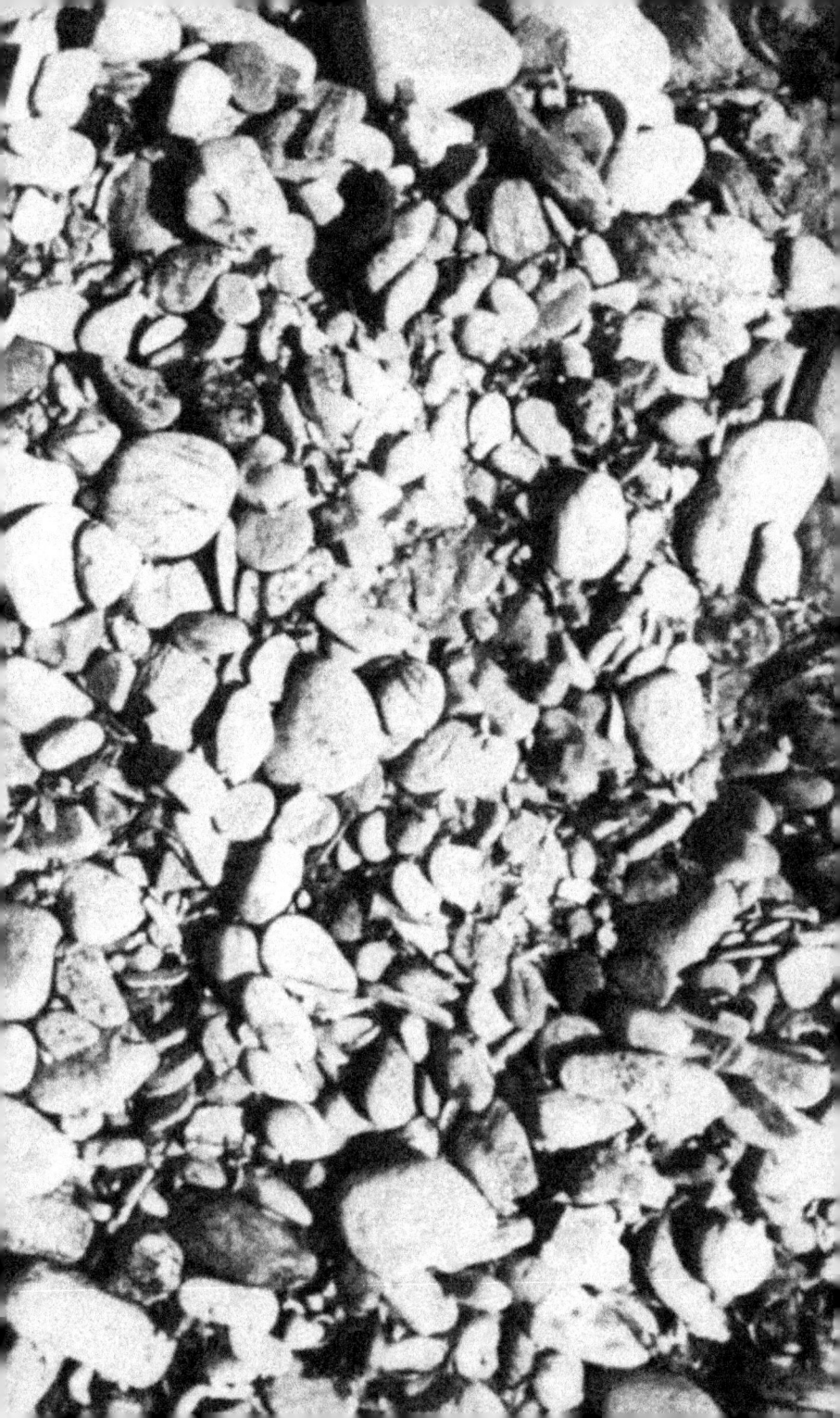

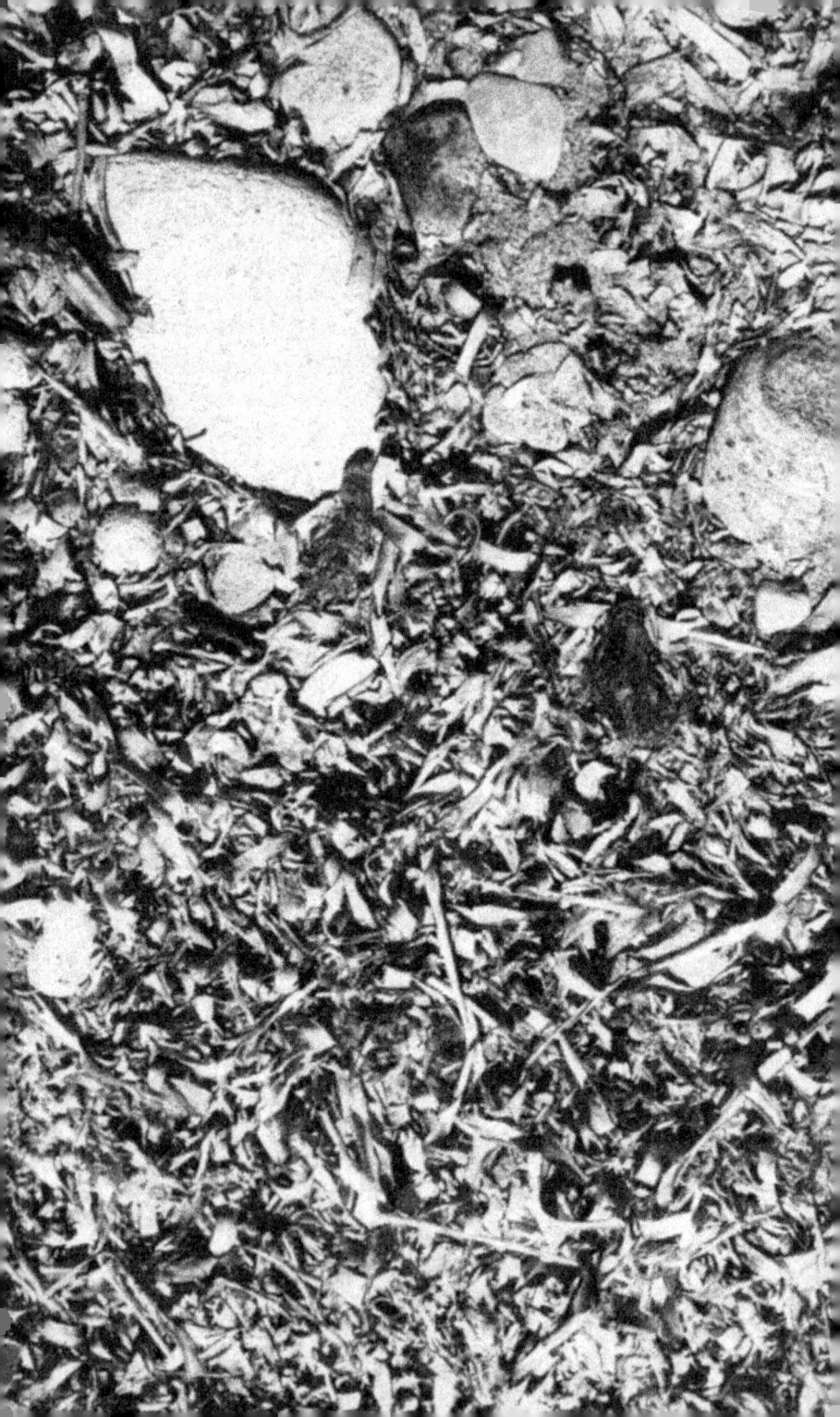

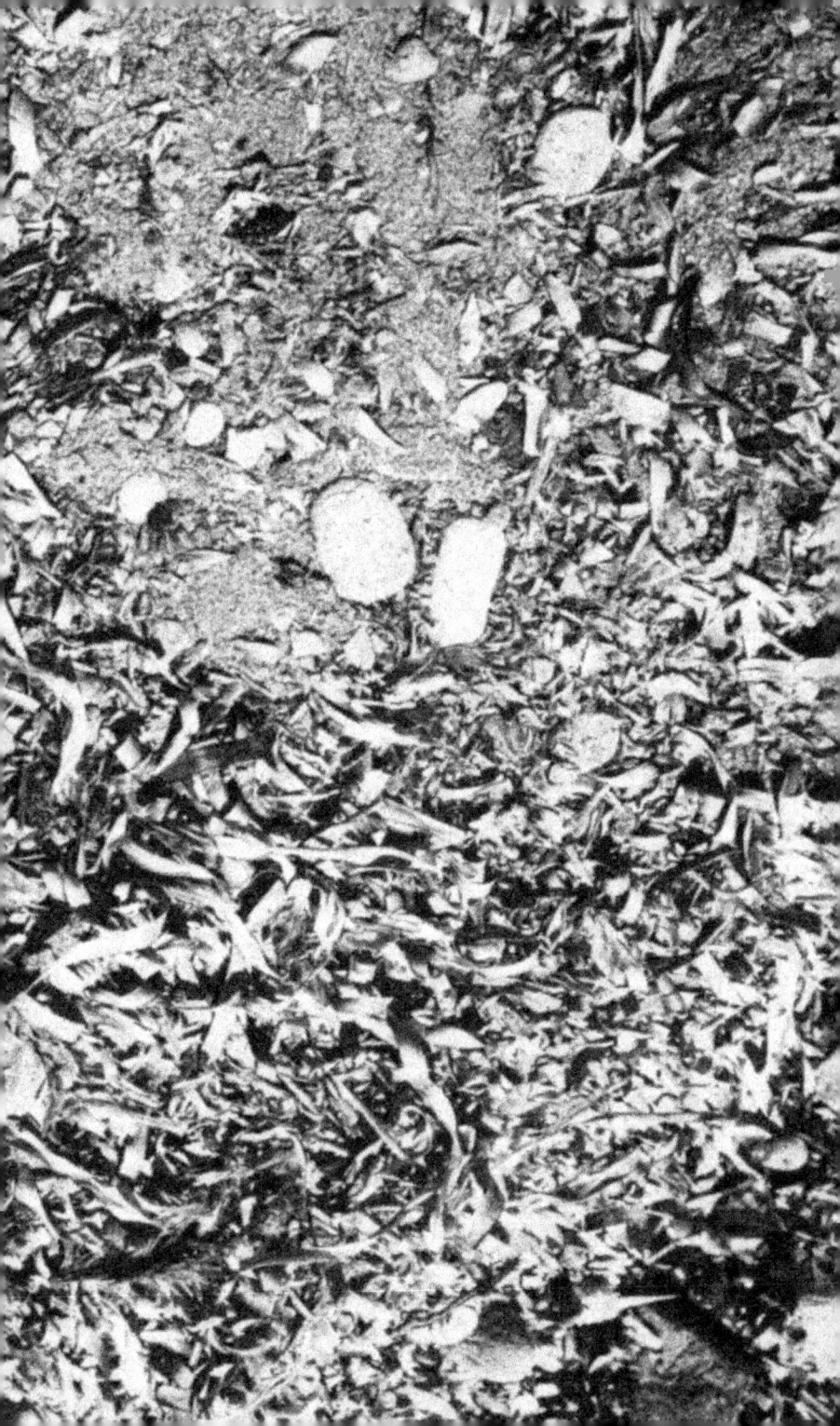

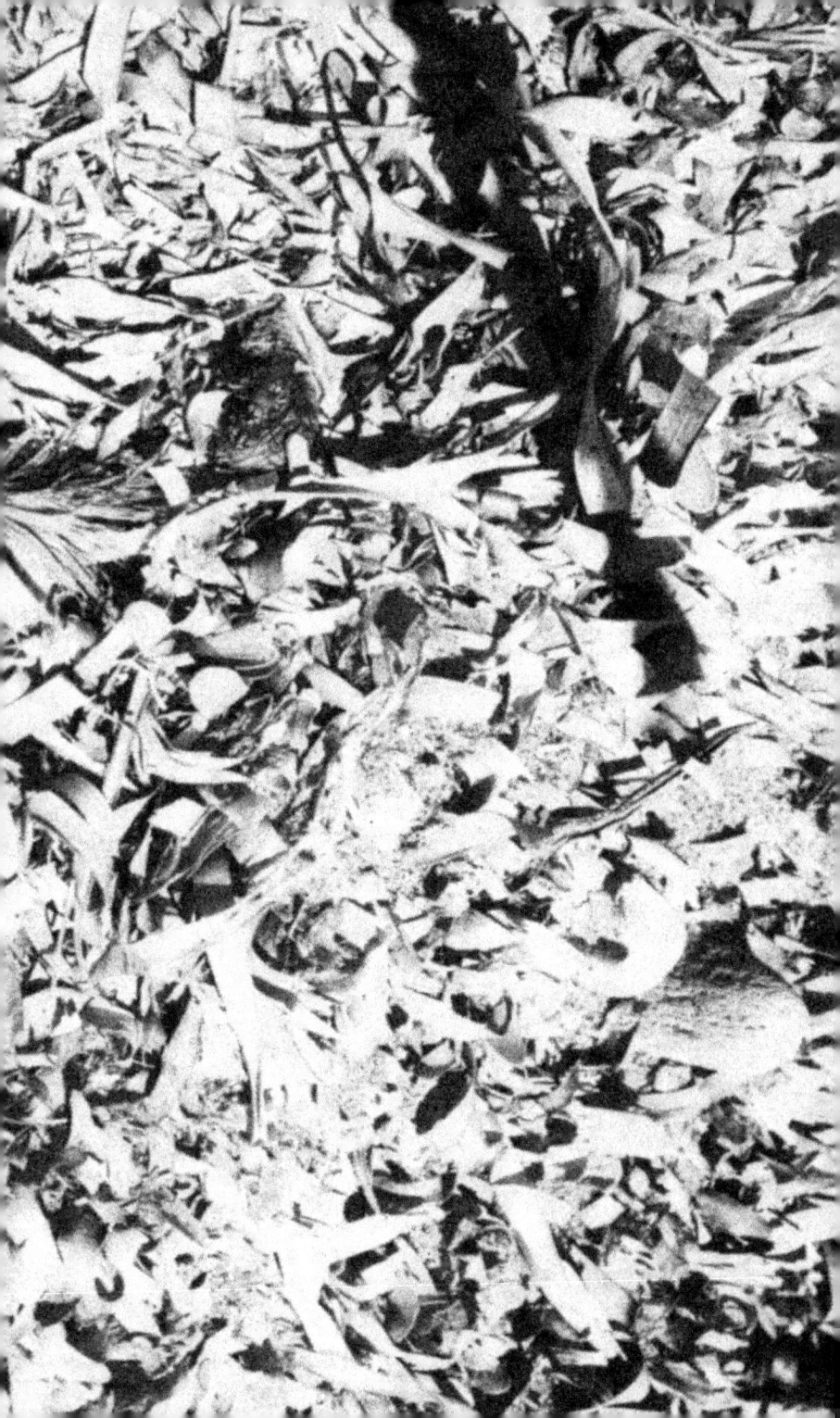

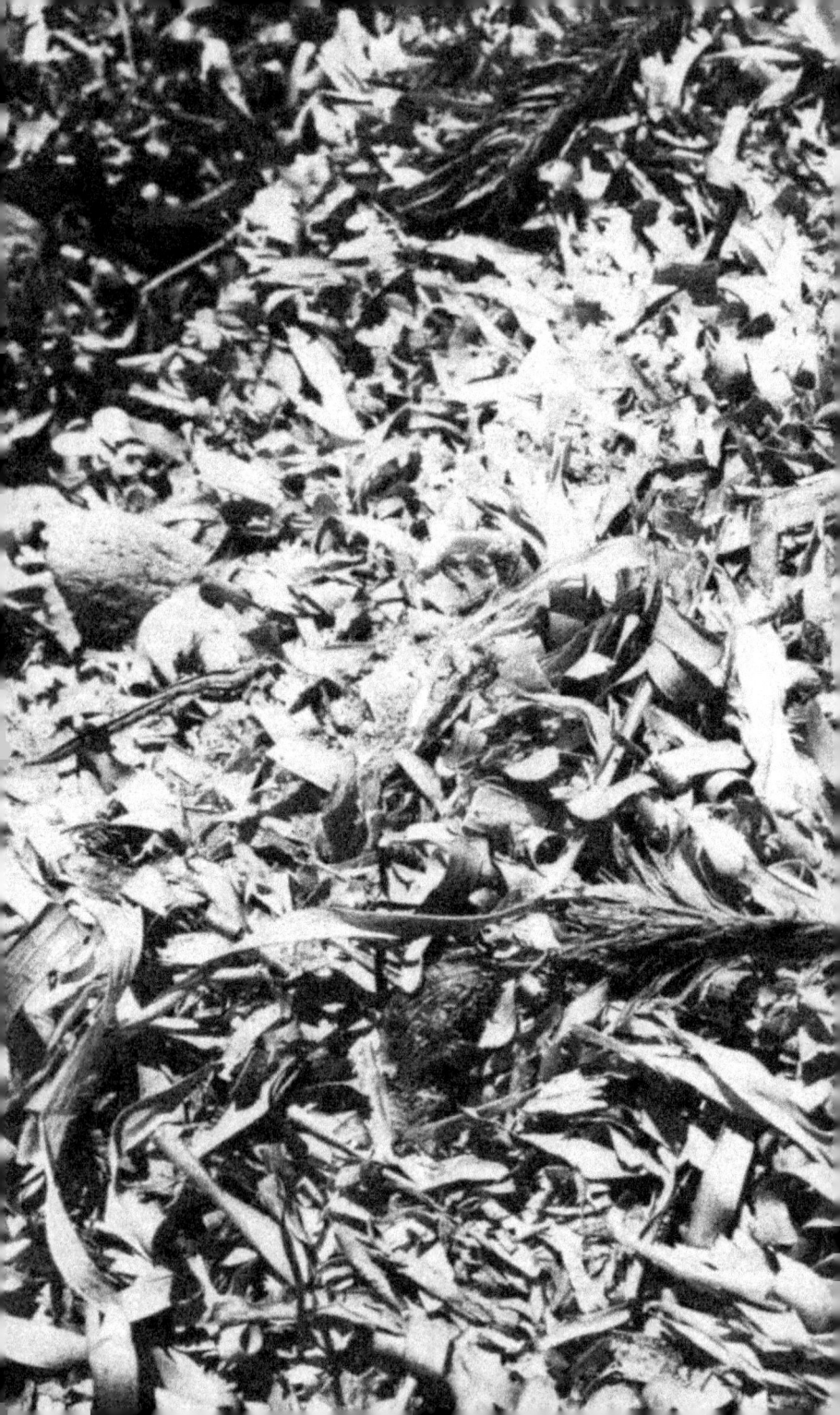

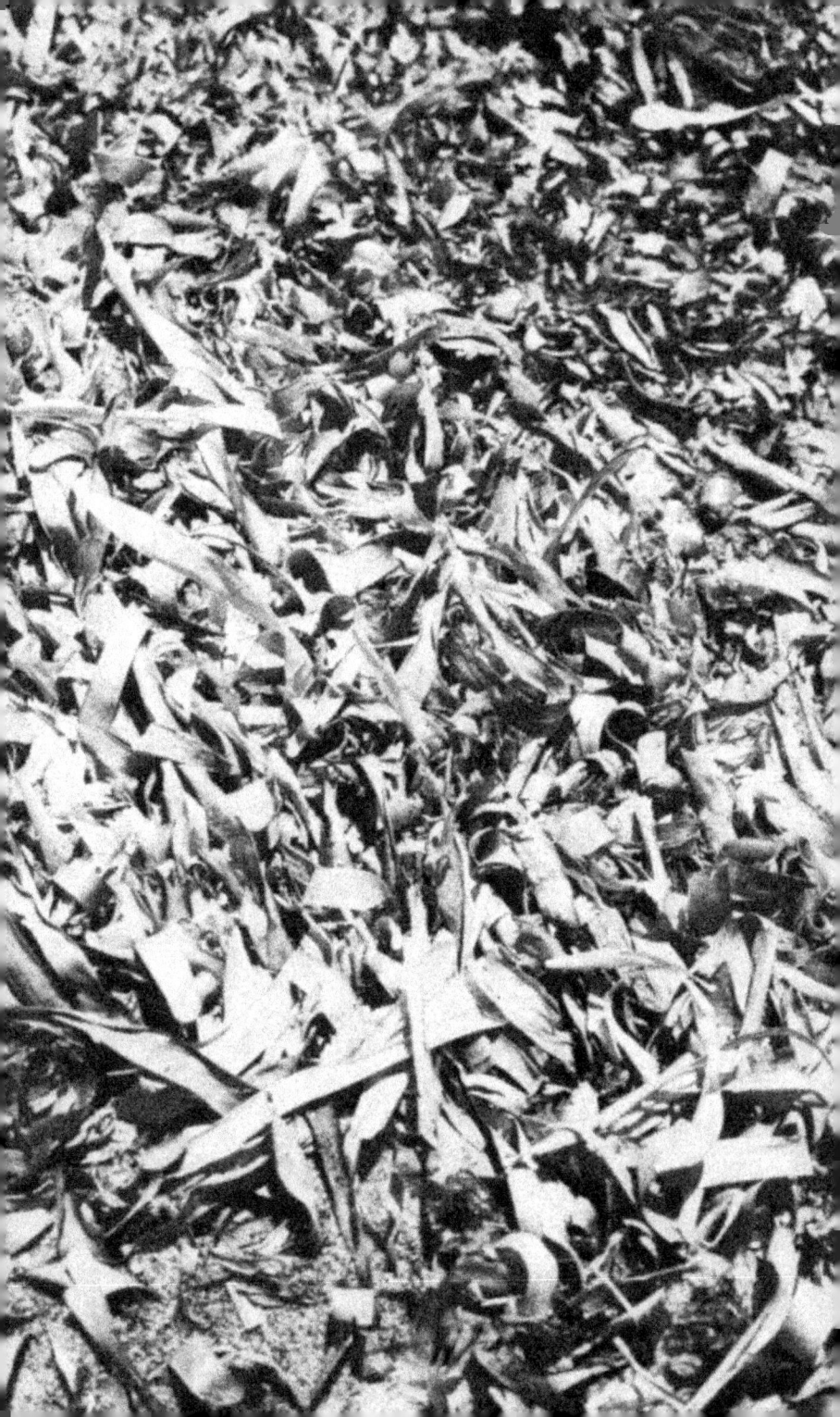

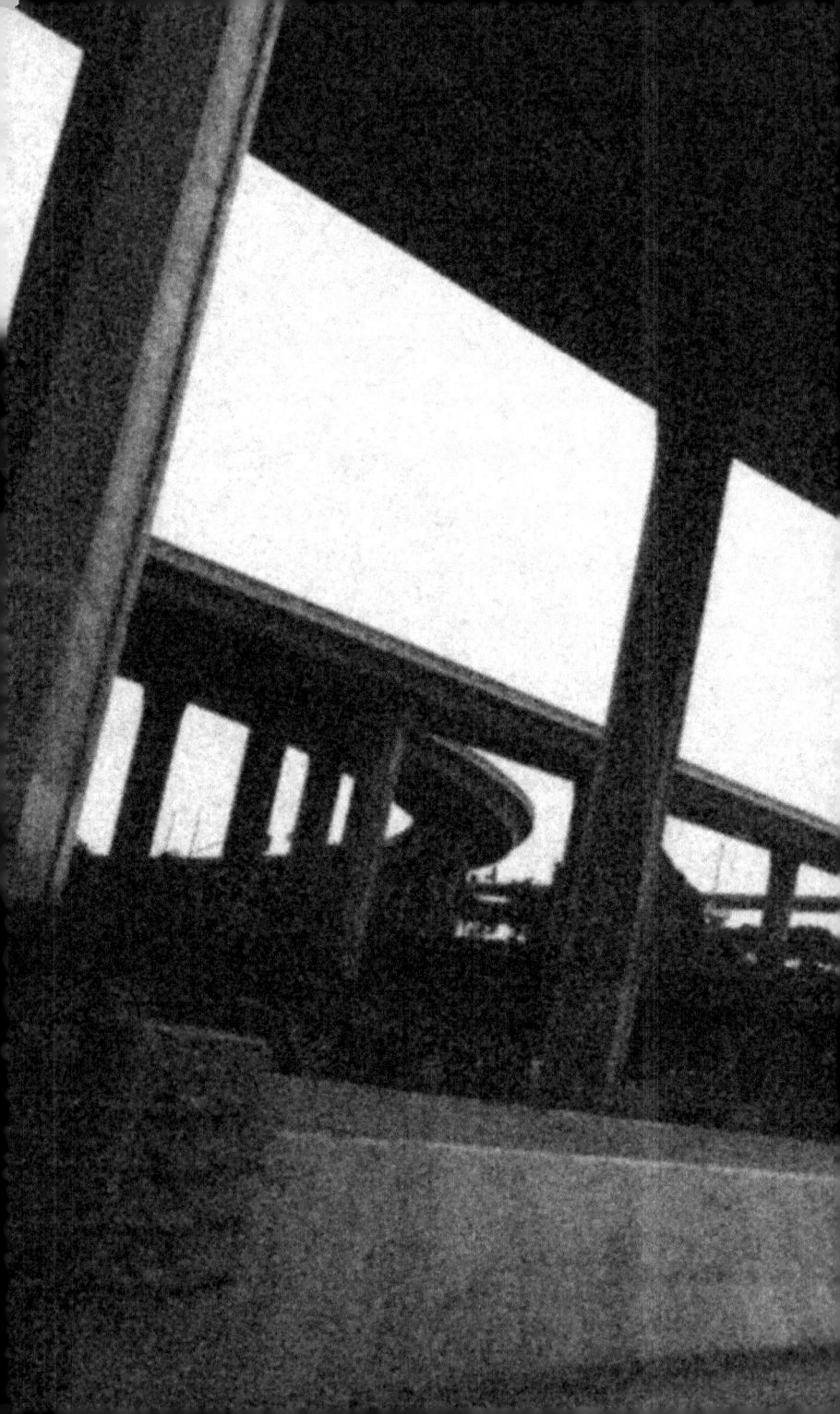

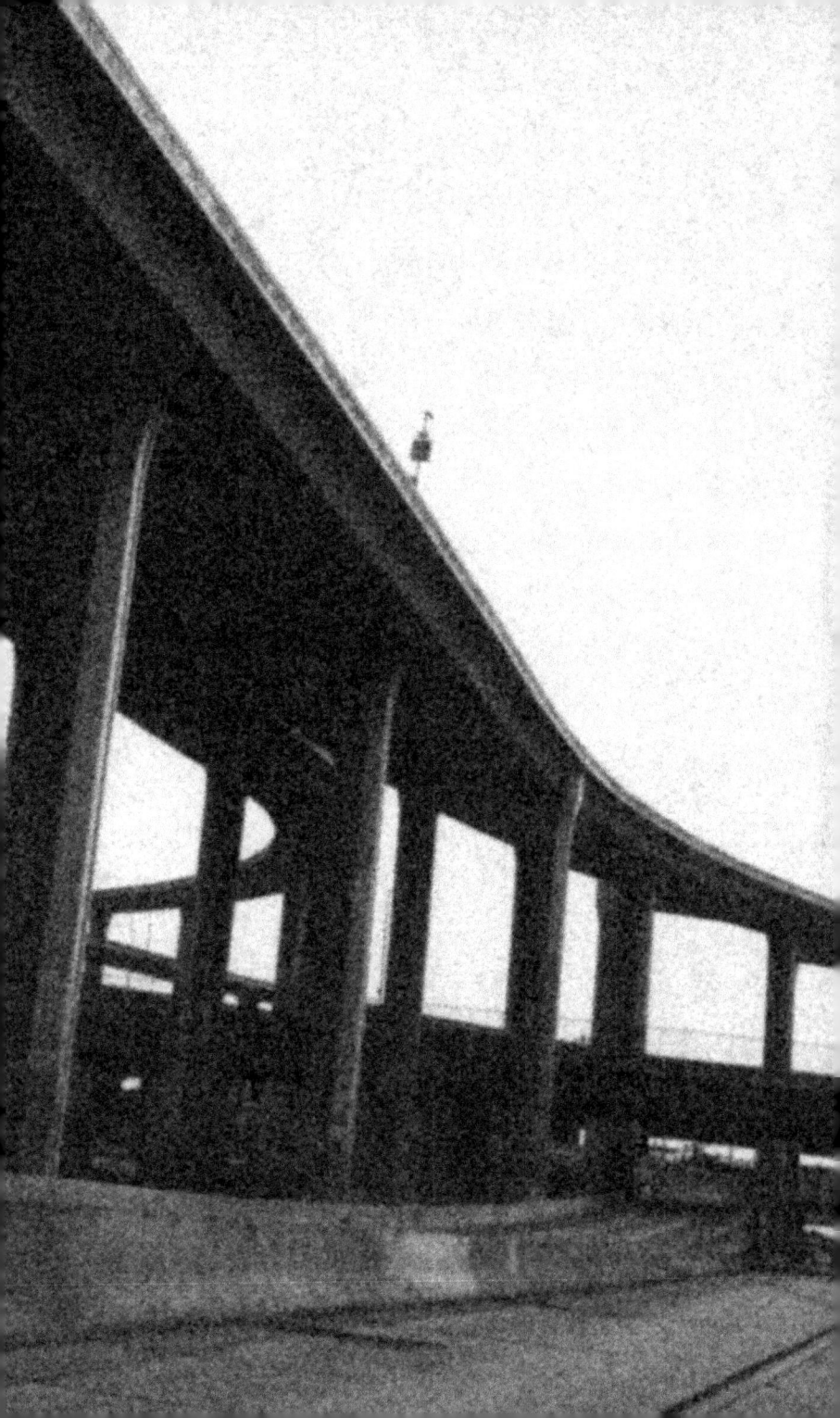

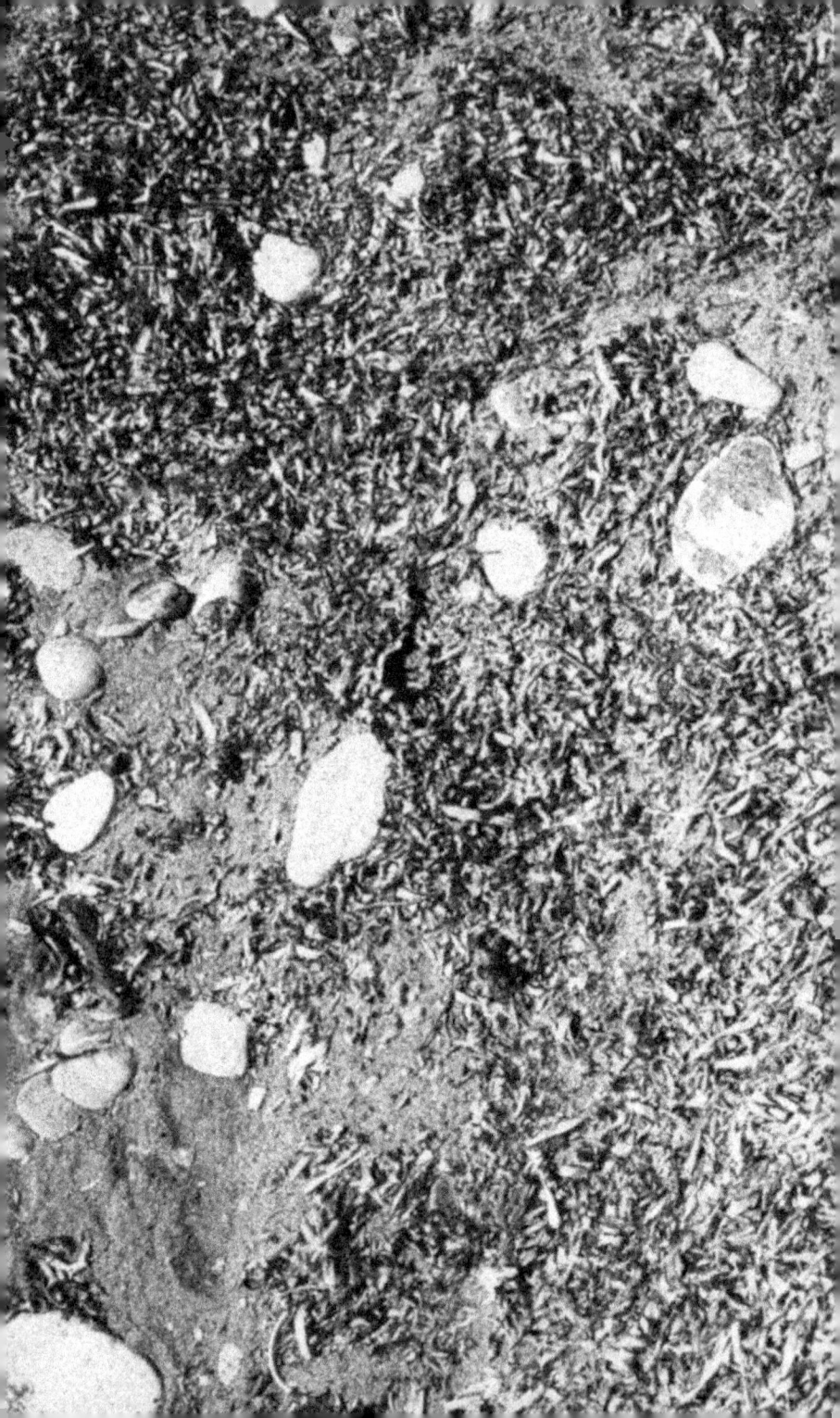

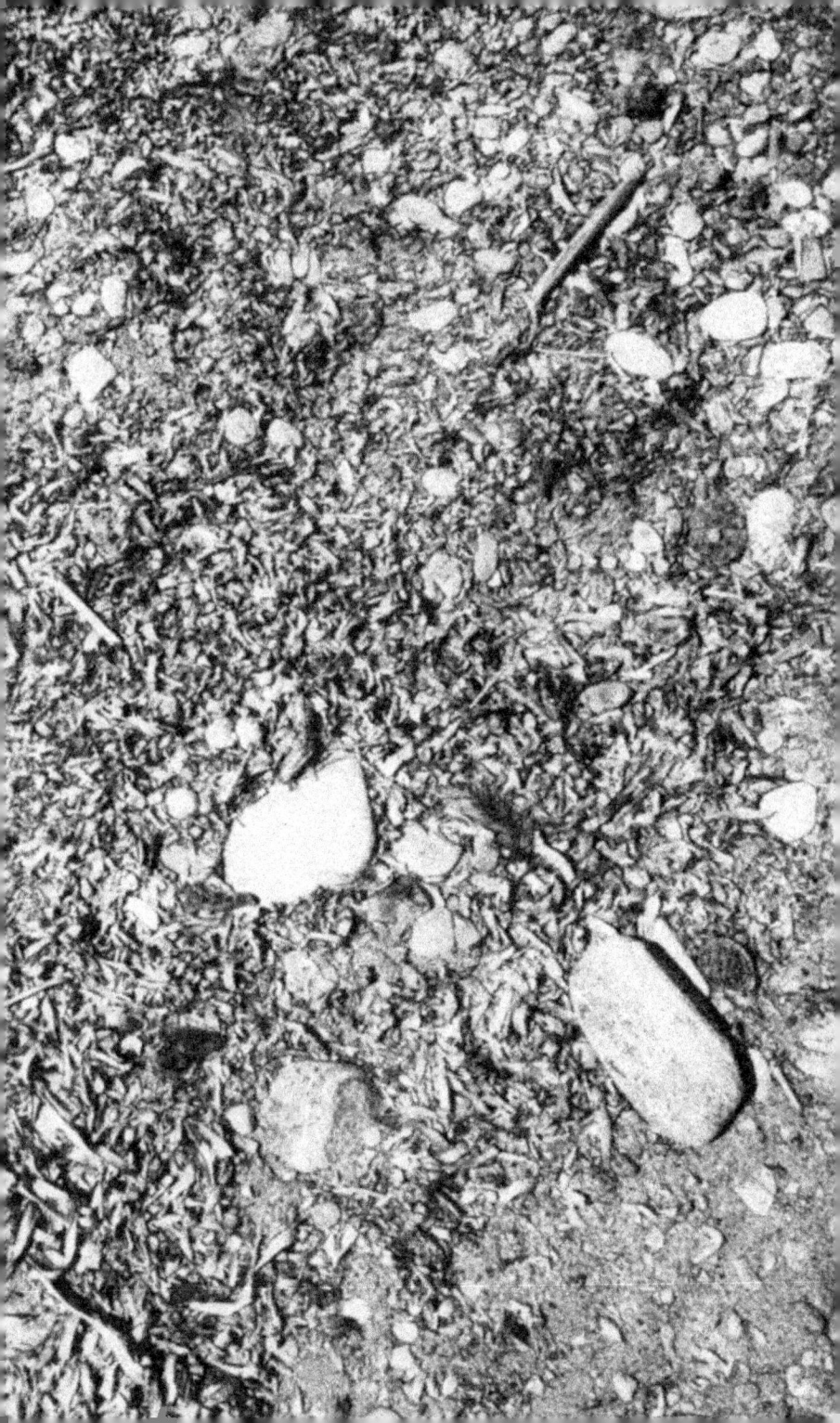

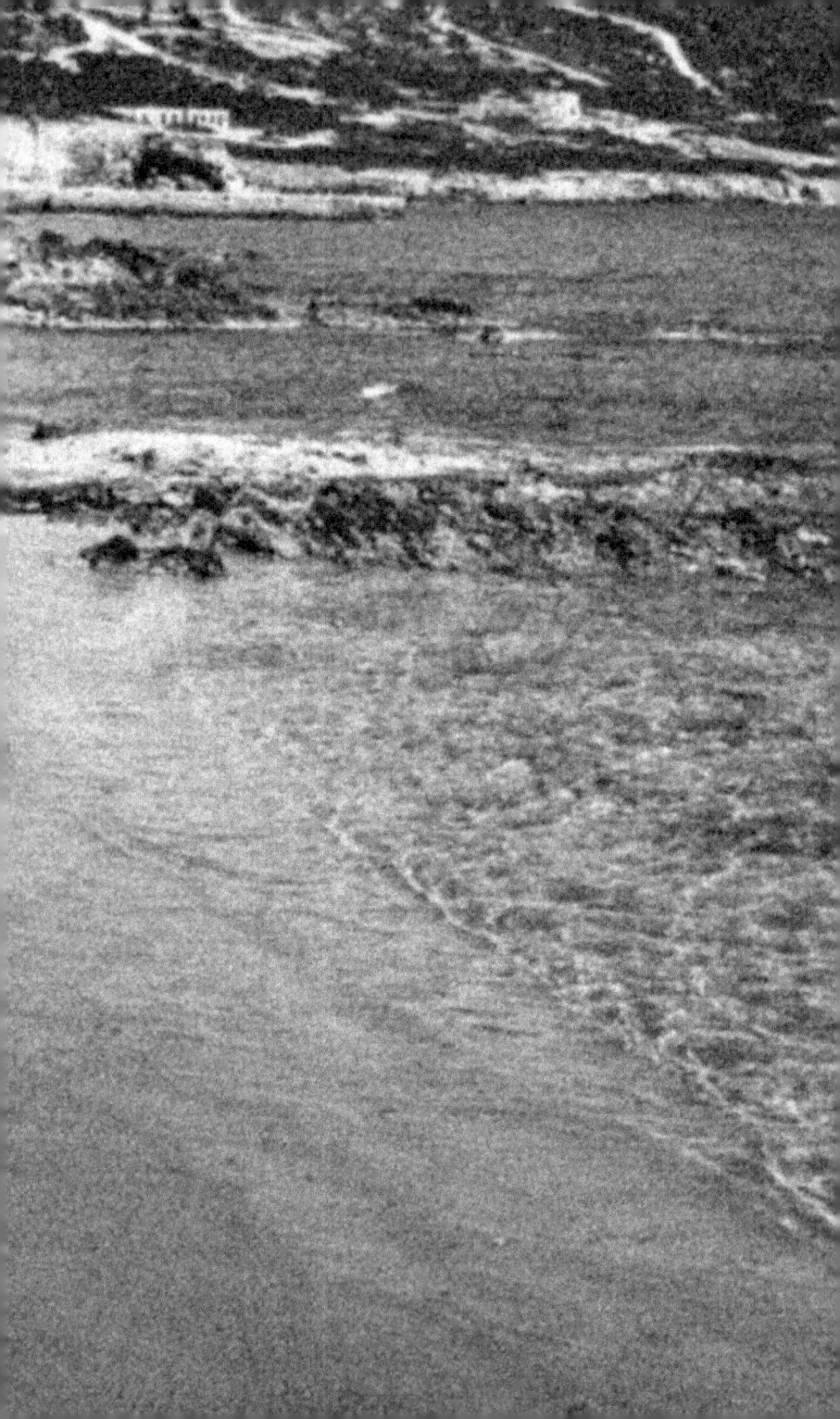

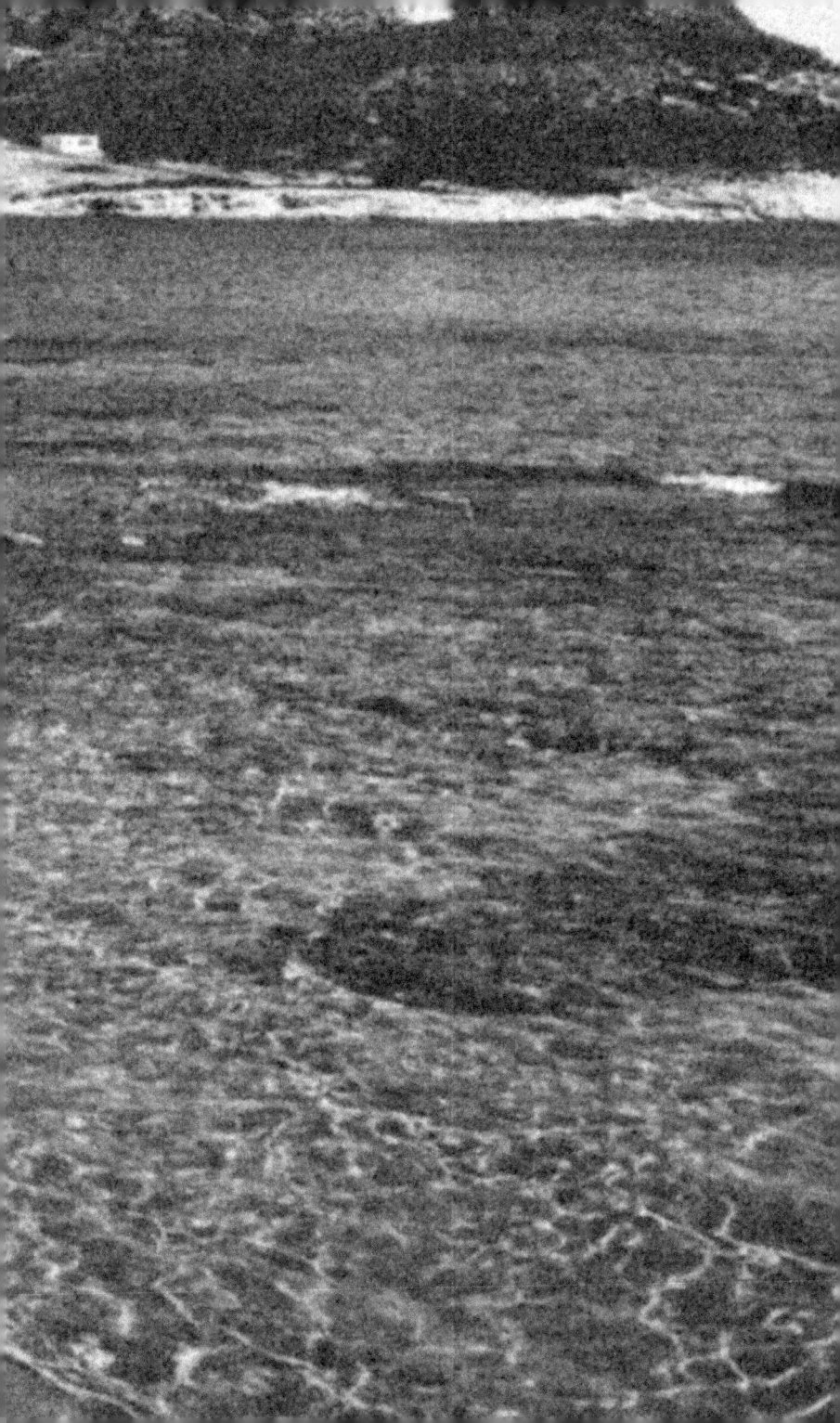

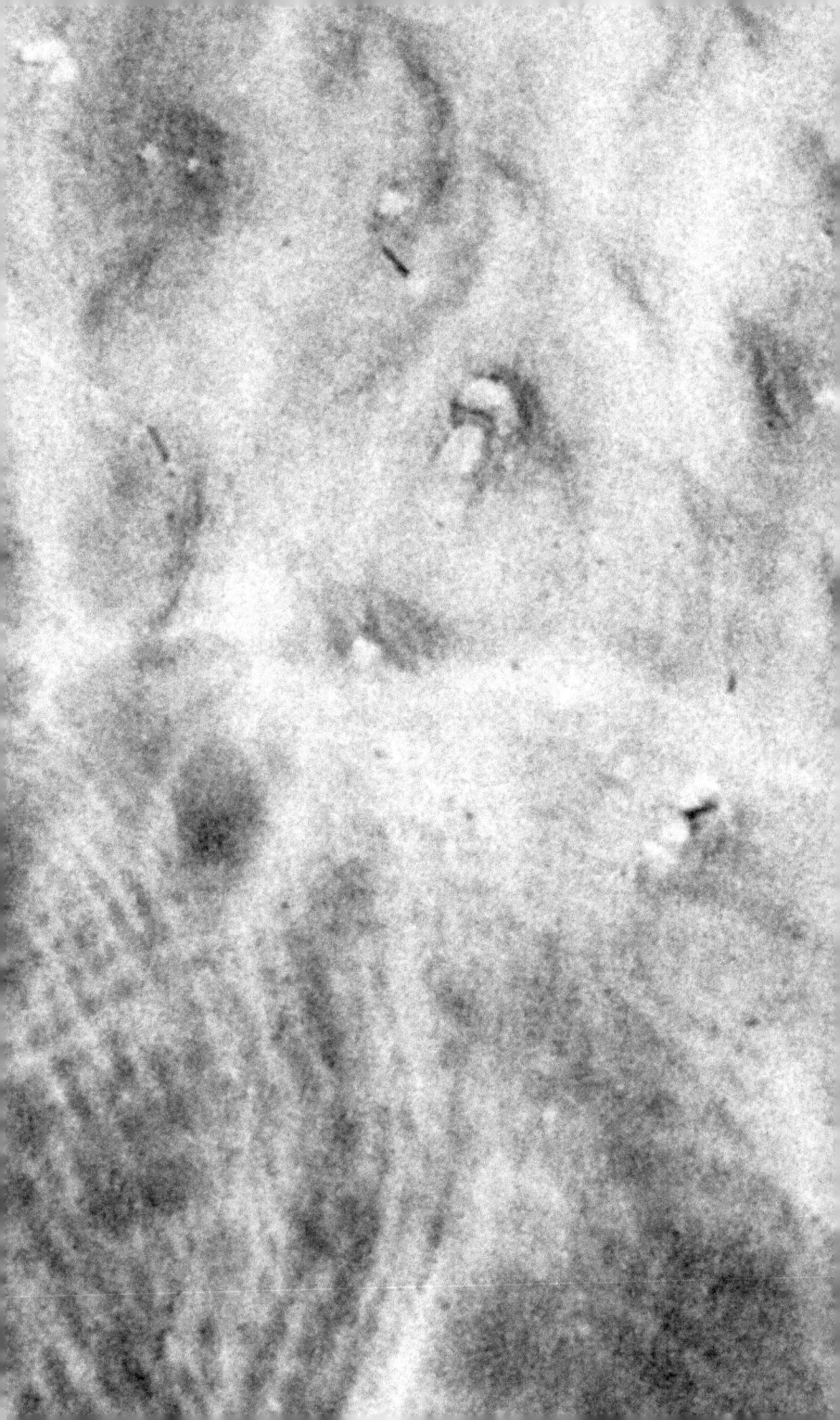

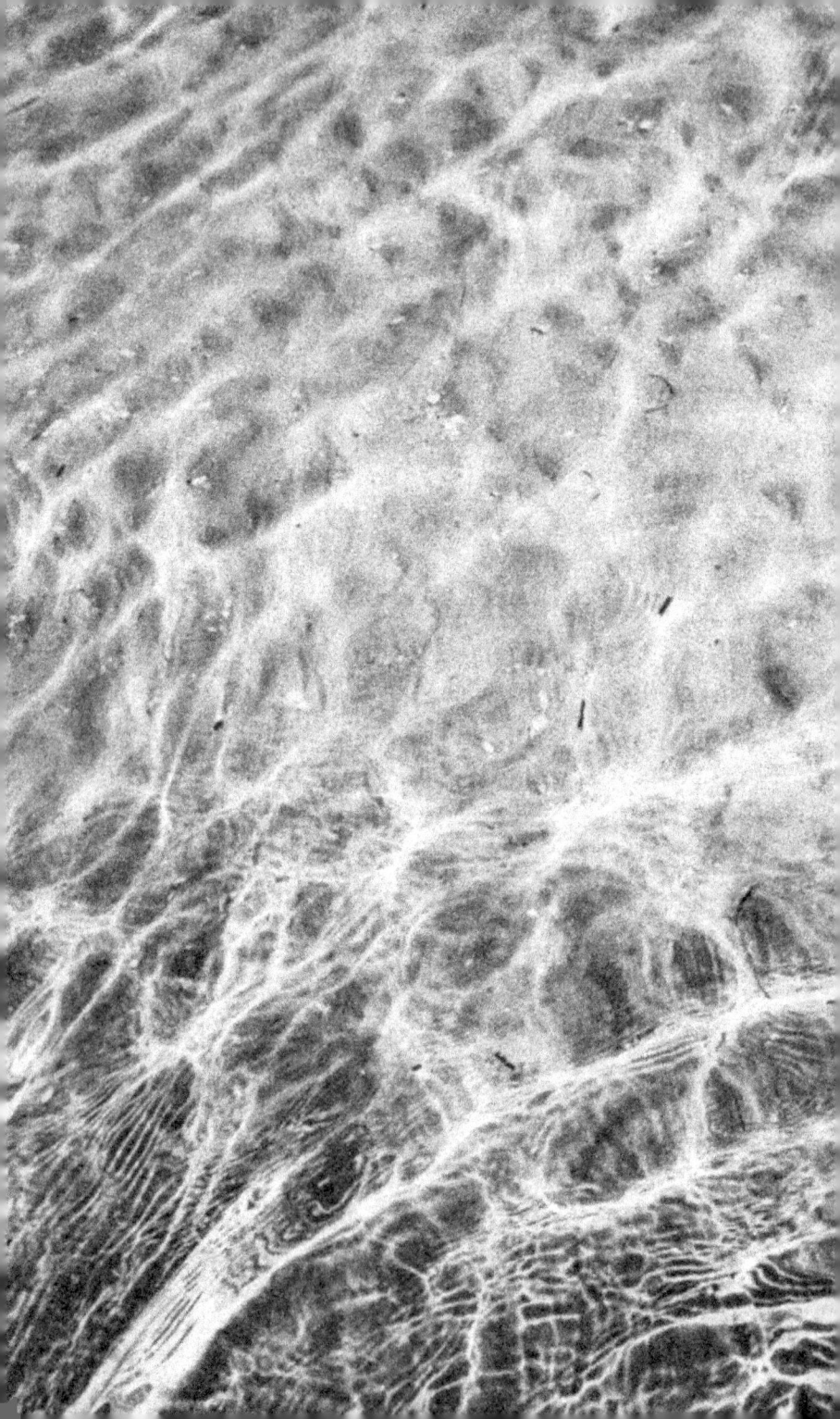

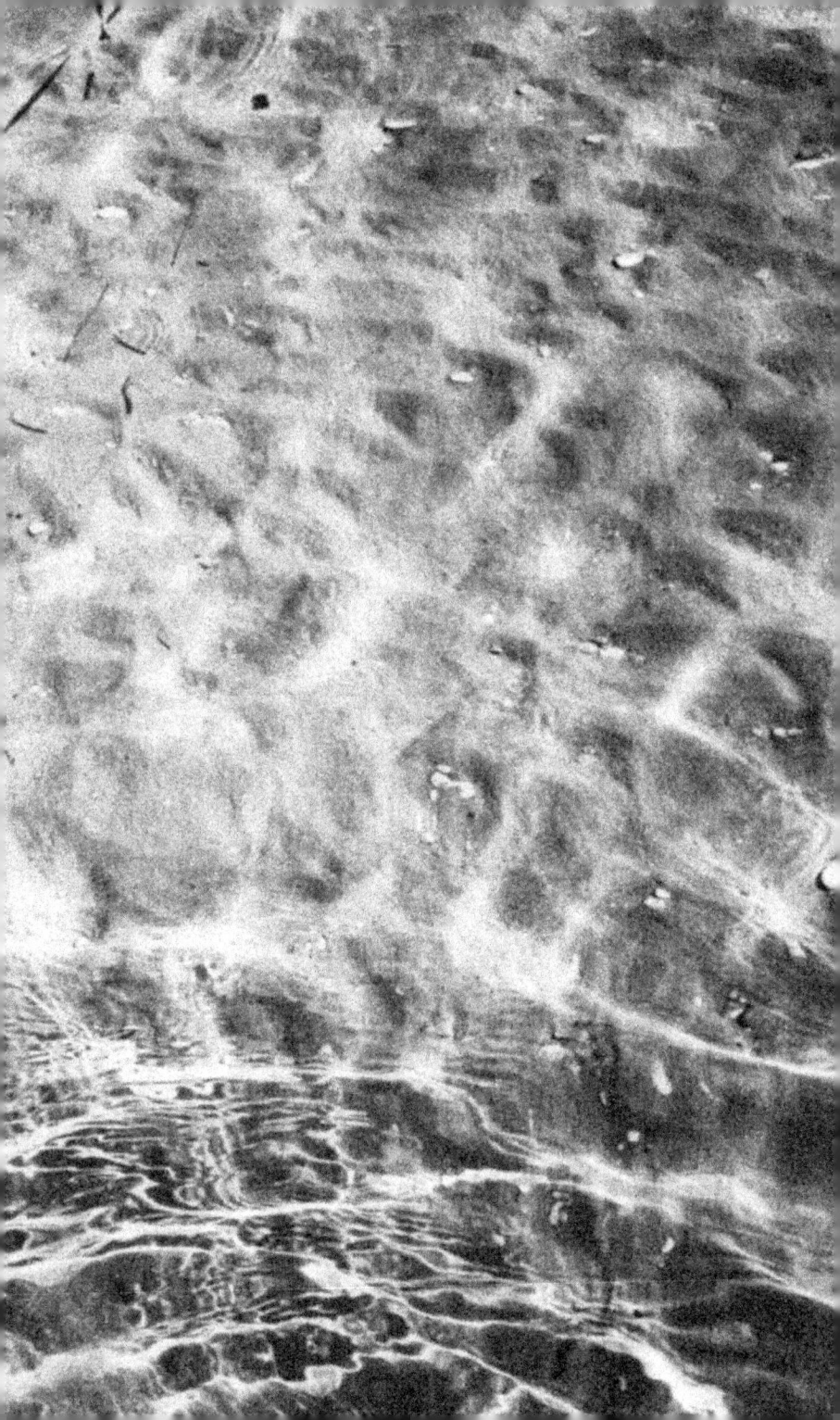

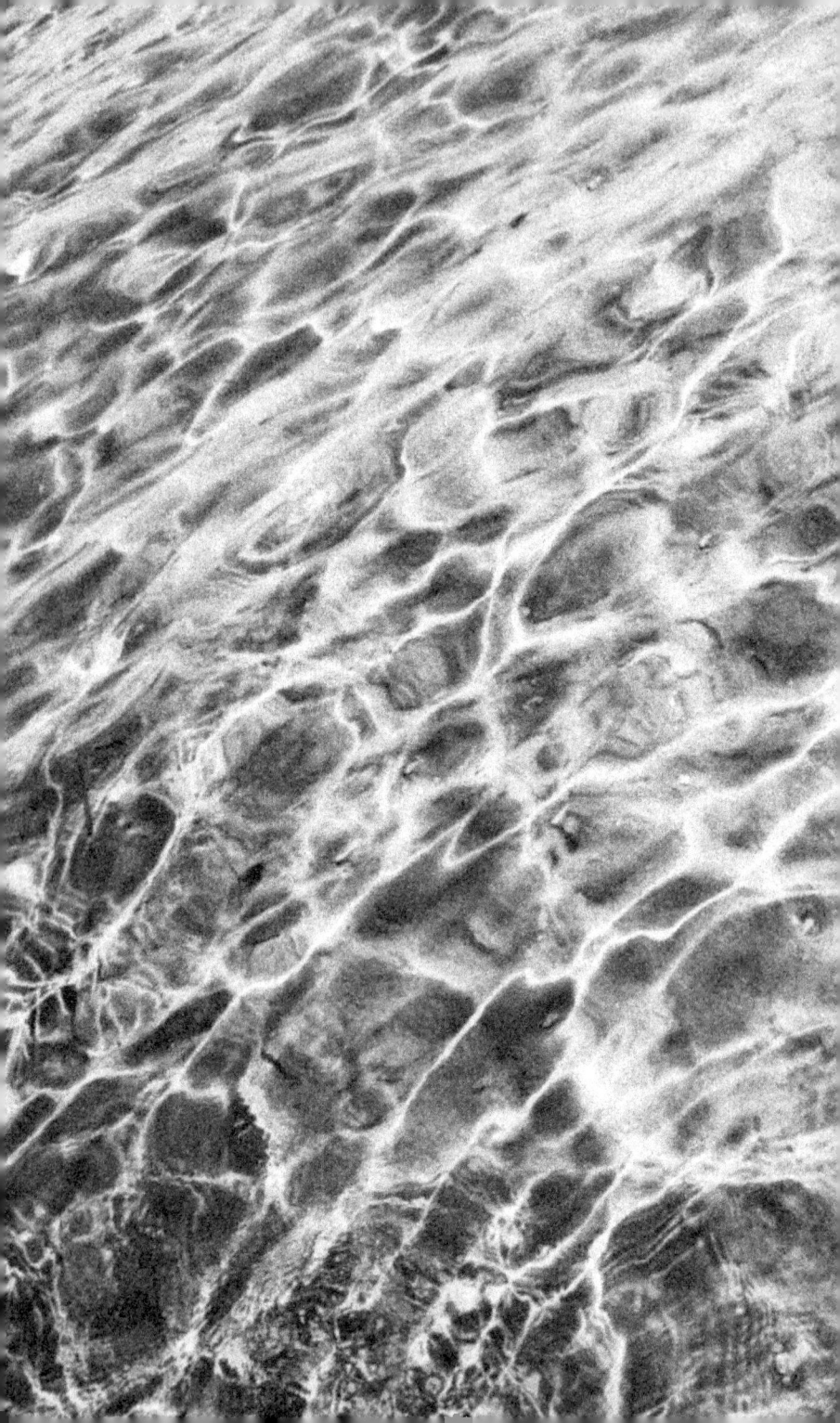

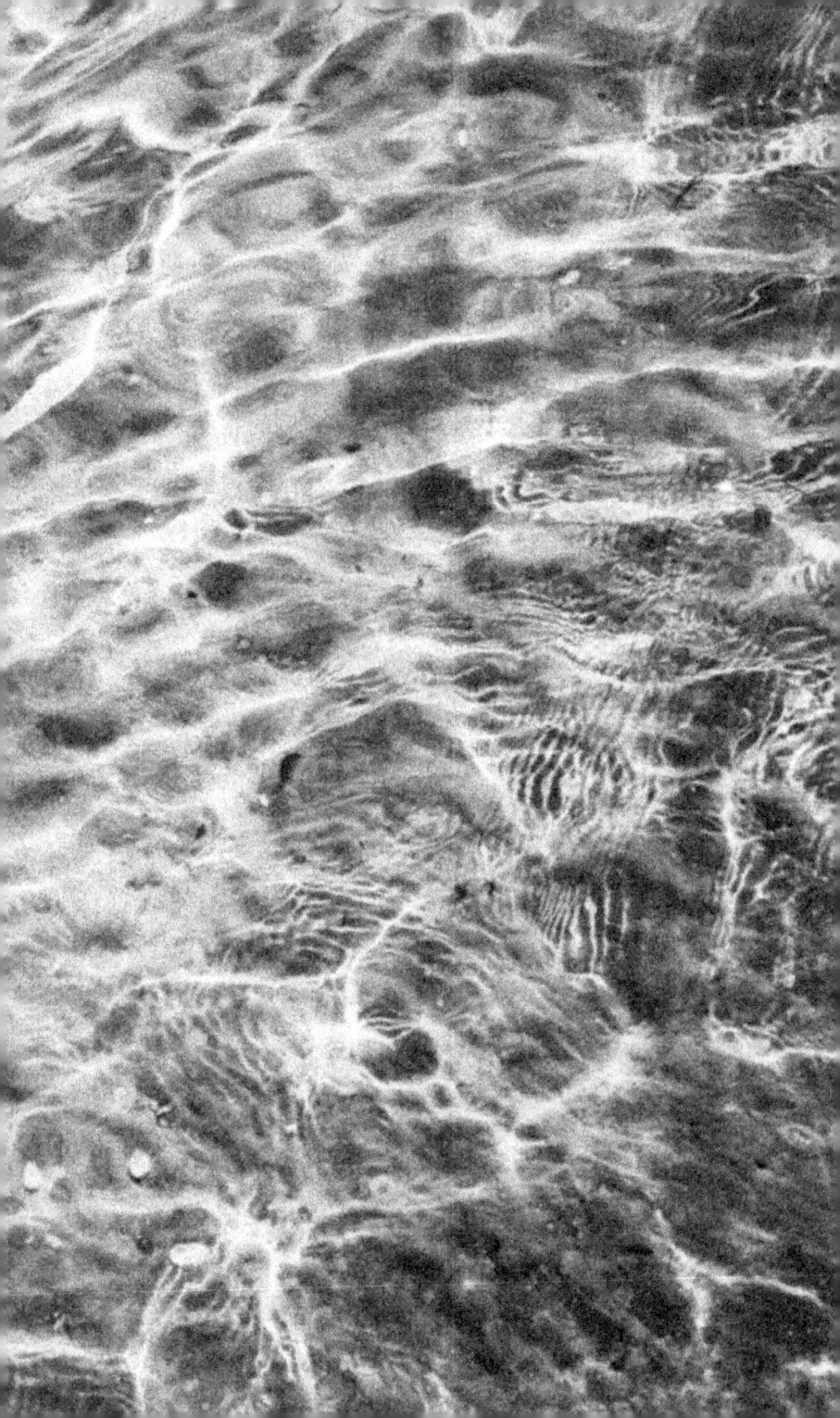

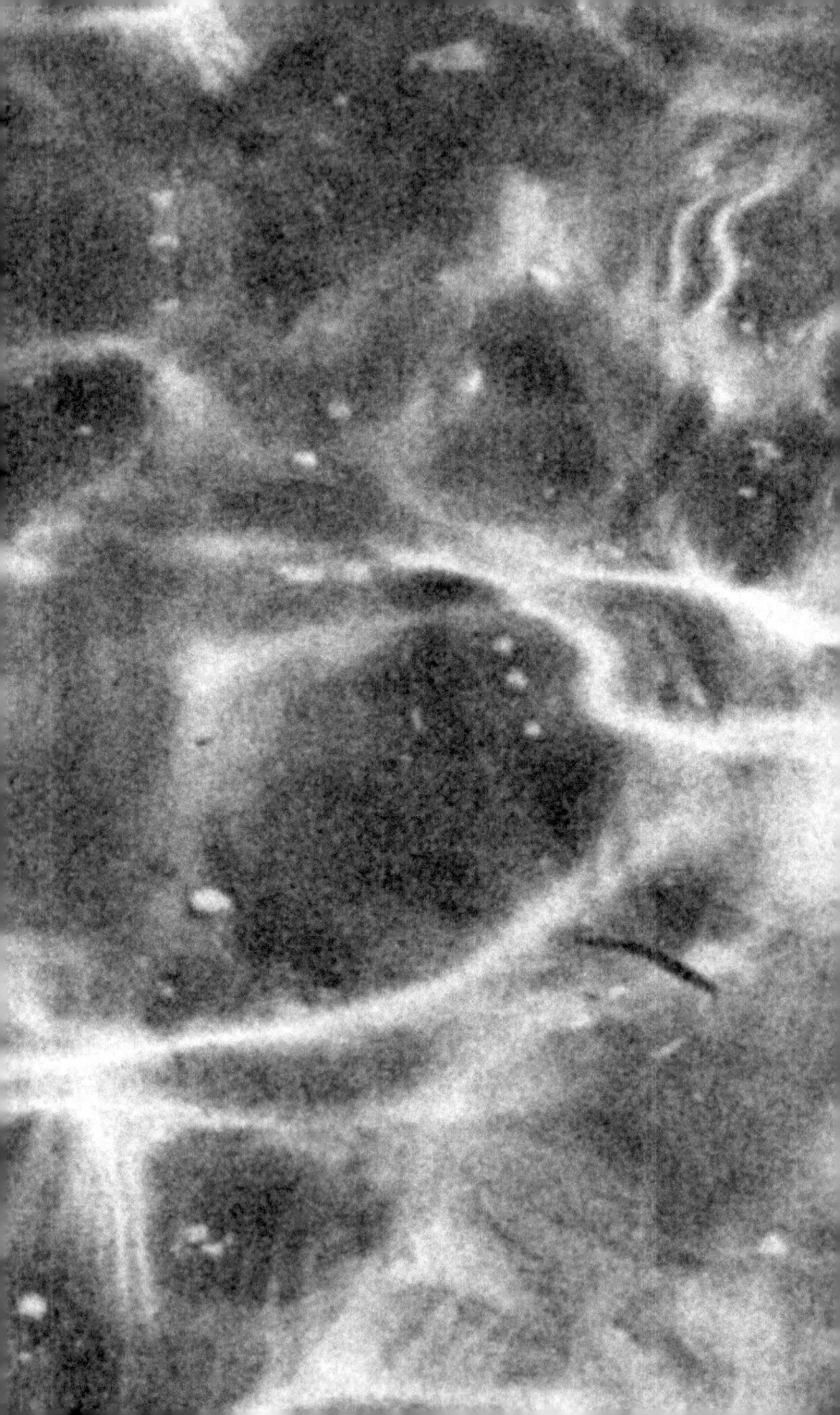

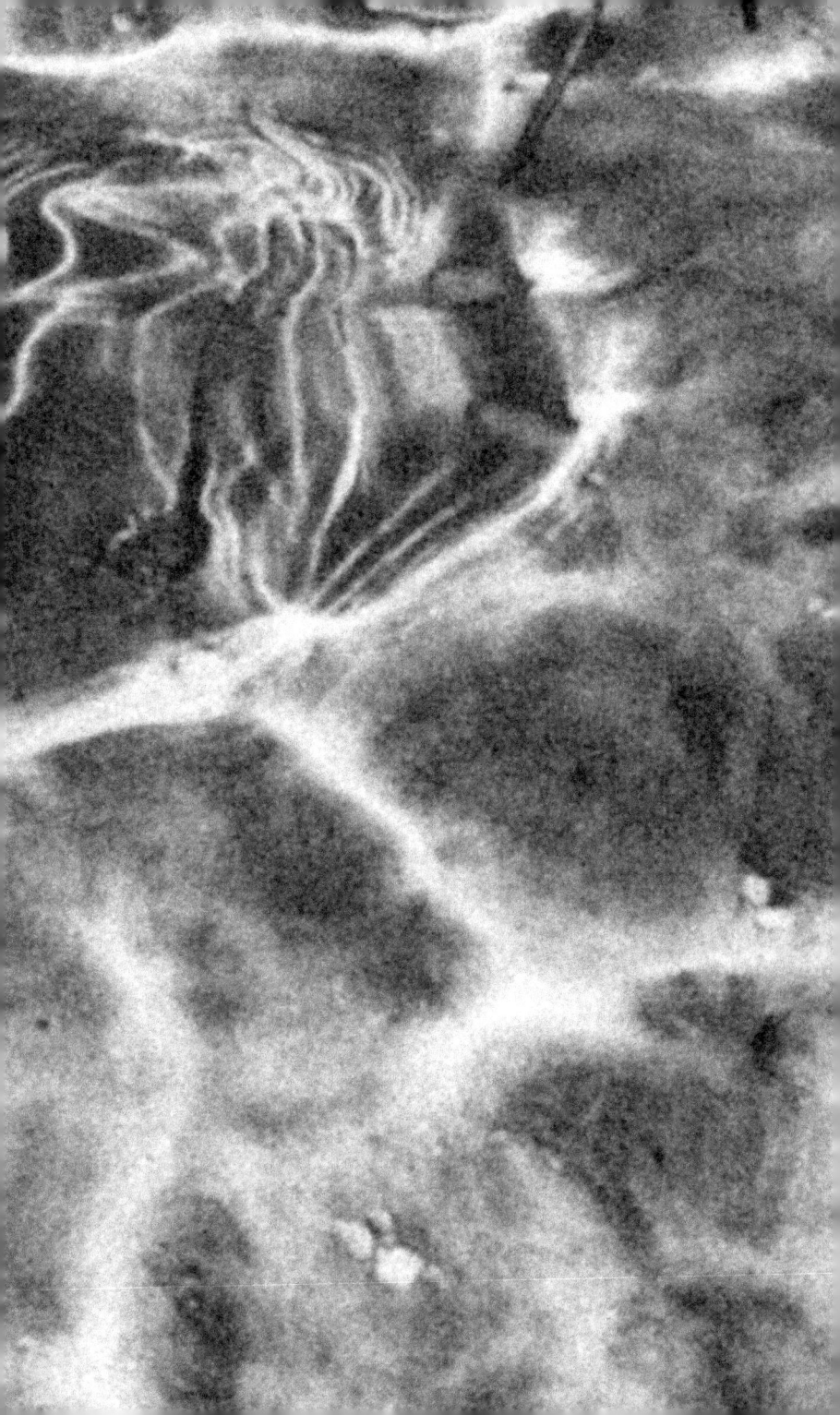

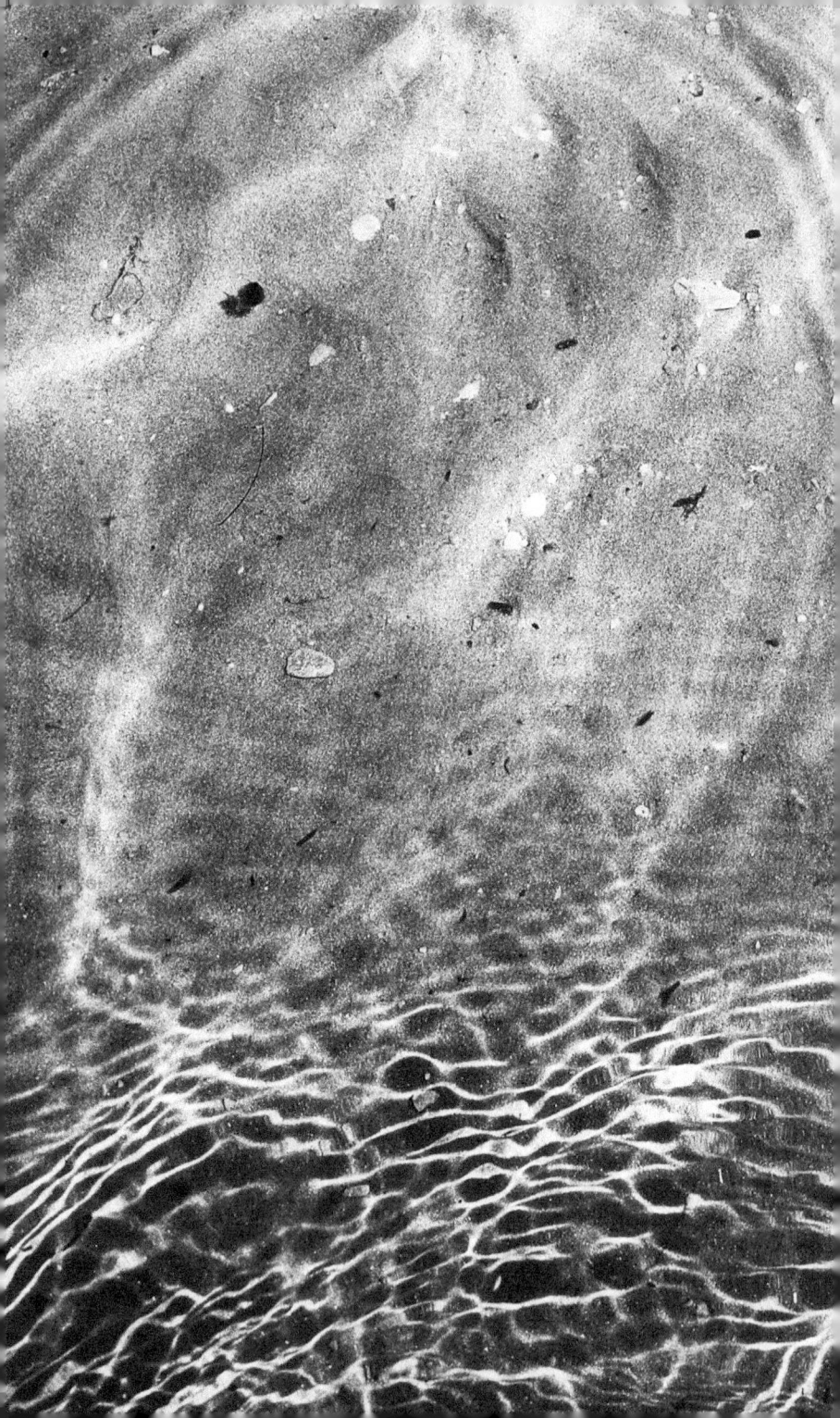

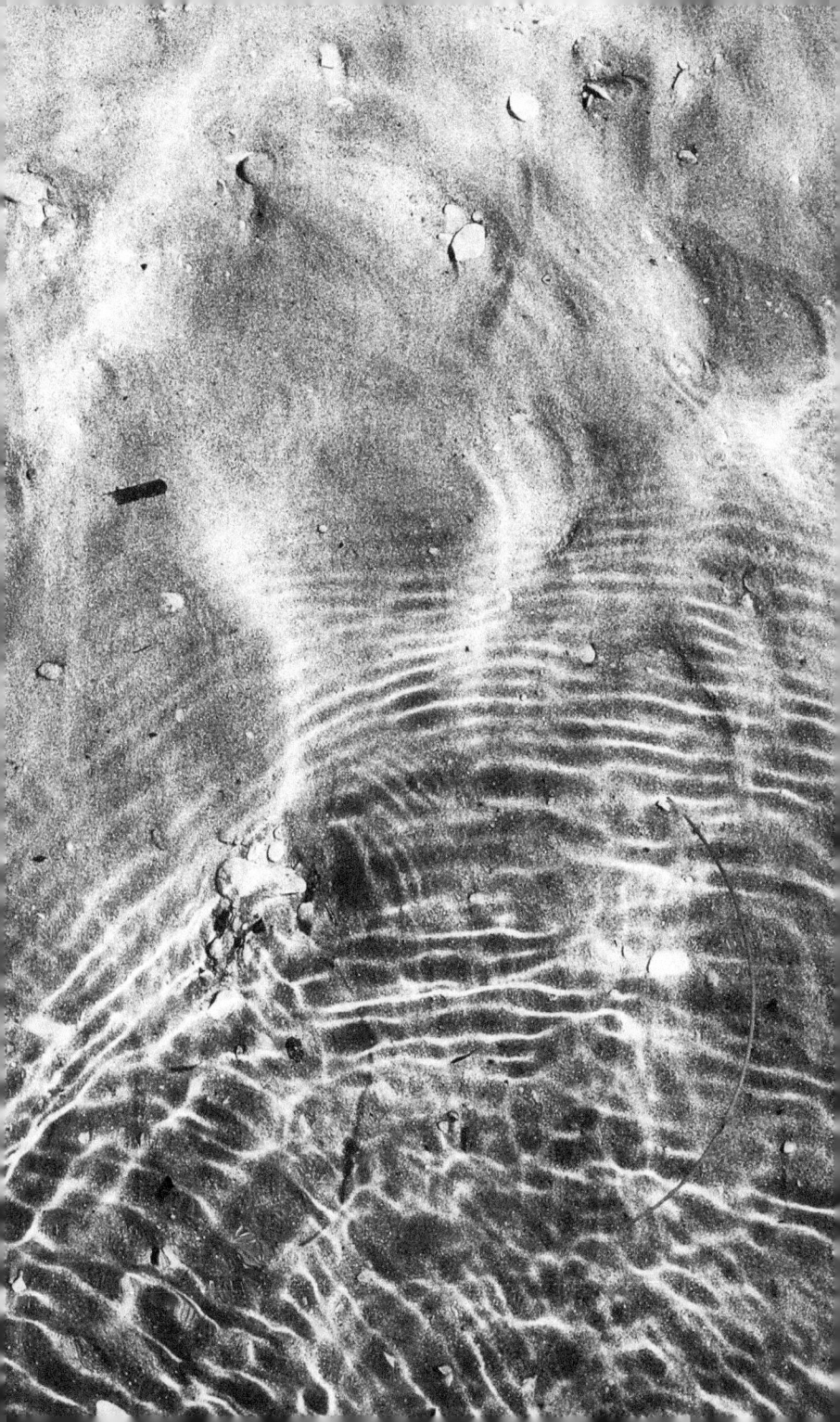

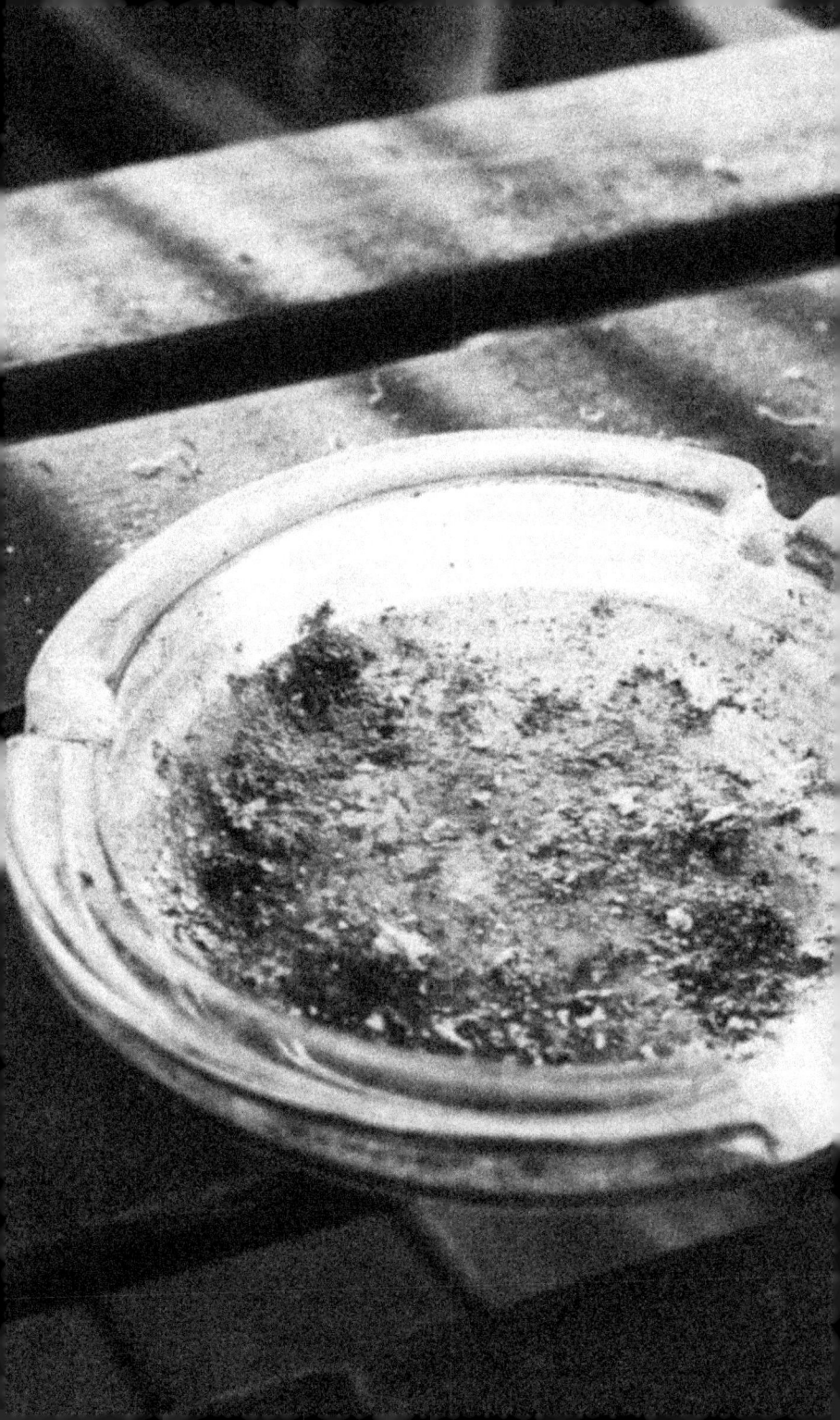

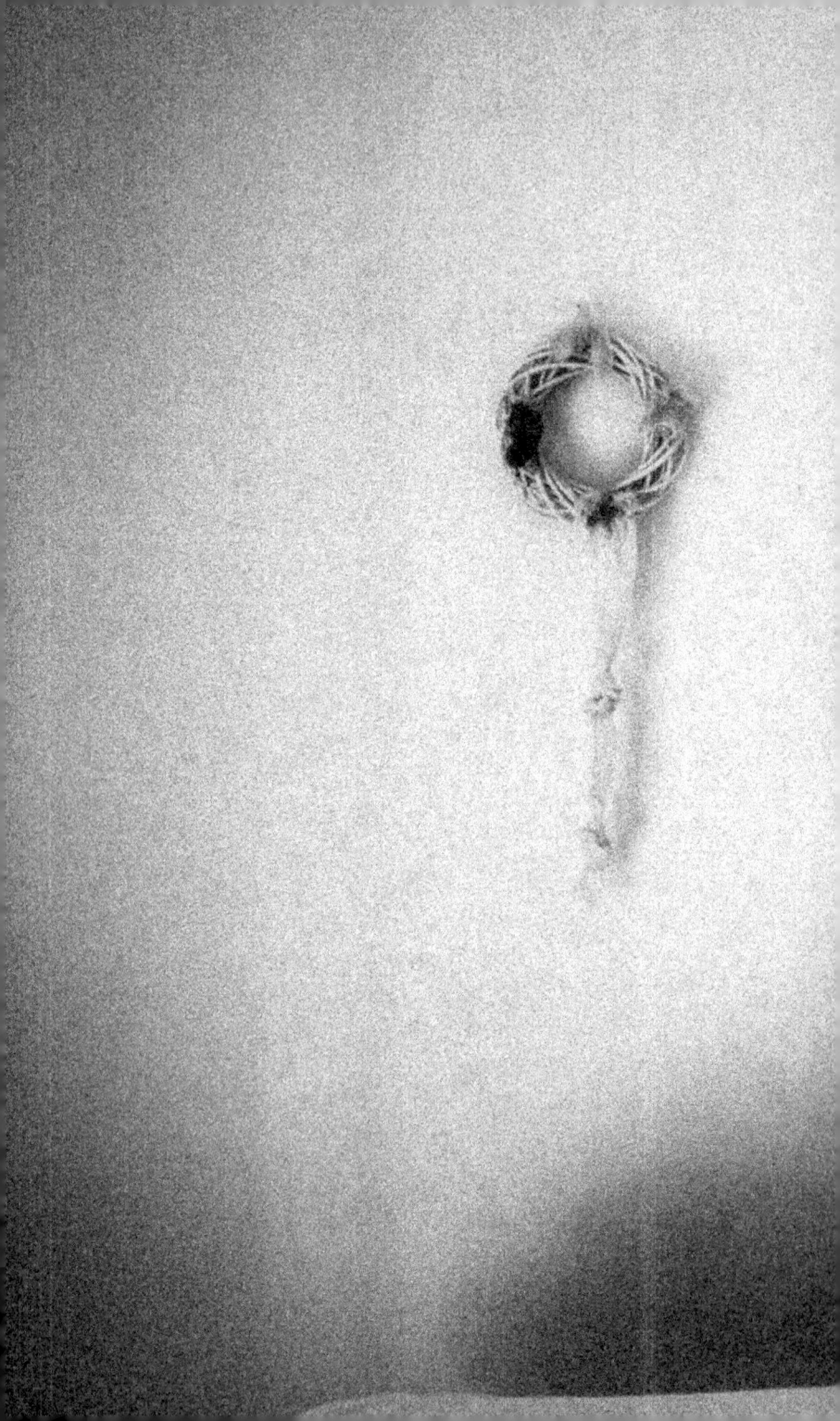

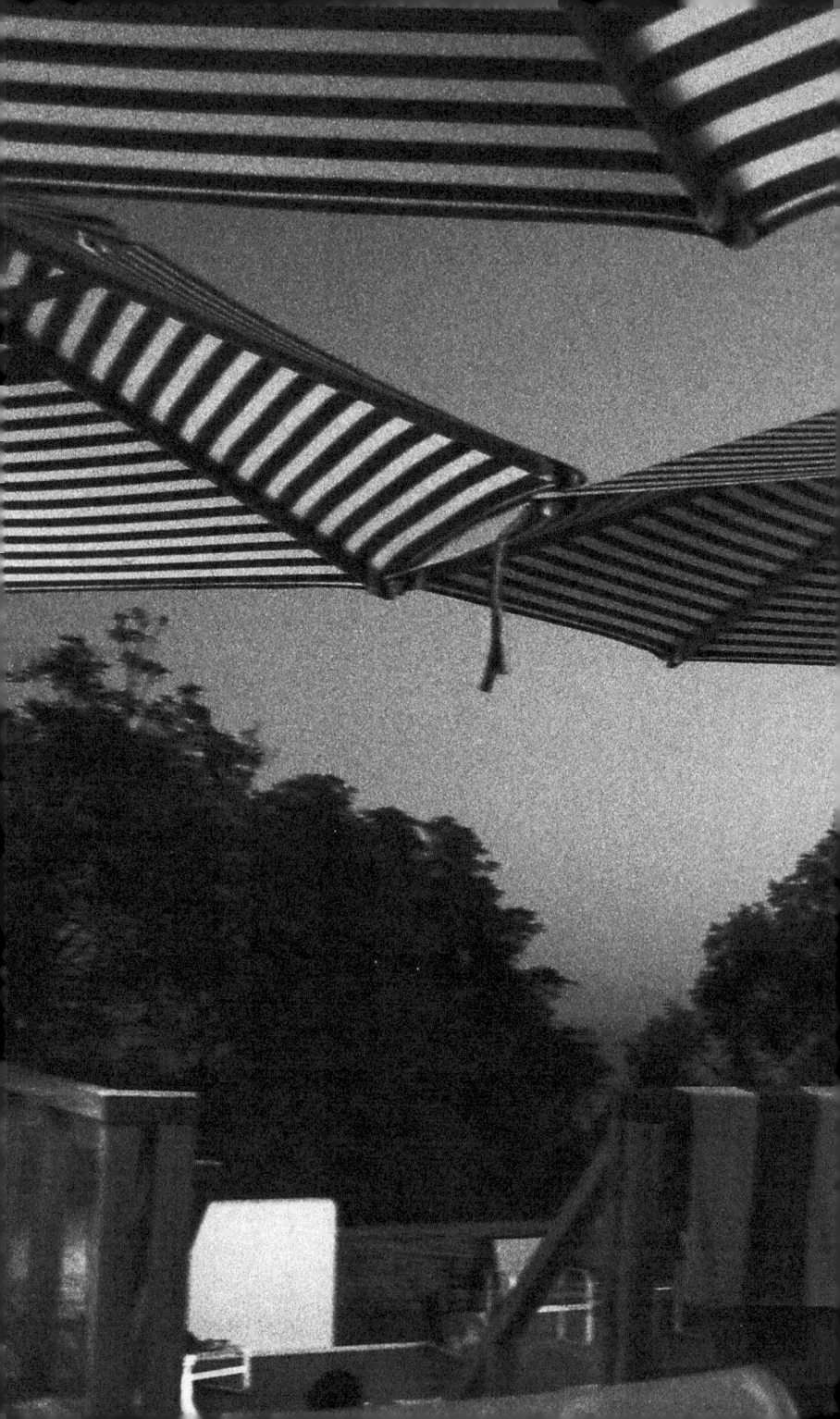

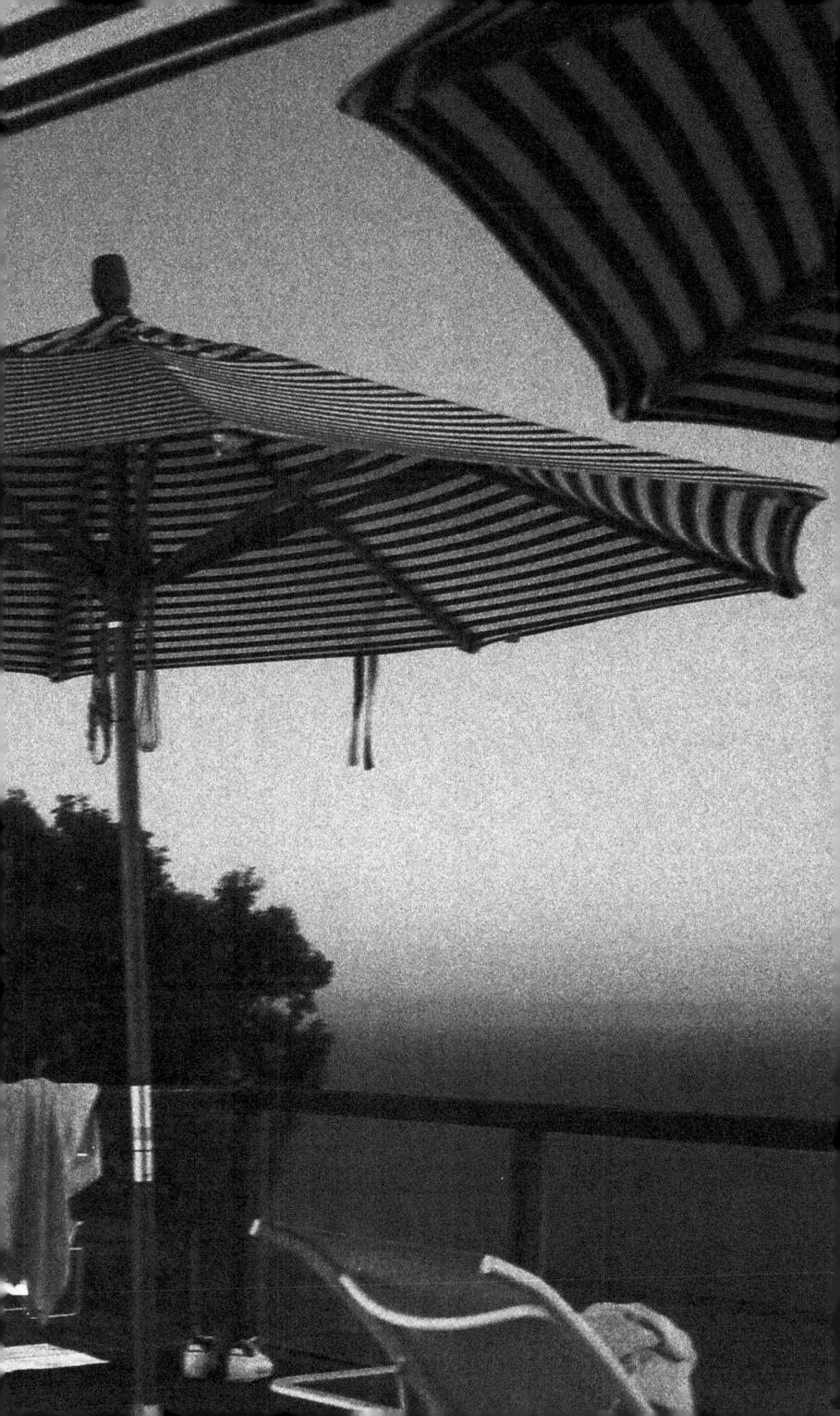

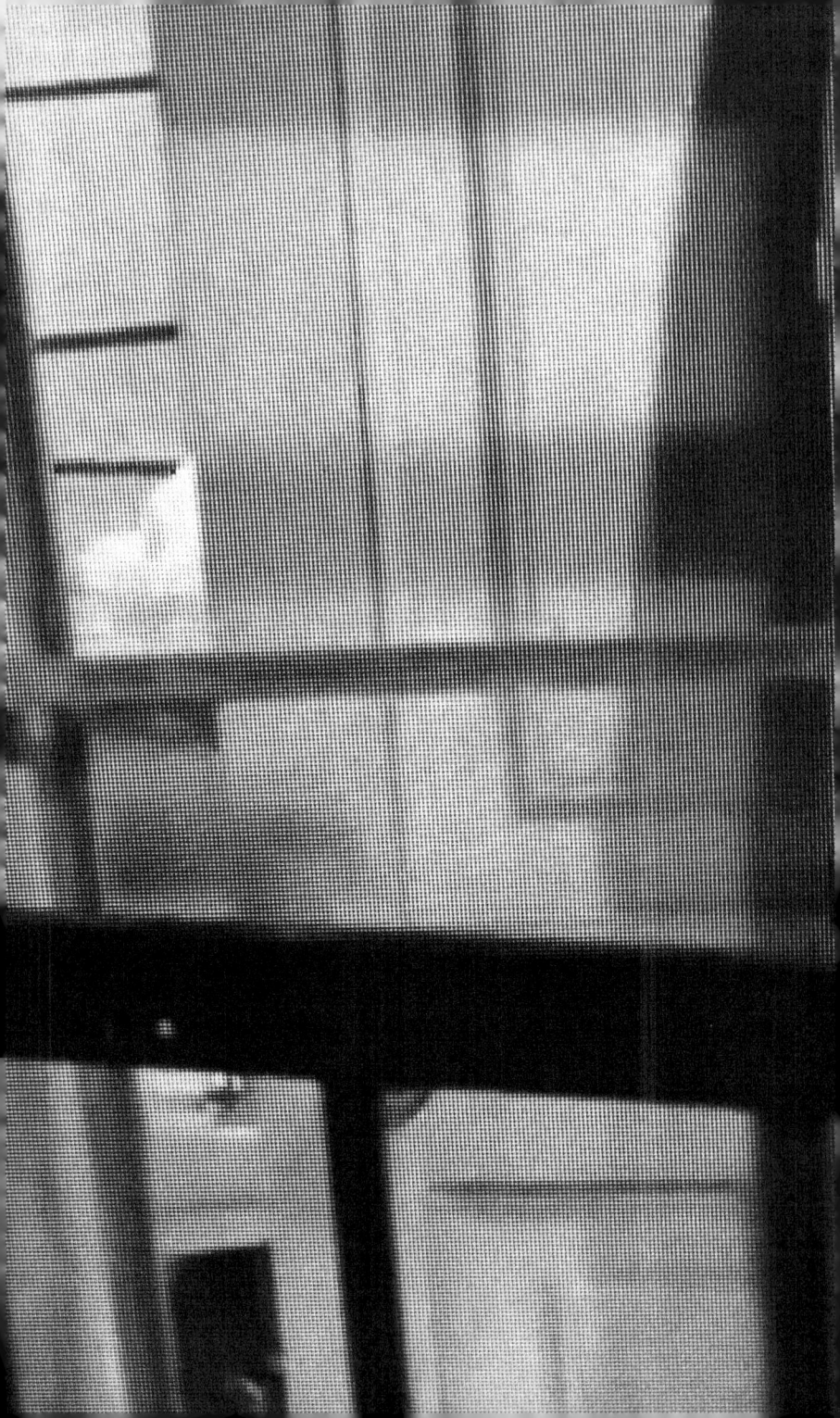

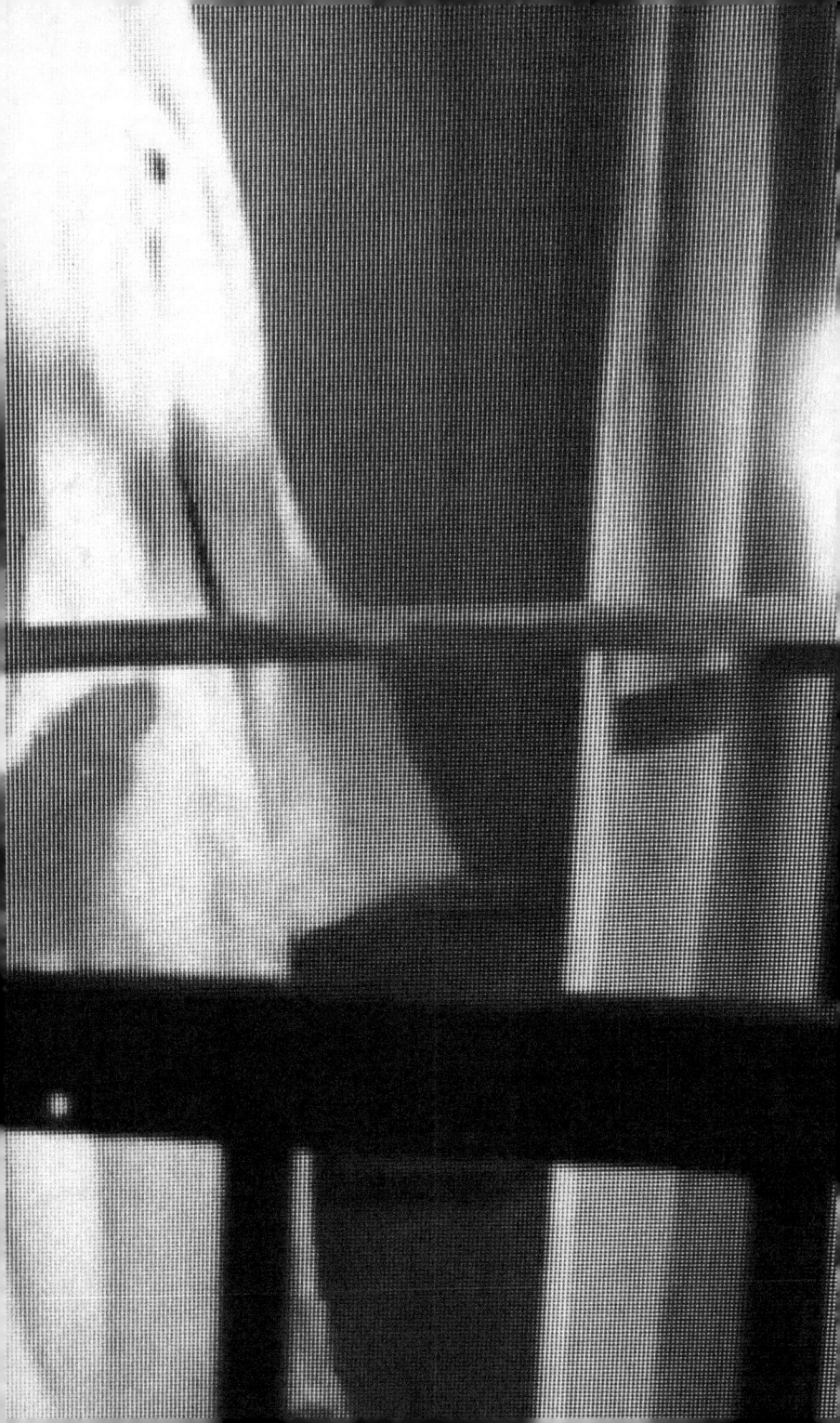

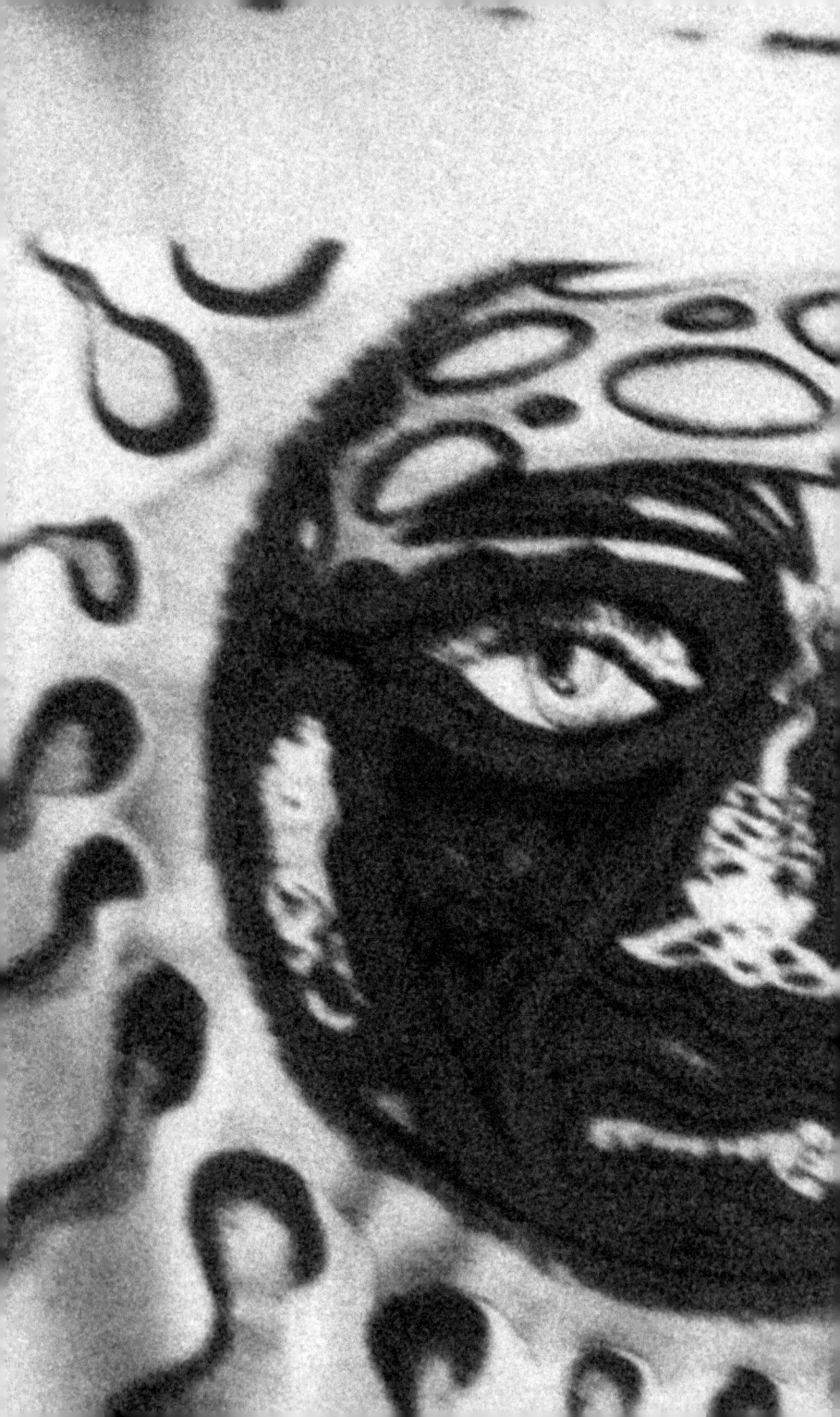

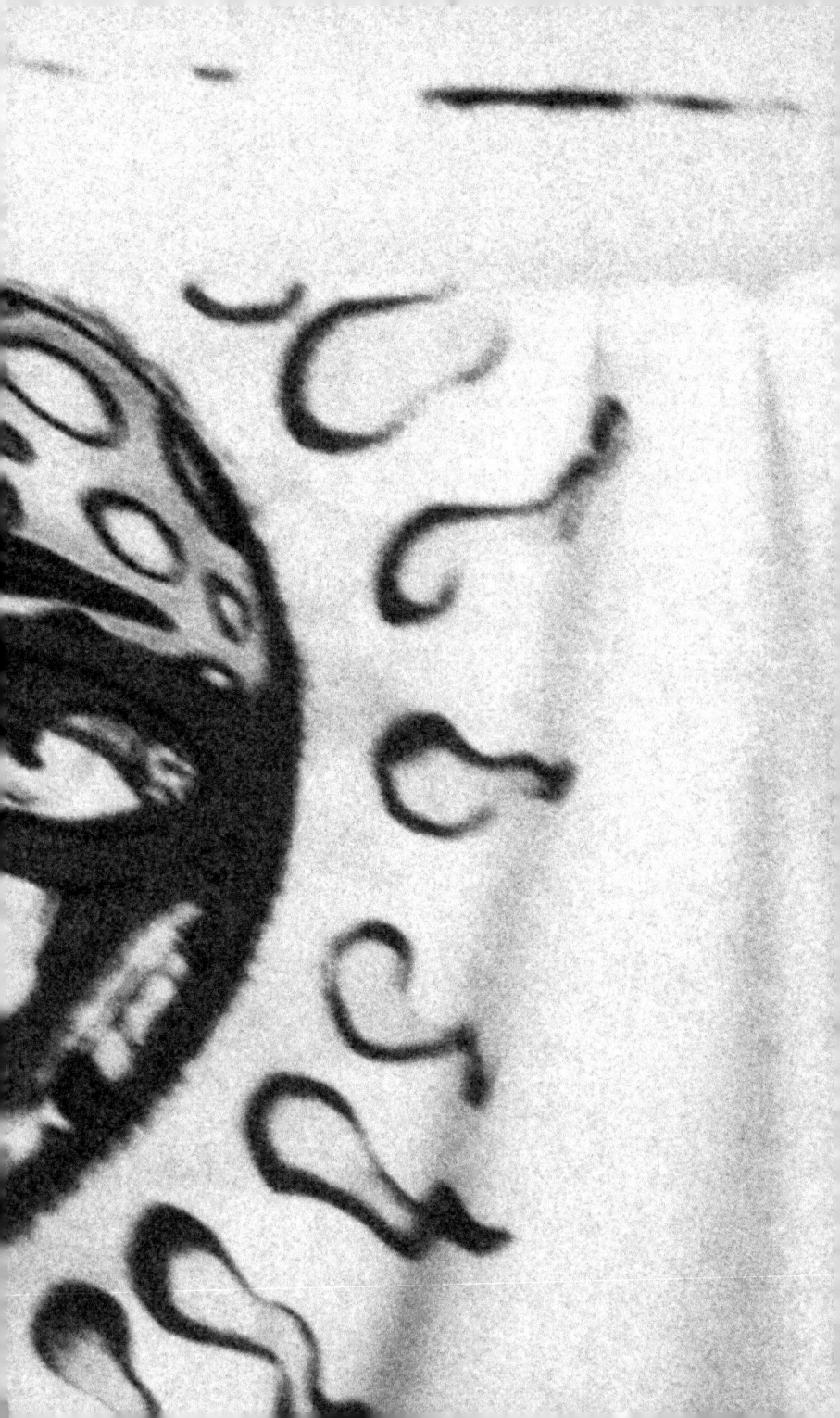

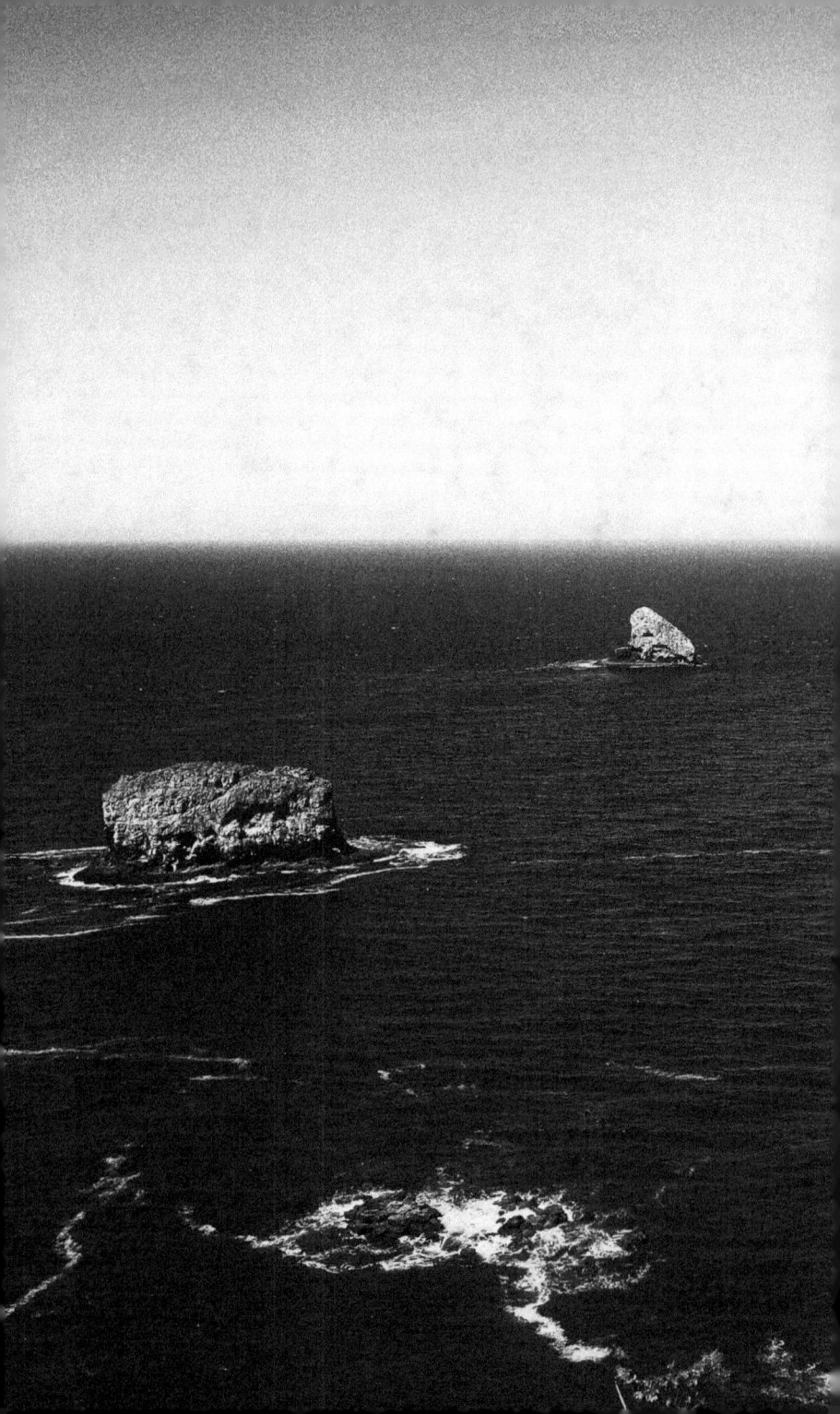

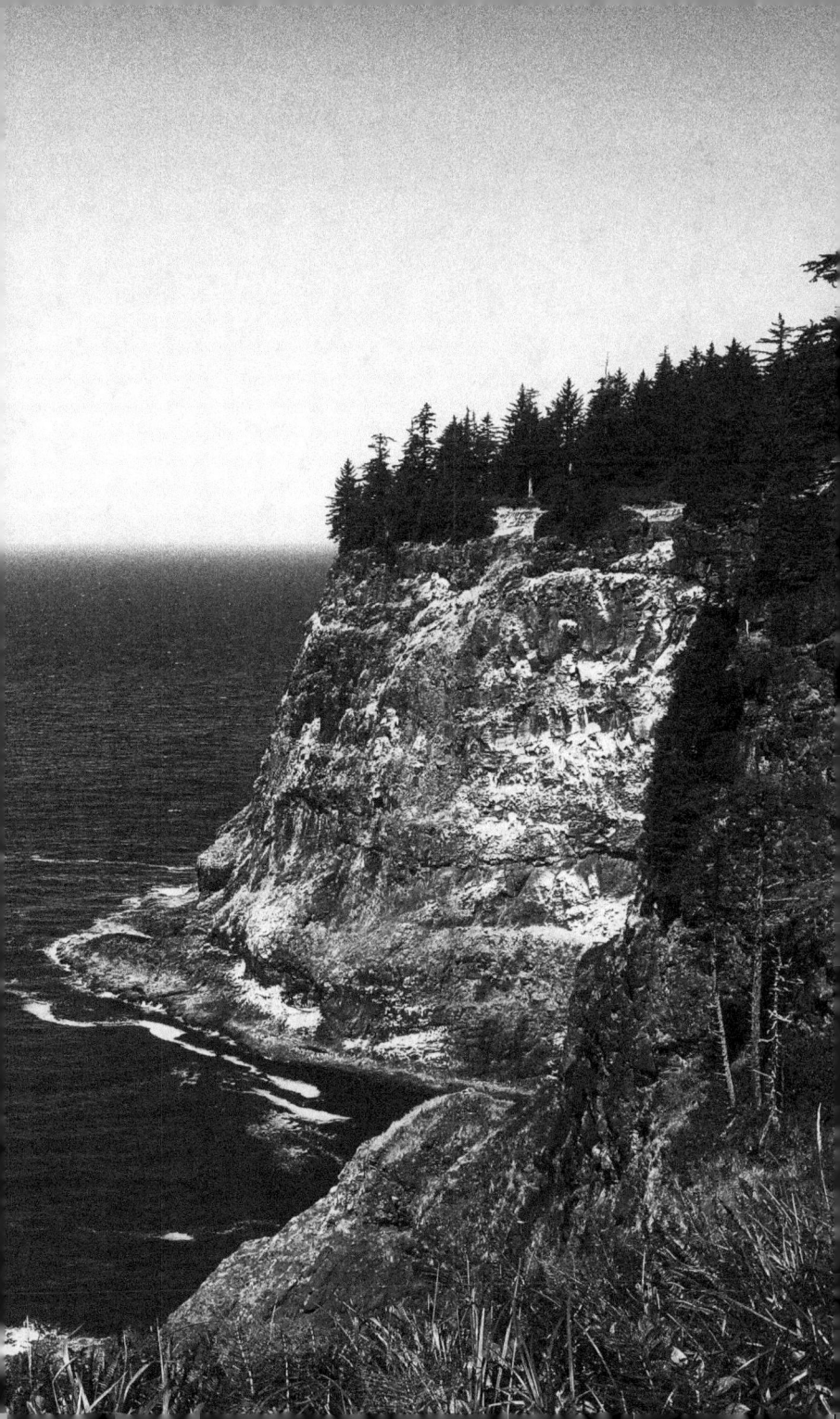

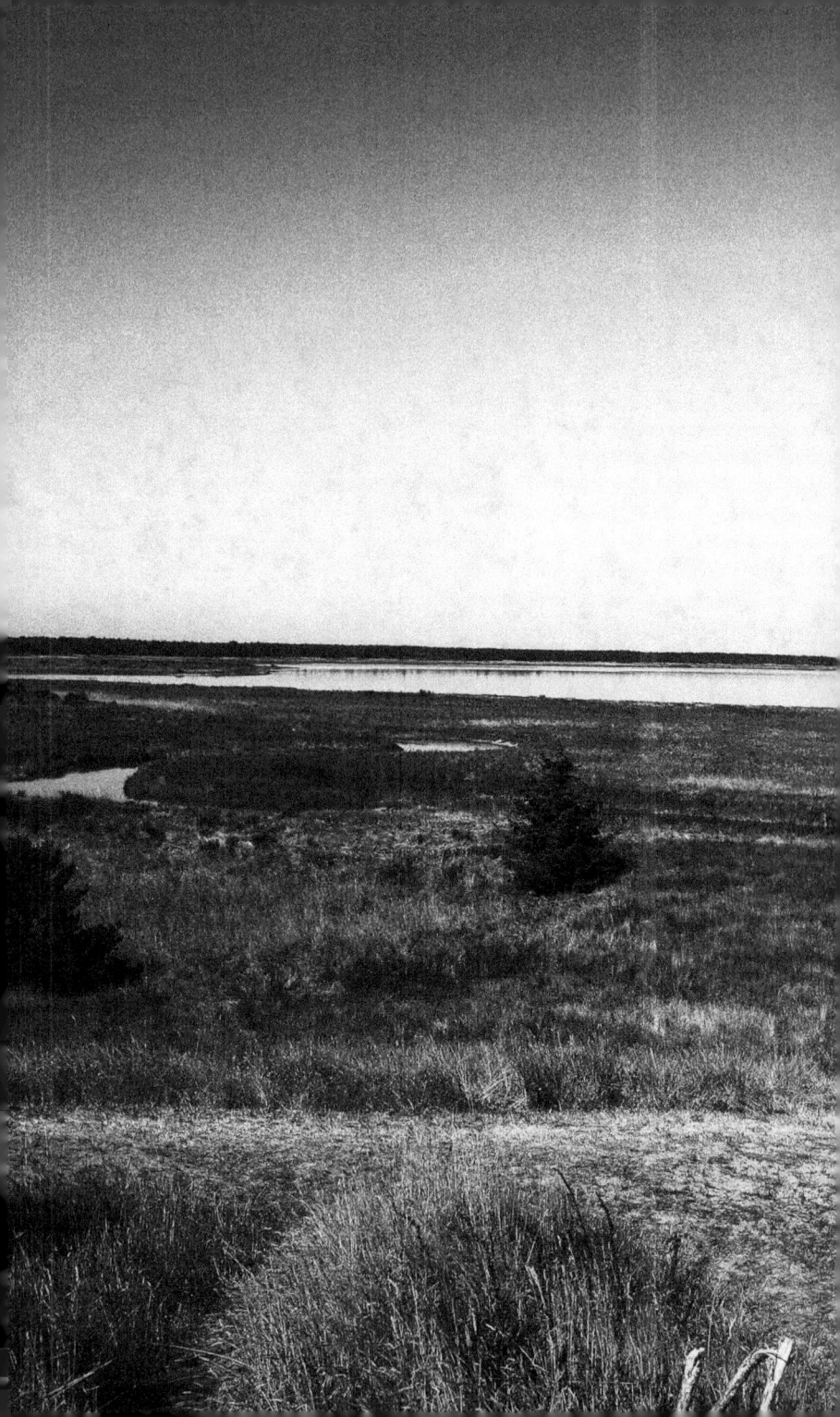

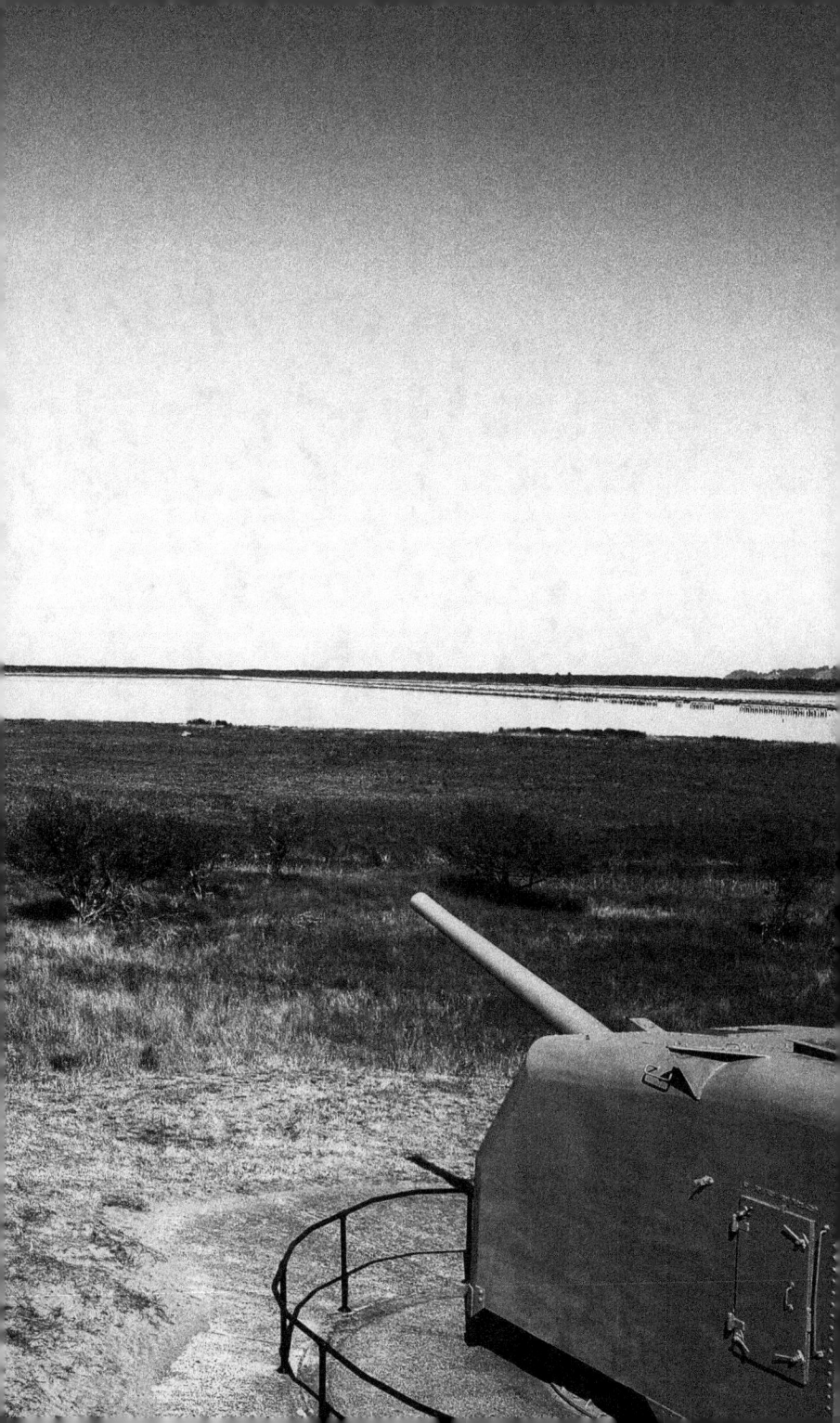

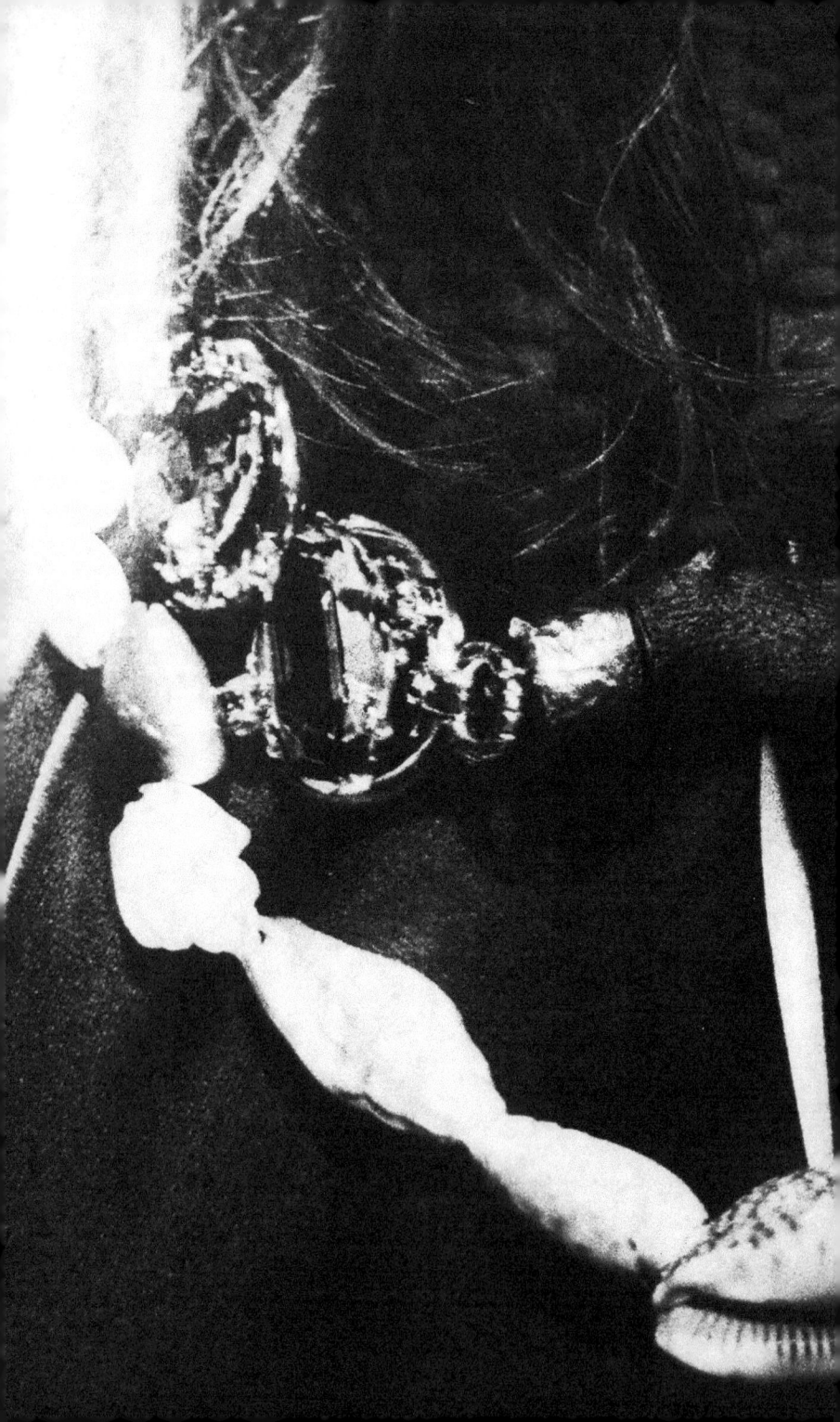

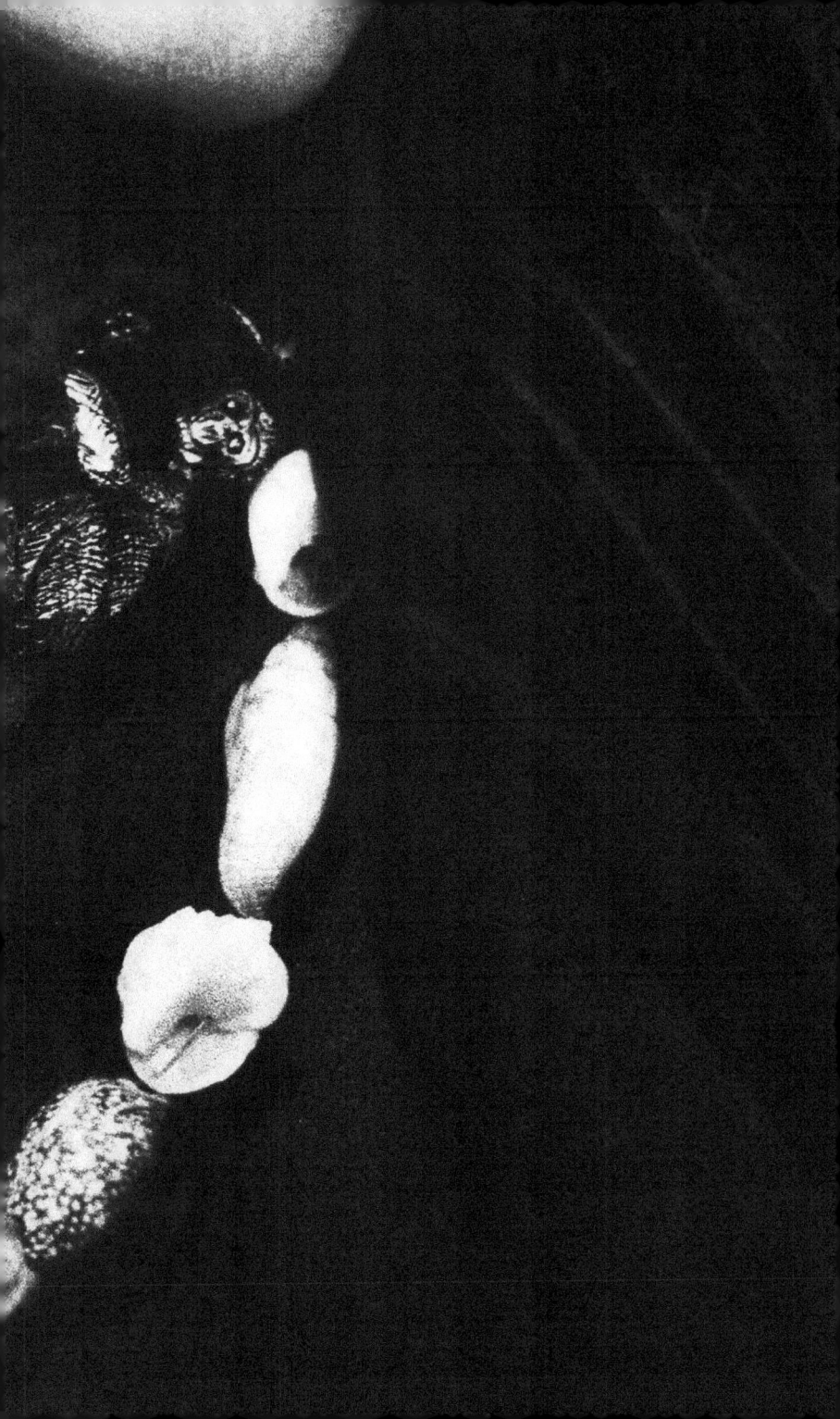

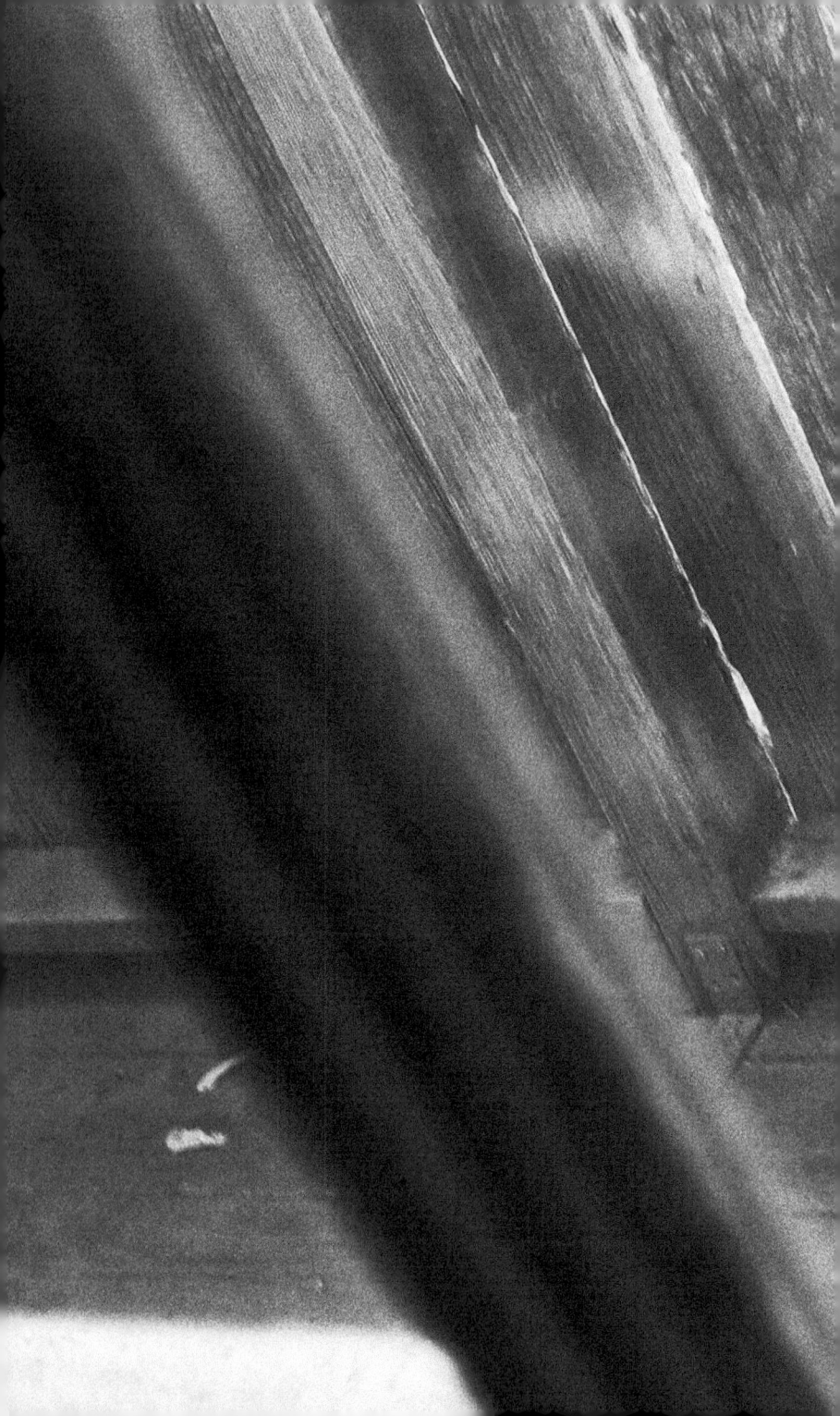

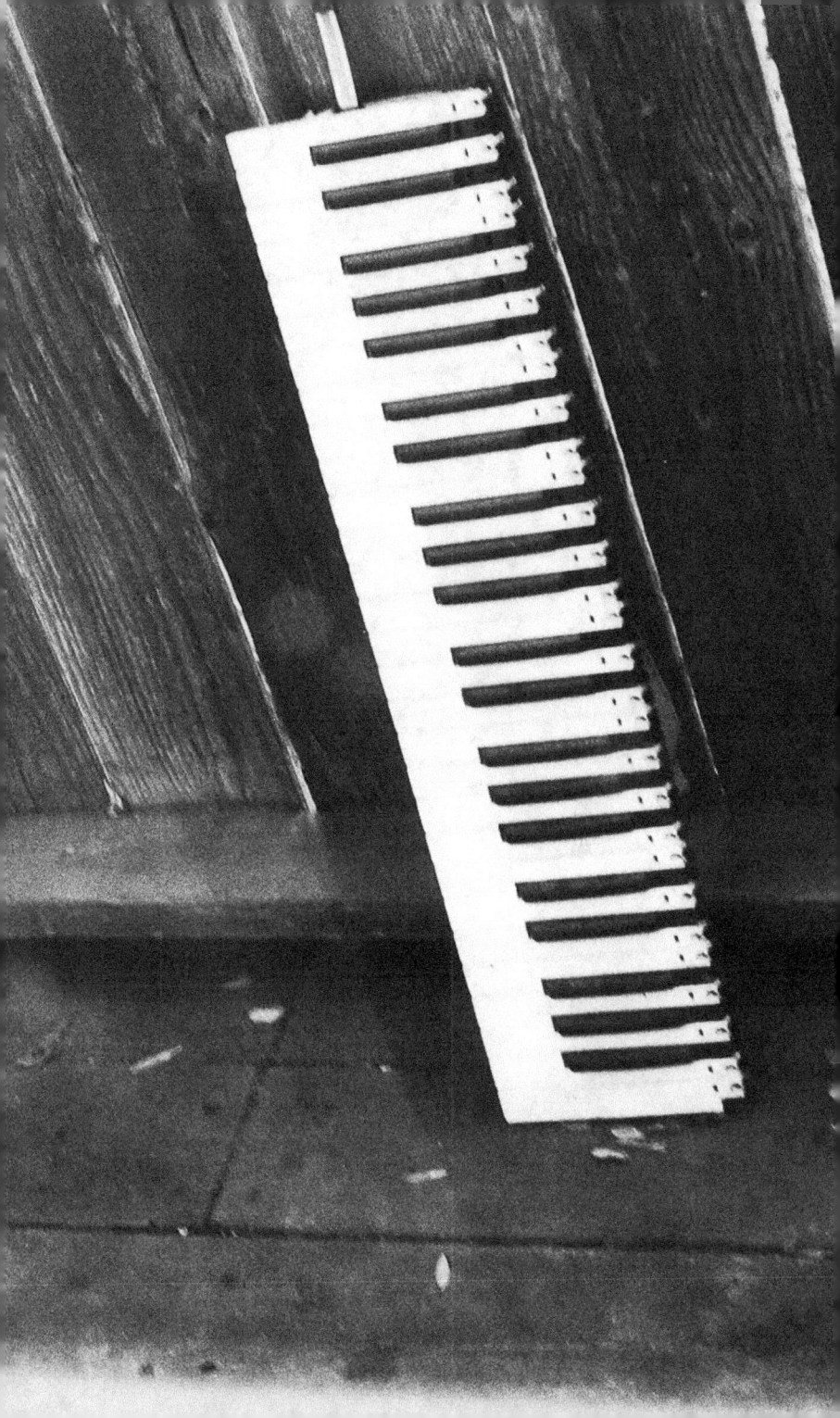

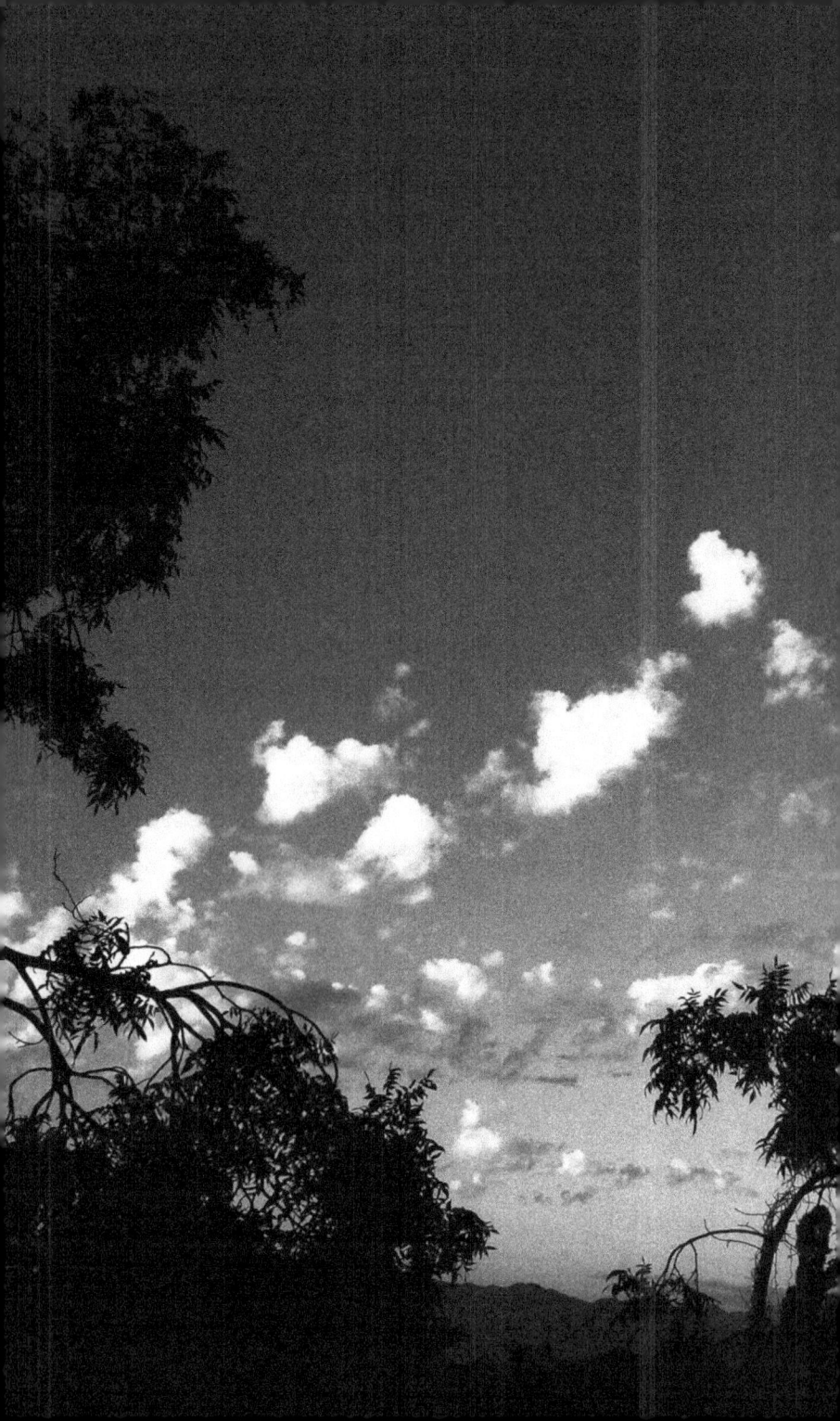

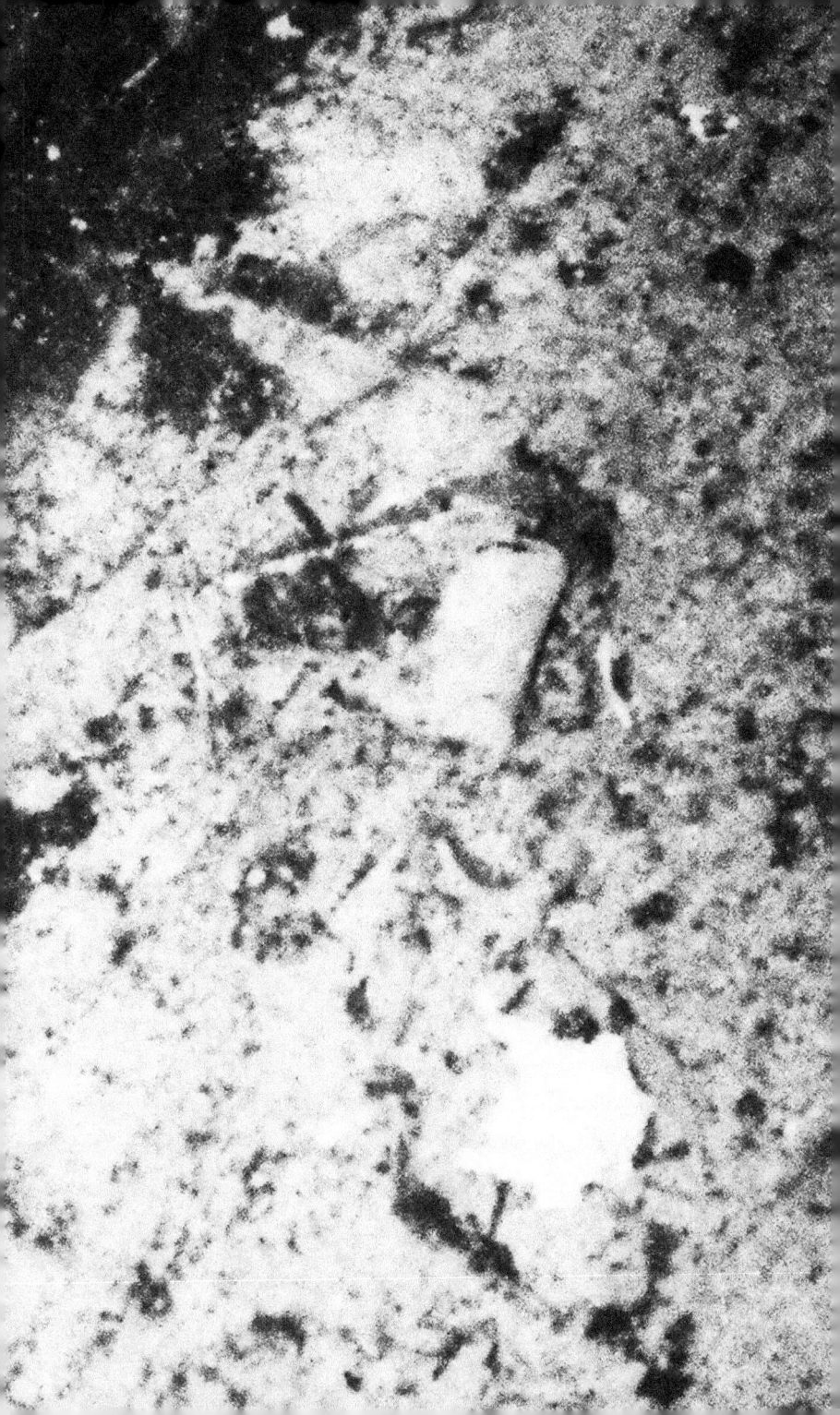

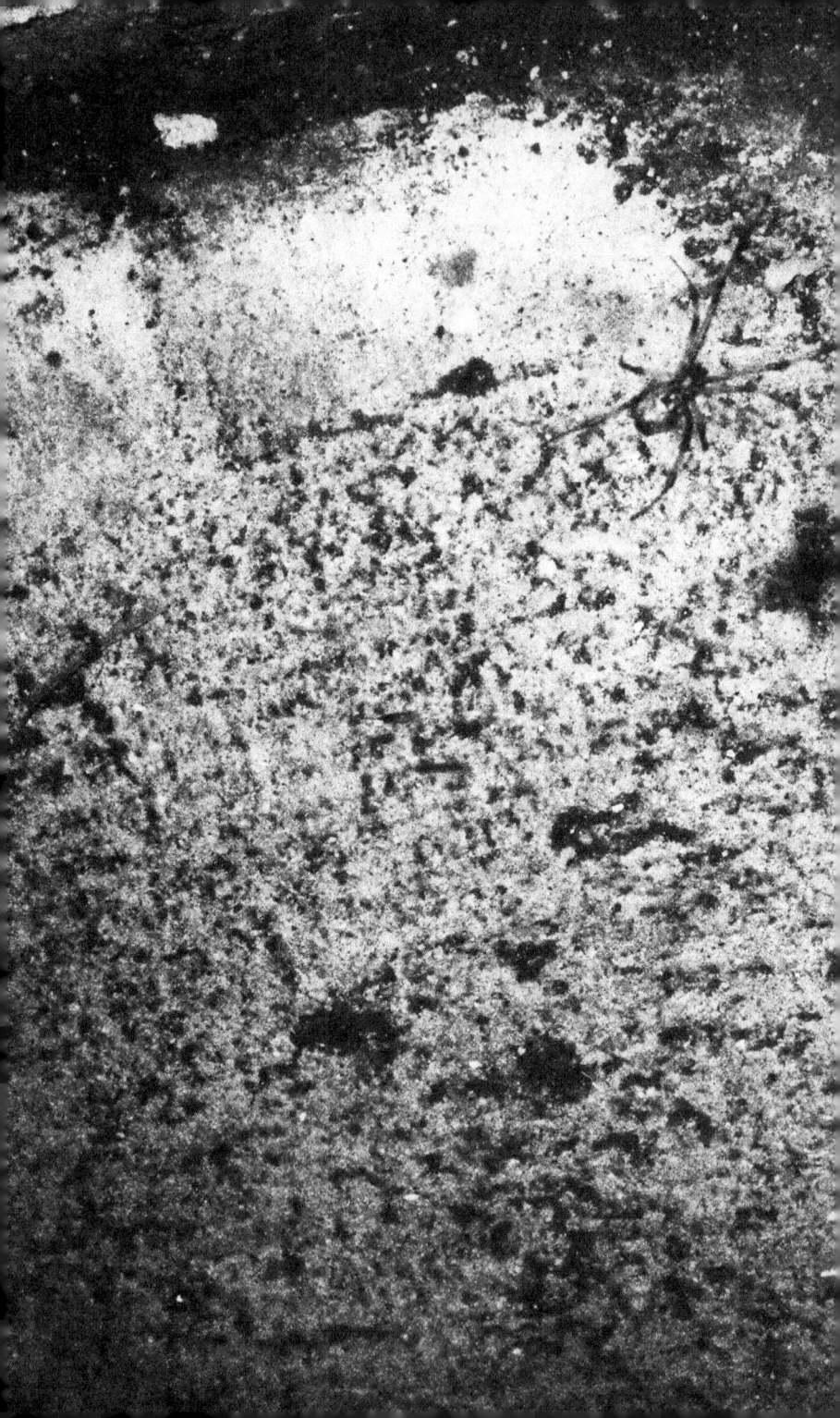

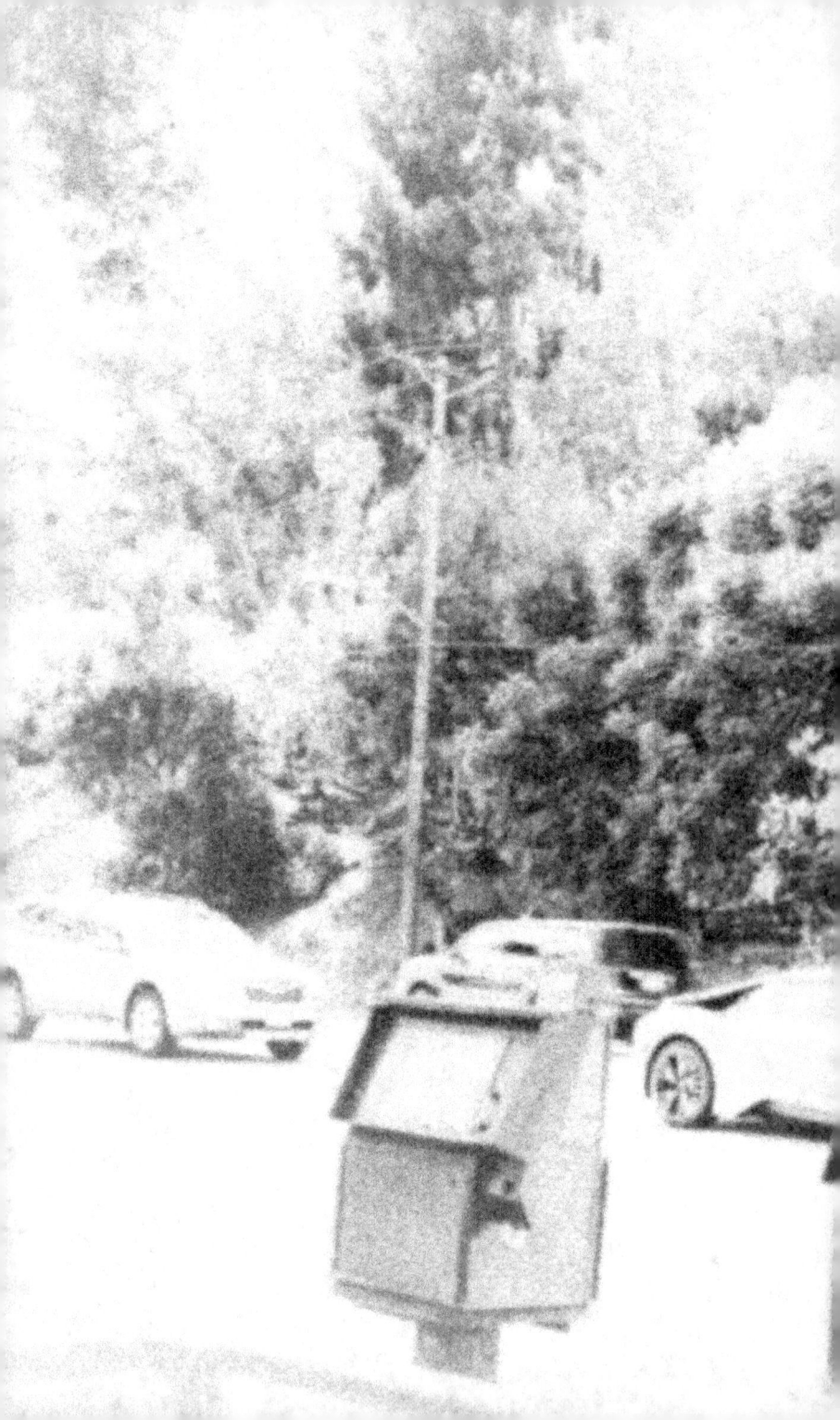

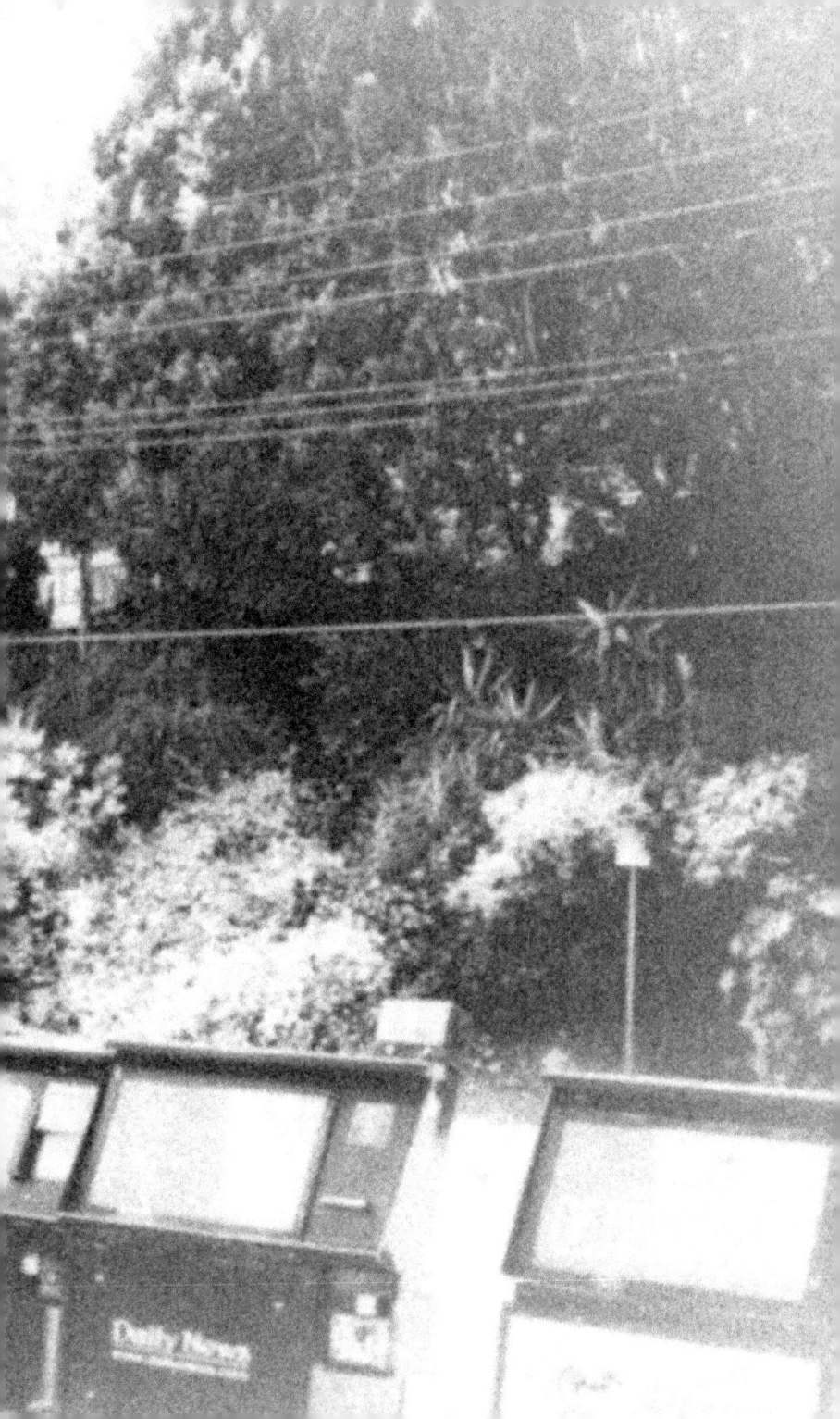

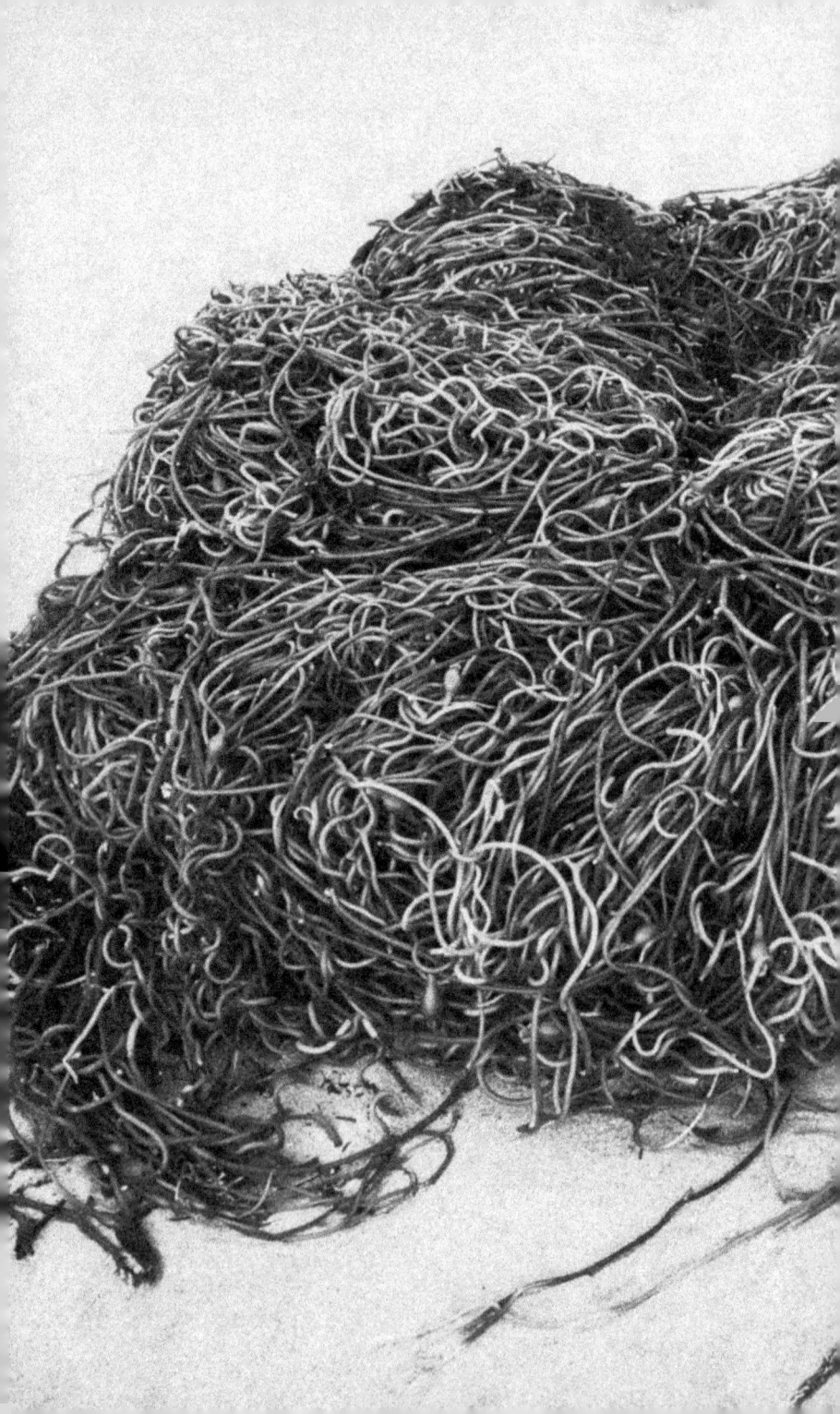

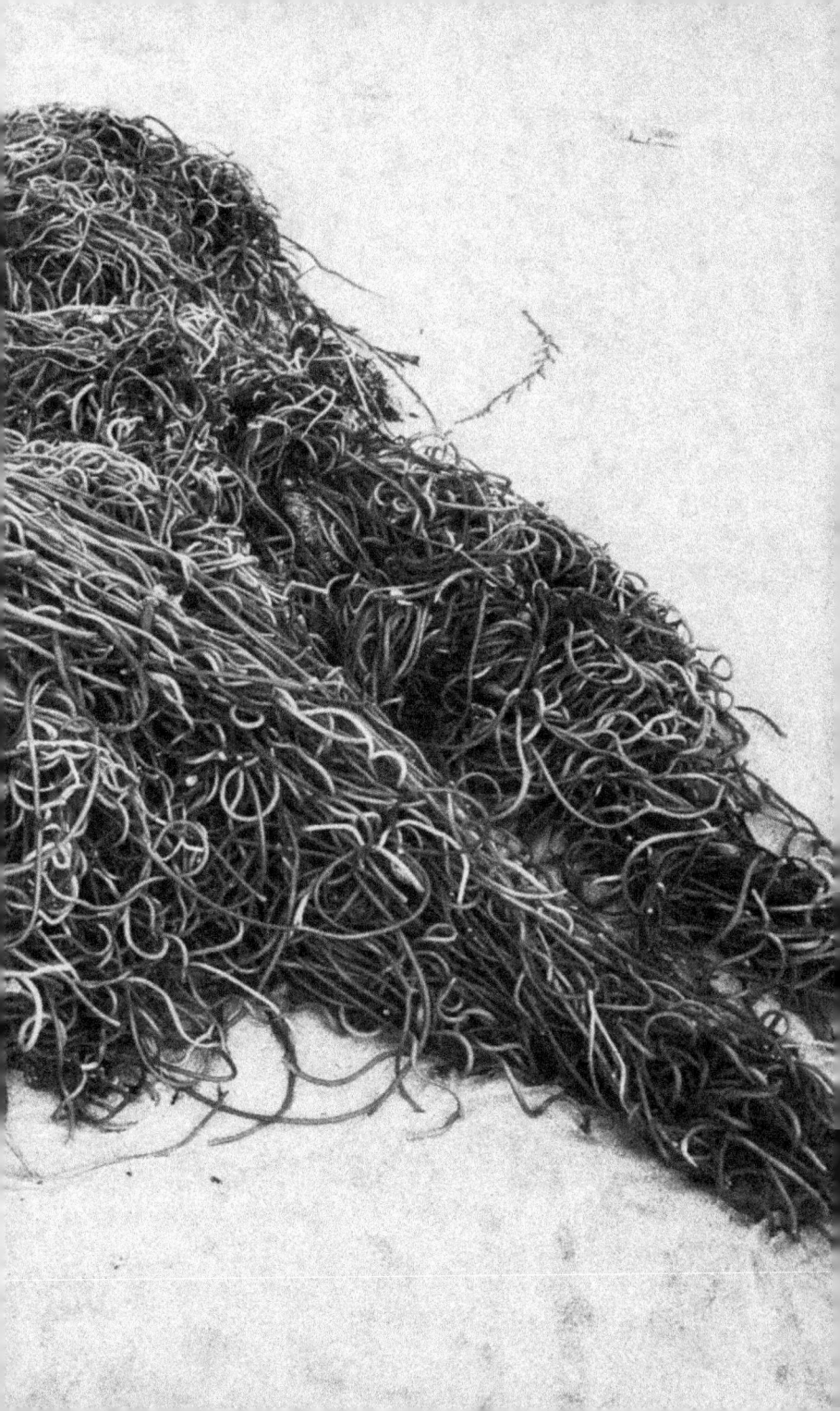

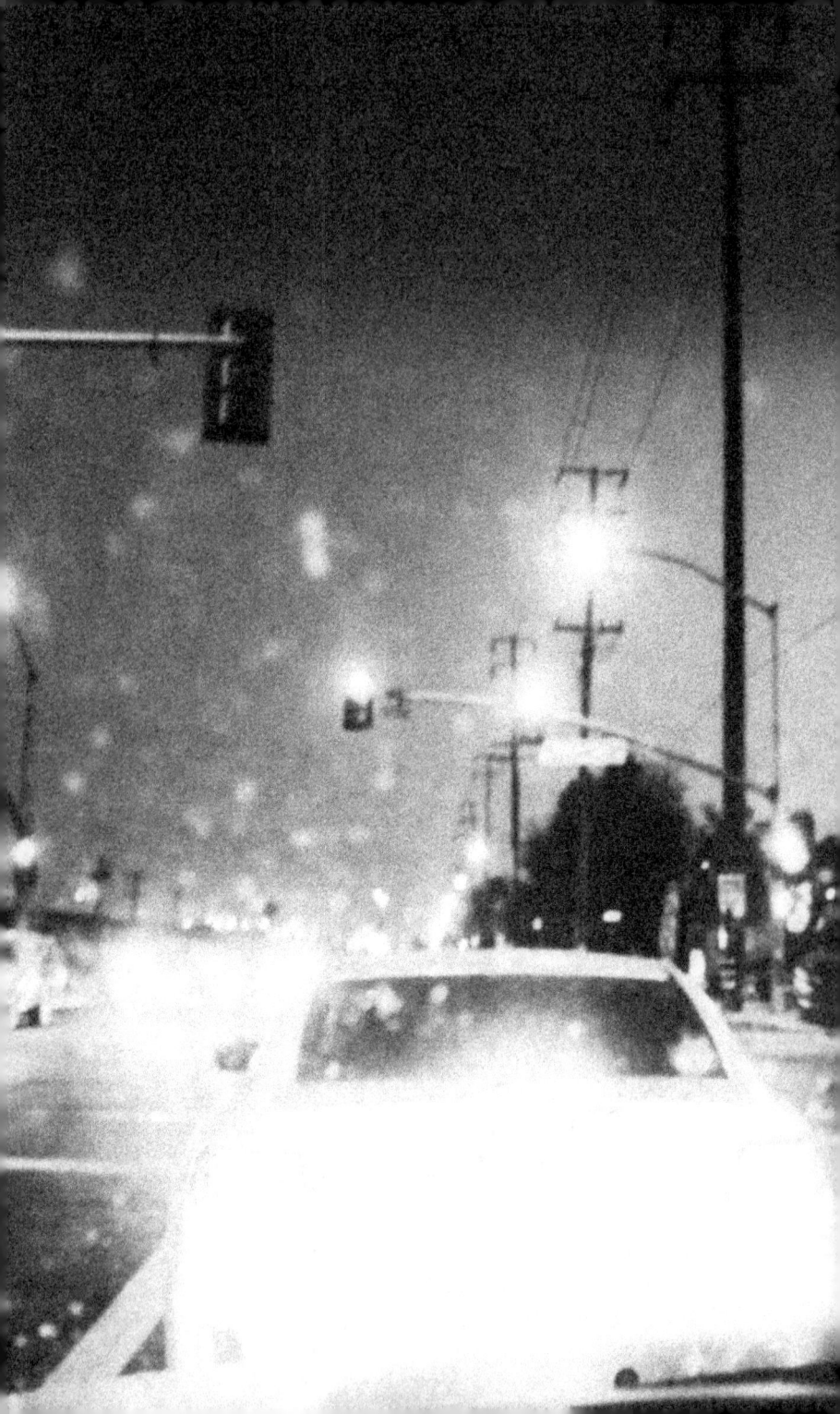

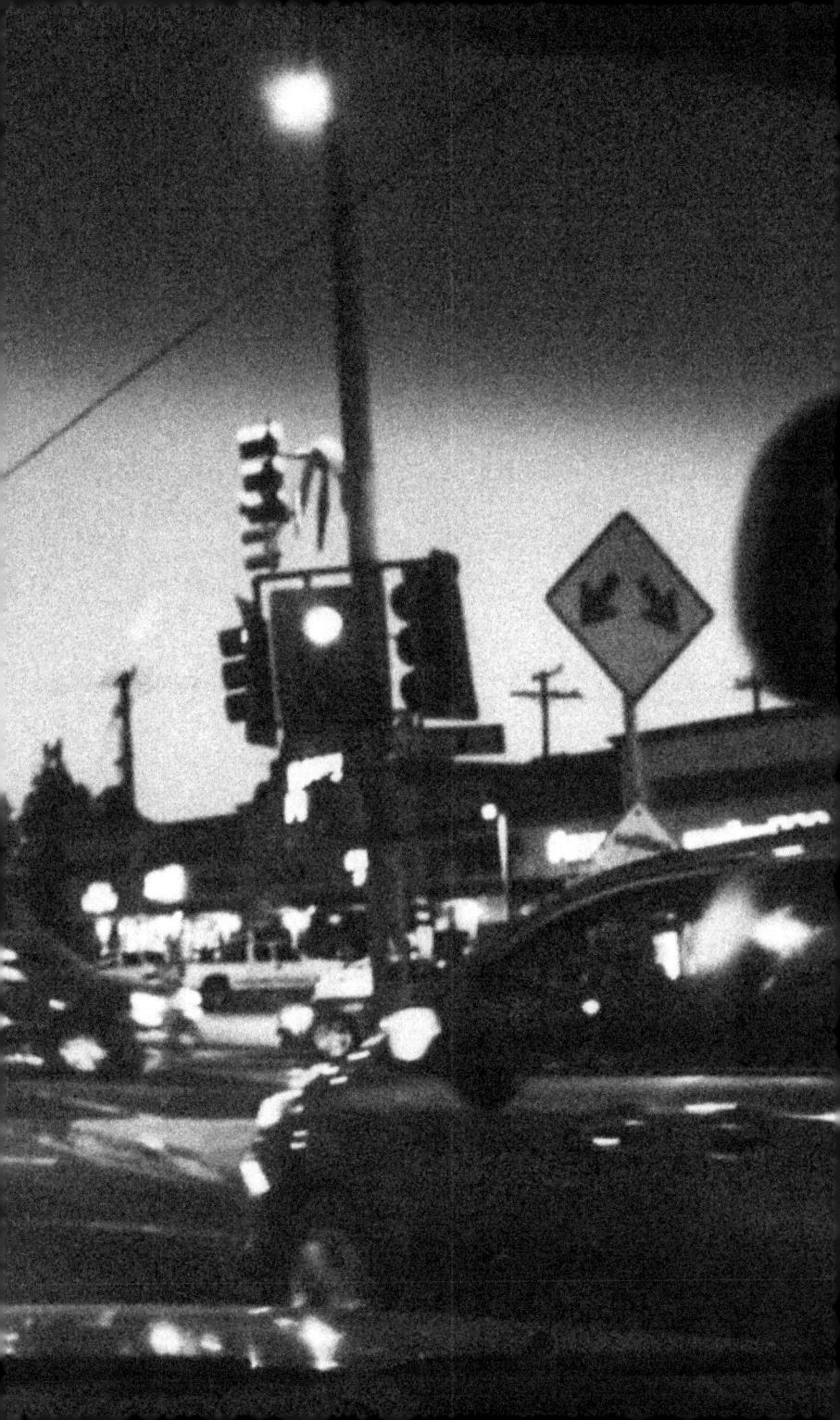

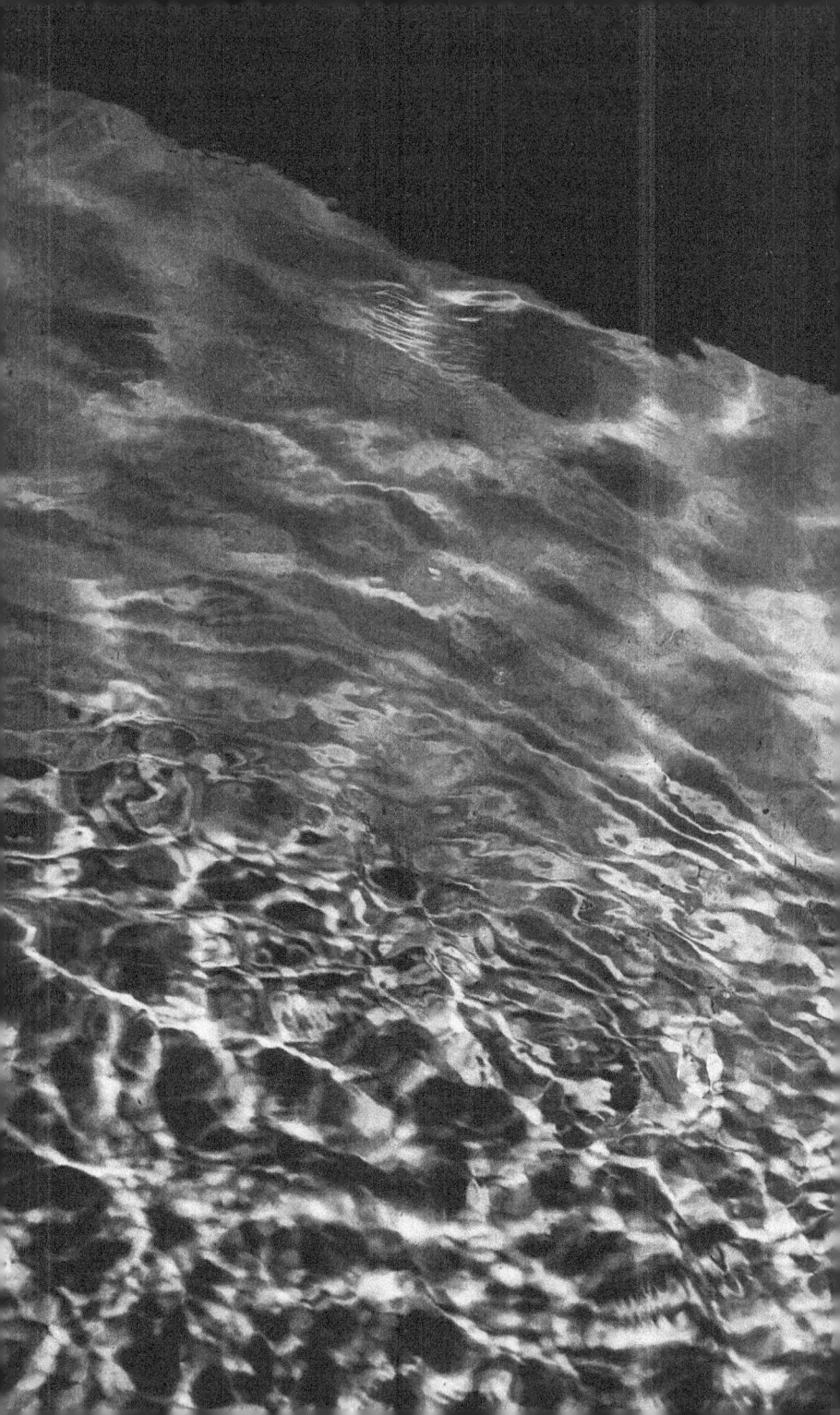

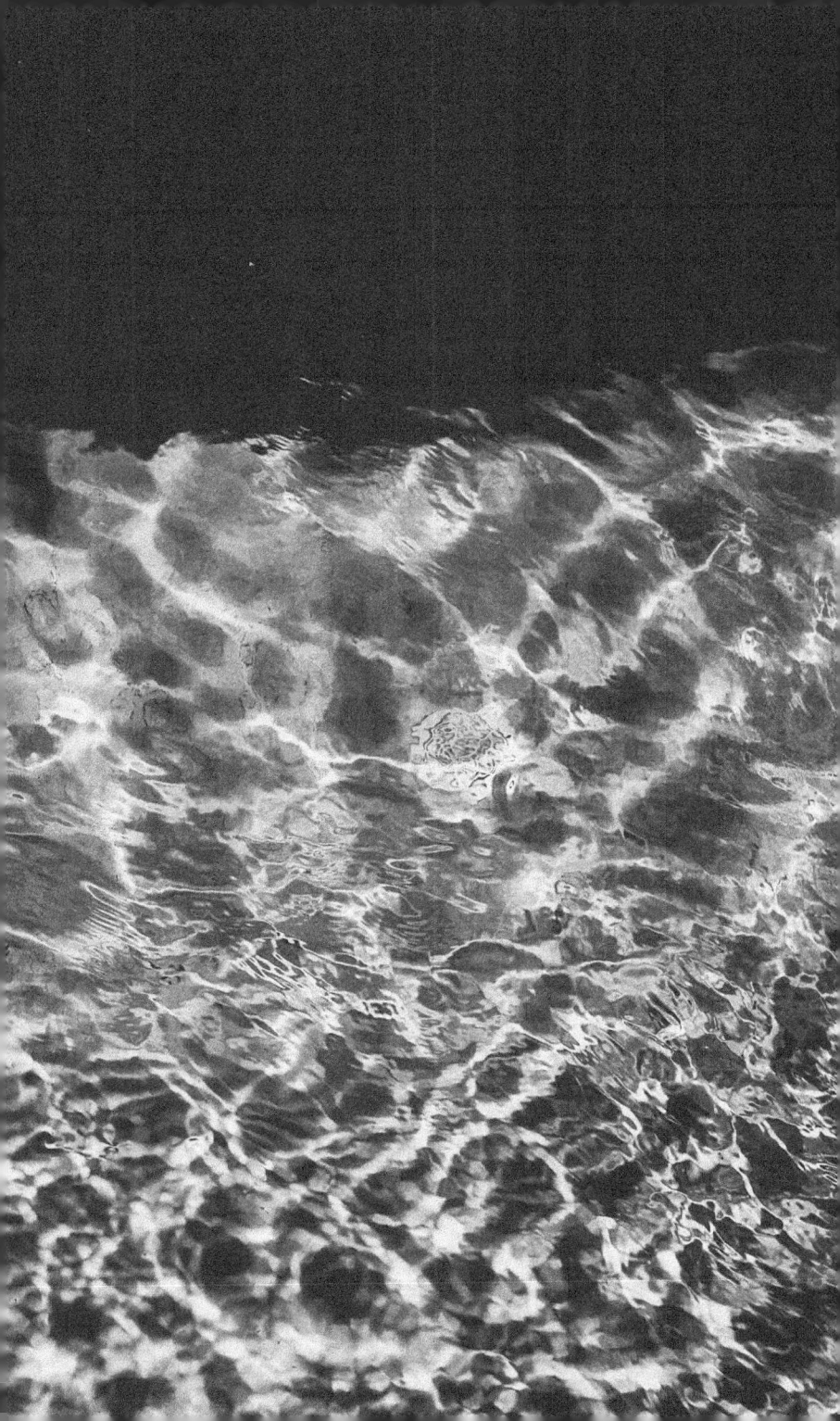

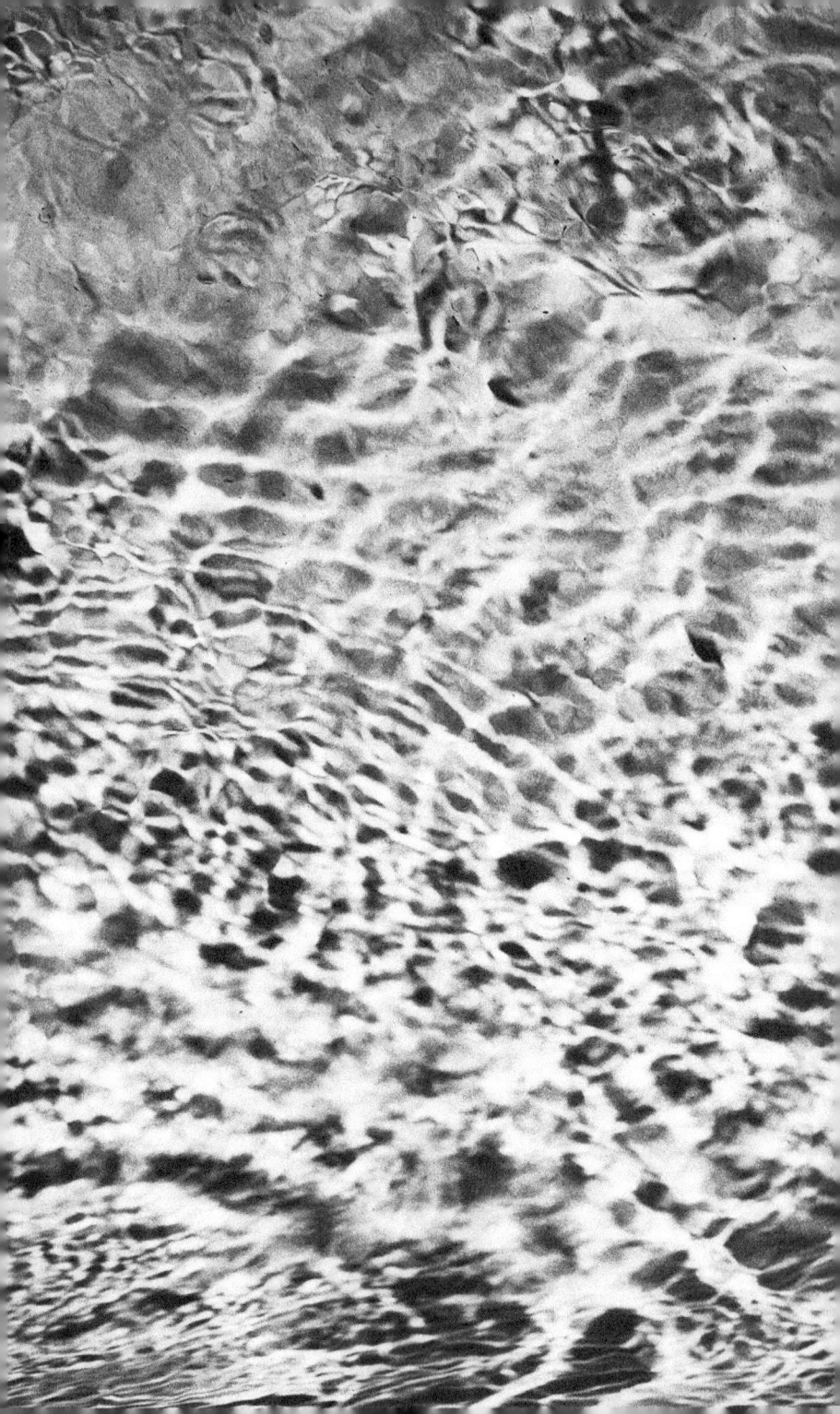

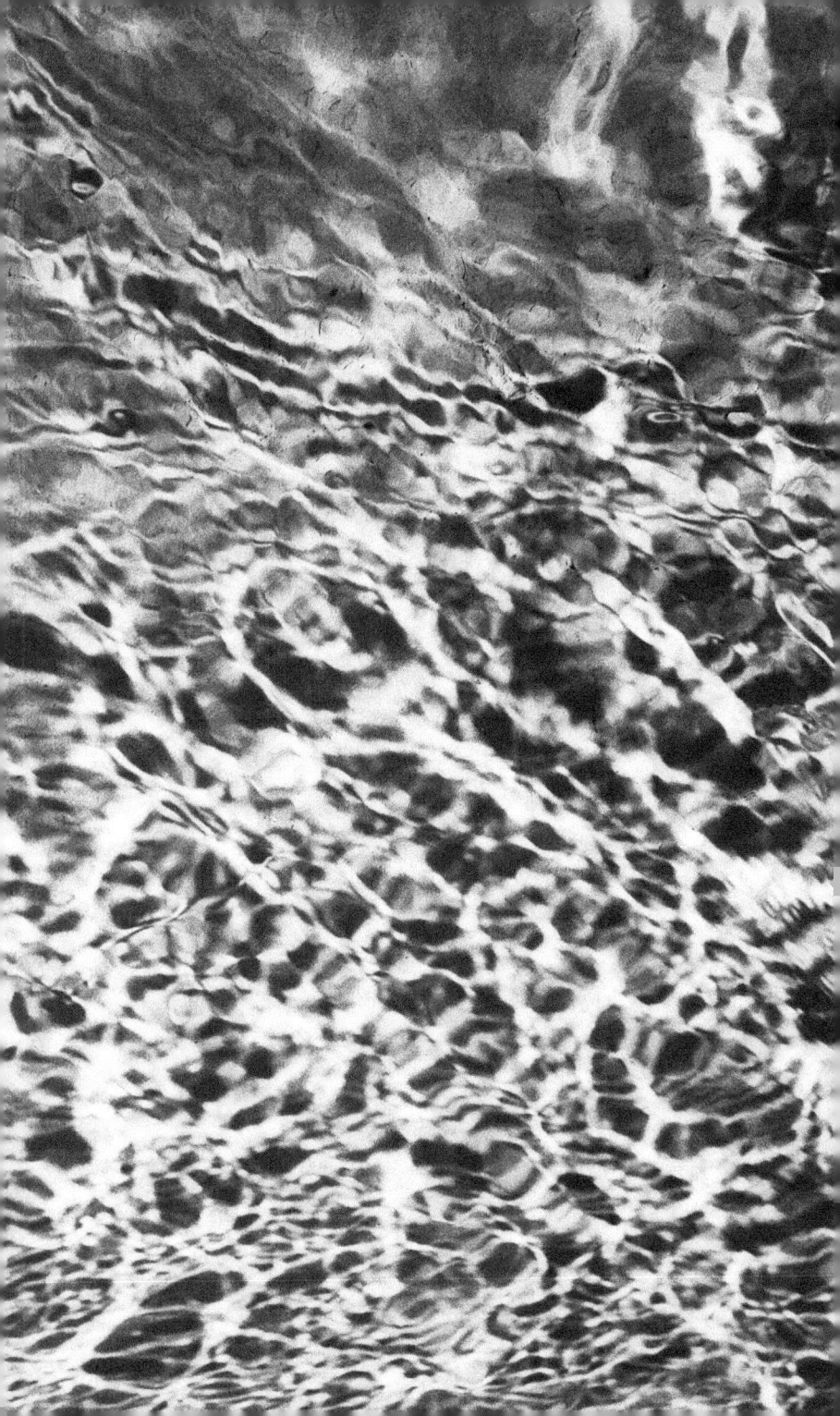

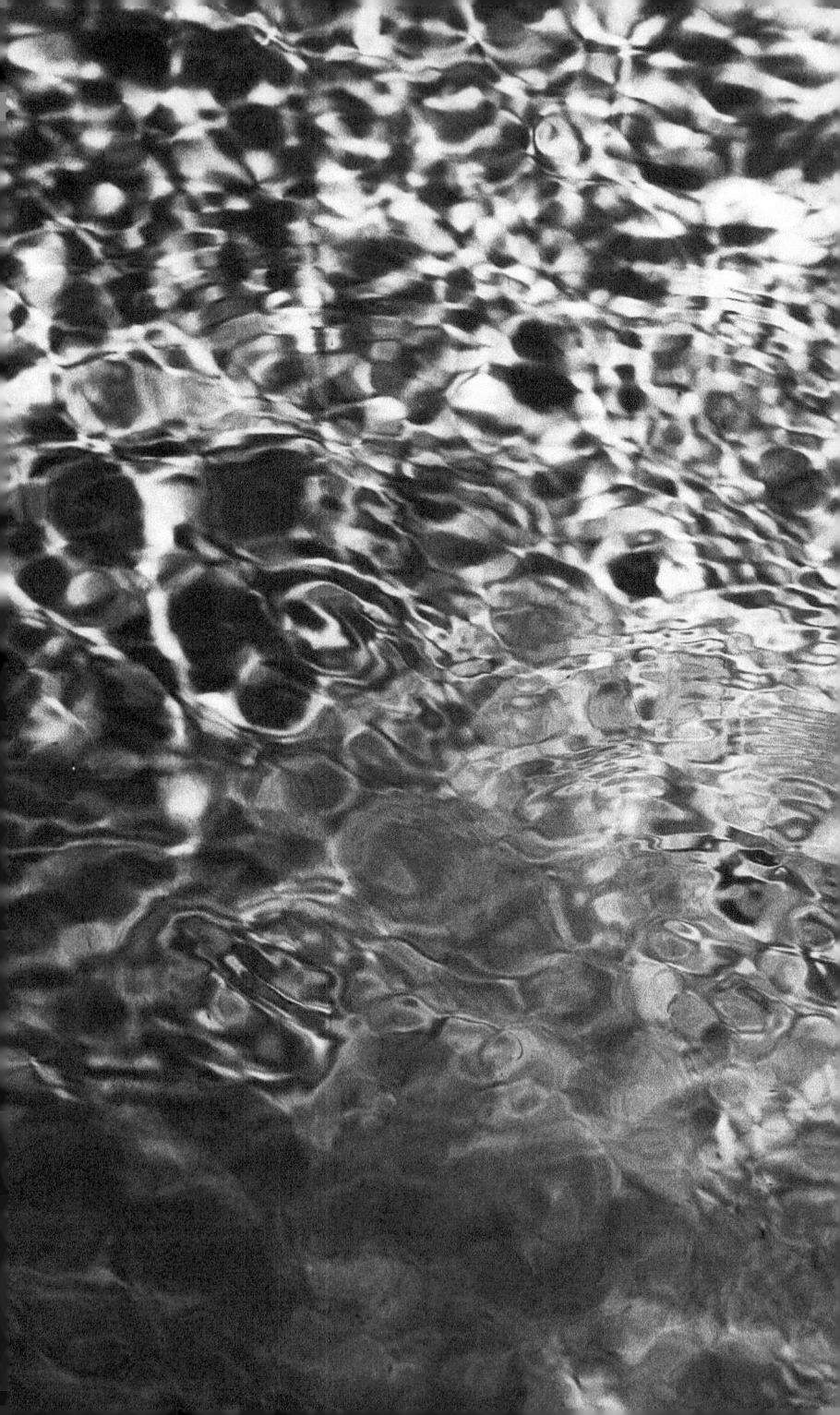

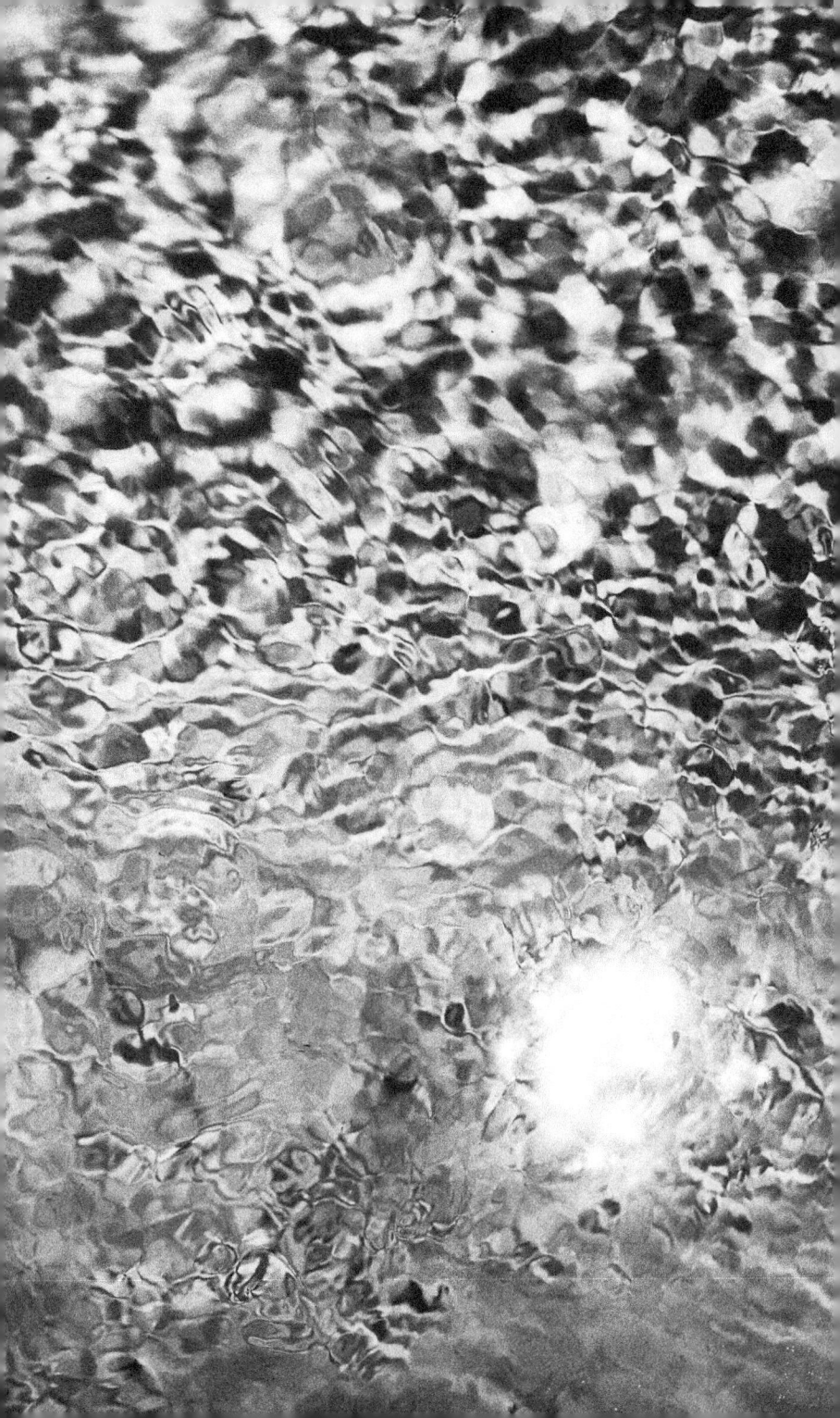

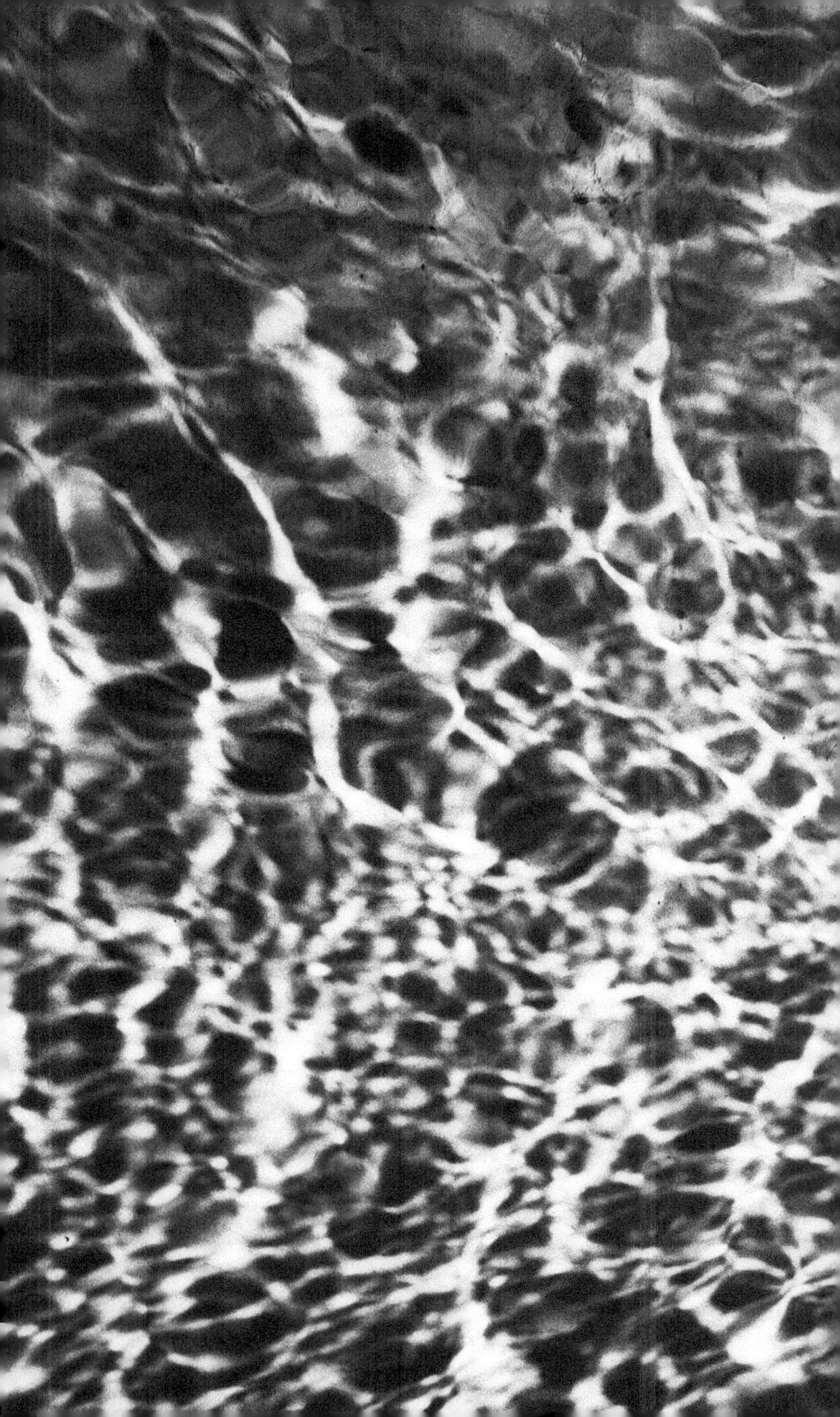

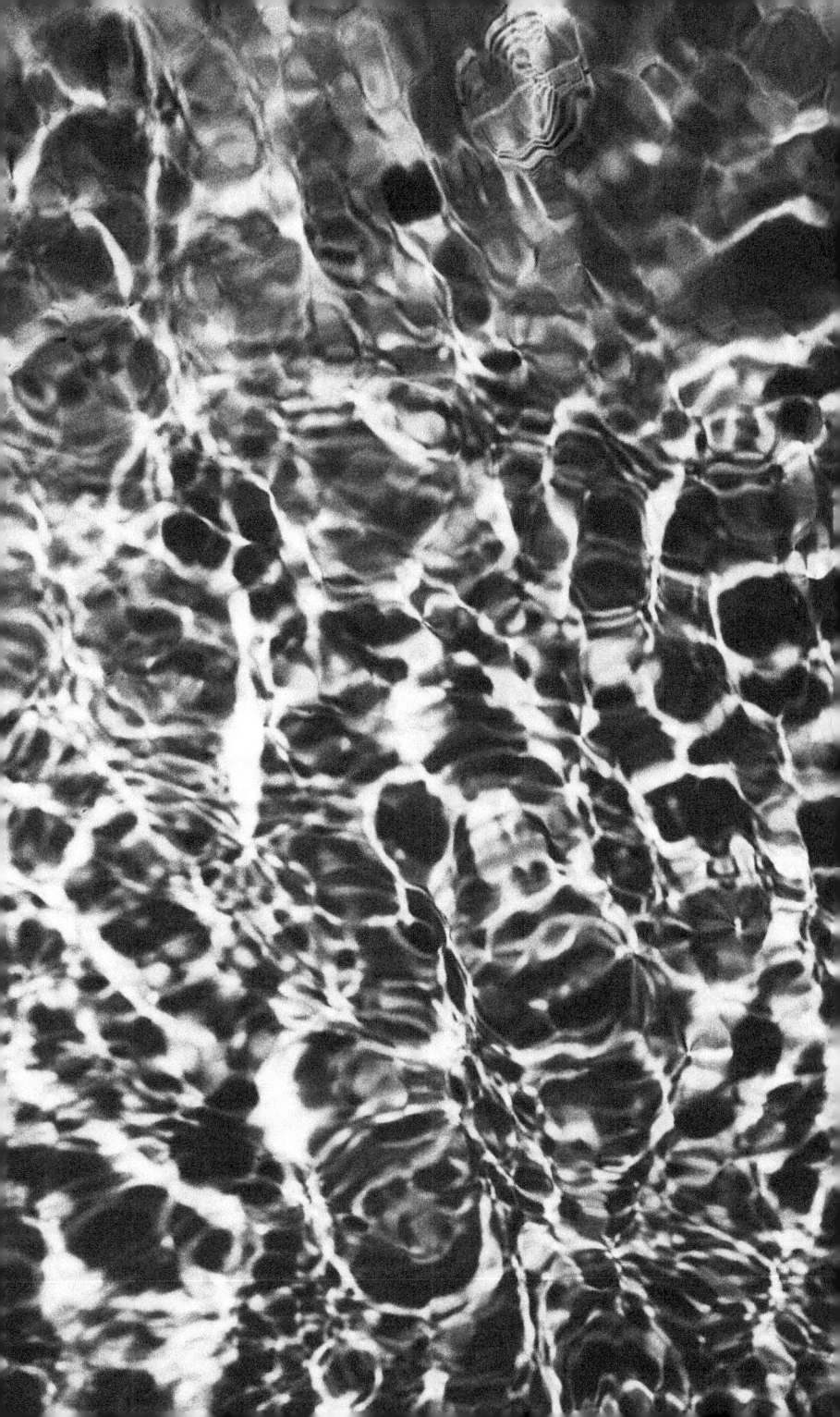

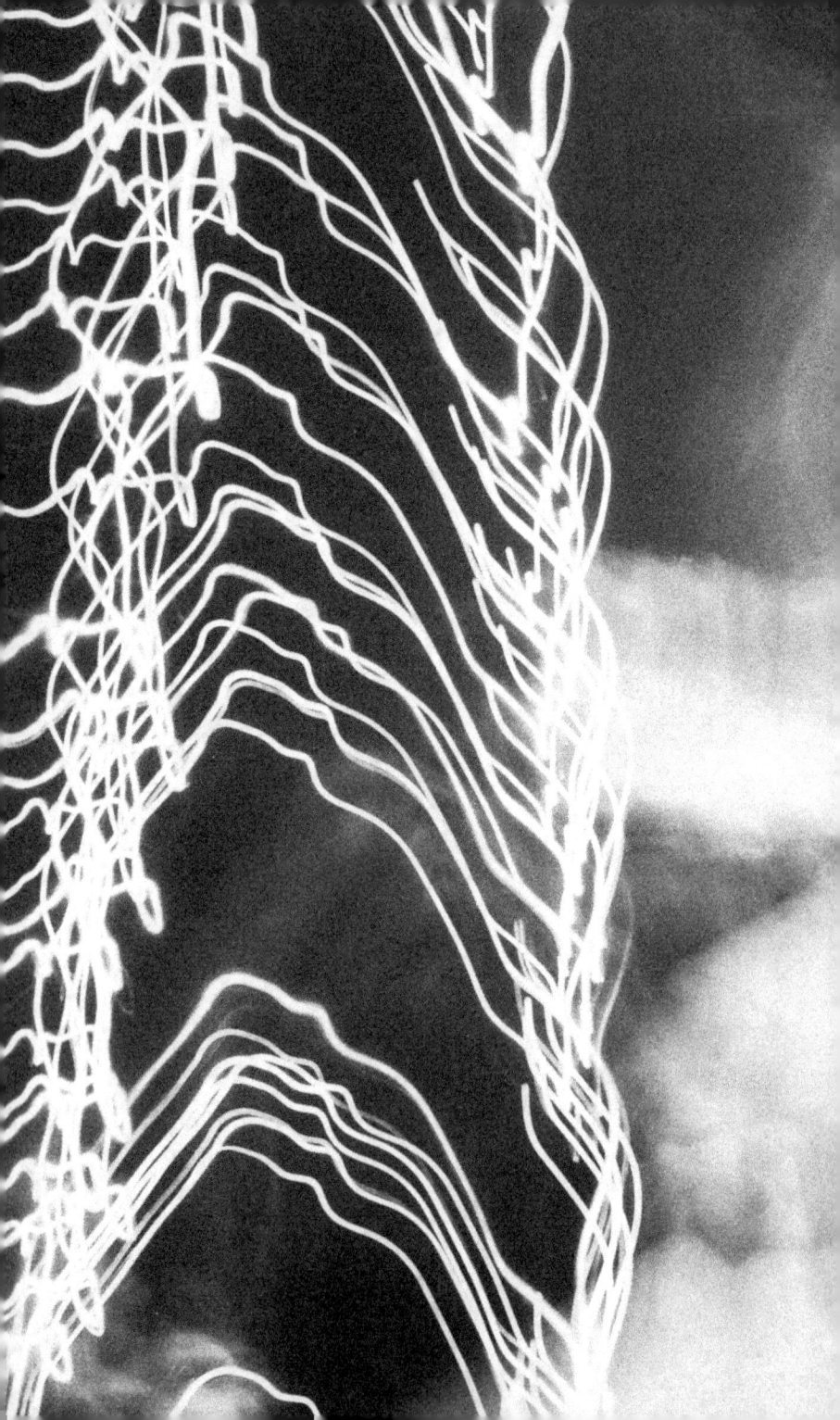

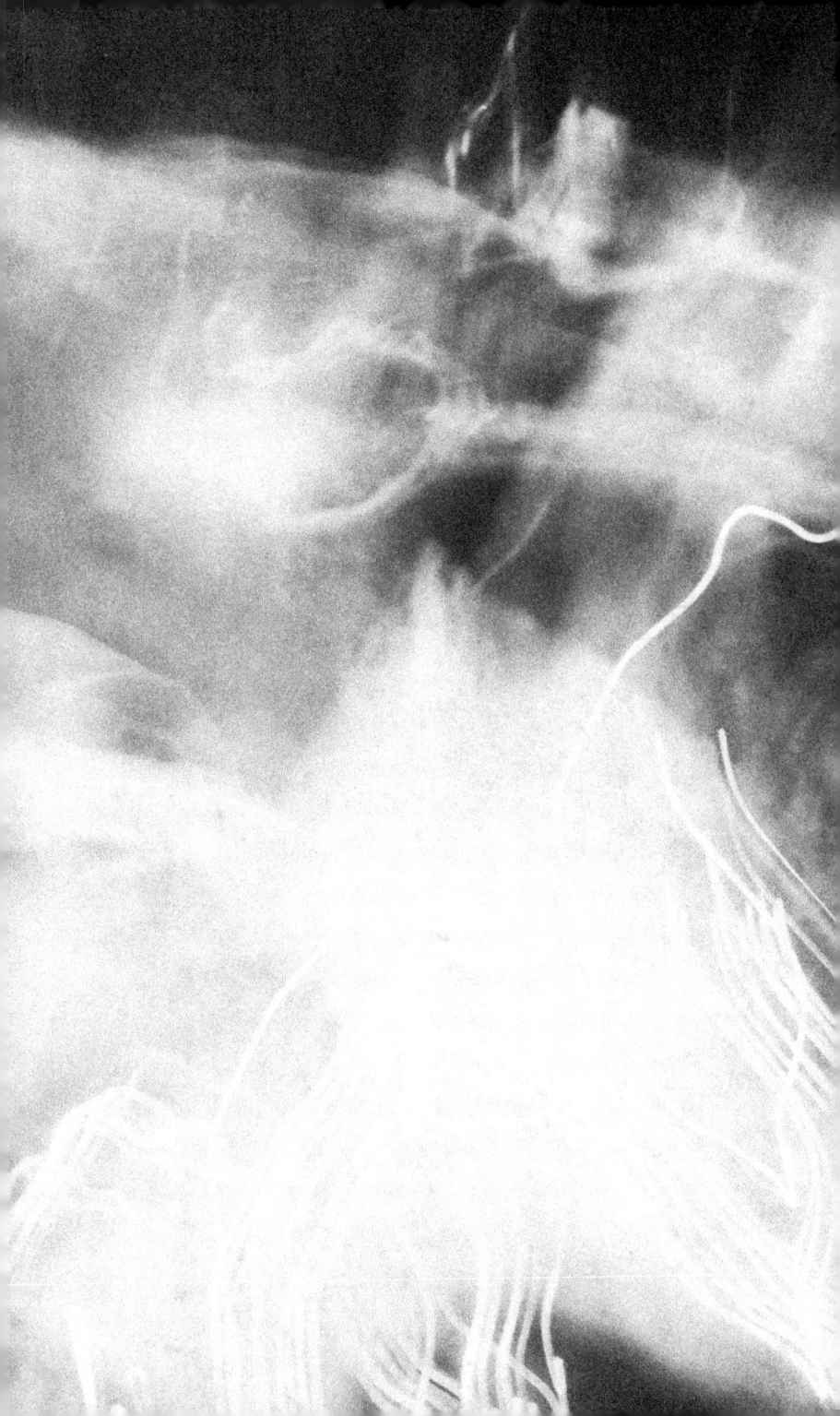

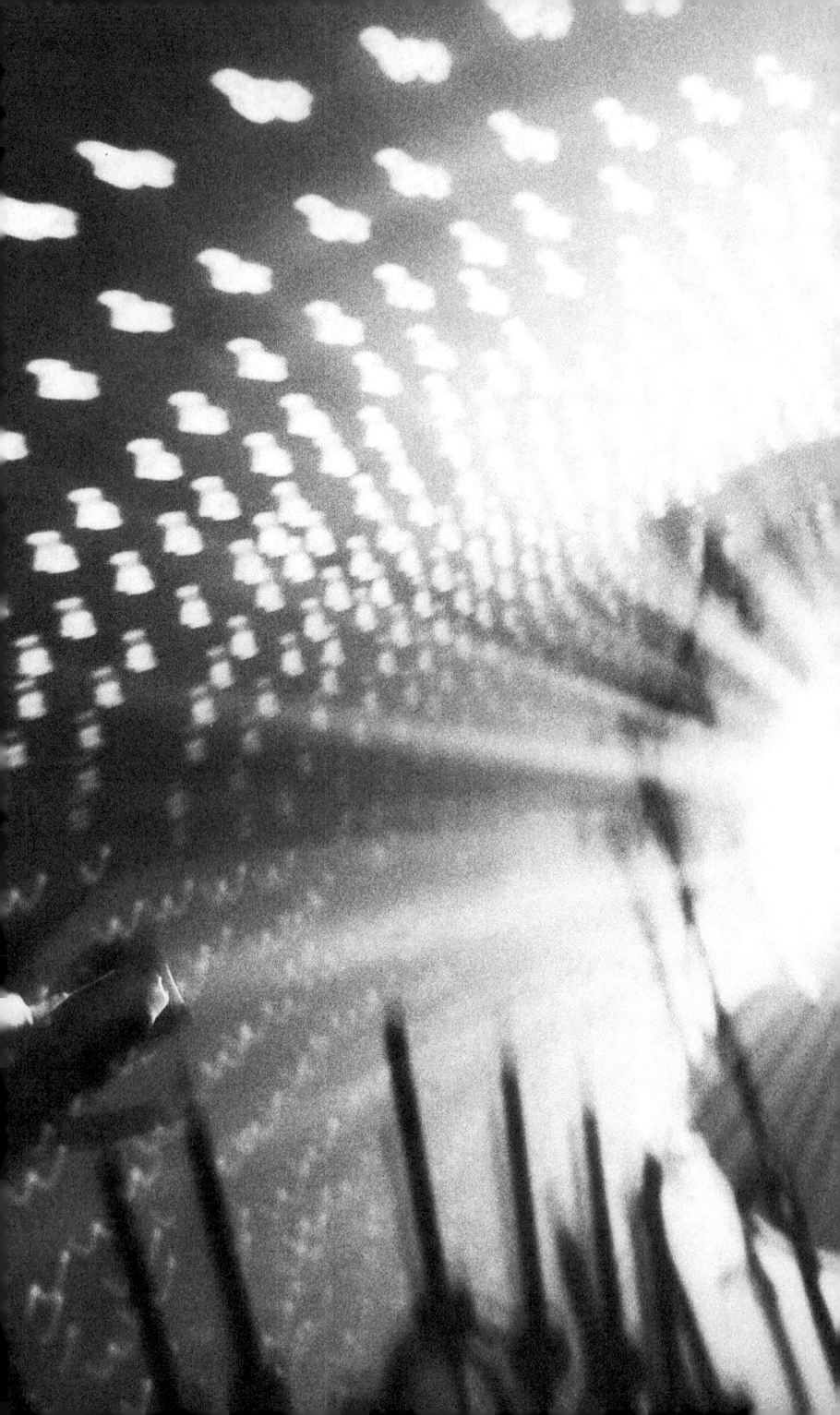

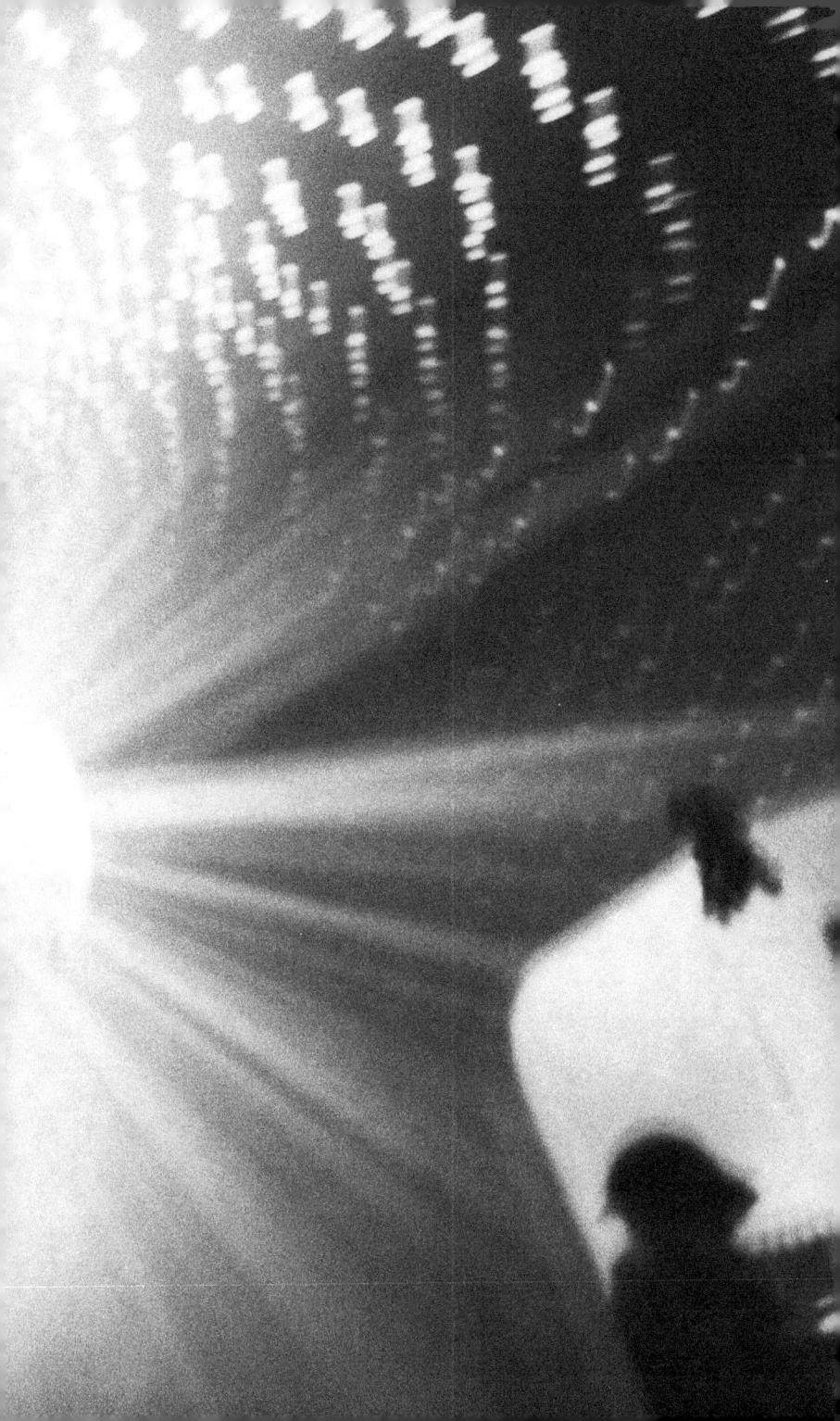

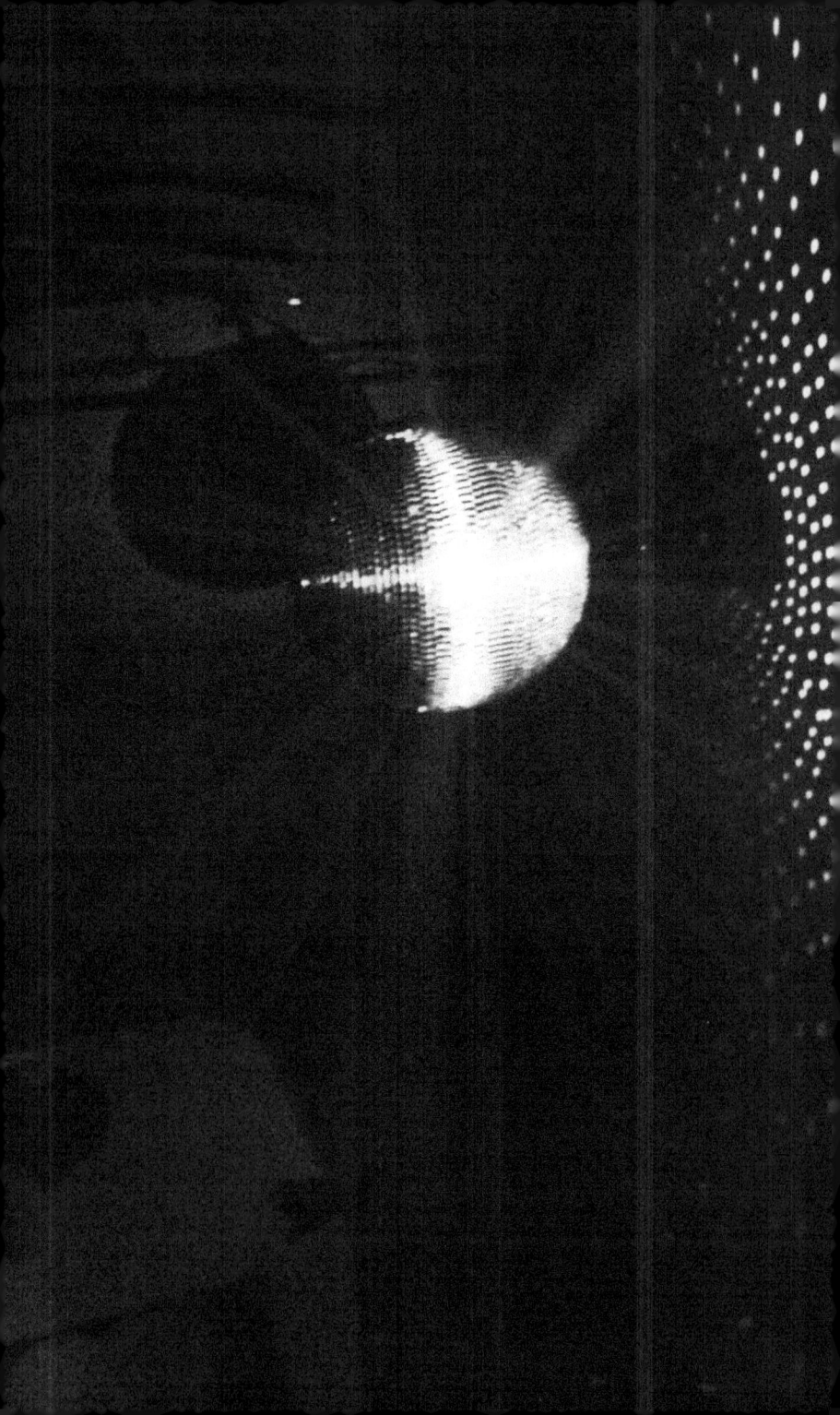

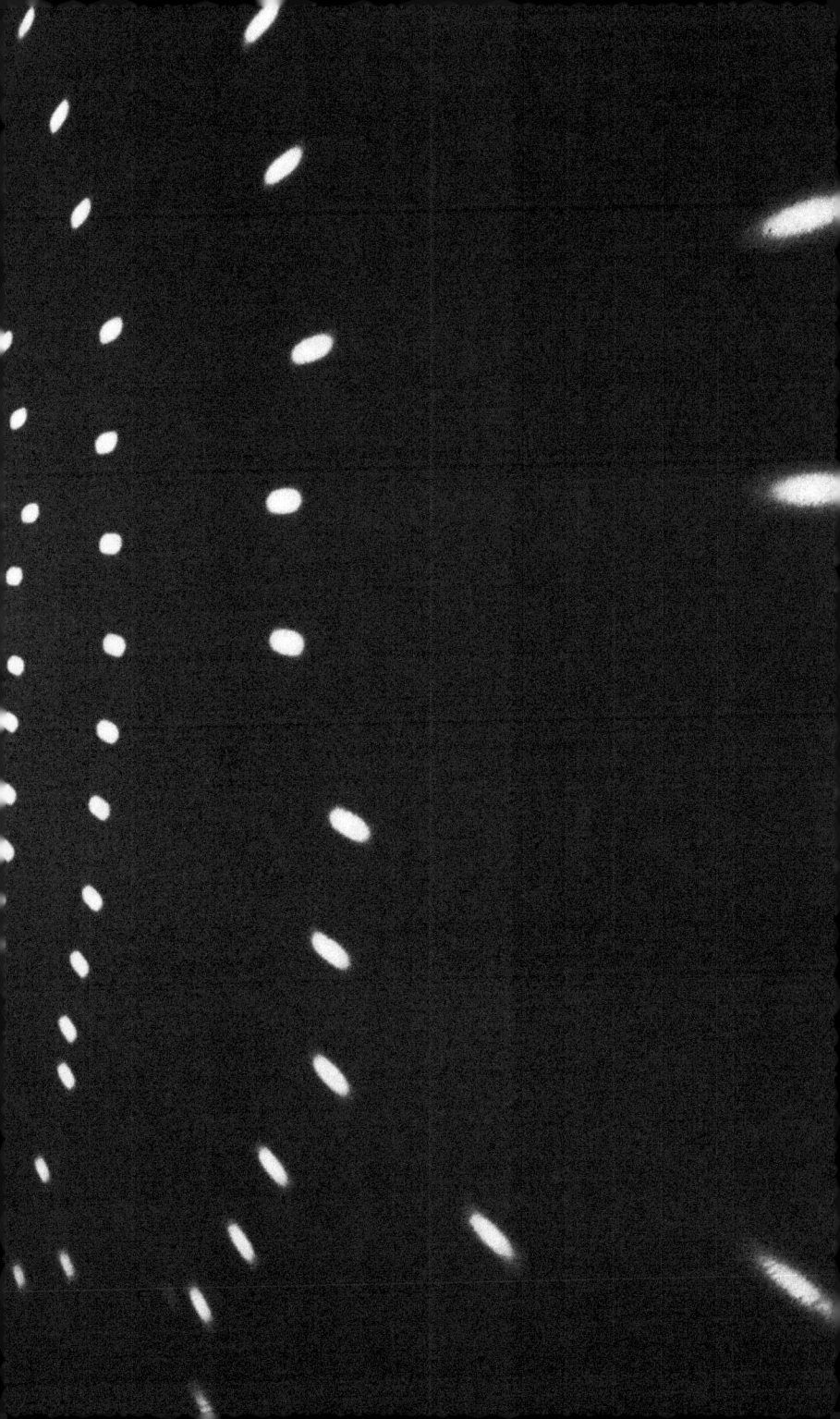

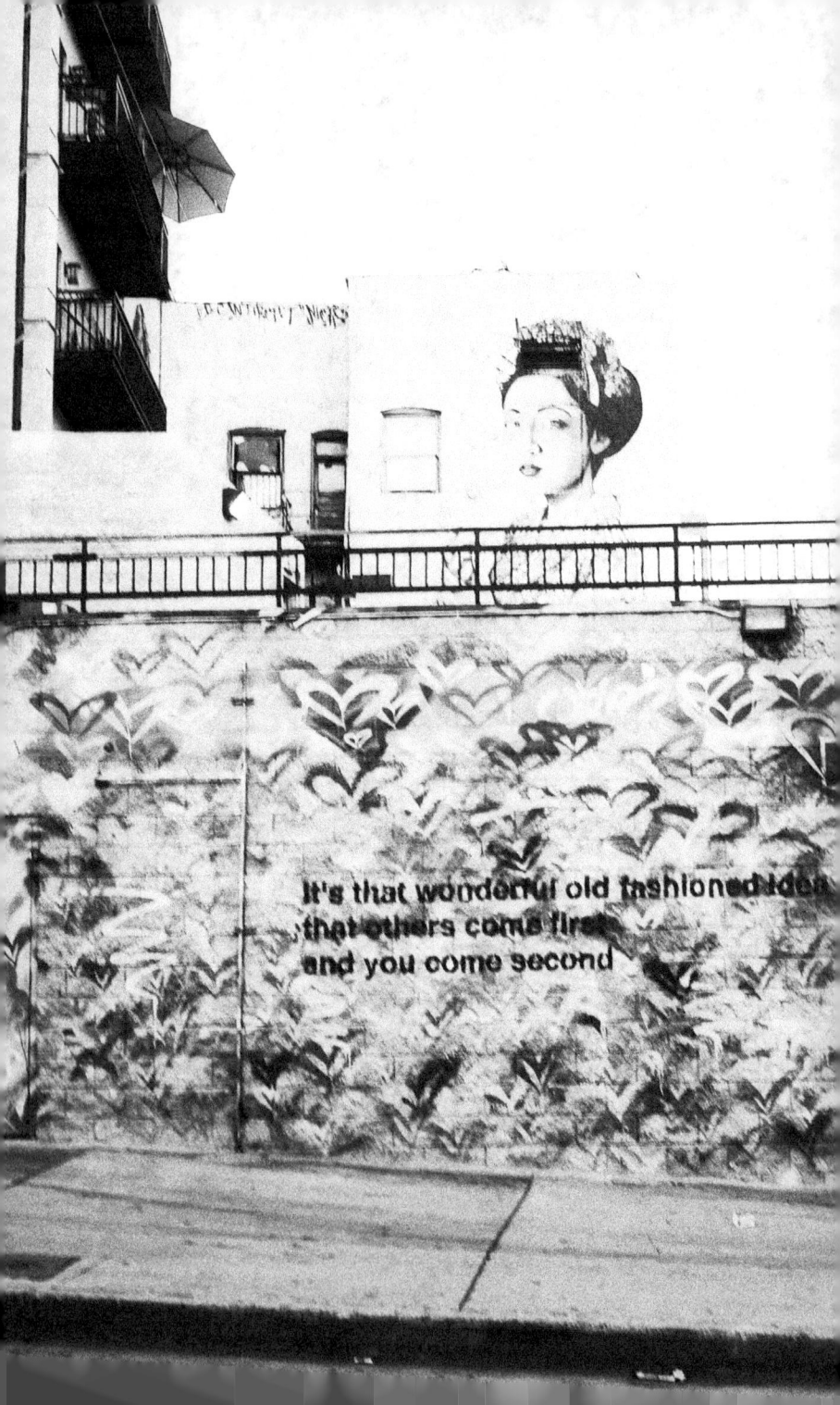

It's that wonderful old fashioned idea
that others come first
and you come second

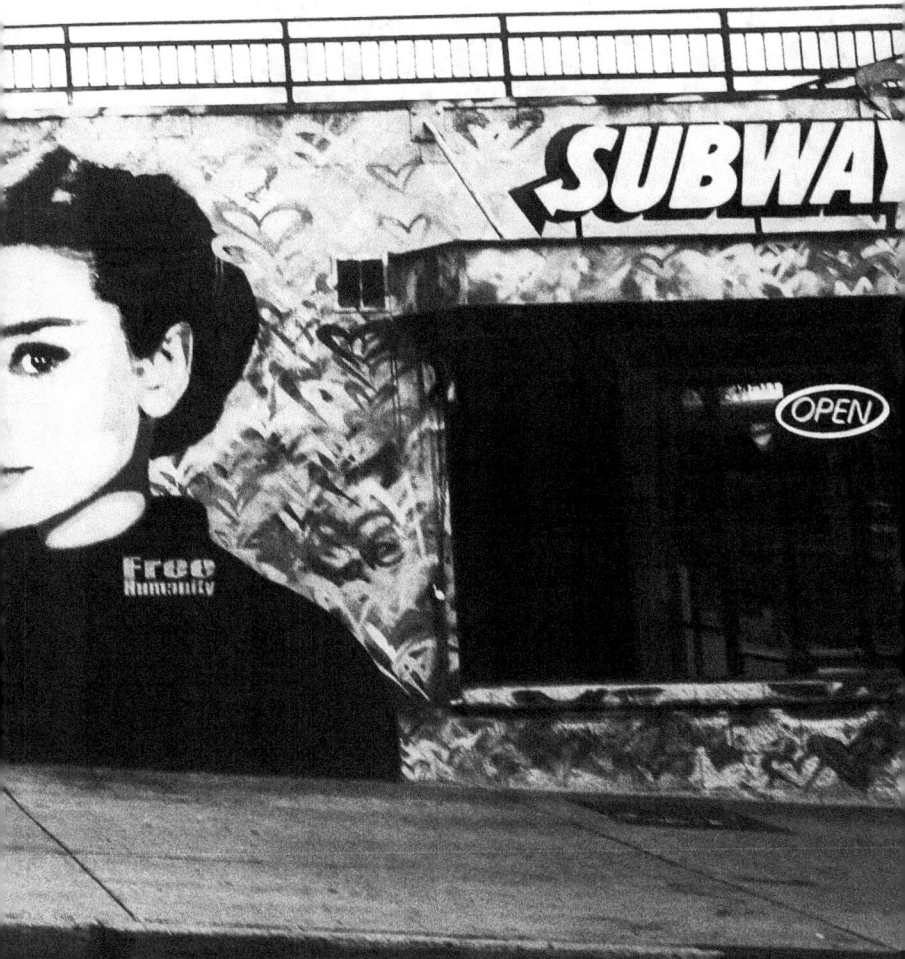

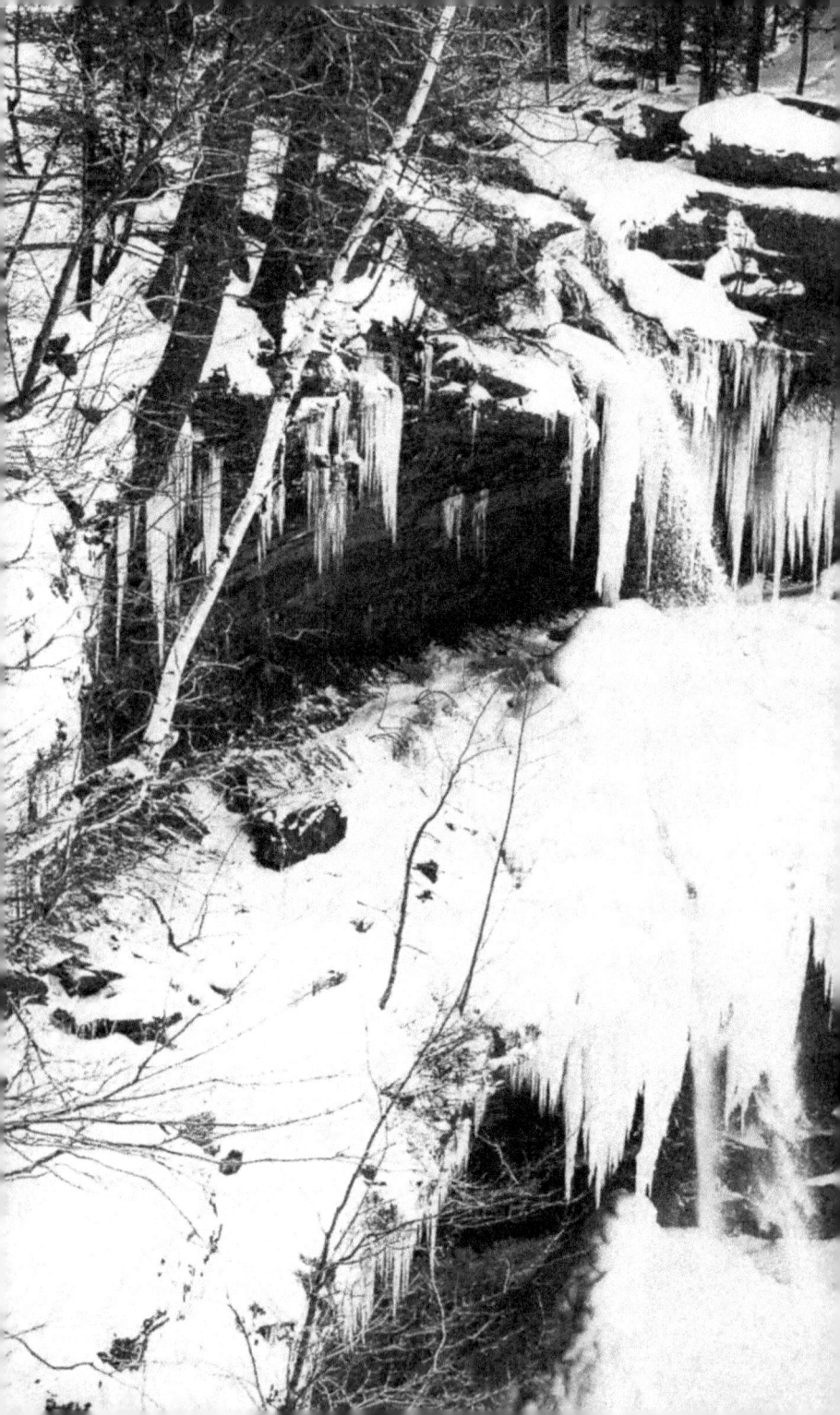

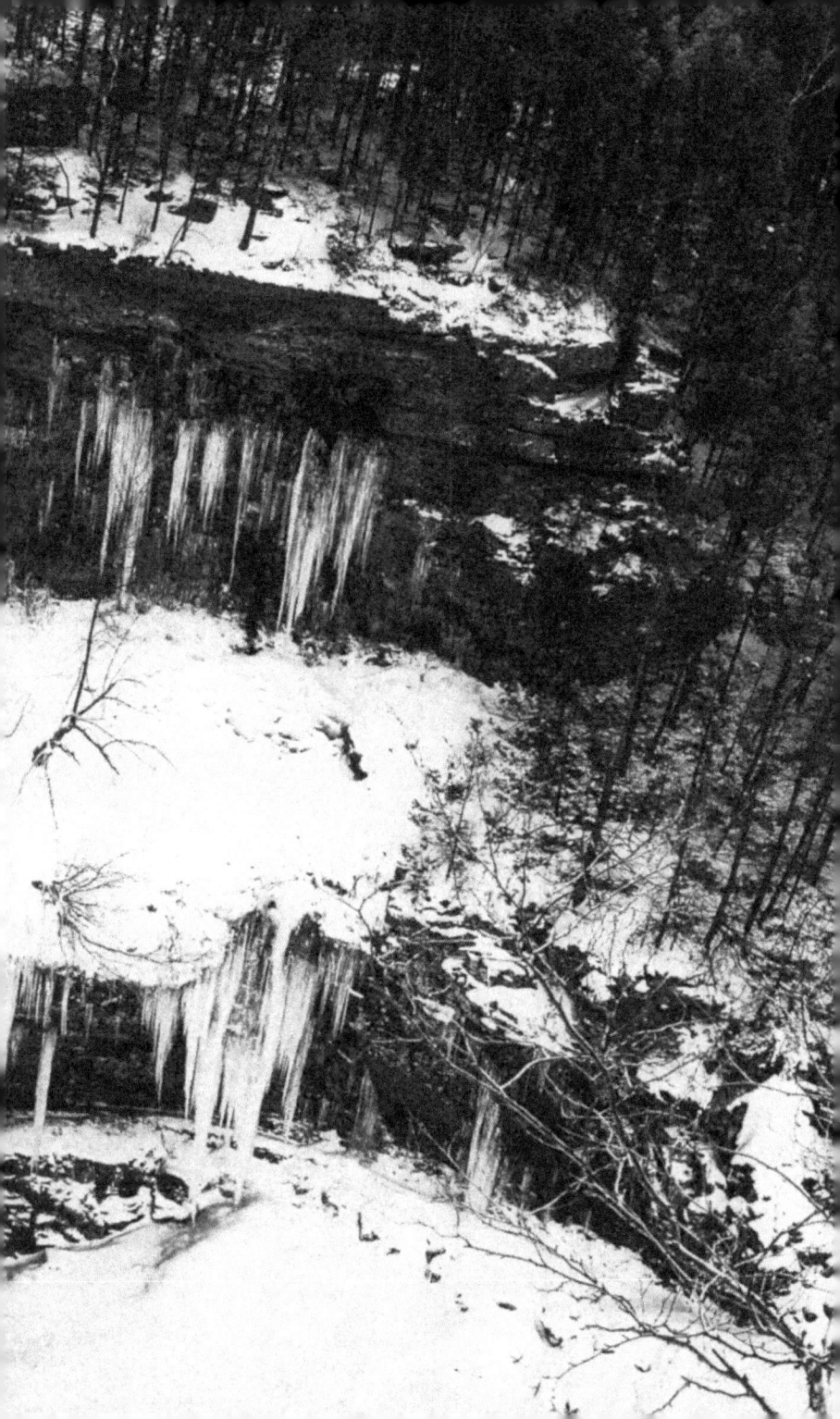

The Total Artist:
Use Your Imagination

Open Edition
V2

Copyright ©2025

The Instrumentals: Song Without Words
Ambient Photographs by Stephen Aldahl

ISBN: 978-1-966326-00-7

AIP 002

For catalog and sticker send SASE to:
American International Pictures
P.O. Box 1261
Hollywood, CA 90078

www.americaninternationalpictures.com

Designed by Blunt Bangs
www.bluntbangs.biz

poems: info@americaninternationalpictures.com
correspondence: editor@americaninternationalpictures.com